ASPECTS of WESTERN CIVILIZATION

Problems and Sources in History

Volume II

Fourth Edition

Edited by

PERRY M. ROGERS

The Ohio State University

Prentice Hall, Upper Saddle River, New Jersey 07458

Library of Congress Cataloging-in-Publication Data

Aspects of Western civilization: problems and sources in history /
    edited by Perry M. Rogers. —4th ed.
        p. cm.
    Vols. 1 and 2.
    ISBN 0-13-083202-2 (vol. 1).—ISBN 0-13-083203-0 (vol. 2)
        1. Civilization, Western—History. 2. Civilization, Western—
    History—Sources.   I. Rogers, Perry McAdow.
    CB245.A86   2000
    909′.09812—dc21   99–26935
                                                           CIP

Editor-in-chief: Charlyce Jones-Owen
Acquisitions editor: Todd Armstrong
Assistant editor: Emsal Hasan
Editorial assistant: Holly Jo Brown
Managing editor: Jan Stephan
Production liaison: Fran Russello
Editorial/production supervision: Bruce Hobart (Pine Tree Composition)
Prepress and manufacturing buyer: Lynn Pearlman
Cover director: Jayne Conte
Cover designer: Kiwi Design
Cover art: De Architectura di Vitruvio by Leonardo da Vinci/Art Resource, NY.
Director, Image Resource Center: Melinda Lee Reo
Manager, rights & permissions: Kay Dellosa
Image specialist: Beth Boyd
Photo researcher: Teri Stratford
Marketing manager: Sheryl Adams

This book was set in 10/11½ Baskerville by Pine Tree Composition, Inc.,
and was printed and bound by Courier Companies, Inc.
The cover was printed by Phoenix Color Corp.

Printed in the United States of America

10   9   8   7   6   5   4

Reprinted with corrections May, 2000.

ISBN 0-13-083203-0

Prentice-Hall International (UK) Limited, *London*
Prentice-Hall of Australia Pty. Limited, *Sydney*
Prentice-Hall Canada Inc., *Toronto*
Prentice-Hall Hispanoamericana, S.A., *Mexico*
Prentice-Hall of India Private Limited, *New Delhi*
Prentice-Hall of Japan, Inc., *Tokyo*
Pearson Education Asia Pte. Ltd., *Singapore*
Editora Prentice-Hall do Brasil, Ltda., *Rio de Janeiro*

For Ann
Elisa, Kit, and Tyler

Brief Contents

Contents

SECTION II: THE ENLIGHTENMENT *52*

Thoughts on the Human Condition and Human Progress *52*

Thoughts on Religion *59*

Thoughts on Education *63*

Thoughts on Government: The Political Framework *70*

Thoughts on Women: The Social Framework *80*

The Urban Landscape   172

Reaction and Reform   186

5 Nationalism and Imperialism: The Motives and Methods of Expansion   208

Nationalism   212

9   The "Good War": World War II (1939–1945)   405

The Road to War (1936–1939)   *409*

Preface

The Roman orator Cicero once remarked that "History is the witness of the times, the torch of truth, the life of memory, the teacher of life, the messenger of antiquity." In spite of these noble words, historians have often labored under the burden of justifying the study of events that are over and done. Human beings are practical, more concerned with their present and future than with their past. And yet the study of history provides us with unique opportunities for self-knowledge. It teaches us what we have done and therefore helps define what we are. On a less abstract level, the study of history enables us to judge present circumstance by drawing on the laboratory of the past. Those who have lived and died, through their recorded attitudes, actions, and ideas, have left a legacy of experience.

One of the best ways to travel through time and perceive the very "humanness" of history is through the study of primary sources. These are the documents, coins, letters, inscriptions, and monuments of past ages. The task of historians is to evaluate this evidence with a critical eye and then construct a narrative that is consistent with the "facts" as they have been established. Such interpretations are inherently subjective and open to dispute. History is thus filled with controversy as historians argue their way toward the truth. The only effective way to understand the past is through personal examination of the primary sources.

Yet, for the beginning student, this poses some difficulties. Such inquiry casts the student adrift from the security of accepting the "truth" as revealed in a textbook. In fact, history is too often presented in a deceptively objective manner; one learns facts and dates in an effort to obtain the right answers for multiple-choice tests. But the student who has wrestled with primary sources and has experienced voices from the past on a more intimate level accepts the responsibility of evaluation and judgment. He or she understands that history does not easily lend itself to right answers, but demands reflection on the problems that have confronted past societies and are at play even in our contemporary world.

Aspects of Western Civilization offers the student an opportunity to evaluate the primary sources of the past in a structured and organized format. The documents provided include state papers, secret dispatches, letters, diary accounts, poems, newspaper articles, papal encyclicals, propaganda fliers, and even wall graffiti. Occasionally, the assessments of modern historians are included. Yet this two-volume book has been conceived as more than a simple compilation of sources. The subtitle of the work, *Problems and Sources in History*, gives true indication of the nature of its premise. Students learn from the past most effectively when faced with problems that have meaning for their own lives. In evaluating the material from *Aspects of Western Civilization*, the student will discover that issues are not nearly as simple as they may appear at first glance. Historical sources often contradict each other, and truth then depends upon logic and upon one's own experience and outlook on life. Throughout these volumes, the student is confronted with basic questions regarding historical development, human nature, moral action, and practical necessity. The text is therefore broad in its scope, incorporating a wide variety of political, social, economic, religious, intellectual, and scientific issues. It is internally organized around eight major themes that provide direction and cohesion while allowing for originality of thought in both written and oral analysis:

1. *Imperialism.* How has imperialism been justified throughout Western history, and what are the moral implications of gaining and maintaining empire? Is defensive imperialism a practical foreign policy option? This theme is often juxtaposed with subtopics of nationalism, war, altruism, and human nature.

2. *Church/State Relationships.* Is there a natural competition between these two controlling units in society? Which is more influential, which legacy more enduring? How has religion been used as a means of securing political power or of instituting social change?

3. *Beliefs and Spirituality.* The Judeo-Christian heritage of Western Civilization forms the basis of this theme. How have religious values and moral attitudes affected the course of Western history? To what extent have spiritual reform movements resulted in a change of political or social policy? Are ideas more potent than any army? Why have so many people died fighting for religions that abhor violence? Does every society need a spiritual foundation?

4. *Systems of Government.* This theme seeks to introduce the student to the various systems of rule that have shaped Western Civilization: classical democracy, representative democracy (republican government), oligarchy, constitutional monarchy, divine-right monarchy, theocracy, and dictatorship (especially fascism and totalitarian rule). What are the advantages and drawbacks to each? This rubric also includes the concepts of balance of power and containment, principles of succession, geopolitics, and social and economic theories such as capitalism, communism, and socialism.

5. *Revolution.* This theme seeks to define and examine the varieties of revolution: political, intellectual, economic, and social. What are the underlying and precipitating causes of political revolution? How essential is the intellectual foundation? Are social demands and spontaneity more important elements in radical action?

6. *Propaganda.* What is the role of propaganda in history? Many sections examine the use and abuse of information, often in connection with absolute government, revolution, imperialism, or genocide. How are art and architecture, as well as the written word, used in the "creation of belief"? This theme emphasizes the relativity of truth and stresses the responsibility of the individual in assessing the validity of evidence.

7. *Women in History.* The text intends to help remedy the widespread omission of women from the history of Western society and to develop an appreciation of their contributions to the intellectual and political framework of Western Civilization. At issue is how women have been viewed—or rendered invisible—throughout history and how individually and collectively their presence is inextricably linked with the development and progress of civilization. This inclusive approach stresses the importance of achieving a perspective that lends value and practical application to history.

8. *Historical Change and Transition.* What are the main determinants of change in history? How important is the individual in effecting change, or is society regulated by unseen social and economic forces? What role does chance play? What are the components of civilization, and how do we assess progress or decline? Are civilizations biological in nature? Is a crisis/response theory of change valid? This theme works toward providing the student with a philosophy of history and against the tendency to divide history into strict periods. It stresses the close connection between the past and the present.

Structure of the Book

Each chapter begins with a *time-line chronology* so that students may visualize the historical parameters of the chapter. This is followed by *a series of quotations* from various historians, diplomats, philosophers, literary figures, or religious spokespersons who offer insight on the subject matter of the chapter. These quotations may well be used in conjunction with the study questions at the end of the unit. After the quotations, *chapter themes* are listed and framed by several questions that direct the reader to broader issues and comparative perspectives with ideas and events in other chapters. This feature acknowledges the changing perspectives of different eras while linking historical problems that emphasize the continuity of history. A *general introduction* then provides a brief historical background and focuses the themes or questions to be discussed in the chapter.

Following this general introduction, the primary sources are presented with extensive direction for the student. A *headnote* explains in more detail the historical or biographical background for each primary source and focuses attention on themes or interrelationships with other sources. Each chapter concludes with a *chronology* designed to orient the student to the broader context of history, and a series of *study questions* that can form the basis of oral discussion or written analysis. The questions do not seek mere regurgitation of information, but demand a more thoughtful response based on reflective analysis of the primary sources.

Use of the Book

Aspects of Western Civilization offers the instructor a wide variety of didactic applications. The chapters fit into a more or less standard lecture format and are ordered chronologically. An entire chapter may be assigned for oral discussion, or sections from each chapter may satisfy particular interests or requirements. Some of the chapters provide extensive treatment of a broad historical topic ("The Sword of Faith: Western Civilization During the Middle Ages"; "'Dare to Know!': The Revolution of the Mind in the Seventeenth and Eighteenth Centuries"; "'Liberty, Equality, Fraternity!': Romanticism and Revolution"). In order to make them manageable and effective, I have grouped them into topical sections (with correspondingly labeled study questions) that can be utilized separately, if so desired.

The chapters may also be assigned for written analysis. One of the most important concerns of both instructor and student in an introductory class is the written assignment. *Aspects of Western Civilization* has been designed to provide self-contained topics that are problem-oriented, promote reflection and analysis, and encourage responsible citation of particular primary sources. The study questions for each chapter should generally produce an eight- to ten-page paper.

Acknowledgments

I would particularly like to thank friends and colleagues at Columbus School for Girls who contributed their expertise and enthusiasm to this book. Susan Altan lent her perspective and sensitive awareness of women's issues at critical moments when new avenues of thought were most needed. Daniel Hall and Thomas Tappan advised me on several scientific and technological matters that broadened the scope of the text immeasurably. Anne Lodge and Mary Ann Leonard offered their unique perspectives regarding ethical issues that often caused me to pause and certainly forced the introduction of new questions into the discussion. Mary Alice Fite provided me with material and literary insight that added greatly to the accuracy of the text, and Jack Guy and Patricia Niehoff-Smith read drafts of some chapters, offering sterling commentary throughout. Thanks also to the students of Columbus School for Girls, who continue to "test" the chapters in this book with their typical diligence and hard work; the final product has benefitted greatly from their suggestions and ideas. This revision has also benefited from the insight and suggestions of Eleanor McCluskey, Broward Community College, Florida and Charles Parker, University of St. Louis, who reviewed the text in its preliminary stages. Finally, I owe an immeasurable debt to my wife, Ann, who suffered all the outrageous fortune and disruption that goes into writing a book of this kind over a period of years—she did it with me.

P. M. R.

PART I

FOUNDATIONS OF THE MODERN WORLD

1

"I Am the State": The Absolutism of Louis XIV

Death of Queen Elizabeth of England 1603

Reign of French King Louis XIII managed by Cardinal Richelieu 1610-1643

English Civil War 1642-1646

Commonwealth of England 1649-1653

King Louis XIV revokes the Edict of Nantes 1685

1600 · 1625 · 1650 · 1675 · 1700 · 1725 · 1750

Reign of King James I of England 1603-1625

Reign of King Charles I of England 1625-1649

Reign of Sun King Louis XIV of France 1643-1715

England ruled by Lord Protector Oliver Cromwell 1653-1658

Restoration of the English monarchy under King Charles II 1660-1685

Glorious Revolution in England 1688-1689

It is atheism and blasphemy to dispute what God can do; so it is presumption and contempt to dispute what a king can do, or say that a king cannot do this or that.

—James I

It is in my person alone that ultimate power resides. It is from me alone that my courts derive their authority. It is to me alone that the power to make law belongs, without any dependence and without any division. The whole public order comes from me, and the rights and interests of the nation are necessarily joined with mine and rest only in my hands.

—Louis XIV

Resistance on the part of people to the supreme legislative power of the state is never legitimate; it is the duty of the people to bear any abuse of the supreme power.

—Immanuel Kant

Every subject's duty is the king's, but every subject's soul is his own.

—William Shakespeare

———⌇⊚⌇———

CHAPTER THEMES

- *Systems of Government:* How would you define the term "absolute monarchy"? Is it the most efficient form of government? Can an absolute monarch be compared to a dictator? What is the difference between the two?

- *Propaganda:* How did Louis XIV use court painters and historians, as well as the Palace of Versailles, to create an image that would benefit him politically? Does it follow that the image of government is more important than the substance of government?

- *Church/State Relationships:* How would you best define the phrase "divine-right monarchy"? Did Louis XIV really consider himself divine, and how did this connection serve to strengthen his political authority? Can one be an absolute monarch without being a divine-right monarch?

- *Revolution:* It has been asserted that the seeds of the French Revolution of 1789 were sown during the monarchies of Louis XIV and his immediate successors. For all his glory and prestige, was Louis XIV's reign disastrous for France economically and militarily? Are revolutions dependent on contemporary precipitating causes, or do revolutions have broadly based underlying causes without which political and social change could not be possible?

- *The Big Picture:* Are societies that have a large gap between an elite class and the poor doomed to fail eventually? How important is the presence of a strong middle class? Does the authority of a state's leader increase the more removed he is from the people he rules? Or can governments maintain control over citizens through image alone? Does modern technology change the equation in any way?

It has often been said that the primary purpose of government is to create and maintain a stable domestic environment. Only through such stability and domestic tranquility can a government establish a strong defense against threatening foes and also pursue a successful foreign policy.

When the state is divided against itself into several political, social, or economic factions, it is weak and thus susceptible to invasion or revolution. This is a rather conservative opinion, and others throughout the years have argued that a state based primarily on efficiency and security does not tolerate new ideas or respond quickly to the needs of its citizens; in essence, such a state is not progressive in outlook, but seeks only to maintain the status quo. At the root of these different ideas lies a basic problem: To what extent are citizens of a state able to rule themselves? Is democracy a "noble experiment" that errs by ascribing extraordinary possibilities to ordinary people? Indeed, is progress best served when a citizen body is directed and controlled by a monarch or even a dictator who uses all the resources of the state to achieve his goals? These questions form the basis of political theory in the Western world. How best should humans organize society in order to provide stability, security, and happiness?

During the fifteenth through the eighteenth centuries, these questions were fundamentally important. As the Middle Ages blended into the Renaissance, decentralized feudalism gave way to more structured monarchies in France, England, and Spain. The modern State was forming under the control of kings who had relatively few restrictions on their authority. The major exception to this was England, whose monarch had coexisted since the thirteenth century with a developing Parliament, or representative body, and was beholden to certain laws and decrees (such as the Magna Carta of 1215) that guaranteed basic civil rights for Englishmen. It is perhaps because of this long tradition of more or less shared power and responsibilities that England was the first major state to experience the conflicts that inevitably resulted from such an arrangement.

Between 1603 and 1715, England experienced the most tumultuous years of its long history. The glorious reign of Queen Elizabeth I (1558–1603) gave way to increasing religious dissension under her successor, James I (1603–1625). The new king, who hailed from Scotland, lacked tact and was ignorant of English institutions. More seriously, he advocated absolute, divine-right monarchy. According to this theory, the authority of a king was unlimited and could not be challenged because it was sanctioned by God. The reign of James I began a breach between the monarchy and Parliament that was eventually to result in a civil war (1642–1646) between supporters of the Parliament (Roundheads) and those of the king (Cavaliers). The victory of Parliament was crowned with the beheading of King Charles I (1649), an act without precedent in English history. After this, the government was controlled first by Parliament alone and then under the direction of Oliver Cromwell, who was determined to give England efficient rule as Lord Protector (1653–1658). On Cromwell's death, the monarchy was restored under Charles II (1660–1685), but it was conciliatory to the will of Parliament. The final breach occurred when King James II (1685–1688) once again tried to assert authority as an absolute monarch. Parliament deposed him, banned his Catholic relatives from succession, and invited the popular Dutch Protestant leader William of Orange and his wife Mary to rule as monarchs (1688). This "Glorious Revolution" was bloodless and resulted in a Bill of Rights that limited the powers of the monarchy; henceforward the king would rule with the consent of Parliament.

Seventeenth-century France, in contrast to England, saw representative government crushed by the success of absolute monarchy. It was Henry IV (1589–1610) who began the process of establishing a strong centralized state by curtailing the privileges of the nobility and restricting provincial governors and regional councils called parlements. Henry and his finance minister, the Duke of Sully (1560–1641), also sought to control the finances of the state by establishing government monopolies on gunpowder, mines, and salt. When Henry IV was assassinated in 1610, he was succeeded by his son, Louis XIII (1610–1643). Since Louis was only nine years old at the time of his father's death, France was ruled by his mother, Marie de Medici, who sought internal security by promoting Cardinal Richelieu (1585–1642) as chief advisor to the king. Richelieu, an efficient and shrewd counselor, sought to make France the dominant European power by consolidating the domestic authority of the king. There was to be but one law—that of the king. To this end, Richelieu imprisoned and executed recalcitrant nobles; indeed, the French nobility eventually became docile in their subservience at court. Richelieu was succeeded in 1642 by another cardinal named Mazarin (1602–1661), who acted as regent for the young monarch, Louis XIV. Because of the strict policies of Richelieu and Mazarin, Louis XIV inherited a basic foundation for absolute rule.

The reign of Louis XIV (1643–1715) was fundamentally important for the establishment of France both as the supreme political power on the Continent and as the dominant cultural influence throughout Europe. The sun shone brightly on the fortunes of France in the seventeenth and eighteenth centuries, and Louis, or the Sun King as he was called, became the model of stable, secure rule. His control over his subjects was absolute, subject to no authority except that of God. God had appointed Louis, and God alone could judge his actions. Thus, all political, social, economic, and military decisions were made by the king and his various advisors without interference or input from the people of France. Collectively, his subjects were Louis's children and as such were expected to follow the policies of their "father." Louis's famous comment, "I am the state," was the essence of French divine-right monarchy.

This period of history, however, was not in any sense tranquil. For over half a century before Louis's accession, France had been disrupted by religious wars between Catholics, whom the French monarchy supported, and the Huguenots or French Protestants. The wars had secured certain political and military privileges for the Huguenots that were scarcely compatible with the ideal of a strong, centralized monarchy. When Louis assumed control of the government in 1661 after his eighteen-year minority, the Huguenots were still an independent religious group, officially tolerated by the crown, but an embarrassment nonetheless. Finally, in 1685, Louis demanded conformity to Catholic doctrine and revoked the Edict of Nantes (1598), which had granted religious toleration to the Huguenots.

Another major threat to the tranquility of the state and the supremacy of royal power came from the nobility. During the minority of Louis XIV, France had lapsed into civil war, fomented by nobles who were jealous of the increasing power of the monarchy and particularly its close financial support from an active middle class. To many, the chaos of such disturbances was a greater fear than the existence of a strong, centralized monarchy that could ensure domestic tranquility and external security. This fear of chaos and desire for order probably lay behind popular support of Louis's divine-right monarchy. The longevity and relative harmony of his reign demonstrates Louis's successful disarming of the nobility. His magnificent palace at Versailles, testimony to his pursuit of order, not only was an enduring artistic legacy of his reign, but also served a practical purpose: Louis could house all his important nobles at the palace and thus maintain close control over their activities. Louis reserved high government positions for hand-picked members of the aristocracy and aspiring middle class, who thus owed their success to him; this in turn assured their loyalty.

In the late-seventeenth and early-eighteenth centuries, France was the envy and terror of Europe, its most powerful state and cultural center. Other monarchs imitated Louis's court at Versailles and even the palace itself. His army was perhaps the best trained and best supplied military force of its day, and his diplomatic service proved to be a model of excellence. The French language became accepted as the common tongue among diplomats. French dominance of European affairs was cultural as well as political.

The purpose of this chapter is to examine the theory and practice of absolute rule, especially as it was experienced in England, and as applied quite differently in France under Louis XIV. Is absolute monarchy a natural form of government, in keeping with the human desire to follow, and to be taken care of? Or do you resist this idea? To what extent is absolutism, whether justified by God or by force of arms, different from tyranny? Is a competent, even enlightened despot more attractive than divisive democracy? Charles I, Oliver Cromwell, and Louis XIV were all assertive rulers who struggled to define and maintain their dominant positions. Indeed, Louis sought glory in foreign wars and domestic stability under the motto "one King, one law, one faith." The formula is simplistic, yet the policy was effective. To his admirers, Louis represented the quintessential monarch. Yet, the Sun King was certainly not without his critics. And Oliver Cromwell, in the fluid political environment of seventeenth-century England, can be seen variously as the "caretaker of democracy," as well as the "scourge of freedom." Each would have you believe that his actions were in accordance with the preference of his particular political community and required by the necessities of state. But voices of dissent must also be heard for a balanced assessment of absolutism.

THE THEORY OF ABSOLUTE MONARCHY
The English Model

"The Mortal God": Leviathan (1651)
THOMAS HOBBES

Thomas Hobbes was one of the great political philosophers of the seventeenth century. His major work, entitled Leviathan, *was published in 1651 and reflects the insecurity and fear of the English Revolution that had resulted in civil war (1642–1646) and had just seen the decapitation of a sovereign monarch in 1649. Hobbes himself, because of his aristocratic associations, had been forced to flee England. Not surprisingly,* Leviathan *is a treatise that advocates political absolutism. Its theme is power, and it justifies absolute rule as necessary in order to subdue man's violent nature and promote a reasonable existence. For Hobbes, the authority of the absolute monarch did not lie in hereditary right or in divine sanction, but only in his ability to achieve power and maintain it. In this sense, Hobbes borrowed much from the Renaissance political philosopher Niccolò Machiavelli. But Hobbes went much further by providing an integrated social and political philosophy of government.*

Nature has made men so equal, in the faculties of the body and mind; as that though there be found one man sometimes manifestly stronger in body, or of quicker mind than another; yet when all is reckoned together, the differences between man and man, is not so considerable. . . . For as to the strength of body, the weakest has strength enough to kill the strongest, either by secret machination, or by confederacy with others, that are in the same danger with himself. And as to the faculties of the mind . . . I find yet a greater equality among men, than that of strength. . . . Such is the nature of men, that howsoever they may acknowledge many others to be more witty, or more eloquent, or more learned; yet they will hardly believe there are many so wise as themselves; for they see their own wit at hand, and other men's at a distance. . . .

From this equality of ability, arises equality of hope in the attaining of our ends. And therefore if any two men desire the same thing, which nevertheless they cannot both enjoy, they become enemies; and in the way to their end, which is principally their own conservation . . . endeavour to destroy, or subdue one another. And from hence it comes to pass, that . . . an invader has no more to fear than another man's single power; if one plant, sow, build, and possess a convenient seat, others may probably be expected to come prepared with forces

"The Mortal God: Leviathan" is from W. Molesworth, ed., *The English Works of Thomas Hobbes*, vol. 3 (London: John Bohn, 1839), from chapters 13 and 17, pp. 110–113, 153, 157–158. Text modernized by the editor.

Von est potestas Super Terram quæ Comparetur ei Iob. 41. 24.

This illustration from the title page to *Leviathan* captures the essence of Thomas Hobbes's philosophy: The ruler is embodied by individuals who consent to his dominance for the general welfare. All look to him and in the process lose their individual authority, but gain stability and security. The Latin quotation reads, "Upon the earth, there is not his like." (*Bettmann*)

united, to dispossess, and deprive him, not only of the fruit of his labour, but also of his life, or liberty. And the invader again is in the like danger of another. . . . [Thus], men have no pleasure, but on the contrary a great deal of grief, in keeping company, where there is no power able to over-awe them all. . . .

So that in the nature of man, we find three principal causes of quarrel. First, competition; secondly, insecurity; thirdly, glory.

The first, makes men invade for gain; the second, for safety; and the third, for reputation. The first use violence, to make themselves master of other men's persons, wives, children, and cattle; the second, to defend them; the third, for trifles, as a word, a smile, a different opinion, and any other sign of undervalue, either direct in their persons, or by reflection in their kindred, their friends, their nation, their profession, or their name.

[Therefore, it is clear] that during the time men live without a common power to keep them all in awe, they are in that condition which is called war; and such a war is of every man, against every man. . . . In such condition, there is no place for industry; because the fruit thereof is uncertain: and consequently no culture of the earth; no navigation, nor use of the commodities that may be imported by sea; no commodious building; no instruments of moving, and removing, such things as require much force; no knowledge of the face of the earth; no account of time; no arts; no letters; no society; and which is worst of all, continual fear, and danger of violent death; and the life of man, solitary, poor, nasty, brutish, and short. . . .

The final cause, end, or design of men, who naturally love liberty, and dominion over others, [is] the introduction of that restraint upon themselves, [by] which we see them live in commonwealths. . . . The only way to erect such a common power, as may be able to defend them from the invasion of foreigners, and the injuries of one another, and thereby to secure them in such sort, as that by their own industry, and by the fruits of the earth, they may nourish themselves and live contentedly; is, to confer all their power and strength upon one man, or upon one assembly of men, that may reduce all their wills, by plurality of voices, unto one will. . . . [All men shall] submit their wills . . . to his will, and their judgments, to his judgment. This is more than consent, or concord; it is a real unity of them all, in one and the same person, made by covenant of every man with every man, in such manner, as if every man should say to every man, I authorize and give up my right of governing myself, to this man, or to this assembly of men, on this condition, that you give up your right to him, and authorize all his actions in like manner. This done, the multitude so united in one person, is called a COMMON-WEALTH. . . . This is the generation of that great LEVIATHAN, or rather, to speak more reverently, of that mortal god, to which we own under the immortal God, our peace and defence. For by this authority, given him by every particular man in the commonwealth, he hath the use of so much power and strength conferred on him, that by terror thereof, he is enabled to perform the wills of them all, to peace at home, and mutual aid against their enemies abroad. And in him consists the essence of the commonwealth; which, to define it, is one person of whose acts a great multitude, by mutual covenants one with another, have made themselves every one the author, to the end he may use the strength and means of them all, as he shall think expedient, for their peace and common defence.

And . . . this person, is called SOVEREIGN, and said to have sovereign power; and every one besides, his SUBJECT.

The Theory of Divine-Right Monarchy

The stable monarchy that Louis XIV inherited was largely the product of two master political craftsmen, cardinals Richelieu and Mazarin. These statesmen actually ran the day-to-day affairs of the French state under Louis XIII and during Louis XIV's minority, respectively. Under their strict control, the French nobility was subdued and made to realize that the king was absolute in his authority and would tolerate no defiance. It was under their direction, from 1610 to 1661, that absolutism was advanced out of the realm of theory and made a part of the political life of France.

The practical rule of any government must be justified through some doctrine, whether it be a devotion to the principles of democracy or to the more blatant dictum "might makes right." Louis XIV justified his absolutism through the belief that God so willed it. Such a "divine-right" monarch ruled with the authority of God and was beholden to no power except that of God. For his part, the king was accountable to God and was expected to rule with the best interests of his people at heart.

The following selections explain the theoretical basis of Louis's absolutism. The first is by Jean Domat (1624–1696), one of the most renowned jurists and legal scholars of his age. He was responsible for a codification of French law that was sponsored by the king himself. The selection presented is from his treatment of French public law and may be regarded as the official statement of divine-right absolutism. The second excerpt is from a treatise by Jacques Bénigne Bossuet (1627–1704), bishop and tutor to Louis XIV's heir. An eloquent political writer, Bossuet justified divine-right monarchy by basing his support on direct evidence from the Bible. The treatise, entitled Politics Drawn from the Very Words of Scripture, *was directed specifically at Louis's son and successor, the Dauphin.*

The Ideal Absolute State (1697)
JEAN DOMAT

All men being equal by nature because of the humanity that is their essence, nature does not cause some to be inferior to others. But in this natural equality, they are separated by other principles that render their conditions unequal and give rise to relationships and dependencies that determine their varying duties toward others and render government necessary. . . .

The first distinction that subjects some persons to others is that which birth introduces between parents and children. . . . The second distinction among persons is that which requires different employments in society and unites all in the body of which each is a member. . . . And it is these varying occupations and dependencies that create the ties that form society among men, as those of its members form a body. This renders it necessary that a head coerce and rule the body of society and maintain order among those who should give the public the benefit of the different contributions that their stations require of them. . . .

Since government is necessary for the common good and God himself established it, it follows that those who are its subjects must be submissive and obedient. For otherwise they would resist God, and the government which should be the source of the peace and unity that make possible the public good would suffer from dissension and trouble that would destroy it. . . .

As obedience is necessary to preserve the order and peace that unite the head and members of the body of the state, it is the universal obligation of all

"The Ideal Absolute State" is from William F. Church, ed. and trans., *The Impact of Absolutism in France: National Experience under Richelieu, Mazarin and Louis XIV* (New York: John Wiley & Sons, 1969), pp. 377–381. Copyright © 1969 John Wiley & Sons, Inc. Reprinted by permission of John Wiley & Sons, Inc.

subjects in all cases to obey the ruler's orders without assuming the liberty of judging them. For otherwise each man would be master because of his right to examine what might be just or unjust, and this liberty would favor sedition. Thus every man owes obedience even to unjust laws and orders, provided that he may execute and obey them without injustice. And the only exception that may exempt him from this obligation is limited to cases in which he may not obey without violating divine law. . . .

According to these principles, which are the natural foundations of the authority of those who govern, their power should have two essential attributes: first, to cause justice to rule without exception and, second, to be as absolute as the rule of justice, that is, as absolute as the rule of God Himself who is justice, rules according to its principles, and desires rulers to do likewise. . . .

Since the power of princes comes to them from God and is placed in their hands as an instrument of his providence and his guidance of the states that He commits to their rule, it is clear that princes should use their power in proportion to the objectives that providence and divine guidance seek . . . and that power is confided to them to this end. This is without doubt the foundation and first principle of all the duties of sovereigns that consist of causing God Himself to rule, that is, regulating all things according to His will, which is nothing more than justice. The rule of justice should be the glory of the rule of princes. . . .

The power of sovereigns includes the authority to exercise the functions of government and to use the force that is necessary to their ministry. For authority without force would be despised and almost useless, while force without legitimate authority would be mere tyranny. . . .

There are two uses of sovereign power that are necessary to the public tranquillity. One consists of constraining the subjects to obey and repressing violence and injustice, the other of defending the state against the aggressions of its enemies. Power should be accompanied by the force that is required for these two functions.

The use of force for the maintenance of public tranquillity within the state includes all that is required to protect the sovereign himself from rebellions that would be frequent if authority and force were not united, and all that is required to keep order among the subjects, repress violence against individuals and the general public, execute the orders of the sovereign, and effect all that is required for the administration of justice. Since the use of force and the occasions that require it are never-ending, the government of the sovereign must maintain the force that is needed for the rule of justice. This requires officials and ministers in various functions and the use of arms whenever necessary. . . .

One should include among the rights that the law gives the sovereign that of acquiring all the evidences of grandeur and majesty that are needed to bring renown to the authority and dignity of such great power and to instill awe in the minds of the subjects. For although the latter should view royal power as from God and submit to it regardless of tangible indications of grandeur, God accompanies his own power with a visible majesty that extends over land and sea. . . . When He wishes to exercise his August power as lawgiver, He proclaims his laws with prodigies that inspire reverence and unspeakable terror. He is therefore willing that sovereigns enhance the dignity of their power . . . in such manner as to win the respect of the people. . . .

The general duties . . . of those who have sovereign authority include all that concern the administration of justice, the general polity of the state, public order, tranquillity of the subjects, security of families, attention to all that may contribute to the general good, the choice of skillful ministers who love justice and truth . . . discrimination between justice and clemency whenever justice might suffer from relaxation of its rigor, wise distribution of benefits, rewards, exemptions, privileges and other concessions, wise administration of the public funds, prudence regarding foreigners, and all that may render government agreeable to the good, terrible to the wicked, and entirely worthy of the divine function of ruling men by wielding power that comes only from God and is a participation in his own.

As the final duty of the sovereign, one may add the following which stems from the administration of justice and includes all others. Although his power seems to place him above the law, since no man has the right to call him to account for his conduct, he should observe the laws that concern himself not only because he should be an example to his subjects and render their duty pleasant but because he is not dispensed from his own duty by his sovereign power. On the contrary, his rank obliges him to subordinate his personal interests to the general good of the state, which it is his glory to regard as his own.

Politics and Scripture (1679)

JACQUES BÉNIGNE BOSSUET

Monarchical government is the best form: If it is the most natural, it is therefore the most enduring, and in consequence the strongest form of government.

It is also the best defense against division, which is the deadliest disease of states, and the most certain cause of their downfall. "Every kingdom divided against itself is brought to desolation; and every city or house divided against itself shall not stand." . . . [Matt. 12:25]

The purpose of founding states is unity, and there is no greater unity than being under one ruler. There is also no greater strength, for all [the wills] occur. . . .

Kings should respect their powers and only employ them for the general good: Since their power comes from above, as has been stated, they should not believe that they are masters of it and may use it just as they please; they should exercise it with fear and restraint, as a thing conferred on them by God, for which they are answerable to Him. "Hear therefore, O ye Kings, and understand; learn, ye that be judges of the ends of the earth. Give ear, ye that rule the people, and glory in the multitude of nations. For power is given you of the

"Politics and Scripture" is reprinted with permission of The Free Press, a Division of Simon & Schuster, from *The Seventeenth Century*, edited by Andrew Lossky, section Bossuet, translated by Geoffrey W. Symcox, pp. 221–222, 224–225, 227, 229, 233–234, 250. Copyright © 1967 by The Free Press.

Lord, and sovereignty from the Highest, who shall try your works and search out your counsels. Because, being ministers of His kingdom, ye have not judged aright, not kept the law, nor walked after the counsel of God. Horribly and speedily shall He come upon you: for a sharp judgment shall be to them that are in high places. . . . " [Wis. 6]

Kings should therefore tremble to exercise the power which God has given to them, and remember how terrible a sacrilege it is to abuse the power which comes from God.

We have seen kings seated on the throne of the Lord, holding in their hand the sword which He has committed to their charge. What blasphemy and presumption it is for an unjust ruler to occupy the throne of God and give judgments contrary to His law, to wield the sword which He has placed in their hands to oppress and destroy His children!

There is no higher judgment than that of the prince: Kings are gods, and partake in some measure of the independence of God: "I have said, Ye are gods; and all of you are children of the most High." [Ps. 82:6]

From this we conclude that he who refuses obedience to the prince is not to be referred to another judgment, but condemned to death without appeal, as an enemy of the public peace and of human society. . . .

The prince can correct himself, when he knows that he has erred; but against his authority there can be no redress save in that authority itself.

Kings are not therefore above the law: Kings are therefore, as others, subject to the equity of the laws, both because they are bound to act justly, and because they owe it to the people to set an example of fairness. But they are not liable to the penalties of the law: or, in the language of theology, princes are subject to the laws in their directive, but not in their coercive function.

Definition of majesty: Nothing is more majestic than all-embracing goodness: and there is no greater debasement of majesty than misery brought upon subjects by the prince. . . .

God is the essence of holiness, goodness, power, reason. In these consists the divine majesty. In their reflection consists the majesty of the prince.

So great is this majesty that its source cannot be found to reside in the prince: it is borrowed from God, who entrusts it to the prince for the good of his people, to which end it is well that it be restrained by a higher power. . . .

O kings, be bold therefore in the exercise of your power; for it is divine and beneficial to the human race; but wield it with humility. It is conferred on you from without. It leaves you in the end weak and mortal, it leaves you still sinners: and it lays upon you a heavier charge to render to God.

On arbitrary government which is not found among us in well-ordered states: It is one thing for a government to be absolute, and quite another for it to be arbitrary. It is absolute in that it is not liable to constraint, there being no other power capable of coercing the sovereign, who is in this sense independent of all human authority. But it does not follow from this that the government is arbitrary, for besides the fact that all is subject to the judgment of God (which is also true of those governments we have just called arbitrary), there are also [fundamental] laws, in such empires, so that whatever is done contrary to them is null in a legal sense; moreover, there is always an opportunity for redress, either at other times or in other conditions. Thus each man remains the legitimate owner of his property. . . .

This is what is termed legitimate government, by its very nature the opposite of arbitrary government.

The Practice of Absolute Rule

Letters to His Heirs: "Allow Good Sense to Act"

KING LOUIS XIV

In this selection, drawn from Louis's memoirs, the king himself gives practical advice to his heirs concerning the demands and duties of absolute monarchy.

Two things without doubt were absolutely necessary: very hard work on my part, and a wise choice of persons capable of seconding it.

As for work, it may be, my son, that you will begin to read these Memoirs at an age when one is far more in the habit of dreading than loving it, only too happy to have escaped subjection to tutors and to have your hours regulated no longer, nor lengthy and prescribed study laid down for you.

On this heading I will not warn you solely that it is none the less toil *by which* one reigns, and *for which* one reigns, and that the conditions of royalty, which may seem to you sometimes hard and vexatious in so lofty a position, would appear pleasant and easy if there was any doubt of your reaching it.

There is something more, my son, and I hope that your own experience will never teach it to you: nothing could be more laborious to you than a great amount of idleness if you were to have the misfortune to fall into it through beginning by being disgusted with public affairs, then with pleasure, then with idleness itself, seeking everywhere fruitlessly for what can never be found, that is to say, the sweetness of repose and leisure without having the preceding fatigue and occupation.

I laid a rule on myself to work regularly twice every day, and for two or three hours each time with different persons, without counting the hours which I passed privately and alone, nor the time which I was able to give on particular occasions to any special affairs that might arise. There was no moment when I did not permit people to talk to me about them, provided that they were urgent; with the exception of foreign ministers who sometimes find too favourable moments in the familiarity allowed to them, either to obtain or to discover something, and whom one should not hear without being previously prepared.

"Letters to His Heirs" is from Jean Longnon, ed., *A King's Lessons in Statecraft: Louis XIV*, trans. H. Wilson (London: T. Fisher Unwin Ltd., 1924), pp. 48–53, 149.

Louis XIV, the Sun King (Bernini, Gian Lorenzo, Roman (1598–1680). Louis XIV. Bronze, 33⅛ × 39⅜ × 17 (0.842 × 1.00 × 0.432). Samuel H. Kress Collection 1943. (*National Gallery of Art, Washington*)

I cannot tell you what fruit I gathered immediately I had taken this resolution. I felt myself, as it were, uplifted in thought and courage; I found myself quite another man, and with joy reproached myself for having been too long unaware of it. This first timidity, which a little self-judgment always produces and which at the beginning gave me pain, especially on occasions when I had to speak in public, disappeared in less than no time. The only thing I felt then was that I was King, and born to be one. I experienced next a delicious feeling, hard to express, and which you will not know yourself except by tasting it as I have done. For you must not imagine, my son, that the affairs of State are like some obscure and thorny path of learning which may possibly have already wearied you, wherein the mind strives to raise itself with effort above its purview, more often to arrive at no conclusion, and whose utility or apparent utility is repugnant to us as much as its difficulty. The function of Kings consists principally in allowing good sense to act, which always acts naturally and without effort. What we apply ourselves to is sometimes less difficult than what we do only for our amusement. Its usefulness always follows. A King, however skillful and enlightened be his ministers, cannot put his own hand to the work without its effects being seen. Success, which is agreeable in everything, even in the smallest matters, gratifies us in these as well as in the greatest, and there is no satisfaction to equal that of noting every day some progress in glorious and lofty enterprises, and in the happiness of the people which has been planned and thought out by oneself. All that is most necessary to this work is at the same time agreeable, for; in a word, my son, it is to have one's eyes open to the whole earth; to learn each hour the news concerning every province and every nation, the secrets of every court, the mood and the weaknesses of each Prince and of every foreign minister; to be well-informed on an infinite number of matters about which we are supposed to know nothing; to elicit from our subjects what they hide from us with the greatest care; to discover the most remote opinions of our own courtiers and the most hidden interests of those who come to us with quite contrary professions. I do not know of any other pleasure we would not renounce for that, even if curiosity alone gave us the opportunity. . . .

* * *

I gave orders to the four Secretaries of State no longer to sign anything whatsoever without speaking to me; likewise to the Controller, and that he should authorise nothing as regards finance without its being registered in a book which must remain with me, and being noted down in a very abridged abstract form in which at any moment, and at a glance, I could see the state of the funds, and past and future expenditure. . . .

* * *

Regarding the persons whose duty it was to second my labours, I resolved at all costs to have no prime minister; and if you will believe me, my son, and all your successors after you, the name shall be banished for ever from France, for there is nothing more undignified than to see all the administration on one side, and on the other, the mere title of King.

To effect this, it was necessary to divide my confidence and the execution of my orders without giving it entirely to one single person, applying these different people to different spheres according to their diverse talents, which is perhaps the first and greatest gift that Princes can possess.

I also made a resolution on a further matter. With a view the better to unite in myself alone all the authority of a master, although there must be in all affairs a certain amount of detail to which our occupations and also our dignity do not permit us to descend as a rule, I conceived the plan, after I should have made choice of my ministers, of entering sometimes into matters with each one of them, and when they least expected it, in order that they might understand that I could do the same upon other subjects and at any moment. Besides, a knowledge of some small detail acquired only occasionally, and for amusement rather than as a regular rule, is instructive little by little and without fatigue, on a thousand things which are not without their use in general resolutions, and which we ought to know and do ourselves were it possible that a single man could know and do everything.

• • •

I have never failed, when an occasion has presented itself, to impress upon you the great respect we should have for religion, and the deference we should show to its ministers in matters specially connected with their mission, that is to say, with the celebration of the Sacred Mysteries and the preaching of the doctrine of the Gospels. But because people connected with the Church are liable to presume a little too much on the advantages attaching to their profession, and are willing sometimes to make use of them in order to whittle down their most rightful duties, I feel obliged to explain to you certain points on this question which may be of importance.

The first is that Kings are absolute *seigneurs* [Lords], and from their nature have full and free disposal of all property both secular and ecclesiastical, to use it as wise dispensers, that is to say, in accordance with the requirements of their State. . . .

The Revocation of the Edict of Nantes (1685)
KING LOUIS XIV

On October 22, 1685, Louis XIV annulled the Edict of Nantes, which had provided political and religious freedom for the French Protestants, or Huguenots, since 1598. Louis was determined to control a nation that was unified politically under his rule and religiously under his faith; Catholicism was to be the only accepted religion for the French people. The revocation was hailed by Catholics but was not without its critics even at court, as reflected in the opinion of the duke of Saint-Simon, which follows the text of the treaty.

I.   Be it known that [with] . . . our certain knowledge, full power, and royal authority, we have, by this present perpetual and irrevocable edict, suppressed and revoked . . . the edict of our said grandfather, [Henry IV], null

"The Revocation of the Edict of Nantes" is from James H. Robinson, ed., *Readings in European History,* vol. 2 (Boston: Ginn and Company, 1906), pp. 288–291.

and void, together with all concessions . . . in favor of the said persons of the [Reformed religion], . . . and it is our pleasure, that all the temples of those of the said [Reformed religion] situate in our kingdom, countries, territories, and the lordships under our crown, shall be demolished without delay.

II. We forbid our subjects of the [Reformed religion] to meet any more for the exercise of the said religion in any place or private house, under any pretext whatever. . . .

III. We likewise forbid all noblemen . . . to hold such religious exercises in their houses or fiefs, under penalty . . . of imprisonment and confiscation.

IV. We enjoin all ministers of the said [Reformed religion], who do not choose to become converts and to embrace the Catholic, apostolic, and Roman religion, to leave our kingdom and the territories subject to us within a fortnight of the publication of our present edict . . . on pain of being sent to the gallows. . . .

VII. We forbid private schools for the instruction of children of the said [Reformed religion], and in general all things whatever which can be regarded as a concession of any kind in favor of the said religion.

VIII. As for children who may be born of persons of the said [Reformed religion], we desire that from henceforth they be baptized by the parish priests. We enjoin parents to send them to the churches for that purpose, under penalty of five hundred livres fine . . . and thereafter the children shall be brought up in the Catholic, apostolic, and Roman religion, which we expressly enjoin the local magistrates to see done.

X. We repeat our most express prohibition to all our subjects of the said [Reformed religion], together with their wives and children, against leaving our kingdom, lands, and territories subject to us, or transporting their goods and effect therefrom under penalty, as respects the men, of being sent to the gallows, and as respects the women, of imprisonment and confiscation.

XII. As for the rest, liberty is granted to the said persons of the [Reformed religion], pending the time when it shall please God to enlighten them as well as others to remain in the cities and places of our kingdom, lands, and territories subject to us, and there to continue their commerce, and to enjoy their possessions, without being subjected to molestation . . . on condition of not engaging in the exercise of the said religion. . . .

"A Frightful Plot": Results of the Revocation
THE DUKE OF SAINT-SIMON

The revocation of the Edict of Nantes, without the slightest pretext of necessity, and the various proscriptions that followed it, were the fruits of a frightful plot, in which the new spouse was one of the chief conspirators, and which depopulated a quarter of the realm; ruined its commerce; weakened it

"'A Frightful Plot'" is from James H. Robinson, ed., *Readings in European History,* vol. 2 (Boston: Ginn and Company, 1906), pp. 291–293.

in every direction; gave it up for a long time to the public and avowed pillage of the dragoons; authorized torments and punishments by which many innocent people of both sexes were killed by thousands; ruined a numerous class; tore in pieces a world of families; armed relatives against relatives, so as to seize their property and leave them to die in hunger; banished our manufactures to foreign lands; made those lands flourish and overflow at the expense of France, and enabled them to build new cities; gave to the world the spectacle of a prodigious population proscribed without crime, stripped, fugitive, wandering, and seeking shelter far from their country; sent to the galleys nobles, rich old men, people carefully nurtured, weak, and delicate;—and all solely on account of religion. . . .

The king congratulated himself on his power and his piety. He believed himself to have brought back the days of the apostles, and attributed to himself all the honor. The bishops wrote panegyrics of him; the Jesuits made the pulpit resound with his praise. All France was filled with horror and confusion; and yet there was never such triumph and joy, such boundless laudation of the king.

The Sighs of Enslaved France (1690)
PIERRE JURIEU

As a result of the revocation of the Edict of Nantes, the persecution of Huguenots began in earnest. The author of the following memoirs cannot be positively identified, but they are probably from the pen of Pierre Jurieu, a Calvinist pastor who had fled to Holland. Louis endured much criticism from such dissidents in exile. Jurieu's memoirs are among the most provocative because they characterize Louis's absolutism as oppressive and responsible for many of the ills of France.

The oppression of the people is caused primarily by the prodigious number of taxes and excessive levies of money that are everywhere taken in France. Taxes and finance are a science today, and one must be skilled to speak knowledgeably of them, but it suffices for us to relate what we all feel and what the people know of the matter. There are the personal and [land taxes]. There are taxes on salt, wine, merchandise, principal, and revenue. This miserable century has produced a flood of names [of taxes], most of which were unknown to our ancestors or, if some were known, they were not odious because of the moderation with which they were imposed and levied. . . . It does not serve my purpose to acquaint you with the details of these taxes so that you may feel their weight and injustice. It will suffice to enable you to understand the horrible oppression of these taxes by showing (1) the immense

"The Sighs of Enslaved France" is from William F. Church, ed. and trans., *The Impact of Absolutism in France: National Experience under Richelieu, Mazarin and Louis XIV* (New York: John Wiley & Sons, 1969), pp. 102–105. Copyright © 1969 John Wiley & Sons, Inc. Reprinted by permission of John Wiley & Sons, Inc.

sums that are collected, (2) the violence and abuses that are committed in levying them, (3) the bad use that is made of them, and (4) the misery to which the people are reduced.

First, dear unfortunate compatriots, you should realize that the taxes that are taken from you comprise a sum perhaps greater than that which all the other princes of Europe together draw from their states. One thing is certain, that France pays two hundred million in taxes of which about three-fourths go into the coffers of the king and the rest to expenses of collection, tax-farmers, officials, keepers, receivers, the profits of financiers, and new fortunes that are created in almost a single day. For the collection of the salt tax alone, there is a great army of officers and constables. . . .

If tyranny is clear and evident in the immense sums that are levied in France, it is not less so in the manner of collecting them. Kings were established by the people to preserve their persons, lives, liberty, and properties. But the government of France has risen to such excessive tyranny that the prince today regards everything as belonging to him alone. He imposes taxes at will without consulting the people, the nobles, the Estates, or the Parlements. I shall tell you something that is true and that thousands know but most Frenchmen do not. During Colbert's ministry [supervisor of the royal finances] it was discussed whether the king should take immediate possession of all real and personal property in France and reduce it to royal domain, to be used and assigned to whomever the court judged appropriate without regard for former possession, heredity, or other rights. . . .

How much abuse and violence is committed in the collection of taxes? The meanest agent is a sacred person who has absolute power over gentlemen, the judiciary, and all the people. A single blow is capable of ruining the most powerful subject. They confiscate houses, furnishings, cattle, money, grain, wine, and everything in sight. The prisons are full of wretches who are responsible for sums that they impose upon other wretches who cannot pay what is demanded of them. Is there anything more harsh and cruel than the salt tax? They make you buy for ten or twelve sous per pound something that nature, the sun, and the sea provide for nothing and may be had for two farthings. Under pretext of exercising this royal right, the realm is flooded with a great army of scoundrels called constables of the *gabelle* [salt tax] who enter houses, penetrate the most secret places with impunity, and do not fail to find unauthorized salt wherever they think there is money. They condemn wretches to pay huge fines, cause them to rot in prison, and ruin families. They force salt upon people everywhere and give each family more than three times as much as they can consume. In the provinces by the sea, they will not permit a poor peasant to bring home salt water; they break jugs, beat people, and imprison them. In a word, every abuse is committed in levying this and other taxes which is done with horrible expense, seizures, imprisonments, and legal cases before the collectors and courts with costs far above the sums involved. . . .

This is how all of France is reduced to the greatest poverty. In earlier reigns, that is, during the ministries of Cardinal Richelieu and Cardinal

Mazarin, France was already burdened with heavy taxes. But the manner of collecting them, although not entirely just, nevertheless exhausted the realm much less than the way in which they are collected today. . . . The government of today has changed all of this. M. de Colbert made a plan to reform the finances and applied it to the letter. But what was this reformation? It was not the diminution of taxes in order to relieve the people. . . . He increased the king's revenue by one half. . . .

After this, if we examine the use that is made of these immense sums that are collected with such abuses and extortion, we shall find all the characteristics of oppression and tyranny. It sometimes happens that princes and sovereigns exact levies that appear excessive and greatly inconvenience individuals, but are required by what are called the needs and necessities of the state. In France there is no such thing. There are neither needs nor state. As for the state, earlier it entered into everything; one spoke only of the interests of the state, the needs of the state, the preservation of the state, and the service of the state. To speak this way today would literally be a crime of lese majesty [treason]. The king has taken the place of the state. It is the service of the king, the interest of the king, the preservation of the provinces and wealth of the king. Therefore the king is all and the state nothing. And these are no mere figures of speech but realities. At the French court, no interest is considered but the personal interest of the king, that is, his grandeur and glory. He is the idol to which are sacrificed princes, great men and small, families, provinces, cities, finances and generally everything. Therefore, it is not for the good of the state that these horrible exactions are made, since there is no more state. . . .

This money is used solely to nourish and serve the greatest self-pride and arrogance that ever existed. It is so deep an abyss that it would have swallowed not only the wealth of the whole realm but that of all other states if the king had been able to take possession of it as he attempted to do. The king has caused himself to receive more false flattery than all the pagan demi-gods did with true flattery. Never before was flattery pushed to this point. Never has man loved praise and vainglory to the extent that this prince has sought them. In his court and around himself he supports a multitude of flatterers who constantly seek to outdo each other. He not only permits the erection of statues to himself, on which are inscribed blasphemies in his honor and below which all the nations of the earth are shown in chains; he causes himself to be represented in gold, silver, bronze, copper, marble, silk, in paintings, arches of triumph, and inscriptions. He fills all Paris, all his palaces, and the whole realm with his name and his exploits, as though he far surpasses the Alexanders, the Caesars, and all the heroes of antiquity.

Louis XIV: The Sun King

"Vanity Was His Ruin"

THE DUKE OF SAINT-SIMON

The Duke of Saint-Simon (1675–1755) was a rather indifferent soldier and diplomat, but he was a passionate observer of affairs at Louis's court and has provided us with our most vivid account of the king and his activities. Saint-Simon was typical of the feudal nobility that Louis was trying to control, and thus this account, from his memoirs, was by no means free from prejudice.

Portrait of the King

Louis XIV was made for a brilliant Court. In the midst of other men, his figure, his courage, his grace, his beauty, his grand mien, even the tone of his voice and the majestic and natural charm of all his person, distinguished him till his death as the King Bee, and showed that if he had only been born a simple private gentleman, he would equally have excelled in fetes, pleasures, and gallantry, and would have had the greatest success in love. . . . Vanity, this unmeasured and unreasonable love of admiration, was his ruin. His ministers, his generals, his mistresses, his courtiers, soon perceived his weakness. They praised him with emulation and spoiled him. Praises, or to say the truth, flattery, pleased him to such an extent, that the coarsest was well received, the vilest even better relished. It was the sole means by which you could approach him. Those whom he liked owed his affection for them, to their untiring flatteries. This is what gave his ministers so much authority, and the opportunities they had for adulating him, of attributing everything to him, and of pretending to learn everything from him. Suppleness, meanness, an admiring, dependent, cringing manner—above all, an air of nothingness—were the sole means of pleasing him. . . .

Though his intellect, as I have said, was beneath mediocrity, it was capable of being formed. He loved glory, was fond of order and regularity; was by disposition prudent, moderate, discreet, master of his movements and his tongue. Will it be believed? He was also by disposition good and just! God had sufficiently gifted him to enable him to be a good King; perhaps even a tolerably great King! All the evil came to him from elsewhere. His early education was so neglected that nobody dared approach his apartment. He has often been heard to speak of those times with bitterness, and even to relate that, one evening he was found in the basin of the Palais Royale garden fountain, into which he had fallen! He was scarcely taught how to read or write, and remained so ignorant, that the most familiar historical and other facts

"'Vanity Was His Ruin'" is from Bayle St. John, ed., *The Memoirs of the Duke of Saint-Simon*, vol. 2 (New York: James Pott and Co., 1901), pp. 202–203, 214–219, 226–227, 231–232, 273–276.

were utterly unknown to him! He fell, accordingly, and sometimes even in public, into the grossest absurdities. . . .

Louis XIV took great pains to be well informed of all that passed everywhere; in the public places, in the private homes, in society and familiar intercourse. His spies and tell-tales were infinite. He had them of all species; many who were ignorant that their information reached him; others who knew it; others who wrote to him direct, sending their letters through channels he indicated; and all these letters were seen by him alone, and always before everything else; others who sometimes spoke to him secretly in his cabinet, entering by the back stairs. These unknown means ruined an infinite number of people of all classes, who never could discover the cause; often ruined them very unjustly; for the King, once prejudiced, never altered his opinion, or so rarely, that nothing was more rare. He had, too, another fault, very dangerous for others and often for himself, since it deprived him of good subjects. He had an excellent memory; in this way, that if he saw a man who, twenty years before, perhaps, had in some manner offended him, he did not forget the man, though he might forget the offence. This was enough, however, to exclude the person from all favour. The representations of a minister, of a general, of his confessor even, could not move the King. He would not yield.

The most cruel means by which the King was informed of what was passing—for many years before anybody knew it—was that of opening letters. The promptitude and dexterity with which they were opened passes understanding. He saw extracts from all the letters in which there were passages that the chiefs of the post-office, and then the minister who governed it, thought ought to go before him; entire letters, too, were sent to him, when their contents seemed to justify the sending. Thus the chiefs of the post, nay, the principal clerks were in a position to suppose what they pleased and against whom they pleased. A word of contempt against the King or the government, a joke, a detached phrase, was enough. It is incredible how many people, justly or unjustly, were more or less ruined, always without resource, without trial, and without knowing why. The secret was impenetrable; for nothing ever cost the King less than profound silence and dissimulation. . . .

The King loved air and exercise very much, as long as he could make use of them. He had excelled in dancing, and at tennis and mall. On horseback he was admirable, even at a late age. He liked to see everything done with grace and address. To acquit yourself well or ill before him was a merit or fault. He said that with things not necessary it was best not to meddle, unless they were done well. He was fond of shooting, and there was not a better or more graceful shot than he. . . .

He liked splendour, magnificence, and profusion in everything: you pleased him if you shone through the brilliancy of your houses, your clothes, your table, your equipages. Thus a taste for extravagance and luxury was disseminated through all classes of society; causing infinite harm, and leading to general confusion of rank and to ruin.

The King's Day

At eight o'clock the chief valet de chambre on duty, who alone had slept in the royal chamber, and who had dressed himself, awoke the King. The chief physician, the chief surgeon, and the nurse (as long as she lived), entered at the same time. The latter kissed the King; the others rubbed and often changed his shirt, because he was in the habit of sweating a great deal. At the quarter, the grand chamberlain was called (or, in the absence, the first gentleman of the chamber), and those who had what was called the grandes entrées. The chamberlain (or chief gentleman) drew back the curtains which had been closed again, and presented the holy-water from the vase, at the head of the bed. . . . Then all passed into the cabinet of the council. A very short religious service being over, the King called, they reentered. The same officer gave him his dressing-gown; immediately after, other privileged courtiers entered, and then everybody, in time to find the King putting on his shoes and stockings, for he did almost everything himself and with address and grace. Every other day we saw him shave himself; and he had a little short wig in which he always appeared, even in bed, and on medicine days. He often spoke of the chase, and sometimes said a word to somebody. No toilette table was near him; he had simply a mirror held before him.

As soon as he was dressed, he prayed to God, at the side of his bed, where all the clergy present knelt, the cardinals without cushions, all the laity remaining standing; and the captain of the guards came to the balustrade during the prayer, after which the King passed into his cabinet.

He found there, or was followed by all who had the *entrée*, a very numerous company, for it included everybody in any office. He gave orders to each for the day; thus within a half a quarter of an hour it was known what he meant to do; and then all this crowd left directly. The bastards, a few favorites, and the valets alone were left. It was then a good opportunity for talking with the King; for example, about plans of gardens and buildings; and conversation lasted more or less according to the person engaged in it. . . .

On Sunday, and often on Monday, there was a council of state; on Tuesday a finance council; on Wednesday council of state; on Saturday finance council. Rarely were two held in one day or any on Thursday or Friday. Once or twice a month there was a council of despatches on Monday morning. . . .

The dinner was always *au petit couvert*, that is the King ate by himself in his chamber upon a square table in front of the middle window. It was more or less abundant, for he ordered in the morning whether it was to be "a little," or "very little" service. But even at this last, there were always many dishes, and three courses without counting the fruit.

The King's Diet

As during the last year of his life the King became more and more costive, Fagon [the court physician] made him eat at the commencement of his repasts many iced fruits, that is to say, mulberries, melons, and figs rotten from ripeness; and at his dessert many other fruits, finishing with a surprising quantity of sweetmeats. All the year round he ate at supper a prodigious quantity of salad. His soups, several of which he partook of morning and evening, were full of gravy, and were of exceeding strength, and everything that was served to him was full of spice, to double the usual extent, and very strong also. . . .

This summer he redoubled his regime of fruits and drinks. At last the former clogged his stomach, taken after soup, weakened the digestive organs and took away his appetite, which until then had never failed him all his life, though however late dinner might be delayed he never was hungry or wanted to eat. But after the first spoonfuls of soup, his appetite came, as I have several times heard him say, and he ate so prodigiously and so solidly morning and evening that no one could get accustomed to see it. So much water and so much fruit unconnected by anything spirituous, turned his blood into gangrene; while those forced night sweats diminished its strength and impoverished it; and thus his death was caused, as was seen by the opening of his body. The organs were found in such good and healthy condition that there is reason to believe he would have lived beyond his hundredth year. His stomach above all astonished, and also his bowels by their volume and extent, double that of the ordinary, whence it came that he was such a great yet uniform eater.

The King's Death

Friday, August the 30th, was a bad day preceded by a bad night. The King continually lost his reason. About five o'clock in the evening Madame de Maintenon left him, gave away her furniture to the domestics, and went to Saint-Cyr never to leave it.

On Saturday, the 31st of August, everything went from bad to worse. The gangrene had reached the knee and all the thigh. Towards eleven o'clock at night the King was found to be so ill that the prayers for the dying were said. This restored him to himself. He repeated the prayers in a voice so strong that it rose above all the other voices. At the end he recognised Cardinal de Rohan, and said to him, "These are the last favours of the Church." This was the last man to whom he spoke. He repeated several times, *Nunc et in hora mortis* ["And now in the hour of death"], then said, "Oh, my God, come to my aid: hasten to succour me."

These were his last words. All the night he was without consciousness and in a long agony, which finished on Sunday, the 1st September, 1715, at a quarter past eight in the morning, three days before he had accomplished his seventy-seventh year, and in the seventy-second of his reign. He had survived all his sons and grandsons, except the King of Spain. Europe never saw so long a reign or France a King so old.

The Palace of Versailles:
"A Celebration of Greatness"
JEAN COLBERT

In 1661, Louis XIV began constructing his famous palace at Versailles, about twenty miles from Paris. By 1668, two shifts of laborers were working constantly, and by 1682, enough of the palace had been completed to warrant Louis's move from Paris. Amid the construction that continued until 1710, Louis lived, along with most of the French aristocracy, entertaining lavishly and administering the affairs of state.

The expense of the palace was indeed a concern, especially to Jean Colbert, who supervised the royal finances. Still, in 1665, Colbert did not doubt that such a venture was an essential component of Louis's monarchy. In the second selection, Louis himself reveals the necessity of a palace on such a scale as Versailles.

If Your Majesty desires to discover where in Versailles are the more than 500,000 ecus spent there in two years, he will have great difficulty in finding them. Will he also deign to reflect that the Accounts of the Royal Buildings will always record the evidence that, during the time he has lavished such vast sums on this mansion, he has neglected the Louvre, which is assuredly the most superb palace in the world and the one worthiest of Your Majesty's greatness. . . . And God forbid that those many occasions which may impel him to go to war, and thus deprive him of the financial means to complete this superb building, should give him lasting occasion for regret at having lost the time and opportunity.

Your Majesty knows that, apart from glorious actions of war, nothing celebrates so advantageously the greatness and genius of princes than buildings, and all posterity measures them by the yardstick of these superb edifices which they have erected during their life. O what pity were the greatest and most virtuous of kings, of that real virtue which makes the greatest princes, to be measured by the scale of Versailles!

Visible Majesty
KING LOUIS XIV

Those who imagine that these are merely matters of ceremony are gravely mistaken. The peoples over whom we reign, being able to apprehend the basic reality of things, usually derive their opinion from that they can see with their eyes.

"The Palace of Versailles" is from Gilette Ziegler, ed., *The Court of Versailles in the Reign of Louis XIV,* trans. Simon Watson Taylor (London: George Allen and Unwin, Ltd., 1966), p. 26. Reprinted by permission of the publisher.

"Visible Majesty" is from Gilette Ziegler, ed., *The Court of Versailles in the Reign of Louis XIV,* trans. Simon Watson Taylor (London: George Allen and Unwin, Ltd., 1966), p. 26. Reprinted by permission of the publisher.

A full view of Versailles as it appeared after its expansion from a hunting lodge to the royal residence and seat of government (ca. 1682). A center of culture, the palace also served as propaganda, being symbolic of the absolute authority of the Sun King. (*The New York Public Library Picture Collection*)

CHRONOLOGY: "I Am the State": The Absolutism of Louis XIV

1558–1603   Reign of Queen Elizabeth of England, last Tudor monarch.

1589–1610   Foundations of centralized monarchy in France established by King Henry IV and his finance minister, the duke of Sully, through royal monopolies.

1610–1643   Reign of Louis XIII of France. The crown is managed by the king's advisor, Cardinal Richelieu, who further secures the foundation of French absolutism by indoctrinating the French with propaganda and spectacle.

1625–1649   Reign of Charles I of England. Confrontation with Parliament over specific power of king to raise funds on his own authority.

1642–1646   English civil war between royal forces led by Charles (Cavaliers) and parliamentary forces (Roundheads) ultimately led by Oliver Cromwell.

1643–1715   Reign of the Sun King, Louis XIV. Construction begins on the royal palace at Versailles in 1661.

1649–1652   Outbreak of the Fronde in France: a series of widespread rebellions by segments of the French nobility and townspeople to stop the drift toward absolute monarchy in France. Young Louis XIV flees until the revolt collapses for lack of organization. Louis XIV convinced never to be a "king of straw" and is confirmed in the rightness of absolute rule.

1649   Execution of Charles I on charges of high treason.

1649–1653   The Commonwealth of England is established "for the good of the people."

1660–1685   Restoration of the English monarchy under the rule of Charles II.

1685   Louis XIV revokes the Edict of Nantes, which had protected the religious freedoms and civil rights of French Protestants since 1598.

1688–1689   Parliament deposes James II and invites Protestant leader William of Orange and his wife, Mary, to rule England jointly in what is termed the Glorious Revolution.

1680–1700   Theory of absolute monarchy in France refined by Jean Domat and Jacques Bénigne Bossuet.

1715   Death of Louis XIV. Succeeded by his great-grandson, who ruled ineffectively from 1715 to 1774 as Louis XV.

STUDY QUESTIONS

1. Discuss the ideas of Thomas Hobbes contained in the excerpt entitled *Leviathan*. What is his view of human nature, and how does he justify absolute monarchy? Be specific in your assessment. How does Hobbes's *Leviathan* reflect the uncertainty of the time?

2. Louis XIV was a divine-right monarch. What does this mean, and how did Louis use religion to strengthen his political position in the state? How compelling in support of absolutism are the arguments of Jean Domat on "The Ideal Absolute State" and Jacques Bénigne Bossuet on "Politics and Scripture"? What are the responsibilities of the king and the political advantages of absolute rule?

3. What is the difference between tyranny and the absolutism of Louis XIV's monarchy? What were the advantages and disadvantages of absolute rule for the different classes of French society? Who profited the most?

4. What was the Edict of Nantes? Why was it invoked in 1598 and why did Louis XIV revoke it? Was this a wise move politically? Are you persuaded by the Duke of Saint-Simon's criticism? If you accept his criticism as valid, then how would you characterize the absolute rule of Louis XIV? Was he a tyrant—or a wise monarch?

5. Was Louis XIV a responsible monarch? From the accounts in his own memoirs and those of the Duke of Saint-Simon, do you think that Louis worked hard at his job? How did he view his duties as king? Do the criticisms of Pierre Jurieu in "The Sighs of Enslaved France" seem valid to you? Why should a historian be somewhat careful in the judgments drawn from this evidence?

6. Look closely at the picture of Louis's palace at Versailles at the beginning of the section. In what ways did this structure reflect the character of Louis's monarchy? According to the comments contained about Versailles, was the palace an effective propaganda medium? Why?

7. To what extent do you think absolute rule is a "natural" form of government, generally acceptable to most people, especially if it is benign or even enlightened so that the best interests of citizens are promoted? Do people want a government that provides for their security and happiness but prevents the participation and personal responsibility that a democracy demands? What are your own opinions on the subject?

2

"Dare to Know!": The Revolution of the Mind in the Seventeenth and Eighteenth Centuries

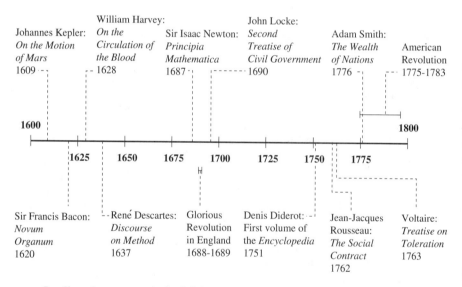

Johannes Kepler:
On the Motion of Mars
1609

William Harvey:
On the Circulation of the Blood
1628

Sir Isaac Newton:
Principia Mathematica
1687

John Locke:
Second Treatise of Civil Government
1690

Adam Smith:
The Wealth of Nations
1776

American Revolution
1775-1783

1600

1800

1625   1650   1675   1700   1725   1750   1775

Sir Francis Bacon:
Novum Organum
1620

René Descartes:
Discourse on Method
1637

Glorious Revolution in England
1688-1689

Denis Diderot:
First volume of the *Encyclopedia*
1751

Jean-Jacques Rousseau:
The Social Contract
1762

Voltaire:
Treatise on Toleration
1763

Intellect does not attain its full force unless it attacks power.

—Madame de Staël

Reason is the greatest enemy that faith has. It never comes to the aid of spiritual things, but ... struggles against the divine Word, treating with contempt all that emanates from God.

—Martin Luther

I respect faith, but doubt is what gets you an education.

—Wilson Mizner

He who desires to have understanding must be free in mind.

—Alcinous

All nature and nature's law lay hid in night / God said let Newton be and all was light.

—Alexander Pope

The real and legitimate goal of the sciences, is the endowment of human life with new inventions and riches.

—Francis Bacon

Science has done more for the development of western civilization in one hundred years than Christianity has done in eighteen hundred years.

—John Burroughs

CHAPTER THEMES

- *Beliefs and Spirituality:*   The advancements of Scientific Revolution were the result of a spirit of rational inquiry and confidence in the ability of human beings to understand and improve their world. Do the demands of science necessarily preclude the validity of religion? Can science and religion coexist with mutual respect and even admiration?

- *Women in History:*   How important were the contributions of women to the enlightened thought of the eighteenth century? What were salons, and how did they allow women to compete with men on an equal intellectual footing?

- *Historical Change and Transition:*   Why do certain eras of history seem to explode with creativity and intellectual risk while others stagnate? What do the Scientific Revolution and the Enlightenment have in common with the spirit of fifth-century Athens or the Renaissance era? Do we live in an age of intellectual enlightenment or stagnation?

- *The Big Picture:*   Why must one "dare to know"? Does intellectual inquiry require risk and even courage, or are these matters confined to political and military concerns? Is human progress more dependent on the mind than on the sword?

When the great eighteenth-century thinker Immanuel Kant challenged his contemporaries to "Dare to Know!" he was also voicing a classic intellectual defiance of authority. The origin of the phrase can be traced to the Roman poet Horace, but nearly every era has possessed those individuals who are not satisfied with maintaining adherence to the "established doctrine" as defined by those in positions of authority. One must be bold in seeking knowledge, for there are many impediments to its attainment. Ideas have power. If successfully transmitted and accepted by the general population, they threaten the status quo, whatever its nature. This makes the pursuit of ideas a risky business that requires an intangible confidence, a willingness to gamble on the potential of an uncertain future. Curiosity and determination, therefore, coupled with a measure of defiance, are the essential components of progress.

Just as the individual in our modern society struggles to define and seek personal knowledge in order to make rational judgments independent of advertisers, politicians, and television preachers, so too did individuals in the seventeenth and eighteenth centuries struggle against similar constraints imposed on them by secular and spiritual institutions. Despite the condemnation of the Catholic Church and the intimidation of the Inquisition, people gradually changed the way they viewed the world around them. The long religious wars between Catholics and Protestants had ended by 1648, leaving people disillusioned and repulsed. Their belief had been shaken by the mindless fighting of the Thirty Years' War. Instead, many invested their confidence in a new association between Protestantism and monarchy. The compatibility between the Calvinists and commerce allowed the developing middle class to seek godly profit and at the same time build the economic foundations of a strong, centralized state. Contemporary with these political and economic developments was the rising influence of philosophers and writers whose primary concern lay within the realm of science and letters. With the aid of hindsight that only history can afford, we can now ascertain that most of the intellectual, political, economic, and social characteristics associated with the modern world came into being during the seventeenth and eighteenth centuries.

The human experience in Europe was indeed transformed. In the *salons* of Paris, in the coffee houses of London, the talk was of machines and the heavens, of natural laws and moral responsibility, of education and the purpose of religion. The ideals of reform captured the imagination and directed the energy of many writers, who exported great advancements in science and political thought throughout the world.

In the interest of understanding more fully the broad dimensions of this complex period, the chapter has been divided into two sections: the Scientific Revolution of the sixteenth and seventeenth centuries, and the Enlightenment of the eighteenth century. Although the study of ideas does not so easily lend itself to chronological arrangement as does political history, it is still possible to see intellectual development over time. The Enlightenment movement drew confidence from the scientific worldview that had developed as a result of the efforts and sacrifices of the pioneers of modern science.

Juxtaposed with the chaos of religious warfare and its attendant human destruction during the seventeenth century was an intellectual attempt to foster progress in the realm of science. Sweeping changes took place in humanity's conception of the universe and of one's place in it. Although the movement has been called the Scientific Revolution, the changes were not rapid, nor did they involve large numbers of people. On the contrary, the revolution evolved slowly, through experimentation, often in makeshift laboratories. Yet great thinkers such as Sir Isaac Newton, René Descartes, and Francis Bacon attempted to discover the physical and natural laws of the universe and to organize and criticize that diverse body of knowledge. Thus did Descartes champion the principles of deduction and invent analytical geometry; so too did Newton seek to explain motion in the universe through observation, experimentation, and induction. Others, like John Locke, even endeavored to explain human relationships through such rational thought.

The eighteenth century has been called the Age of Reason, or the Enlightenment. The writers and thinkers of this time, following precedents set in the preceding century, were convinced that natural laws governed the universe and that a human, essentially a rational creature, could further discover and apply those laws in the world. These intellectuals, called *philosophes*, examined and challenged the economic theories and political and religious assumptions of the day. The *philosophes* were diverse in their thought and often contended among themselves, but they were united by the conviction that one had natural rights (defined by political philosopher John Locke as life, liberty, and property) and that one must control one's own destiny for the sole purpose of a better life on earth. Thus the political divine-right absolutism of King Louis XIV (1643–1715), although providing security, could not be tolerated by many philosophes because it curtailed individual liberty. Similarly, the *philosophes* were generally opposed to the accepted economic theory of mercantilism, which sought complete government control of the national economy and especially promoted the establishment of foreign trading monopolies. The production and distribution of goods in colonial markets were therefore regulated for the benefit of the mother country. The theory of capitalism was born as a reaction to this strict economic regulation by the state. Adam Smith, in his treatise *The Wealth of Nations* (1776), argued that such a rigid monopolistic policy restricted individual initiative and the natural pursuit of profit. In spiritual matters as well, the *philosophes* regarded religion, especially Christianity, as fantasy that drew humanity away from the rational world into a realm of hope and belief in a nonexistent life beyond. The spiritual world was not subject to reason or proof and therefore drew scorn from the *philosophes*. Indeed, they contended that organized religion sought to control thought and was therefore anathema to true intellectual freedom.

But the rationalists of the Enlightenment were also adamant that knowledge must have practical purpose and inquiry must yield useful knowledge. Perhaps the best-known and most influential *philosophe* of them all, Voltaire, exclaimed: "What light has burst over Europe within the last few years! It is the light of common sense." Reason was synonymous with common sense. To the intellectuals of the time, anyone who could rid the mind of the chains of thought and social constraints established by the political and religious institutions of the day could possess reason.

Yet there is a certain naïveté in this relationship between reason and common sense that also characterized the *philosophes*. This naïveté appears most clearly in their conception of "progress." They professed a profound faith in the future and some even predicted a united era of peace and prosperity by the dawn of the twenty-first century. When one compares George Orwell's dire predictions in his novel *1984,* the contrast between the cockiness of the Age of Reason and the brutal realities of the twentieth century is staggering. The *philosophes* had none of the fear and distrust of human nature and technology that has been reflected in our experience with poisonous gas and nuclear destruction. For the enlightened thinker, education in the simple laws of nature, technological progress, and increased production could only bring increased happiness. And for the eighteenth century, that was enough. Humankind was breaking its medieval chains, discarding archaic attitudes, and taking the risks requisite of a new era where religion was but a personal choice, and monarchs seemingly embodied Plato's ideal of philosopher-kings. It was therefore reasonable to think that happiness was in the offing.

This chapter introduces some of the most important personalities, ideas, and attitudes of this remarkable period. In so many ways, by "daring to know," the scientists and philosophers of the seventeenth and eighteenth centuries picked up the gauntlet laid down by the thinkers of the Renaissance and provided the intellectual challenge for future generations.

SECTION I:
THE SCIENTIFIC REVOLUTION

The New Scientific Method

Sir Francis Bacon (1561–1626)

Sir Francis Bacon was born in London in 1561. Educated at Cambridge in law and science, he was an Englishman of almost universal accomplishment. He rose quickly as a lawyer during the reign of Queen Elizabeth I and was knighted in 1603 before being named chancellor by King James I in 1618. His career took a tragic turn in 1621 when he was charged with financial corruption, expelled from Parliament, and briefly imprisoned before his death in 1626. Throughout his career as a royal official, he wrote histories, moral essays, and philosophical treatises. But he never lost his interest in scientific studies, and, although not a scientist except in an amateur sense, he has traditionally been regarded as the father of scientific empiricism, the doctrine that all knowledge is derived from sense experience, observation, and experimentation. In books such as The Advancement of Learning *(1605) and* Novum Organum *(1620), he set the tone for a new standard of scientific inquiry and attacked the medieval Scholastic belief that most truth had already been discovered by calling into question the tradi-tional reverence for the authority of the ancient authors. Bacon urged his contem-poraries to have confidence in their own abilities and see change as desirable.*

The following excerpts focus on the goals of Bacon's new methods of scientific inquiry and offer some of his thoughts on the relationship between religion and science.

"I Have Made a Beginning of the Work": *Novum Organum* (1620)

SIR FRANCIS BACON

For my own part at least, in obedience to the everlasting love of truth, I have committed myself to the uncertainties and difficulties and solitudes of the ways, and relying on the divine assistance have upheld my mind both against the shocks and embattled ranks of opinion, and against my own private and inward hesitations and scruples, and against the fogs and clouds of nature, and the phantoms flitting about on every side; in the hope of providing at last for the present and future generations guidance more faithful and secure. Wherein if I have made any progress, the way has been opened to me by no other means than the true and legitimate humiliation of the human spirit. For all those who before me have applied themselves to the invention of arts have but cast a glance or two upon facts and examples and experience, and straightway proceeded . . . to invoke their own spirits to give them oracles. I on the contrary, dwelling purely and constantly among the facts of nature, withdraw my intellect from them no further than may suffice to let the im-ages and rays of natural objects meet in a point, as they do in the sense of vi-sion. . . . And by these means I suppose that I have established for ever a true and lawful marriage between the empirical and the rational faculty, the un-kind and ill-starred divorce and separation of which has thrown into confu-sion all the affairs of the human family. . . . I have sought on all sides dili-gently and faithfully to provide helps for the sense—substitutes to supply its failures, rectifications to correct its errors; and this I endeavour to accom-plish not so much by instruments as by experiments. For the subtlety of ex-periments is far greater than that of the sense itself, even when assisted by ex-quisite instruments; such experiments, I mean, as are skillfully and artificially devised for the express purpose of determining the point in question. To the immediate and proper perception of the sense therefore I do not give much weight; but I contrive that the office of the sense shall be only to judge of the experiment, and that the experiment itself shall judge of the thing.

But I design not only to indicate and mark out the ways, but also to enter them. And therefore the third part of the work embraces the Phenomena of

"'I Have Made a Beginning'" is from J. Spedding *et al.*, *The Works of Francis Bacon* (Boston: Tag-gard and Thompson, 1863), vol. 8, pp. 31–34, 44–47, 53.

the Universe; that is to say, experience of every kind. . . . Those who aspire not to guess and divine, but to discover and know; who propose not to devise mimic and fabulous worlds of their own, but to examine and dissect the nature of this very world itself; must go to facts themselves for everything. . . . This therefore we must have, or the business must be forever abandoned. But up to this day such has been the condition of men in this matter, that it is no wonder if nature will not give herself into their hands. . . .

I have made a beginning of the work—a beginning, as I hope, not unimportant. . . . For the matter in hand is no mere felicity of speculation, but the real business and fortunes of the human race, and all power of operation. For man is but the servant and interpreter of nature: what he does and what he knows is only what he has observed of nature's order in fact or in thought; beyond this he knows nothing and can do nothing. For the chain of causes cannot by any force be loosed or broken, nor can nature be commanded except by being obeyed. And so those twin objects, human Knowledge and human Power, do really meet in one; and it is from ignorance of causes that operation fails.

The Advancement of Learning (1605)
SIR FRANCIS BACON

Lastly, some are weakly afraid lest a deeper search into nature should transgress the permitted limits of sober-mindedness, wrongfully wresting and transferring what is said in Holy Writ against those who pry into sacred mysteries to the hidden things of nature, which are barred by no prohibition. Others, with more subtlety, surmise and reflect that if the secondary causes are unknown, everything can be more readily referred to divine hand and rod—a point in which they think religion greatly concerned; which is, in fact, nothing else but to seek to gratify God with a lie. Others fear from past example that movements and changes in philosophy will end in assaults on religion; and others again appear apprehensive that in the investigation of nature something may be found to subvert, or at least shake, the authority of religion, especially with the unlearned.

But these two last fears seem to me to savor utterly of carnal wisdom; as if men in the recesses and secret thoughts of their hearts doubted and distrusted the strength of religion, and the empire of faith over the senses, and therefore feared that the investigation of truth in nature might be dangerous to them. But if the matter be truly considered, natural philosophy is, after the word of God, at once the surest medicine against superstition and the most approved nourishment for faith; and therefore she is rightly given to religion as her most faithful handmaid, since the one displays the will of God, the other his power.

"The Advancement of Learning" is from James H. Robinson and Charles A. Beard, eds., *Readings in Modern European History*, vol. 1 (Boston: Ginn and Company, 1908), p. 176.

René Descartes (1596–1650)

René Descartes was born in 1596 in western France but lived primarily in Holland for the last twenty years of his life. He attended Jesuit schools and graduated in law from the university in Poitiers. He was not attracted to a legal career, however, and became a soldier in the German wars of the time. It was while he was billeted in a German town that he had an intellectual revelation akin, as he later maintained, to a religious conversion. He had a vision of the great potential for progress, if mathematical method were to be applied to all fields of knowledge. He thus pursued a career devoted to the propagation of a strict method, best exemplified by his invention of analytical geometry. Descartes believed that human beings were endowed by God with the ability to reason and that God served as the guarantor of the correctness of clear ideas. The material world could thus be understood through adherence to mathematical laws and methods of inquiry. Descartes championed the process of deductive reasoning whereby specific information could be logically deduced from general information. His method was influential well into the eighteenth century, when it was supplanted by the method of scientific induction, whereby generalizations could be drawn from the observation of specific data.

The following selection is drawn from Descartes's most famous work, Discourse on the Method of Rightly Conducting the Reason *(1636).*

"I Think, Therefore I Am":
Discourse on Method (1637)
RENÉ DESCARTES

As a multitude of laws often furnishes excuses for vice, so that a state is much better governed when it has but few, and those few strictly observed, so in place of the great number of precepts of which logic is composed, I believed that I should find the following four sufficient, provided that I made a firm and constant resolve not once to omit to observe them.

The first was, never to accept anything as true when I did not recognize it clearly to be so, that is to say, to carefully avoid precipitation and prejudice, and to include in my opinions nothing beyond that which should present itself so clearly and so distinctly to my mind that I might have no occasion to doubt it.

The second was, to divide each of the difficulties which I should examine into as many parts as were possible, and as should be required for its better solution.

The third was, to conduct my thoughts in order, by beginning with the simplest objects, and those most easy to know, so as to mount little by little, as

"'I Think, Therefore I Am'" is from René Descartes, *The Discourse on Method and Metaphysical Meditations*, trans. G. B. Rawlings (London: Walter Scott, 1901), pp. 32–35, 60–61, 75–76.

René Descartes. The great champion of deductive reasoning, Descartes believed that because the world operated according to mathematical laws, it could be understood by the human mind. (*Corbis*)

if by steps, to the most complex knowledge, and even assuming an order among those which do not naturally precede one another.

And the last was, to make everywhere enumerations so complete, and reviews so wide, that I should be sure of omitting nothing. . . .

I had long remarked that, in conduct, it is sometimes necessary to follow opinions known to be very uncertain, just as if they were indisputable, as has been said above; but then, because I desired to devote myself only to the research of truth, I thought it necessary to do exactly the contrary, and reject as absolutely false all in which I could conceive the least doubt, in order to see if afterwards there did not remain in my belief something which was entirely indisputable. Thus, because our senses sometimes deceive us, I wanted to suppose that nothing is such as they make us imagine it; and because some men err in reasoning . . . and judging that I was as liable to fail as any other, I rejected as false all the reasons which I had formerly accepted as [true]; . . . I resolved that everything which had ever entered into my mind was no more true than the illusions of my dreams. But immediately afterwards I observed that while I thus desired everything to be false, I, who thought, must of necessity [exist]; and remarking that this truth, I think, therefore I am, was so firm and so assured that all the most extravagant suppositions of the skeptics were unable to shake it, I judged that I could unhesitatingly accept it as the first principle of the philosophy I was seeking. . . .

After this, and reflecting upon the fact that I doubted, and that in consequence my being was not quite perfect (for I saw clearly that to know was a greater perfection than to doubt), I [wondered where] I had learned to think of something more perfect than I; and I knew for certain that it must be from some nature which was in reality more perfect. [And I clearly recognized that] this idea . . . had been put in me by a nature truly more perfect than I, which had in itself all perfections of which I could have any idea; that is, to explain myself in one word, God. . . .

Finally, whether awake or asleep, we ought never to allow ourselves to be persuaded of the truth of anything unless on the evidence of our Reason. And it must be noted that I say of our Reason, and not of our imagination or of our senses: thus, for example, although we very clearly see the sun, we ought not therefore to determine that it is only of the size which our sense of sight presents; and we may very distinctly imagine the head of a lion joined to the body of a goat, without being therefore shut up to the conclusion that a chimaera exists; for it is not a dictate of Reason that what we thus see or imagine is in reality existent; but it plainly tells us that all our ideas or notions contain in them some truth; for otherwise it could not be that God, who is wholly perfect and veracious, should have placed them in us.

Science and the Church

Nicolaus Copernicus (1473–1543)

One of the most important and fundamental areas of investigation during the Scientific Revolution was astronomy. For centuries, humans had subscribed to a geocentric theory that placed earth at the center of the universe with all the planets orbiting around it. This theory, ascribed to the Egyptian astronomer Ptolemy (fl. 150 C.E.) and supported by Aristotelian physics, maintained that the earth had to be the center of the universe because of its heaviness and that the stars and other planets existed in surrounding crystalline spheres. Beyond these crystalline spheres lay the realm of God and the angels. This view was supported by the Catholic Church, which saw humanity as the central focus of God's creation and therefore at the epicenter of all existence. Biblical support for the geocentric theory included Psalm 104: "Thou didst set the earth on its foundation, so that it should never be shaken." Still, there were mathematical problems associated with this theory. For one, it was difficult to explain the motion of the planets, which seemed to be moving in noncircular patterns around the earth. At times the planets actually appeared to be going backward. This was explained by epicycles. Ptolemy maintained that planets make a second revolution in an orbit tangent to the first. It was therefore difficult to predict the location of a planet at any given time. A Polish astronomer named Nicolaus Copernicus (1473–1543) attempted to eliminate many of the mathematical inconsistencies by proposing that the sun, not the earth, was the center of the universe. In most other ways, including the acceptance of epicycles and the circular orbit of planets, Copernicus's system was still Ptolemaic. Yet Copernicus freed scientists from a rigid conception of cosmic structure and in essence proposed the empirical evidence of mathematics as the cornerstone of scientific thought.

The first selection is the simple statement by Copernicus proposing the heliocentric theory; it is excerpted from a letter entitled Commentariolus, *written sometime after 1520. In 1543, Copernicus published* On the Revolutions of the Heavenly Spheres. *The second excerpt is from the preface of that work and was addressed to Pope Paul III. In it, Copernicus explains why he questioned the geocentric theory.*

The Heliocentric Statement (ca. 1520)
NICOLAUS COPERNICUS

What appears to us as motions of the sun arise not from its motion but from the motion of the earth and our sphere, with which we revolve about the sun like any other planet. The earth has, then, more than one motion.

On the Movement of the Earth (1543)
NICOLAUS COPERNICUS

I may well presume, most Holy Father, that certain people, as soon as they hear that in this book about the Revolutions of the Spheres of the Universe I ascribe movement to the earthly globe, will cry out that, holding such views, I should at once be hissed off the stage. . . .

So I should like your Holiness to know that I was induced to think of a method of computing the motions of the spheres by nothing else than the knowledge that the mathematicians [who had previously considered the problem] are inconsistent in these investigations.

For, first, the mathematicians are so unsure of the movements of the Sun and Moon that they cannot even explain or observe the constant length of the seasonal year. Secondly, in determining the motions of these and of the other five planets, they use neither the same principles and

"The Heliocentric Statement" is from Copernicus, *Three Copernican Treatises*, trans. Edward Rosen (New York: Columbia University Press, 1939), p. 58. Copyright © 1939, Columbia University Press. Reprinted by permission.

"On the Movement of the Earth" is from Copernicus, *De Revolutionibus Orbium Caelestium* (1543), trans. John F. Dobson and Selig Brodetsky, published in Occasional Notes of the Royal Astronomical Society, vol. 2, no. 1 (London: Royal Astronomical Society, 1947), excerpts from the preface and Book I.

hypotheses nor the same demonstrations of the apparent motions and revolutions. . . . Nor have they been able thereby to discern or deduce the principal thing—namely the shape of the Universe and the unchangeable symmetry of its parts. . . .

I pondered long upon this uncertainty of mathematical tradition in establishing the motions of the system of the spheres. At last I began to chafe that philosophers could by no means agree on any one certain theory of the mechanism of the Universe, wrought for us by a supremely good and orderly Creator. . . . I therefore took pains to read again the works of all the philosophers on whom I could lay hand to seek out whether any of them had even supposed that the motions of the spheres were other than those demanded by the [Ptolemaic] mathematical schools. I found first in Cicero that Hicetas [of Syracuse, fifth century B.C.E.] had realized that the Earth moved. Afterwards I found in Plutarch that certain others had held the like opinion. . . .

Thus assuming motions, which in my work I ascribe to the Earth, by long and frequent observations I have at last discovered that, if the motions of the rest of the planets be brought into relation with the circulation of the Earth and be reckoned in proportion to the circles of each planet, . . . the orders and magnitudes of all stars and spheres, nay the heavens themselves, become so bound together that nothing in any part thereof could be moved from its place without producing confusion of all the other parts of the Universe as a whole.

Galileo Galilei (1564–1642)

After Copernicus, the quest for rational truth was continued by Tycho Brahe, who compiled accurate tables of astronomical observations, and Johannes Kepler, who analyzed these tables and posited the elliptical orbits of planets. And yet this progress in scientific thought was to encounter various roadblocks beyond the difficulties of gathering and interpreting data. For the Catholic Church, the question was not one of empirical evidence and rational inquiry but rather of faith and authority. During the sixteenth century, the church established an organization that was designed to maintain purity of doctrine and authority over the faithful. The Inquisition, as it came to be called, was administered by Dominican friars, whose responsibilities had always involved the explanation of doctrine to those who had strayed from the path. Now they actively sought those whose deeds and ideas seemed to contradict established Catholic doctrine. The Inquisition became a vehicle for reform through coercion, with allegiance being obtained through argument, intimidation, and torture if necessary.

During the seventeenth century, the church found itself embroiled in events that again threatened its established authority. The attack was now centered on the new scientific theories that challenged Catholic doctrine and were being pursued and advocated independently of church control. At the forefront of the controversy was one of the most influential scientists in history—Galileo Galilei. Galileo was born in Pisa, Italy, in the year of Shakespeare's birth and Michelangelo's death (1564). He had much in common with these great men since he played the lute, painted, wrote poetry, and enjoyed polemics and satire. In 1592, Galileo was appointed professor of mathematics at the University of Padua, and he remained in this position for eighteen years, supporting a mistress, two daughters, a son, and a widowed mother on a small income supplemented by tutoring. During this time, Galileo came to doubt the teachings of Aristotle and other ancient philosophers and scientists, which were accepted by the church as being consistent with Catholic doctrine. Galileo had admired the mathematical aesthetics of the Copernican theory and became even more confirmed in his support of this thesis after viewing the heavens through a new instrument that he had recently improved—the telescope. Galileo considered himself a devout and obedient son of the church, but he believed that the Bible conveyed truth figuratively as well as literally. He argued that scientific facts must first be discovered, then interpreted according to observation. As Galileo noted, "The Bible shows the way to go to Heaven, not the way the heavens go." No one, not even the pope, could alter the facts.

Galileo's response to charges that the ideas of Copernicus contradicted the Bible is contained in the following letter to the Grand Duchess of Tuscany in 1615. Nevertheless, the next year the heliocentric theory was condemned as formally heretical. For his impertinence and continuing adherence to the Copernican theory, Galileo was twice ordered to appear before the Inquisition, though he was a frail man of seventy. Under threat of torture, he finally recanted his position. Only in 1992 was Galileo formally absolved from his sin by Pope John Paul II.

Science and the Bible: Letter to the Grand Duchess of Tuscany (1615)

GALILEO GALILEI

Some years ago, as Your Serene Highness well knows, I discovered in the heavens many things that had not been seen before our own age. The novelty of these things, as well as some consequences which followed from them in contradiction to the physical notions commonly held among academic

"Science and the Bible" is from *Discoveries and Opinions of Galileo by Galileo Galilei*, pp. 175, 177–179, 181–184, 189–190, 194–195. Copyright © 1957 by Stillman Drake. Used by permission of Doubleday, a division of Bantam, Doubleday, Dell Publishing Group, Inc.

philosophers, stirred up against me no small number of professors—as if I had placed these things in the sky with my own hands in order to upset nature and overturn the sciences. . . .

Showing a greater fondness for their own opinions than for truth, they sought to deny and disprove the new things which, if they had cared to look for themselves, their own senses would have demonstrated to them. To this end they hurled various charges and published numerous writings filled with vain arguments, and they made the grave mistake of sprinkling these with passages taken from places in the Bible which they had failed to understand properly, and which were ill suited to their purposes. . . .

Persisting in their original resolve to destroy me and everything mine by any means they can think of, these men . . . know that as to the arrangement of the parts of the universe, I hold the sun to be situated motionless in the center of the revolution of the celestial orbs while the earth rotates on its axis and revolves about the sun. They know also that I support this position not only by refuting the arguments of Ptolemy and Aristotle, but by producing many counter-arguments; in particular, some which relate to physical effects whose causes can perhaps be assigned in no other way. In addition there are astronomical arguments derived from many things in my new celestial discoveries that plainly confute the Ptolemaic system while admirably agreeing with and confirming the contrary hypothesis. . . . These men have resolved to fabricate a shield for their fallacies out of the mantle of pretended religion and the authority of the Bible. These they apply, with little judgment, to the refutation of arguments that they do not understand and have not even listened to.

First they have endeavored to spread the opinion that such propositions in general are contrary to the Bible and are consequently damnable and heretical. . . . Next, becoming bolder, and hoping (though vainly) that this seed which first took root in their hypocritical minds would send out branches and ascend to heaven, they began scattering rumors among the people that before long this doctrine would be condemned by the supreme authority. . . .

They go about invoking the Bible, which they would have minister to their deceitful purposes. Contrary to the sense of the Bible and the intention of the holy Fathers, if I am not mistaken, they would extend such authorities until even in purely physical matters—where faith is not involved—they would have us altogether abandon reason and the evidence of our senses in favor of some biblical passage, though under the surface meaning of its words this passage may contain a different sense. . . .

I think in the first place that it is very pious to say and prudent to affirm that the holy Bible can never speak untruth—whenever its true meaning is understood. But I believe nobody will deny that it is often very abstruse, and may say things which are quite different from what its bare words signify. . . .

This being granted, I think that in discussion of physical problems we ought to begin not from the authority of scriptural passages, but from sense-experiences and necessary demonstrations; for the holy Bible and the phenomena of nature proceed alike from the divine Word, the former as the dictate of the Holy Ghost and the latter as the observant executrix of God's commands. It is necessary for the Bible, in order to be accommodated to the understanding of every man, to speak many things which appear to differ from the absolute truth so far as the bare meaning of the words is concerned. But Nature, on the other hand, is inexorable and immutable; she never transgresses the laws imposed upon her, or cares a whit whether her abstruse reasons and methods of operation are understandable to men. For that reason it appears that nothing physical which sense-experience sets before our eyes, or which necessary demonstrations prove to us, ought to be called in question (much less condemned) upon the testimony of biblical passages which may have some different meaning beneath their words. For the Bible is not chained in every expression to conditions as strict as those which govern all physical effects; nor is God any less excellently revealed in Nature's actions than in the sacred statements of the Bible. . . .

From this I do not mean to infer that we need not have an extraordinary esteem for the passages of holy Scripture. On the contrary, having arrived at any certainties in physics, we ought to utilize these as the most appropriate aids in the true exposition of the Bible and in the investigation of those meanings which are necessarily contained therein for these must be concordant with demonstrated truths. I should judge the authority of the Bible was designed to persuade men of those articles and propositions which, surpassing all human reasoning, could not be made credible by science, or by any other means than through the very mouth of the Holy Spirit. . . .

But I do not feel obliged to believe that the same God who had endowed us with senses, reason, and intellect has intended to forgo their use and by some other means to give us knowledge which we can attain by them.

The Resolution: "Science and Faith Are Both Gifts from God" (1993)
POPE JOHN PAUL II

The papacy, which played such a fundamental role in the Middle Ages, declined in international authority after the Protestant Reformation. However, with the emergence of twentieth-century leaders such as John XXIII, Paul VI, and John Paul II, the papacy has played an important role in international affairs apart from the eight hundred million Catholics it represents. For example, John Paul II

"Science and Faith Are Both Gifts from God" is from Pope John Paul II's address delivered to the international scientific community at the Ettore Maiorana Research Centre on May 8, 1993, contained in *The Pope Speaks*, vol. 38 (1993), pp. 296–300.

(1978–) was a formidable figure in defying Soviet threats to invade his native Poland in 1980; his knowledge of languages and frequent travel have made him a vital force, especially in Third World countries. The following address of John Paul II to the international scientific community discusses the relationship between science and faith, which he believes can be mutually supportive. This relationship had been strained since the sixteenth century when Galileo was condemned by the church as a heretic for his scientific theories. This concession of the pope indicates a new tolerance between rational scientific methods and the realm of faith.

From the beginning of my pontificate I have taken pains to emphasize that the dialogue between science and faith is not merely possible, but essential. I have been committed to removing the obstacles which could still impair its constant development. In that regard it seemed important to resolve, once and for all, some perennial controversies which unfortunately have undermined the good understanding between the Church and the scientific community. I am referring, in particular, to regrettable past events of history, such as the "Galileo case." On November 19, 1979, in an address to the Pontifical Academy of Sciences on the occasion of the commemorations marking the centenary of the birth of Albert Einstein, I suggested an objective review of the Copernican-Ptolemaic controversy of the 17th century. On that occasion I said: "I give all my support to this task which could do honor to the truth of the faith and of science and open the doors for future collaboration." I wanted to emphasize the same urgency in a message for the 300th anniversary of Isaac Newton's publication of the *Philosophiae Naturalis Principia Mathematica*, recalling that science and religion are at the service of the human community, and expressing the wish for a common search based on critical frankness and an exchange that will not only continue but also grow in quality and scope. . . .

However, what direction will the dialogue between science and faith take in the future? My reflection takes its cue from the bronze inscription unveiled here today: "Science and faith are both gifts of God."

This terse statement not only excludes the idea that science and faith must view one another with mutual suspicion, but also shows the deepest reason calling them to establish a constructive and cordial relationship: God, the common foundation of both; God, the ultimate reason for the logic of creation which science explores, and the source of the Revelation by which He freely gives himself to man, calling him to faith, in order to make him a son instead of a creature, and opening to him the gates of intimacy with Him. The light of reason, which makes science possible, and the light of Revelation, which makes faith possible, emanate from a single source. They are two distinct, autonomous trajectories, but by their very nature they are never on a collision course. Whenever some type of friction is noted, it is the symptom of an unfortunate pathological condition. . . .

In what sense is science a "gift" of God? Such a statement could seem ambiguous, even provocative, to a person without faith if it were to be understood as playing down the natural capacity of the mind to grasp reality by means of a rigorous logical and cognitive procedure. Such a sense, however, is quite far from the thinking of the Church, which even in the realm of faith rejects a blind "fideism." There is even greater reason to acknowledge the human mind's natural capacity to obtain truth in its own areas of experience and knowledge of the world.

The dialogue between science and faith, each respecting the other's areas, is doubly necessary in the domain of applied science. . . . If human life is at enormous risk today, it is not because of the truth discovered through scientific research but because of the deadly applications made of it on the technological level. . . . Both of them, however, must take on a precise ethical responsibility in regard to their relationships and applications. The stakes are too high to be taken lightly. . . .

In recent years we have witnessed rapid and surprising social transformation. Among these, how can we fail to mention overcoming the rigid division of the world into opposite ideological, political and military blocs? It is because of this event that the threat of the "nuclear holocaust" has been removed, at least to a large degree. In this same span of time, however, other emergencies of a planetary nature have reached levels of extreme danger, making us see the risk of a type of "environmental holocaust" due to the careless destruction of vital ecological resources and the increase of ever more insidious attacks on the defense of and respect for human life. The unbridled race by the few and privileged to hoard and exploit the earth's resources is laying the foundations of another form of cold war, this time between the planet's North and South, between the highly industrialized countries and the poor nations, which cannot be ignored by those who take the world's fate to heart. Threatening clouds are once again gathering on mankind's horizon. . . .

Whenever scientific activity has a positive effect on respect for and protection of human dignity, it contributes significantly to building peace. Therefore it is necessary to be tireless in promoting a scientific culture capable of looking always at "the whole person" and at "the whole of peoples," serving the universal good and solidarity. In this regard, great importance is attached to making progress in the dialogue between science and faith. We must work together to reestablish the connection between truth and values, between science and ethical commitment. We must all be truly convinced that progress is really such if it is at the service of the true and total well-being of individuals and of the whole human family. I am therefore compelled to emphasize once again what I have stressed more than once, namely, that although science's main task is to seek the truth in the free and legitimate liberty belonging to it, scientists are nevertheless not permitted to prescind from the ethical implications concerning the means of their research and the use of the truths they discover. Ethical goodness is simply another name for truth sought by the practical intellect.

The Foundations of Modern Science

Sir Isaac Newton (1642–1727)

Sir Isaac Newton was perhaps the most brilliant scientist in an age of genius. He drew on the work of his predecessors and his own vast mental abilities to devise a system of physical laws that have endured for more than 250 years. Newton reasoned that the planets and all other material objects in the universe moved in an orderly regimen, dictated by the principles of gravity and mutual attraction. Newton made no attempt to explain the nature of gravity itself, but he did demonstrate the principles mathematically. He adopted the methods of empirical observation established by Francis Bacon a half-century earlier and championed inductive reasoning as the primary method for scientific inquiry. With the work of Newton, the immense universe became rational and knowable, a realm of regularity, subject to immutable laws. Humankind no longer lived in a haphazard and chaotic universe, dependent on the intervention of spirits and angels for its regulation. And yet, Newton was no atheist. The new universe simply demanded a new conception of God. For Newton, science and faith could not only be reconciled but were mutually dependent. The following selection from his Optics *(1704) gives evidence of this important concept.*

Principles of Analysis—Induction and God: *Optics* (1704)

SIR ISAAC NEWTON

All these things being considered, it seems probable to me, that God in the Beginning formed Matter in solid, massy, hard, impenetrable, moveable Particles, of such Sizes and Figures, and with such other Properties, and in such Proportion to Space, as most conduced to the End for which he formed them; and that these primitive Particles being Solids, are incomparably harder than any porous Bodies compounded of them; even so very hard, as never to wear or break in pieces; no ordinary Power being able to divide what God himself made one in the first Creation. . . .

To derive two or three general Principles of Motion from Phaenomena, and afterwards to tell us how the Properties and Actions of all corporeal Things follow from those manifest Principles, would be a very great step in

---

"Principles of Analysis" is from Sir Isaac Newton, *Optics* (London: W. & J. Innys, 1721), pp. 344–345, 375–381. Text modernized by the editor.

Philosophy, though the Causes of those Principles were not yet discovered: And therefore, I scruple not to propose the Principles of Motion . . . and leave their Causes to be found out.

Now by the help of these Principles, all material Things seem to have been composed of the hard and solid Particles above-mentioned, variously associated in the first Creation by the Counsel of an intelligent Agent. For it became him who created them to set them in order. And if he did so, it's unphilosophical to seek for any other Origin of the World, or to pretend that it might arise out of a Chaos by the mere Laws of Nature; though being once formed, it may continue by those Laws for many Ages. For while Comets move in very eccentric orbits in all manner of Positions, blind Fate could never make all the Planets move one and the same way in concentric orbits, some inconsiderable Irregularities excepted, which may have risen from the mutual Actions of Comets and Planets upon one another, and which will be apt to increase, till this System wants a Reformation. Such a wonderful Uniformity in the Planetary System must be allowed the Effect of Choice. And so must the Uniformity in the Bodies of Animals, they having generally a right and a left side shaped alike, and on either side of their Bodies two Legs behind, and either two Arms, or two legs, or two Wings before upon their Shoulders, and between their Shoulders a Neck running down into a Backbone, and a Head upon it; and in the Head two Ears, two Eyes, a Nose, a Mouth, and a Tongue, alike situated . . . and the Instinct of Brutes and Insects, can be the effect of nothing else than the Wisdom and Skill of a powerful ever-living Agent, who being in all Places, is more able by his Will to move the Bodies within his boundless uniform Sensorium, and thereby to form and reform the Parts of the Universe, than we are by our Will to move the Parts of our own Bodies. And yet we are not to consider the World as the Body of God, or the several Parts thereof, as the Parts of God. He is a uniform Being, void of Organs, Members or Parts, and they are his Creatures subordinate to him, and subservient to his Will. . . .

And since Space is divisible in infinitum, and Matter is not necessarily in all places, it may be also allowed that God is able to create Particles of Matter of several Sizes and Figures, and in several Proportions to Space, and perhaps of different Densities and Forces, and thereby to vary the Laws of Nature, and make Worlds of several sorts in several Parts of the Universe. At least, I see nothing of Contradiction in all this.

As in Mathematics, so in Natural Philosophy, the Investigation of difficult Things by the Method of Analysis, ought ever to precede the Method of Composition. This Analysis consists in making Experiments and Observations, and in drawing general Conclusions from them by Induction, and admitting of no Objections against the Conclusions, but such as are taken from Experiments, or other certain Truths. For Hypotheses are not to be regarded in experimental Philosophy. And although the arguing from Experiments and Observations by Induction be no Demonstration of general Conclusions; yet it is the best way of arguing which the Nature of Things admits of. . . . By this way of Analysis, we may proceed from Compounds to Ingredients, and from

Motions to the Forces producing them; and in general, from Effects to their Causes, and from particular Causes to more general ones, till the Argument end in the most general. This is the Method of Analysis: And the Synthesis consists in assuming the Causes discovered, and established as Principles, and by them explaining the Phaenomena proceeding from them, and proving the Explanations.

William Harvey (1578–1657)

William Harvey has been termed the father of modern physiology. He was heir to a legacy of interest in the internal workings of the human body that had been most recently in evidence among artists during the Renaissance. But whereas Michelangelo studied the body to better represent the human form, Harvey sought to discover the internal workings on their own scientific merit. In this, he was more closely akin to the earlier scientific studies of Leonardo da Vinci. Harvey built upon the work of the Greek physician Galen (fl. 150 c.e.), who demonstrated that the arteries carried blood instead of air. Harvey's exacting methods set the pattern of scientific research for generations. In the following selection, which was an address to the Royal College of Physicians in 1628, he gave the results of his methodical dissections and experiments.

"I Learn and Teach from the Fabric of Nature": On the Circulation of the Blood (1628)
WILLIAM HARVEY

As this book alone declares the blood to course and revolve by a new route, very different from the ancient and beaten pathway trodden for so many ages, and illustrated by such a host of learned and distinguished men, I was greatly afraid lest I might be charged with presumption did I lay my work before the public at home, or send it beyond seas for impression, unless I had first proposed its subject to you, had confirmed its conclusions by ocular demonstrations in your presence, had replied to your doubts and objections, and secured the assent and support of our distinguished President. For I was most intimately persuaded, that if I could make good my proposition before you and our College, . . . I had less to fear from others. . . . For true philosophers, who are only eager for truth and knowledge, never regard themselves

---

"'I Learn and Teach from the Fabric of Nature'" is from R. Willis, trans., *The Works of William Harvey* (London: Sydenham Society, 1847), pp. 5–7, 31–32, 45–47.

as already so thoroughly informed, but that they welcome further information from whomsoever and from whencesoever it may come; nor are they so narrow-minded as to imagine any of the arts or sciences transmitted to us by the ancients, in such a state of forwardness or completeness, that nothing is left for the ingenuity and industry of others. . . . Neither do they swear such fealty to their mistress Antiquity, that they openly, and in sight of all, deny and desert their friend Truth. . . .

My dear colleagues . . . I profess both to learn and to teach anatomy, not from books, but from dissections; not from the positions of philosophers, but from the fabric of nature. . . .

From these and other observations of the like kind, I am persuaded it will be found that the motion of the heart is as follows:

First of all, the auricle contracts, and in the course of its contraction throws the blood, (which it contains in ample quantity as the head of the veins, the store-house and cistern of the blood,) into the ventricle, which being filled, the heart raises itself straightway, makes all its fibers tense, contracts the ventricles, and performs a beat, by which beat it immediately sends the blood supplied to it by the auricle into the arteries; the right ventricle sending its charge into the lungs by the vessel which is called vena arteriosi, but which, in structure and function, and all things else, is an artery; the left ventricle sending its charge into the aorta, and through this by the arteries to the body at large. . . .

Thus far I have spoken of the passage of the blood from the veins into the arteries, and of the manner in which it is transmitted and distributed by the action of the heart. . . . But what remains to be said upon the quantity and source of the blood which thus passes, is of so novel and unheard-of character, that I not only fear injury to myself from the envy of a few, but I tremble lest I have mankind at large for my enemies. . . . Still, the die is cast, and my trust is in my love of truth, and the candor that inheres in cultivated minds. And when I surveyed my mass of evidence, . . . I revolved in my mind, what might be the quantity of blood which was transmitted, in how short a time its passage might be effected, and the like; . . . I began to think whether there might not be A MOTION, AS IT WERE, IN A CIRCLE. Now this I afterwards found to be true; and I finally saw that the blood, forced by the action of the left ventricle into the arteries, was distributed to the body at large . . . impelled by the right ventricle . . . through the veins, and so round to the left ventricle in the manner already indicated. . . .

The heart, consequently, is the beginning of life; the sun of the microcosm, even as the sun in his turn might well be designated the heart of the world; for it is the heart by whose virtue and pulse the blood is moved, perfected, made apt to nourish, and is preserved from corruption and coagulation; it is the household divinity which, discharging its function, nourishes, cherishes, quickens the whole body, and is indeed the foundation of life, the source of all action.

SECTION II: THE ENLIGHTENMENT

Thoughts on the Human Condition and Human Progress

John Locke (1632–1704)

John Locke was one of the most important figures of this period of scientific dis-
covery and reason. He initiated the Age of Enlightenment in England and
France, was an inspirer of the U.S. Constitution, and remains a powerful influ-
ence on the life and thought of Western Civilization. Locke was educated at Ox-
ford, where he was fascinated with experimental science. He became a physician
but was particularly attracted to human relationships concerning how people
learn, and how they are best governed. Well known in the academic circles of
England and France, his political philosophy was to provide a confirmation of
the Glorious Revolution of 1688 and a framework for the American and French
revolutions of 1776 and 1789.

The following selection from one of his primary works investigates a seminal
question debated in the Enlightenment: Are children born with any innate ideas
that have been inherited from parents, or are all ideas products of associations
within society? This work extended empirical investigation into the realm of the
human mind and reveals Locke's inquiring nature and intellectual depth.

The Blank Slate of the Mind: *An Essay Concerning Human Understanding* (1690)

JOHN LOCKE

It is established opinion among some men, that there are in the understanding certain innate principles; some primary notions, characters, as it were
stamped upon the mind of man, which the soul receives in its very first being,
and brings into the world with it. It would be sufficient to convince unprejudiced readers of the falseness of this supposition, if I should only show . . .
how men, barely by the use of their natural faculties, may attain to all the
knowledge they have, without the help of any innate impressions; and may arrive at certainty, without any such original notions or principles. . . .

Let us then suppose the mind to be, as we say, white paper, void of all characters, without any ideas:—How comes it to be furnished? Whence comes it

"The Blank Slate of the Mind" is from John Locke, *An Essay Concerning Human Understanding*,
ed. A. D. Fraser (Oxford: Clarendon Press, 1894), vol. 1, pp. 37–38, 121–124.

by that vast store which the busy and boundless fancy of man has painted on it with an almost endless variety? Whence has it all the materials of reason and knowledge? To this I answer, in one word, EXPERIENCE. In that all our knowledge is founded; and from that it ultimately derives itself. Our observation employed either, about external sensible objects, or about the internal operations of our minds perceived and reflected on by ourselves, is that which supplies our understandings with all the materials of thinking. These two are the fountains of knowledge, from whence all the ideas we have, or can naturally have, do spring. . . .

The understanding seems to me not to have the least glimmering of any ideas which it does not receive from [sensation or reflection]. External objects furnish the mind with the ideas of sensible qualities, which are all those different perceptions they produce in us; and the mind furnishes the understanding with ideas of its own operations.

He that attentively considers the state of a child at his first coming into the world, will have little reason to think him stored with plenty of ideas that are to be the matter of his future knowledge. It is by degrees [that] he comes to be furnished with them. . . . But all that are born into the world being surrounded with bodies that perpetually and diversely affect them, variety of ideas, whether care be taken about it or not, are imprinted on the minds of children. Light and colors are busy at hand everywhere when the eye is but open; sounds and some tangible qualities fail not to solicit their proper senses; but yet I think it will be granted easily, that if a child were kept in a place where he never saw any other but black and white till he were a man, he would have no more ideas of scarlet or green than he that from his childhood never tasted an oyster or a pineapple has of those particular relishes. . . .

Marquis de Condorcet (1743–1794)

Marie-Jean-Antoine-Nicolas de Caritat, best known by the rather imposing title Marquis de Condorcet, was descended from an ancient French family. He was educated at Rheims and Paris, where he showed ability in mathematics under the tutelage of the famous philosophe Jean Le Rond d'Alembert. A frequent contributor to the Encyclopedia *of Diderot, Condorcet was a zealous propagator of the progressive views of the Enlightenment. He was one of the guiding minds behind the French Revolution in 1789, becoming secretary of the National Assembly and primary architect of the reform of the French educational system. His independent attitude flew in opposition to the radical policies of Robespierre, and he became a hunted man, hiding in thickets and quarries in the countryside of France before being captured and imprisoned. Two days later he was found dead in his cell, perhaps by poison.*

The following passage is from his most famous work, Outlines of a Historical View of the Progress of the Human Mind. *Its fundamental idea is that of the continual progress of the human race to an ultimate perfection. Wholly a man of the Enlightenment, an advocate of economic freedom, religious toleration, and legal and educational reform, Condorcet sought to apply reason to social affairs. In this, he became a precursor to the discipline of sociology.*

The Progress of the Human Mind (1795)
MARQUIS DE CONDORCET

All the causes which contribute to the improvement of the human species, all the means we have enumerated that insure its progress, must, from their very nature, exercise an influence always active, and acquire an extent forever increasing. . . .

And it cannot be doubted that the progress of the sanative art, that the use of more wholesome food and more comfortable habitations, . . . shall develop the physical powers by exercise, without at the same time impairing them by excess. . . . It is manifest that the improvement of the practice of medicine, become more efficacious in consequence of the progress of reason and the social order, must [put an end] to transmissible or contagious disorders as well to those general maladies resulting from climate, ailments, and the nature of certain occupations. Nor would it be difficult to prove that this hope might be extended to almost every other malady, of which it is probable we shall hereafter discover the most remote causes. Would it even be absurd to suppose this quality of melioration in the human species as susceptible of an indefinite advancement; to suppose that a period must one day arrive when death will be nothing more than the effect either of extraordinary accidents, or of the flow and gradual decay of the vital powers; and that the duration of the middle space, of the interval between the birth of man and this decay, will itself have no assignable limit? Certainly man will not become immortal; but may not the distance between the moment in which he draws his first breath and the common term when, in the course of nature, without malady, without accident, he finds it impossible any longer to exist, be necessarily protracted? . . .

May we not include in the same circle the intellectual and moral faculties? May not our parents, who transmit to us the advantages or defects of their conformation, and from whom we receive our features and shape, as well as our propensities to certain physical affections, transmit to us also that part of organization upon which intellect, strength of understanding, energy of soul or moral sensibility depend? Is it not probable that education by improving these qualities will at the same time have an influence upon, will modify and improve this organization itself? Analogy, an investigation of the human faculties, and even some facts, appear to authorize these conjectures, and thereby to enlarge the boundary of our hopes. . . .

"The Progress of the Human Mind" is from Marquis de Condorcet, *Outlines of a Historical View of the Progress of the Human Mind* (Philadelphia: M. Carey, 1796), pp. 289–293.

And how admirably calculated is this view of the human race, emancipated from its chains, released alike from the dominion of chance, as well as from that of the enemies of its progress, and advancing with a firm and indeviate step in the parts of truth, to console the philosopher lamenting the errors, the flagrant acts of injustice, the crimes with which the earth is still polluted? It is the contemplation of this prospect that rewards him for all his efforts to assist the progress of reason and the establishment of liberty.

Cesare Beccaria (1738–1794)

Cesare Beccaria was the son of a Milanese aristocrat of modest means. He was educated initially at a Jesuit school, an experience that he later described as "fanatical" and stifling to "the development of human feelings." At the age of twenty-six, he became an international celebrity with the publication of his work on criminal law in 1764. Translated into several languages, it enjoyed a remarkable success in France, where it went through seven editions in six months. In it, Beccaria lashed out against the barbarities of the day, including the torture of prisoners in order to induce confession, the corruption of judges, and degrading and brutal punishments. Penalties, he concluded, should be scaled to the offense. Beccaria was the first modern writer to advocate the complete abolition of capital punishment, and his treatise remains the most important and influential volume written on criminal justice.

"The Greatest Happiness of the Greatest Number": *On Crimes and Punishments* (1764)

CESARE BECCARIA

If we look into history, we shall find that laws, which are, or ought to be, conventions between men in a state of freedom, have been, for the most part the work of the passions of a few, or the consequences of a fortuitous or temporary necessity; not dictated by a cool examiner of human nature, who knew how to collect in one point the actions of a multitude, and had only this end in view, the greatest happiness of the greatest number. . . .

Observe that by justice I understand nothing more than that bond which is necessary to keep the interest of individuals united, without which men would return to their original state of barbarity. All punishments which exceed the necessity of preserving this bond are in their nature unjust. . . .

"'The Greatest Happiness of the Greatest Number'" is from Cesare Beccaria, *An Essay on Crimes and Punishments,* trans. E. D. Ingraham (Philadelphia: H. Nicklin, 1819), pp. xii, 18–19, 47, 59–60, 93–94, 104–105, 148–149.

The end of punishment, therefore, is no other than to prevent the criminal from doing further injury to society, and to prevent others from committing the like offence. Such punishments, therefore, and such a mode of inflicting them ought to be chosen, as will make the strongest and most lasting impressions on the minds of others, with the least torment to the body of the criminal.

The torture of a criminal during the course of his trial is a cruelty consecrated by custom in most nations. It is used with an intent either to make him confess his crime, or to explain some contradiction into which he had been led during his examination, or discover his accomplices, or for some kind of metaphysical and incomprehensible purgation of infamy, or, finally, in order to discover other crimes of which he is not accused, but of which he may be guilty.

No man can be judged a criminal until he be found guilty; nor can society take from him the public protection until it have been proved that he has violated the conditions on which it was granted. What right, then, but that of power, can authorise the punishment of a citizen so long as there remains any doubt of his guilt? This dilemma is frequent. Either he is guilty, or not guilty. If guilty, he should only suffer the punishment ordained by the laws, and torture becomes useless, as his confession is unnecessary. If he be not guilty, you torture the innocent; for in the eye of the law, every man is innocent whose crime has not been proved. . . .

Crimes are more effectually prevented by the certainty than by the severity of punishment. . . . In proportion as punishments become more cruel, the minds of men, as a fluid rises to the same height with that which surrounds it, grow hardened and insensible; and the force of the passions still continuing, in the space of an hundred years the wheel [torture device] terrifies no more than formerly the prison. That a punishment may produce the effect required, it is sufficient that the evil it occasions should exceed the good expected from the crime, including in the calculation the certainty of the punishment, and the privation of the expected advantage. All severity beyond this is superfluous, and therefore tyrannical.

The punishment of death is pernicious to society, from the example of barbarity it affords. If the passions, or the necessity of war, have taught men to shed the blood of their fellow creatures, the laws, which are intended to moderate the ferocity of mankind, should not increase it by examples of barbarity, them more horrible as this punishment is usually attended with formal pageantry. Is it not absurd, that the laws, which detest and punish homicide, should, in order to prevent murder, publicly commit murder themselves? . . .

It is better to prevent crimes than to punish them. This is the fundamental principle of good legislation, which is the art of conducting men to the maximum of happiness, and to the minimum of misery, if we may apply this mathematical expression to the good and evil of life. . . .

Would you prevent crimes? Let the laws be clear and simple, let the entire force of the nation be united in their defence, let them be intended rather to favour every individual than any particular classes of men; let the laws be feared, and the laws only. The fear of the laws is salutary, but the fear of men is a fruitful and fatal source of crimes.

Immanuel Kant (1724–1804)

Immanuel Kant was a German philosopher whose comprehensive and systematic work in the theory of knowledge, ethics, and aesthetics greatly influenced subsequent philosophy. Kant's entire life was spent in Königsberg, where he was educated and served as a popular teacher and lecturer at the local university. In his writings, he hoped to avoid the confusion of earlier thinkers by examining the possibilities and limitations of applied reason. He sought to accept the rationalism of the Enlightenment while still preserving a belief in human freedom, immortality, and the existence of God. In fact, Kant found the world open to pure reason to be quite limited and postulated a sphere of moral reality known only by "practical reason and conscience." Although he hoped to raise philosophy to the level of a science, he believed that all things could not be proved by discursive reasoning—God and eternal life among them.

In the following selection, Kant seeks to define the Enlightenment by empowering the individual to break away from a somnolent dependence, toward an active intellectual existence. Only through such personal initiative could one attain true enlightenment.

What Is Enlightenment? (1784)

IMMANUEL KANT

Enlightenment is man's release from his self-incurred tutelage. Tutelage is man's inability to make use of his understanding without direction from another. Self-incurred is this tutelage when its cause lies not in lack of reason but in lack of resolution and courage to use it without direction from another. Dare to Know! Have courage to use your own reason!—that is the motto of enlightenment.

Laziness and cowardice are the reasons why so great a portion of mankind, after nature has long since discharged them from external direction, nevertheless remains under lifelong tutelage, and why it is so easy for others to set themselves up as their guardians. It is so easy not to be of age. If I have a book

---

"What Is Enlightenment?" is from Immanuel Kant, *Foundations of the Metaphysics of Morals, What Is Enlightenment?*, 2nd ed., trans. and ed. Lewis White Beck, (New York: Macmillan Publishing Company, 1990), pp. 83–85, 88. Copyright © 1990 by Macmillan Publishing Company. Reprinted by permission of the publisher.

which understands for me, a pastor who has a conscience for me, a physician who decides my diet, and so forth, I need not trouble myself. I need not think, if I can only pay—others will readily undertake the irksome work for me.

That the step to competence is held to be very dangerous by the far greater portion of mankind (and by the entire fair sex)—quite apart from its being arduous—is seen to by those guardians who have so kindly assumed superintendence over them. After the guardians have first made their domestic cattle dumb and have made sure that these placid creatures will not dare take a single step without the harness of the cart to which they are confined, the guardians then show them the danger which threatens if they try to go alone. Actually, however, this danger is not so great, for by falling a few times they would finally learn to walk alone. But an example of this failure makes them timid and ordinarily frightens them away from all further trials.

For any single individual to work himself out of the life under tutelage which has become almost his nature is very difficult. He has come to be fond of this state, and he is for the present really incapable of making use of his reason, for no one has ever let him try it out. Statutes and formulas, those mechanical tools of the rational employment or rather misemployment of his natural gifts, are the fetters of an everlasting tutelage. Whoever throws them off makes only an uncertain leap over the narrowest ditch because he is not accustomed to that kind of free motion. Therefore, there are only few who have succeeded by their own exercise of mind both in freeing themselves from incompetence and in achieving a steady pace.

But that the public should enlighten itself is more possible; indeed, if only freedom is granted, enlightenment is almost sure to follow. For there will always be some independent thinkers, even among the established guardians of the great masses, who, after throwing off the yoke of tutelage from their own shoulders, will disseminate the spirit of the rational appreciation of both their own worth and every man's vocation for thinking for himself. . . .

For this enlightenment, however, nothing is required but freedom, and indeed the most harmless among all the things to which this term can properly be applied. It is the freedom to make public use of one's reason at every point. But I hear on all sides, "Do not argue!" The officer says: "Do not argue but drill!" The tax collector: "Do not argue but pay!" The cleric: "Do not argue but believe!" Only one prince in the world [Frederick the Great of Prussia] says, "Argue as much as you will, and about what you will, but obey!" Everywhere there is restriction on freedom. . . .

If we are asked, "Do we now live in an enlightened age?" the answer is, "No," but we do live in an age of enlightenment. As things now stand, much is lacking which prevents men from being, or easily becoming, capable of correctly using their own reason in religious matters with assurance and free from outside direction. But, on the other hand, we have clear indications that the field has now been opened wherein men may freely deal with these things and that the obstacles to general enlightenment or the release from self-imposed tutelage are gradually being reduced. In this respect, this is the age of enlightenment, or the century of Frederick.

Thoughts on Religion

Baron d'Holbach (1723–1789)

Paul-Henri Dietrich, Baron d'Holbach, was a naturalized French citizen who was best known for his radical atheism. Some of the most esteemed and even the more radicalized of the philosophes, *including d'Alembert and Rousseau, reportedly withdrew from his gatherings, frightened by the audacity of their speculations. A major contributor of over 375 articles on chemistry and related topics to Diderot's* Encyclopedia, *Holbach held views on atheism that represent an extreme in the critical analysis of the Age of Reason.*

God—"A Cause Contradicted by Its Effects": *Common Sense* (1770)

BARON D'HOLBACH

Morality and virtue are totally incompatible with the idea of a God, whose ministers and interpreters have painted him in all countries as the most fantastic, the most unjust, and the most cruel of tyrants, whose pretended wishes are to serve as rules and laws for the inhabitants of the earth. To discover the true principles of morality, men have no need of theology, of revelation, or of Gods; they need but common sense; they have only to look within themselves, to reflect upon their own nature, to consult their obvious interests, to consider the object of society and of each of the members who compose it, and they will easily understand that virtue is an advantage, and that vice is an injury to beings of their species.

By metaphysics, God is made a pure spirit, but has modern theology advanced one step further than the theology of the barbarians? They recognized a grand spirit as master of the world. The barbarians, like all ignorant men, attribute to spirits all the effects of which their inexperience prevents them from discovering the true causes. Ask a barbarian what causes your watch to move, he will answer, "a spirit!" Ask our philosophers what moves the universe, they will tell you "it is a spirit."

Is it not more natural and more intelligible to deduce all which exists, from the bosom of matter, whose existence is demonstrated by all our senses, whose effects we feel at every moment, which we see act, move, communicate, motion, and constantly bring living beings into existence, than to attribute the formation of things to an unknown force, to a spiritual being, who cannot draw from his ground that which he has not himself, and who, by the

---

"God—'A Cause Contradicted by Its Effects'" is from Baron d'Holbach, *Common Sense,* trans. Anna Knoop (New York: Miss A. Knoop, 1884), pp. 43, 55–56, 63–65, 69–70.

spiritual essence claimed for him, is incapable of making anything, and of putting anything in motion?

We are assured that the wonders of nature are sufficient to a belief in the existence of a God, and to convince us fully of this important truth. . . . The unprejudiced philosopher sees nothing in the wonders of nature but permanent and invariable law; nothing but the necessary effects of different combinations of diversified substance.

Whence comes man? What is his origin? Is he the result of the fortuitous meeting of atoms? Was the first man formed of the dust of the earth? I do not know! Man appears to me to be a production of nature like all others she embraces. I should be just as much embarrassed to tell you whence came the first stones, the first trees, the first elephants, the first ants, the first acorns, as to explain the origin of the human species. Recognize, we are told, the hand of God, of an infinitely intelligent and powerful workman, in a work so wonderful as the human machine. I would admit without question that the human machine appears to me surprising; but since man exists in nature, I do not believe it right to say that his formation is beyond the forces of nature. . . . I see that this admirable machine is subject to derangement; that at that time this wonderful intelligence is disordered, and sometimes totally disappears; from this I conclude that human intelligence depends upon a certain disposition of the material organs of the body, and that, because man is an intelligent being, it is not well to conclude that God must be an intelligent being, any more than because man is material, we are compelled to conclude that God is material. The intelligence of man no more proves the intelligence of God than the malice of men proves the malice of this God, of whom they pretend that man is the work. In whatever way theology is taken, God will always be a cause contradicted by its effects, or of whom it is impossible to judge by His works. We shall always see evil, imperfections, and follies resulting from a cause claimed to be full of goodness, or perfections, and of wisdom.

François-Marie Arouet, Voltaire (1694–1778)

The Enlightenment is often characterized as an era of empirical reasoning and critical thought, of doubt and skepticism, of individual assertion at the expense of formal control by the state or church. For the most part, this is a fair assessment. God, if he existed, was prone to be antiseptic, the "great clock-winder," who created the universe and then sat back, uninvolved in the lives of his creations. This philosophy, called "deism," generally prevailed among the philosophes. *It did not deny the existence of God, but it gave virtually no support to organized religion. The deists particularly denounced the mysteries of the Christian religion such as the Trinity, and miracles like the Virgin Birth and the Eucharist. Since God was disinterested in the affairs of the world, formal prayers were useless.*

Deism enabled many of the philosophes *to effect a reconciliation between a perfect God and an imperfect world.*

Voltaire was the quintessential personality of the Enlightenment. An author of dramas, histories, and scathing satires, his wit and intellectual power dominated the age. Voltaire adamantly opposed organized religion but enthusiastically advocated religious toleration and the deist viewpoint. The first selection is from his famous Treatise on Toleration. *In the letter that follows, Voltaire argues for the logic and necessity of a supreme deity. His ideas are generally representative of the enlightened thinkers of the age.*

On Universal Toleration

VOLTAIRE

It does not require any great art or studied elocution to prove that Christians ought to tolerate one another. Nay, I shall go still farther and say that we ought to look upon all men as our brethren. How! Call a Turk, a Jew, and a Siamese, my brother? Yes, doubtless; for are we not all children of the same parent, and the creatures of the same Creator?

But these people hold us in contempt, and call us idolaters! Well, then, I should tell them that they were to blame. And I fancy that I could stagger the headstrong pride of an imam, or a talapoin [religious leaders], were I to address them in the following manner:

"This little globe, which is no more than a point, rolls, together with many other globes, in that immensity of space in which we are all alike confounded. Man, who is an animal, about five feet high, is certainly a very inconsiderable part of the creation; but one of those hardly visible beings says to others of the same kind inhabiting another spot of the globe: Hearken to me, for the God of all these worlds has enlightened me. There are about nine hundred millions of us little insects who inhabit the earth, but my ant-hill is alone cherished by God, who holds all the rest in horror and detestation; those who live with me upon my spot will alone be happy, and all the rest eternally wretched."

They would here stop me short and ask, "What madman could have made so ridiculous a speech?" I should then be obliged to answer them, "It is yourselves." . . .

O you different worshippers of a God of mercy! If you have cruel hearts, if, while you adore that Deity who has placed the whole of His law in these few words, "Love god and you neighbor," you have loaded that pure and holy law with sophistical and unintelligible disputes, if you have lighted the flames of discord sometimes for a new word, and at others for a single letter only; if you have annexed eternal punishment to the omission of some few words, or of

"On Universal Toleration," is from Tobias Smollett, ed., *The Works of Voltaire* (London: E. R. DuMont, 1901), vol. 4, pp. 272–273, 275–276, 278. Text modernized by the editor.

certain ceremonies which other people cannot comprehend, I must say to you with tears of compassion for mankind: "Transport yourselves with me to that great instant in which all men are to receive judgment from the hand of God, who will then do unto every one according to their works, and with me behold all the dead of past ages appearing in His presence. Are you very sure that our heavenly Father and Creator will say to the wise and virtuous Confucius, to the great legislator Solon, to Pythagoras, Socrates, Plato, the divine Antoninus, the good Trajan, to Titus, the delight of humankind, and to many others who have been the models of humankind: 'Depart from me, wretches! into torments that know neither alleviation nor end; but are, like Himself, everlasting.'"

I think I see you start with horror at these words. . . .

May all men remember that they are brethren! May they alike abhor that tyranny which seeks to subject the freedom of the will, as they do the rapine which tears from the arms of industry the fruits of its peaceful labors! And if the scourge of war is not to be avoided, let us not mutually hate and destroy each other in the midst of peace; but rather make use of the few moments of our existence to join in praising, in a thousand different languages, from one extremity of the world to the other, Thy goodness, O all-merciful Creator, to whom we are indebted for that existence!

"If God Did Not Exist, He Would Have to Be Invented"
VOLTAIRE

To Frederick William, Prince of Prussia:
Monseigneur, the royal family of Prussia has excellent reasons for not wishing the annihilation of the soul. It has more right than anyone to immortality.

It is very true that we do not know any too well what the soul is: no one has ever seen it. All that we do know is that the eternal Lord of nature has given us the power of thinking, and of distinguishing virtue. It is not proved that this faculty survives our death: but the contrary is not proved either. It is possible, doubtless, that God has given thought to a particle to which, after we are no more, He will still give the power of thought: there is no inconsistency in this idea.

In the midst of all the doubts which we have discussed for four thousand years in four thousand ways, the safest course is to do nothing against one's conscience. With this secret, we can enjoy life and have nothing to fear from death.

"'If God Did Not Exist, He Would Have to Be Invented,'" is from S. G. Tallentyre, trans., *Voltaire in His Letters* (New York: G. P. Putnam's Sons, 1919).

There are some charlatans who admit no doubts. We know nothing of first principles. It is surely very presumptuous to define God, the angels, spirits, and to pretend to know precisely why God made the world, when we do not know why we can move our arms at our pleasure. Doubt is not a pleasant condition, but certainty is an absurd one.

What is most repellent in the System of Nature [by the Baron d'Holbach] . . . is the audacity with which it decides that there is no God, without even having tried to prove the impossibility. There is some eloquence in the book: but much more rant, and no sort of proof. It is a pernicious work, alike for princes and people: "Si Dieu n'existait pas, il faudrait l'inventer." [If God did not exist, he would have to be invented].

But all nature cries aloud that He does exist: that there is a supreme intelligence, an immense power, an admirable order, and everything teaches us our own dependence on it.

From the depth of our profound ignorance, let us do our best: this is what I think, and what I have always thought, amid all the misery and follies inseparable from seventy-seven years of life. . . . I am, with deep respect, Voltaire

Thoughts on Education

The scholars of the Enlightenment did not simply seek knowledge for their own personal joy, but rather planned for the aggrandizement of humankind in a larger sense. Perhaps the most laborious endeavor was the compilation of knowledge in comprehensive dictionaries or encyclopedias. Voltaire wrote a philosophical dictionary, as he termed it, wherein he defined certain concepts from faith and natural law to government and kissing, all with his inimitable flair and personal bias. Some excerpts appear in the first selection.

One of the most ambitious and dramatic accomplishments of the Enlightenment was the publication of the Encyclopedia, *a work of twenty-one volumes of text, twelve of plates illustrating the trades and mechanical arts, and two of index. The aim of the work was to provide a summary of human knowledge—a task that had been attempted before on a smaller scale, but with uneven and disappointing results.*

The mindset and guiding influence behind the Encyclopedia *was a young, little-known journalist named Denis Diderot (1713–1784). Together with the renowned mathematician Jean Le Rond d'Alembert, he directed the project from the publication of the first volume in 1745 to its completion thirty-five years later in 1780. Diderot solicited the most accomplished scholars of the age to contribute articles on their research and to offer theories and opinions on a wide variety of topics. The task of distillation and compilation was formidable, and Diderot was constantly engaged in disputes with scholars, publishers, and the Catholic Church in bringing the project to its remarkable conclusion. Apart from the impressive body of knowledge contained in the* Encyclopedia, *it stands as the quintessential expression of the ideals and attitudes of the Enlightenment. The next excerpt in this section is from the introduction to the first volume. The last passage recounts the dedication of Diderot in overcoming opposition to his grand project.*

A Philosophical Dictionary (1764)
VOLTAIRE

Astrology

Astrology might rest on a better foundation than magic. For if no one has seen goblins, or lemurs, . . . or demons, the predictions of astrologers have often been found true. Let two astrologers be consulted on the life of an infant, and on the weather; if one of them says that the child shall live to manhood, the other that he shall not; if one foretells rain and the other fair weather, it is quite clear that [one of them] will be a prophet.

One of the most famous mathematicians of Europe, named Stöffler, who flourished in the fifteenth and sixteenth centuries, foretold a universal flood for the year 1524. The deluge was to happen in the month of February, and nothing can be more plausible, for Saturn, Jupiter, and Mars were in conjunction in the sign of Pisces. Every nation in Europe, Asia, and Africa that heard of the prediction was worried. The whole world expected the flood, in spite of the rainbow. . . . Each [person] provided himself with a boat to serve as an ark. . . . At last the month of February arrived, and not a drop of rain fell, never was a month more dry, never were the astrologers more embarrassed. However, we neither discouraged nor neglected them; almost all our princes continued to consult them.

I have not the honor to be a prince; nevertheless, the celebrated Count de Boulainvilliers and an Italian, named Colonna, who had great reputation at Paris, both foretold to me that I should assuredly die at the age of thirty-two. I have already been malicious enough to [outwit] them by thirty years in their calculation—for which I most humbly ask their pardon.

Authority

Miserable human beings, whether in green robes or in turbans, whether in black gowns or in [cloaks or clerical bands], never seek to use authority where nothing but reason will do, unless they wish to be [scorned] in all ages as the most impertinent of men, as well as to endure public hatred as the most unjust.

You have been told a hundred times of the insolent absurdity with which you condemned Galileo, and I speak to you of it for the hundred and first. I would have it inscribed over the door of your holy office.

"A Philosophical Dictionary" is from Tobias Smollett, ed., *The Works of Voltaire* (London: E. R. DuMont, 1901), vol. 6, pp. 93, 95–96, 178–179; vol. 8, pp. 260–266. Text modernized by the editor.

Seven cardinals, assisted by certain minor friars, threw into prison the master of thinking in Italy, at the age of seventy; and made him live upon bread and water because he instructed mankind in that of which they were ignorant. . . .

Further, a [university] Faculty, which possessed very small faculties, made a decree against innate ideas, and afterwards another for them, without the said Faculty being informed, except by its [officials] what an idea was.

In neighboring schools legal proceedings were commenced against the circulation of the blood. A process was issued against inoculation, and the parties [subpoenaed]. Twenty-one folio volumes were seized in which it was wickedly and falsely said that triangles have always three angles; that a father was older than his son; that Rhea Silvia lost her virginity before [giving birth to her child]; and that flour differs from oak leaves!

Democracy

There is ordinarily no comparison to be made between the crimes of the great, who are always ambitious, and those of the people, who never desire and who never can desire, anything but liberty and equality. These two sentiments, "liberty and equality," do not necessarily lead to slander, rapine, assassination, poisoning, and devastation of the lands of neighbors; but, the towering ambition and thirst for power of the great [plunge] them head-long into every kind of crime in all times and places. . . .

Popular government, therefore, is in itself . . . less abominable than monarchical despotism. The great vice of democracy is certainly not tyranny and cruelty. . . . [But] democracy seems to suit only a very small country and one that is fortunately situated. Small as it may be, it will commit many faults, because it will be composed of men. Discord will prevail in it, . . . but there will be no St. Bartholomews there, no Irish massacre, . . . no Inquisition, no condemnation to the galleys for having taken water from the ocean without paying for it—unless it be a republic of devils, established in some corner of hell. . . .

Every day we are asked which is better, a republic or a monarchy? The dispute always ends in agreeing that the government of men is exceedingly difficult. The Jews had God himself for their master; yet observe the events of their history. They have almost always been trampled upon and enslaved, and even today what a wretched figure they make!

Equality

Nothing can be clearer than that men, enjoying the faculties of their common nature, are in a state of equality; they are equal when they perform their animal functions, and exercise their understandings. . . . All animals of each species are on an equality with one another. . . .

It is impossible in our unhappy world to prevent men living in society from being divided into two classes, one of the rich who command, the other of the poor who obey, and these two are subdivided into various others, which have also their respective shades of difference. . . .

All the poor are not unhappy. The majority are born in that state, and constant labor prevents them from too sensibly feeling their situation; but when they do strongly feel it, then come wars such as those of the popular party against the senate at Rome, and those of the peasantry in Germany, England, and France. All these wars ended sooner or later with the subjection of the people, because the great have money, and money in a state commands everything; I say in a state, for the case is different between nation and nation. That nation which makes the best use of [the sword] will always subjugate another that has more gold but less courage.

Every man is born with an eager inclination for power, wealth, and pleasure, and also with a great taste for indolence. Every man, consequently, would wish to possess the fortunes and the wives or daughters of others, to be their master, to retain them in subjection to his whims, and to do nothing, or at least nothing but what is perfectly agreeable. You clearly perceive that with such amiable dispositions, it is as impossible for men to be equal as for two preachers or theology professors not to be jealous of each other.

The human race, constituted as it is, cannot exist unless there be an infinite number of useful individuals possessed of no property at all, for most certainly a man who is well off will not leave his own land to come and cultivate yours; and if you want a pair of shoes you will not get a lawyer to make them for you. Equality, then, is at the same time the most natural and the most implausible thing possible.

As men carry everything to excess if they have it in their power to do so, this inequality has been pushed too far; it has been maintained in many countries that no citizen has a right to [renounce the country of his birth]. The meaning of such a law must evidently be: "This country is so badly governed that we forbid every man from leaving for fear that everyone will leave it." Do better: excite in all your subjects a desire to stay with you, and in foreigners a desire to come and settle among you.

Every man has a right to [think himself equal] to other men, but it does not follow that a cardinal's cook should [order] his master to prepare his dinner. The cook, however, may say: "I am a man as well as my master; I was born like him crying, and shall like him die in anguish, attended by the same common ceremonies. We both perform the same animal functions. If the Turks get possession of Rome, and I then become a cardinal and my master a cook, I will take him into my service." This language is perfectly reasonable and just, but, while waiting for the Grand Turk to get possession of Rome, the cook is bound to do his duty, or all human society is subverted.

With respect to a man who is neither a cardinal's cook nor invested with any office whatever in the state—with respect to an individual who has no connections, and is disgusted at always being [patronized or scorned], who sees quite clearly that many men of quality and title have no more knowledge, wit, or virtue than himself, and is bored at waiting in their antechambers—what ought such a man to do? He ought to leave.

Introduction to the *Encyclopedia* (1751)

JEAN LE ROND D'ALEMBERT

The *Encyclopedia* is, as its title proclaims, the work of a company of men of letters. Were we not one of them, we might venture to claim that they have, or are worthy of having, a good reputation. But without wishing to anticipate a judgment which scholars alone may form, it is at least our duty to set aside, before everything else, the objection most capable of prejudicing the success of such a vast enterprise. We declare, therefore, that we have by no means had the temerity to take upon ourselves alone a burden so far beyond our capabilities, and that our role as editors consists principally in putting in order materials of which the greater part was supplied to us. . . .

The work which we are beginning (and wish to complete) has two aims: as an encyclopedia, its purpose is to set forth, as well as possible, the order and continuity of human knowledge; as an analytical dictionary of the arts, the sciences, and the professions, its purpose is to contain, for each science and each art, whether liberal or mechanical, the general principles on which it is based and the most essential details which make up its body and substance. These two points of view, of encyclopedia and of analytical dictionary, will therefore dictate the outline and the division of this preliminary discourse. We will consider them, pursue them one after the other, and report on the means by which we have attempted to satisfy this double aim.

If one has ever reflected at all on the connections between discoveries, it is easy to realize that the arts and sciences lend each other mutual assistance that there is consequently a chain which joins them. But it is often difficult to reduce to a small number of rules or general ideas each particular science or art; it is no less difficult to enclose in a unified system the infinitely varied branches of human knowledge.

The first step we have to take in this research is to examine . . . the genealogy of our knowledge and the relationships within it, the causes which must have led to its birth and the nature that distinguishes it—in brief, to go back to the origin and generation of our ideas. Aside from the benefits we will reap from examining this encyclopedic enumeration of the arts and sciences, this will not be out of place at the head of an analytical dictionary of human knowledge.

We can divide all our knowledge into direct knowledge and reasoned knowledge. Direct knowledge is that which we receive immediately without an operation of our will, which finding open . . . all of the doors of our soul, enters it without resistance and without effort. Reasoned knowledge is that which the mind acquires in operating on direct knowledge, in uniting and combining it.

"Introduction to the Encyclopedia" is from Nina B. Gunzenhauser, trans., in *Major Crises in Western Civilization*, vol. 2 (New York: Harcourt Brace and World, 1965), pp. 13–14.

Denis Diderot, above, and Jean Le Rond d'Alembert, below, surrounded by the principle contributors to the *Encyclopedia*. One of the most ambitious accomplishments of the Enlightenment, the *Encyclopedia* was condemned by both church and state. (*Giraudon/Art Resource*)

All of our direct knowledge can be reduced to that which we receive through the senses; from which it follows that we owe all our ideas to our sensations. The system of innate ideas, tempting in many respects . . . after having reigned for a long time [still] has some partisans; with such difficulty does truth [gain] its place. . . . At last, quite recently, there has been almost universal consensus that [innate ideas do not exist].

"We Did Not Live Entirely in Vain" (1764)
DENIS DIDEROT

The public has judged the first seven volumes; we ask for the current batch only the same indulgence. . . . From the point where we started to the point we have reached the distance was tremendous. . . . Thanks to our labor, those who come after us will be able to go further. Without declaring what they have yet to do, we will turn over to them at least the best book on tools and machines that ever existed . . . and an infinite number of precious morsels concerning all the sciences. O compatriots and contemporaries! With whatever severity you judge this work, remember that it was undertaken, continued, completed by a small number of isolated men, thwarted in their views, shown in the worst light, slandered and insulted in the most atrocious manner, having no other encouragement than the love of the good, no other support than several commendations, no other help but that which they found in the confidence of three or four tradesmen!

Our main purpose was to collect the discoveries of preceding centuries. . . . Should a revolution, the germ of which is forming perhaps in some unknown canton of the earth or incubating secretly in the very center of the civilized world, break out in time, destroy the cities, scatter the nations once again, and bring back ignorance and darkness; if one single complete set of this work survives, all will not be lost.

At least it cannot be contested, I think, that our work is on a level with our century, and that is something. The most enlightened man will find in it ideas that were unfamiliar to him and facts he did not know. If only general education could advance at such a rapid rate that twenty years from now there would be, out of a thousand of our pages, scarcely a single line that was not popular knowledge! It is up to the rulers of the world to hasten that happy revolution; it is they who expand or contract the sphere of enlightenment. Happy the time when they will all have understood that their security consists in commanding educated men! The major crimes have never been attempted by any except blinded fanatics. . . . [We hope that] we led our fellow men to love each other, to tolerate each other and to recognize at last the

---

"'We Did Not Live Entirely in Vain'" is from Nina B. Gunzenhauser, trans., in *Major Crises in Western Civilization*, vol. 2 (New York: Harcourt Brace and World, 1965), pp. 35–37.

superiority of universal ethics over all the particular morals that inspire hatred and disorder and that break or relax the general and common bond. Such was our aim throughout. . . .

If one adds to the years of our life that had passed at the time we planned this work those we have given to its accomplishment, one will easily realize that we have lived more years than we have left. But we shall have received the compensation that we look for from our contemporaries and our descendants if we make them say one day that we did not live entirely in vain.

Thoughts on Government: The Political Framework

The following selections present a theoretical foundation for the political structure of human society and present justification for the elimination of absolute monarchy. John Locke *(1632–1704) was an English political philosopher whose* Second Treatise of Civil Government *(1690) later influenced both the French and American revolutions. It is also the first philosophical statement of liberalism, a doctrine that sought the limitation of the arbitrary power of government and the establishment of legal equality, religious toleration, and freedom of the press.* Baron de Montesquieu *(1689–1755) was one of the most penetrating political analysts of his age. The selection from* The Spirit of the Laws *was published in 1748, about forty years before the French Revolution broke out. The third selection is from* The Social Contract *(1762) by Jean-Jacques Rousseau (1712–1778). Although Rousseau spent much of his life in intimate contact with the* philosophes, *he rejected their attitude that the human being is a rational creature whose confidence in reason would result in liberty and equality. Rousseau advocated the elimination of political despotism and the introduction of a new social order in which only the authority of the "general will" of the governed placed limits on individual freedom. His ideas provided the most inspirational justification for revolutionary action during the eighteenth century.*

Second Treatise of Civil Government (1690)
JOHN LOCKE

Political power, then, I take to be a right of making laws with penalties of death, and consequently all less penalties, for the regulating and preserving of property, and of employing the force of the community, in the execution

"Second Treatise of Civil Government" is from John Locke, *The Treatises of Government* (London, 1694).

of such laws, and in the defence of the commonwealth from foreign injury; and all this only for the public good.

Chapter II: Of the State of Nature

To understand political power right, and derive it from its original, we must consider what state all men are naturally in, and that is, a state of perfect freedom to order their actions and dispose of their possessions and persons, as they think fit, within the bounds of the law of nature; without asking leave, or depending upon the will of any other man.

A state also of equality, wherein all the power and jurisdiction is reciprocal, no one having more than another; there being nothing more evident, than that creatures of the same species and rank, promiscuously born to all the same advantages of nature, and the use of the same faculties, should also be equal one amongst another without subordination or subjection; unless the lord and master of them all should, by any manifest declaration of his will, set one above another, and confer on him, by an evident and clear appointment, an undoubted right to dominion and sovereignty. . . .

But though this be a state of liberty, yet it is not a state of license: though man in that state has an uncontrollable liberty to dispose of his person or possessions, yet he has not liberty to destroy himself, or so much as any creature in his possession, but where some nobler use than its bare preservation call for it. The state of nature has a law of nature to govern it, which obliges every one: and reason, which is that law, teaches all mankind, who will but consult it, that being equal and independent, no one ought to harm another in his life, health, liberty, or possessions: for men being all the workmanship of one omnipotent and infinitely wise Maker; all the servants of one sovereign master, sent into the world by his order, and about his business; they are his property, whose workmanship they are, made to last during his, not another's pleasure: and being furnished with like faculties, sharing all in one community of nature, there cannot be supposed any such subordination among us, that may authorize us to destroy another, as if we were made for one another's uses, as the inferior ranks of creatures are for ours. Every one, as he is bound to preserve himself, . . . ought he, as much as he can, to preserve the rest of mankind, and may not, unless it be to do justice to an offender, take away or impair the life, or what tends to the preservation of life, the liberty, health, limb, or goods of another.

And that all men may be restrained from invading others' rights, and from doing hurt to one another, and the law of nature be observed, which willeth the peace and preservation of all mankind, the execution of the law of nature is, in that state, put into every man's hands, whereby every one has a right to punish the transgressors of that law to such a degree as may hinder its violation: for the law of nature would, as all other laws that concern men in this world, be in vain, if there were nobody that in the state of nature had a power to execute the law, and thereby preserve the innocent and restrain offenders. And if any one in the state of nature may punish another for any evil he has done, every one may do so: for in that state of perfect equality, where naturally there is no superiority or jurisdiction of one over another, what any may do in prosecution of that law, every one must needs have a right to do.

And thus, in the state of nature, "one man comes by a power over another"; but yet this is not an absolute or arbitrary power. . . .

Chapter III: Of the State of War

[It is reasonable and just that . . .] I should have a right to destroy that which threatens me with destruction; for, by the fundamental law of nature, man being to be preserved as much as possible, when all cannot be preserved, the safety of the innocent is to be preferred: and one may destroy a man who makes war upon him, or has discovered an enmity to his being, for the same reason that he may kill a wolf or a lion; because such men are not under the ties of the common law of reason, have no other rule, than that of force and violence, and so may be treated as beasts of prey, those dangerous and noxious creatures, that will be sure to destroy him whenever he falls into their power.

And hence it is, that he who attempts to get another man into his absolute power, does thereby put himself into a state of war with him; it being to be understood as a declaration of a design upon his life: for I have reason to conclude, that he who would get me into his power without my consent, would use me as he pleased when he got me there, and destroy me too when he had a fancy to it; for nobody can desire to have me in his absolute power, unless it be to compel me by force to that which is against the right of my freedom, i.e., make me a slave. To be free from such force is the only security of my preservation; and reason bids me look on him, as an enemy to my preservation, who would take away that freedom which is the fence to it; so that he who makes an attempt to enslave me, thereby puts himself into a state of war with me. He that, in the state of nature, would take away the freedom that belongs to any one in that state, must necessarily be supposed to have a design to take away everything else, that freedom being the foundation of all the rest; as he that, in the state of society, would take away the freedom belonging to those of that society or commonwealth, must be supposed to design to take away from them every thing else, and so be looked on as in a state of war. . . .

Chapter IV: Of Slavery

The natural liberty of man is to be free from any superior power on earth, and not to be under the will or legislative authority of man, but to have only the law of nature for his rule. The liberty of man, in society, is to be under no other legislative power, but that established, by consent, in the commonwealth; nor under the dominion of any will, or restraint of any law, but what that legislative shall enact, according to the trust put in it. Freedom then is not what Sir Robert Filmer tells us, "a liberty for every one to do what he lists, to live as he pleases, and not to be tied by any laws": but freedom of men under government is, to have a standing rule to live by, common to every one of that society, and made by the legislative power erected in it; a liberty to follow my own will in all things, where the rule prescribes not; and not to be subject to the inconstant, uncertain, unknown, arbitrary will of another man: as freedom of nature is, to be under any other restraint but the law of nature.

This freedom from absolute, arbitrary power, is so necessary to, and closely joined with a man's preservation, that he cannot part with it, but by what forfeits his preservation and life together.

Chapter VIII: Of the Beginning of Political Societies

Men being, as has been said by nature, all free, equal, and independent, no one can be put out of this estate, and subjected to the political power of another, without his own consent. The only way, whereby any one divests himself of his natural liberty, and puts on the bonds of civil society, is by agreeing with other men to join and unite into a community, for their comfortable, safe, and peaceable living one amongst another, in a secure enjoyment of their properties, and a greater security against any, that are not of it. This any number of men may do, because it injures not the freedom of the rest; they are left as they were in the liberty of the state of nature. When any number of men have so consented to make one community or government they are thereby presently incorporated, and make one body politic, wherein the majority have a right to act and conclude the rest.

For, when any number of men have, by the consent of every individual, made a community, they have thereby made that community one body, with a power to act as one body, which is only by the will and determination of the majority: . . . or else it is impossible that it should act or continue as one body, one community, which the consent of every individual that united into it, agreed that it should; and so every one is bound by that consent to be concluded by the majority. . . .

And thus every man, by consenting with others to make one body politic under one government, puts himself under an obligation, to every one of that society, to submit to the determination of the majority, and to be concluded by it; or else this original compact, whereby he with others incorporate into one society, would signify nothing, and be no compact, if he be left free, and under no other ties than he was in before in the state of nature.

Chapter IX: Of the Ends of Political Society and Government

If man in the state of nature be so free, as has been said: if he be absolute lord of his own person and possessions, equal to the greatest, and subject to nobody, why will he part with his freedom? why will he give up his empire, and subject himself to the dominion and control of any other power? To which it is obvious to answer, that though in the state of nature he hath such a right, yet the enjoyment of it is very uncertain, and constantly exposed to the invasion of others; for all being kings as much as he, every man his equal, and the greater part no strict observers of equity and justice, the enjoyment of the property he has in this state is very unsafe, very unsecure. This makes him willing to quit a condition, which however free, is full of fears and continual dangers: and it is not without reason, that he seeks out, and is willing to join in society with others, who are already united, or have a mind to unite, for the mutual preservation of their lives, liberties, and estates, which I call by the general name, property.

The great and chief end, therefore, of men's uniting into commonwealths, and putting themselves under government, is the preservation of their property. To which in the state of nature there are many things wanting. . . .

Chapter XV: Of Despotical Power

Despotical power is an absolute, arbitrary power one man has over another, to take away his life whenever he pleases; and this is a power which neither Nature gives, for it has made no such distinction between one man and another, nor compact can convey. . . . For having quitted reason, which God has given to be the rule betwixt man and man, and the peaceable ways which that teaches, and made use of force to compass his unjust ends upon another where he has no right, he renders himself liable to be destroyed by his adversary whenever he can, as any other noxious and brutish creature that is destructive to his being. . . .

Chapter XIX: Of the Dissolution of Government

The reason why men enter into society, is the preservation of their property; and the end why they choose and authorize a legislative, is, that there may be laws made, and rules set, as guards and fences to the properties of all the members of the society: to limit the power, and moderate the dominion, of every part and member of the society: for since it can never be supposed to be the will of the society, that the legislative should have a power to destroy that which every one designs to secure by entering into society, and for which the people submitted themselves to legislators of their own making; whenever the legislators endeavour to take away and destroy the property of the people, or to reduce them to slavery under arbitrary power, they put themselves into a state of war with the people, who are thereupon absolved from any farther obedience, and are left to the common refuge, which God hath provided for all men, against force and violence. Whensoever therefore the legislative shall transgress this fundamental rule of society; and either by ambition, fear, folly or corruption, endeavour to grasp themselves, or put into the hands of any other, an absolute power over the lives, liberties, and estates of the people, by this breach of trust they forfeit the power the people had put into their hands for quite contrary ends, and it devolves to the people, who have a right to resume their original liberty, and, by the establishment of a new legislative, (such as they shall think fit) provide for their own safety and security, which is the end for which they are in society. What I have said here, concerning the legislative in general holds true also concerning the supreme executor, who having a double trust put in him, both to have a part in the legislative, and the supreme execution of the law, acts against both, when he goes about to set up his own arbitrary will as the law of the society. . . .

Whosoever uses force without right, as every one does in society, who does it without law, puts himself into a state of war with those against whom he so used it; and in that state all former ties are cancelled, all other rights cease, and every one has a right to defend himself, and to resist the aggressor.

The Spirit of the Laws (1748)
BARON DE MONTESQUIEU

When the legislative and executive powers are united in the same person, or in the same body of magistrates, there can be no liberty; because apprehensions may arise lest the same monarch or senate should enact tyrannical laws to execute them in a tyrannical manner.

Again there is no liberty if the power of judging be not separated from the legislative and executive powers. Were it joined with the legislature, the life and liberty of the subject would be exposed to arbitrary control; for the judge would be then the legislator. Were it joined to the executive power, the judge might behave with all the violence of an oppressor.

There would be an end of everything were the same man or the same body, whether of the nobles or of the people, to exercise those three powers, that of enacting the laws, that of executing the public resolutions, and that of judging the crimes or differences of individuals.

Most kingdoms of Europe enjoy a moderate government because the prince who is invested with the two first powers leaves the third to his subjects. In Turkey, where these three powers are united in the sultan's person, the subjects groan under the weight of the most frightful oppression.

In the republics of Italy, where these three powers are united, there is less liberty than in our monarchies. Hence their government is obliged to have recourse to as violent methods for its support as even that of the Turks; witness the state inquisitors (at Venice), and the lion's mouth into which every informer may at all hours throw his written accusations.

What a situation must the poor subjects be in, under those republics! The same body of magistrates are possessed, as executors of the laws, of the whole power they have given themselves in quality of legislators. They may plunder the state by their general determination, and as they have likewise the

"The Spirit of the Laws" is from Baron de Montesquieu (Charles de Secondat), *The Spirit of the Laws*, 2 vols. (London, 1758), pp. 216–217.

judiciary power in their hands, every private citizen may be ruined by their particular decisions.

The whole power is here united in one body; and though there is no external pomp that indicates a despotic sway, yet the people feel the effects of it every moment.

Hence it is that many of the princes of Europe, whose aim has been levelled at arbitrary power, have constantly set out with uniting in their own persons all the branches of magistracy, and all the great offices of the state.

The Social Contract (1762)

JEAN JACQUES ROUSSEAU

Of the Social Compact

We will suppose that men in a state of nature are arrived at that crisis when the strength of each individual is insufficient to defend him from the attacks he is subject to. This primitive state can therefore subsist no longer; and the human race must perish, unless they change their manner of life.

As men cannot create for themselves new forces, but merely unite and direct those which already exist, the only means they can employ for the preservation is to form by aggregation an assemblage of forces that may be able to resist all assaults, be put in motion as one body, and act in concert upon all occasions.

This assemblage of forces must be produced by the concurrence of many: as the force and the liberty of a man are the chief instruments of his preservation, how can he engage them without danger, and without neglecting the care which is due to himself? This doubt, which leads directly to my subject, may be expressed in these words:

Where shall we find a form of association which will defend and protect with the whole aggregate force the person and the property of each individual; and by which every person, while united with ALL, shall obey only HIMSELF, and remain as free as before the union? Such is the fundamental problem, of which the Social Contract gives the solution.

The articles of this contract are so unalterably fixed by the nature of the act, that the least modification renders them vain and of no effect. They are the same everywhere, and are everywhere understood and admitted, even though they may never have been formally announced: so that, when once the social pact is violated in any instance, all obligations it created cease; and each individual is restored to his original rights, and resumes native liberty, as the consequence of losing that conventional liberty for which he exchanged them.

"The Social Contract" is from Jean-Jacques Rousseau, *An Inquiry into the Nature of the Social Contract* (London, 1791), pp. 33–49.

Jean-Jacques Rousseau brilliantly challenged the established thought of his day and even alienated several philosophes. He outlined a political structure that he hoped would nurture human virtue. *(Library of Congress)*

All the articles of the social contract will, when clearly understood, be found reducible to this single point—THE TOTAL ALIENATION OF EACH ASSOCIATE, AND ALL HIS RIGHTS, TO THE WHOLE COMMUNITY. For every individual gives himself up entirely—the condition of every person is alike; and being so, it would not be the interest of anyone to render himself offensive to others.

Moreover, the alienation is made without any reserve; the union is as complete as it can be, and no associate has a claim to anything; for if any individual was to retain rights not enjoyed in general by all, as there would be no common superior to decide between him and the public, each person being in some points his own proper judge, would soon pretend to be so in everything; and thus would the state of nature be revived, and the association become tyrannical or be annihilated.

Finally, each person gives himself to ALL, but not to any INDIVIDUAL: and as there is no one associate over whom the same right is not acquired which is ceded to him by others, each gains an equivalent for what he loses, and finds his force increased for preserving that which he possesses.

If, therefore, we exclude from the social compact all that is not essentially necessary, we shall find it reduced to the following terms:

"We each of us place, in common, his person, and all his power, under the supreme direction of the general will; and we receive into the body each member as an indivisible part of the whole."

From that moment, instead of so many separate persons as there are contractors, this act of association produces a moral collective body, composed of as many members as there are voices in the assembly; which from this act receives its unity, its common self, its life, and its will. This public person, which is thus formed by the union of all the private persons, took formerly the name of city, and now takes that of republic or body politic. It is called by its members state when it is passive, and sovereign when in activity: and whenever it is spoken of with other bodies of a similar kind, it is denominated power. The associates take collectively the name of people, and separately that of citizens, as participating in the sovereign authority: they are also styled subjects, because they are subjected to the laws. But these terms are frequently confounded, and used one for the other; and a man must understand them well to distinguish when they are properly employed.

Of the Sovereign Power

It appears from this form that the act of association contains a reciprocal engagement between the public and individuals; and that each individual contracting as it were with himself, is engaged under a double character that is, as a part of the sovereign power engaging with individuals, and as a member of the state entering into a compact with the sovereign power. But we cannot apply here the maxim of civil right, that no person is bound by any engagement which he makes with himself; for there is a material difference between an obligation contracted towards one's self individually, and towards a collective body of which one's self constitutes a part.

It is necessary to observe here that the will of the public, expressed by a majority of votes—which can enforce obedience from the subjects to the sovereign power in consequence of the double character under which the members of that body appear—cannot bind the sovereign power to itself; and that it is against the nature of the body politic for the sovereign power to impose any one law which it cannot alter. Were they to consider themselves as acting under one character only, they would be in the situation of individuals forming each a contract with himself: but this is not the case; and therefore there can be no fundamental obligatory law established for the body of the people, not even the social contract. But this is of little moment, as that body could not very well engage itself to others in any manner which would not derogate from the contract. With respect to foreigners, it becomes a single being, an individual only.

But the body politic, or sovereign power, which derives its existence from the sacredness of the contract, can never bind itself, even towards others, in any thing that would derogate from the original act; such as alienating any portion of itself, or submitting to another sovereign; for by violating the contract its own existence would be at once annihilated, and by nothing nothing can be performed.

As soon as the multitude is thus united in one body, you cannot offend one of its members without attacking the whole; much less can you offend the whole without incurring the resentment of all the members. Thus duty and interest equally oblige the two contracting parties to lend their mutual aid to each other; and the same men must endeavour to unite under this double character all the advantages which attend it.

The sovereign power being formed only of the individuals which compose it, neither has, or can have, any interest contrary to theirs; consequently the sovereign power requires no guarantee towards its subjects, because it is impossible that the body should seek to injure all its members: and shall see presently that it can do no injury to any individual. The sovereign power by its nature must, while it exists, be everything it ought to be: it is not so with subjects towards the sovereign power; to which, notwithstanding the common interest subsisting between them, there is nothing to answer for the performance of their engagements, if some means is not found of ensuring their fidelity.

In fact, each individual may, as a man, have a private will, dissimilar contrary to the general will which he has as a citizen. His own particular interest may dictate to him very differently from the common interest; his mind, naturally and absolutely independent, may regard what he owes to the common cause as a gratuitous contribution, the omission of which would be less injurious to others than the payment would be burdensome to himself; and considering the moral person which constitutes the state as a creature of the imagination, because it is not a man, he may wish to enjoy the rights of a citizen, without being disposed to fulfill the duties of a subject: an injustice which would in its progress cause the ruin of the body politic.

In order therefore to prevent the social compact from becoming an empty formula, it tacitly includes this premise, which alone can give effect to the others—That whoever refuses to obey the general will, shall be compelled to it by the whole body, which is in fact only forcing him to be free; for this is the condition which guarantees his absolute personal independence to every citizen of the country: a condition which gives motion and effect to the political machine; which alone renders all civil engagements legal; and without which they would be absurd, tyrannical, and subject to the most enormous abuses.

Of the State

agree

The passing from a state of nature to a civil state, produces in man a very remarkable change, by substituting justice for instinct, and giving to his actions a moral character which they wanted before.

It is at the moment of that transition that the voice of duty succeeds to physical impulse; and a sense of what is right, to the incitements of appetite. The man who had till then regarded none but himself, perceives that he must act on other principles, and learns to consult his reason before he listens to his propensities.

Thoughts on Women: The Social Framework

Jean-Jacques Rousseau's radical stance on nature and the establishment of the civil state was viewed as dangerous by many philosophes. *Voltaire, in a horrified state of mind, wrote to him: "Never has anyone employed so much genius to make us into beasts. When one reads your book, one is seized at once with a desire to go down on all fours." Indeed, under Rousseau, the social contract theory was limited in its application. Both Thomas Hobbes and John Locke advocated a government predicated on equality of human rights. Although Rousseau never mentioned women in his treatise* The Social Contract, *his many other works defined more exactly the particular role he assigned them in society. Rousseau's woman knew her place. He urged that women be "trained to bear the yoke from the first, so that they may not feel it." The first selection is from* Emile *(1762), his treatise on education.*

The events of 1789 were to bring into focus many of the philosophical arguments concerning natural rights presented in the previous section. But the emphasis was on the rights of male citizens. Many accepted the views of Rousseau that women were not rational creatures and lacked the capacity for understanding the abstract tenets of the Enlightenment. Mary Wollstonecraft, an English writer and early disciple of Rousseau's political views, nevertheless took him to task in the second selection. In her work A Vindication of the Rights of Women *(1792), she extended the call for political liberty into the social realm. Her arguments gave justification to a different kind of revolution between the sexes.*

Woman: "Especially Constituted to Please Man"
JEAN JACQUES ROUSSEAU

A perfect man and a perfect woman ought no more to resemble each other in mind than in features. . . . In the union of the sexes each contributes equally toward the common end, but not in the same way. Hence arises the

---

"Woman: 'Especially Constituted to Please Man'" is from W. H. Payne, ed., Rousseau's *Emile* (New York: D. Appleton and Co., 1895), pp. 260–263, 281, 303.

first assignable difference among their moral relations. One must be active and strong, the other passive and weak. One must needs have power and will, while it suffices that the other have little power of resistance.

This principle once established, it follows that woman is especially constituted to please man. If man ought to please her in turn, the necessity for it is less direct. His merit lies in his power; he pleases simply because he is strong. I grant that this is not the law of love, but it is the law of Nature, which is anterior even to love. . . .

The moment it is demonstrated that man and woman are not and ought not to be constituted in the same way, either in character or in constitution, it follows that they ought not to have the same education. In following the directions of Nature they ought to act in concert, but they ought not to do the same things; their duties have a common end, but the duties themselves are different, and consequently the tastes which direct them. After having tried to form the natural man, let us also see, in order not to leave our work incomplete, how the woman is to be formed who is befitting to this man. . . .

Woman is worth more as a woman, but less as a man; wherever she improves her rights she has the advantage, and wherever she attempts to usurp ours she remains inferior to us. Only exceptional cases can be urged against this general truth—the usual mode of argument adopted by the gallant partisans of the fair sex. . . .

Does it follow that she ought to be brought up in complete ignorance, and restricted solely to the duties of the household? . . . No, doubtless. . . . They ought to learn multitudes of things, but only those which it becomes them to know. . . . The whole education of women ought to be relative to men. To please them, to be useful to them, to make themselves loved and honored by them, to educate them when young, to care for them when grown, to counsel them, to console them, and to make life agreeable and sweet to them—these are the duties of women at all times, and what should be taught them from their infancy. . . .

The search for abstract and speculative truths, principles, and scientific axioms, whatever tends to generalize ideas, does not fall within the compass of women; all their studies ought to have reference to the practical; it is for them to make the application of the principles which man has discovered. . . . She must therefore make a profound study of the mind of man, not the mind of man in general, through abstraction, but the mind of the men who surround her, the mind of the men to whom she is subject, either by law or by opinion. She must learn to penetrate their feelings through their conversation, their actions, their looks, and their gestures. Through her conversations, her actions, her looks, and her gestures she must know how to give them the feelings which are pleasing to her, without even seeming to think of them. . . .

A woman of wit is the scourge of her husband, her children, her friends, her servants, of everybody. . . . If all the men in the world were sensible, every girl of letters would remain unmarried all her life.

A Vindication of the Rights of Women (1792)

MARY WOLLSTONECRAFT

But what have women to do in society? . . . Women might certainly study the art of healing, and be physicians as well as nurses. . . . They might also study politics, and settle their benevolence on the broadest basis. . . . Business of various kinds, they might likewise pursue, if they were educated in a more orderly manner, which might save many from common and legal prostitution. Women would not then marry for a support . . . nor would an attempt to earn their own subsistence . . . sink them almost to the level of those poor abandoned creatures who live by prostitution. . . . The few employments open to women, so far from being liberal, are menial; and when a superior education enables them to take charge of the education of children as governesses, they are not treated like the tutors of sons. . . . But as women educated like gentlewomen, are never designed for the humiliating situation which necessity sometimes forces them to fill; these situations are considered in the light of a degradation; and they know little of the human heart, who need to be told, that nothing so painfully sharpens sensibility as such a fall in life.

How many women thus waste life away the prey of discontent, who might have practised as physicians, regulated a farm, managed a shop, and stood erect, supported by their own industry, instead of hanging their heads surcharged with the dew of sensibility, that consumes the beauty to which it at first gave lustre; nay, I . . . have seldom seen much compassion excited by the helplessness of females unless they were fair; then, perhaps pity was the soft handmaid of love, or the harbinger of lust. How much more respectable is the woman who earns her own bread by fulfilling any duty, than the most accomplished beauty!

Proud of their weakness, however, [some women believe] they must always be protected, guarded from care, and all the rough toils that dignify the mind. If this be the fiat of fate, if they will make themselves insignificant and contemptible, sweetly to waste "life away," let them not expect to be valued when their beauty fades, for it is the fate of the fairest flowers to be admired and pulled to pieces by the careless hand that plucked them. In how many ways do I wish, from the purest benevolence, to impress this truth on my sex; yet I fear that they will not listen to a truth that dear bought experience has brought home to many an agitated bosom, nor willingly resign the privileges of rank and sex for the privileges of humanity, to which those have no claim who do not discharge its duties. . . .

"A Vindication of the Rights of Women" is from Mary Wollstonecraft, *A Vindication of the Rights of Women*, 2nd ed. (London: J. Johnson, 1792), chapter 9.

Would men but generously snap our chains, and be content with rational fellowship instead of slavish obedience, they would find us more observant daughters, more affectionate sisters, more faithful wives, more reasonable mothers—in a word, better citizens. We should then love them with true affection, because we should learn to respect ourselves; and the peace of mind of a worthy man would not be interrupted by the idle vanity of his wife, nor the babes sent to nestle in a strange bosom, having never found a home in their mother's. . . .

It is time to effect a revolution in female manners—time to restore to them, as a part of the human species, labour by reforming themselves to reform the world. It is time to separate unchangeable morals from local manners. . . .

I wish to sum up what I have said in a few words, for I here throw down my gauntlet, and deny the existence of sexual virtues, not excepting modesty. For man and woman, truth, if I understand the meaning of the word, must be the same; yet the fanciful female character, so prettily drawn by poets and novelists, demanding the sacrifice of truth and sincerity, virtue becomes a relative idea, having no other foundation than utility, and of that utility men pretend arbitrarily to judge, shaping it to their own convenience.

Women, I allow, may have different duties to fulfill; but they are human duties, and the principles that should regulate the discharge of them, I sturdily maintain, must be the same.

To become respectable, the exercise of their understanding is necessary, there is no other foundation for independence of character; I mean explicitly to say that they must only bow to the authority of reason, instead of being the modest slaves of opinion.

In the superior ranks of life how seldom do we meet with a man of superior abilities, or even common acquirements? The reason appears to me clear: the state they are born in was an unnatural one. The human character has ever been formed by the employments the individual or class pursues; and if the faculties are not sharpened by necessity, they must remain obtuse. The argument may fairly be extended to women; for, seldom occupied by serious business, the pursuit of pleasure gives that insignificancy to their character which renders the society of the great so insipid. . . . Such are the blessings of civil governments, as they are at present organized, that wealth and female softness equally tend to debase mankind, and are produced by the same cause; but allowing women to be rational creatures, they should be incited to acquire virtues which they may call their own, for how can a rational being be ennobled by anything that is not obtained by its own exertions? . . .

There must be more equality established in society, or morality will never gain ground, and this virtuous equality will not rest firmly even when founded on a rock, if one half of mankind be chained to its bottom by fate, for they will be continually undermining it through ignorance or pride.

The Parisian Salon of an "Indispensable Woman"

The Parisian salons during the Enlightenment brought writers together for elegant, stylized conversation. It was in the salon, a rather formal reception room of a private home, where the intellectual elite congregated to spend the evening engaged in disputation, storytelling, timely debate over the latest issues of the day, or relaxed musing about the potentials of the future. Good conversation flourished under the guidance of an elegant hostess, who often directed the debate, smoothed ruffled feathers, and generally maintained an atmosphere conducive to discovery and pleasant conversation. It was in this setting that women not only competed with men on an equal intellectual footing but assumed a leading role by organizing and conducting the proceedings. In the process, women often became the arbiters of good taste and the dispensers of merit.

The following selection gives testimony to one of the most remarkable women of the Age of Reason, Julie de Lespinasse. Note carefully why others regarded her as an indispensable woman.

From Memoir of Baron de Grimm

Her circle met daily from five o'clock until nine in the evening. There we were sure to find choice men of all orders in the State, the Church, the Court,—military men, foreigners, and the most distinguished men of letters. Every one agrees that though the name of M. d'Alembert may have drawn them, it was she alone who kept them there. Devoted wholly to the care of preserving that society, of which she was the soul and the charm, she subordinated to this purpose all her tastes and all her personal intimacies. She seldom went to the theatre or into the country, and when she did make an exception to this rule it was an event of which all Paris was notified in advance.... Politics, religion, philosophy, anecdotes, news, nothing was excluded from the conversation, and, thanks to her care, the most trivial little narrative gained, as naturally as possible, the place and notice it deserved. News of all kinds was gathered there in its first freshness.

From Memoir of Marmontel

The circle was formed of persons who were not bound together. She had taken them here and there in society, but so well assorted were they that once there they fell into harmony like the strings of an instrument touched by an able hand. Following out that comparison, I may say that she played the instrument with an art that came of genius; she seemed to know what tone each string would yield before she touched it; I mean to lay that our minds and our natures were so well known to her that in order to bring them into play she had but to say a word.

"The Parisian Salon of an 'Indispensable Woman'" is from Katherine P. Wormley, trans., *Letters of Julie de Lespinasse* (Boston: Hardy, Pratt and Co., 1903), pp. 34–35, 75.

Nowhere was conversation more lively, more brilliant, or better regulated than at her house. It was a rare phenomenon indeed, the degree of tempered, equable heat which she knew so well how to maintain, sometimes by moderating it, sometimes by quickening it. The continual activity of her soul was communicated to our souls, but measurably; her imagination was the mainspring, her reason the regulator. Remark that the brains she stirred at will were neither feeble nor frivolous: the Coudillacs and Turgots were among them; d'Alembert was like a simple, docile child beside her. Her talent for casting out a thought and giving it for discussion to men of that class, her own talent in discussing it with precision, sometimes with eloquence, her talent for bringing forward new ideas and varying the topic—always with the facility and ease of a fairy, who, with one touch of her wand, can change the scene of her enchantment—these talents, I say, were not those of an ordinary woman. It was not with the follies of fashion and vanity that daily, during four hours of conversation, without languor and without vacuum, she knew how to make herself interesting to a wide circle of strong minds.

Thoughts on Commerce: The Economic Framework

Since the Renaissance, Europeans had sought new economic horizons. The commercial revolution of the sixteenth century and the exploration of the Americas had resulted in the establishment of colonies that engendered competition among imperial powers. Dominance and success in this commercial rivalry required that nations such as Spain, France, Great Britain, and the Netherlands become efficient producers and resourceful traders. To this end, governments focused their domestic economies and strictly regulated their foreign colonies in order to produce profit at each turn. This was especially important because these powers were constantly at war with each other in the eighteenth century, often squandering the precious wealth that they had accumulated.

To the extent that there was any formal economic theory behind this process of accumulating wealth, it was called mercantilism. Mercantilism gradually became a structured economic system based on the notion that the world was an arena of scarce resources. Since gold, silver and other products were limited, governments had to regulate trade with protective tariffs, navigation laws that restricted trade with rivals, and domestic monopolies on salt and gunpowder. Mercantilist statesmen believed that their economies could grow only at the expense of others.

Although this economic system developed in the seventeenth century, it became more pronounced in the eighteenth as the wars in Europe and North America forced each country to become even more heavy-handed. The first selection by Sir William Keith encapsulates the tenets of mercantilism. But there were also critics and the reaction to this economic regulation reached a climax in the late eighteenth-century with the ideas of Adam Smith.

Adam Smith can rightly be considered one of the most influential thinkers of the Enlightenment. He studied moral philosophy at Oxford and in his mid-twenties conceived of an economic philosophy of "the obvious and simple system of natural liberty," which the world would come to know as capitalism. In response to the restrictive emphasis of mercantilism, Smith conceived of an expansive universe, full of opportunity for the individual or nation to exercise initiative, accumulate wealth, and serve others in the process.

The second selection is an excerpt from his major work, The Wealth of Nations. *It focuses on Smith's view of human nature and the "invisible hand" of competition as guide to an economic system based on individual self-interest. If one views the Industrial Revolution of the early-nineteenth century and the birth of Marxism in 1848 as being directly influenced by Smith's theories, then his impact on the history of the twentieth century is immeasurable.*

Economic Regulation:
"The Maxim of All Polite Nations"
SIR WILLIAM KEITH

When either by conquest or increase of people, foreign provinces are possessed, and colonies planted abroad, it is convenient, and often necessary, to substitute little dependant provincial governments, whose people being enfranchised, and made partakers of the liberties and privileges belonging to the original Mother State, are justly bound by its laws, and become subservient to its interests, as the true end of their incorporation.

Every act of a dependant provincial government therefore ought to terminate in the advantage of the Mother State, unto whom it woes its being, and by whom it is protected in all its valuable privileges: hence it follows, that all advantageous projects, or commercial gains in any colony, which are truly prejudicial to, and inconsistent with the interest of the Mother State, must be understood to be illegal, and the practice of them unwarrantable, because they contradict the end for which the colony had a being, and are incompatible with the terms on which the people claim both privilege and protection. . . .

It has ever been the Maxim of all polite nations, to regulate their government to the best advantage of their trading interest. . . . By this short view of trade in general we may plainly understand that those colonies can be very beneficially employed both for Great Britain and themselves, without interfering with any of the staple manufactures in England.

But in order to set this point yet in a clearer light, we will proceed to consider some of the obvious regulations on the American trade, for rendering the colonies truly serviceable to Great Britain.

"Economic Regulation" is from Sir William Keith, *A Collection of Papers and Other Tracts, Written Occasionally on Various Subjects* (London: J. Mechell, 1740), pp. 169–170, 173–175.

1. That all the product of the colonies, for which the manufacture and trade of Britain has a constant demand, be enumerated among the goods which by law must be first transported to Britain, before they can be carried to any other market.

2. That all kinds of woollen manufactures for which the colonies have a demand, shall continue to be brought from Britain only, and linens from Great Britain and Ireland.

3. All other European commodities to be carried to the colonies, (salt excepted) entry thereof to be first made in Britain, before they can be transported to any of the English colonies.

4. The colonies to be absolutely restrained in their several governments from laying any manner of duties on shipping or trade from Europe, or upon European goods transported from one colony to another.

Supposing these things to be done, it will evidently follow in that the more extensive the trade of the colonies is, the greater will be the advantages accruing to Great Britain therefrom; and consequently, that the enlargement of the colonies, and the increase of their people, would still be an addition to the national strength. . . .

From what has been said of the nature of colonies, and the restriction that ought to be laid on their trade, it is plain that none of the English plantation in America can with any reason or good sense pretend to claim an absolute legislative power with themselves; so that let their several Constitutions be founded by Charters, Royal Patents, . . . or what other legal authority you please; yet still they cannot be possessed of any rightful capacity to contradict, or evade the true intent and force of any Act of Parliament, wherewith the wisdom of Great Britain may think fit to affect them from time to time.

The Wealth of Nations (1776)
ADAM SMITH

Human Nature and the Division of Labor

This division of labour, from which so many advantages are derived, is not originally the effect of any human wisdom, which foresees and intends that general opulence to which it gives occasion. It is the necessary, though very slow and gradual, consequence of a certain propensity in human nature which has in view no such extensive utility; the propensity to truck, barter, and exchange one thing for another.

Whether this propensity be one of those original principles in human nature, of which no further account can be given; or whether, as seems more

"The Wealth of Nations" is from Adam Smith, *An Inquiry into the Nature and Causes of the Wealth of Nations*, ed. Edwin A. Seligman (London: J. M. Dent, 1901), pp. 12–15, 400–401, 436–437.

probable, it be the necessary consequence of the faculties of reason and speech, it belongs not to our present subject to enquire. It is common to all men, and to be found in no other race of animals, which seem to know neither this nor any other species of contracts. . . . In civilized society, [man] stands at all times in need of the cooperation and assistance of great multitudes, while his whole life is scarce sufficient to gain the friendship of a few persons. In almost every other race of animals each individual, when it is grown up to maturity, is entirely independent, and in its natural state has occasion for the assistance of no other living creature. But man has almost constant occasion for the help of his brethren, and it is in vain for him to expect it from their benevolence only. He will be more likely to prevail if he can interest their self-love in his favour, and show them that it is for their own advantage to do for him what he requires of them. Whoever offers to another a bargain of any kind, proposes to do this. Give me that which I want, and you shall have this which you want, is the meaning of every such offer; and it is in this manner that we obtain from one another the far greater part of those good offices which we stand in need of. It is not from the benevolence of the butcher, the brewer, or the baker, that we expect our dinner, but from their regard to their own interest. We address ourselves, not to their humanity but to their self-love, and never talk to them of our own necessities but of their advantages. . . .

The difference of natural talents in different men is, in reality, much less than we are aware of; and the very different genius which appears to distinguish men of different professions, when grown up to maturity, is not upon many occasions so much the cause, as the effect of the division of labour. The difference between the most dissimilar characters, between a philosopher and a common street porter, for example, seems to arise not so much from nature, as from habit, custom, and education. When they came into the world, and for the first six or eight years of their existence, they were, perhaps, very much alike, and neither their parents nor playfellows could perceive any remarkable difference. About that age, or soon after, they come to be employed in very different occupations. The difference of talents comes then to be taken notice of, and widens by degrees, till at last the vanity of the philosopher is willing to acknowledge scarce any resemblance. . . . By nature a philosopher is not in genius and disposition half so different from a street porter, as a mastiff is from a greyhound, or a greyhound from a spaniel, or this last from a shepherd's dog. . . . Among men, on the contrary, the most dissimilar geniuses are of use to one another; the different produces of their respective talents, by the general disposition to truck, barter, and exchange, being brought, as it were, into a common stock, where every man may purchase whatever part of the produce of other men's talents he has occasion for. . . .

The Invisible Hand

As every individual, therefore, endeavors as much as he can both to employ his capital in the support of domestic industry, and so to direct that industry that its produce may be of the greatest value; every individual necessarily labours to render the annual revenue of the society as great as he can. He generally, indeed, neither intends to promote the public interest, nor knows how much he is promoting it. . . . He intends only his own security; and by directing that industry in such a manner as its produce may be of the greatest value, he intends only his own gain, and he is in this, as in many other cases, led by an invisible hand to promote an end which was no part of his intention. Nor is it always the worse for the society that it was no part of it. By pursuing his own interest he frequently promotes that of the society more effectually than when he really intends to promote it. I have never known much good done by those who affected to trade for the public good. . . . The statesman, who should attempt to direct private people in what manner they ought to employ their capitals, would not only load himself with a most unnecessary attention, but assume an authority which could safely be trusted, not only to no single person, but to no council or senate whatever, and which would nowhere be so dangerous as in the hands of a man who had folly and presumption enough to fancy himself fit to exercise it.

Unreasonableness of Restraints

Each nation has been made to look with an invidious eye upon the prosperity of all nations with which it trades, and to consider their gain as its own loss. Commerce, which ought naturally to be, among nations, as among individuals, a bond of union and friendship, has become the most fertile source of discord and animosity. . . . The violence and injustice of the rulers of mankind is an ancient evil, for which, I am afraid, the nature of human affairs can scarce admit of a remedy. But the mean rapacity, the monopolising spirit of merchants and manufacturers, who neither are, nor ought to be, the rulers of mankind, though it cannot perhaps be corrected, may very easily be prevented from disturbing the tranquility of anybody but themselves.

That it was the spirit of monopoly which originally both invented and propagated this doctrine cannot be doubted; and they who first taught it were by no means such fools as they who believed it. In every country it always is and must be the interest of the great body of the people to buy whatever they want of those who sell it cheapest. The proposition is so very manifest that it seems ridiculous to take any pains to prove it; nor could it have ever been called in question had not the interested sophistry of merchants and manufacturers confounded the common sense of mankind. Their interest is, in this respect, directly opposite to that of the great body of the people. As it is the interest of the freemen of a [guild] to hinder the rest of the inhabitants from employing any workmen but themselves, so it is the interest of the merchants and manufacturers of every country to secure to themselves the monopoly of the home market. Hence in Great Britain, and in most other European countries, the extraordinary duties upon almost all goods imported by alien merchants. Hence the high duties and prohibitions upon all those foreign manufactures which can come into competition with our own.

Hence, too, the extraordinary restraints upon the importation of almost all sorts of goods from those countries . . . whom national animosity happens to be most violently inflamed. . . . This very competition, however, is advantageous to the great body of the people, who profit greatly besides by the good market which the great expense of such a nation affords them in every other way. . . .

CHRONOLOGY: "Dare to Know!": The Revolution of the Mind in the Seventeenth and Eighteenth Centuries

1543	Nicolaus Copernicus: *On the Revolutions of the Heavenly Spheres*
1605	Sir Francis Bacon: *The Advancement of Learning*
1609	Johannes Kepler: *On the Motion of Mars*
1620	Sir Francis Bacon: *Novum Organum*
1628	William Harvey: *On the Circulation of the Blood*
1632	Galileo Galilei: *Dialogues on the Two Chief Systems of the World*
1637	René Descartes: *Discourse on Method*
1682–1725	Reign of Peter the Great of Russia. In 1697, the Tsar visits western Europe to study the skills necessary to build Russia into a strong, modern state.
1687	Sir Isaac Newton: *Principia Mathematica*
1688–1689	Glorious Revolution in England
1690	John Locke: *Essay Concerning Human Understanding; Second Treatise of Civil Government*
1693	John Locke: *Some Thoughts Concerning Education*
1713–1740	Frederick William I builds up the military power of Prussia.
1740–1748	Maria Theresa succeeds to the Austrian throne. War of the Austrian Succession: Frederick II of Prussia invades Austrian province of Silesia in violation of Pragmatic Sanction; Maria Theresa fights Frederick to a stalemate, but loses Silesia in the Treaty of Aix-la-Chapelle.
1748	The Baron de Montesquieu: *The Spirit of the Laws*
	David Hume: *Inquiry into Human Nature*
1751	Denis Diderot: First volume of the *Encyclopedia* appears
1756–1763	Seven Years War: France, Austria, Sweden, and Russia versus Prussia (supported financially by Great Britain)

STUDY QUESTIONS

Section I: The Scientific Revolution

1. What did Sir Francis Bacon contribute to the Scientific Revolution? What specific ideas does he offer about scientific method in *Novum Organum*?
2. How do some of Descartes's ideas on scientific method show the influence of Sir Francis Bacon? What did Descartes mean by the phrase "I think, therefore I am"? Why was this so fundamental to his method? Reconstruct his logic for the existence of God. Do you find it compelling?
3. Read Copernicus's statement on the movement of the sun and earth. What reasons does he give for supporting the heliocentric theory? Is he convincing? Why is it significant that Copernicus refers to ancient authors like Cicero and Plutarch?
4. What were Galileo's specific ideas regarding the relationship between science and the Bible? Be particular in your analysis. Why were Galileo's ideas considered dangerous by the Inquisition? Did the Inquisition do the church more harm than good?
5. How would you define the process of induction as championed by Sir Isaac Newton? How does he specifically demonstrate this principle in his work on *Optics*? If Newton was such a methodical scientist, why did he accept the compatibility of science and God in the pursuit of empirical truth? What does Sir Francis Bacon say about this compatibility in his selection on the *Advancement of Learning* (1605)?
6. Consider the words of Martin Luther quoted at the beginning of this chapter: "Reason is the greatest enemy that faith has. It never comes to the aid of spiritual things, but . . . struggles against the divine Word, treating with contempt all that emanates from God." Does it surprise you that this statement comes from the leader of the Protestant Reformation? Discuss the compatibility of science and religion in light of this quotation.
7. What are some of the current areas of tension between science and religion? In our quest for knowledge and understanding about the world around us and our place in it, must one choose between the mind and the spirit? What did Pope John Paul II say about this?

8. Where does "greatness" lie? In the conquests of men like Julius Caesar or Alexander the Great, the political leadership of Augustus or Oliver Cromwell, or in the intellectual influence of Isaac Newton? Is knowledge the most powerful force in the secular world?

9. Why did William Harvey want to present his findings in an address before the Royal College of Physicians? What was he afraid of? Why were his discoveries about the heart and circulation of blood so important and perhaps so threatening?

Section II: The Enlightenment

10. Do you find Locke's assertion that the mind is a blank slate at birth and that there are no innate ideas to be a compelling argument? What does Voltaire think? This still remains a disputed issue in modern psychology—can you solve it? What notions and actions are instinctive to human beings and what is learned through experience?

11. What did Marquis de Condorcet think about the progress of humankind? Have some of his predictions come true? Can they ever come true?

12. What mathematical equation did Cesare Beccaria apply to "the good and evil of life"? How do you think he might have reacted to our modern concern over capital punishment? Ultimately, how does a society prevent crime?

13. How does Immanuel Kant answer the question "What is Enlightenment?" In what ways do you see his views on freedom and risk in evidence throughout this chapter? Select four other thinkers and demonstrate specifically how Kant's attitude applies to the tenor of their writings.

14. Carefully scrutinize the arguments of Baron d'Holbach. Does his atheism seem well supported by his argument? What does he mean by denoting God as "a cause contradicted by its effects"? Why was toleration so important to Voltaire? Do you regard him as a religious individual? Why is deism a comfortable philosophy? Are you persuaded by Voltaire's arguments in opposition to the Baron d'Holbach as expressed in his letter to Frederick William of Prussia?

15. Carefully read Voltaire's entries in his *Philosophical Dictionary*. Are any of his personal biases evident? Can you discern his view of human nature? What does he mean when he says that equality "is the most natural and the most implausible thing possible"?

16. Why did Denis Diderot think his encyclopedia necessary and reflective of the Age of Enlightenment? What was the method that Diderot employed in obtaining articles for the *Encyclopedia*? According to d'Alembert, what were the aims of the *Encyclopedia*? What is the difference between reasoned knowledge and direct knowledge?

17. In the selection "We Did Not Live Entirely in Vain," Diderot expressed some of the general attitudes of the Enlightenment. He mentions the topics of toleration, education, progress, and ethics. Choose the specific writers and documents from this chapter that best represent Diderot's generalized comments. Defend your choices.

18. What are the arguments used by Locke, Montesquieu, and Rousseau to justify revolution? Who or what is the "sovereign power" Rousseau mentions? Comment in particular on Rousseau's belief that "whoever refuses to obey the general will shall be compelled to it by the whole body." Isn't this a form of tyranny?

19. Note the excerpts under the section "The Political Framework." In order to be enduring, must revolutions have precedents for action (like the Glorious Revolution or the American Revolution)? Must they have some philosophical justification?

20. Compare the views of Rousseau and Mary Wollstonecraft on the education and abilities of women. In what ways do Wollstonecraft's arguments mirror the ideals of the Enlightenment? In this regard, does Rousseau appear somewhat hypocritical? Or can one rationalize his arguments?

21. What talents did Julie de Lespinasse possess that made her indispensable to the success of her salon? How did women of her social class and education contribute to the progress of this age? Do you think that hers was an important function, or would this type of social/intellectual discussion have taken place without hostesses of such talent and ability? What does this say about the role of women during the Enlightenment?

22. What are the primary tenets of mercantilism as noted by Sir William Keith in the selection "The Maxim of All Polite Nations"? As the ruler of a state, would you find his arguments impressive? What was Adam Smith's view of human nature as expounded in the selection entitled "The Wealth of Nations"? Do you find his thoughts on self-interest to be compelling? Does his belief negate the sincerity of altruism? What are the primary ingredients of success in the world? How do you define the principle of the "invisible hand?" How do you interpret his phrase: "I have never known much good done by those who affected to trade for the public good"? Smith foresaw a "mean rapacity" of merchants and manufacturers that "perhaps cannot be corrected." Why was he so sure that it could "very easily be prevented from disturbing the tranquility of anybody but themselves"?

PART II

THE ERA OF REVOLUTION

3

"Liberty, Equality, Fraternity!": Romanticism and Revolution

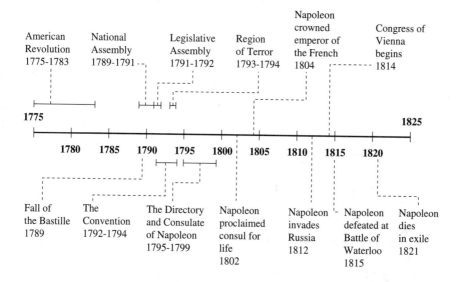

A time of revolution is not the season of true liberty. Alas! the obstinacy and perversion of men is such that she is too often obliged to borrow the very arms of despotism to overthrow him, and in order to reign in peace must establish herself by violence.

—William Wordsworth

The greatest dangers to liberty lurk in insidious encroachment by men of zeal—well-meaning, but without understanding.

—Justice Louis D. Brandeis

Extremism in the defense of liberty is no vice. And . . . moderation in the pursuit of justice is no virtue.

—Barry Goldwater

True tragedy arises when the idea of "justice" appears to be leading to the destruction of higher values.

—Max Scheler

What is the throne?—a bit of wood gilded and covered with velvet. I am the state—I alone am the representative of the people. . . . France has more need of me than I of France.

—Napoleon Bonaparte (1814)

Do you know what astounds me most about the world? It is the impotence of force to establish anything. In the end, the sword is always conquered by the mind.

—Napoleon Bonaparte (1808)

Men of genius are meteors destined to be consumed in lighting up their century.

—Napoleon Bonaparte (1791)

CHAPTER THEMES

- *Systems of Government:* Did the French Revolution result in a democratic system of government for France or in the tyranny of Napoleon? How easily can the process of democracy degenerate into extremism? Is freedom, most importantly, just a state of mind?

- *Revolution:* To what extent is a successful revolution more dependent on the foundation of ideas than on the leadership of fanatics? Without the ideas of Locke, Rousseau, and other thinkers of the Enlightenment, would the French Revolution have succeeded?

- *Imperialism:* Many eighteenth-century French statesmen believed that it was important to export the ideals of the French Revolution through war and imperialism. Is this a valid goal? Can one impose the ideals of democracy on other people? How important is foreign war to the success of a domestic revolution?

- *Women in History:* The French Revolution was a measurable step in the evolution of human freedom. Did women benefit from the experience and gain political advantages within France? What role did women play in the French Revolution?

• **Church/State Relationships:** How did the leaders of the French Revolution suppress the Catholic Church and then use religion to their advantage? Does a revolution produce its own pantheon of gods which is syncretized with the political leadership thus rendering a church/state relationship unnecessary? To what extent was Napoleon a spiritual leader?

• **Propaganda:** Was Napoleon's rise from soldier to emperor primarily the result of his military ability, his luck, or the cultivation of his image? Does one gain power through military or political ability and maintain power through creation of belief? Did the painter Jacques-Louis David actually create the image of Napoleon for posterity? Was it real?

• **Historical Change and Transition:** How important is the "hero" in history? Did Robespierre and Napoleon "create" and control the French Revolution? Or was it created by social and economic forces? Must every revolution go through a violent phase that devours its leaders before another "hero" arrives to create stability? Is history thus a contest between the forces of revolution and reaction?

• **The Big Picture:** To what extent does revolution depend on a fortuitous blend of popular anger and resentment, philosophical ideas, and fanatical leadership? How would you compare these elements in the French Revolution with the American Revolution or the Russian Revolution? Are the political, social, and economic elements of all revolutions interchangeable? Can one predict when a revolution will occur? What is the value of history?

One of the most exciting periods of change and development in Western Civilization occurred during the seventeenth and eighteenth centuries. The attitudes and ideas that flourished during this time have formed the intellectual and political bases of our modern Western world.

Although the writers and thinkers of·this period, often called *philosophes,* generally advocated intellectual freedom and political equality, it should be added that the eighteenth-century Enlightenment was not initially a concerted effort, but took shape in individual minds over several generations; it did not become a conscious movement until about 1750. Yet the ideas of such important figures as John Locke, the Baron de Montesquieu, Voltaire, Denis Diderot, and Jean-Jacques Rousseau were to be influential apart from the theoretical and abstract world of thought. They were to give philosophical justification to the notion that it was proper and desirable to remove a monarch who was incompetent or inattentive to the needs of the people. Revolution often requires philosophical inspiration in order to succeed; without the underlying attitude that revolution can be a proper and progressive act, perhaps the French middle class would not have been motivated to lead a revolt against the established order.

And yet the French Revolution in 1789 did not simply happen as a result of intellectual commitment to abstract principles. In fact, there existed more tangible evidence that revolution could succeed and produce desired results. The precedents were clear. In 1649, the English executed their monarch, Charles I, for his autocratic behavior, and in 1688, Parliament established itself as the supreme depository of law and the "popular will" by restricting monarchical authority. It should be remembered, however, that the English had a long tradition of representative government and monarchical limitation dating back most importantly to the Magna Carta in 1215. The French lacked this tradition, and their representative institution, the Estates-General, had not met in 175 years. More recent precedent for French revolutionary action existed in the American example. In 1776, the American colonies declared their independence from Britain and were supported in this venture by the French government itself.

There were also economic problems that moved France toward revolution. The wars and extravagance of Louis XIV had sent France to the brink of bankruptcy by 1715—and Louis was a competent and diligent administrator. His heirs, on the other hand, were not particularly dedicated to the governance of France. Louis XV (1715–1774) was poorly educated and preferred to allow his mistresses (one of whom had been a Parisian prostitute) to control the politics of state. Louis XVI (1774–1792) was well educated but more interested in hunting than in administration. From 1715 to 1789, the French economy spiraled into chaos. With the nobility and church exempt from taxation, the burden fell upon the Third Estate.

The French Revolution drew much of its support from the Third Estate, a conglomeration of middle-class professionals, artisans, and peasants. As a group, the middle class or bourgeoisie was ambitious, educated, and competent. Could they be expected to sit idly by while the nobility held offices that should have been theirs? Inspired by philosophical ideals as well as by potential economic and social advantages, they provided the leadership for the revolution. Lower members of the Third Estate, the artisans and peasants, generally could not read and were not concerned with philosophical justifications. It was the peasantry that labored under intolerable taxes, rents, and *corvées* (feudal services), which they were forced to undertake by the nobility without payment. What were their demands in 1789? Did their needs justify revolution?

The first part of this chapter will explore some of the ideological and social origins of the French Revolution, as well as some of its most important events, such as the storming of the Bastille, the execution of Louis XVI, and the Terror. Revolutions generally go through conservative and radical phases. Differences among revolutionaries often result in violence. The path toward freedom or despotism is littered with bodies and bloodshed. And in the power vacuum created by such chaos, the door is left open for a transfer of power. During the French Revolution, an individual seized the initiative, filled the power vacuum, and altered its course. His name was Napoleon Bonaparte.

The mere name of Napoleon (1769–1821) evokes a wide array of emotions. As is the case with most influential individuals, he inspires controversy. Some historians have described him as a force for good, a lawgiver and reformer who spread revolutionary ideals throughout Europe. Others have viewed him as an egomaniac whose lust for conquest overshadowed any other secondary achievements. Whatever final judgment one may make, it is clear that Napoleon Bonaparte had a brilliant mind, equally at home in the context of law and military strategy.

Napoleon was born in 1769 to a poor family of lesser nobility on the island of Corsica. The "little Corporal," as he was called, went to French schools and obtained a commission as a French artillery officer. He was enthusiastic about the revolution of 1789 and was rewarded for his military service against the British with a promotion to brigadier general. After the fall of Robespierre in 1794, Napoleon's radical political associations threatened his career, but he was able to convince the new government of his loyalty. This government was called the Directory, and it was composed of people who had benefitted from the recent revolution and whose major goal was to perpetuate their own rule. Their chief opposition came from royalists, who supported a monarch as head of France and who had won a majority of the seats in the legislature in 1797. With the aid of Napoleon, the Directory succeeded in overthrowing the elected officials and placed their own supporters in the legislature. Napoleon then received a command against the Austrians and Sardinians that resulted in a swift victory for the French and eventual annexation of Italy. Napoleon was hailed as a hero and decided to sail to Egypt, there to fight the British fleet and, it was hoped, cut off British contact and trade with her colonies in the East. However, the invasion of Egypt (1798) was a failure for the French; Napoleon abandoned his troops and returned to Paris, where he overthrew the Directory that he had once championed (November 10, 1799). Establishing a new government called the Consulate, he then issued the Constitution for the Year VIII (December 1799), which promoted liberal ideas such as universal manhood suffrage and a system of governmental checks and balances, but in reality granted Napoleon virtual dictatorial power as first consul. His position was confirmed by a plebiscite that approved the new constitution by a vote of 3,011,077 to 1,567. Both the middle and lower classes seemed satisfied to accept the security that Napoleon offered.

Napoleon then quickly consolidated his rule by achieving peace with Austria and Britain and by restoring order at home. In 1801, he concluded a concordat with the Catholic Church, which in fact resulted in the subordination of the church to the state; there would be no controversy between secular and religious authority in Napoleonic France. So satisfied were French citizens that in 1802 they voted Napoleon consul for life. In 1804, there was simply no one with enough authority to grant him the final accolade, so Napoleon crowned himself Napoleon I, Emperor of the French. The pope sat nearby, watching the ceremony. Napoleon had achieved the ultimate authority, which had escaped even Charlemagne.

In his decade as emperor, Napoleon conquered most of Europe, spreading France's revolutionary ideals. It was at this time, too, that he paid great attention to domestic concerns and soon instituted reforms and programs, including a codification of laws known as the Napoleonic Code. His glory came to an end in 1814 when he was finally defeated by a coalition of European powers. Napoleon's brief return from exile was unsuccessful and resulted in his defeat by Lord Wellington at Waterloo. The victors agreed at the Congress of Vienna in 1815 that no single state should dominate Europe—power must be balanced. Another Napoleon would not be tolerated. The great general was ingloriously exiled to St. Helena, an isolated and inaccessible rock in the Atlantic. He died there in 1821 of stomach cancer or, as some modern researchers advocate, the victim of gradual poisoning. Even in death, Napoleon remains a controversial figure.

In the second part of this chapter, we will look at Napoleon's rise to power and especially his reforms and attempts to consolidate his position. Napoleon was certainly a military leader of genius, but his achievements often inspire philosophical analysis. His career raises questions about the nature of power and the ability of the individual to change the course of history. Is history motivated by social and economic forces over which individuals have no control? Or does the "hero" actually change history by force of personality and ability? Did Napoleon make France a great nation through his reforms and conquests? If so, does progress come about because of the imposition of reforms upon a people? Was Napoleon, who overthrew the legitimate, elected government of France and installed a dictatorship, necessary for the progress of a revolution dedicated to liberty and equality?

In the third section, we will look at the artistic and literary movement called Romanticism that existed contemporaneously with these political events. This was a revolutionary period in art, poetry, music, and literature as great creative figures such as Johann von Goethe, Ludwig van Beethoven, and Eugene Delacroix broke through the boundaries of established forms and created new standards of artistic expression. This was a movement inspired by the beauty and power of nature, the confidence in personal intuition and validity of the senses, and finally in the passion of nationalism.

The French Revolution presents historians with complex problems of great importance. This chapter will focus on the components of revolution, the relationship between power and progress, and factors of historical change. Finally, did the French Revolution succeed in realizing its ideals of liberty, equality, and fraternity and how were these visions of independent thought reflected in the arts and literature of the Romantic movement?

SECTION I:
THE FRENCH REVOLUTION

Conditions of Society on the Eve of Revolution

France was composed of three main classes, which were divided on the basis of occupation and ancient privilege. The First Estate consisted of the clergy, the Second Estate of the nobility, and the Third Estate of everyone else. Within the estates themselves there were also social divisions. The following selections relate many of the problems and criticisms of the time.

The Nobility

Corruption of the French Court
MARQUIS D'ARGENSON

Marquis d'Argenson was minister of foreign affairs under Louis XV. He claimed he "loved both royalty and the people."

The court! The court! In that single word lies all the nation's misfortune. . . . It is the court that corrupts the morals of the nation by its luxury, its extravagance, its artificial manners, its ignorance, and its intrigue in place of emulation. All places, positions, and grades in the army go to the courtiers through favoritism; hence there is no longer any attempt to rise by merit.

In the finances everything is sold; all the money of the provinces goes to Paris never to return; all the people go there to make fortunes by intrigue. . . .

Justice cannot be administered with integrity; the judges fear the grandees, and base their hopes only upon favor. In short, the king no longer reigns, and disregards even the virtues that he has.

Those are the fruits of the establishment by Louis XIV of a capital at Versailles expressly for the court. He was still powerful and gave authority to his ministers. But these are not supported under Louis XV, who distrusts them and prefers his courtiers and favorites. There is, as a result, anarchy and an oligarchy of satraps. Favor means influence, and the possession of favor is more important than the rights of authority.

"Corruption of the French Court" is from E. L. Higgins, ed., *The French Revolution as Told by Contemporaries* (Boston: Houghton Mifflin, 1966), p. 10. Copyright © 1938, renewed 1966 by Houghton Mifflin Company. Used by permission of the publisher.

"Ancient Oaks Mutilated by Time"

MARQUIS DE BOUILLE

Marquis de Bouille was a noble, general, governor, and trusted advisor to Louis XVI.

The nobility had undergone still greater changes; it had lost, not only its ancient splendor, but almost its existence, and had entirely decayed. There had been in France nearly eighty thousand noble families. . . . Included in this numerous nobility were about a thousand families whose origin dated from the earliest times of the monarchy. Among these there were scarcely two or three hundred who had escaped poverty and misfortune. There could still be found at court a few great names which brought to mind the noted personages who had made them illustrious, but which too often were brought into disrepute by the vices of those who had inherited them. There were a few families in the provinces who had continued to exist and command respect. . . . The remainder of this ancient nobility languished in poverty, and resembled those ancient oaks mutilated by time, where nothing remains except the ravaged trunks. No longer convoked either for military service or for the provincial or national assemblies, they had lost their ancient hierarchy. If honorary titles remained to some illustrious or ancient families, they were also held by a multitude of newly created nobles who had acquired by their riches the right to assume them arbitrarily. . . . The nobility, in short, were not distinguishable from the other classes of citizens, except by the arbitrary favors of the court, and by the exemptions from imposts, less useful to them than onerous to the state and shocking to the people. They had conserved nothing of their ancient dignity and consideration; they retained only the hate and jealousy of the plebeians. Such was the situation of the nobility of the kingdom.

The Indifferent Nobility

COMPTE DE SÉGUR

Compte de Ségur was a liberal noble in favor at Louis XVI's court, a diplomatist, and a historian.

The heads of the old noble families, believing themselves as unshakable as the monarchy, slept without fear upon a volcano. The exercise of their charges; royal promotions, favors, or rebuffs; and the nomination or dismissal of ministers, were the sole objects of their attention, the motives of their movements, and the subjects of their conversations. Indifferent to the real affairs of state as to their own they allowed themselves to be governed, some by the intendants of the provinces, others by their own intendants; but they regarded with a chagrined and scornful eye the changes in costumes which were being introduced, the abandonment of liveries, the vogue of dress-coats and English styles.

The Superficial Education of the Nobility
MME DE STAËL

Mme de Staël was an author and a liberal member of the nobility.

The great nobles in France were not very well informed, because they had nothing to gain by being so. Grace in conversation, which would please at court, was the surest means of arriving at honors. This superficial education was one cause of the downfall of the nobles: they could no longer fight against the intelligence of the third estate; they should have tried to surpass it. The great lords would have by degrees gained supremacy in the primary assemblies through their knowledge of administration, as formerly they had acquired it by their swords; and the public mind would have been prepared for the establishment of free institutions in France.

The Clergy
"Luxury, Debauchery, and Lavish Expenditure"
MARQUIS DE FERRIERÈS

Marquis de Ferrierès was a conservative noble, yet still a severe critic of the monarchy, the nobility, and revolutionaries.

There were dioceses which contained fifteen hundred square leagues, and others which contained only twenty; parishes which were ten leagues in circumference, and others which had scarcely fifteen families. Among the priests there were some whose allowances scarcely reached seven hundred livres; while in their neighborhood were benefices of ten and twelve thousand livres income, possessed of ecclesiastics who performed no function in the cult and who,

"The Superficial Education of the Nobility" is from E. L. Higgins, ed., *The French Revolution as Told by Contemporaries* (Boston: Houghton Mifflin, 1966), p. 20. Copyright © 1938, renewed 1966 by Houghton Mifflin Company. Used by permission of the publisher.

"'Luxury, Debauchery, and Lavish Expenditure'" is from E. L. Higgins, ed., *The French Revolution as Told by Contemporaries* (Boston: Houghton Mifflin, 1966), pp. 15–16. Copyright © 1938, renewed 1966 by Houghton Mifflin Company. Used by permission of the publisher.

residing elsewhere, carried away the revenue of these benefices, dissipating it in luxury, debauchery, and lavish expenditure. . . . Inasmuch as the appointment of bishops had been concentrated in the hands of the king, or rather in the hands of the ministers, too often the choice fell, not upon him who possessed the most apostolic virtues, but upon him whose family enjoyed the greatest influence. What evils have not resulted from this! Most of the bishops, incapable of fulfilling their duties, entered upon them with insuperable distaste. This distaste extended even to the places where they were to exercise their functions, and had become so general that the small number of prelates who remained were cited as models. The same abuses reigned in the selection of the grand vicars: all thought more of soliciting favors than of deserving them. Totally abandoned by those who were supposed to administer them, the dioceses remained in the hands of obscure secretaries.

The Middle Class

The following is a cahier de doleance, *a list of grievances, complaints and protests of the Third Estate in the district of Carcassonne in southern France. Cahiers were frank expressions of reform and demonstrate a willingness of the middle class to demand (albeit tempered by respect) political and social changes from their king.*

The Grievances of Carcassonne

The third estate of the electoral district of Carcassonne, desiring to give to a beloved monarch, and one so worthy of our affection, the most unmistakable proof of its love and respect, of its gratitude and fidelity, desiring to cooperate with the whole nation in repairing the successive misfortunes which have overwhelmed it, and with the hope of reviving once more its ancient glory, declares that the happiness of the nation must, in their opinion, depend upon that of its king, upon the stability of the monarchy, and upon the preservation of the orders which compose it and of the fundamental laws which govern it. . . .

The third estate of the electoral district of Carcassonne very humbly petitions his Majesty to take into consideration these several matters, weigh them in his wisdom, and permit his people to enjoy, as soon as may be, fresh proofs of that benevolence which he has never ceased to exhibit toward them and which is dictated by his affection for them:

1. Public worship should be confined to the Roman Catholic apostolic religion, to the exclusion of all other forms of worship; . . . nevertheless the civil

"The Grievances of Carcassonne" is from James H. Robinson and Charles A. Beard, eds., *Readings in Modern European History*, vol. 1 (Boston: Ginn and Company, 1908), pp. 249–250.

rights of those of the king's subjects who are not Catholics should be confirmed, and they should be admitted to positions and offices in the public administration, without however extending this privilege—which reason and humanity alike demand for them—to judicial or police functions or to those of public instruction.

8. Among these rights the following should be especially noted: the nation should hereafter be subject only to such laws and taxes as it shall itself freely ratify.

9. The meetings of the Estates General of the kingdom should be fixed for definite periods, and the subsidies judged necessary for the support of the State and the public service should be voted for no longer a period than to the close of the year in which the next meeting of the Estates General is to occur.

10. In order to assure to the third estate the influence to which it is entitled in view of the number of its members, the amount of its contributions to the public treasury, and the manifold interests which it has to defend or promote in the national assemblies, its votes in the assembly should be taken and counted by head.

11. No order, corporation, or individual citizen may lay claim to any monetary exemptions. . . . All taxes should be assessed on the same system throughout the nation.

12. The general or particular regulations should be abolished which exclude members of the third estate from certain positions, offices, and ranks which have hitherto been bestowed on nobles either for life or hereditarily. A law should be passed declaring members of the third estate qualified to fill all such offices for which they are judged to be personally fitted.

13. Since individual liberty is intimately associated with national liberty, his Majesty is hereby petitioned not to permit that it be hereafter interfered with by arbitrary orders for imprisonment. . . .

14. Freedom should be granted also to the press, which should however be subjected, by means of strict regulations, to the principles of religion, morality, and public decency.

The Peasantry

Beggars, Rags, and Misery

ARTHUR YOUNG

Arthur Young was an English writer on agricultural subjects who traveled through France before and during the revolution.

"Beggars, Rags, and Misery" is from Arthur Young, *Travels in France During the Years 1781, 1788, 1789,* 3rd ed. (London: George Bell and Sons, 1889), pp. 19, 27.

1787

The same wretched country continues to La Loge; the fields are scenes of pitiable management, as the houses are of misery. Yet all this country is highly improveable, if they knew what to do with it: the property, perhaps, of some of those glittering beings, who figured in the procession the other day at Versailles. Heaven grant me patience while I see a country thus neglected—and forgive me the oaths I swear at the absence and ignorance of the possessors. . . .

Pass Payrac, and meet many beggars, which we had not done before. All the country, girls and women, are without shoes or stockings; and the ploughmen at their work have neither sabots nor feet to their stockings. This is a poverty, that strikes at the root of national prosperity; a large consumption among the poor being of more consequence than among the rich the wealth of a nation lies in its circulation and consumption; and the case of poor people abstaining from the use of manufacturers of leather and wool ought to be considered as an evil of the first magnitude. It reminded me of the misery of Ireland.

1788

To Montauban. The poor people seem poor indeed; the children terribly ragged, if possible worse clad than if with no clothes at all; as to shoes and stockings they are luxuries. A beautiful girl of six or seven years playing with a stick, and smiling under such a bundle of rags as made my heart ache to see her: they did not beg and when I gave them any thing seemed more surprised than obliged. One third of what I have seen of this province seems uncultivated, and nearly all of it in misery. What have kings, and ministers, and parliaments, and states, to answer for their prejudices, seeing millions of hands that would be industrious, idle and starving, through the execrable maxims of despotism, or the equally detestable prejudices of a feudal nobility. . . .

The Outbreak of Revolution (1789–1791)

The Domestic Crisis

"What Is the Third Estate?" (January 1789)
THE ABBÉ SIEYÈS

By August 1788, Louis XVI had decided to summon the Estates-General, a convocation of the three estates, which had not met since 1614, in order to solve the government's financial problems. Louis was in debt, and he wanted the Estates-

General to raise new taxes. This pamphlet by the Abbé Sieyès (1748–1836) was issued in January 1789, before the Estates-General met. It was intended to unite the various interests within the Third Estate toward a common cause: reform of the unequal voting procedure that gave advantage to the first two estates.

What Does the Third Estate Demand? To Become Something

The true petitions of this order may be appreciated only through the authentic claims directed to the government by the large municipalities of the kingdom. What is indicated therein? That the people wishes to be something, and, in truth, the very least that is possible. It wishes to have real representatives in the Estates General, that is to say, deputies drawn from its order, who are competent to be interpreters of its will and defenders of its interests. But what will it avail it to be present at the Estates General if the predominating interest there is contrary to its own! Its presence would only consecrate the oppression of which it would be the external victim. Thus, it is indeed certain that it cannot come to vote at the Estates General unless it is to have in that body an influence at least equal to that of the privileged classes; and it demands a number of representatives equal to that of the first two orders together. Finally, this equality of representation would become completely illusory if every chamber voted separately. The third estate demands, then, that votes be taken by head and not by order. This is the essence of those claims so alarming to the privileged classes, because they believed that thereby the reform of abuses would become inevitable. The real intention of the third estate is to have an influence in the Estates General equal to that of the privileged classes. I repeat, can it ask less?

What Remains to Be Done: Development of Some Principles

The time is past when the three orders, thinking only of defending themselves from ministerial despotism, were ready to unite against the common enemy. . . .

• • •

The third estate awaits, to no purpose, the meeting of all classes, the restitution of its political rights, and the plenitude of its civil rights; the fear of seeing abuses reformed alarms the first two orders far more than the desire for liberty inspires them. Between liberty and some odious privileges, they have chosen the latter. Their soul is identified with the favors of servitude. Today they dread this Estates General which but lately they invoked so ardently. All is well with them; they no longer complain, except of the spirit of innovation. They no longer lack anything; fear has given them a constitution.

The third estate must perceive in the trend of opinions and circumstances that it can hope for nothing except from its own enlightenment and courage. Reason and justice are in its favor; . . . there is no longer time to work for the conciliation of parties. What accord can be anticipated between the energy of the oppressed and the rage of the oppressors?

They have dared pronounce the word secession. They have menaced the King and the people. Well! Good God! How fortunate for the nation if this desirable secession might be made permanently! How easy it would be to dispense with the privileged classes! How difficult to induce them to be citizens!

● ● ●

In vain would they close their eyes to the revolution which time and force of circumstances have effected; it is none the less real. Formerly the third estate was serf, the noble order everything. Today the third estate is everything, the nobility but a word. . . .

In such a state of affairs, what must the third estate do if it wishes to gain possession of its political rights in a manner beneficial to the nation? There are two ways of attaining this objective. In following the first, the third estate must assemble apart: it will not meet with the nobility and the clergy at all; it will not remain with them, either by order or by head. I pray that they will keep in mind the enormous difference between the assembly of the third estate and that of the other two orders. The first represents 25,000,000 men, and deliberates concerning the interests of the nation. The two others, were they to unite, have the powers of only about 200,000 individuals, and think only of their privileges. The third estate alone, they say, cannot constitute the Estates General. Well! So much the better! It will form a National Assembly.

Women of the Third Estate (January 1789)

Juxtaposed with the famous document just presented is the little-known petition from the women of the Third Estate. The petitioners were women of humble origin who sought not political equality, but dignity and the opportunity to improve themselves. It is important to note that they did not conceive of themselves as part of the political process but appealed directly to the king to improve the conditions of their lives.

Sire,

At a time when the various orders of the state are busy with their interests, when everyone is trying to assert his titles and his rights, when some people are worrying about recalling centuries of servitude and anarchy, when others are making every effort to shake off the last links which still bind them to the imperious remains of the feudal system, women—continual objects of the admiration and scorn of men—women, wouldn't it be possible for them also to make their voice heard amidst this general agitation?

Excluded from the national assemblies by laws too well consolidated for them to hope to break, they do not ask, Sire, for your permission to send their deputies to the Estates General. . . . We prefer, Sire, to place our cause at your feet; not wishing to obtain anything except from your heart, we address our complaints and confide our miseries to it.

The women of the Third Estate are almost all born without fortune; their education is very neglected or very defective. . . . If nature has refused them beauty, they get married without dowry to unfortunate artisans, lead aimless, difficult lives stuck away in the provinces, and give birth to children they are incapable of raising. If, on the contrary, they are born pretty, without culture, without principles, without any idea of morals, they become the prey of the first seducer, commit a first sin, come to Paris to bury their shame, end by losing it altogether, and die victims of licentious ways. . . .

Also, several, solely because they are born girls, are disdained by their parents, who refuse to set them up, preferring to concentrate their fortune on the head of a son whom they designate to carry on their name in the capital; for it is good that Your Majesty understands that we also have names to keep up. Or, if old age finds them spinsters, they spend it in tears and see themselves the object of the scorn of their nearest relatives. . . .

We ask to be enlightened, to have work, not in order to usurp men's authority, but in order to be better esteemed by them, so that we might have the means of living out of the way of misfortune and so that poverty does not force the weakest among us . . . to join the crowd of unfortunate beings who overpopulate the streets and whose debauched audacity is a disgrace to our sex and to the men who keep them company. . . .

We implore you, Sire, to set up free schools where we could learn our language on the basis of principles and religion and ethics. . . .

We ask to come out of the state of ignorance, to be able to give our children a sound and reasonable education so as to make of them subjects worthy of serving you. We will teach them to cherish the beautiful name of Frenchmen [and] we will transmit to them the love we have for Your Majesty.

The Tennis Court Oath (June 20, 1789)

From the outset, the Estates-General was hampered by organizational disputes. After several weeks of frustration, the Third Estate invited the clergy and nobility to join them in organizing a new legislative body. Only a few of the lower clergy accepted, but the National Assembly was thus formed on June 17, 1789. Three days later, they were accidentally locked out of their usual meeting place, and they marched to a nearby tennis court, where they took an oath to draft a new

"The Tennis Court Oath" is reprinted with permission of Macmillan Publishing Company from *A Documentary Survey of the French Revolution*, edited by John Hall Stewart, p. 88. Copyright 1951 by Macmillan Publishing Company, renewed 1979 by John Hall Stewart.

The Oath of the Tennis Court by Jacques-Louis David. Having pledged their cooperation in the establishment of the National Assembly, members from the different estates took the famous oath to write a new constitution for France. (*Giraudon/Art Resource, NY*)

constitution for France. This is one of the most important documents of the revolution. The oath was taken orally and individually with but one vote in dissension. The president of the National Assembly was barely able to save the dissenter from bodily harm.

The National Assembly, considering that it has been summoned to establish the constitution of the kingdom, to effect the regeneration of public order, and to maintain the true principles of monarchy; that nothing can prevent it from continuing its deliberations in whatever place it may be forced to establish itself; and, finally, that wheresoever its members are assembled, there is the National Assembly;

Decrees that all members of this Assembly shall immediately take a solemn oath not to separate, and to reassemble wherever circumstances require, until the constitution of the kingdom is established and consolidated upon firm foundations; and that, the said oath taken, all members and each one of them individually shall ratify this steadfast resolution by signature.

The Fall of the Bastille (July 14, 1789)

The Bastille was a fortress built to protect the eastern gates of Paris. It had also been used as a prison for political offenders of the Old Regime. Hence, it served as a symbol of monarchical despotism. On July 14, 1789, a mob, irritated at the dismissal of a popular minister of the king, paraded through the streets of Paris, searching for arms and clashing with the military. They stormed the Bastille and slaughtered many of its small garrison. Although this act yielded few political prisoners of the king, the event would provide a catalyst to the revolution and is commemorated today in France with special reverence. Louis XVI, however, did not view it with such import. The entry in his diary for July 14, 1789, was "rien" (nothing), signifying that he failed to kill any game in his hunt that day. The following accounts of the fall of the Bastille are drawn from various witnesses and contemporaries of the event.

The Surrender

It was then that M. de Launay [commander of the forces of the Bastille] asked the garrison what course should be followed, that he saw no other than to blow himself up rather than to expose himself to having his throat cut by the people, from the fury of which they could not escape; that they must remount the towers, continue to fight, and blow themselves up rather than surrender.

The soldiers replied that it was impossible to fight any longer, that they would resign themselves to everything rather than destroy such a great

The fortress of the Bastille. When King Louis XVI was informed that the Bastille had been stormed by a Parisian crowd on July 14, 1789, he said, "It is then a revolt." "No, Sire," replied the duke. "It is a revolution." *(Robert, Hubert "Demolition of the Bastille." 1789. Musee de la Ville de Paris, Musee Carnavalet, Paris, France, Giraudon/Art Resource)*

number of citizens, that it was best to put the drummer on the towers to beat the recall, hoist a white flag, and capitulate. The governor, having no flag, gave them a white handkerchief. An officer wrote out the capitulation and passed it through the hole, saying that they desired to render themselves and lay down their arms, on condition of a promise not to massacre the troop; there was a cry of, "Lower your bridge; nothing will happen to you!"

•   •   •

The little drawbridge of the fort being first opened, Elie [one of the leaders of the attacking force] entered with his companions, all brave and honorable men, and fully determined to keep his word. On seeing him the governor went up to him, embraced him, and presented him with his sword, with the keys of the Bastille.

"I refused his sword," said Elie to me, "and took only the keys." His companions received the staff and the officers of the garrison with the same cordiality, swearing to serve them as guard and defense; but they swore in vain.

As soon as the great bridge was let down (and it is not known by what hand that was done) the people rushed into the court of the castle and, full of fury, seized on the troop of Invalides. Elie and the honest men who had entered with him exerted all their efforts to tear from the hands of the people the victims which they themselves had delivered to it. Ferocity held obstinately attached to its prey. Several of these soldiers, whose lives had been promised them, were assassinated; others were dragged like slaves through the streets of Paris. Twenty-two were brought to the Grève, and, after humiliations and inhuman treatment, they had the affliction of seeing two of their comrades hanged. When they were presented at the Hotel de Ville, a furious madman said to them: "You deserve to be hanged; and you shall be so presently." De Launay, torn from the arms of those who wished to save him, had his head cut off under the walls of the Hotel de Ville. In the midst of his assassins, he defended his life with the courage of despair; but he fell under their number. De Losme-Salbray, his major, was murdered in the same manner. The adjutant, Mirai, had been so, near the Bastille. Pernon, an old lieutenant of the Invalides, was assassinated on the wharf Saint-Paul, as he was going to the hall. Another lieutenant, Caron, was covered with wounds. The head of the Marquis de Launay was carried about Paris by this same populace that he would have crushed had he not been moved to pity. Such were the exploits of those who have since been called the heroes and conquerors of the Bastille.

The King Informed of the Fall of the Bastille

When M. de Liancourt had made known to the king the total defection of his guards, the taking of the Bastille, the massacres that had taken place, the rising of two hundred thousand men, after a few moments' silence the king said, "It is then a revolt." "No, Sire," replied the duke. "It is a revolution."

Declaration of the Rights of Man
(August 27, 1789)

The Declaration of the Rights of Man, issued by the National Assembly on August 27, 1789, served as a preamble to the French constitution, which was as yet unwritten. Its articles detail abuses of the Old Regime and were imitative of American bills of rights that had been attached to state constitutions. The declaration in turn influenced several European constitutions in the nineteenth century.

"Declaration of the Rights of Man" is from James H. Robinson and Charles A. Beard, eds., *Readings in Modern European History*, vol. 1 (Boston: Ginn and Company, 1908), pp. 260–262.

The representatives of the French people, organized as a National Assembly, believing that the ignorance, neglect, or contempt of the rights of man are the sole causes of public calamities and of the corruption of governments, have determined to set forth in a solemn declaration the natural, inalienable, and sacred rights of man, in order that this declaration, being constantly before all the members of the social body, shall remind them continually of their rights and duties; in order that the acts of the legislative power, as well as those of the executive power, may be compared at any moment with the objects and purposes of all political institutions and may thus be more respected; and, lastly, in order that the grievances of the citizens, based hereafter upon simple and incontestable principles, shall tend to the maintenance of the constitution and redound to the happiness of all. Therefore the National Assembly recognizes and proclaims, in the presence and under the auspices of the Supreme Being, the following rights of man and of the citizen:

Article 1. Men are born and remain free and equal in rights. Social distinctions may be founded only upon the general good.

2. The aim of all political association is the preservation of the natural and imprescriptible rights of man. These rights are liberty, property, security, and resistance to oppression.

3. The principle of all sovereignty resides essentially in the nation. No body nor individual may exercise any authority which does not proceed directly from the nation.

4. Liberty consists in the freedom to do everything which injures no one else; hence the exercise of the natural rights of each man has no limits except those which assure to the other members of the society the enjoyment of the same rights. These limits can only be determined by law.

5. Law can only prohibit such actions as are hurtful to society. Nothing may be prevented which is not forbidden by law, and no one may be forced to do anything not provided for by law.

6. Law is the expression of the general will. Every citizen has a right to participate personally, or through his representative, in its formation. It must be the same for all, whether it protects or punishes. All citizens, being equal in the eyes of the law, are equally eligible to all dignities and to all public positions and occupations, according to their abilities, and without distinction except that of their virtues and talents.

7. No person shall be accused, arrested, or imprisoned, except in the cases and according to the forms prescribed by law. Any one soliciting, transmitting, executing, or causing to be executed, any arbitrary order, shall be punished. But any citizen summoned or arrested in virtue of the law shall submit without delay, as resistance constitutes an offense.

8. The law shall provide for such punishments only as are strictly and obviously necessary, and no one shall suffer punishment except it be legally inflicted in virtue of a law passed and promulgated before the commission of the offense.

9. As all persons are held innocent until they shall have been declared guilty, if arrest shall be deemed indispensable, all harshness not essential to the securing of the prisoner's person shall be severely repressed by law.

10. No one shall be disquieted on account of his opinions, including his religious views, provided their manifestation does not disturb the public order established by law.

11. The free communication of ideas and opinions is one of the most precious of the rights of man. Every citizen may, accordingly, speak, write, and print with freedom, but shall be responsible for such abuses of this freedom as shall be defined by law.

12. The security of the rights of man and of the citizen requires public military forces. These forces are, therefore, established for the good of all and not for the personal advantage of those to whom they shall be entrusted.

13. A common contribution is essential for the maintenance of the public forces and for the cost of administration. This should be equitably distributed among all the citizens in proportion to their means.

14. All the citizens have a right to decide, either personally or by their representatives, as to the necessity of the public contribution; to grant this freely; to know to what uses it is put; and to fix the proportion, the mode of assessment and of collection and the duration of the taxes.

15. Society has the right to require of every public agent an account of his administration.

16. A society in which the observance of the law is not assured, nor the separation of powers defined, has no constitution at all.

17. Since property is an inviolable and sacred right, no one shall be deprived thereof except where public necessity, legally determined, shall clearly demand it, and then only on condition that the owner shall have been previously and equitably indemnified.

Reflections on the Revolution (1790)
EDMUND BURKE

Edmund Burke (1729–1797) was a respected member of the English Parliament who gained extraordinary influence in public affairs through his writings. The following selection from his most famous work, Reflections on the Revolution in France *(1790), gives evidence of his regret concerning the changes that had taken place during the first year of the revolution. Burke left a legacy of conservative thought that proved a solace to many whose status was jeopardized by revolutionary action. Burke's contributions to conservative political theory would provide a serious challenge to liberalism in the nineteenth century.*

"Reflections on the Revolution" is from Edmund Burke, *Reflections on the Revolution in France,* in *The Works of the Right Honourable Edmund Burke,* vol. 2 (London: Henry G. Bohn, 1864), pp. 515–516.

When I see the spirit of liberty in action, I see a strong principle at work; and this, for a while, is all I can possibly know of it. The wild gas, the fixed air is plainly broke loose: but we ought to suspend our judgment until the first effervescence is a little subsided, till the liquor is cleared, and until we see something deeper than the agitation of a troubled and frothy surface. I must be tolerably sure, before I venture publicly to congratulate men upon a blessing, that they have really received one. Flattery corrupts both the receiver and the giver; and adulation is not of more service to the people than to kings. I should therefore suspend my congratulations on the new liberty of France, until I was informed how it had been combined with government; with public force; with the discipline and obedience of armies; with the collection of an effective and well-distributed revenue; with morality and religion; with the solidity for property; with peace and order; with civil and social manners. All these (in their way) are good things too; and, without them, liberty is not a benefit while it lasts, and is not likely to continue long. The effect of liberty to individuals is, that they may do what they please: we ought to see what it will please them to do, before we risk congratulations, which may soon be turned into complaints. Prudence would dictate this in the case of separate insulated private men; but liberty, when men act in bodies, is power. Considerate people, before they declare themselves, will observe the use which is made of power; and particularly of so trying a thing as new power in new persons, of whose principles, tempers, and dispositions, they have little or no experience, and in situations where those who appear the most stirring in the scene may possibly not be the real movers. . . .

The age of chivalry is gone.—That of sophisters, economists, and calculators, has succeeded; and the glory of Europe is extinguished for ever. Never, never more, shall we behold that generous loyalty to rank and sex, that proud submission, that dignified obedience, that subordination of the heart, which kept alive, even in servitude itself, the spirit of an exalted freedom. The unbought grace of life, the cheap defense of nations, the nurse of manly sentiment and heroic enterprise is gone! It is gone, that sensibility of principle, that chastity of honour, which felt a stain like a wound, which inspired courage while it mitigated ferocity, which ennobled whatever it touched, and under which vice itself lost half its evil, by losing all its grossness. . . .

But now all is to be changed. All the pleasing illusions, which made power gentle, and obedience liberal, which harmonized the different shades of life, and which, by a bland assimilation, incorporated into politics the sentiments which beautify and soften private society, are to be dissolved by this new conquering empire of light and reason. All the decent drapery of life is to be rudely torn off. All the super-added ideas, furnished from the wardrobe of a moral imagination, which the heart owns, and the understanding ratifies, as necessary to cover the defects of our naked shivering nature, and to raise it to dignity in our own estimation, are to be exploded as a ridiculous, absurd, and antiquated fashion.

On this scheme of things, a king is but a man; a queen is but a woman; a woman is but an animal; and an animal not of the highest order. . . . On the scheme of this barbarous philosophy, which is the offspring of cold hearts and muddy understandings, and which is as void of solid wisdom, as it is destitute of all taste and elegance, laws are to be supported only by their own terrors, and by the concern, which each individual may find in them, from his own private speculations, or even spare to them from his own private interests. In the groves of their academy, at the end of every vista, you see nothing but the gallows. . . . When the old feudal and chivalrous spirit of Fealty, which, by freeing kings from fear, freed both kings and subjects from the precautions of tyranny, shall be extinct in the minds of men, plots and assassinations will be anticipated by preventive murder and preventive confiscation, and that long roll of grim and bloody maxims, which form the political code of all power, not standing on its own honour, and the honour of those who are to obey it. Kings will be tyrants from policy when subjects are rebels from principle. . . .

To make a government requires no great prudence. Settle the seat of power; teach obedience: and the work is done. To give Freedom is still more easy. It is not necessary to guide; it only requires to let go the rein. But to form a free government; that is, to temper together these opposite elements of liberty and restraint in one consistent work, requires much thought, deep reflection, a sagacious, powerful, and combining mind. This I do not find in those who take the lead in the National Assembly. Perhaps they are not so miserably deficient as they appear. I rather believe it. It would put them below the common level of human understanding. But when the leaders choose to make themselves bidders at an auction of popularity, their talents, in the construction of the state, will be of no service. They will become flatterers instead of legislators; the instruments, not the guides, of the people. If any of them should happen to propose a scheme of liberty, soberly limited, and defined with proper qualifications, he will be immediately outbid by his competitors, who will produce something more splendidly popular. Suspicions will be raised of his fidelity to his cause. Moderation will be stigmatized as the virtue of cowards; and compromise as the prudence of traitors; until, in hopes of preserving the credit which may enable him to temper, and moderate, on some occasions, the popular leader is obliged to become active in propagating doctrines, and establishing powers, that will afterwards defeat any sober purpose at which he ultimately might have aimed.

The improvements of the National Assembly are superficial, their errors fundamental.

The Clerical Oath of Loyalty (November 27, 1790)

The serious financial crisis that had existed before the revolution and had actually resulted in the calling of the Estates-General persisted. In order to pay off the national debt, the Assembly took decisive action and confiscated church lands. Such a radical act required an ecclesiastical reconstruction. In July 1790, the National Assembly issued the Civil Constitution of the Clergy. This placed the Roman Catholic Church under the direct control of the secular state. Bishops and priests were reduced in number and became salaried employees of the state. In this move, the Assembly consulted neither the pope nor the French clergy. It was a major blunder which divided the clergy and brought condemnation from the pope; many devout Catholics were then forced to choose between their loyalties to the revolution and to the church. This domination of the French state over the Catholic Church was to continue under Napoleon and resulted in a papal offensive against liberalism throughout the nineteenth century. The following selection is a decree that was designed to test the loyalty of the clergy to the religious reorganization of the state.

Bishops and former archbishops and curés maintained in office, [directors of seminaries, . . . teachers in seminaries and colleges, and all other ecclesiastical public functionaries], shall be required to take, if they have not done so, the oath to which they are subject by article 39 of the decree . . . concerning the Civil Constitution of the Clergy. Accordingly, by virtue of this latter decree, they shall swear to watch carefully over the faithful of the diocese or parish entrusted to them, to be faithful to the nation, to the law, and to the King, and to maintain with all their power the Constitution decreed by the National Assembly and accepted by the King. . . .

In case the said bishops, former archbishops, curés, and other ecclesiastical public functionaries, after having taken their respective oaths, fail therein, either by refusing to obey the decrees of the National Assembly accepted or sanctioned by the King, or by constituting or instigating opposition to their execution, they shall be prosecuted in the district courts as rebels resisting the law, and punished by deprivation of their stipend, and, moreover, they shall be declared to have forfeited the rights of active citizenship and to be ineligible for any public office. Consequently, provision shall be made for their replacement, according to the said decree [Civil Constitution of the Clergy]. . . .

All ecclesiastical or lay persons who unite to contrive a refusal to obey the decrees of the National Assembly accepted or sanctioned by the King, or to constitute or instigate opposition to the execution thereof, likewise shall be prosecuted as disturbers of public order, and punished according to the rigor of the laws.

The Radicalization of the Revolution (1792–1794)

The Fall of Louis XVI

On June 20, 1791, the royal family managed to get out of Paris. Traveling in disguise with false passports, they were detained and arrested in Varennes, about 150 miles from Paris. The king was disgraced, and the monarchy suffered a humiliating blow. The months following the king's flight from Paris were tense and saw the eventual erosion of royalist support and the abolition of the monarchy in September 1792. Louis was indicted on December 11, 1792.

The first selection indicates that he was being tried for treason. The king de-nied most of the charges and blamed the rest on others. Nevertheless, a small majority of votes in the Assembly sent him to the guillotine. The second excerpt is an eyewitness account of the execution by Henry Edgeworth de Firmont, the king's confessor, who accompanied Louis to the scaffold. Justification for regi-cide came two days later by way of a proclamation of the government to the French people. The last selection is from the memoirs of Mme Roland, a guid-ing spirit of the revolutionary Girondist faction who was eventually impris-oned and sent to the guillotine herself.

The Indictment of Louis XVI (December 11, 1792)

Louis, the French people accuses you of having committed a multitude of crimes in order to establish your tyranny by destroying its liberty.

1. On 20 June, 1789, you attacked the sovereignty of the people by sus-pending the assemblies of its representatives and by driving them by violence from the place of their sessions. . . .

2. On 23 June you wished to dictate laws to the nation; you surrounded its representatives with troops; you presented them with two royal declarations, subversive of every liberty, and you ordered them to separate. Your declara-tions and the minutes of the Assembly establish these outrages undeniably.

3. You caused an army to march against the citizens of Paris; your satellites caused their blood to flow, and you withdrew this army only when the capture of the Bastille and the general insurrection apprised you that the people were victorious. . . .

6. For a long time you contemplated flight; . . . but on 21 June [1791] you made your escape with a false passport; you left a declaration against those same constitutional articles; you ordered the ministers not to sign any docu-ments emanating from the National Assembly, and you forbade the Minister of Justice to deliver the Seals of State. The people's money was wasted in achieving the success of this treason. . . .

7. On 14 September you apparently accepted the Constitution; your speeches announced a desire to maintain it, and you worked to overthrow it before it even was achieved.

15. Your brothers, enemies of the state, have rallied the émigrés [French nobility in self-imposed exile] under their colors; they have raised regiments, borrowed money, and contracted alliances in your name; you disavowed them only when you were quite certain that you could not harm their plans. . . .

"The Indictment of Louis XVI" is reprinted with permission of Macmillan Publishing Com-pany from *A Documentary Survey of the French Revolution*, edited by John Hall Stewart, pp. 386–389, 391. Copyright 1951 by Macmillan Publishing Company, renewed 1979 by John Hall Stewart.

30. You tried to bribe, with considerable sums, several members of the Constituent and Legislative Assemblies. . . .

31. You allowed the French nation to be disgraced in Germany, in Italy, and in Spain, since you did nothing to exact reparation for the ill treatment which the French experienced in those countries.

32. On 10 August you reviewed the Swiss Guards at five o'clock in the morning; and the Swiss Guards fired first on the citizens.

33. You caused the blood of Frenchmen to flow.

The Execution of Louis XVI (January 21, 1793)
HENRY EDGEWORTH DE FIRMONT

The carriage arrived . . . in the greatest silence, at the Place Louis XV, and came to a halt in the middle of a large empty space that had been left around the scaffold. This space was bordered with cannon; and beyond, as far as the eye could reach, was a multitude in arms. . . .

As soon as the king descended from the carriage, three executioners surrounded him and wished to take off his coat. He repulsed them with dignity and took it off himself. The executioners, whom the proud bearing of the king had momentarily disconcerted, seemed then to resume their audacity and, surrounding him again, attempted to tie his hands. "What are you trying to do?" asked the king, withdrawing his hands abruptly.

"Tie you," replied one of the executioners.

"Tie me!" returned the king in an indignant tone. "No, I will never consent; do what you are ordered to do, but I will not be tied; renounce that idea." The executioners insisted, they lifted their voices, and seemed about to call for help in order to use force. . . .

"Sire," I said to him with tears, "in this new outrage I see only a final resemblance between Your Majesty and the Saviour who is to reward you."

At these words he lifted his eyes to heaven with a sorrowing look that I cannot describe . . . and, turning to the executioners, said: "Do what you wish; I will drain the cup to the dregs."

The steps that led to the scaffold were extremely steep in ascent. The king was obliged to hold to my arm, and by the pains he seemed to take, feared that his courage had begun to weaken; but what was my astonishment when, upon arriving at the last step, I saw him escape, so to speak, from my hands, cross the length of the scaffold with firm step to impose silence, by a single glance, upon ten or fifteen drummers who were in front of him, and with a voice so strong that it could be heard at the Pont-Tournant, distinctly pronounce these words forever memorable: "I die innocent of all the crimes

"The executioners seized [Louis XVI's head] by the hair, and showed it to the multitude, whose cries of 'Long live the Republic!' resounded to the very bosom of the Convention."—Henry Edgeworth de Firmont. (*Bibliotheque Nationale de France*)

imputed to me. I pardon the authors of my death, and pray God that the blood you are about to shed will never fall upon France."

• • •

The executioners seized him, the knife struck him, his head fell at fifteen minutes after ten. The executioners seized it by the hair, and showed it to the multitude, whose cries of "Long live the Republic!" resounded to the very bosom of the Convention, whose place of meeting was only a few steps from the place of execution.

Thus died, at the age of thirty-eight years, four months, and twenty-eight days, Louis, sixteenth of his name, whose ancestors had reigned in France for more than eight hundred years. . . .

Immediately after the execution, the body of Louis was transported to the cemetery of the ancient Church of the Madeleine. It was placed in a pit six feet square, close to the wall of the Rue d'Anjou, and dissolved instantly by a great quantity of quicklime with which they took the precaution to cover it.

Proclamation of the Convention to the French People (January 23, 1793)

Citizens, the tyrant is no more. For a long time the cries of the victims, whom war and domestic dissensions have spread over France and Europe, loudly protested his existence. He has paid his penalty, and only acclamations for the Republic and for liberty have been heard from the people.

We have had to combat inveterate prejudices, and the superstition of centuries concerning monarchy. Involuntary uncertainties and inevitable disturbances always accompany great changes and revolutions as profound as ours. This political crisis has suddenly surrounded us with contradictions and tumults.

But the cause has ceased, and the motives have disappeared; respect for liberty of opinion must cause these tumultuous scenes to be forgotten; only the good which they have produced through the death of the tyrant and of tyranny now remains, and this judgment belongs in its entirety to each of us, just as it belongs to the entire nation. The National Convention and the French people are now to have only one mind, only one sentiment, that of liberty and civic fraternity.

Now, above all, we need peace in the interior of the Republic, and the most active surveillance of the domestic enemies of liberty. Never did circumstances more urgently require of all citizens the sacrifice of their passions and their personal opinions concerning the act of national justice which has just been effected. Today the French people can have no other passion than that for liberty.

Reflections on Louis XVI

MME ROLAND

Louis XVI was not exactly the man they were interested in painting in order to discredit him. He was neither the stupid imbecile that they presented for the disdain of the people, nor the fine, judicious, virtuous man that his friends described. Nature had made him an ordinary man, who would have done well in some obscure station. He was ruined in being educated for the throne, and lost through mediocrity in a difficult period when he could have been saved only through genius and strength. An ordinary mind, brought up near the throne and taught from infancy to dissemble, acquires many advantages for dealing with people; the art of letting each see only what is suitable

"Proclamation of the Convention to the French People" is from E. L. Higgins, ed., *The French Revolution* as Told by Contemporaries (Boston: Houghton Mifflin, 1966), p. 392. Copyright © 1938, renewed 1966 by Houghton Mifflin Company. Used by permission of the publisher.

"Reflections on Louis XVI" is from E. L. Higgins, ed., *The French Revolution as Told by Contemporaries* (Boston: Houghton Mifflin, 1966), pp. 13–14. Copyright © 1938, renewed 1966 by Houghton Mifflin Company. Used by permission of the publisher.

for him to see is for it only a habit to which practice gives an appearance of cleverness: one would have to be an idiot to appear stupid in such a situation. Louis XVI had moreover, a good memory and much activity; he never remained idle, and read a great deal. He knew well the various treaties made by France with the neighboring powers, and he was the best geographer in his kingdom. The knowledge of names, the exact application to the faces of the court personages to whom they belonged, of anecdotes personal to them, had been extended by him to all the individuals who appeared in some manner in the Revolution. But Louis XVI, without elevation of soul, without boldness of mind, without strength of character, still had his ideas narrowed and his sentiments perverted, so to say, by religious prejudices and jesuitical principles. . . . If he had been born two centuries earlier, and if he had had a reasonable wife, he would have made no more noise in the world than many other princes of his race who have passed across the stage without having done much good or much harm.

Reality Check: An Update on the Political Rights of Women (1793)

In the midst of the revolution, with the recent execution of the king and the various political groups scrambling to consolidate their power, the official government (called the Convention) was presented with a complaint regarding the impending dissolution of the Society of Revolutionary Republican Women. An investigation was ordered, and the Committee of General Security presented the following recommendations to the Convention. The Convention subsequently voted to outlaw "women's societies and popular clubs." Note carefully the committee's reasons for rejecting of the organization.

The Committee thought it should carry its investigation further. It raised the following questions: . . . (1) Can women exercise political rights and take an active part in affairs of government? (2) Can they deliberate together in political associations or popular societies? With respect to these two questions, the Committee decided in the negative. . . .

We are going to put forward a few ideas which may shed light on [these questions]. In your wisdom you will know how to submit them to a thorough examination.

1. Should women exercise political rights and meddle in affairs of government? To govern is to rule the commonwealth by laws, the preparation of

"Reality Check: An Update on the Political Rights of Women" is from Darline Gay Levy et al., eds., *Women in Revolutionary Paris 1789–1795* (Urbana: University of Illinois Press, 1979), pp. 214–216. Copyright © 1979 by the Board of Trustees of the University of Illinois. Used with the permission of the author and the University of Illinois Press.

which demands extensive knowledge, unlimited attention and devotion, a strict immovability, and self-abnegation; again, to govern is to direct and ceaselessly to correct the action of constituted authorities. Are women capable of these cares and of the qualities they call for? In general, we can answer, no. Very few examples would contradict this evaluation.

The citizen's political rights are to debate and to have resolutions drawn up, by means of comparative deliberations, that relate to the interest of the state, and to resist oppression. Do women have the moral and physical strength which the exercise of one and the other of these rights calls for? Universal opinion rejects this idea.

2. Should women meet in political associations? The goal of popular associations is this: to unveil the maneuvers of the enemies of the commonwealth; to exercise surveillance both over citizens as individuals and over public functionaries—even over the legislative body; to excite the zeal of one and the other by the example of republican virtues; to shed light by public and in-depth discussion concerning the lack or reform of political laws. Can women devote themselves to these useful and difficult functions? No, because they would be obliged to sacrifice the more important cares to which nature calls them. The private functions for which women are destined by their very nature are related to the general order of society; this social order results from the differences between man and woman. . . .

Man is strong, robust, born with great energy, audacity, and courage; he braves perils [and] the intemperance of seasons because of his constitution; he resists all the elements; he is fit for the arts, difficult labors; and as he is almost exclusively destined for agriculture, commerce, navigation, voyages, war—everything that calls for force, intelligence, capability, so in the same way, he alone seems to be equipped for profound and serious thinking which calls for great intellectual effort and long studies which it is not granted to women to pursue.

What character is suitable for woman? Morals and even nature have assigned her functions to her. To begin educating men, to prepare children's minds and hearts for public virtues, to direct them early in life towards the good, to elevate their souls, to educate them in the political cult of liberty; such are their functions, after household cares. . . . When they have fulfilled all these obligations, they will have deserved well of the Fatherland. . . .

We must say that this question is related essentially to morals, and without morals, no republic. Does the honesty of woman allow her to display herself in public and to struggle against men? to argue in full view of a public about questions on which the salvation of the republic depends? In general, women are ill suited for elevated thoughts and serious meditations, and if, among ancient peoples, their natural timidity and modesty did not allow them to appear outside their families, then in the French Republic do you want them to be seen coming into the gallery to political assemblies as men do? abandoning both reserve—source of all the virtues of their sex—and the care of their family? . . .

We believe, therefore, that a woman should not leave her family to meddle in affairs of government.

The Reign of Terror

One of the most dramatic personalities of the French Revolution was Maximilien Robespierre (1758–1794), who dominated the principal policy-making body in the state, the Committee of Public Safety. An ardent democrat, Robespierre believed in a republic of virtue that demanded selfless adherence to republican ideals. Those who supported the monarchy or were more moderate in their republican zeal became threats to the success of the revolution and had to be eliminated. Terror, according to Robespierre, was "swift, inflexible justice" and therefore virtuous. The Reign of Terror, which lasted from 1793 to 1794, saw the execution by the guillotine of more than 25,000 people, from both the political left and right, many without proper trials.

Perhaps the most amiable of the radical political leaders was Camille Desmoulins. Although he was one of the first to preach and write about republican ideals, he harbored none of the fanaticism or cruelty that so energized and blinded his friend Robespierre. In the first selection, Desmoulins pleads for clemency and an end to the Terror. Ultimately, his voice threatened the authority of Robespierre, who sent Desmoulins, Danton, and other former adherents to the guillotine three months later.

The aims of the revolution are presented in the second selection by Robespierre. The next document is a law that transferred the administration of the Terror from the Convention to the Committee of Public Safety. This enactment provided a general definition of an "enemy of the Republic" and increased the number of victims sacrificed to the purity of the revolution. Historians generally agree that this law not only damaged the ideals of the French Revolution, but also was the ultimate cause of Robespierre's downfall. He fell victim to colleagues who feared his menacing power, and was himself executed a month and a half after the law was ratified. With Robespierre's death, the Terror came to an end. The revolution continued, but without the bloodshed that had devoured its own children.

"You Would Exterminate All Your Enemies by the Guillotine!" (December 20, 1793)

CAMILLE DESMOULINS

Is this liberty that we desire a mere empty name? Is it only an opera actress carried about with a red cap on, or even that statue, forty-six feet high, which David proposes to make? If by liberty you do not understand, as I do, great principles, but only a bit of stone, there never was idolatry more stupid and expensive than ours. . . . No, heaven-born liberty is no nymph of the opera, nor a red liberty cap, nor a dirty shirt and rags. Liberty is happiness, reason, equality, justice, the Declaration of Rights, your sublime constitution.

"'You Would Exterminate All Your Enemies by the Guillotine!'" is from James H. Robinson and Charles A. Beard, eds., *Readings in Modern European History*, vol. 1 (Boston: Ginn and Company, 1908), pp. 307–308.

Would you have me recognize this liberty, have me fall at her feet, and shed all my blood for her? Then open the prison doors to the two hundred thousand citizens whom you call suspects, for in the Declaration of Rights no prisons for suspicion are provided for, only places of detention. Suspicion has no prison, but only the public accuser; there are no suspects, but only those accused of offenses established by law.

Do not think that such a measure would be fatal to the republic. It would, on the contrary, be the most revolutionary that you have adopted. You would exterminate all your enemies by the guillotine! But was there ever greater madness? Can you possibly destroy one enemy on the scaffold without making ten others among his family and friends? Do you believe that those whom you have imprisoned—these women and old men, these stragglers of the Revolution—are really dangerous? Only those among your enemies have remained among you who are cowardly or sick. The strong and courageous have emigrated. They have perished at Lyons or in the Vendee. The remnant which still lingers does not deserve your anger. . . .

Moreover, it has not been love of the republic, but curiosity, which has every day attracted multitudes to the Place de la Revolution [site of the executions]; it was the new drama which was to be enacted but once. . . .

I am of a very different opinion from those who claim that it is necessary to leave Terror as the order of the day. I am confident . . . that liberty will be assured and Europe conquered as soon as you have a Committee of Clemency. This committee will complete the Revolution, for clemency is itself a Revolutionary measure, the most efficient of all when it is wisely dealt out.

"Virtue and Terror": Speech to the Convention (February 5, 1794)

MAXIMILIEN ROBESPIERRE

What is the aim we want to achieve? The peaceful enjoyment of liberty and equality, the reign of that eternal justice whose laws have been engraved, not in stone and marble, but in the hearts of all men, even in the heart of the slave who forgets them or of the tyrant who denies them.

We want a state of affairs where all despicable and cruel passions are unknown and all kind and generous passions are aroused by the laws; where ambition is the desire to deserve glory and to serve the fatherland; where distinctions arise only from equality itself; where the citizen submits to the magistrate, the magistrate to the people and the people to justice; where the fatherland guarantees the well-being of each individual, and where each individual enjoys with pride the prosperity and the glory of the fatherland; where all souls elevate themselves through constant communication of republican sentiments and through the need to deserve the esteem of a great people;

"'Virtue and Terror'" is from Richard W. Lyman and Lewis W. Spitz, eds., *Major Crises in Western Civilization*, vol. 2 (New York: Harcourt, Brace & World, 1965), pp. 71–72.

where the arts are the decorations of liberty that ennobles them, where commerce is the source of public wealth and not only of the monstrous opulence of a few houses.

In our country we want to substitute morality for egoism, honesty for honor, principles for customs, duties for decorum, the rule of reason for the tyranny of custom, the contempt of vice for the contempt of misfortune, pride for insolence, magnanimity for vanity, love of glory for love of money, good people for well-bred people, merit for intrigue, genius for wit, truth for pompous action, warmth of happiness for boredom of sensuality, greatness of man for pettiness of the great; a magnanimous, powerful, happy people for a polite, frivolous, despicable people—that is to say, all the virtues and all the miracles of the Republic for all the vices and all the absurdities of the monarchy.

In one word, we want to fulfill the wishes of nature, accomplish the destiny of humanity, keep the promises of philosophy, absolve Providence from the long reign of crime and tyranny.

What kind of government can realize these marvels? Only a democratic or republican government.

But what is the fundamental principle of the democratic or popular government, that is to say, the essential strength that sustains it and makes it move? It is virtue: I am speaking of the public virtue which brought about so many marvels in Greece and Rome and which must bring about much more astonishing ones yet in republican France; of that virtue which is nothing more than love of the fatherland and of its laws.

If the strength of popular government in peacetime is virtue, the strength of popular government in revolution is both virtue and terror; terror without virtue is disastrous, virtue without terror is powerless. Terror is nothing but prompt, severe, and inflexible justice; it is thus an emanation of virtue; it is less a particular principle than a consequence of the general principle of democracy applied to the most urgent needs of the fatherland. It is said that terror is the strength of despotic government. Does ours then resemble despotism? Yes, as the sword that shines in the hands of the heroes of liberty resemble the one with which the satellites of tyranny are armed. Let the despot govern his brutalized subjects through terror; he is right as a despot. Subdue the enemies of liberty through terror and you will be right as founders of the Republic. The government of revolution is the despotism of liberty against tyranny.

The Administration of Terror (June 10, 1794)

1. In the Revolutionary Tribunal there shall be a president and four vice-presidents, one public prosecutor, four substitutes for the public prosecutor, and twelve judges.

2. The jurors shall be fifty in number.

4. The Revolutionary Tribunal is instituted to punish the enemies of the people.

5. The enemies of the people are those who seek to destroy public liberty, either by force or by cunning.

6. The following are deemed enemies of the people: those who have instigated the re-establishment of monarchy, or have sought to disparage or dissolve the National Convention and the revolutionary and republican government of which it is the center;

Those who have betrayed the Republic in the command of places and armies, or in any other military function, carried on correspondence with the enemies of the Republic, labored to disrupt the provisioning or the service of the armies;

Those who have supported the designs of the enemies of France, either by countenancing the sheltering and the impunity of conspirators and aristocracy, by persecuting and calumniating patriotism, by corrupting the mandataries of the people, or by abusing the principles of the Revolution or the laws or measures of the government by false and perfidious applications;

Those who have deceived the people or the representatives of the people, in order to lead them into undertakings contrary to the interests of liberty;

Those who have sought to inspire discouragement, in order to favor the enterprises of the tyrants leagued against the Republic;

Those who have disseminated false news in order to divide or disturb the people;

Those who have sought to mislead opinion and to prevent the instruction of the people, to deprave morals and to corrupt the public conscience, to impair the energy and the purity of revolutionary and republican principles, or to impede the progress thereof, either by counter-revolutionary or insidious writings, or by any other machination; . . .

Finally, all who are designated in previous laws relative to the punishment of conspirators and counter-revolutionaries, and who, by whatever means or by whatever appearances they assume, have made an attempt against the liberty, unity, and security of the Republic, or labored to prevent the strengthening thereof.

7. The penalty provided for all offences under the jurisdiction of the Revolutionary Tribunal is death.

8. The proof necessary to convict enemies of the people comprises every kind of evidence, whether material or moral, oral or written, which can naturally secure the approval of every just and reasonable mind; the rule of judgments is the conscience of the jurors, enlightened by love of the Patrie; their aim, the triumph of the Republic and the ruin of its enemies; the procedure, the simple means which good sense dictates in order to arrive at a knowledge of the truth, in the forms determined by law.

9. Every citizen has the right to seize conspirators and counter-revolutionaries, and to arraign them before the magistrates. He is required to denounce them as soon as he knows of them.

The Execution of Robespierre (July 28, 1794)

DURAND DE MAILLANE

Robespierre's turn had come at last. By fawning upon the people he had become their idol, and this will happen to any man who declaims against the rich, causing the people to hope for a division of the spoils. Through the populace, he ruled the Jacobin Club; through the Jacobin Club, the Convention and through the Convention, France. He dictated decrees and directed the administration. Nothing was done except by his orders or with his approval. His caprices were flattered, and his very manias were praised. The tribunal beheaded those he designated without investigation. His power seemed too terrible to his accomplices as it did to his victims. A number had been sacrificed already and others feared the same fate. They banded together to pull down the idol they themselves had set up.

• • •

[The committee of general security] ordered that he [Robespierre] be taken to the prison of the Conciergerie. His trial was short. On the following day he was guillotined, together with Saint-Just, Couthon, and his other accomplices. It was quite a distance from the Palais de Justice to the scaffold, and the immensity of the long Rue Saint-Honore had to be traversed. Along the whole course, the people pursued Robespierre with hoots and maledictions. He had been given a conspicuous place in the tumbril, his face half covered by a dirty, bloodstained cloth which enveloped his jaw. It may be said that this man, who had brought so much anguish to others, suffered during these twenty-four hours all the pain and agony that a mortal can experience.

SECTION II: THE NAPOLEONIC ERA

The Rise of Napoleon

The Will to Power (1799–1802)

After the Reign of Terror, the French Revolution entered a moderate period that retreated from the violent radicalism of Robespierre. A new government called the Directory was formed, and it governed the French Republic rather ineffectively until 1799. In that year, Napoleon Bonaparte, who had supported the Directory and had earned fame as the military protector of the Republic, returned to Paris

"The Execution of Robespierre" is from E. L. Higgins, ed., *The French Revolution as Told by Contemporaries* (Boston: Houghton Mifflin, 1966), pp. 346, 361. Copyright © 1938, renewed 1966 by Houghton Mifflin Company. Used by permission of the publisher.

from his Egyptian campaign and promptly overthrew the government. In its place, he established the Consulate. Napoleon, as first consul, was given significant power over his other two colleagues. On December 15, 1799, the Consulate proclaimed the end of the French Revolution. The ideals that founded the Republic ostensibly had not changed, but the leadership certainly had. The first excerpt is from a conversation Napoleon had with one of his confidants in 1796, three years before coming into power. The second document is a proclamation to the French people that explains Napoleon's role in the overthrow of the Directory and the establishment of the Consulate. It is a fine example of effective propaganda. Both excerpts reveal much about Napoleon's ambition.

On the Realities of Power (1796)
NAPOLEON BONAPARTE

What I have done so far is nothing. I am but at the opening of the career I am to run. Do you suppose that I have gained my victories in Italy in order to advance the lawyers of the Directory? Do you think, either, that my object is to establish a Republic? What a notion! A republic of thirty million people, with our morals and vices! How could that ever be? It is a chimera with which the French are infatuated but which will pass away in time like all others. What they want is glory and the gratification of their vanity; as for liberty, of that they have no conception. Look at the army! The victories which we have just gained have given the French soldier his true character. I am everything to him. Let the Directory attempt to deprive me of my command and they will see who is master. The nation must have a head, a head rendered illustrious by glory and not by theories of government, fine phrases, or the talk of idealists, of which the French understand not a whit. Let them have their toys and they will be satisfied. They will amuse themselves and allow themselves to be led, provided the goal is cleverly disguised.

The First Consul: "A Citizen Devoted to the Republic" (November 10, 1799)
NAPOLEON BONAPARTE

On my return to Paris [from Egypt] I found division among all authorities, and agreement upon only one point, namely, that the Constitution was half destroyed and was unable to save liberty.

"On the Realities of Power" is from *Memoires of Miot de Melito*, in James H. Robinson, ed., *Translations and Reprints from the Original Sources of European History*, rev. ed., vol. 2, pt. 2 (Philadelphia: University of Pennsylvania Press, 1900), pp. 2–3.

"The First Consul" is reprinted with permission of Macmillan Publishing Company from *A Documentary Survey of the French Revolution*, edited by John Hall Stewart, pp. 763–765. Copyright 1951 by Macmillan Publishing Company, renewed 1979 by John Hall Stewart.

All parties came to me, confided to me their designs, disclosed their secrets, and requested my support; I refused to be the man of a party.

The Council of Elders summoned me; I answered its appeal. A plan of general restoration had been devised by men whom the nation has been accustomed to regard as the defenders of liberty, equality, and property; this plan required an examination, calm, free, exempt from all influence and all fear. Accordingly, the Council of Elders resolved upon the removal of the Legislative Body to Saint-Cloud; it gave me the responsibility of disposing the force necessary for its independence. I believe it my duty to my fellow citizens, to the soldiers perishing in our armies, to the national glory acquired at the cost of their blood, to accept the command.

The Councils assembled at Saint-Cloud; republican troops guaranteed their security from without, but assassins created terror within. Several deputies of the Council of Five Hundred, armed with stilettos and firearms, circulated threats of death around them.

The plans which ought to have been developed were withheld, the majority disorganized, the boldest orators disconcerted, and the futility of every wise proposition was evident.

I took my indignation and grief to the Council of Elders. I besought it to assure the execution of its generous designs; I directed its attention to the evils of the Patrie [Fatherland] . . . ; it concurred with me by new evidence of its steadfast will.

I presented myself at the Council of Five Hundred, alone, unarmed, my head uncovered, just as the Elders had received and applauded me; I came to remind the majority of its wishes, and to assure it of its power.

The stilettos which menaced the deputies were instantly raised against their liberator; twenty assassins threw themselves upon me and aimed at my breast. The grenadiers of the Legislative Body whom I had left at the door of the hall ran forward, placed themselves between the assassins and myself. One of these brave grenadiers had his clothes pierced by a stiletto. They bore me out.

At the same moment cries of "Outlaw" were raised against the defender of the law. It was the fierce cry of assassins against the power destined to repress them.

They crowded around the president, uttering threats, arms in their hands; they commanded him to outlaw me; I was informed of this: I ordered him to be rescued from their fury, and six grenadiers of the Legislative Body secured him. Immediately afterwards some grenadiers of the Legislative Body charged into the hall and cleared it.

The factions, intimidated, dispersed and fled. The majority, freed from their attacks, returned freely and peaceably into the meeting hall, listened to the proposals on behalf of public safety, deliberated, and prepared the salutary resolution which is to become the new and provisional law of the Republic.

Frenchmen, you will doubtless recognize in this conduct the zeal of a soldier of liberty, a citizen devoted to the Republic. Conservative, tutelary, and liberal ideas have been restored to their rights through the dispersal of the rebels who oppressed the Councils.

Napoleon's Consolidation of His Rule

In order to consolidate the new regime, Napoleon sought to control the flow of information in the state. In the first document, note the reasons given for suppression of the newspapers. Between July 1801 and April 1802, Napoleon sought to reorganize the religious institutions of France. The second document is the agreement between France and the papacy, which controlled the position of the Roman Catholic Church in France until 1905. The third selection is a legislative act of state that was promulgated without the pope's consent, but enforced nevertheless. There were other similar pronouncements for Protestants (1802) and Jews (1808).

Suppression of the Newspapers (1800)

The consuls of the Republic, considering that a part of the newspapers which are printed in the department of the Seine are instruments in the hands of the enemies of the Republic; that the government is particularly charged by the French people to look after their security, orders as follows:

1. The minister of police shall permit to be printed, published, and circulated during the whole course of the war only the following newspapers: . . . [Here follows the names of thirteen newspapers], and newspapers devoted exclusively to science, arts, literature, commerce, announcements and notices.

2. The minister of the general police shall immediately make a report upon all the newspapers that are printed in the other departments.

3. The minister of the general police shall see that no new newspaper be printed in the department of the Seine, as well as in all the other departments of the Republic.

4. The proprietors and editors of the newspapers preserved by the present order shall present themselves to the minister of the police in order to attest their character as French citizens, their residences and signatures, and they shall promise fidelity to the constitution.

5. All newspapers which shall insert articles opposed to the respect that is due to the social compact, to the sovereignty of the people and the glory of the armies, or which shall publish invectives against the governments and nations who are the friends or allies of the Republic, even when these articles may be extracts from foreign periodicals, shall be immediately suppressed.

6. The minister of the general police is charged with the execution of the present order, which shall be inserted in the Bulletin of the Laws.

"Suppression of the Newspapers" is from Frank M. Anderson, ed., *The Constitutions and Other Illustrative Documents of the History of France*, 2nd ed., revised (New York: Russell and Russell, 1908), p. 282.

Reorganization of Religion: Convention Between the French Government and His Holiness Pope Pius VII (1802)

The government of the French Republic recognizes that the Roman, catholic and apostolic religion is the religion of the great majority of French citizens.

His Holiness likewise recognizes that this same religion has derived and in this moment again expects the greatest benefit and grandeur from the establishment of catholic worship in France and from the personal profession of it which the consuls of the Republic make. In consequence, after this mutual recognition, as well for the benefit of religion as for the maintenance of internal tranquility, they have agreed as follows:

1. The catholic, apostolic and Roman religion shall be freely exercised in France: its worship shall be public, and in conformity with the police regulations which the government shall deem necessary for the public tranquility.

4. The First Consul of the Republic shall make appointments, within the three months which shall follow the publication of the bull of His Holiness to the archbishoprics and bishoprics of the new circumscription. His Holiness shall confer the canonical institution, following the forms established in relation to France before the change of government.

6. Before entering upon their functions, the bishops shall take directly, at the hands of the First Consul, the oath of fidelity which was in use before the change of government, expressed in the following terms:

"I swear and promise to God, upon the holy scriptures, to remain in obedience and fidelity to the government established by the constitution of the French Republic. I also promise not to have any intercourse, nor to assist by any counsel, nor to support any league, either within or without, which is inimical to the public tranquility; and if, within my diocese or elsewhere, I learn that anything to the prejudice of the state is being contrived, I will make it known to the government."

Articles for the Catholic Church (1802)

1. No bull, brief, rescript, decree, injunction, provision, signature serving as a provision, nor other documents from the court of Rome, even concerning individuals only, can be received, published, printed, or otherwise put into effect, without the authorization of the government.

"Reorganization of Religion" is from Frank M. Anderson, ed., *The Constitutions and Other Illustrative Documents of the History of France*, 2nd ed., revised (New York: Russell and Russell, 1908), pp. 296–297.

"Articles for the Catholic Church" is from Frank M. Anderson, ed., *The Constitutions and Other Illustrative Documents of the History of France*, 2nd ed., revised (New York: Russell and Russell, 1908), p. 299.

4. No national or metropolitan council, no diocesan synod, no deliberative assembly, shall take place without the express permission of the government.

6. There shall be recourse to the Council of State in every case of abuse on the part of the Superiors and other ecclesiastical persons.

The cases of abuse are usurpation or excess of power, contravention of the laws and regulations of the Republic, infraction of the rules sanctioned by the canons received in France, attack upon the liberties, privileges and customs of the Gallican church, and every undertaking or any proceeding which in the exercise of worship can compromise the honor of the citizens, disturb arbitrarily their consciences, or degenerate into oppression or injury against them or into public scandal.

The Dominance and Fall of Napoleon

Napoleon's Reforms and Institutions

Although Napoleon's rise was extraordinary and, some would say, not in keeping with the spirit of a free republic, it is true that the programs he advocated were progressive and contributed to the stability and morale of the French state. Of the many reforms and institutions created by Napoleon, the provisions for education and the Legion of Honor are among the most characteristic and enduring. Apart from these official decrees, note some of Napoleon's personal comments on the same topics, as excerpted from his diary.

General Provisions on Education (May 1, 1802)

143. The Imperial University and its grand master, charged exclusively by us with the care of education and public instruction in all the empire, shall aim without respite to improve the instruction of all sorts, and to favor the composition of classical works; they shall particularly take care that the instruction of the sciences shall always be upon the level of acquired knowledge and that the spirit of system shall never arrest their progress.

"General Provisions on Education" is from Frank M. Anderson, ed., *The Constitutions and Other Illustrative Documents of the History of France*, 2nd ed., revised (New York: Russell and Russell, 1908), p. 323.

The Legion of Honor (May 19, 1802)

Each person admitted to the legion shall swear upon his honor to devote himself to the service of the Republic, to the preservation of its territory in its integrity, to the defense of its government, its laws and the properties which they have consecrated; to combat with all the means that justice, reason and the laws authorise, every undertaking having a tendency to reestablish the feudal regime, or to reproduce the titles and qualities which were symbolical of it; lastly, to assist with all his power in the maintenance of liberty and equality.

All military men who have received arms of honor are members of the legion. The military men who have rendered important services to the state in the war for liberty;

The citizens who by their knowledge, their talents or their virtues, have contributed to the establishment or defense of the principles of the Republic, or have made justice or the public administration loved and respected shall be eligible for appointment.

In times of peace one must have had twenty-five years of military service in order to be appointed a member of the legion; the years of service in time of war shall count double and each campaign of the last war shall count for four years.

Great services rendered to the state in legislative functions, diplomacy, administration, justice or the sciences, shall also be titles for admission, provided the person who shall have rendered them has made part of the national guard of the place of his domicile.

Comments on Reform from Napoleon's Diary

NAPOLEON BONAPARTE

On Honors (May 14, 1802):

Where is the republic, ancient or modern, that has not granted honours? Call them trifles if you like, but it is by trifles that men are influenced. I would not utter such a sentiment as this in public, but here, among statesmen and thinkers, things should be spoken of as they are. In my opinion the French do not care for liberty and equality; they have but one sentiment, that of honour. Therefore, that sentiment must be gratified; they must be given distinctions. Do you suppose you can persuade men to fight by a process of analysis?

"The Legion of Honor" is from Frank M. Anderson, ed., *The Constitutions and Other Illustrative Documents of the History of France*, 2nd ed., revised (New York: Russell and Russell, 1908), p. 337.

"Comments on Reform from Napoleon's Diary" is from R. M. Johnston, ed., *The Corsican: A Diary of Napoleon's Life in His Own Words* (Boston: Houghton Mifflin, 1910), pp. 160, 226, 469.

Never! That process is valid only for the man of science in his study. The soldier demands glory, distinction, rewards.

On the Education of Women (March 1, 1806):

I think it is unnecessary to take into consideration a system of education for girls, they can get no better teaching than that of their mothers. A public education does not suit them, for the reason that they are not called on to live in public; for them habit is everything, and marriage is the goal.

If we are to establish the nation, we must hasten to regulate by means of codes the principal fields of legislation. The Civil Code, though imperfect, has done much good. Everyone is familiar now with the first principles of conduct, and governs his property and business accordingly.

On Crime and Shakespeare (November 29, 1815):

My [Civil] Code alone, because of its simplicity, has done more good in France than the sum total of all the laws that preceded it. My schools are preparing unknown generations. And so during my reign, crime diminished rapidly, while on the contrary among our neighbours in England it increased with frightful rapidity. And that is enough, I think, to give a clear judgment on the two governments.

People take England on trust, and repeat that Shakespeare is the greatest of all authors. I have read him; there is nothing that compares with Racine or Corneille: his plays are unreadable, pitiful.

Napoleon Becomes Emperor (1804)

Five years after Napoleon became head of the French government as First Consul, then as Consul for Life, he moved to expand his power. On May 18, 1804, the Senate decreed that he should be made Emperor of the French. The people of France overwhelmingly approved of this measure through a plebiscite. Napoleon now had complete control of France's government and fate.

In the first excerpt, given before the legislative body of December 31, 1804, Napoleon recounts the reasons for establishing the government of the Empire in place of the Consulate. Note the importance of having the pope "officiate" at the coronation. In fact, Napoleon crowned himself emperor since he did not recognize the pope's authority as superior to his own. But why did the French people willingly submit to the despotism of Napoleon? In the second selection, the Comtesse de Rémusat (1780–1821), lady-in-waiting to Napoleon's wife, Josephine, and the author of some lively memoirs, gives her assessment. Appropriately, Napoleon found divine sanction for his power. The third offering recounts a catechism written during the reign of Louis XIV and modified to meet Napoleon's particular needs. Its questions and answers address the duties of French citizens toward their emperor.

The Coronation of Josephine by Jacques-Louis David. Having executed King Louis XVI in 1793 in support of republican government, the French overwhelmingly accepted Napoleon as emperor in 1804. Did France have more need of Napoleon than did he for France? *(Giraudon/Art Resource, NY)*

Reasons for Establishing the Empire (December 1804)

NAPOLEON BONAPARTE

The internal situation of France is today as calm as it has ever been in the most peaceful periods. There is no agitation to disturb the public tranquility, no suggestion of those crimes which recall the Revolution. Everywhere useful enterprises are in progress, and the general improvements, both public and private, attest the universal confidence and sense of security. . . .

A plot conceived by an implacable government was about to replunge France into the abyss of civil war and anarchy. The discovery of this horrible crime stirred all France profoundly, and anxieties that had scarcely been calmed again awoke. Experience has taught that a divided power in the state is impotent and at odds with itself. It was generally felt that if power was delegated for short periods only, it was so uncertain as to discourage any prolonged undertakings or wide-reaching plans. If vested in an individual for life, it would lapse with him, and after him would prove a source of anarchy and discord. It was clearly seen that for a great nation the only salvation lies in hereditary power, which can alone assure a continuous political life which may endure for generations, even for centuries.

The Senate, as was proper, served as the organ through which this general apprehension found expression. The necessity of hereditary power in a state as vast as France had long been perceived by the First Consul. He had endeavored in vain to avoid this conclusion; but the public solicitude and the hopes of our enemies emphasized the importance of his task, and he realized that his death might ruin his whole work. Under such circumstances, and with such a pressure of public opinion, there was no alternative left to the First Consul. He resolved, therefore, to accept for himself, and two of his brothers after him, the burden imposed by the exigencies of the situation.

After prolonged consideration, repeated conferences with the members of the Senate, discussion in the councils, and the suggestions of the most prudent advisers, a series of provisions was drawn up which regulate the succession to the imperial throne. These provisions were decreed by a senatus consultus of the 28th Floreal last. The French people, by a free and independent expression, then manifested its desire that the imperial dignity should pass down in a direct line through the legitimate or adopted descendants of Napoleon Bonaparte, or through the legitimate descendants of Joseph Bonaparte, or of Louis Bonaparte.

From this moment Napoleon was, by the most unquestioned of titles, emperor of the French. No other act was necessary to sanction his right and consecrate his authority. But he wished to restore in France the ancient forms

"Reasons for Establishing the Empire" is from James H. Robinson and Charles A. Beard, eds., *Readings in Modern European History*, vol. 1 (Boston: Ginn and Company, 1908), pp. 334–336.

and recall those institutions which divinity itself seems to have inspired. He wished to impress the seal of religion itself upon the opening of his reign. The head of the Church, in order to give the French a striking proof of his paternal affection, consented to officiate at this August ceremony. What deep and enduring impressions did this leave on the mind of Napoleon and in the memory of the nation! What thoughts for future races! What a subject of wonder for all Europe!

In the midst of this pomp, and under the eye of the Eternal, Napoleon pronounced the inviolable oath which assures the integrity of the empire, the security of property, the perpetuity of institutions, the respect for Law, and the happiness of the nation. The oath of Napoleon shall be forever the terror of the enemies of France. If our borders are attacked, it will be repeated at the head of our armies, and our frontiers shall never more fear foreign invasion.

Why the French Submitted to Napoleon's Rule (1804)
COMTESSE DE RÉMUSAT

I can understand how it was that men worn out by the turmoil of the Revolution, and afraid of that liberty which had long been associated with death, looked for repose under the dominion of an able ruler on who Fortune was seemingly resolved to smile. I can conceive that they regarded his elevation as a decree of destiny and fondly believed that in the irrevocable they should find peace. I may confidently assert that those persons believed quite sincerely that Bonaparte, whether as Consul or Emperor, would exert his authority to oppose the intrigues of faction and would save us from the perils of anarchy.

None dared to utter the word "republic," so deeply had the Terror stained that name; and the government of the Directory had perished in the contempt with which its chiefs were regarded. The return of the Bourbons could only be brought about by the aid of a revolution; and the slightest disturbance terrified the French people, in whom enthusiasm of every kind seemed dead. Besides, the men in whom they had trusted had one after the other deceived them; and as, this time, they were yielding to force, they were at least certain they were not deceiving themselves.

The belief, or rather the error, that only despotism could at that epoch maintain order in France was very widespread. It became the mainstay of Bonaparte; and it is due to him to say that he also believed it. The factions played into his hands by imprudent attempts which he turned to his own

"Why the French Submitted to Napoleon's Rule" is from James H. Robinson and Charles A. Beard, eds., *Readings in Modern European History*, vol. 1 (Boston: Ginn and Company, 1908), pp. 333–334.

advantage. He had some grounds for his belief that he was necessary; France believed it, too; and he even succeeded in persuading foreign sovereigns that he constituted a barrier against republican influences, which, but for him, might spread widely. At the moment when Bonaparte placed the imperial crown upon his head there was not a king in Europe who did not believe that he wore his own crown more securely because of that event. Had the new emperor granted a liberal constitution, the peace of nations and of kings might really have been forever secured.

The Imperial Catechism (April 1806)

Question: What are the duties of Christians toward those who govern them, and what in particular are our duties towards Napoleon I, our emperor?

Answer: Christians owe to the princes who govern them, and we in particular owe to Napoleon I, our emperor, love, respect, obedience, fidelity, military service, and the taxes levied for the preservation and defense of the empire and of his throne. We also owe him fervent prayers for his safety and for the spiritual and temporal prosperity of the state.

Question: Why are we subject to all these duties toward our emperor?

Answer: First, because God, who has created empires and distributes them according to his will, has, by loading our emperor with gifts both in peace and in war, established him as our sovereign and made him the agent of his power and his image on earth. To honor and serve our emperor is therefore to honor and serve God himself. Secondly, because our Lord Jesus Christ himself, both by his teaching and his example, has taught us what we owe to our sovereign. Even at his very birth he obeyed the edict of Caesar Augustus; he paid the established tax; and while he commanded us to render to God those things which belong to God, he also commanded us to render unto Caesar those things which are Caesar's.

Question: Are there not special motives which should attach us more closely to Napoleon I, our emperor?

Answer: Yes, for it is he whom God has raised up in trying times to reestablish the public worship of the holy religion of our fathers and to be its protector; he has reestablished and preserved public order by his profound and active wisdom; he defends the state by his mighty arm; he has become the anointed of the Lord by the consecration which he has received from the sovereign pontiff, head of the Church universal.

Question: What must we think of those who are neglecting their duties toward our emperor?

"The Imperial Catechism" is from James H. Robinson and Charles A. Beard, eds., *Readings in Modern European History*, vol. 1 (Boston: Ginn and Company, 1908), pp. 351–352.

Answer: According to the apostle Paul, they are resisting the order established by God himself, and render themselves worthy of eternal damnation.

The Military Genius

Beginning in 1792 and continuing throughout much of the revolution, France was at war against various coalitions of European nations. Revolutionary ideology was exportable and threatened the very foundation of enlightened despotism. As the French revolutionaries attacked the church, monarchy, and aristocracy, most of Europe, including Great Britain, reacted by repressing liberal reform movements. These wars at once threatened the revolution and also granted it purpose and unity. Napoleon, a military commander of genius and overreaching ambition, capitalized on this French "spirit of the times" and sought first to link himself with the revolutionary forces within the state and then, as Consul and Emperor, to dominate Europe both militarily and culturally from 1803 to his final defeat at Waterloo in 1815. In the process, he inspired France and certainly changed the course of history. Napoleon believed that his actions were directed toward a destiny that he was compelled to achieve by fate. The first selection is a good example of this belief. It is an address to Dutch representatives upon the annexation of Holland to the French empire in 1810.

The image of Napoleon and his glorious reputation as a military genius was cultivated through the paintings of Jacques Louis David and the memoirs of Napoleon's commanders. Without doubt, Napoleon demonstrated organizational ability and strategic brilliance. This, coupled with a nearly limitless supply of well-trained French soldiers, allowed him to dominate and expand his control over the European continent.

Napoleon's grand ambitions, however, proved his undoing during his famous invasion of Russia through Poland in June, 1812. The second selection is Napoleon's proclamation to his Grand Army at the outset of the Russian campaign. His boastful words turned to disaster as Napoleon was unable to engage the Russian army on favorable terms and left a burning Moscow to be dogged by constant surprise attacks, the ravages of hunger, and the devastation of the harsh Russian winter. The section ends with an account of the disaster from the memoirs of one of Napoleon's commanders, Wairy Louis Constant.

"An End to the Woes of Anarchy" (1810)
NAPOLEON BONAPARTE

When Providence elevated me to the first throne in the world it became my duty, while establishing forever the destinies of France, to determine the fate of all those people who formed a part of the empire, to insure for all the benefits of

---

"'An End to the Woes of Anarchy'" is from James H. Robinson and Charles A. Beard, eds., *Readings in Modern European History*, vol. 1 (Boston: Ginn and Company, 1908), pp. 355–356.

stability and order, and to put an end everywhere to the woes of anarchy. I have done away with the uncertainty in Italy by placing upon my head the crown of iron. . . .

I gave you a prince of my own blood to govern you. . . . I have opened the continent to your industry, and the day will come when you shall bear my eagles upon the seas which your ancestors have rendered illustrious. You will then show yourself worthy of them and of me. . . .

The Invasion of Russia (1812)
NAPOLEON BONAPARTE

Soldiers, the second war of Poland has commenced. The first was brought to a close at Friedland and Tilsit. At Tilsit, Russia swore eternal alliance with France and war with England. She now violates her oaths, she refuses to give any explanation of her strange conduct, except on condition that the eagles of France shall repass the Rhine, leaving, by such a movement, our allies at her mercy. Russia is dragged along by a fate. Her destinies must be accomplished. Shall she then consider us degenerate? Are we no longer to be looked upon as the soldiers of Austerlitz [a Napoleonic victory]? She offers us the alternative of dishonor or war. The choice does not admit of hesitation. Let us march forward. Let us pass the Nieman [River]. Let us carry war into her territory. The second war of Poland will be as glorious to the French arms as was the first; but the peace which we shall conclude will be its own guaranty and will put an end to the proud and haughty influence which Russia has for fifty years exercised in the affairs of Europe.

At Our Headquarters at Wilkowiski
June 22,1815

"Everything Had Failed Us"
WAIRY LOUIS CONSTANT

The emperor awaited daylight in a poor hut, and in the morning said to Prince Berthier, "Well, Berthier, how can we get out of this?" He was seated in his room, great tears flowing down his cheeks, which were paler than usual; and the prince was seated near him. They exchanged few words, and the emperor appeared overcome by his grief. I leave to the imagination what was passing in his soul. . . .

On the 29th the emperor quitted the banks of the Beresina and we slept at Kamen, where his Majesty occupied a poor wooden building which the

"The Invasion of Russia" is from James H. Robinson and Charles A. Beard, eds., *Readings in Modern European History*, vol. 1 (Boston: Ginn and Company, 1908), pp. 356–357.

"'Everything Had Failed Us'" is from James H. Robinson and Charles A. Beard, eds., *Readings in Modern European History*, vol. 1 (Boston: Ginn and Company, 1908), pp. 357–360.

icy air penetrated from all sides through the windows, for nearly all the glass was broken. We closed the openings as well as we could with bundles of hay. A short distance from us, in a large lot, were penned up the wretched Russian prisoners whom the army drove before it. I had much difficulty in comprehending the delusion of victory which our poor soldiers still kept up by dragging after them this wretched luxury of prisoners, who could only be an added burden, as they required constant surveillance. When the conquerors are dying of famine, what becomes of the conquered? These poor Russians, exhausted by marches and hunger, nearly all perished that night. . . .

On the 3rd of December we arrived at Malodeczno. During the whole day the emperor appeared thoughtful and anxious. . . . At two leagues from Smorghoni, the duke of Vicenza summoned me and told me to go on in front and give orders to have the six best horses harnessed to my carriage, which was the lightest of all, and keep them in constant readiness. I reached Smorghoni before the emperor, who did not arrive until the following night. . . . After supper the emperor ordered Prince Eugene to read the twenty-ninth bulletin and spoke freely of his plans, saying that his departure was essential in order to send help to the army. . . .

The emperor left in the night. By daybreak the army had learned the news, and the impression it made cannot be depicted. Discouragement was at its height, and many soldiers cursed the emperor and reproached him for abandoning them.

This night, the 6th, the cold increased greatly. Its severity may be imagined, as birds were found on the ground frozen stiff. Soldiers seated themselves with their heads in their hands and bodies bent forward in order thus to feel less the emptiness of their stomachs. . . . Everything had failed us. Long before reaching Vilna, the horses being dead, we received orders to burn our carriages and all their contents.

Exile and Death: The Hero in History

After the victory of the Duke of Wellington over the French forces at Waterloo in 1815, Napoleon was sentenced to permanent exile on the South Atlantic island of St. Helena. The first selection from his diary gives indication of his dominant personality and spirit. However, he remained on this isolated rock until his death in 1821.

Yet, what is the role of the "great man" or "hero" in history? Can the course of history be changed by a dynamic individual of ability and resolve? Or does history progress by uncontrollable economic and social "forces"? The last selection is by G. W. F. Hegel, a German philosopher who believed that "heroes" such as Caesar, Alexander, and Napoleon were unconscious instruments of a "world spirit" (Zeitgeist) *that lay behind the development of human history. The chosen passage reveals Hegel's thoughts about how heroes could change the course of history. Hegel is representative of the romantic belief, current in the early nineteenth century, that human history was connected with much larger spiritual forces.*

Napoleon in Exile: "We Stand as Martyrs to an Immortal Cause!"

NAPOLEON BONAPARTE

What infamous treatment they have held in store for us! This is the agony of death! To injustice, to violence, they add insult and slow torture! If I was so dangerous, why didn't they get rid of me? A few bullets in my heart or in my head would have settled it; there would have been some courage at least in such a crime! How can the Sovereigns of Europe permit the sacred nature of sovereignty to be attainted in me? Can't they see that they are killing themselves at St. Helena? I have entered their capitals as a conqueror; had I been moved by such motives, what would have become of them? They all called me their brother, and I had become so by the will of the people, the sanction of victory, the character of religion, the alliances of policy and of family. . . . Apart from that, who has there been in history with more partisans, more friends? Who has been more popular, more beloved? Who ever left behind more ardent regrets? Look at France: might not one say that from this rock of mine I still reign over her? . . .

Our situation may even have good points! The Universe watches us! We stand as martyrs to an immortal cause! Millions of men weep with us, our country sighs, and glory has put on mourning! We struggle here against the tyranny of the gods, and the hopes of humanity are with us! Misfortune itself knows heroism, and glory! Only adversity was wanting to complete my career! Had I died on the throne, in the clouds of my almightiness, I would have remained a problem for many; as it is, thanks to my misfortunes, I can be judged naked.

The Role of Great Men in History

G. W. F. HEGEL

Such are all great historical men—whose own particular aims involve those large issues which are the will of the World-Spirit. They may be called Heroes, inasmuch as they have derived their purposes and their vocation, not from the calm, regular course of things, sanctioned by the existing order: but from

---

" 'We Stand as Martyrs to an Immortal Cause!' " is from R. M. Johnston, ed., *The Corsican: A Diary of Napoleon's Life in His Own Words* (Boston: Houghton Mifflin, 1910), pp. 468–469.

"The Role of Great Men in History" is from G. W. F. Hegel, *The Philosophy of History*, trans. J. Sibree (New York: Dover, 1956), pp. 30–31. Reprinted by permission of the publisher.

a concealed fount—one which has not attained to phenomenal, present existence—from that inner Spirit, still hidden beneath the surface, which, impinging on the outer world as on a shell, bursts it in pieces, because it is another kernel than that which belonged to the shell in question. They are men, therefore, who appear to draw the impulse of their life from themselves; and whose deeds have produced a condition of things and a complex of historical relations which appear to be only their interest, and their work.

Such individuals had no consciousness of the general idea they were unfolding, while prosecuting those aims of theirs; on the contrary, they were practical, political men. But at the same time they were thinking men, who had an insight into the requirements of the time—what was ripe for development. This was the very Truth for their age, for their world: the species next in order, so to speak, and which was already formed in the womb of time. It was theirs to know this nascent principle; the necessary, directly sequent step in progress, which their world was to take; to make this their aim, and to expend their energy in promoting it. World-historical men—the Heroes of an epoch—must, therefore, be recognized as its clear-sighted ones: their deed, their words are the best of that time.

SECTION III: THE ROMANTIC MOVEMENT

The dramatic events from the French Revolution in 1789 to the fall of Napoleon in 1815 transformed European social and political realities, and also found expression in the art and literature of the day. The term, Romanticism, refers to an intellectual and cultural movement that was current from about 1780 to 1830 and beyond. It was in many ways a reaction to the structured rationalism of the Enlightenment and focused instead on passionate individualism and on the world of nature. The philosophes *of the Enlightenment had sought to understand the natural world and were confident that phenomena could be explained through theory and experimentation. But the Romantic viewed the world differently. Natural beauty was to be engaged, not explained, and knowledge was more a matter of sense experience than of intellectual fortitude. Intuition, in fact, was more essential to understanding a world in flux than was an established method of inquiry. Romantic writers, artists, and musicians sought to break through established norms in search of new possibilities. In so many ways, the Romantic movement in the arts and literature paralleled the new political opportunities that were unfolding.*

In order to understand Romanticism, one must be willing to suspend logic, trust intuition, and enter a world of natural beauty and foreboding terror, of idealistic passion fueled by the conviction that there is more to the world than can be explained.

The Evocation of Nature

The fascination with and evocation of the power and beauty of nature was an important theme during the Romantic period. One of the founders of the English Romantic movement, William Wordsworth (1770–1850), once defined poetry as the "spontaneous overflow of powerful feelings." In the first selection from one of his most famous poems entitled "Lines Composed a Few Miles Above Tintern Abbey" (1798), he evokes the beauty of a pastoral scene that suspends the realities of his adult perspective, and defines the moment by recapturing his childhood with new insight.

In the second selection, another leading English poet, Percy Bysshe Shelley (1792–1822), reiterates the Romantic vision of nature in his "Ode to the West Wind." One feels the "wild spirit" of the West Wind—it is the only way to understand and truly know it.

"The Language of the Sense, the Anchor of My Purest Thoughts"
WILLIAM WORDSWORTH

Five years have past; five summers, with the length
Of five long winters! And again I hear
These waters, rolling from their mountain-springs
With a soft inland murmur.—Once again
do I behold these steep and lofty cliffs,
That on a wild secluded scene impress
Thoughts of more deep seclusion; and connect
The landscape with the quiet of the sky.
The day is come when I again repose
Here, under this dark sycamore, and view
These plots of cottage-ground, these orchard-tufts,
Which at this season, with their unripe fruits,
Are clad in one green hue, and lose themselves
'Mid groves and copses. Once again I see
These hedge-rows, hardly hedge-rows, little lines
Of sportive wood run wild: these pastoral farms,
Green to the very door; and wreaths of smoke
Sent up, in silence from among the trees!
With some uncertain notice, as might seem
Of vagrant dwellers in the houseless woods,
Or of some Hermit's cave, where by his fire
The Hermit sits alone. . . .

"The Language of the Sense" is from H. T. Tuckerman, ed., *The Poems of William Wordsworth* (New York: C. S. Francis, 1855).

And now, with gleams of half-extinguished thought,
With many recongitions dim and faint,
And somewhat of a sad perplexity,
The picture of the mind revives again:
While here I stand, not only with the sense
Of present pleasure, but with pleasing thoughts
For future years. And so I dare to hope,
Though changed, no doubt, from what I was when first
I bounded o'er the mountains, by the sides
Of the deep rivers, and the lonely streams,
Wherever nature led: more like a man
Flying from something that he dreads, than one
Who sought the thing he loved. For nature then
(The coarser pleasures of my boyish days,
And their glad animal movements all gone by)
To me was all in all.—I cannot paint
What then I was. The sounding cataract
Haunted me like a passion: the tall rock,
The mountain, and the deep and gloomy wood,
Their colors and their forms, were then to me
An appetite; a feeling and a love,
That had no need of a remoter charm,
By thought supplied, nor any interest
Unborrowed from the eye.—that time is past,
And all its aching joys are now no more,
And all its dizzy raptures. Not for this
Faint I, nor mourn nor murmur; other gifts
Have followed; for such loss, I would believe,
Abundant recompense. For I have learned
To look on nature, not as in the hour
Of thoughtless youth; but hearing oftentimes
The still, sad music of humanity,
Nor harsh nor grating, though of ample power
To chasten and subdue. And I have felt
A presence that disturbs me with the joy
Of elevated thoughts; a sense sublime
Of something far more deeply interfused,
Whose dwelling is the light of setting suns,
And the round ocean and the living air,
And the blue sky, and in the mind of man;
A motion and a spirit, that impels
All thinking things, all objects of all thought,
And rolls through all things. Therefore am I still
A lover of the meadows and the woods,
And mountains; and of all that we behold
From this green earth; of all the mighty world

Of eye, and ear,—both what they half create,
And what perceive; well pleased to recognise
In nature and the language of the sense,
The anchor of my purest thoughts, the nurse,
The guide, the guardian of my heart, and soul
Of all my moral being. . . .

Ode to the West Wind (1820)

PERCY BYSSHE SHELLEY

O, wild West Wind, thou breath of Autumn's being,
Thou, from whose unseen presence the
leaves dead
Are driven, like ghosts from an enchanter
fleeing,

Yellow, and black, and pale, and hectic red,
Pestilence-stricken multitudes: O, thou,
Who chariotest to their dark wintry bed

The winged seeds, where they lie cold and
low,
Each like a corpse within its grave, until
thine azure sister of the spring shall blow

Her clarion o'er the dreaming earth, and
fill
(Driving sweet buds like flocks to feed in
air)
With living hues and odors plain and hill:

Wild Spirit, which art moving every where;
Destroyer and preserver; hear, O, Hear! . . .

Make me thy lyre, even as the forest is:
What if my leaves are falling like its won!
The tumult of thy mighty harmonies

Will take from both a deep autumnal
tone,

"Ode to the West Wind" is from H. Buxton Foreman, ed., *Complete Poetical Works of Percy Bysshe Shelley*. 8 vols. (Boston: Houghton Mifflin, 1892).

Sweet though in sadness. Be thou, spirit
    fierce,
My spirit! Be thou me, impetuous one!

Drive my dead thoughts over the universe
Like withered leaves to quicken a new
    birth!
And, by the incantation of this verse,

Scatter, as from an unextinguished hearth
Ashes and sparks, my words among man-
    kind!
Be through my lips to unawakened earth

the trumpet of a prophecy! O, wind,
If Winter comes, can Spring be far be-
    hind?

Terror and the Macabre

The Romantic fascination with the natural world was accompanied by an expansive and creative vision of the potential of nature and the forces that existed beyond the limits of the human realm. This was an emotional response, a desire to participate in the fantastic, the forbidden, and the macabre forces that danced in the dreams and preyed on the fears of humankind.

Nowhere was this obsession with the occult so pronounced as in the work of Johann Wolfgang von Goethe (1749–1832). Goethe was perhaps the greatest creative force in German literature. His poetry, essays, and dramas brought him national fame and reverence. Goethe began work on the poetic drama Faust *in his early twenties and finished Part I in 1808 and Part II in 1831, a year before his death at eighty-two.*

The Faust legend of a person making a pact with the devil abounds in folklore and literature. It is a tale of a learned doctor named Johannes Faustus who in the end throws away the rationality contained in his books and forms a pact with the devil, whereby he is able to enjoy all the sensual pleasures of the world in exchange for his soul. Goethe transforms this morality tale into a passionate search by the human spirit for the Infinite.

The second selection entitled "The Erlking" is Goethe's disturbing poem about a father and his son riding through the darkness of a storm toward the safety of home. All the Romantic elements are present: the power of nature, the beckoning of magical forces, the emotional link between father and son, the demon threat, and the final tragedy. So powerful was the evocative force of this poem that the great German composer Franz Schubert (1797–1828) heightened its intensity by

Monastery, Cemetary in the Snow by Caspar David Friedrich, destroyed 1945, Berlin, National Gallery. "And the roots like wondrous snakes/Rise from rock and sandy soil/Rise to fright us in the brakes/Quick to catch us in a coil."—Johann Wolfgang von Goethe *(Bildarchiv Foto Marburg/Art Resource, NY).*

using the text as lyrics to a song. The musical accompaniment truly plays on the emotions of foreboding and fear.

Faust: "Into Witchery and Dreams . . ."
JOHANN WOLFGANG VON GOETHE

Now we wend our way, it seems,
Into witchery and dreams.
Prove your worth, good flickering guide,
Swiftly bringing us to glide
Through the vast and mournful spaces.
    See, the pillared forest races
Tree on tree in vision reeling,
Cliffs that curtsey in their wheeling,

"Faust" is from Johann Wolfgang Goethe, *Faust, Part One,* trans. Phillip Wayne (Baltimore, Md., and Harmondsworth, Middlesex: Penguin Books, 1949), pp. 168–169. Copyright © The Estate of Phillip Wayne, 1949. Reprinted by permission.

Snouted rocks in gulches roaring,
Hear their snarling and their snoring!
    Through the rocks and meads come pouring
Brooks and rivers downward streaming.
Songs are these? In murmurs dreaming?
Airs are these of lovers' yearning,
Voices of the heavenly morning?
All we long for, hoping, aching!
Echo comes in power returning,
Legendary things redeeming,
    Uhoo! Shuhoo! Floating over
Come the cries of owl and plover,
With the jay: they all are waking.
What are those, in thickets crawling?
Salamanders, belly-sprawling?
And the roots like wondrous snakes
Rise from rock and sandy soil,
Rise to fright us in the brakes,
Quick to catch us in a coil;
Knotted gnarls to catch at us
Wreathe their strands of polypus.
Fearful faring! And the swarming
Rodents run, their squadrons forming,
Black and blonde, through moss and heather,
While the glow-worms paint the weather,
In their crowded ranks providing
Craze escort for our guiding.
    Nay, but tell me, in our traces
Are we standing or advancing?
All is whirling, swimming, dancing,
Fell and forest, full of faces,
Mock at us. The wild-fires, flying,
Menace in their multiplying. . . .

The Erlking

JOHANN WOLFGANG VON GOETHE

Who rides so late through night and
    wind?
It is the father with his
    child.

"The Erlking" is from N.H. Flower, *Franz Schubert, The Man and His Circle* (New York: Tudor), 1922.

He holds the boy within his
	arm,
He clasps him tight, he keeps him
	warm.

"My son, why hide your face in
	fear?"
"See, father, the Erlking's
	near.
The Erlking with crown and
	wand."
"Dear son, 'tis but a misty
	cloud."

"Ah, sweet child, come with
	me!
Such pleasant games I'll play with
	thee!
Such pleasant flowers bloom in the
	field,
My mother has many a robe of
	gold."

"Oh father, father, do you not
	hear
What the Erlking whispers in my
	ear?"
"Be still, my child, be
	calm;
'Tis but the withered leaves in the
	wind."

"My lovely boy, wilt go with
	me?
My daughters fair shall wait on
	thee,
My daughters nightly revels
	keep,
They'll sing and dance and rock thee to
	sleep."

"Oh father, father, see you
	not
The Erlking's daughters in yon dark
	spot?"
"My son, my son, the thing you
	see

Is only the old gray willow
    tree."

"I love thee, thy form enflames my
    sense;
And art thou not willing, I'll take thee
    hence."
"Oh father, father, he grasps my
    arm,
The Erlking has done me
    harm!"

The father shudders, he speeds
    ahead,
He clasps to his bosom the sobbing
    child,
He reaches home with pain and
    dread;
In his arms the child lay
    dead!

Frankenstein (1818)

MARY WOLLSTONECRAFT SHELLEY

Mary Shelley (1797–1851) was the daughter of the political philosopher William Godwin and the women's rights advocate, Mary Wollstonecraft. She married the poet Percy Bysshe Shelley in 1814 and was introduced to his circle of literary friends. The idea of Frankenstein came to her during a vacation in Switzerland with her husband and the poet Lord Byron. Byron suggested that they write ghost stories. Her astonishing tale of an ambitious young scientist, Victor Franken- stein, and the monster he unleashes questions the very principles of life and the mysteries of nature. It forces us to consider ethical and religious issues, but more importantly we are introduced to the terror of the soul, the limits of the human mind, and the pathos of creation and destruction. Enter the laboratory of Dr. Frankenstein as he encounters his unnatural creation for the first time. . . .

It was on a dreary night of November that I beheld the accomplishment of my toils. With an anxiety that almost amounted to agony, I collected the in- struments of life around me, that I might infuse a spark of being into the life- less thing that lay at my feet. It was already one in the morning: the rain pat- tered dismally against the panes, and my candle was nearly burnt out, when,

"Frankenstein" is from Mary Shelley, *Frankenstein, Or the Modern Prometheus* (London, 1818).

by the glimmer of the half-extinguished light, I saw the dull yellow eye of the creature open; it breathed hard, and a convulsive motion agitated its limbs.

How can I describe my emotions at this catastrophe, or how delineate the wretch whom with such infinite pains and care I had endeavoured to form? His limbs were in proportion, and I had selected his features as beautiful. Beautiful! Great God! His yellow skin scarcely covered the work of muscles and arteries beneath; his hair was of a lustrous black, and flowing; his teeth of pearly whiteness; but these luxuriances only formed a more horrid contrast with his watery eyes, that seemed almost of the same colour as the dun-white sockets in which they were set, his shrivelled complexion and straight black lips.

The different accidents of life are not so changeable as the feelings of human nature. I had worked hard for nearly two years, for the sole purpose of infusing life into an inanimate body. For this I had deprived myself of rest and health. I had desired it with an ardour that far exceeded moderation; but now that I had finished, the beauty of the dream vanished, and breathless horror and disgust filled my heart. Unable to endure the aspect of the being I had created, I rushed out of the room and continued a long time traversing my bedchamber, unable to compose my mind to sleep. At length lassitude succeeded to the tumult I had before endured, and I threw myself on the bed in my clothes, endeavouring to seek a few moments of forgetfulness. But it was in vain; I slept, indeed, but I was disturbed by the wildest dreams. . . .

I thought that I held the corpse of my dead mother in my arms; a shroud enveloped her form, and I saw the grave-worms crawling in the folds of the flannel. I started from my sleep with horror; a cold dew covered my forehead, my teeth chattered, and every limb became convulsed; when by the dim and yellow light of the moon, as it forced its way through the window shutters, I beheld the wretch—the miserable monster whom I had created. He held up the curtain of the bed; and its eyes, if eyes they may be called, were fixed on me. His jaws opened and he muttered some inarticulate sounds, while a grin wrinkled his cheeks. He might have spoken, but I did not hear; one hand was stretched out, seemingly to detain me, but I escaped and rushed downstairs. I took refuge in the courtyard belonging to the house which I inhabited, where I remained during the rest of the night, walking up and down in the greatest agitation, listening attentively, catching and fearing each sound as if it were to announce the approach of the demoniacal corpse to which I had so miserably give life.

Art and Ideas

The dynamics of this revolutionary period, with its social upheaval and its rapidly changing political and industrial scenes, confronted artists with new realities and opportunities to work within broadened parameters. The shift of wealth from the landed aristocracy to the growing middle class resulted in a change of patrons who commissioned the art, architecture and music. The arts were no longer produced for a small but sophisticated aristocracy who had particular tastes and demands.

Artists now had to appeal to a wider audience, one that wanted to be charmed and astonished by new techniques and subject matter. Instead of one patron, artists had to adapt to the varying tastes and styles of many clients.

The consequences of these changes profoundly impacted the arts. It was no longer enough for an artist to be a fine craftsman, he now had to be a great personality, who could hold his own in a dynamic environment, and who espoused epic, often nationalistic causes. The artistic media became allied as painting, music, and literature shared a common vocabulary of Romanticism. For example, "artistic color" referred to the subtle nuances in a work that produced specific emotional responses. So poetry began to depend on the sounds of words and their appeal to the senses. In painting, color evoked intensity of expression, and in music the tone color of particular instruments connoted subtle images of nature.

Romantic ideas flowed from the alliance of the arts, from concepts of individualism, nationalism and the exotic. In many ways, Romanticism was a psychological escapism from the increasingly industrialized and mechanized world.

Ode to Napoleon Bonaparte (1814)
LORD BYRON

The image of Napoleon loomed large in the Romantic mind. His passionate call to arms and the ensuing spirit of nationalism that he evoked charged the French imagination and gave a new focus to the revolution. But after Napoleon's defeat in 1815 and subsequent exile, an exhausted Europe seemed to celebrate his departure and condemned his excesses. The first selection is by the English poet Lord Byron (1788–1824). Himself an ardent nationalist, Byron hurried to Greece in support of the 1820 liberation movement from Turkish control. He died there in 1824 of disease.

'Tis done—but yesterday a king!
    And armed with kings to strive—
And now thou art a nameless thing:
    So abject—yet alive! ˙
Is this the man of thousand thrones,
Who strewed our earth with hostile bones,
    And can he thus survive?
Since he, miscalled the Morning Star,
Nor man nor fiend hath fallen so far.

Ill-minded man! Why scourge thy kind
    Who bowed so low the knee?
By gazing on thyself grown blind,
    Thou taught'st the rest to see.

"Ode to Napoleon" is from *The Works of Lord Byron* (London: J. Murray, 1903).

With might unquestioned,—power to
    save,—
Thine only gift hath been the grave,
    to those that worshipped thee;
Nor till thy fall could mortals guess
Ambition's less than littleness!

Thanks for that lesson—it will teach
    To after-warriors more,
Than high philosophy can preach,
    And vainly preached before.
That spell upon the minds of men
Breaks never to unite again,
    That led them to adore
Those things of sabre sway
With fronts of brass, and feet of clay . . .

The desolator desolate!
    The victor overthrown!
The arbiter of other's fate
    A suppliant for his own!
Is it some yet imperial hope
That with such change can calmly cope?
    Or dread of death alone?
To die a prince—or live a slave—
Thy choice is most ignobly brave! . . .

The Third of May, 1808

FRANCISCO GOYA

The contempt for Napoleon and the cruelties of war can also be seen in the paint-ing entitled "The Third of May, 1808" by Francisco Goya (1746–1828). Depict-ing the execution of Spanish patriots at the hands of Napoleon's troops in 1808, the victims are each differentiated by writhing gestures of despair. In contrast, the faceless soldiers, seen only from behind, are lined up like automatons, denoting the inhuman nature of their task. Our attention is immediately drawn to the man with outstretched arms, almost like Christ at the crucifixion. Below him, lying face down in a pool of blood also with his arms spread in supplication, is a twisted corpse. Goya sought the commission to paint this scene from the Spanish king, Ferdinand VII, asking to commemorate the "most notable and heroic ac-tions or scenes of our glorious insurrection against the tyrant of Europe." Both the previous poem by Byron and this painting by Goya were produced in the year of Napoleon's defeat, 1814–1815.

The Third of May, 1808 by Francisco Goya. *(The Prado, Madrid, Scala/Art Resource, NY)*

Liberty Leading the People (1830)
EUGÈNE DELACROIX

Perhaps the leading representative of Romantic painting was Eugène Delacroix (1798–1863). His imagination had been haunted by Goethe's Faust *since he first saw it in London, and he produced several lithographs connected to the text. Delacroix also focused on classical subjects ("Dante and Vergil in Hell," 1822) and on exotic material ("Algerian Women in Their Harem," 1834). But his most inspirational work revealed a disposition for liberal political causes that were threatened by the conservative forces of reaction.*

The following painting, entitled "Liberty Leading the People" (1830), depicts the July Revolution of 1830 in Paris that led to the fall of the reactionary Bourbon monarch, Charles X, and the institution of a new monarchy under Louis Philippe, the "Citizen King." This was a middle-class revolution with an idealized focus. Two main social classes are represented: On the extreme left is a proletarian figure with a saber, while in front of him toward the center is a bourgeois gentleman with top hat, sideburns, and frock coat. The allegorical female figure

Liberty Leading the People, 1830 by Eugene Delacroix (© *Photograph by Erich Lessing/ Art Resource, NY*)

of Liberty as the spirit of the French people is portrayed as serene and determined in the midst of the danger. She has purpose and an aura of power in depicting the energetic reincarnation of the spirit of 1789.

CHRONOLOGY: "Liberty, Equality, Fraternity!": Romanticism and Revolution

May 1789– June 1789	**ESTATES-GENERAL:** Monarchy still in control of the government. War is the expected foreign policy of the ancien régime.
1789–1791	**NATIONAL ASSEMBLY:** Nominal absolute monarchy. State church exists with priests paid by the state.

June 20, 1789:	Tennis Court Oath.
July 14, 1789:	Fall of Bastille.
August 27, 1789:	Declaration of the Rights of Man.

	July 12, 1790:	Civil Constitution of the Clergy adopted.
	June 24, 1791:	Louis XVI and family are caught trying to flee France.

1791–1792   **LEGISLATIVE ASSEMBLY:** Constitutional monarchy. War is promoted to solve domestic problems. State church.

	October 1, 1791:	Legislative Assembly convenes.
	September 2, 1792:	The September Massacres.

1792–1794   **THE CONVENTION:** Committee of Public Safety administers government. Universal manhood suffrage. Cult of Reason promoted. Reign of Terror (1793–1794).

	September 21, 1792:	The Convention meets and the monarchy is abolished.
	January 21, 1793:	Louis XVI is executed.
	July, 1793:	Robespierre enters the Committee of Public Safety.
	October 16, 1793:	Queen Marie-Antoinette is executed.
	November 10, 1793:	The Cult of Reason is proclaimed.
	April 6, 1794:	Execution of Danton and Desmoulins.
	May 7, 1794:	Cult of the Supreme Being proclaimed.
	June 10, 1794:	Law of 22 Prairial is adopted (Administration of Terror).
	July 28, 1794:	Execution of Robespierre.

1795–1799   **THE DIRECTORY AND CONSULATE:** Thermidorian Reaction. Restricted franchise. Separation of church and state promoted.

	August 22, 1795:	Directory established.

1798   English Romantic poet William Wordsworth writes "Lines Composed a Few Miles Above Tintern Abbey."

	November 10, 1799:	Consulate established with Napoleon as first consul.
	December 15, 1799:	Consulate proclaims end of French Revolution.

1802   Napoleon concludes a concordat with Pope Pius VII: Clergy must swear loyalty oath to the state,

1802   Napoleon proclaimed consul for life.

1804   Napoleon crowned emperor of the French; Civil Code issued.

1805   Nelson defeats French fleet at Trafalgar; Napoleon's victory at Austerlitz.

1806	Napoleon's victory at Jena.
1808	German Romantic poet Johann Wolfgang von Goethe completes *Faust Part I.*
1812	Invasion of Russia and French defeat at Borodino.
1813	French defeat at Leipzig (Battle of Nations).
1814	Congress of Vienna convenes in September.
1815	Napoleon escapes from Elba and returns to Paris. The Duke of Wellington commands coalition forces in victory over Napoleon at Waterloo.
1818	Mary Wollstonecraft Shelley publishes *Frankenstein.*
1821	Napoleon dies in exile on South Atlantic island of St. Helena.
1827	Eugène Delacroix paints "Greece Dying on the Ruins of Missolonghi" in commemoration of the Greek nationalist defeat in 1820.
1830	Delacroix paints "Liberty Leading the People, 1830" in support of the July Revolution that toppled the Bourbon monarchy and ushered in the Citizen King, Louis Philippe.

STUDY QUESTIONS

Section I: The French Revolution

1. What is a revolution? How do you distinguish it from a riot or a rebellion? What political, social, or economic conditions existed in eighteenth-century France that contributed to the French Revolution? In a general sense, do you think that difficult conditions precede any successful revolution?

2. What were the specific demands made by the Third Estate? Do they seem reasonable to you? Compare the demands made by the Abbé Sieyès with the requests made by the women of the Third Estate to the king. Assess the progress made by 1793 for women to achieve political equality as noted in the document "Update on the Political Rights of Women." Do you find it hypocritical that in a period where the "rights of man" are hotly contested, they don't apply to women?

3. Read the Tennis Court Oath carefully. Does it call for radical action? Why is it considered to be one of the most important documents of the French Revolution?

4. Why was the fall of the Bastille such an important event? After reading the pertinent selections, discuss how important violence is in a revolution. Do most successful revolutions promote violence to some degree?

5. What are the most important ideas contained in the Declaration of the Rights of Man? Why was it essential to the French Revolution? What does it tell you about the Old Regime of Louis XVI and his predecessors? Do you believe (as did most of the philosophes) that there are "natural rights" for all human beings

and that a government should protect these rights? How is this "natural rights" argument reflected in the various documents of the revolution?

6. What were Edmund Burke's main criticisms of the revolution in France? Why did Burke anticipate plots, assassinations, and a "long roll of bloody maxims"? Was he right?

7. Is the "Indictment of Louis XVI" a truthful or exaggerated account of the king's actions? To what extent, then, were the revolutionaries justified in executing Louis XVI as a tyrant and traitor to the revolution?

8. Analyze the speech of Robespierre. How did he justify the use of terror in the promotion of revolution? Note, in particular, the juxtaposition of virtue and terror. In an ethical sense, can virtue ever be promoted by terror?

Section II: The Napoleonic Era

9. How did Napoleon come to power in 1799? Carefully read the statement he made on becoming consul. Pay particular attention to the vocabulary. How did Napoleon justify his overthrow of the Directory? Balance this public statement with the attitude found in the preceding excerpt "On the Realities of Power." What does this say about Napoleon's commitment to democratic ideals? At the time, though, to progress as a nation did France need less ideal and more practical inspiration and leadership? Was Napoleon a hypocrite who saved France from chaos? If so, do you condemn him for his hypocrisy?

10. On becoming first consul, Napoleon consolidated his position by suppressing the newspapers and reorganizing the state's religious institutions. Read these selections. Are these actions consistent with democratic government? From Napoleon's perspective, why were these actions essential to the stability of the state?

11. Look carefully at the statements concerning the reform of education and establishing the Legion of Honor. What special traits or characteristics of French citizens was Napoleon trying to reward or inspire in these measures? Were these reforms progressive and healthy for the French state? Why? Do Napoleon's revealing diary accounts on these topics detract from the reform ideals he set forth publicly? Note in particular Napoleon's comment from his diary regarding the education of women. What does this say about Napoleon as an enlightened reformer?

12. In 1804, Napoleon became emperor of the French by decree of the senate. How does this position differ from that of first consul for life? Compare the reasons that Napoleon gives for assuming this position with those given when he became first consul. Is there any pattern of justification? Note that the people of France approved of Napoleon's rise to power and his assumption of titles by supporting him with plebiscites. Were they in fact limiting their own freedom? Is freedom, most importantly, just a state of mind? Does progress often depend on a restriction of freedom in the interests of stability and security?

13. Compare the provisions for Napoleon's reorganization of the church in 1802 with the imperial catechism of 1806. What comment can you make regarding Napoleon and religion? Was he a divine-right monarch? What role did religion

play in the establishment of Napoleon's political power? In this sense, note also the "Clerical Oath of Loyalty" (1790). Why is it essential in time of revolution for the state to control religious organization?

14. Was Napoleon an absolute monarch in the tradition of Louis XIV? Was he a democrat, or the first of the "modern dictators" in the fascist mold of Mussolini and Hitler? Does the distinction between a democrat and a dictator blur when one is trying to achieve and consolidate power?

15. Napoleon has been called a "military genius" and indeed his conquest of a large part of Europe would support that judgement. But after reading the accounts of his invasion and retreat from Russia, what perspective can you give on his character and qualities of leadership? Did he sacrifice the lives of soldiers in order to satiate his ego, or was his vision of a French empire worth dying for? Why did the soldiers of France support him even during his darkest days?

16. Note Napoleon's view of his destiny, entitled "An End to the Woes of Anarchy," and his comments in exile on St. Helena. Was he a progressive or destructive force in French history? Did he embody Hegel's conception of the term "hero"? How? Was the philosophy of Jean-Jacques Rousseau every bit as much a force for the promotion of historical change as were the actions of Napoleon Bonaparte?

Part III: The Romantic Movement

17. How would you define the concept of "Romanticism"? What were the primary characteristics of the Romantic movement? Was it a revolution of sorts in the arts?

18. How does the poem by William Wordsworth capture the essence of the Romantic vision? What are the specific images that he evokes? Compare "Ode to the West Wind" by Percy Bysshe Shelley. How would you interpret the last line: "O, Wind/If Winter comes, can Spring be far behind?"

19. How does Goethe's excerpt from *Faust* play on the emotions? What images does he evoke and how does he use words and sounds to heighten the sense of place and foreboding? Identify the Romantic elements within Goethe's poem, "The Erlking." Why is this such an effective piece? How does the excerpt from Mary Shelley's *Frankenstein* create the sense of dread and terror? What larger human themes does she propose? How has the concept of the reanimation of "dead" tissue progressed from a Romantic idea to a reality in contemporary society? Can scientists now defy nature, create life and redefine death as did Dr. Frankenstein?

20. After reading Lord Byron's poem and viewing Francisco Goya's painting in condemnation of Napoleon, would you conclude that Romantic artists and writers were unsupportive of nationalism? Are these pieces propagandistic in nature and produced only after Napoleon was defeated and safely in exile? How do the paintings of Eugène Delacroix inspire nationalistic sentiment? Why has he been considered the greatest of French Romantic painters?

4

"A World to Win!": The Industrial Revolution

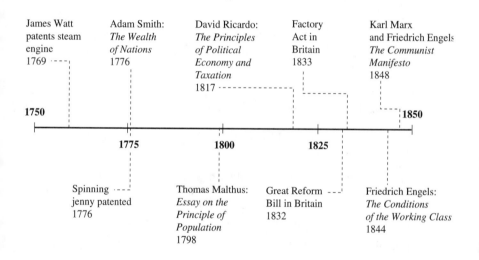

James Watt patents steam engine 1769

Adam Smith: *The Wealth of Nations* 1776

David Ricardo: *The Principles of Political Economy and Taxation* 1817

Factory Act in Britain 1833

Karl Marx and Friedrich Engels *The Communist Manifesto* 1848

1750

1850

1775

1800

1825

Spinning jenny patented 1776

Thomas Malthus: *Essay on the Principle of Population* 1798

Great Reform Bill in Britain 1832

Friedrich Engels: *The Conditions of the Working Class* 1844

Two nations between whom there is no intercourse and no sympathy; who are as ignorant of each other's habits, thoughts and feelings as if they were . . . inhabitants of different planets; who are formed by a different breeding, are fed by a different food, are ordered by different manners, and are not governed by the same laws—the rich and the poor.

—Benjamin Disraeli

The inherent vice of capitalism is the unequal sharing of blessings; the inherent virtue of socialism is the equal sharing of miseries.

—Winston Churchill

The worth of a State, in the long run, is the worth of the individuals composing it.

—John Stuart Mill

Man is born free and everywhere he is in chains.

—Jean-Jacques Rousseau

CHAPTER THEMES

- **Revolution:** What defines an economic or social revolution as opposed to a political revolution? Does one generally cause the other, or do all revolutions depend on a complex relationship between various elements? Can we define the Industrial Revolution as primarily technological in nature?

- **Women in History:** How did the Industrial Revolution change the social relationships within the family and alter the nature of the workforce? Was this a progressive period for women?

- **Church/State Relationships:** What role did the Catholic Church play in addressing the struggle between capitalists and workers in the state? Does the church's social involvement represent a revitalization of the church and strike a new relationship between church and state in the modern world?

- **Beliefs and Spirituality:** How would you define Marxism? Why did it become a popular social and economic policy in the nineteenth century? Although Marx repudiated religion, he became a spiritual leader for thousands of people. Can you explain this phenomenon?

- **Historical Change and Transition:** How did the Industrial Revolution forever change the history of humankind? What were its social and economic consequences, and how are they still felt today? Have the transistor and microchip created a second Industrial Revolution with similar social and economic impact?

- **The Big Picture:** In order for civilization to progress, to move forward technologically, must there always be a price to pay in human suffering and abuse? Is it worth it?

The word "revolution" implies drastic change, most often of a political nature, which results in a new form of government. There are other types of revolution as well. From the late-eighteenth century to the late-nineteenth century, Europe underwent a social and economic revolution that was the result of technological progress inspired by inventive minds. No longer would humans be harnessed to the land, completely dependent on the vicissitudes of nature for their livelihood; a new world was dawning, based in the city and filled with the prospect of employment and new lives. But this was not a move toward economic independence, for humans would soon be harnessed to an even more exacting master than the land—the machine.

Historically, the process of industrialization was a gradual one. The first stage of the Industrial Revolution began slowly, about 1760, and was made possible by several factors. First, Europe had reaped the benefits of an age of discovery during the sixteenth and seventeenth centuries. This fostered a commercial revolution that resulted in substantial economic growth. Indeed, the economic benefits of exploration were evident as nations sought to organize and compete on a grand scale. In addition, the English and French political revolutions of the seventeenth and eighteenth centuries began the ascendency of the middle class, which furnished the investment capital and expansive leadership necessary for the inception of the Industrial Revolution. At the same time, the population of Europe was growing dramatically, so much so that a rural-based economy simply could not support the growing tax requirements of governments and employ all who sought jobs.

These conditions were especially evident in England, where rural unemployment had been exacerbated by a conscious decision on the part of the wealthy landowners and the government itself to "enclose" farmland, release the tenantry from the security of farm labor, and use the land as pasture for sheep. Great profits were to be made in the textile trade, but the resulting displacement of the yeoman farmer added to the rural dilemma.

Yet England in the mid-eighteenth century was generally prosperous since it had developed a solid colonial foundation that provided ready markets for its goods. These markets were served by a maritime commercial and military fleet without peer and were supported by growing domestic production. This increase in the productive capacity of domestic industry resulted in large part from English ingenuity. The development of the flying shuttle, spinning jenny, and power loom in the mid-eighteenth century bespoke English technical superiority and advancement. The English had other natural advantages as well. Blessed with the existence of large quantities of coal and iron in close proximity, the English developed techniques for reducing the impurities in iron, thereby stimulating production; this eventually led to the development of the railroad in the mid-nineteenth century.

These new technologies were harnessed and organized in the factory. Men, women, and children were employed to keep the machines running, and the factory system was established to provide the greatest efficiency of material and labor, at the least expensive cost.

To many, industrialization became synonymous with progress. Increased production of goods meant greater potential for export, and this in turn created greater profit for the individual and government alike. The cultivation of new markets inspired competition among nations, exploration of new lands, and efficient management of time and labor. Yet industrialization, for all its glorification of the genius of the human mind, was never without its critics. It solved certain problems, but created others. What, for instance, should be done with those people who moved to the city in search of factory employment and found themselves among the "technologically unemployed," looking for jobs that simply did not exist? And what of those who were fortunate enough to find work in the mills or the mines? The dull monotony and danger of their occupations, not to mention their subsistence living conditions, made life depressing. Factory workers dreaded unemployment, yet could do little to change their condition. As long as competition, efficiency, and profit were the primary catalysts of the Industrial Revolution, the laborer would have to be sacrificed.

The conflicts raised by industrialization were all the more bewildering because they were unprecedented. How, for example, was government to respond to the complex problems created by industrial progress? This question was of primary importance for Britain, the first industrial area and the subject of this chapter. British industrialization was stimulated in the nineteenth century by the needs of national defense in view of the threat imposed by Napoleon. Criticism by reformers was not tolerated by the government, which viewed such acts as unpatriotic and incendiary. By the 1820s, however, tentative reforms were made that led to a rather prolonged debate resulting in the Reform Bill of 1832. This ensured that most middle-class British subjects would receive parliamentary representation and opened the franchise to some of the new industrial towns whose populations had never before been represented. In the following years, further reforms were legislated, such as the Factory Act of 1833, which limited the working hours of women and children in the textile mills and provided government inspection of the workplace. Still, reform was not won without struggle. In the 1830s and 1840s, writers and literary figures such as Charles Dickens and historian Thomas Carlyle and political organizations such as the Chartists advocated constitutional and social change. Liberalism was born as a political philosophy, and intellectuals such as John Stuart Mill (1806–1873) advocated workers' cooperatives, unions, and even women's suffrage.

Change was advocated from other directions as well. It was during this time that Karl Marx and Friedrich Engels observed the conditions of the working class in England and composed one of the most influential documents of the modern world—*The Communist Manifesto* (1848). According to Marx, the true revolutionary force in society was the workers (proletarians) who were dominated and abused by capitalists interested in profit at the workers' expense. As Marx wrote: "Let the ruling classes tremble at a Communist revolution. The proletarians have nothing to lose but their chains. They have a world to win." Other socialists less radical than Marx preached the need and inevitability of change to a more balanced society, based less on privilege and more on equality of opportunity.

The Industrial Revolution can thus be viewed in two ways: as a force for progress, an example of human ability to mold the environment, and as a demonstration of man's abuse of man, for the Industrial Revolution intensified class animosities and provided the catalyst for social change. The questions that emerge from this chapter are thus philosophical in nature yet practical in application. In order for civilization to progress, to move forward technologically, must there always be a price to pay in human suffering or abuse? And if that is the case, is it worth it? What indeed constitutes "progress"? The twentieth century has experienced some of the greatest technological change, from the invention of the automobile to the exploration of space. Have we too paid a price?

Rural and Urban Transformations

During the eighteenth century, England was at the center of both the agricultural and industrial revolutions. This was a time of great change and social upheaval as the introduction of new fertilizers and the process of crop rotation allowed farmers to produce crops more efficiently and in greater abundance. Landed aristocrats began to "engross" or add to their holdings and to enclose this property for more efficient pasturage. As a result, the rural peasantry were often turned off the land and wandered the countryside with little hope of gainful employment. Increasing numbers of these "dependant poor" required charitable assistance and often drifted to the cities in search of new lives.

But in the urban factories, a parallel process occurred as the development of new machinery produced goods more economically and in greater quantity than ever before. Many artisans could not compete and were displaced from skilled positions. Workers protested these changes in the patterns of labor by demonstrating and even by destroying the new machinery they found so threatening to their livelihood.

The first selection is an analysis of the plight of the agricultural laborers. The second is a petition from the Leeds Woollen Workers who demanded that machines not be used to prepare wool for spinning. The fear and frustration of trying to provide for a family in the face of such technological change fueled an ongoing debate on the nature of public assistance and the price to be paid for progress.

The Dependent Poor (1795)
DAVID DAVIES

III. The practice of enlarging and engrossing of farms, and especially that of depriving the peasantry of all landed property, have contributed greatly to increase the number of dependent poor.

"The Dependent Poor" is from David Davies, *The Case of Labourers in Husbandry Stated and Considered* (London, 1795), pp. 55–56.

The Land-owner, to render his income adequate to the increased expense of living, unites several small farms into one, raises the rent to the utmost, and avoids the expense of repairs. The rich farmer also engrosses as many farms as he is able to stock; lives in more credit and comfort than he could otherwise do; and out of the profits of *several farms*, makes an ample provision for *one family*. Thus thousands of families, which formerly gained an independent livelihood on those separate farms, have been gradually reduced to the class of day-laborers. But day-laborers are sometimes in want of work, and are sometimes unable to work; and in either case their sole resource is the parish. It is a fact, that thousands of parishes have not now half the number of farmers which they had formerly. And in proportion as the number of poor families has increased.

Thus depriving the peasantry of all landed property has beggared multitudes. It is plainly agreeable to sound policy, that as many individuals as possible in a state should possess an interest in the soil; because this attaches them strongly to the country and its constitution, and makes them zealous and resolute in defending them. But the gentry of this kingdom seem to have lost sight of this wise and salutary policy. Instead of giving to laboring people a valuable stake in the soil, the opposite measure has so long prevailed, that but few cottages, comparatively, have now *any* land about them. Formerly many of the lower sort of people occupied tenements of their own, with parcels of land about them, or they rented such of others. On these they raised for themselves a considerable part of their subsistence, without being obliged, as now, to buy all they want at shops. And this kept numbers from coming to the parish. But since those small parcels of ground have been swallowed up in the contiguous farms and inclosures, and the cottages themselves have been pulled down; the families which used to occupy them are crowded together in decayed farm-houses, with hardly ground enough about them for a cabbage garden: and being thus reduced to be *mere* hirelings, they are of course very liable to come to want. And not only the *men* occupying those tenements, but *their wives and children* too, could formerly, when they wanted work abroad, employ themselves profitably at home; whereas now, few of *these* are constantly employed, except in harvest; so that almost the whole burden of providing for their families rests upon the *men*. Add to this, that the former occupiers of small farms and tenements, though poor themselves, gave away something in alms to their poorer neighbors; a resource which is now much diminished.

Thus an amazing number of people have been reduced from a comfortable state of partial independence to the precarious condition of hirelings, who, when out of work, must immediately come to their parish. And the great plenty of working hands always to be had when wanted, having kept down the price of labor below its proper level, the consequence is universally felt in the increased number of dependent poor.

"How Are Men to Provide for Their Families?": A Workers' Petition (1786)

To the Merchants, Clothiers and all such as wish well to the Staple Manufactory of this Nation:

The Humble ADDRESS and PETITION of Thousands, who labour in the Cloth Manufactory.

SHEWETH, That the Scribbling-Machines have thrown thousands of your petitioners out of employ, whereby they are brought into great distress, and are not able to procure a maintenance for their families, and deprived them of the opportunity of bringing up their children to labour: We have therefore to request, that prejudice and self-interest may be laid aside, and that you may pay that attention to the following facts, which the nature of the case requires.

The number of Scribbling-Machines extending about seventeen miles south-west of Leeds, exceed all belief, being no less than *one hundred and seventy!* And as each machine will do as much work in twelve hours, as ten men can in that time do by hand, (speaking within bounds) and they working night and day, one machine will do as much work in one day as would otherwise employ twenty men.

As we do not mean to assert anything but what we can prove to be true, we allow four men to be employed at each machine twelve hours, working night and day, will take eight men in twenty-four hours; so that, upon a moderate computation twelve men are thrown out of employ for every single machine used in scribbling; and as it may be supposed the number of machines in all the other quarters together, nearly equal those in the South-West, full four thousand men are left to shift for a living how they can, and must of course fall to the Parish, if not timely relieved. Allowing one boy to be bound apprentice from each family out of work, eight thousand hands are deprived of the opportunity of getting a livelihood.

We therefore hope, that the feelings of humanity will lead those who have it in their power to prevent the use of those machines, to give every discouragement they can to what has a tendency so prejudicial to their fellow-creatures.

This is not all; the injury to the Cloth is great, in so much that in Frizing, instead of leaving a nap upon the cloth, the wool is drawn out, and the Cloth is left thread-bare.

Many more evils we could enumerate, but we would hope, that the sensible part of mankind, who are not biased by interest, must see the dreadful tendency of their continuance; a depopulation must be the consequence; trade being then lost, the landed interest will have no other satisfaction but that of being *last devoured . . . .*

"How Are Men to Provide for Their Families?" is from J. F. C. Harrison, *Society and Politics in England, 1780–1960* (New York: Harper & Row, 1965), pp. 70–72.

How are those men, thus thrown out of employ to provide for their families;—and what are they to put their children apprentice to, that the rising generation may have something to keep them at work, in order that they may not be like vagabonds strolling about in idleness? Some say, Begin and learn some other business.—Suppose we do; who will maintain our families, while we undertake the arduous task; and when we have learned it, how we have served our second apprenticeship, another machine may arise, which may take away that business also; so that our families, being half pined while we are learning how to provide them with bread, will be wholly so during the period of our third apprenticeship.

But what are our children to do; are they to be brought up in idleness? Indeed as things are, it is no wonder to hear of so many executions; for our parts, though we may be thought illiterate men, our conceptions are, that bringing children up to industry, and keeping them employed, is the way to keep them from falling into those crimes, which an idle habit naturally leads to.

These things impartially considered will we hope, be strong advocates in our favor; and we conceive that men of sense, religion and humanity, will be satisfied of the reasonableness, as well as necessity of this address, and that their own feelings will urge them to espouse the cause of us and our families.

Signed, in behalf of THOUSANDS, by

Joseph Hepworth	Thomas Lobley
Robert Wood	Thomas Blackburn

The Urban Landscape

The Factory System

Sybil (1845)
BENJAMIN DISRAELI

One of the most ardent reformers who criticized working conditions was Benjamin Disraeli. A novelist and politician, he served as prime minister of Britain from 1867 to 1868 and from 1874 to 1880. His most famous novel, Sybil, or the Two Nations, *vividly describes working and living conditions in factory towns. Disraeli hoped to gain working-class support for a group of reforming aristocrats in his Tory party. The following selection from this novel demonstrates the power of his prose.*

"Sybil" is from Benjamin Disraeli, *Sybil, or the Two Nations* (New York: M. Walter Dunne, 1904), pp. 199–200.

They come forth: the mine delivers its gang and the pit its bondsmen, the forge is silent and the engine is still. The plain is covered with the swarming multitude: bands of stalwart men, broad-chested and muscular, wet with the toil, and black as the children of the tropics; troops of youth, alas! of both sexes, though neither their raiment nor their language indicates the difference; all are clad in male attire; and oaths that men might shudder at issue from lips born to breathe words of sweetness. Yet these are to be, some are, the mothers of England! But can we wonder at the hideous coarseness of their language, when we remember the savage rudeness of their lives? Naked to the waist, an iron chain fastened to a belt of leather runs between their legs clad in canvas trousers, while on hands and feet an English girl, for twelve, sometimes for sixteen hours a day, hauls and hurries tubs of coals up subterranean roads, dark, precipitous, and plashy; circumstances that seem to have escaped the notice of the Society for the Abolition of Negro Slavery. Those worthy gentlemen, too, appear to have been singularly unconscious of the sufferings of the little trappers, which was remarkable, as many of them were in their own employ.

See, too, these emerge from the bowels of the earth! Infants of four and five years of age, many of them girls, pretty and still soft and timid; entrusted with the fulfillment of responsible duties, the very nature of which entails on them the necessity of being the earliest to enter the mine and the latest to leave it. Their labour indeed is not severe, for that would be impossible, but it is passed in darkness and in solitude. They endure that punishment which philosophical philanthropy has invented for the direst criminals, and which those criminals deem more terrible than the death for which it is substituted. Hour after hour elapses, and all that reminds the infant trappers of the world they have quitted, and that which they have joined, is the passage of the coal-wagons for which they open the air-doors of the galleries, and on keeping which doors constantly closed, except at this moment of passage, the safety of the mine and the lives of the persons employed in it entirely depend.

Testimony Before the Sadler Committee (1832)

In 1831 and 1832, the British government was under popular pressure to regulate factories and protect men, women, and children from abusive working conditions. The Sadler Committee was established and heard testimony from both workers and factory owners. The following selection clearly describes working conditions in a flax mill.

What age are you?—Twenty-three.
Where do you live?—At Leeds.

"Testimony before the Sadler Committee" is from *Parliamentary Papers, Reports from Committees, XV, "Labour of Children in Factories 1831–1832"* (London, 1932).

What time did you begin to work at a factory?—When I was six years old.

At whose factory did you work?—At Mr. Busk's.

What kind of mill is it?—Flax-mill.

What was your business in that mill?—I was a little doffer.

What were your hours of labour in that mill?—From 5 in the morning till 9 at night, when they were thronged.

For how long a time together have you worked that excessive length of time?—For about half a year.

What were your usual hours of labour when you were not so thronged?—From 6 in the morning till 7 at night.

What time was allowed for your meals?—Forty minutes at noon.

Had you any time to get your breakfast or drinking?—No, we got it as we could.

And when your work was bad, you hardly had anytime to eat at all?—No; we were obliged to leave it or take it home, and when we did not take it, the overlooker took it, and gave it to his pigs.

Do you consider doffing a laborious employment?—Yes.

Explain what it is you had to do?—When the frames are full, they have to stop the frames, and take the flyers off, and take the full bobbins off, and carry them to the roller; and then put empty ones on, and set the frame going again.

Does that keep you constantly on your feet?—Yes, there are so many frames, and they run so quick.

Your labour is very excessive?—Yes; you have not time for anything.

Suppose you flagged a little, or were too late, what would they do?—Strap us.

Are they in the habit of strapping those who are last in doffing?—Yes.

Constantly?—Yes.

Have you ever been strapped?—Yes.

Severely?—Yes.

Is the strap used so as to hurt you excessively?—Yes, it is.

Were you strapped if you were too much fatigued to keep up with the machinery?—Yes; the overlooker I was under was a very severe man, and when we have been fatigued and worn out, and had not baskets to put the bobbins in, we used to put them in the window bottoms, and that broke the panes sometimes, and I broke one one time, and the overlooker strapped me on the arm, and it rose a blister, and I ran home to my mother.

How long did you work at Mr. Busk's?—Three or four years.

Where did you go to then?—Benyon's factory.

That was when you were about 10 years?—Yes.

What were you then?—A weigher in the card-room.

How long did you work there?—From half-past 5 till 8 at night.

Was that the ordinary time?—Till 9 when they were thronged.

What time was allowed for meals at that mill?—Forty minutes at noon.

Any time at breakfast or drinking?—Yes, for the card-rooms, but not for the spinning-rooms, a quarter of an hour to get their breakfast.

And the same for their drinking?—Yes.

So that the spinners in that room worked from half-past 5 till 9 at night?—Yes.

Having only forty minutes' rest?—Yes.

The carding-room is more oppressive than the spinning department?—Yes, it is so dusty they cannot see each other for dust.

It is on that account they are allowed a relaxation of those few minutes?—Yes; the cards get so soon filled up with waste and dirt, they are obliged to stop them, or they would take fire.

There is a convenience in that stoppage?—Yes, it is as much for their benefit as for the working people.

When it was not necessary no such indulgence was allowed?—No.

Never?—No.

Were the children beat up to their labour there?—Yes.

With what?—A strap; I have seen the overlooker go to the top end of the room, where the little girls hug the can to the backminders; he has taken a strap, and a whistle in his mouth, and sometimes he has got a chain and chained them, and strapped them all down the room.

All the children?—No, only those hugging the cans.

What was his reason for that?—He was angry.

Had the children committed any fault?—They were too slow.

Were the children excessively fatigued at that time?—Yes, it was in the afternoon.

Were the girls so struck as to leave marks upon their skin?—Yes, they have had black marks many times, and their parents dare not come to him about it, they were afraid of losing their work.

If the parents were to complain of this excessive ill-usage, the probable consequence would be the loss of the situation of the child?—Yes.

In what part of the mill did you work?—In the card-room.

It was exceedingly dusty?—Yes.

Did it affect your health?—Yes; it was so dusty, the dust got upon my lungs, and the work was so hard; I was middling strong when I went there, but the work was so bad; I got so bad in health, that when I pulled the baskets down, I pulled my bones out of their places.

You dragged the baskets?—Yes; down the rooms to where they are worked.

And as you had been weakened by excessive labour, you could not stand that labour?—No.

It has had the effect of pulling your shoulders out?—Yes; it was a great basket that stood higher than this table a good deal.

How heavy was it?—I cannot say; it was a very large one, that was full of weights up-heaped, and pulling the basket pulled my shoulders out of its place, and my ribs have grown over it.

You continued at that work?—Yes.

You think that work is too much for children?—Yes.

It is woman's work, not fit for children?—Yes.

Is that work generally done by women?—Yes.

How came you to do it?—There was no spinning for me.

Did they give you women's wages?—They gave me 5s. and the women had 6s. 6d.

What wages did you get as a spinner?—Six shillings.

Did you perceive that many other girls were made ill by that long labour?—Yes, a good many of them.

So that you were constantly receiving fresh hands to supply the places of those that could no longer bear their work?—Yes, there were fresh hands every week; they could not keep their hands.

Did they all go away on account of illness?—They were sick and ill with the dust.

Do you know whether any of them died in consequence of it?—No, I cannot speak to that.

You do not know what became of them?—No, we did not know that.

If a person was to take an account of a mill, and the hands in it that were ill, they would know very little of those who had suffered from their labour; they would be elsewhere?—Yes.

But you are sure of this, that they were constantly leaving on account of the excessive labour they had to endure?—Yes.

And the unhealthy nature of their employment?—Yes.

Did you take any means to obviate the bad effects of this dust?—No.

Did it make you very thirsty?—Yes, we drank a deal of water in the room.

Were you heated with your employment at the same time?—No, it was not so very hot as in the summer time; in the winter time they were obliged to have the windows open, it made no matter what the weather was, and sometimes we got very severe colds in frost and snow.

You were constantly exposed to colds, and were made ill by that cause also?—Yes.

You are considerably deformed in your person in consequence of this labour?—Yes, I am.

At what time did it come on?—I was about 13 years old when it began coming, and it has got worse since. . . .

Do you know of any body that has been similarly injured in their health?—Yes, in their health, but not many deformed as I am.

You are deformed in the shoulders?—Yes.

It is very common to have weak ankles and crooked knees?—Yes, very common indeed.

That is brought on by stopping the spindle?—Yes.

Do you know anything of wet-spinning?—Yes, it is very uncomfortable; I have stood before the frame till I have been wet through to my skin; and in winter time, when we have gone home, our clothes have been frozen, and we have nearly caught our death of cold.

Conditions in the mines were dismal and dangerous. Children were often used to "hurry coal" through low shafts, as shown in this drawing of 1842. *(Library of Congress)*

Child Labor

Children were an integral part of the factory system. Mine owners depended on small boys to enter and work in restrictive areas that could not accommodate adults. The mills were common sources of employment for children who were good with their hands. Many parents condoned this and often forced their children to work, since they depended on their children's wages to live at subsistence level. The following accounts were excerpted from various liberal journals such as the Edinburgh Review, *the* Westminster Review, *and* Fraser's Magazine; *they reveal the social conscience of Victorian England.*

With regard to the hours of work, the commissioners state, that when the work-people are in full employment, the regular hours of work for children and young persons are rarely less than eleven; more often they are twelve; in some districts they are thirteen; and in one district they are generally fourteen and upwards. Certainly, unless upon the ample testimony produced by the Commission, it would not be credible that there is one district in the centre of England in which children are regularly required to pursue the labours of the mine for fourteen and sixteen hours daily; but in Derbyshire, south of Chesterfield, from thirteen to sixteen hours are considered a day's work; from eleven to twelve hours are reckoned three quarters of a day's work; and eight hours make half a day's work.

"John Hawkins, eight years of age:—'Has worked in Sissons Pit, a year and a half; lives a mile from the pit; goes down from five to nine;' that is, this child, eight years old, is employed in the pit at work from five o'clock in the morning to nine at night, a period of 16 hours.—John Houghton, nine years old:—'Goes down from six to eight—it has been ten:' that is, this child is regularly employed at work in the pits 14 hours, and occasionally 16 hours.—Ephraim Riley, eleven years old:—'Had three miles to walk to the pit; left home at five o'clock, winter and summer, and did not get home

"Child Labor" is from John Saville, ed., *Working Conditions in the Victorian Age* (Westmead, England: Gregg International Publishers Limited, 1973), pp. 130–132, 378–380. Reprinted by permission of the publisher.

again until nine o'clock at night (16 hours); his legs and thighs hurt him so with working so much that he remains in bed on Sunday mornings.'—John Chambers, thirteen years old:—'Has worked in pits since he was seven; works from six to nine or ten (from 15 to 16 hours). When first he worked in a pit he felt so tired, and his legs, arms, and back ached so much, that his brother has had to help him home many times. He could not go to school on a Sunday morning, he has been so stiff; he felt these pains until about a year since; he now feels tired, but his limbs do not ache as they did.'—James Creswell, fourteen years old:—'Has worked in pits four or five years; goes down at half-past six to nine, has this winter been after ten; half-days half-past six to three or four.'

"Of the fatigue of such labour, so protracted and carried on in such places of work, the following evidence exhibits a striking picture, and it will be observed that the witnesses of every class, children, young persons, colliers, underground stewards, agents, parents, teachers, and ministers of religion, all concur in making similar statements.

"John Bostock, aged seventeen, Babbington:—'Has often been made to work until he was so tired as to lie down on his road home until 12 o'clock, when his mother has come and led him home; he has done so many times when he first went to the pits; he has sometimes been so fatigued that he could not eat his dinner, but has been beaten and made to work until night; he never thought to play, was always too anxious to get to bed; is sure this is all true.'—John Leadbeater, aged eighteen, Babbington:—'Has two miles to go to the pit, and must be there before six, and works until eight; he has often worked all night, and been made by the butties to work as usual the next day; has often been so tired that he has lain in bed all Sunday. He knows no work so bad as that of a pit lad.'—Samuel Radford, aged nineteen, New Birchwood:—'Has been a week together and never seen daylight but on a Sunday, and not much then, he was so sleepy.'"

An imperfect abstract from the registration of deaths for the year 1838, gives a total, in England alone, of 349 deaths by violence in coal mines, and shows the most common causes of them:—

Cause of death	Under 13 years of age	13 and not exceeding 18 years of age	Over 18 years of age
Fell down the shafts	13	12	31
Fell down the shaft from the rope breaking	1	—	2
Fell out when ascending	—	—	3
Drawn over the pulley	3	—	3
Fall of stone out of a skip down the shaft	1	—	3
Drowned in the mines	3	4	15
Fall of stones, coal, and rubbish in the mines	14	14	69

Cause of death	Under 13 years of age	13 and not exceeding 18 years of age	Over 18 years of age
Injuries in coal-pits, the nature of which is not specified	6	3	32
Crushed in coal-pits	—	1	1
Explosion of gas	13	18	49
Suffocation of choke-damp	—	2	6
Explosion of gunpowder	—	1	3
By tram-wagons	4	5	12
Total	58	60	229

We proceed now to notice the great Metal Manufactures and their influence upon the health and well being of the children and youths employed in them. . . . In the blast-furnaces, mills, and forges, great numbers of children and youths are employed in night sets, between 6 P.M. and 6 A.M.; and in the miscellaneous trades overtime is very common, a great number of children working as long as the men, viz. from 6 A.M. to 11 P.M. Little girls are employed in bellows-blowing (very hard work for children) for fourteen hours a-day, standing on platforms to enable them to reach the handle of the bellows. Night work, overtime, and the very nature of the employment, cannot but have a very disastrous influence on their health. The foundry-boys, it is admitted by the masters themselves, commence work at much too early an age, and are taxed far beyond their strength; and the children who work at home, in the various domestic manufactures, are so injured by premature labour, often commencing from the age of seven, that, as a rule, they are stunted, dwarfed, or deformed. An instance is given of a father having worked his three young boys from four in the morning until twelve at night for weeks together, until the other men 'cried shame upon him'. . . . Two girls, nine and ten years of age, were working as 'strikers' and a little girl of eight, occasionally relieved by a still younger one of six, was working the bellows. The gross earnings of this man amounted to two guineas per week. It may be doubted whether the world could not produce a more revolting instance of parental oppression than the spectacle of these two young girls, whose little hands would have been appropriately employed in hemming a kerchief or working a sampler, begrimed with the smoke, stifled with the heat and stunned with the din morning till night. A single instance of oppression has often had a greater effect in rousing indignation than the most powerful denunciation of a general wrong. The picture of these little Staffordshire girls thus unsexed by an imperious taskmaster, and that taskmaster their parent, is well adapted to expose for universal reprobation a system under which such an enormity could be possible, and to prove the necessity of immediate legislative interference.

A Defense of the Factory System (1835)
ANDREW URE

The factory system was not without its advocates. One of the most influential was Andrew Ure, a professor of applied science at the University of Glasgow. He was supportive of the efficiency and productive capabilities of mechanized manufacturing. Note how the major criticisms of the reformers (child labor, degrading and unhealthy work conditions, etc.) are methodically countered. Ure argued that the owners of the mills and mines were not devils, but were actually abused themselves by the demands of the workers.

Proud of the power of malefaction, many of the cotton-spinners, though better paid, as we have shown, than any similar set of artisans in the world, organized the machinery of strikes through all the gradations of their people, terrifying or cajoling the timid or the passive among them to join their vindictive union. They boasted of possessing a dark tribunal, by the mandates of which they could paralyze every mill whose master did not comply with their wishes, and so bring ruin on the man who had given them profitable employment for many a year. By flattery or intimidation, they levied contributions from their associates in the privileged mills, which they suffered to proceed, in order to furnish spare funds for the maintenance of the idle during the decreed suspension of labour. In this extraordinary state of things, when the inventive head and the sustaining heart of trade were held in bondage by the unruly lower members, a destructive spirit began to display itself among some partisans of the union. Acts of singular atrocity were committed, sometimes with weapons fit only for demons to wield, such as the corrosive oil of vitriol, dashed in the faces of most meritorious individuals, with the effect of disfiguring their persons, and burning their eyes out of the sockets with dreadful agony.

The true spirit of turn-outs [strikes] among the spinners is well described in the following statement made on oath to the Factory Commission, by Mr. George Royle Chappel, a manufacturer of Manchester, who employs 274 hands, and two steam-engines of sixty-four horse power.

"I have had several turn-outs, and have heard of many more, but never heard of a turn-out for short time. I will relate the circumstances of the last turn-out, which took place on the 16th October, 1830, and continued till the 17th January, 1831. The whole of our spinners, whose average (weekly) wages were 2£. 13s. 5d., turned out at the instigation, as they told us at the time, of the delegates of the union. They said they had no fault to find with their wages, their work, or their masters, but the union obliged them to turn out. The same week three delegates from the spinners' union waited upon us at our mill, and dictated certain advances in wages, and other regulations, to

"A Defense of the Factory System" is from Andrew Ure, *The Philosophy of Manufactures* (London: Charles Knight, 1835), pp. 282–284, 290, 300–301, 309–311, 398–399.

"[The children] seemed to be always cheerful and alert, taking pleasure in the light play of their muscles, enjoying the mobility natural to their age."—Andrew Ure, *The Philosophy of Manufactures* (1835). *(Hein/Corbis)*

which, if we would not adhere, they said neither our own spinners not any other should work for us again! Of course we declined, believing our wages to be ample, and our regulations such as were necessary for the proper conducting of the establishment. The consequences were, they set watches on every avenue to the mill, night and day, to prevent any fresh hands coming into the mill, an object which they effectually attained, by intimidating some, and promising support to others (whom I got into the mill in a caravan), if they would leave their work. Under these circumstances, I could not work the mill, and advertised it for sale, without any applications, and I also tried in vain to let it. At the end of twenty-three weeks the hands requested to be taken to the mill again on the terms that they had left it, declaring, as they had done at first, that the union alone had forced them to turn out. . . ."

Nothing shows in a clearer point of view the credulity of mankind in general, and of the people of these islands in particular, than the ready faith which was given to the tales of cruelty exercised by proprietors of cotton-mills towards young children. The systems of calumny somewhat resembles that brought by the Pagans against the primitive Christians, of enticing children into their meetings in order to murder and devour them. . . .

No master would wish to have any wayward children to work within the walls of his factory, who do not mind their business without beating, and he therefore usually fines or turns away any spinners who are known to mal-treat their assistants. Hence, ill-usage of any kind is a very rare occurrence. I have visited many factories, both in Manchester and in the surrounding districts, during a period of several months, entering the spinning rooms, un-expectedly, and often alone, at different times of the day, and I never saw a single instance of corporal chastisement inflicted on a child, nor indeed did I ever see children in ill-humour. They seemed to be always cheerful and alert, taking pleasure in the light play of their muscles, enjoying the mobility natural to their age. The scene of industry, so far from exciting sad emotions in my mind, was always exhilarating. It was delightful to observe the nimbleness with which they pieced the broken ends, as the mule-carriage began to recede from the fixed roller-beam, and to see them at leisure, after a few seconds' exercise of their tiny fingers, to amuse them-selves in any attitude they chose, till the stretch and winding-on were once more completed. The work of these lively elves seemed to resemble a sport, in which habit gave them a pleasing dexterity. Conscious of their skill, they were delighted to show it off to any stranger. As to exhaustion by the day's work, they evinced no trace of it on emerging from the mill in the evening; for they immediately began to skip about any neighbouring playground, and to commence their little amusements with the same alacrity as boys is-suing from a school. It is moreover my firm conviction, that if children are not ill-used by bad parents or guardians, but receive in food and raiment the full benefit of what they earn, they would thrive better when employed in our modern factories, than if left at home in apartments too often ill-aired, damp, and cold. . . .

Of all the common prejudices that exist with regard to factory labour, there is none more unfounded than that which ascribes to it excessive te-dium and irksomeness above other occupations, owing to its being carried on in conjunction with the "unceasing motion of the steam-engine." In an establishment for spinning or weaving cotton, all the hard work is per-formed by the steam-engine, which leaves for the attendant no hard labour at all, and literally nothing to do in general; but at intervals to perform some delicate operation, such as joining the threads that break, taking the cops off the spindle, &c. And it is so far from being true that the work in a factory is incessant, because the motion of the steam-engine is incessant, that the fact is, that the labour is not incessant on that very count, because it is performed in conjunction with the steam-engine. Of all manufacturing employments, those are by far the most irksome and incessant in which steam-engines are not employed, as in lace-running and stocking-weaving; and the way to prevent an employment from being incessant, is to

introduce a steam-engine into it. These remarks certainly apply more especially to the labour of children in factories. Three-fourths of the children so
employed are engaged in piecing at the mules. "When the carriages of
these have receded a foot and a half or two feet from the rollers," says Mr.
Tufnell, "nothing is to be done, not even attention is required from either
spinner or piecer." Both of them stand idle for a time, and in fine spinning
particularly, for three-quarters of a minute, or more. Consequently, if a
child remains at this business twelve hours daily, he has nine hours of inac-
tion. And though he attends two mules, he has still six hours of non-
exertion. Spinners sometimes dedicate these intervals to the perusal of
books. The scavengers, who, in Mr. Sadler's report, have been described as
being "constantly in a state of grief, always in terror, and every moment they
have to spare stretched all their length upon the floor in a state of perspira-
tion," may be observed in cotton factories idle for four minutes at a time, or
moving about in a sportive mood, utterly unconscious of the tragical scenes
in which they were dramatized. . . .

Mr. Hutton, who has been in practice as a surgeon at Stayley Bridge upwards of thirty-one years, and, of course, remembers the commencement,
and has had occasion to trace the progress and effect, of the factory system,
says that the health of the population has much improved since its introduction, and that they are much superior in point of comfort to what they
were formerly. He also says that fever has become less common since the
erection of factories, and that the persons employed in them were less attacked by the influenza in 1833, than other classes of work-people. Mr.
Bott, a surgeon, who is employed by the operatives in Messrs. Lichfield's
mills to attend them in all cases of sickness or accident, at the rate of one
halfpenny a week (a sum which indicates pretty distinctly their small
chances of ailment), says that the factory workmen are not so liable to epi-
demics as other persons; and that though he has had many cases of typhus
fever in the surrounding district, nearly all the mill-hands have escaped,
and not one was attacked by the cholera during its prevalence in the neigh-
bourhood.

Living Conditions

*The living conditions of workers in urban industrial settings were a popular sub-
ject for reformers. One of the most important reformers, Friedrich Engels
(1820–1895), was born to a family of German textile manufacturers. Engels
was a keen observer of society and a talented, urbane writer. His close friendship
and collaboration with Karl Marx were instrumental in the dissemination and
success of communist ideology. In the first selection, Engels describes the condition of the working class in Manchester, the primary manufacturing town in
England. In the second, he exposes the threat to women and the family engendered by the factory system.*

The Condition of the Working Class in England (1844)

FRIEDRICH ENGELS

Above Ducie Bridge, the left bank grows more flat and the right bank steeper, but the condition of the dwellings on both banks grows worse rather than better. He who turns to the left here from the main street, Long Millgate, is lost; he wanders from one court to another, turns countless corners, passes nothing but narrow, filthy nooks and alleys, until after a few minutes he has lost all clue, and knows not whither to turn. Everywhere half or wholly ruined buildings, some of them actually uninhabited, which means a great deal here; rarely a wooden or stone floor to be seen in the houses, almost uniformly broken, ill-fitting windows and doors, and a state of filth! Everywhere heaps of debris, refuse, and offal; standing pools for gutters, and a stench which alone would make it impossible for a human being in any degree civilised to live in such a district. The newly-built extension of the Leeds railway, which crosses the Irk here, has swept away some of these courts and lanes, laying others completely open to view. Immediately under the railway bridge there stands a court, the filth and horrors of which surpass all the others by far, just because it was hitherto so shut off, so secluded that the way to it could not be found without a good deal of trouble. I should never have discovered it myself, without the breaks made by the railway, though I thought I knew this whole region thoroughly. Passing along a rough bank, among stakes and washing-lines, one penetrates into this chaos of small one-storied, one-roomed huts, in most of which there is no artificial floor; kitchen, living and sleeping-room all in one. In such a hole, scarcely five feet long by six broad, I found two beds—and such bedsteads and beds!—which, with a staircase and chimney-place, exactly filled the room. In several others I found absolutely nothing, while the door stood open, and the inhabitants leaned against it. Everywhere before the doors refuse and offal; that any sort of pavement lay underneath could not be seen but only felt, here and there with the feet. This whole collection of cattle-sheds for human beings was surrounded on two sides by houses and a factory, and on the third by the river, and besides the narrow stair up the bank, a narrow doorway alone led out into another almost equally ill-built, ill-kept labyrinth of dwellings. . . .

Such is the Old Town of Manchester, and on re-reading my description, I am forced to admit that instead of being exaggerated, it is far from black enough to convey a true impression of the filth, ruin, and uninhabitableness, the defiance of all considerations of cleanliness, ventilation, and health which characterise the construction of this single district, containing at least twenty to thirty thousand inhabitants. And such a district exists in the heart of the second city of England, the first manufacturing city of the world. If any one wishes to see in how little space a human being can move, how little air—and such air!—he can breathe, how little civilisation he may share and yet live, it is only necessary to travel hither. True, this is the Old Town, and the people of Manchester

"The Condition of the Working Class in England" is from Friedrich Engels, *The Condition of the Working Class in England in 1844* (London: Sonenschein & Co., 1892), pp. 51–53.

This 1872 engraving of Gustave Doré's *Over London by Rail* shows the crowded, polluted, urban living conditions that had developed during the Industrial Revolution. Friedrich Engels noted: "Everywhere heaps of debris, refuse and offal; standing pools for gutters, and a stench which alone would make it impossible for a human being . . . to live in such a district." (*Bibliotheque Nationale, Paris/Giraudon/Art Resource, NY*)

emphasise the fact whenever any one mentions to them the frightful condition of this Hell upon Earth; but what does that prove? Everything which here arouses horror and indignation is of recent origin, belongs to the industrial epoch.

The Impact of the Factory System on Women and the Family

FRIEDRICH ENGELS

The employment of women at once breaks up the family; for when the wife spends twelve or thirteen hours every day in the mill, and the husband works the same length of time there or elsewhere, what becomes of the children? They grow up like wild weeds; they are put out to nurse for a shilling or eighteenpence a week, and how they are treated may be imagined. . . . That the general mortality among young children must be increased by the employment of the mothers is self-evident, and is placed beyond all doubt by notorious facts.

Women often return to the mill three or four days after confinement [for childbirth], leaving the baby, of course; in the dinner hour they must hurry

"The Impact of the Factory System on Women and the Family" is from Friedrich Engels, *The Condition of the Working Class in England in 1844* (London: Sonnenschein & Co., 1892).

home to feed the child and eat something, and what sort of suckling that can be is also evident.

Lord Ashley repeats the testimony of several workwomen:

"M. H., twenty years old, has two children, the youngest a baby, that is tended by the other, a little older. The mother goes to the mill shortly after five o'clock in the morning, and comes home at eight at night; all day the milk pours from her breasts so that her clothing drips with it."

"H. W. has three children, goes away Monday morning at five o'clock, and comes back Saturday evening; has so much to do for the children then that she cannot get to bed before three o'clock in the morning; often wet through to the skin, and obliged to work in that state. She said: 'My breasts have given me the most frightful pain, and I have been dripping wet with milk.'"

The use of narcotics to keep the children still is fostered by this infamous system, and has reached a great extent in the factory districts. Dr. Johns, Registrar in Chief for Manchester, is of opinion that this custom is the chief source of the many deaths from convulsions. The employment of the wife dissolves the family utterly and of necessity, and this dissolution, in our present society, which is based upon the family, brings the most demoralizing consequences for parents, as well as children. . . .

Yet the working man cannot escape from the family, must live in the family, and the consequence is a perpetual succession of family troubles, domestic quarrels, most demoralizing for parents and children alike. Neglect of all domestic duties, neglect of the children, especially, is only too common among English working people, and only too vigorously fostered by the existing institutions of society. And children growing up in this savage way, amidst these demoralizing influences, are expected to turn out goody-goody and moral in the end! Verily the requirements are naive which the self-satisfied bourgeois makes upon the working man!

Reaction and Reform

Law and Liberty

The Iron Law of Wages (1817)

DAVID RICARDO

The Industrial Revolution began to develop in England while the economic practice of mercantilism was still widespread. Proponents of mercantilism argued that colonies existed for the benefit of the mother country, and indeed all economic activity should be regulated by the state for the good of the state. This concept was

"The Iron Law of Wages" is from David Ricardo, *The Principles of Political Economy and Taxation* (London: J. M. Dent & Sons, Ltd., 1911), pp. 57, 61–63.

not in harmony with the rise of industrial capitalism. Adam Smith, in his important treatise The Wealth of Nations *(1776), advocated the economic doctrine of laissez-faire. He contended that every human being is motivated primarily by self-interest and that the marketplace is regulated by its own competitive laws of supply and demand, profit and loss. Therefore, the market must be left alone (hence the name laissez-faire) and free from government controls and monopolies. Adam Smith soon became the "Patron Saint of Free Enterprise," and capitalism as a theory was born.*

Two of the most important "classical economists" who subscribed to Smith's ideas were Thomas Malthus (1766–1834) and David Ricardo (1772–1823). Malthus employed statistics to develop the Malthusian doctrine: The world's population, unless checked by war, disease, famine, late marriage, or moral restraint, grows at a higher rate than the means of subsistence, resulting in a doubling of the population every twenty-five years. His prediction for world famine was pessimistic indeed. David Ricardo, who had made a fortune on the London Stock Exchange, developed a theory, based to some extent on Malthus's analysis, that later came to be called the Iron Law of Wages. Ricardo believed that the wages of laborers must necessarily remain at a subsistence level because of the working class's unchecked rate of reproduction, which would continuously keep the supply of labor excessive. Ricardo advocated a restriction of "poor laws" that were enacted by Parliament in the early-nineteenth century to relieve the poor through governmental assistance. Ricardo thus became a champion of the rising industrial capitalists. A selection from his treatise The Principles of Political Economy and Taxation *(1817) follows.*

The friends of humanity cannot but wish that in all countries the labouring classes should have a taste for comforts and enjoyments, and that they should be stimulated by all legal means in their exertions to procure them. There cannot be a better security against a superabundant population. In those countries where the labouring classes have the fewest wants, and are contented with the cheapest food, the people are exposed to the greatest vicissitudes and miseries. They have no place or refuge from calamity; they cannot seek safety in a lower station; they are already so low that they can fall no lower. On any deficiency of the chief article of their subsistence there are few substitutes of which they can avail themselves and dearth to them is attended with almost all the evils of famine.

In the natural advance of society, the wages of labour will have a tendency to fall, as far as they are regulated by supply and demand; for the supply of labourers will continue to increase at the same rate, while the demand for them will increase at a slower rate. . . . I say that, under these circumstances, wages would fall if they were regulated only by the supply and demand of labourers; but we must not forget that wages are also regulated by the prices of the commodities on which they are expended.

As population increases, these necessaries will be constantly rising in price, because more labour will be necessary to produce them. If, then, the money wages of labour should fall, while every commodity on which the wages of labour were expended rose, the labourer would be doubly affected, and would be soon totally deprived of subsistence. . . . These, then, are the laws by which wages are regulated, and by which the happiness of far the greatest part of every community is governed. Like all other contracts, wages should be left to the fair and free competition of the market, and should never be controlled by the interference of the legislature.

The clear and direct tendency of the poor laws is in direct opposition to those obvious principles: it is not, as the legislature benevolently intended, to amend the condition of the poor, but to deteriorate the condition of both poor and rich; instead of making the poor rich, they are calculated to make the rich poor; and while the present laws are in force, it is quite in the natural order of things that the fund for the maintenance of the poor should progressively increase till it has absorbed all the net revenue of the country, or at least so much of it as the state shall leave to us, after satisfying its own never-failing demands for the public expenditure.

This pernicious tendency of these laws is no longer a mystery, since it has been fully developed by the able hand of Mr. Malthus; and every friend to the poor must ardently wish for their abolition. Unfortunately, however, they have been so long established, and the habits of the poor have been so formed upon their operation, that to eradicate them with safety from our political system requires the most cautious and skillful management. It is agreed by all who are most friendly to a repeal of these laws that, if it be desirable to prevent the most overwhelming distress to those for whose benefit they were erroneously enacted, their abolition should be effected by the most gradual steps.

It is a truth which admits not a doubt that the comforts and well-being of the poor cannot be permanently secured without some regard on their part, or some effort on the part of the legislature, to regulate the increase of their numbers, and to render less frequent among them early and improvident marriages. The operation of the system of poor laws has been directly contrary to this. They have rendered restraint superfluous, and have invited imprudence, by offering it a portion of the wages of prudence and industry.

The nature of the evil points out the remedy. By gradually contracting the sphere of the poor laws; by impressing on the poor the value of independence, by teaching them that they must look not to systematic or casual charity, but to their own exertions for support, that prudence and forethought are neither unnecessary nor unprofitable virtues, we shall by degrees approach a sounder and more healthful state.

No scheme for the amendment of the poor laws merits the least attention which has not their abolition for its ultimate object; and he is the best friend of the poor, and to the cause of humanity, who can point out how this end can be attained with the most security, and at the same time with the least violence. It is not by raising in any manner different from the present the fund from which the poor are supported that the evil can be mitigated. It would not only be no improvement, but it would be an aggravation of the distress which we wish to see removed, if the fund were increased in amount or were levied according to some late proposals, as a general fund from the country at large. . . . If by law every human being wanting support could be sure to obtain it, and obtain it in such a degree as to make life tolerably comfortable, theory would lead us to expect that all other taxes together would be light compared with the single one of poor rates. The principle of gravitation is not more certain than the tendency of such laws to change wealth and power into misery and weakness; . . . to confound all intellectual distinction; to busy the mind continually in supplying the body's wants; until at last all classes should be infected with the plague of universal poverty. Happily these laws have been in operation during a period of progressive prosperity, when the funds for the maintenance of labour have regularly increased, and when an increase of population would be naturally called for. But if our progress should become more slow; if we should attain the stationary state, from which I trust we are yet far distant, then will the pernicious nature of these laws become more manifest and alarming; and then, too, will their removal be obstructed by many additional difficulties.

The Chartist Demands (1838)

Although the Factory Act of 1833 resulted in an improvement in factory working conditions and in restrictions on child labor, many critics favored more radical reform. The Chartist movement in Great Britain, which was popular in the 1840s, sought political participation and especially universal manhood suffrage as means of improving the living conditions of the working poor. The following is an excerpt from the People's Petition of 1838, which articulated Chartist demands to the British House of Commons.

We, your petitioners, dwell in a land whose merchants are noted for enterprise, whose manufacturers are very skillful, and whose workmen are proverbial for their industry.

The land itself is goodly, the soil rich, and the temperature wholesome; it is abundantly furnished with the materials of commerce and trade; it has numerous and convenient harbours; in facility of internal communication it exceeds all others. For three-and-twenty years we have enjoyed a profound peace.

"The Chartist Demands" is from *The Life and Struggles of William Lovett* (New York: Knopf, 1920), pp. 478–481.

Yet, with all these elements of national prosperity, and with every disposition and capacity to take advantage of them, we find ourselves overwhelmed with public and private suffering.

We are bowed down under a load of taxes; which, notwithstanding, fall greatly short of the wants of our rulers; our traders are trembling on the verge of bankruptcy; our workmen are starving; capital brings no profit, and labour no remuneration; the home of the artificer is desolate, and the warehouse of the pawnbroker is full; the workhouse is crowded, and the manufactory is deserted. . . .

It was the found expectation of the people that a remedy for the greater part, if not for the whole, of their grievances, would be found in the Reform Act of 1832.

They were taught to regard that Act as a wise means to a worthy end; as the machinery of an improved legislation, when the will of the masses would be at length potential.

They have been bitterly and basely deceived.

The fruit which looked so fair to the eye has turned to dust and ashes when gathered.

The Reform Act has effected a transfer of power from one domineering faction to another, and left the people as helpless as before. . . .

Required as we are, universally, to support and obey the laws, nature and reason entitle us to demand, that in the making of the laws, the universal voice shall be implicitly listened to.

We perform the duties of freemen; we must have the privileges of freemen.

WE DEMAND UNIVERSAL SUFFRAGE

The suffrage to be exempt from the corruption of the wealthy, and the violence of the powerful, must be secret. . . .

WE DEMAND THE BALLOT

The connection between the representatives and the people, to be beneficial must be intimate. . . . To public safety as well as public confidence, frequent elections are essential.

WE DEMAND ANNUAL PARLIAMENTS

With power to choose, and freedom in choosing, the range of our choice must be unrestricted.

We are compelled, by the existing laws, to take for our representatives, men who are incapable of appreciating our difficulties, or who have little sympathy with them; merchants who have retired from trade, and no longer feel its harassings; proprietors of land who are alike ignorant of its evils and their cure; lawyers, by whom the honours of the senate are sought after only as means of obtaining notice in the courts. . . .

We demand that in the future election of members of you Hounourable House, the approbation of the constituency shall be the sole qualification; and that to every representative so chosen shall be assigned, out of the public taxes, a fair and adequate remuneration for the time which he is called upon to devote to the public service.

Finally, we would most earnestly impress on your Honourable House, that this petition has not been dictated by an idle love of change; that it springs out of no inconsiderate attachment to fanciful theories; but that it is the result of much and long deliberation, and of convictions, which the events of each succeeding year tend more and more to strengthen.

A Middle-Class Perspective (1859)

SAMUEL SMILES

The classical economists such as Adam Smith and David Ricardo stressed the need for free enterprise in the marketplace and defied regulation by government. Other theoreticians accepted these principles of self-interest and self-determination and yet applied them more specifically to the social and political world. Jeremy Bentham (1748–1832) advocated a principle called "utilitarianism," whereby all things could be judged on twin concepts of utility and happiness. The best government, for example, was one that ensured the greatest happiness for the greatest number of people. These utilitarians were also referred to as "philosophical radicals" because they lacked all reverence for tradition and believed that political, social, and encomic problems could be addressed rationally, without reference to privilege or special interests. They were popularly characterized as unemotional intellectuals without a practical understanding of humanity.

Yet for many members of the growing middle class, the Victorian Age was not characterized by the slums of Glasgow or the dirt of industry—or even by mathematical ratios between utility and happiness. To their thinking, perseverance and hard work resulted in a better life and were always rewarded. In his book Self-Help *(1859), Samuel Smiles emphasized this principle through a series of biographies of men who had risen to fame and fortune. The guiding idea was that "the most important results in daily life are to be obtained, not through the exercise of extraordinary powers, such as genius and intellect, but through the energetic use of simple means and ordinary qualities with which nearly all human individuals have more or less been endowed." One was responsible for one's own fate; it was up to the individual to change a bad situation if so desired.*

The object of the book briefly is, to re-inculcate these old-fashioned but wholesome lessons—which perhaps cannot be too often urged,—that youth must work in order to enjoy,—that nothing creditable can be accomplished without application and diligence,—that the student must not be daunted by difficulties, but conquer them by patience and perseverance,—and that,

---

"A Middle-Class Perspective" is from Samuel Smiles, *Self-Help* (London: John Murray, 1882), pp. v, 1, 4.

above all, he must seek elevation of character, without which capacity is worthless and worldly success is naught. If the author has not succeeded in illustrating these lessons, he can only say that he has failed in his object.

"Heaven helps those who help themselves" is a well-tried maxim, embodying in a small compass the results of vast human experience. The spirit of self-help is the root of all genuine growth in the individual; and, exhibited in the lives of many, it constitutes the true source of national vigour and strength. Help from without is often enfeebling in its effects, but help from within invariably invigorates. Whatever is done for men or classes, to a certain extent takes away the stimulus and necessity of doing for themselves; and where men are subjected to over-guidance and over-government, the inevitable tendency is to render them comparatively helpless.

Even the best institutions can give a man no active help. Perhaps the most they can do is, to leave him free to develop himself and improve his individual condition. But in all times men have been prone to believe that their happiness and well-being were to be secured by means of institutions rather than by their own conduct. Hence the value of legislation as an agent in human advancement has usually been much over-estimated. To constitute the millionth part of a Legislature, by voting for one or two men once in three or five years, however conscientiously this duty may be performed, can exercise but little active influence upon any man's life and character. Moreover, it is every day becoming more clearly understood, that the function of Government is negative and restrictive, rather than positive and active; being resolvable principally into protection—protection of life, liberty, and property. Laws, wisely administered, will secure men in the enjoyment of the fruits of their labour, whether of mind or body, at a comparatively small personal sacrifice; but no laws, however, stringent, can make the idle industrious, the thriftless provident, or the drunken sober. Reforms can only be effected by means of individual action, economy, and self-denial; better habits, rather than by greater rights. . . .

Daily experience shows that it is energetic individualism which produces the most powerful effects upon the life and action of others, and really constitutes the best practical education. Schools, academies, and colleges, give but the merest beginnings of culture in comparison with it. Far more influential is the life-education daily given in our homes, in the streets, behind counters, in workshops, at the loom and the plough, in counting-houses and manufactories, and in the busy haunts of men. This is that finishing instruction as members of society, which Schiller designated "the education of the human race," consisting in action, conduct, self-culture, self-control,—all that tends to discipline a man truly, and fit him for the proper performance of the duties and business of life,—a kind of education not to be learnt from books, or acquired by any amount of mere literary training. With his usual weight of words Bacon observes, that "Studies teach not their own use; but that is a wisdom without them, and above them, won by observation"; a remark that holds true of actual life, as well as of the cultivation of the intellect itself. For all experience serves to illustrate and enforce the lesson, that a man perfects himself by work more than by reading,—that it is life rather than literature, action rather than study, and character rather than biography, which tend perpetually to renovate mankind.

Visions of a New World
Utopian Socialism (1816)
ROBERT OWEN

One of the great personal success stories of the nineteenth century was Robert Owen. Born the son of a saddle maker, Owen left school at the age of nine and went to work in a draper's shop. At the age of eighteen, he borrowed money and set up a small cotton mill in Manchester. Within ten years, he was very wealthy and was joint owner of the New Lanark mills, the largest textile operation in Scotland. But Robert Owen was possessed with a desire to improve the lot of humanity. He provided higher wages and better working conditions for his employees and established free schools for their children. The New Lanark mills also returned a handsome profit. Owen sought government intervention and regulation to change conditions in industry. He could not understand why all factories could not be run on his utopian model. He is generally accepted in England as the founder of British socialism. The following address was delivered in 1816 on the opening of an "Institution for the Formation of Character" at New Lanark. Note the emphasis on morality as an essential ingredient of change.

Every society which exists at present, as well as every society which history records, has been formed and governed on a belief in the following notions, assumed as *first principles*:

First,—That it is in the power of every individual to form his own character.

Hence the various systems called by the name of religion, codes of law, and punishments. Hence also the angry passions entertained by individuals and nations towards each other.

Second,—That the affections are at the command of the individual. Hence insincerity and degradation of character.

Hence the miseries of domestic life, and more than one-half of all the crimes of mankind.

Third,—That it is necessary that a large portion of mankind should exist in ignorance and poverty, in order to secure to the remaining part such a degree of happiness as they now enjoy.

"Utopian Socialism" is from Robert Owen, *Address to the Workers of New Lanark* (1816).

The factory school at New Lanark mills. Robert Owen, a successful businessman and utopian socialist, believed that a humane working environment need not be sacrificed in order to maintain a fine profit. His industrial community included free schooling for the children of his workers. (*Mansell Collection / Time Life Syndication, Time, Inc.*)

Hence a system of counteraction in the pursuits of men, a general opposition among individuals to the interests of each other, and the necessary effects of such a system,—ignorance, poverty, and vice.

Facts prove, however—

First,—That character is universally formed *for*, and not *by*, the individual.

Second,—That *any* habits and sentiments may be given to mankind.

Third,—That the affections are not under the control of the individual.

Fourth,—That every individual may be trained to produce far more than he can consume, while there is a sufficiency of soil left for him to cultivate.

Fifth,—That nature has provided means by which population may be at all times maintained in the proper state to give the greatest happiness to every individual, without one check of vice or misery.

Sixth,—That any community may be arranged, on a due combination of the foregoing principles, in such a manner, as not only to withdraw vice, poverty, and, in a great degree, misery, from the world, but also to place *every* individual under circumstances in which he shall enjoy more permanent happiness than can be given to *any* individual under the principles which have hitherto regulated society.

Seventh,—That all the assumed fundamental principles on which society has hitherto been founded are erroneous, and may be demonstrated to be contrary to fact. And—

Eighth,—That the change which would follow the abandonment of those erroneous maxims which bring misery into the world, and the adoption of principles of truth, unfolding a system which shall remove and for ever exclude that misery, may be effected without the slightest injury to any human being.

Here is the groundwork,—these are the data, on which society shall ere long be re-arranged; and for this simple reason, that it will be rendered evident that it will be for the immediate and future interest of every one to lend his most active assistance gradually to reform society on this basis. I say gradually, for in that word the most important considerations are involved. Any sudden and coercive attempt which may be made to remove even misery from men will prove injurious rather than beneficial. Their minds must be gradually prepared by an essential alteration of the circumstances which surround them, for any great and important change and amelioration in their condition. They must be first convinced of their blindness: this cannot be effected, even among the least unreasonable, or those termed the best part of mankind, in their present state, without creating some degree of irritation. This irritation, must then be tranquillized before another step ought to be attempted; and a general conviction must be established of the truth of the principles on which the projected change is to be founded. Their introduction into practice will then become easy,—difficulties will vanish as we approach them,—and, afterwards, the desire to see the whole system carried immediately into effect will exceed the means of putting it into execution.

The principles on which this practical system is founded are not new; separately, or partially united, they have been often recommended by the sages of antiquity, and by modern writers. But it is not known to me that they have ever been thus combined. Yet it can be demonstrated that it is only by their being *all brought into practice together* that they are to be rendered beneficial to mankind; and sure I am that this is the earliest period in the history of man when they could be successfully introduced into practice.

The Communist Manifesto (1848)
KARL MARX AND FRIEDRICH ENGELS

The Communist Manifesto, *written by Karl Marx (1818–1883) and Friedrich Engels in 1848, is the fundamental declaration of communist ideology. Marx was concerned with the process of change in history (dialectic). A keen observer of the industrial world around him, Marx saw the oppression of the worker (proletarian) by those who owned the means of production (bourgeoisie). Marx advocated a society that was devoid of capitalistic oppression, a society in which workers actually controlled the factories and regulated their own working*

"The Communist Manifesto" is from Karl Marx and Friedrich Engels, *The Communist Manifesto,* trans. Samuel Moore (New York: Socialist Labor Party, 1888).

conditions and environment. His call to revolution had little influence on the protests of 1848, but his ideas would serve as the foundation for the Russian Revolution in 1917 and are of great importance today.

Bourgeoisie and Proletariat

The history of all hitherto existing society is the history of class struggles.

Freeman and slave, patrician and plebeian, lord and serf, guildmaster and journeyman, in a word, oppressor and oppressed, stood in constant opposition to one another, carried on an uninterrupted, now hidden, now open fight, a fight that each time ended, either in a revolutionary reconstitution of society at large, or in the common ruin of the contending classes.

In the earlier epochs of history, we find almost everywhere a complicated arrangement of society into various orders, a manifold graduation of social rank. In ancient Rome we have patricians, knights, plebeian, slaves; in the Middle Ages, feudal lords, vassals, guildmasters, journeymen, apprentices, serfs; in almost all of these classes, again, subordinate gradations.

The modern bourgeois society that has sprouted from the ruins of feudal society, has not done away with class antagonisms. It has but established new classes, new conditions of oppression, new forms of struggle in place of the old ones.

Our epoch, the epoch of the bourgeoisie, possesses, however, this distinctive feature: it has simplified the class antagonisms. Society as a whole is more and more splitting up into two great hostile camps, into two great classes directly facing each other: Bourgeoisie and Proletariat. . . .

Each step in the development of the bourgeoisie was accompanied by a corresponding political advance of the class. An oppressed class under the sway of the feudal nobility, an armed and self-governing association in the medieval commune, here independent urban republic (as in Italy and Germany), there taxable "third estate" of the monarchy (as in France), afterwards, in the period of manufacture proper, serving either the semifeudal or the absolute monarchy as a counterpoise against the nobility, and in fact, corner stone of the great monarchies in general, the bourgeoisie has at last, since the establishment of Modern Industry and of the world-market, conquered for itself, in the modern representative State, exclusive political sway. The executive of the modern State is but a committee for managing the common affairs of the whole bourgeoisie. . . .

The need of a constantly expanding market for its products chases the bourgeoisie over the whole surface of the globe. It must nestle everywhere, establish connections everywhere. . . .

The bourgeoisie, during its rule of scarce one hundred years, has created more massive and more colossal productive forces than have all preceding generations together. Subjection of Nature's forces to man, machinery, application of chemistry to industry and agriculture, steam-navigation, railways, electric telegraphs, clearing of whole continents for cultivation, canalization of rivers, whole populations conjured out of the ground—what earlier

The grave memorial of Karl Marx at Highgate Cemetery in London: "The proletarians have nothing to lose but their chains. They have a world to win. Workers of the world, unite!" *(Perry M. Rogers)*

century had even a presentiment that such productive forces slumbered in the lap of social labor? . . .

In proportion as the bourgeoisie, i.e., capital, is developed, in the same proportion is the proletariat, the modern working-class, developed, a class of laborers, who live only so long as they find work, and who find work only so long as their labor increases capital. These laborers, who must sell themselves piecemeal, are a commodity, like every other article of commerce, and are consequently exposed to all the vicissitudes of competition, to all the fluctuations of the market.

Owing to the extensive use of machinery and to division of labor, the work of the proletarians has lost all individual character, and, consequently, all charm for the workman. He becomes an appendage of the machine, and it is only the most simple, most monotonous, and most easily acquired knack that is required of him. Hence, the cost of production of a workman is restricted, almost entirely, to the means of subsistence that he requires for his maintenance, and for the propagation of his race. But the price of commodity, and also of labor, is equal to its cost of production. In proportion, therefore, as the repulsiveness of the work increases, the wage decreases. Nay more, in proportion as the use of the machinery and division of labor increases, in the same proportion the burden of toil also increases, whether by prolongation of the working hours, by increase of the work enacted in a given time, or by increased speed of the machinery, etc.

Modern industry has converted the little workshop of the patriarchal master into the great factory of the industrial capitalist. Masses of laborers, crowded into the factory, are organized like soldiers. As privates of the industrial army they are placed under the command of a perfect hierarchy of officers and sergeants. Not only are they the slaves of the bourgeois class, and of the bourgeois State, they are daily and hourly enslaved by the machine, by the over-looker, and, above all, by the individual bourgeois manufacturer himself. The more openly despotism proclaims gain to be its end and aim, the more petty, the more hateful and the more embittering it is.

The less the skill and exertion or strength implied in manual labor, in other words, the more modern industry becomes developed, the more is the labor of men superseded by that of women. Differences of age and sex have no longer any distinctive social validity for the working class. All are instruments of labor, more or less expensive to use, according to their age and sex.

No sooner is the exploitation of the laborer by the manufacturer, so far at an end, that he receives his wages in cash, than he is set upon by the other portions of the bourgeoisie, the landlord, the shopkeeper, the pawnbroker, etc. . . .

But with the development of industry the proletariat not only increases in number, it becomes concentrated in greater masses, its strength grows, and it feels that strength more. The various interests and conditions of life within the ranks of the proletariat are more and more equalized, in proportion as machinery obliterates all distinctions of labor, and nearly everywhere reduces wages to the same low level. The growing competition among the bourgeois, and the resulting commercial crises, make the wages of the workers ever more fluctuating. The unceasing improvement of machinery, ever more rapidly developing, makes their livelihood more and more precarious; the collisions between individual workmen and individual bourgeois take more and more the character of collisions between two classes. Thereupon the workers begin to form combinations (Trades' Unions) against the bourgeois; they club together in order to keep up the rate of wages; they found permanent associations in order to make provision beforehand for these occasional revolts. Here and there the contest breaks out into riots.

Now and then the workers are victorious, but only for a time. The real fruit of their battle lies, not in the immediate result, but in the ever expanding union of the workers. This union is helped on by the improved means of communications that are created by modern industry, and that places the workers of different localities in contact with one another. It was just this contact that was needed to centralize the numerous local struggles, all of the same character, into one national struggle between classes. But every class struggle is a political struggle. . . .

This organization of the proletarians into a class, and consequently into a political party, is continually being upset again by the competition between the workers themselves. But it ever rises up again, stronger, firmer, mightier. It compels legislative recognition of particular interests of the workers, by taking advantage of the divisions among the bourgeoisie itself. Thus the ten-hour bill in England was carried. . . .

The essential condition for the existence, and for the sway of the bourgeois class, is the formation and augmentation of capital; the condition for capital is wage-labor. Wage-labor rests exclusively on competition between the laborers. The advance of industry, whose involuntary promoter is the bourgeoisie, replaces the isolation of the laborers, due to competition, by their revolutionary combination, due to association. The development of Modern Industry, therefore, cuts from under its feet the very foundation on which the bourgeoisie produces and appropriates products. What the bourgeoisie therefore produces, above all, are its own gravediggers. Its fall and the victory of the proletariat are equally inevitable.

Proletarians and Communists

In what relation do the Communists stand to the proletarians as a whole?

The Communists do not form a separate party opposed to other working class parties.

They have no interests separate and apart from those of the proletariat as a whole.

They do not set up any sectarian principles of their own, by which to shape and mould the proletarian movement.

The Communists are distinguished from the other working class parties by this only: 1. In the national struggles of the proletarians of the different countries, they point out and bring to the front the common interests of the entire proletariat independently of all nationality. 2. In the various stages of development which the struggle of the working class against the bourgeoisie has to pass through, they always and everywhere represent the interests of the movement as a whole.

The Communists, therefore, are on the one hand, practically, the most advanced and resolute section of the working class parties of every country, that section which pushes forward all other; on the other hand, theoretically, they have over the great mass of the proletariat the advantage of clearly understanding the line of march, the conditions, and the ultimate general results of the proletarian movement.

The immediate aim of the Communists is the same as that of all the other proletarian parties: formation of the proletariat into a class, overthrow of the bourgeois supremacy, conquest of political power by the proletariat.

The theoretical conclusions of the Communists are in no way based on ideas or principles that have been invented, or discovered, by this or that would-be universal reformer.

They merely express, in general terms, actual relations springing from an existing class struggle, from a historical movement going on under our very eyes. The abolition of existing property relations is not at all a distinctive feature of Communism.

All property relations in the past have continually been subject to historical change consequent upon the change in historical conditions.

The French Revolution, for example, abolished feudal property in favor of bourgeois property.

The distinguishing feature of Communism is not the abolition of property generally, but the abolition of bourgeois property. But modern bourgeois private property is the final and most complete expression of the system of producing and appropriating products, that is based on class antagonism, on the exploitation of the many by the few.

In this sense, the theory of the Communists may be summed up in the single sentence: Abolition of private property. . . .

The Communist revolution is the most radical rupture with traditional property-relations; no wonder that its development involves the most radical rupture with traditional ideas.

But let us have done with the bourgeois objections to Communism.

We have seen above, that the first step in the revolution by the working class, is to raise the proletariat to the position of ruling class, to win the battle of democracy.

The proletariat will use its political supremacy, to wrest, by degrees, all capital from the bourgeoisie, to centralize all instruments of production in the hands of the State, i.e., of the proletariat organized as the ruling class; and to increase the total of productive forces as rapidly as possible.

Of course, in the beginning, this cannot be effected except by means of despotic inroads on the rights of property, and on the conditions of bourgeois production; by means of measures, therefore, which appear economically insufficient and untenable, but which, in the course of the movement, outstrip themselves, necessitate further inroads upon the old social order, and are unavoidable as a means of entirely revolutionizing the mode of production.

These measures will of course be different in different countries.

Nevertheless in the most advanced countries the following will be pretty generally applicable:

1. Abolition of property in land and application of all rents of land to public purposes.
2. A heavy progressive or graduated income tax.

3. Abolition of all rights of inheritance.
4. Confiscation of the property of all emigrants and rebels.
5. Centralization of credit in the hands of the state, by means of a national bank with State capital and an exclusive monopoly.
6. Centralization of the means of communication and transport in the hands of the State.
7. Extension of factories and instruments of production owned by the State; the bringing into cultivation of waste lands, and the improvement of the soil generally in accordance with a common plan.
8. Equal liability of all to labor. Establishment of industrial armies, especially for agriculture.
9. Combination of agriculture with manufacturing industries; gradual abolition of the distinction between town and country, by a more equable distribution of population over the country.
10. Free education for all children in public schools. Abolition of children's factory labor in its present form. Combination of education with industrial production, etc., etc.

When, in the course of development, class distinctions have disappeared, and all production has been concentrated in the hands of a vast association of the whole nation, the public power will lose its political character. Political power, properly so called, is merely the organized power of one class for oppressing another. If the proletariat during its contest with the bourgeoisie is compelled, by the force of circumstances, to organize itself as a class, if, by means of a revolution, it makes itself the ruling class, and, as such, sweeps away by force the old conditions of production, then it will, along with these conditions, have swept away the conditions for the existence of class antagonisms, and of class generally, and will thereby have abolished its own supremacy as a class.

In place of the old bourgeois society, with its classes and class antagonisms, we shall have an association, in which the free development of each is the condition for the free development of all. . . .

In short, the Communists everywhere support every revolutionary movement against the existing social and political order of things.

In all these movements they bring to the front, as the leading question in each, the property question, no matter what its degree of development at the time.

Finally, they labor everywhere for the union and agreement of the democratic parties of all countries.

The Communists disdain to conceal their views and aims. They openly declare that their ends can be attained only by the forcible overthrow of all existing social conditions. Let the ruling classes tremble at a Communistic revolution. The proletarians have nothing to lose but their chains. They have a world to win.

Workers of the world, unite!

Rerum Novarum (1891)

POPE LEO XIII

One of the more influential associations against the abuses of industrialism was the Christian Socialist movement. It began in England about 1848 and stressed that one could overcome the evils of industrialism by following Christian principles: Brotherly love was preferable to ruthless competition and exploitation. Quite apart from this movement, but adhering to the same basic principles, was the Catholic Church. Pope Leo XIII was an active commentator on political power and human liberty. In 1891, he issued the encyclical Rerum Novarum, *which addressed the continuing struggle between capitalists and workers. This official opinion of the pope demonstrates the church's continuing interest in the affairs of the secular world.*

Rights and Duties of Capital Labor

That the spirit of revolutionary change, which has long been disturbing the nations of the world, should have passed beyond the sphere of politics and made its influence felt in the cognate sphere of practical economics is not surprising. The elements of the conflict now raging are unmistakable, in the vast expansion of industrial pursuits and the marvelous discoveries of science; in the changed relations between masters and workmen; in the enormous fortunes of some few individuals, and the utter poverty of the masses; in the increased self-reliance and closer mutual combination of the working classes; as also, finally, in the prevailing moral degeneracy. The momentous gravity of the state of things now obtaining fills every mind with painful apprehension; wise men are discussing it; practical men are proposing schemes; popular meetings, legislatures, and rulers of nations are all busied with it—actually there is no question which has taken a deeper hold on the public mind.

Therefore, . . . We thought it expedient now to speak on the condition of the working classes. It is a subject on which We have already touched more than once, incidentally. But in the present letter, the responsibility of the apostolic office urges Us to treat the question of set purpose and in detail, in order that no misapprehension may exist as to the principles which truth and justice dictate for its settlement. The discussion is not easy, nor is it void of danger. It is no easy matter to define the relative rights and mutual duties of the rich and of the poor, of capital and of labor. And the danger lies in this, that crafty agitators are intent on making use of these differences of opinion to pervert men's judgments and to stir up the people to revolt.

In any case we clearly see, and on this there is general agreement, that some opportune remedy must be found quickly for the misery and wretchedness pressing so unjustly on the majority of the working class: for the ancient

"Rerum Novarum" is from Claudia Carlen Ihm, ed., *The Papal Encyclicals, 1878–1903*, vol. 2 (New York: McGrath Publishing Company, 1981), pp. 241–242, 244–246, 248, 255–256.

working-men's guilds were abolished in the last century, and no other protective organization took their place. . . . Hence, by degrees it has come to pass that working men have been surrendered, isolated and helpless, to the hardheartedness of employers and the greed of unchecked competition. The mischief has been increased by rapacious usury, which, although more than once condemned by the Church, is nevertheless, under a different guise, but with like injustice, still practiced by covetous and grasping men. To this must be added that the hiring of labor and the conduct of trade are concentrated in the hands of comparatively few; so that a small number of very rich men have been able to lay upon the teeming masses of the laboring poor a yoke little better than that of slavery itself.

To remedy these wrongs the socialists, working on the poor man's envy of the rich, are striving to do away with private property, and contend that individual possessions should become the common property of all, to be administered by the State or by municipal bodies. They hold that by thus transferring property from private individuals to the community, the present mischievous state of things will be set to rights, inasmuch as each citizen will then get his fair share of whatever there is to enjoy. But their contentions are so clearly powerless to end the controversy that were they carried into effect the working man himself would be among the first to suffer. They are, moreover, emphatically unjust, for they would rob the lawful possessor, distort the functions of the State, and create utter confusion in the community. . . .

What is of far greater moment, however, is the fact that the remedy they propose is manifestly against justice. For, every man has by nature the right to possess property as his own. This is one of the chief points of distinction between man and the animal creation, for the brute has no power of self-direction, but is governed by two main instincts, which keep his powers on the alert, impel him to develop them in a fitting manner, and stimulate and determine him to action without any power of choice. One of these instincts is self-preservation, the other the propagation of the species. Both can attain their purpose by means of things which lie within range; beyond their verge the brute creation cannot go, for they are moved to action by their senses only, and in the special direction which these suggest. But with man it is wholly different. He possesses, on the one hand, the full perfection of the animal being, and hence enjoys at least as much as the rest of the animal kind, the fruition of things material. But animal nature, however perfect, is far from representing the human being in its completeness, and is in truth but humanity's humble handmaid, made to serve and to obey. It is the mind, or reason, which is the predominate element in us who are human creatures; it is this which renders a human being human, and distinguishes him essentially from the brute. And on this very account—that man alone among the animal creation is endowed with reason—it must be within his right to possess things not merely for temporary and momentary use, as other living things do, but to have and to hold them in stable and permanent possession. . . .

The contention, then, that the civil government should at its option intrude into and exercise intimate control over the family and the household is a great and pernicious error. True, if a family finds itself in exceeding distress, utterly deprived of the counsel of friends, and without any prospect of extricating itself, it is right that extreme necessity be met by public aid, since each family is a part of the commonwealth. In like manner, if within the precincts of the household there occur grave disturbance of mutual rights, public authority should intervene to force each party to yield to the other its proper due; for this is not to deprive citizens of their rights, but justly and properly to safeguard and strengthen them. But rulers of the commonwealth must go no further; here, nature bids them stop. Paternal authority can be neither abolished nor absorbed by the State; for it has the same source as human life itself. . . . The socialists, therefore, in setting aside the parent and setting up a State supervision, act against natural justice, and destroy the structure of the home. . . .

The great mistake in regard to the matter now under consideration is to take up with the notion that class is naturally hostile to class, and that the wealthy and the working men are intended by nature to live in mutual conflict. So irrational and so false is this view that the direct contrary is the truth. Just as the symmetry of the human frame is the result of the suitable arrangement of the different parts of the body, so in a State is it ordained by nature that these two classes should dwell in harmony and agreement, so as to maintain the balance of the body politic. Each needs the other: capital cannot do without labor, nor labor without capital. Mutual agreement results in the beauty of good order, while perpetual conflict necessarily produces confusion and savage barbarity. Now, in preventing such strife as this, and in uprooting it, the efficacy of Christian institutions is marvelous and manifold. First of all, there is no intermediary more powerful than religion (whereof the Church is the interpreter and guardian) in drawing the rich and the working class together, by reminding each of its duties to the other, and especially of the obligations of justice.

Of these duties, the following bind the proletarian and the worker: fully and faithfully to perform the work which has been freely and equitably agreed upon; never to injure the property, nor to outrage the person, of an employer; never to resort to violence in defending their own cause, nor to engage in riot or disorder; and to have nothing to do with men of evil principles, who work upon the people with artful promises of great results, and excite foolish hopes which usually end in useless regrets and grievous loss. The following duties bind the wealthy owner and the employer: not to look upon their work people as their bondsmen, but to respect in every man his dignity as a person ennobled by Christian character. They are reminded that, according to natural reason and Christian philosophy, working for gain is creditable, not shameful, to a man, since it enables him to earn an honorable livelihood; but to misuse men as though they were things in the pursuit of gain, or to value them solely for their physical powers—that is truly shameful and inhuman. Again justice demands that, in dealing with the working man, religion and the good of his soul must be kept in mind. Hence, the employer is bound to see that the worker has time for his religious duties; that he be not exposed to corrupting influences and dangerous occasions; and that he be not led away to neglect his home and family, or to squander his earnings. Furthermore, the employer must never tax his work people beyond their strength, or employ them in work unsuited to their sex and age. His great and principal duty is to give every one what is just. Doubtless, before deciding whether wages are fair, many things have to be considered; but wealthy owners and all masters of labor should be mindful of this—that to exercise pressure upon the indigent and the destitute for the sake of gain, and to gather one's profit out of the need of another, is condemned by all laws, human and divine. To defraud any one of wages that are his due is a great crime which cries to the avenging anger of Heaven. . . .

To sum up, then, We may lay it down as a general and lasting law that working men's associations should be so organized and governed as to furnish the best and most suitable means for attaining what is aimed at, that is to say, for helping each individual member to better his condition to the utmost in body, soul, and property. It is clear that they must pay special and chief attention to the duties of religion and morality, and that social betterment should have this chiefly in view; otherwise they would lose wholly their special character, and end by becoming little better than those societies which take no account whatever of religion. What advantage can it be to a working man to obtain by means of a society material well-being, if he endangers his soul for lack of spiritual food? "What doth it profit a man, if he gains the whole world and suffer the loss of his soul?" This, as our Lord teaches, is the mark of character that distinguishes the Christian from the heathen. . . . Let the working man be urged and led to the worship of God, to the earnest practice of religion. . . . Let him learn to reverence and love holy Church, the common Mother of us all; and hence to obey the precepts of the Church, . . . since they are the means ordained by God for obtaining forgiveness of sin and for leading a holy life. . . .

CHRONOLOGY: "A World to Win!": The Industrial Revolution

1733	James Kay invents flying shuttle, which increases productive capacity of weavers.
1769	James Watt patents steam engine, which provided for the first time in history a steady and unlimited source of inanimate power.
1769	Richard Arkwright patents water frame, which permits the production of a purely cotton fabric, thus allowing large-scale textile manufacturing in factories.
1770	James Hargreaves patents spinning jenny, which allows for faster production of thread.

1776   Adam Smith publishes *The Wealth of Nations,* which develops the theory of capitalism, an economic system based on individual self-interest.

1787   Edmund Cartwright invents the power loom for machine, rather than hand, weaving.

1798   Thomas Malthus writes *Essay on the Principle of Population,* which contended that the plight of the working class could only become worse because the human population must eventually outstrip the food supply.

1817   David Ricardo's *Principles of Political Economy and Taxation* fashioned Malthus's theories into the "Iron Law of Wages."

1825   Death of Count Claude Henri de Saint-Simon, the earliest of socialist pioneers: private wealth, property, and enterprise should be subject to regulation.

1832   Great Reform Bill passed by British Parliament: eliminated "rotten boroughs" and extended franchise to a greater proportion of the middle class.

1833   Factory Act passed by British Parliament: limited the working hours of women and children in the textile mills and provided government inspection of the workplace.

1844   *The Conditions of the Working Class in England, in 1844* by Friedrich Engels, appears.

1848   *The Communist Manifesto,* by Karl Marx and Friedrich Engels, is published. Revolutions throughout Europe in support of liberal agendas are unsuccessful.

1858   Death of Robert Owen, a "Utopian Socialist," who believed that a proper working environment would improve human character. Through enlightened management, his New Lanark textile mills were successful and humanely operated.

1891   Pope Leo XIII issues the encyclical *Rerum Novarum,* which addresses the continuing struggle between capitalists and workers: brotherly love was preferable to ruthless competition and exploitation.

STUDY QUESTIONS

1. Discuss the plight of agricultural laborers as noted in the selection, "The Dependant Poor." How did displacement from the land affect the security of the family? What are the arguments of the Leeds Woollen Workers? Do you find them compelling? If you were a Leeds woollen merchant, how would you counter the workers' claims?

2. What was the "factory system"? How and why did it originate? What was it intended to do?

3. Do the descriptions of child labor and the testimony about degrading working conditions constitute a realistic and accurate portrayal of urban life during the Industrial Revolution? Or is this portrait an exaggeration? How does Engels's description of the impact of the factory system on women and the family seem to reflect some of the concerns of our contemporary society?

4. How does Andrew Ure defend the factory system? What specific points does he address? Are his arguments persuasive? Why or why not?

5. Discuss David Ricardo's ideas on the wages of laborers. Why were the poor laws to be regarded as destructive to the basic economic health of the state? Do you find his argument logical and compelling? Can you apply it to our contemporary society?

6. Who were the Chartists and what were their demands for reform? Was this a political or social reform program?

7. What was the attitude of Samuel Smiles toward the plight of the working class? Why would this opinion be considered "middle class"? What do you think of the principle of "self-help"?

8. What do you consider to be the most important ideas or statements that can be found in the excerpt on *The Communist Manifesto*? Why is this considered one of the most influential documents in Western Civilization?

9. What is Pope Leo XIII's basic argument concerning the relationship between capital and labor? What specific measures does he advocate? How do his ideals compare with those of Karl Marx or Robert Owen? Note especially his statement: "The great mistake . . . is to take up with the notion that class is naturally hostile to class, and that the wealthy and the working men are intended by nature to live in mutual conflict." Is this a naïve statement, or does the pope give a strong supporting argument?

10. How do you view the Industrial Revolution? Was it a progressive time that demonstrated human creativity, or was it born of human greed and exploitation of others who were less fortunate or less conscientious and determined to succeed? Is there always a price to pay in human suffering for a civilization to progress? How can you apply your ideas to our contemporary age?

5

Nationalism and Imperialism: The Motives and Methods of Expansion

Crimean War 1854-1856

Victor Emmanuel II proclaimed king of Italy 1861

Dual monarchy established in Austria-Hungary 1867

Franco-Prussian War 1870

Ministry of Disraeli in Britain 1874-1880

France controls Algeria 1882

Boer War in South Africa 1899

1850 — 1855 1860 1865 1870 1875 1880 1885 1890 1895 1900

Charles Darwin: *The Origin of Species* 1859

Otto von Bismarck becomes prime minister of Prussia 1862

Proclamation of German Empire at Versailles 1871

Ministry of Gladstone in Britain 1868-1874

Britain controls Suez 1875

Spanish-American War 1898

No other factor in history, not even religion, has produced so many wars as has the clash of national egotisms sanctified by the name of patriotism.

—Preserved Smith

Lust for dominion inflames the heart more than any other passion.

—Tacitus

The Englishman does everything on principle. He fights you on patriotic principles; he robs you on business principles; he enslaves you on imperial principles. . . . His watchword is always Duty; and he never forgets that the nation which lets its duty get on the side opposite to its interest is lost.

—Napoleon Bonaparte

The right of conquest has no foundation other than the right of the strongest.

—Jean Jacques Rousseau

When any group sees itself as the bearer of civilization, this very belief will betray it into behaving barbarously at the first opportunity.

—Simone Weil

CHAPTER THEMES

- *Imperialism:* How did the "New Imperialism" of the late-nineteenth century differ from the colonialism of the fifteenth through eighteenth centuries? What political conditions had changed which compelled European nations to establish their control abroad?

- *Church/State Relationships:* How did religious organizations encourage and support the various imperial efforts of European nations? What were the religious motives for controlling foreign populations? Was this blatantly hypocritical?

- *Beliefs and Spirituality:* How did nationalism and the fervent belief in the sanctity of one's national and ethnic origins both contribute to the progress of a unified Europe and lead to the degeneration of personal freedom?

- *Propaganda:* How was propaganda used to create images of peoples in Africa, India, and Asia that allowed European and American governments to justify their imperialistic control? How was science in particular distorted to create a new ethical perspective that made such expansion not just tolerable, but socially responsible?

- *Historical Change and Transition:* Are nationalism and imperialism such a part of human nature and social organization that they will always exist in some form? Is "extreme nationalism" a dangerous concept which led to World Wars I and II? To what extent are these elements at work in Serbia today?

- **The Big Picture:**   What is the relationship between nationalism and imperialism? Are they inextricably linked, and does one fuel the other? Are they progressive elements in history, or will they inevitably lead to a decline of Western Civilization?

Nationalism and imperialism were two of the most important factors that shaped the nineteenth century. These terms, however, are difficult to define and have been used so loosely as nearly to be deprived of meaning. Nationalism involves devotion, a patriotism that implies unity and constructive action in the service of one's country. Imperialism is a policy of extending a nation's authority by establishing political or economic control over another area or people. It is important to note that nationalism need not cause imperialism, but it promotes domestic unity, which is necessary for successful expansion. The term "expansion" is basically benign, connoting progress and dedication, but "imperialism" is often pejorative in connotation and recalls economic exploitation, racial prejudice, and even war. This chapter will seek to define more clearly the nature of nationalism and imperialism and to demonstrate how the two were inextricably linked during the nineteenth century.

Imperialism and nationalism were certainly not introduced in the nineteenth century. During the Renaissance and Reformation eras in the fifteenth and sixteenth centuries, countries such as Spain, France, and England, which had heretofore been decentralized feudal areas, were united under the leadership of strong monarchs. Although this unity was often achieved initially by the sword, the benefits of centralized rule soon became apparent. Unity fostered pride and cooperation among compatriots and soon provided the energy and direction that made possible an age of exploration and discovery.

In essence, the establishment of colonial empires was profitable and patriotic. But by the nineteenth century, the age of colonial empire-building was at an end. Spain, Portugal, and France had lost much of their old empires, Great Britain had lost her American colonies, and Germany was too divided internally to attempt to acquire new territory. Of the continental powers, only France under Napoleon was somewhat successful in establishing overseas colonies but realized only small gains. From 1800 to 1870, Britain acquired New Zealand, central Canada, and western Australia; however, these territories generally were contiguous to areas Britain already held. There was a great deal of missionary activity from Christian organizations but little overt government support.

This period of relative disinterest did not last long. Suddenly, between 1870 and 1900, there was a general outburst of imperialistic activity among the nations of Europe. France, Belgium, Britain, and Portugal made extensive gains, especially in Africa. By 1871, both Italy and Germany had been born as nations under the aggressive political and military leadership of Camillo Cavour (1810–1861) and Giuseppe Garibaldi (1807–1882) in the case of Italy, and Otto von Bismarck (1815–1898), the first chancellor of the German Empire. Appealing to abstractions such as "fate" and "duty," politicians immediately sought new territories that would keep them economically and politically competitive with the other nations of Europe. It has been estimated that in this thirty-year period from 1870 to 1900, Europeans expanded their colonial empires by over ten million square miles and nearly 150 million people. These intense economic rivalries were often expressed as well in political alliances. In 1882, the Triple Alliance was formed among Germany, Austria-Hungary, and Italy; in 1907, Great Britain, France, and Russia fashioned the Triple Entente. Such organized competition resulted in a polarization of European nations that contributed to the outbreak of World War I in 1914.

This drive for colonial acquisition was not limited to European powers, however. The United States had come of age in the mid-nineteenth century by expanding to its "natural boundaries" of Mexico and the Pacific. Impelled by the dictates of a policy called "manifest destiny," American settlers moved west in quest of new lives as farmers or in pursuit of gold in California. They were supported militarily by the American government and ideologically by Christian missionaries who saw westward expansion as the fulfillment of the destiny of the United States, so ordained by God. Thus were Indians dehumanized and sent to reservations, and thus was Texas taken from Mexico in 1845. This expansion, however, was essentially "domestic." The United States did not become involved in foreign adventures until 1898, when the Spanish-American War resulted in the cession of the Philippines. The same arguments used by Europeans to legitimate their rule were now employed by the United States.

The imperialism of the late-nineteenth century differed somewhat from the colonialism of the fifteenth to the eighteenth centuries. Earlier, nations had seized land with the intention of settling it with colonists or using it as a base from which to exploit the area economically. The "New Imperialism," as it was called, retained some of these goals, but also introduced new ones. European nations now invested capital in a "backward region" and set about building productive enterprises while also improving the area with hygienic and transportation facilities. In so doing, the colonial powers employed native labor and made cooperative arrangements with local rulers (through either enrichment or intimidation). Their main purpose was to control the region, and if such arrangements proved inadequate, the colonial power had other options, which frequently resulted in full annexation.

Our twentieth century has also seen its share of imperialism. Determined to secure Germany's "place in the sun," Kaiser Wilhelm II led Germany to war in 1914. Adolf Hitler resurrected a moribund German people, reminded them of their national heritage, gave them self-respect, and promised them more living space through expansion to "natural boundaries." Hitler's territorial demands could not be satisfied and became one of the primary causes of World War II. After Hitler's defeat in 1945, the Soviet Union and the United States moved from their role as allies to rivals in the scramble for territory and influence in the remains of war-ravaged Europe. In a more contemporary setting, the United States fought a war in Vietnam to maintain "principles of democracy" in a country seventy-five hundred miles from home. In 1979, the Soviet Union invaded Afghanistan and offered as justification the explanation that it was "asked in" by the Afghan people. In 1982, the Israelis invaded southern Lebanon in an attempt to eliminate dangerous Palestinian bases in the area; they ended up controlling Beirut itself. The United States in 1983 not only rescued American students from the perils of a coup d'état on the Caribbean island of Grenada, but also stayed to ensure the establishment of a democratic regime. Most recently, Panama was liberated from its dictator, Manuel Noriega, by U.S. forces in 1989, as was Kuwait from Saddam Hussein in 1991. The questions abound: What are the responsibilities of great powers? Impelled by their concept of rightness and geopolitical advantage, do "superpowers" constitute forces for civilization or obstructions to the principle of self-determination? Are they vanguards of freedom in crisis areas like Kosovo, or proponents of narrowly defined self-interest? It is important to gain the perspective that history offers.

Nationalism

The Unification of Italy

The Duties of Man
GIUSEPPE MAZZINI

Before Italy finally became a single, independent state under the pragmatic leadership of Count Camillo Cavour, unification was an ideal kept alive through the liberal beliefs of advocates such as Giuseppe Mazzini. Active in the 1830s and 1840s, Mazzini, through his writings, helped define a basis for unification and proved influential in establishing a liberal constitutional monarchy in Italy by 1870. The following selection is from his address to Italian workers.

Your first duties—first as regards importance—are, as I have already told you, towards Humanity. You are men before you are either citizens or fathers. Embrace the whole human family in your affection. Bear witness to your belief in the Unity of that family, consequent upon the Unity of God, and in that fraternity among the peoples which is destined to reduce that unity of action. . . .

But what can each of you, singly, do for the moral improvement and progress of Humanity? You can from time to time give sterile utterance to your belief; you may, on some rare occasions, perform some act of charity towards a brother man not belonging to your own land;—no more. But charity is not the watchword of the Faith of the Future. The watchword of the faith of the future is Association, and fraternal co-operation of all towards a common aim; and this is as far superior to all charity, as the edifice which all of you should unite to raise would be superior to the humble hut each one of you might build alone, or with the mere assistance of lending, and borrowing stone, mortar, and tools.

But, you tell me, you cannot attempt united action, distinct and divided as you are in language, customs, tendencies, and capacity. The individual is too insignificant, and Humanity too vast. . . .

This means was provided for you by God when he gave you a country; when, even as a wise overseer of labour distributes the various branches of

---

"The Duties of Man" is from Emilie Ashurst Venturi, *Joseph Mazzini: A Memoir* (London: Alexander and Shepherd, 1875), pp. 312–315.

employment according to the different capacities of the workmen, he divided Humanity into distinct groups or nuclei upon the face of the earth, thus creating the germ of Nationalities. Evil governments have disfigured the divine design. Nevertheless you may still trace it, distinctly marked out. . . . They have disfigured it by their conquests, their greed, and their jealousy even of the righteous power of others; disfigured it so far that if we except England and France—there is not perhaps a single country whose present boundaries correspond to that design.

These governments did not, and do not, recognize any country save their own families or dynasty, the egotism of caste. But the Divine design will infallibly be realized. Natural divisions, and the spontaneous, innate tendencies of the peoples, will take the place of the arbitrary divisions sanctioned by evil governments. The map of Europe will be re-drawn. The countries of the Peoples, defined by the vote of free men, will arise upon the ruins of the countries of kings and privileged castes, and between these countries harmony and fraternity will exist. And the common work of Humanity, of general amelioration and the gradual discovery and application of its Law of life, being distributed according to local development and advance. Then may each one of you, fortified by the power and the affection of many millions, all speaking the same language, gifted with the same tendencies, and educated by the same historical tradition, hope, even by your own single effort, to be able to benefit all Humanity.

O my brothers, love your Country! Our country is our Home, the house that God has given us, placing therein a numerous family that loves us, and whom we love; a family with whom we sympathise more readily, and whom we understand more quickly than we do others; and which, from its being centered round a given spot, and from the homogeneous nature of its elements, is adapted to a special branch of activity. Our country is our common workshop, whence the products of our activity are sent forth for the benefit of the whole world; wherein the tools and implements of labour we can most usefully employ are gathered together: nor may we reject them without disobeying the plan of the Almighty, and diminishing our own strength.

Proclamation for the Liberation of Sicily (1860)
GIUSEPPE GARIBALDI

One of Mazzini's most devoted disciples was Giuseppe Garibaldi (1807–1882). A man of action, he was also an adventurer of military ability who succeeded in gaining military support for the king of Piedmont, Victor Emmanuel. In 1860, he organized a volunteer force to invade Sicily and offered the following appeal to the people. Note the emphasis on goals that transcend the individual boundaries and responsibilities of the small regions that heretofore composed Italy. Garibaldi successfully gained control of both Sicily and Naples.

"Proclamation for the Liberation of Sicily" is from *Public Documents, The Annual Register, 1860* (London: 1861), pp. 281–282.

Italians!—The Sicilians are fighting against the enemies of Italy, and for Italy. It is the duty of every Italian to succour them with words, money, and arms, and, above all, in person.

The misfortunes of Italy arise from the indifference of one province to the fate of the others.

The redemption of Italy began from the moment that men of the same land ran to help their distressed brothers.

Left to themselves, the brave Sicilians will have to fight, not only the mercenaries of the Bourbon, but also those of Austria and the Priest of Rome.

Let the inhabitants of the free provinces lift their voices in behalf of their struggling brethren, and impel their brave youth to the conflict.

Let the Marches, Umbria, Sabina, Rome, the Neapolitan, rise to divide the forces of our enemies.

Where the cities suffice not for the insurrection, let them send bands of their bravest into the country.

The brave man finds an arm everywhere. Listen not to the voice of cowards, but arm, and let us fight for our brethren, who will fight for us tomorrow.

A band of those who fought with me the country's battles marches with me to the fight. Good and generous, they will fight for their country to the last drop of their blood, nor ask for other reward than a clear conscience.

"Italy and Victor Emmanuel!" they cried, on passing the Ticino. "Italy and Victor Emmanuel!" shall re-echo in the blazing caves of Mongibello.

At this cry, thundering from the great rock of Italy to the Tarpeian, the rotten Throne of tyranny shall crumble, and, as one man, the brave descendants of Vespro shall rise.

To Arms! Let me put an end, once and for all, to the miseries of so many centuries. Prove to the world that it is no lie that Roman generations inhabited this land.

Address to Parliament (1871)
KING VICTOR EMMANUEL

Through years of idealistic and impassioned speeches by people like Giuseppe Mazzini, diplomatic maneuvering by Camillo Cavour, and the exercise of military might by Giuseppe Garibaldi, Italy became a unified, independent state in 1870 under the leadership of Victor Emmanuel (1820–1878), former king of Piedmont. This excerpt from his address to the Italian Parliament in 1871 discusses some of the challenges that a new nation must face.

Senators and Deputies, gentlemen!

The work to which we consecrated our life is accomplished. After long trials of expiation Italy is restored to herself and to Rome. Here, where our

"Address to Parliament" is from Christine Walsh, ed., *Prologue: A Documentary History of Europe: 1846–1960.* Originally published by Cassell Australia Ltd. (1968), pp. 103–104. Reprinted by permission of Macmillan Publishing Company.

people, after centuries of separation, find themselves for the first time solemnly reunited in the person of their representatives: here where we recognize the fatherland of our dreams, everything speaks to us of greatness; but at the same time it all reminds us of our duties. The joy that we experience must not let us forget them. . . .

We have proclaimed the separation of Church and State. Having recognized the absolute independence of the spiritual authority, we are convinced that Rome, the capital of Italy, will continue to be the peaceful and respected seat of the Pontificate. . . .

Economic and financial affairs, moreover, claim our most careful attention. Now that Italy is established, it is necessary to make it prosperous by putting in order its finances; we shall succeed in this only by persevering in the virtues which have been the source of our national regeneration. Good finances will be the means of re-enforcing our military organization. Our most ardent desire is for peace, and nothing can make us believe that it can be troubled. But the organization of the army and the navy, the supply of arms, the works for the defense of the national territory, demand long and profound study. . . .

Senators and deputies, a vast range of activity opens before you; the national unity which is today attained will have, I hope, the effect of rendering less bitter the struggles of parties, the rivalry of which will have henceforth no other end than the development of the productive forces of the nation.

I rejoice to see that our population already gives unequivocal proofs of its love of work. The economic awakening is closely associated with the political awakening. The banks multiply, as do the commercial institutions, the expositions of the products of art and industry, and the congresses of the learned. We ought, you and I, to favor this productive movement while giving to professional and scientific education more attention and efficiency, and opening to commerce new avenues of communication and new outlets. . . .

A brilliant future opens before us. It remains for us to respond to the blessings of Providence by showing ourselves worthy of bearing among the nations the glorious names of Italy and Rome.

The Unification of Germany
The People and the Fatherland (1807–1808)
JOHANN GOTTLIEB FICHTE

Like Italy, Germany did not achieve unification until 1871. But there were those who provided the philosophical and idealistic foundation for later policies that would prove more practical. Johann Gottlieb Fichte delivered a series of addresses in 1807–1808 that disclose the frustration of German disunity and presage the

"The People and the Fatherland" is from Guy Carelton Lee, ed., *The World's Orators*, vol. 2 (New York: G. P. Putnam's Sons, 1900), pp. 190–193.

intense nationalism that was to erupt in the latter part of the nineteenth century, propelling Germany toward what Kaiser Wilhelm II would later call her "place in the sun."

Our oldest common ancestors, the original people of the new culture, the Teutons, called Germans by the Romans, set themselves bravely in opposition to the overwhelming worldwide rule of the Romans. Did they not see with their own eyes the finest blossom of the Roman provinces beside them, the finer enjoyment in the same, together with laws, courts of justice, lictors' staves and axes in superabundance? Were not the Romans ready and generous enough to let them share in all these benefits? Did they not see proof of the famous Roman clemency in the case of several of their own princes, who allowed themselves to think that war against such benefactors of the human race was rebellion? For the compliant were decorated with the title of king and rewarded with posts of importance as leaders in the Roman army, with Roman sacrificial wreaths; and when they were expelled by their countrymen, the Romans furnished them with a refuge and support in their colonies. Had they no appreciation of the advantages of Roman culture, for better organization of their armies, for example, in which even Arminius himself did not refuse to learn the art of war? It cannot be charged against them that in any one of these respects they were ignorant. Their descendants have appropriated that culture, as soon as they could do so without loss of their own freedom, and as far as it was possible without loss of their distinctive character. Wherefore, then, have they fought for so many generations in bloody wars which have been repeatedly renewed with undiminished fury? A Roman writer represents their leaders as asking if anything else remained for them but to maintain their freedom or to die before they became slaves. Freedom was their possession, that they might remain Germans, that they might continue to settle their own affairs independently and originally and in their own way, and at the same time to advance their culture and to plant the same independence in the hearts of their posterity. Slavery was what they called all the benefits which the Romans offered them, because through them they would become other than Germans, they would have to become semi-Romans. It was perfectly clear, they assumed, that every man, rather than become this, would die, and that a true German could wish to live only to be and to remain a German, and to have his sons the same.

They have not all died; they have not seen slavery; they have bequeathed freedom to their children. To their constant resistance the whole new world owes that it is as it is. Had the Romans succeeded in subjugating them also, and, as the Romans everywhere did, destroying them as a nation, the entire development of the human race would have taken a different direction, and it cannot be thought a better one. We who are the nearest heirs of their land, their language, and their sentiments, owe to them that we are still Germans, that the stream of original and independent life still bears us on; to them we owe that we have since then become a nation; to them, if now perhaps it is not at an end with us and the last drops of blood inherited from them are not dried in our veins, we owe all that which we have become. To them, even the other tribes, who have become to us aliens but through them our brethren, owe their existence; when they conquered eternal Rome, there were no others of all those peoples present; at that time was won for them the possibility of their future origin. . . .

These orations have attempted, by the only means remaining after others have been tried in vain, to prevent this annihilation of every noble action that may in the future arise among us, and this degradation of our entire nation. They have attempted to implant in your minds the deep and immovable foundations of the true and almighty love of the fatherland, in the conception of our nation as eternal and the people as citizens of our own eternity through the education of all hearts and minds.

"We Germans Fear God, and Naught Else in the World": Speech to the Reichstag (1888)
OTTO VON BISMARCK

In 1862, Otto von Bismarck was appointed prime minister of Prussia. At that time he declared that German unity would be realized "not by speeches and majorities . . . but by blood and iron." By 1871, after several wars, Bismarck had formed the unified fatherland of which Fichte had dreamed: The nation of Germany existed under the leadership of Kaiser Wilhelm I. The following excerpt is from Bismarck's speech to the Reichstag (parliament) in 1888. Unity demands great goals.

Great complications and all kinds of coalitions, which no one can foresee, are constantly possible, and we must be prepared for them. We must be so strong, irrespective of momentary conditions, that we can face any coalition with the assurance of a great nation which is strong enough under circumstances to take her fate into her own hands. We must be able to face our fate placidly with that self-reliance and confidence in God which are ours when we are strong and our cause is just. And the government will see to it that the German cause will be just always.

We must, to put it briefly, be as strong in these times as we possibly can be, and we can be stronger than any other nation of equal numbers in the world. I shall revert to this later—but it would be criminal if we were not to make use of our opportunity. If we do not need our full armed strength, we need not summon it. The only problem is the not very weighty one of money—not very weighty I say in passing, because I have no wish to enter upon a discussion of the financial and military figures, and of the fact that France has spent

"Speech to the Reichstag" is from pp. 290–293 of *The Age of Bismarck: Documents and Interpretations*, edited by T. S. Hamerow. Copyright © 1973 by T. S. Hamerow. Reprinted by permission of Harper & Row, Publishers, Inc.

Otto von Bismarck was a ruthless genius whose policy of German unification by "blood and iron" proved to have tremendous implications for the future. As Bismarck warned: "Attack the German nation anywhere, and you will find it armed to a man, and every man with the firm belief in his heart: God will be with us." (*Hader/Corbis*)

three milliards for the improvement of her armaments these last years, while we have spent scarcely one and one half milliards, including what we are asking of you at this time. But I leave the elucidation of this to the minister of war and the representatives of the treasury department.

When I say that it is our duty to endeavor to be ready at all times and for all emergencies, I imply that we must make greater exertions than other people for the same purpose, because of our geographical position. We are situated in the heart of Europe, and have at least three fronts open to an attack. France has only her eastern, and Russia only her western frontier where they may be attacked. We are also more exposed to the dangers of a coalition than any other nation, as is proved by the whole development of history, by our geographical position, and the lesser degree of cohesiveness, which until now has characterized the German nation in comparison with others. God has placed us where we are prevented, thanks to our neighbors, from growing lazy and dull. He has placed by our side the most warlike and restless of all nations, the French, and He has permitted warlike inclinations to grow strong in Russia, where formerly they existed to a lesser degree. Thus we are given the spur, so to speak, from both sides, and are compelled to exertions which we should perhaps not be making otherwise. The pikes in the European carp-pond are keeping us from being carps by making us feel their teeth on both sides. They also are forcing us to an exertion which without them we might not make, and to a union among us Germans, which is abhorrent to us at heart. By nature we are rather tending away, the one from the other. But the Franco-Russian press within which we are squeezed compels us to hold together, and by pressure our cohesive force is greatly increased. This will bring us to that state of being inseparable which all other nations possess, while we do not yet enjoy it. But we must respond to the intentions of Providence by making ourselves so strong that the pikes can do nothing but encourage us. . . .

If we Germans wish to wage a war with the full effect of our national strength, it must be a war which satisfies all who take part in it, all who sacrifice anything for it, in short the whole nation. It must be a national war, a war carried on with the enthusiasm of 1870, when we were foully attacked. I still remember the earsplitting, joyful shouts in the station at Köln. It was the same all the way from Berlin to Köln, in Berlin itself. The waves of popular approval bore us into the war, whether or not we wished it. That is the way it must be, if a popular force like ours is to show what it can do. . . . A war into which we are not borne by the will of the people will be waged, to be sure, if it has been declared by the constituted authorities who deemed it necessary; it will even be waged pluckily, and possibly victoriously, after we have once smelled fire and tasted blood, but it will lack from the beginning the nerve and enthusiasm of a war in which we are attacked. In such a one the whole of Germany from Memel to the Alpine Lakes will flare up like a powder mine; it will be bristling with guns, and no enemy will dare to engage this furor teutonicus which develops when we are attacked. We cannot afford to lose this factor of preeminence even if many military men—not only ours but others as well—believe that today we are superior to our future opponents. Our own officers believe this to a man, naturally. Every soldier believes this. He would almost cease to be a useful soldier if he did not wish for war, and did not believe that we would be victorious in it. If our opponents by any chance are thinking that we are pacific because we are afraid of how the war may end, they are mightily mistaken. We believe as firmly in our victory in a just cause as any foreign lieutenant in his garrison, after his third glass of champagne, can believe in his, and we probably do so with greater certainty. It is not fear, therefore, which makes us pacific, but the consciousness of our strength. We are strong enough to protect ourselves, even if we should be attacked at a less favorable moment, and we are in a position to let divine providence determine whether a war in the meanwhile may not become unnecessary after all.

I am, therefore, not in favor of any kind of an aggressive war, and if war could result only from our attack—somebody must kindle a fire, we shall not kindle it. Neither the consciousness of our strength, which I have described, nor our confidence in our treaties, will prevent us from continuing our former endeavors to preserve peace. In this we do not permit ourselves to be influenced by annoyances or dislikes. The threats and insults, and the challenges, which have been made have, no doubt, excited also with us a feeling of irritation, which does not easily happen with Germans, for they are less prone to national hatred than any other nation. We are, however, trying to calm our countrymen, and we shall work for peace with our neighbors, especially with Russia, in the future as in the past. . . .

We are easily influenced—perhaps too easily—by love and kindness, but quite surely never by threats! We Germans fear God, and naught else in the world! It is this fear of God which makes us love and cherish peace. If in spite of this anybody breaks the peace, he will discover that ardent patriotism . . . has today become the common property of the whole German nation. Attack the German nation anywhere, and you will find it armed to a man, and every man with the firm belief in his heart: God will be with us.

The Motives and Methods of Imperialism

Racism and the Corruption of Science

The Origin of Species (1859)

CHARLES DARWIN

Charles Darwin altered the main currents of human thought when he published The Origin of Species *in 1859. Before Darwin, the public believed that species of plants and animals had been created separately by God when he created the universe. Each species came into existence at once and had not changed since its creation. But Darwin's research led him to conclude that species of plants and animals had evolved by gradual and continuous changes which allowed them to adapt to their changing environments. Those species that were able to adapt were selected for survival, and those that failed simply perished. This thesis of "natural selection" gave rise to a host of popular slogans: "survival of the fittest" and "struggle of life." For some, evolution spelled inevitable progress. "There is warrant for the belief," wrote the influential philosopher Herbert Spencer, "that Evolution can end only in the establishment of the greatest perfection and the most complete happiness." But Darwin's work aroused bitter controversy because it contradicted the story of Genesis in the Bible and led to a continuing dispute between the competing demands of science and faith, which are still at issue today. Already in his* Origin of Species, *Darwin insisted on including humans in his theory. But it was not until 1871 that he published* The Descent of Man, *which bumped humankind from its preeminent position as God's most miraculous creation and connected it more intimately with chimpanzees.*

The following excerpts present Darwin's ideas regarding natural selection and its scientific application to the world at large. These ideas would soon be distorted and misapplied by "Social Darwinists" who sought to confirm racial superiority and to justify imperialism.

"The Origin of Species" is from Charles Darwin, *The Origin of Species* (London, 1859), pp. 606–610, 617–618.

New species have come on the stage slowly and at successive intervals; and the amount of change, after equal intervals of time, is widely different in different groups. The extinction of species and of whole groups of species which has played so conspicuous a part in the history of the organic world, almost inevitably follows from the principle of natural selection; for old forms are supplanted by new and improved forms. Neither single species nor groups of species reappear when the chain of ordinary generation is once broken. . . .

Recent forms are generally looked upon as being, on the whole, higher in the scale of organization than ancient forms; and they must be higher, in so far as the later and more improved forms have conquered the older and less improved forms in the struggle for life; they have also generally had their organs more specialized for different functions. This fact is perfectly compatible with numerous beings still retaining simple and but little improved structures, fitted for simple conditions of life. . . .

Why, it may be asked, until recently did nearly all the most eminent living naturalists and geologists disbelieve in the mutability of species? The belief that species were immutable productions was almost unavoidable as long as the history of the world was thought to be of short duration; and now that we have acquired some idea of the lapse of time, we are too apt to assume, without proof, that the geological record is so perfect that it would have afforded us plain evidence of the mutation of species, if they had undergone mutation.

But the chief cause of our natural unwillingness to admit that one species has given birth to clear and distinct species, is that we are always slow in admitting great changes of which we do not see the steps. . . . The mind cannot possibly grasp the full meaning of the term of even a million years; it cannot add up and perceive the full effects of many slight variations, accumulated during an almost infinite number of generations.

Although I am fully convinced of the truth of the views given in this volume, I by no means expect to convince experienced naturalists whose minds are stocked with a multitude of facts all viewed, during a long course of years, from a point of view directly opposite to mine. It is so easy to hide our ignorance under such expressions as the "plan of creation," "unity of design," etc., and to think that we give an explanation when we only restate a fact. Anyone whose disposition leads him to attach more weight to unexplained difficulties than to the explanation of a certain number of facts will certainly reject the theory. A few naturalists, endowed with much flexibility of mind, and who have already begun to doubt the immutability of species, may be influenced by this volume; but I look with confidence to the future—to young and rising naturalists, who will be able to view both sides of the question with impartiality. Whoever is led to believe that species are mutable will do good service by conscientiously expressing his conviction; for thus only can the load of prejudice by which this subject is overwhelmed be removed. . . .

It is interesting to contemplate a tangled bank, clothed with many plants of many kinds, with birds singing on the bushes, with various insects flitting about, and with worms crawling through the damp earth, and to reflect that these elaborately constructed forms, so different from each other and dependent upon each other in so complex a manner, have all been produced by laws acting around us. . . . Thus, from the war of nature, from famine and death, the most exalted object which we are capable of conceiving, namely, the production of the higher animals, directly follows. There is grandeur in this view of life, with its several powers, having been originally breathed by the Creator into a few forms or into one; and that, while this planet has gone cycling on according to the fixed law of gravity, from so simple a beginning endless forms most beautiful and most wonderful have been, and are being evolved.

The Descent of Man (1871)
CHARLES DARWIN

The main conclusion arrived at in this work, namely that man is descended from some lowly organized form, will, I regret to think be highly distasteful to many. But there can hardly be a doubt that we are descended from barbarians. The astonishment which I felt on first seeing a party of Fuegians on a wild and broken shore will never be forgotten by me, for the reflection at once rushed into my mind—such were our ancestors. These men were absolutely naked and bedaubed with paint, their long hair was tangled, their mouths frothed with excitement, and their expression was wild, startled, and distrustful. They possessed hardly any arts, and like wild animals lived on what they could catch; they had no government, and were merciless to every one not of their own small tribe. He who has seen a savage in his native land will not feel much shame, if forced to acknowledge that the blood of some more humble creature flows in his veins. For my own part I would as soon be descended from that heroic little monkey, who braved his dreaded enemy in order to save the life of his keeper, or from that old baboon, who descending from the mountains, carried away in triumph his young comrade from a crowd of astonished dogs—as from a savage who delights to torture his enemies, offers up bloody sacrifices, practices infanticide without remorse, treats his wives like slaves, knows no decency, and is haunted by the grossest superstitions.

Man may be excused for feeling some pride at having risen, though not through his own exertions, to the very summit of the organic scale; and the fact of his having thus risen, instead of having been aboriginally placed there, may give him hope for a still higher destiny in the distant future. But we are not here concerned with hopes or fears, only with the truth as far as our reason permits us to discover it; and I have given the evidence to the best of my ability. We must, however, acknowledge, as it seems to me, that man with all

"The Descent of Man" is from Charles Darwin, *The Descent of Man*, vol. 2 (New York: P. F. Collier and Son, 1874), pp. 796–797.

his noble qualities, with sympathy which feels for the most debased, with benevolence which extends not only to other men but to the humblest living creature, with his god-like intellect which has penetrated into the movements and constitution of the solar system—with all these exalted powers—Man still bears in his bodily frame the indelible stamp of his lowly origin.

Our Country (1885)
JOSIAH STRONG

In general, imperialistic nations have felt compelled to justify their actions by ex-plaining why they have taken control of territory or populations. One of the most popular justifications has been the policy of Social Darwinism, a vulgarization of the scientific theory of Charles Darwin contained in The Origin of Species *(1859). Social Darwinists held that only the fittest peoples would survive and that "lesser breeds" would of necessity perish or be taken over. Indeed, some ar-gued that an empire was a living organism that must either grow or die. Racism, therefore, provided a potent thrust to imperial expansion. The first selection, by American clergyman Josiah Strong (1847–1916), is typical of the racist argu-ment. The second excerpt is from a lecture delivered in 1900 by the German scien-tist Karl Pearson, who presents racism as being consistent with the directives of nature.*

God, with infinite wisdom and skill, is training the Anglo-Saxon race for an hour sure to come in the world's future. Heretofore there has always been in the history of the world a comparatively unoccupied land westward, into which the crowded countries of the East have poured their surplus popula-tions. But the widening waves of migration, which millenniums ago rolled east and west from the valley of the Euphrates meet to-day on our Pacific coast. There are no more new worlds. . . . The time is coming when the pres-sure of population on the means of subsistence will be felt here as it is now felt in Europe and Asia. Then will the world enter upon a new stage of its his-tory—the final competition of races, for which the Anglo-Saxon is being schooled. Long before the thousand millions are here, the mighty centrifugal tendency, inherent in this stock and strengthened in the United States, will assert itself. Then this race of unequaled energy, with all the majesty of num-bers and the might of wealth behind it—the representative, let us hope, of the largest liberty, the purest Christianity, the highest civilization—having de-veloped peculiarly aggressive traits calculated to impress its institutions upon mankind, will spread itself over the earth. If I read not amiss, this powerful race will move down upon Mexico, down upon Central and South America, out upon the islands of the sea, over upon Africa and beyond. And can any

"Our Country" is from Josiah Strong, *Our Country* (New York: The Baker and Taylor Publish-ing Company, 1885), pp. 174–178.

one doubt that the result of this competition of races will be the "survival of the fittest"? . . . Nothing can save the inferior race but a ready and pliant assimilation. Whether the feebler and more abject races are going to be regenerated and raised up, is already very much of a question. What if it should be God's plan to people the world with better and finer material? Certain it is, whatever expectations we may indulge, that there is a tremendous overbearing surge of power in the Christian nations, which, if the others are not speedily raised to some vastly higher capacity, will inevitably submerge and bury them forever. . . . To this result no war of extermination is needful; the contest is not one of arms, but of vitality and of civilization. "At the present day," says Mr. Darwin, "civilized nations are everywhere supplanting barbarous nations. . . ."

Some of the stronger races, doubtless, may be able to preserve their integrity; but, in order to compete with the Anglo-Saxon, they will probably be forced to adopt his methods and instruments, his civilization and his religion. . . . The contact of Christian with heathen nations is awakening the latter to new life. Old superstitions are loosening their grasp. The dead crust of fossil faiths is being shattered by the movements of life underneath. In Catholic countries, Catholicism is losing its influence over educated minds, and in some cases the masses have already lost all faith in it. Thus, while on this continent God is training the Anglo-Saxon race for its mission, a complemental work has been in progress in the great world beyond. God has two hands. Not only is He preparing in our civilization the die with which to stamp the nations, but . . . he is preparing mankind to receive our impress.

Is there room for reasonable doubt that this race, unless devitalized by alcohol and tobacco, is destined to dispossess many weaker races, assimilate others, and mold the remainder, until, in a very true and important sense, it has Anglo-Saxonized mankind?

The Standpoint of Science (1900)
KARL PEARSON

How many centuries, how many thousand of years, have the Kaffir or the Negro held large districts in Africa undisturbed by the white man? Yet their intertribal struggles have not yet produced a civilization in the least comparable with the Aryan. Educate and nurture them as you will, I do not believe that you will succeed in modifying the stock. History shows me one way, and one way only, in which a high state of civilization has been produced, namely, the struggle of race with race, and the survival of the physically and mentally fitter race. If you want to know whether the lower races of man can evolve a higher type, I fear the only course is to leave them to fight it out among

"The Standpoint of Science" is from Karl Pearson, *National Life from the Standpoint of Science,* 2nd ed. (Cambridge: Cambridge University Press, 1907), pp. 21–25.

themselves, and even then the struggle for existence between individual and individual, between tribe and tribe, may not be supported by that physical selection due to a particular climate on which probably so much of the Aryan's success depended.

If you bring the white man into contact with the black, you too often suspend the very process of natural selection on which the evolution of a higher type depends. You get superior and inferior races living on the same soil, and that coexistence is demoralizing for both. They naturally sink into the position of master and servant, if not admittedly or covertly into that of slave-owner and slave. Frequently they inter-cross, and if the bad stock be raised the good is lowered. Even in the case of Eurasians, of whom I have met mentally and physically fine specimens, I have felt how much better they would have been had they been pure Asiatics or pure Europeans. Thus it comes about that when the struggle for existence between races is suspended, the solution of great problems may be unnaturally postponed; instead of the slow, stern processes of evolution, cataclysmal solutions are prepared for the future. Such problems in suspense, it appears to me, are to be found in the Negro population of the Southern States of America, in the large admixture of Indian blood in some of the South American races, but, above all, in the Kaffir factor in South Africa.

You may possibly think that I am straying from my subject, but I want to justify natural selection to you. I want you to see selection as something which renders the inexorable law of heredity a source of progress which produces the good through suffering, an infinitely greater good which far outbalances the very obvious pain and evil. Let us suppose the alternative were possible. Let us suppose we could prevent the white man, if we liked, from going to lands of which the agricultural and mineral resources are not worked to the full; then I should say a thousand times better for him that he should not go than that he should settle down and live alongside the inferior race. The only healthy alternative is that he should go and completely drive out the inferior race. That is practically what the white man has done in North America. . . . The civilization of the white man is a civilization dependent upon free white labour, and when that element of stability is removed it will collapse like those of Greece and Rome. I venture to assert, then, that the struggle for existence between white and red man, painful and even terrible as it was in its details, has given us a good for outbalancing its immediate evil. In place of the red man, contributing practically nothing to the work and thought of the world, we have a great nation, mistress of many arts, and able, with its youthful imagination and fresh, untrammeled impulses, to contribute much to the common stock of civilized man. Against that we have only to put the romantic sympathy for the Red Indian generated by the novels of Cooper and the poems of Longfellow, and then—see how little it weighs in the balance! . . .

You will see that my view—and I think it may be called the scientific view of a nation—is that of an organized whole, kept up to a high pitch of internal efficiency by insuring that its numbers are substantially recruited from the better stocks, and kept up to a high pitch of external efficiency by contest, chiefly by way of war with inferior races, and with equal races by the struggle for trade-routes and for the sources of raw material and of food supply. This is the natural history view of mankind, and I do not think you can in its main features subvert it. Some of you may refuse to acknowledge it, but you cannot really study history and refuse to see its force. Some of you may realize it, and then despair of life; you may decline to admit any glory in a world where the superior race must either eject the inferior, or, mixing with it, or even living alongside it, degenerate itself. What beauty can there be when the battle is to the stronger, and the weaker must suffer in the struggle of nations and in the struggle of individual men? You may say: Let us cease to struggle; let us leave the lands of the world to the races that cannot profit by them to the full; let us cease to compete in the markets of the world. Well, we could do it, if we were a small nation living off the produce of our own soil, and a soil so worthless that no other race envied it and sought to appropriate it. We should cease to advance; but then we should naturally give up progress as a good which comes through suffering. I say it is impossible for a small rural community to stand apart from the world-contest and to stagnate, if no more powerful nation wants its possessions.

War and Civilization (1895)

CHARLES MORRIS

In the first selection, Charles Morris, a popularizer of Social Darwinist theories, argues that war is a progressive force in civilization. The second account is by Sir Harry Johnston, a British explorer and administrator in central and eastern Africa at the turn of the century, who actually calculated the percentage of "civilization" inherent in various cultures.

It may seem to many readers absurd to speak of war as a helpful agency in civilization. It is the general impression that a state of profound peace, with its consequent agricultural and mechanical industries, is most conducive to human advancement. Warfare is usually looked upon as simply destructive, and as destitute of any redeeming feature; and yet I venture to claim that all the civilizations to-day existing were in their origin largely the results of ancient wars; and that peace, in the long past of the human race, was almost a synonym for social and intellectual stagnation. . . .

If we ask what is the philosophy of this, the answer may not be difficult to reach. Unlike the fixed conservatism of peace, war introduces new conditions, new foundations for human thought, on which the edifice of future civilization may be erected; and, breaking up the isolation of peace, it spreads these conditions throughout the world, making distant nations participants in their influences. The progress of mankind means simply the development of the human mind. Ideas are the seeds of civilization, and under whatever form it appears

"War and Civilization" is from Charles Morris, "War As a Factor in Civilization," *Popular Science Monthly* 47 (1895), pp. 823, 826.

the idea must be born first, the embodiment must come afterward. In seeking for the causes of advancement, then, we must seek for the sources of new ideas; but, as experience lies at the root of ideas, new ideas can only arise from new experiences. Whence, then, do we derive our experiences? No isolated individual can learn much of himself. His own powers of observation and thought are limited. Our minds can only rapidly develop when we avail ourselves of the experience of others. In this way only can they become storehouses of new thoughts. There is a common stock of such thought abroad in the world, from which we derive the great mass of the ideas which we call our own. And, obviously, that mind will be most developed which comes into contact with and assimilates the greatest number of these thoughts.

The same holds good with nations. An isolated nation is in the same position as an isolated individual. Its experiences are limited, its ideas few and narrow in range. Its thoughts move in one fixed channel, and the other powers of its mind are apt to become virtually aborted. An isolated nation, then, is not likely rapidly to gain new ideas. Yet peace, in all barbarian and semicivilized nations, seems to tend strongly toward this condition of isolation; and such isolation in its conservative influence is a fatal bar to any wide or continuous progress. The long persistence of one form of government, of one condition of social customs, of one line of thought, tends to produce that uniformity of character which is so fatally opposed to any width of development of breadth of mental grasp. From uniformity arises stagnation. Its final result is a dead pause in mental advancement. Variety of influences and conditions alone can yield a healthy and vigorous growth of thought. The movement of the national mind in any one line must soon cease. Its limit is quickly reached, unless it be aided by development in other directions.

The Backward Peoples (1920)
SIR HARRY JOHNSTON

[L]et us proceed to define who and what these backward or unprogressive peoples are and to what extent they may be considered to be retrograde and ineffective as compared with the dominating white race. The chief and obvious distinction between the backward and forward peoples is that the former, with the exception of about 20,000,000 in the Mediterranean basin and the Near East, are of coloured skin; while the latter are white-skinned, or, as in the case of the Japanese and the inhabitants of Northern China, nearly white.

I think if we took all the factors into consideration—religion, education (especially knowledge concerning the relations between this planet and the universe of which it is a minute speck, the history and geography of the planet, the sciences that are a part of earth-study), standard of living, respect for sanitation, infant death rate, bodily strength, manner of government,

"The Backward Peoples" is from Sir Harry Johnston, *The Backward Peoples and Our Relations with Them* (London: Oxford University Press, 1920), pp. 7–9.

regard for law and order, position in agriculture and manufactures,—we might appraise mathematically, according to the following ratio, the principal nations and peoples into which humanity is divided:

100 per cent.

1. Great Britain and Ireland, Canada and Newfoundland, White Australia, New Zealand, White South Africa (south of the Zambezi), Malta and Mauritius, United States, France, Corsica, much of Algeria and Tunis, Belgium and Luxembourg, Holland, Germany, Austria, Chekho-Slovakia, Italy, Switzerland, Hungary, Norway, Sweden, Denmark and Iceland, Finland, Estonia, Spain, Chile, Argentina, Japan

98 per cent.

2. Poland and Lithuania, Serbia and Croatia, Bulgaria, Rumania, Portugal, Greece, Cyprus, Brazil, Peru, Colombia, British Guiana, French and Dutch Guiana, British and French West Indies, Cuba and Puerto Rico, Hawaii, Uruguay

97 per cent.

3. Russia, Russian Siberia, Russian Central Asia, the Caucasus, Egypt, British India, French Indo-China, Siam, British Malaysia, Mexico, Central America, Bolivia, Venezuela, Ecuador, Paraguay, Java, . . . Armenia

95 per cent.

4. Albania, Asia Minor, Morocco, Southern Algeria, Tripoli, Palestine, Syria, Persia, China, Tibet, Afghanistan, Zanzibar

90 per cent.

5. Madagascar, Black South Africa, French West Africa, British West Africa, Uganda, British Central and East Africa, Sumatra, Borneo, the Philippines, the Anglo-Egyptian Sudan, Angola, Santo Domingo

80 per cent.

6. Abyssinia, Arabia, Portuguese East Africa, the Belgian Congo, Portuguese Congo, Liberia, Haiti, Celebes, Timor, New Caledonia, British Papas

75 per cent.

7. Dutch New Guinea and New Hebrides, Portuguese Guinea, French Central Africa

This rough estimate of civilization and culture does not imply that the nations or peoples which are classed together resemble one another in all their stages of culture. Some will excel in one direction, some in another. In certain directions a people may be very forward, coupled with retrograde features which reduce their average value.

Obviously, the foremost nations in the world at the present day are Britain and the regions of the British Empire in which the white race predominates; the United States; France; and Germany,—not only by the numbers of their peoples and the degree of their national wealth, but by their industry, commerce and the proportion of educated to uneducated people in the population. In all elements of greatness, but not in potency of numbers, Denmark, Sweden, Norway, Finland, Holland, Luxembourg and Belgium, are on an equal footing. From their magnificent parts in history one would like to class Spain, Portugal and Italy with these powers of the first rank. . . .

It is the peoples of 95 per cent. to 90 per cent. that may be put in the unprogressive or retrograde class, unable at present to govern themselves in a manner conducive to progress; while those that are graded 80 to 75 per cent. still contain in their midst elements of sheer savagery. Such regions, if left alone by the controlling white men, might easily relapse into the unprofitable barbarism out of which they have been lifted with the white man's efforts during the past fifty years.

For God and Country
The Mandate System: Britain's Duty in Egypt (1890)
JOSEPH CHAMBERLAIN

The British in the late-nineteenth century often justified their imperialism on the premise of duty. As a civilized power, it was imperative that they spread God's word and the fruits of civilization to those peoples who were not sufficiently advanced to develop them on their own. In essence, Britain held a nation "in trust" until the backward peoples could be educated and made ready to assume the responsibilities of self-government. The "mandate system," as it came to be called, is described in the following excerpt by the liberal statesman Joseph Chamberlain (1836–1914). The motive for British expansion in Egypt was not completely altruistic, however. Britain also wanted to protect the strategic Suez Canal, which controlled access to the riches of Britain's empire in India and the Far East. In 1882, Britain occupied Cairo and set about reorganizing the country. Chamberlain's address to Parliament must also be viewed in this light.

"The Mandate System: Britain's Duty in Egypt" is from Joseph Chamberlain, *Foreign and Colonial Speeches* (London: George Routledge and Sons, 1897), pp. 41–44.

I want to say a word or two to you about the future. I am going to make a confession. I admit I was one of those—I think my views were shared by the whole Cabinet of Mr. Gladstone—who regretted the necessity for the occupation of Egypt. I thought that England had so much to do, such enormous obligations and responsibilities, that we might well escape, if we could, this addition to them; and, when the occupation was forced upon us, I looked forward with anxiety to an early, it might be even, to an immediate evacuation. The confession I have to make is that having seen what are the results of this occupation, having seen what is the nature of the task we have undertaken, and what progress we have already made towards its accomplishment, I have changed my mind. (Cheers.) I say it would be unworthy of this great nation if we did not rise to the full height of our duty, and complete our work before we left the country. (Cheers.) We have no right to abandon the duty which has been cast upon us, and the work which already shows so much promise for the advantage of the people with whose destinies we have become involved.

This great alteration is due to the influence of a mere handful of your fellow-countrymen. . . . They, by their persevering devotion, and their single-minded honesty, have wrought out this great work, and have brought Egypt from a condition which may fairly be described as one of ruin, to the promise of once more being restored to its ancient prosperity. I hear sometimes of pessimists who think the work of England is accomplished, who will tell you that we have lost the force and the capacity to govern. No; that is not true; and as long as we can spare from our abundance men like these, who, after all, are only ordinary Englishmen—men like these, who are able and willing to carry their zeal and their intelligence wherever it may conduce to the service of humanity, and to the honour of their native land—so long as we can do that we need not despair of the future of the United Kingdom. (Cheers.) But we owe it to them, we owe it to ourselves, that their work shall not be in vain. You cannot revolutionise a country like Egypt—you cannot reform all that is wrong in her system, all that is poor and weak in the character of the people—in a few minutes, or a few years. Egypt has been submitted for centuries to arbitrary despotism. I believe there is hardly any time in her history, even if you go back to almost prehistoric ages, when she has not been in the grasp of some foreign ruler; and, under these circumstances, you cannot expect to find ready to your hands a self-governing people. They are not able—they cannot be able—to stand alone; and they do not wish to stand alone. They ask for your support and assistance, and without it, it is absolutely impossible that their welfare can be secured. If you were to abandon your responsibility, your retirement would be followed by an attempt once more to restore the old arbitrary methods and the old abuses, which in turn would no doubt be followed by anarchy and disorder; and then in time there would be again a foreign intervention, this time the intervention of some other European country. I have too much confidence in the public spirit of the country to believe that it will ever neglect a national duty. (Hear, hear.) A nation is like an individual; it has duties which it must fulfill, or else it cannot live honoured and respected as a nation. (Loud cheers.)

American Imperialism in the Philippines (1900)
ALBERT J. BEVERIDGE

*Through much of the nineteenth century, the United States was involved with es-
tablishing its own borders "from sea to shining sea," but did not try to expand in-
ternationally. In 1898, however, because of the Spanish-American War, the
United States inaugurated a policy of foreign imperialism. One of the Spanish
colonies ceded to the United States was the Philippine Islands. There was a
strong independence movement in the islands, however, and actual warfare
broke out in 1899 between Filipinos and American forces. Congress was divided
about setting up a government for the newly acquired territory. One of the champions of imperialism was Albert J. Beveridge, senator from Indiana. In January
1900, he addressed Congress in support of a resolution that decreed that the
United States "establish and maintain such government control throughout the
archipelago as the situation may demand."*

Mr. President, the times call for candor. The Philippines are ours forever,
"territory belonging to the United States," as the Constitution calls them.
And just beyond the Philippines are China's illimitable markets. We will not
retreat from either. We will not repudiate our duty in the archipelago. We
will not abandon our opportunity in the Orient. We will not renounce our
part in the mission of our race, trustee under God, of the civilization of the
world. And we will move forward to our work, not howling our regrets like
slaves whipped to their burdens, but with gratitude for a task worthy of our
strength, and thanksgiving to Almighty God that He has marked us as His
chosen people, henceforth to lead in the regeneration of the world. . . .

Senators, it would be better to abandon this combined garden and Gibral-
tar of the Pacific, and count our blood and treasure already spent a profitable
loss, than to apply any academic arrangement of self-government to these
children. They are not capable of self-government. How could they be? They
are not of a self-governing race. They are Orientals, Malays, instructed by
Spaniards in the latter's worst estate.

They know nothing of practical government except as they have witnessed
the weak, corrupt, cruel, and capricious rule of Spain. What magic will anyone employ to dissolve in their minds and characters those impressions of
governors and governed which three centuries of misrule have created? What
alchemy will change the Oriental quality of their blood and set the self-
governing currents of the American pouring through their Malay veins? How
shall they, in the twinkling of an eye, be exalted to the heights of self-governing peoples which required a thousand years for us to reach, Anglo-Saxon
though we are? . . .

"American Imperialism in the Philippines" is from *Congressional Record*, vol. 33 (1900), pp.
704–705, 708, 710–712.

Mr. President, self-government and internal development have been the dominant notes of our first century; administration and the development of other lands will be the dominant notes of our second century. And administration is as high and holy a function as self-government, just as the care of a trust estate is as sacred an obligation as the management of our own concerns. . . .

The Declaration of Independence does not forbid us to do our part in the regeneration of the world. If it did, the Declaration would be wrong, just as the Articles of Confederation, drafted by the very same men who signed the Declaration, were found to be wrong. The Declaration has no application to the present situation. It was written by self-governing men for self-governing men. . . .

Mr. President, this question is deeper than any question of party politics; deeper than any question of the isolated policy of our country even; deeper even than any question of constitutional power. It is elemental. It is racial. God has not been preparing the English-speaking and Teutonic peoples for a thousand years for nothing but vain and idle self-contemplation and self-admiration. No! He has made us the master organizers of the world to establish system where chaos reigns. He has given the spirit of progress to overwhelm the forces of reaction throughout the earth. He has made us adept in government that we may administer government among savage and senile peoples. Were it not for such a force as this the world would relapse into barbarism and night. And of all our race He has marked the American people as His chosen nation to finally lead in the regeneration of the world. This is the divine mission of America, and it holds for us all the profit, all the glory, all the happiness possible to man. We are trustees of the world's progress, guardians of its righteous peace. The judgment of the Master is upon us: "Ye have been faithful over a few things; I will make you ruler over many things."

What shall history say of us? Shall it say that we renounced that holy trust, left the savage to his base condition, the wilderness to the reign of waste, deserted duty, abandoned glory, forgot our sordid profit even, because we feared our strength and read the charter of our powers with the doubter's eye and the quibbler's mind? Shall it say that, called by events to captain and command the proudest, ablest, purest race of history in history's noblest work, we declined that great commission? Our fathers would not have had it so. No! They founded no paralytic government, incapable of the simplest acts of administration. They planted no sluggard people, passive while the world's work calls them. They established no reactionary nation. They unfurled no retreating flag. . . .

Blind indeed is he who sees not the hand of God in events so vast, so harmonious, so benign. Reactionary indeed is the mind that perceives not that this vital people is the strongest of the saving forces of the world; that our place, therefore, is at the head of the constructing and redeeming nations of the earth; and that to stand aside while events march on is a surrender of our interests, a betrayal of our duty as blind as it is base. Craven indeed is the heart that fears to perform a work so golden and so noble; that dares not win a glory so immortal. . . .

Mr. President and Senators, adopt the resolution offered, that peace may quickly come and that we may begin our saving, regenerating, and uplifting work. . . . Reject it, and the world, history, and the American people will know where to forever fix the awful responsibility for the consequences that will surely follow such failure to do our manifest duty. How dare we delay when our soldiers' blood is flowing?

The White Man's Burden (1899)

RUDYARD KIPLING

In commemoration of successful U.S. imperialism in the Philippines, the great British poet Rudyard Kipling wrote "The White Man's Burden" in 1899. It reflects a devotion to the demands of empire and the duty of civilized nations. In Kipling's eyes, imperialism was a nationalistic venture—a heroic necessity.

Take up the White Man's burden—
Send forth the best ye breed—
Go bind your sons to exile
To serve your captive's need;
To wait in heavy harness,
On fluttered folk and wild—
Your new-caught, sullen peoples,
Half-devil and half-child.

Take up the White Man's burden—
In patience to abide,
To veil the threat of terror
And check the show of pride;
By open speech and simple,
An hundred times made plain
To seek another's profit,
And work another's gain.

Take up the White Man's burden—
The savage wars of peace—
Fill full the mouth of Famine
And bid the sickness cease;
And when your goal is nearest
The end for others sought,
Watch sloth and heathen Folly
Bring all your hopes to nought.

"The White Man's Burden" is from Rudyard Kipling, *Collected Verse* (New York: Doubleday and Page, 1911), pp. 215–217.

A British Officer in India, ca. 1870: "Take up the White Man's burden / And reap his old reward: / The blame of those ye better, / The hate of those ye guard."—Rudyard Kipling *(Liaison Agency, Inc.)*

Take up the White Man's burden—
No tawdry rule of kings,
But toil of serf and sweeper—
The tale of common things.
The ports ye shall not enter,
The roads ye shall not tread,
Go make them with your living,
And mark them with your dead.

Take up the White Man's burden—
And reap his old reward:
The blame of those ye better,
The hate of those ye guard—
The cry of hosts ye humour
(Ah, slowly!) toward the light:—
'Why brought he us from bondage,
Our loved Egyptian night?'

Take up the White Man's burden—
Ye dare not stoop to less—
Nor call too loud on Freedom
To cloke your weariness;
By all ye cry or whisper,
By all ye leave or do,
The silent, sullen peoples
Shall weigh your gods and you.

Take up the White Man's burden—
Have done with childish days—
The lightly proferred laurel,
The easy, ungrudged praise.
Comes now, to search your manhood
Through all the thankless years,
Cold, edged with dear-bought wisdom,
The judgment of your peers!

The Economic Argument

Probably the most obvious motive for imperialism is in the economic profit to be made from the colonization of territory and the subjugation of people. Sir Frederick Lugard, British soldier and administrator of some of Britain's colonial possessions in the late-nineteenth century, analyzes the "scramble for Africa."

"A Natural Inclination to Submit to a Higher Authority" (1893)

SIR FREDERICK DEALTRY LUGARD

The Chambers of Commerce of the United Kingdom have unanimously urged the retention of East Africa on the grounds of commercial advantage. The Presidents of the London and Liverpool chambers attended a deputation to her Majesty's Minister for Foreign Affairs to urge "the absolute necessity, for the prosperity of this country, that new avenues for commerce such as that in East Equatorial Africa should be opened up, in view of the hostile tariffs with which British manufacturers are being everywhere confronted." Manchester followed with a similar declaration; Glasgow, Birmingham, Edinburgh, and other commercial centres gave it as their opinion that "there is practically no middle course for this country, between a reversal of the freetrade policy to which it is pledged, on the one hand, and a prudent but continuous territorial extension for the creation of new markets, on the other hand. . . ."

The "Scramble for Africa" by the nations of Europe—an incident without parallel in the history of the world—was due to the growing commercial rivalry, which brought home to civilised nations the vital necessity of securing the only remaining fields for industrial enterprise and expansion. It is well, then, to realise that it is for our advantage—and not alone at the dictates of duty—that we have undertaken responsibilities in East Africa. It is in order to

"'A Natural Inclination to Submit to a Higher Authority'" is from Sir Frederick Dealtry Lugard, *The Rise of Our East African Empire*, vol. 1 (London: William Blackwood and Sons, 1893), pp. 379–382.

foster the growth of the trade of this country, and to find an outlet for our manufactures and our surplus energy, that our far-seeing statesmen and our commercial men advocate colonial expansion. . . .

There are some who say we have no right in Africa at all, that "it belongs to the natives." I hold that our right is the necessity that is upon us to provide for our ever-growing population—either by opening new fields for emigration, or by providing work and employment which the development of oversea extension entails—and to stimulate trade by finding new markets, since we know what misery trade depression brings at home.

While thus serving our own interests as a nation, we may, by selecting men of the right stamp for the control of new territories, bring at the same time many advantages to Africa. Nor do we deprive the natives of their birthright of freedom, to place them under a foreign yoke. It has ever been the key-note of British colonial method to rule through and by the natives, and it is this method, in contrast to the arbitrary and uncompromising rule of Germany, France, Portugal, and Spain, which has been the secret of our success as a colonising nation, and has made us welcomed by tribes and peoples in Africa, who ever rose in revolt against the other nations named. In Africa, moreover, there is among the people a natural inclination to submit to a higher authority. That intense detestation of control which animates our Teutonic races does not exist among the tribes of Africa, and if there is any authority that we replace, it is the authority of the Slavers and Arabs, or the intolerable tyranny of the "dominant tribe."

Power and Pride

The next three selections comment on another motive for imperialism. The desire for power can be justified through the pride that one has in one's nation. Nationalism and imperialism seem to be intimately connected. The first selection, by John Louis O'Sullivan, promotes the concept of "manifest destiny," which legitimized the American annexation of land as settlers moved west. The fulfillment of the "destiny" of the nation necessarily involved the sacrifice of Mexican and Indian populations in Texas and throughout the plains.

Manifest Destiny: The Annexation of Texas (1845)
JOHN LOUIS O'SULLIVAN

Texas is now ours. . . . It is wholly untrue, and unjust to ourselves, the pretence that the Annexation has been a measure of spoliation, unrightful and

"Manifest Destiny: The Annexation of Texas" is from *The United States Magazine and Democratic Review*, vol. 17, no. 85 (1845).

unrighteous—of military conquest under forms of peace and law—of territorial aggrandizement at the expense of justice, and justice due by a double sanctity to the weak. This view of the question is wholly unfounded, and has been before so amply refuted in these pages, as well as in a thousand other modes, that we shall not again dwell upon it. The independence of Texas was complete and absolute. It was an independence, not only in fact but of right. . . .

Texas has been absorbed into the Union in the inevitable fulfillment of the general law which is rolling our population westward; the connection of which with that ratio of growth in population which is destined within a hundred years to swell our numbers to the enormous population of two hundred and fifty millions (if not more), is too evident to leave us in doubt of the manifest design of Providence in regard to the occupation of this continent. It was disintegrated from Mexico in the natural course of events, by a process perfectly legitimate on its own part, blameless on ours; and in which all the censures due to wrong, perfidy and folly, rest on Mexico alone. And possessed as it was by a population which was in truth but a colonial detachment from our own, and which was still bound by myriad ties of the very heart-strings to its old relations, domestic and political, their incorporation into the Union was not only inevitable, but the most natural, right and proper thing in the world—and it is only astonishing that there should be any among ourselves to say it nay. . . .

California will, probably, next fall away from the loose adhesion which, in such a country as Mexico, holds a remote province in a slight equivocal kind of dependence on the metropolis. Imbecile and distracted, Mexico never can exert any real governmental authority over such a country. A population will soon be in actual occupation of California, over which it will be idle for Mexico to dream of dominion. They will necessarily become independent. Whether they will then attach themselves to our Union or not, is not to be predicted with any certainty. Unless the projected railroad across the continent to the Pacific be carried into effect, perhaps they may not; though even in that case, the day is not distant when the Empires of the Atlantic and Pacific would again flow together into one, as soon as their inland border should approach each other. . . .

Away then with all idle French talk of balances of power on the American Continent. There is no growth in Spanish America! Whatever progress of population there may be in the British Canada, is only for their own early severance of their present colonial relation to the little island three thousand miles across the Atlantic; soon to be followed by Annexation, and destined to swell the still accumulating momentum of our progress. And whosoever may hold the balance, though they should cast into the opposite scale all the bayonets and cannon, not only of France and England, but of Europe entire, how would it kick the beam against the simple solid weight of the two hundred millions—destined to gather beneath the flutter of the stripes and stars, in the fast hastening year of the Lord 1945!

"Poor, Wicked Nineteenth Century, Farewell!" (1900)

WILFRID SCAWEN BLUNT

The next selection includes entries from the diary of Wilfrid Scawen Blunt (1840–1922), a diplomat and poet who ardently opposed British imperialism in Egypt, India, and Ireland. He was one of several who resisted the attractions of power and glory and advocated the right of national self-determination. His criticism is followed by that of Mark Twain, whose scathing wit and anguish at American imperialism are evident in his reinterpretation of "The Battle Hymn of the Republic" (1900).

22nd Dec., 1900—The old century is very nearly out, and leaves the world in a pretty pass, and the British Empire is playing the devil in it as never an empire before on so large a scale. We may live to see its fall. All the nations of Europe are making the same heel upon earth in China, massacring and pillaging and raping in the captured cities as outrageously as in the Middle Ages. The Emperor of Germany gives the word for slaughter and the Pope looks on and approves. In South Africa our troops are burning farms under Kitchener's command, and the Queen and the two houses of Parliament, and the bench of bishops thank God publicly and vote money for the work. The Americans are spending fifty millions a year on slaughtering Filipinos; the King of the Belgians has invested his whole fortune on the Congo, where he is brutalizing the Negroes to fill his pockets. The French and Italians for the moment are playing a less prominent part in the slaughter, but their inactivity grieves them. The whole white race is reveling openly in violence, as though it had never pretended to be Christian. God's equal curse be on them all! So ends the famous nineteenth century into which we were so proud to have been born. . . .

31st Dec., 1900—I bid good-bye to the old century, may it rest in peace as it has lived in war. Of the new century I prophesy nothing except that it will see the decline of the British Empire. Other worse empires will rise perhaps in its place, but I shall not live to see the day. It all seems a very little matter here in Egypt, with the pyramids watching us as they watched Joseph, when, as a young man four thousand years ago, perhaps in this very garden, he walked and gazed at the sunset behind them, wondering about the future just as I did this evening. And so, poor wicked nineteenth century, farewell!

"Poor, Wicked Nineteenth Century, Farewell!" is from Wilfrid Scawen Blunt, *My Diaries: Being a Personal Narrative of Events 1888–1914*, vol. 1 (New York: Alfred A. Knopf, 1921), pp. 375–377. Reprinted by permission of the publisher.

The Battle Hymn of the Republic (Brought Down to Date)

MARK TWAIN

Mine eyes have seen the orgy of the launching of the
    Sword;
He is searching out the hoardings where the stranger's
    wealth is stored;
He hath loosed his fateful lightnings, and with woe
    and death has scored;
HIS LUST IS MARCHING ON.

I have seen him in the watch-fires of a hundred
    circling camps,
They have builded him an altar in the Eastern dews
    and damps;
I have read his doomful mission by the dim and
    flaring lamps—
HIS NIGHT IS MARCHING ON.

I have read his bandit gospel writ in burnished rows
    of steel:
"As ye deal with my pretensions, so with you my
    wrath shall deal;
Let the faithless son of Freedom crush the patriot
    with his heel;
LO, GREED IS MARCHING ON!"

In a sordid slime harmonious, Greed was born in
    yonder ditch,
With a longing in his bosom—and for others' goods
    an itch—
As Christ died to make men holy, let men die to
    make us rich—
OUR GOD IS MARCHING ON!

"The Battle Hymn of the Republic" is from Mark Twain, *The Complete Works of Mark Twain*, vol. 20 (New York: Harper Brothers, 1917), p. 465.

CHRONOLOGY: Nationalism and Imperialism: The Motives and Methods of Expansion

1854–1856	Crimean War: Britain, France, and the Ottoman Empire vs. Russia. Opposition to Russian expansion in Balkans leads to an ineptly managed war that shatters the invincible image of Russia and the Concert of Europe.
1859	War of Piedmont and France against Austria.
1859	*The Origin of Species* by Charles Darwin is published and promotes the theory of "natural selection."
1860	Garibaldi lands his forces in Sicily and invades southern Italy. These southern states join the northern union forged by Piedmont under the direction of Camillo Cavour.
1861	Victor Emmanuel II proclaimed king of Italy. Cavour dies three months later.
1861	Serfdom abolished in Russia by Tsar Alexander II.
1862	Otto von Bismarck becomes prime minister of Prussia.
1864	Danish-Prussian War results in quick Prussian victory. Prussia and Austria respectively rule Schleswig and Holstein.
1866	Austro-Prussian War breaks out over the Austrian administration of Holstein. Prussian victory in seven weeks: Austria is permanently excluded from German affairs.
1867	Dual monarchy established in a compromise solution between Austria and Hungary.
1868–1874	Liberal ministry of William Gladstone in Great Britain.
1869	Suez Canal completed.
1870	France declares war on Prussia over Ems dispatch. France defeated at Sedan and Emperor Napoleon III captured. Third French Republic proclaimed.
1870	Italian state annexes Rome. Italian unification completed under King Victor Emmanuel II.
1871	Proclamation of the German Empire at Versailles. Paris Commune in existence from March to May with goal to administer Paris separately from the rest of the country. The Commune is suppressed with heavy loss of life.
1874–1880	Ministry of Benjamin Disraeli in Great Britain highlighted by social legislation such as the Public Health Act and Artisans Dwelling Act, both in 1875.

1875	Britain gains control of Suez. Britain begins to establish Protectorate over Egypt.
1882	France controls Algeria.
1884–1885	Germany establishes Protectorate over Southwest Africa, Togoland, Cameroons, and East Africa.
1894	Captain Dreyfus accused of passing secret information to the German army and convicted on forged evidence by a military court. Dreyfus conviction set aside in 1906, but military discredited and France divided politically.
1898	Spanish-American War: United States acquires Puerto Rico, Philippines, Guam; annexes Hawaiian Islands and establishes Protectorate over Cuba.
1899	"Open Door Policy" in the Far East is proposed by the United States.
1899–1902	Britain crushes a rebellion by Dutch farmers in South Africa called the Boer War.

STUDY QUESTIONS

1. What are the main ideas contained in Giuseppe Mazzini's address "The Duties of Man"? This piece was directed toward Italian workers. How does it appeal to them specifically? How does Garibaldi's speech to the Italians differ from that of Mazzini's? How is Garibaldi using nationalism?

2. Why does Johann Gottlieb Fichte refer to Rome and the Germanic tribes to such an extent? What specifically does he demonstrate by these examples? How does he define the German "people"?

3. According to Bismarck, why must Germany be armed? Does Bismarck advocate imperialism? How does he use God in his arguments? How does this relate to nationalism? How is religion (specifically Christianity) used in other sources as justification for imperial expansion?

4. Explain the ideas of Charles Darwin regarding "natural selection" and evolution. How do his theories as contained in *The Origin of Species* demonstrate a scientific approach to the development of nature? How would you explain the term "survival of the fittest"? What is his approach to human development as noted in his work? Why are Darwinist theories considered by some to be dangerous and irreligious?

5. Explain Social Darwinism and give several specific examples from the reading selections that demonstrate its practice and use as justification for imperial expansion. What phrases and ideas are consistently used? What are some of Karl Pearson's arguments? Are they compelling? Do you agree or disagree with the arguments of Charles Morris on war as a factor of civilization? Why? To what

extent is Social Darwinism a corruption of Darwinist theories? Or is it simply a logical extension and application of the theories?

6. Discuss the "mandate system." What was it and how is it evident in the speech by Joseph Chamberlain regarding Britain's duty in Egypt? Cite specific phrases in this regard.

7. Analyze Senator Beveridge's speech on American control of the Philippines. What does he advocate and what are the specific arguments he uses to justify his beliefs? Note especially how he uses the abstraction of "history." Is this a logical, if not satisfying, argument? Why would it be appealing to many? How does Kipling's poem "The White Man's Burden" complement Beveridge's statements? How do this source and other sources in this chapter define imperialism as an agent of "progress and civilization"?

8. How does Sir Frederick Lugard connect nationalism with the economic argument for imperialism? How does he respond to the arguments presented by critics of imperialism? How does he justify his support of imperial expansion?

9. Explain the concept of "manifest destiny." What is "Providence" and how is it used to justify expansion into Indian lands and the annexation of Texas? What other arguments does O'Sullivan use for justification?

10. What does Wilfrid Blunt have to say about the civility of British imperialism, or American or European imperialism, for that matter? What specific justifications for imperialism, presented in earlier accounts, do his comments attack? What do you think of Mark Twain's version of "The Battle Hymn of the Republic"? What point was he trying to make? Compare Twain's poem with Rudyard Kipling's "White Man's Burden." Are they both honest and truthful?

PART III

THE TWENTIETH CENTURY

6

The Great War and the Birth of the Modern Era

Orville and Wilbur Wright successfully fly a powered airplane 1903

S.S. *Titanic* sinks on its maiden voyage 1912

Battle of Verdun (February-December) Battle of the Somme (July-November) 1916

Bolshevik Revolution in Russia (November) 1917

President Wilson issues Fourteen Points (January) 1918

1905 1910 1915 1920 1930

1900 1925

Albert Einstein formulates special theory of relativity 1905

Assassination of Archduke Franz Ferdinand (June) Declarations of war follow (August) 1914

German submarine sinks American ocean liner *Lusitania* 1915

World War I 1914-1918

Treaty of Versailles 1919

Women receive full franchise in the United States 1920

Women receive full franchise in Great Britain 1929

The next dreadful thing to a battle lost is a battle won.

—Arthur Wellesley, Duke of Wellington

Only a general who was a barbarian would send his men to certain death against the concentrated power of my new gun.

—Hiram Maxim (inventor of the machine gun)

Diplomats are just as essential to starting a war as soldiers are for finishing it. . . . You take diplomacy out of war and the whole thing would fall flat in a week.

—Will Rogers

The rain drives on, the stinking mud becomes evilly yellow, the shell holes fill up with green-white water, the roads and tracks are covered in inches of slime, the black, dying trees ooze and sweat and the shells never cease. They alone plunge overhead tearing away the rotting tree stumps. . . . It is unspeakable, Godless, hopeless.

—Paul Walsh

What's the use of worrying, it never was worthwhile/So, pack up your troubles in your old kit bag and smile, smile, smile. . . .

—World War I song

CHAPTER THEMES

- *Imperialism:*   How did the intense economic and political rivalries between European governments lead to war? Was this the kind of war that European leaders expected to fight?

- *Propaganda:*   What propaganda techniques and themes were used by European governments to establish a martial spirit among soldiers? Did soldiers and diplomats actually believe that this was the "war to end all wars"?

- *Women in History:*   It has been said that the real victims of war are not the soldiers who kill and are killed, but the women who support broken families, wander as homeless refugees, and sacrifice their sons and husbands to forces outside of their control. What is your reaction to this idea?

- *Beliefs and Spirituality:*   The twentieth century has been described as a "century of holocaust" wherein the state has dominated the individual and produced an ethical vacuum. Some have asserted that technology has created an impersonal world devoid of spiritual commitment. Do you agree? Is God dead?

- *Historical Change and Transition:*   What impact did new military technology such as the machine gun, tank, airplane, and poisonous gas have on the Great War? Did World War I, World War II, and the Cold War encompass a transitional period between an "old world" where personal valor and courage were esteemed and a "new world" of impersonal, abstract war where the stakes were higher and the destruction of humanity

This landscape of devastation in Belgium gives testimony to the mindless destruction that was such a part of the Great War. *(Reproduced by permission of the Trustees of the Imperial War Museum, London)*

a distinct possibility? Do technological advancements make war more destructive or antiseptic, and therefore more acceptable?

- ***The Big Picture:*** Why did Europe lose an entire generation of men during the Great War? What did they die for? Did the peace settlements at the end of World War I make World War II inevitable? Will the areas of Bosnia, Serbia, and Kosovo lead Europe to war again?

After the defeat of Napoleon at the Battle of Waterloo in 1815, it was decided by the victors at the Congress of Vienna that Europe had to be governed by a policy of deterrence that resisted dominance by any one country. Nations required comparable strength in order to maintain the balance of power and thus preserve the peace. Great Britain led the way and applied this policy successfully throughout the nineteenth century. During this time, however, Europe was changing. The Industrial Revolution had increased the demand for trade, and various countries sought markets in Africa and the East, establishing hegemony over a region by military force. Imperialism and competition abroad affected the sense of security and the balance of power that were crucial to the preservation of peace at home. In addition, new factors were being introduced that further threatened to disrupt the balance.

The first serious threat to the Pax Britannica of the nineteenth century came from the expansion of industry and the accompanying scientific progress. In the first decade of the twentieth century, new weapons were being developed, as were more rapid forms of communication and transportation, including the telegraph, the automobile, the railway, and the steamship. These technological advancements presented new possibilities for highly mobilized warfare that could be better coordinated and managed.

The second serious threat to the balance of European power in the late-nineteenth century was Germany. By 1870, the Prussians had unified north and west Germany through a policy of "blood and iron." The various regions of Germany had always been disunited, defying such masters as the Romans, Charlemagne, the Holy Roman Emperors, and Napoleon. But Kaiser Wilhelm I of Prussia (1797–1888), together with his master statesman Otto von Bismarck (1815–1898) and his general Count Helmut von Moltke, made highly effective use of the military capabilities of a thoroughly disciplined and well-supported army. To achieve unification, Prussia had beaten and humiliated the French in 1870 and succeeded in forging a unified German Reich. The balance of power had been upset and the lesson was clear: No nation in Europe could feel secure without training all of its young men for war, establishing a system of reserves, and creating a general staff that would prepare plans for potential wars and oversee a scheme for mobilization.

The concept of mobilization is very important in understanding why Europe and the world went to war. By 1914, every continental power had a complex plan and timetable for mobilizing against the most likely opponent or combination of enemies. When a country mobilized for war, its reserve troops were called to active duty, placed in the field, and supported with necessary rations, equipment, and armament. Timing was essential. Full mobilization took weeks, and it was important to get the process started before your enemy was ready to commit to such a policy. Hence the beginning of hostilities came when the various chiefs of state were convinced that military "necessity" required a mobilization order and that further delay would spell defeat by allowing the opponent to gain a military advantage that could not be overcome. Since mobilization involved a radical shift of the economy to maximum production and since troop movements could be detected by other nations within hours, the mobilization order could not be rescinded without the prospect of diplomatic and economic disaster. William H. McNeill, in *The Rise of the West*, notes that "the first weeks of World War I presented the amazing spectacle of vast human machines operating in a truly inhuman fashion and moving at least approximately according to predetermined and irreversible plans. The millions of persons composing the rival machines behaved almost as though they had lost individual will and intelligence." The "predetermined and irreversible" plans were centered on a military theory by Karl von Clausewitz that was accepted by all the general staffs of Europe: A swift and decisive battle that led to the initial destruction of the enemy's forces would achieve ultimate success. None planned for a long war—three or four months at most.

Thus, the nations of Europe were powderkegs waiting to go off when in June 1914 the heir to the Austro-Hungarian Empire, the Archduke Franz Ferdinand, was assassinated at Sarajevo. The diplomats talked and then the armies mobilized one by one. The "guns of August" soon enveloped Europe in a war that was to last not four months but four years. Over 8.5 million people were killed, with a total casualty count of over 37.5 million.

This chapter seeks to give an overall picture of World War I, or what has been more accurately called the Great War. This was war on a world scale, involving hostilities in Africa and the Balkans, as well as an American presence. And it was war on some of the cruelest terms. Rules were changing. There were no longer strict orders to exempt the civilian population from harm. Nor were there moral constraints on the use of submarines, machine guns, and poisonous gas; all became permanent fixtures. The Great War stands unequaled in terms of blood sacrificed for miserable accomplishment. To die for a "victory" of a hundred yards of land needed justification, which was rarely forthcoming. The questions are disturbing and perhaps unanswerable: Why did commanders send their men repeatedly "over the top" of the trenches, across "no man's land," and into the bloody rain of machine gun fire? Why was this slaughter of human life condoned by the diplomats and even by the soldiers themselves? Why did Europe lose an entire generation of men?

As we look back on the twentieth century, our perspective is clearly focused at the midpoint, when the threat of fascism and all the attendant horrors of World War II seemed to be the defining moments of an age of anxiety. And yet, many historians believe that our modern world was fashioned at the outset of the century in the trenches of Europe, at the confluence of nineteenth-century arrogance and twentieth-century technology. In 1912, the great ocean liner *Titanic* set sail from Britain to America. It was described as the quintessential expression of human technology—"unsinkable" said its creators. In 1985, the *Titanic* was finally discovered on the bottom of the Atlantic, the victim of a natural disaster on its maiden voyage, when the impact from a collision with an iceberg split the ship in two. More than this, its sinking symbolized an ordered world on the path to destruction. Two years after the *Titanic* vanished, the world went to war, a war unparalleled in its ferocity and barbarism.

This was the birth of the modern world. Europe in 1914 was on the brink of "becoming." In a sense, the transition had been foreshadowed in one of the great cultural moments of the period. In 1913, the young Russian composer Igor Stravinsky premiered his new ballet to elite society in Paris. The "Rite of Spring" was a story of primal ritual, of sacrifice to the earth and the ceremonial renewal of life. The irregular rhythms, dissonant harmonies, and blatant sexuality shocked the crowd, which rioted in response.

The ritual of primal sacrifice would be played out during the next four years as the earth claimed so many human lives. When the war ended in 1918, the world of the nineteenth century had been forever altered. The thin veneer of civilization had been shattered and the nations of Europe had difficulty defining what had happened and why. Europe would be led out of this abyss of disillusionment and despair by those promising order and respect: Benito Mussolini and Adolf Hitler.

—◌◌◌◌—

Fin de Siècle

Anti-Feminism and the Women's Movement

I myself have never been able to find out precisely what feminism is: I
only know that people call me a feminist whenever I express sentiments
that differentiate me from a doormat.

—Rebecca West (1913)

The desire of the man is for the woman, but the desire of the woman is
for the desire of the man.

—Madame de Staël

*Europe at mid-century was a hot-bed of intellectual and political activity. As the
revolutions of 1848 spread throughout the great capitals of Europe, challenging
conservative assumptions and promoting nationalist change, scientists were
challenging the intellectual foundations of society. Charles Darwin's theory of
evolution by natural selection, introduced in the* Origin of Species *(1859),
and applied to human beings in* The Descent of Man *(1871), remained controversial even within the scientific community until the 1920s. In fact, during
the last decade of the nineteenth century, and the first decade of the twentieth
century, philosophers, scientists, psychologists, and artists rejected many of the assumptions that governed the physical universe and the norms of bourgeois morality. The discovery of radium by Marie Curie (1869–1934), the development of
Quantum Theory by Max Planck (1858–1947), and the relativity proposition of
Albert Einstein (1879–1955) forced a reassessment of the nature of physical
reality.*

*But the reassessment taking place in the scientific world in the latter part of
the nineteenth century did not necessarily promote change in social relationships.
The controversy surrounding new ideas in biology, evolution, and reproduction,
led many intellectuals to emphasize the role of women as a constant, stabilizing
force in society. The mothering instinct was elemental to the female and many
writers portrayed women as one-dimensional. Their minds and bodies were simply not equipped for the stress and strain of active political life. They were creatures shackled to their emotions, susceptible to the illogic of feelings and instincts.
Their role was clearly in the smaller world of the home, not in the university, nor
the professions, nor the voting booth.*

*In reaction to such misogynistic attitudes, there arose in the mid-nineteenth
century a feminist movement that concentrated first on achieving the vote for
women. But in the process, female activists raised other questions regarding the
role of women in society, in marriage, in the law courts, and in their general relationship with men.*

The following selections attest to this struggle for recognition and equality. Many of the issues important at the end of the nineteenth century would be revisited in the decades after World War II as women made further strides toward political, economic, legal, and social equality in Western Civilization.

Seneca Falls Declaration (1848)

The Seneca Falls Declaration of Sentiments and Resolutions is the seminal document of the American women's movement in the nineteenth century. The organizer of the conference in Seneca Falls, New York, on July 19, 1848, was Elizabeth Cady Stanton. She had joined with reformer Lucretia Mott and called the meeting to consider the "social, civil, and religious condition and rights of woman." The year 1848 was particularly significant, for Europe was ablaze with revolutions seeking the fulfillment of liberal democratic rights which had been proclaimed in the American and French revolutions of the eighteenth century.

The history of mankind is a history of repeated injuries and usurpations on the part of man toward woman, having in direct object the establishment of an absolute tyranny over her. To prove this, let facts be submitted to a candid world:

• He has never permitted her to exercise her inalienable right to the elective franchise. He has compelled her to submit to laws, in the formation of which she had no voice. He has withheld from her rights which are given to the most ignorant and degraded men—both natives and foreigners. Having deprived her of this first right of a citizen, the elective franchise, thereby leaving her without representation in the halls of legislation, he has oppressed her on all sides.

• He has made her, if married, in the eye of the law, civilly dead. He has taken from her all right in property, even to the wages she earns. . . . In the covenant of marriage, she is compelled to promise obedience to her husband, he becoming, to all intents and purposes, her master—the law giving him power to deprive her of her liberty, and to administer chastisement. . . . After depriving her of all rights as a married woman, if single, and the owner of property, he has taxed her to support a government which recognizes her only when her property can be made profitable to it.

• He has monopolized nearly all the profitable employments, and from those she is permitted to follow, she receives but a scanty remuneration. He closes against her all the avenues to wealth and distinction which he considers most honorable to himself. As a teacher of theology, medicine,

"Seneca Falls Declaration" is from Elizabeth Cady Stanton, Susan B. Anthony, and Matilda Joslyn Gage, *History of Woman Suffrage*, vol. 1 (Rochester, N.Y., 1881).

or law, she is not known. He has denied her the facilities for obtaining a thorough education, all colleges being closed against her. . . . He has endeavored, in every way that he could, to destroy her confidence in her own powers, to lessen her self-respect, and to make her willing to lead a dependent and abject life. . . .

In view of the unjust laws above mentioned, and because women do feel themselves aggrieved, oppressed, and fraudulently deprived of their most sacred rights, we insist that they have immediate admission to all the rights and privileges which belong to them as citizens of the United States.

In entering upon the great work before us, we anticipate no small amount of misconception, misrepresentation, and ridicule; but we shall use every instrumentality within our power to effect our object. We shall employ agents, circulate tracts, petition the State and National legislatures, and endeavor to enlist the pulpit and the press in our behalf. We hope this Convention will be followed by a series of Conventions embracing every part of the country. . . .

"Sisters of America!
Your Sisters of France Are United with You" (1851)
PAULINE ROLAND AND JEANNE DEROINE

This is a letter to the second national convention for women in the United States in 1851 from two French socialist reformers who had been sentenced to six months in the St. Lazare prison in Paris for union agitation. Pauline Roland and Jeanne Deroine decried the lack of progress in equalizing the status of women in France, progress that had been expected from the abortive liberal revolution of 1848.

June 15, 1851

Dear Sisters:

Your courageous declaration of Woman's Rights has resounded even to our prison, and has filled our souls with inexpressible joy.

In France, reaction has suppressed the cry of liberty of women. . . . The darkness of reaction has obscured the sun of 1848, which seemed to rise so radiantly. Why? Because the revolutionary tempest, in overturning at the same time the [French] throne and the scaffold, in breaking the chain of the black slave, forgot to break the chain of the most oppressed of all—of Woman, the pariah of humanity. . . .

But, while those selected by half of the people—by men alone—evoke force to stifle liberty and forge restrictive laws to establish order by compul-

"'Sisters of America!'" is from Elizabeth Cady Stanton, Susan B. Anthony, and Matilda Joslyn Gage, *History of Woman Suffrage,* vol. 1 (Rochester, N.Y., 1881).

sion, woman, guided by fraternity, foreseeing incessant struggles, and in the hope of putting an end to them, makes an appeal to the laborer to found liberty and equality on fraternal solidarity. . . . The laborer recognizes the right of woman, his companion in labor. . . .

Sisters of America! Your socialist sisters of France are united with you in the vindication of the rights of woman to civil and political equality. We have, moreover, the profound conviction that only by the power of association based on solidarity—by the union of the working classes of both sexes to organize labor—can be acquired, completely and pacifically, the civil and political equality of woman, and the social right for all.

It is in this confidence that, from the depths of the jail which still imprisons our bodies without reaching our hearts, we cry to you, Faith, Love, Hope, and send to you our sisterly salutations.

Jeanne Deroine

Pauline Roland

Against Woman Suffrage (1884)
FRANCIS PARKMAN

At the heart of the women's movement during the nineteenth and early-twentieth centuries was the demand for equal voting rights, or women's suffrage. The goal in America had been clearly detailed in a declaration of equal rights established at the Seneca Falls Convention in 1848. By 1852, the movement to secure the vote had picked up momentum. The reaction to such agitation was intense and polarizing. Advocates of the complete equality of women included the English philosopher John Stuart Mill, who together with his wife, Harriet, became a crusader for the cause. His fundamental tracts, On Liberty *(1859) and* The Subjection of Women *(1869), were especially persuasive in advocating voting rights for women. Opposition forces, however, could also claim their intellectual champions.*

The following selection comes from the pen of the great American historian Francis Parkman. A writer of unusual depth and narrative skill, Parkman was universally acknowledged for his ability to characterize the figures of colonial American history. His account of the westward movement, The Oregon Trail, *became one of the most popular personal narratives of the nineteenth century. He wrote this pamphlet against women's suffrage "at the request of an association of women." It reveals the attitudes and fears of conservatives in the face of an established threat to the status quo.*

"Against Woman Suffrage" is from Francis Parkman, *Some of the Reasons Against Woman Suffrage* (Printed at the Request of an Association of Women, 1884), pp. 1–7, 10–16.

It has been said that the question of the rights and employment of women should be treated without regard to sex. It should rather be said that those who consider it regardless of sex do not consider it at all. . . . Whatever liberty the best civilization may accord to women, they must always be subject to restrictions unknown to the other sex, and they can never dispense with the protecting influences which society throws about them. A man, in lonely places, has nothing to lose but life and property; and he has nerve and muscles to defend them. He is free to go whither he pleases, and run what risks he pleases. Without a radical change in human nature, of which the world has never given the faintest sign, women cannot be equally emancipated. . . . Everybody knows that the physical and mental constitution of woman is more delicate than in the other sex; and, we may add, the relations between mind and body are more intimate and subtle. . . . It is these and other inherent conditions, joined to the engrossing nature of a woman's special functions, that have determined through all time her relative position. . . . Men did not make [these limitations], and they cannot unmake them. Through them, God and Nature have ordained that those subject to them shall not be forced to join in the harsh conflicts of the world militant. It is folly to ignore them, or try to counteract them by political and social quackery. . . .

The frequent low state of health among American women is a fact as undeniable as it is deplorable. In this condition of things, what do certain women demand for the good of their sex? To add to the excitements that are wasting them, other and greater excitements, and to cares too much for their strength, other and greater cares. Because they cannot do their own work, to require them to add to it the work of men, and launch them into the turmoil where the most robust sometimes fail. It is much as if a man in a state of nervous exhaustion were told by his physician to enter at once a foot-race or a boxing match.

Woman suffrage must have one of two effects. If, as many of its advocates complain, women are subservient to men, and do nothing but what they desire, then woman suffrage will have no other result than to increase the power of the other sex; if, on the other hand, women vote as they see fit, without regarding their husbands, then unhappy marriages will be multiplied and divorces redoubled. We cannot afford to add to the elements of domestic unhappiness.

One of the chief dangers of popular government is that of inconsiderate and rash legislation. . . . This danger would be increased immeasurably if the most impulsive and excitable half of humanity had an equal voice in the making of laws, and in the administration of them. . . . If the better class of women flatter themselves that they can control the others, they are doomed to disappointment. The female vote . . . is often more numerous, always more impulsive and less subject to reason, and almost devoid of the sense of responsibility. Here the bad politician would find his richest resources. He could not reach the better class of female voters, but the rest would be ready to his hand. Three fourths of them, when not urged by some pressing need or contagious passion, would be moved, not by principles, but by personal predilections.

Again, one of the chief arguments of the agitators is that government without the consent of the governed is opposed to inalienable right. But most women, including those of the best capacity and worth, fully consent that their fathers, husbands, brothers, or friends shall be their political representatives. . . . We venture to remind those who demand woman suffrage as a right that, even if it were so, the great majority of intelligent women could judge for themselves whether to exercise it better than the few who assume to teach them their duty. The agitators know well that, in spite of their persistent importunity, the majority of their sex are averse to the suffrage. . . .

On women of the intelligent and instructed classes depends the future of the nation. If they are sound in body and mind, impart this soundness to a numerous offspring, and rear them to a sense of responsibility and duty, there are no national evils that we cannot overcome. If they fail to do this their part, then the masses of the coarse and unintelligent, always of rapid increase, will overwhelm us and our institutions. When these indispensable duties are fully discharged, then the suffrage agitators may ask with better grace, if not with more reason, that they may share the political functions of men. . . .

Many women of sense and intelligence are influenced by the fact that the woman-suffrage movement boasts itself a movement of progress, and by a wish to be on the liberal or progressive side. But the boast is unfounded. Progress, to be genuine, must be in accord with natural law. If it is not, it ends in failure and in retrogression. To give women a thorough and wholesome training both of body and mind . . . [is] in the way of normal and healthy development: but to plunge them into politics, where they are not needed and for which they are unfit, would be scarcely more a movement of progress than to force them to bear arms and fight. . . .

Suppose, again, a foreign war in which the sympathies of our women were enlisted on one side or the other. Suppose them to vote against the judgment of the men that we should take part in it; or, in other words, that their male fellow citizens should fight whether they like it or not. Would the men be likely to obey?

There is another reason why the giving of the suffrage to women would tend to civil discord. . . . Most of us have had occasion to observe how strong the social rivalries and animosities of women are. They far exceed those of men. . . . The wives and daughters of the poor would bring into the contest a wrathful jealousy and hate against the wives and daughters of the rich, far more vehement than the corresponding passions in their husbands and brothers. . . .

The suffragists' idea of government is not practical, but utterly unpractical. It is not American, but French. It is that government of abstractions and generalities which found its realization in the French Revolution, and its apostle in the depraved and half-crazy man of genius, Jean Jacques Rousseau. The French had an excuse for their frenzy in the crushing oppression they had just flung off and in their inexperience of freedom. We have no excuse. Since the nation began we have been free and our liberty is in danger from nothing but its own excesses. . . .

Neither Congress, nor the States, nor the united voice of the whole people could permanently change the essential relations of the sexes. Universal female suffrage, even if decreed, would undo itself in time; but the attempt to establish it would work deplorable mischief. The question is, whether the persistency of a few agitators shall plunge us blindfold into the most reckless of all experiments; whether we shall adopt this supreme device for developing the defects of women, and demolish their real power to build an ugly mockery instead. For the sake of womanhood, let us hope not.

"The Brain Weight of Women Is Five Ounces Less Than That of Men" (1887)

GEORGE ROMANES

*Parkman's arguments against suffrage included the inability of women to partic-
ipate effectively in the political arena, a world ill-suited to their excitable and passionate nature. Women's physical anatomy and psychological composition underwent even closer scientific scrutiny during the late-nineteenth century. This
study flowed from the resounding confidence of the age in the discipline of science
to solve the dilemmas and mysteries of past decades. Human relationships were
left open to scientific inquiry, often with misleading and damaging results. Thus
were Charles Darwin's theories on natural selection applied quite loosely to the
human realm with the excesses of Social Darwinism the result. It is therefore not
surprising that several fallacious scientific treatises like the following often confirmed in people's minds the inherent genetic inferiority of women. Such attitudes
retarded progress toward social equality and proved influential even late into the
twentieth century in justifying negative perceptions of women's ability to compete
with men on an equal footing.*

I will now briefly enumerate what appear to me the leading features of this distinction in the case of mankind, adopting the ordinary classification of mental faculties as those of intellect, emotion, and will.

Seeing that the average brain-weight of women is about five ounces less than that of men, on merely anatomical grounds we should be prepared to expect a marked inferiority of intellectual power in the former. Moreover, as the general physique of women is less robust than that of men—and therefore less able to sustain the fatigue of serious or prolonged brain action—we should also on physiological grounds be prepared to entertain a similar antic-ipation. In actual fact, we find that the inferiority displays itself most conspic-uously in a comparative absence of originality, and this more especially in the higher levels of intellectual work. In her powers of acquisition [of knowl-edge] the woman certainly stands nearer to the man than she does in her

"'The Brain Weight of Women'" is from George J. Romanes, "Mental Differences Between Men and Women," *Nineteenth Century* 26 (1887), pp. 654–672.

powers of creative thought, although even as regards the former there is a marked difference. The difference, however, is one which does not assert itself till the period of adolescence. . . . But as soon as the brain, and with it the organism as a whole, reaches the stage of full development, it becomes apparent that there is a greater power of amassing knowledge on the part of the male. Whether we look to the general average or to the intellectual giants of both sexes, we are similarly met with the general fact that a woman's information is less wide and deep and thorough than that of a man. What we regard as a highly cultured woman is usually one who has read largely but superficially; and even in the few instances that can be quoted of extraordinary female industry—which on account of their rarity stand out as exceptions to prove the rule—we find a long distance between them and the much more numerous instances of profound erudition among men. . . .

But it is in original work . . . that the disparity is most conspicuous. . . . In no one department of creative thought can women be said to have at all approached men, save in fiction. Yet in poetry, music, and painting, if not also in history, philosophy, and science, the field has always been open to both. For . . . the disabilities under which women have laboured with regard to education, social opinion, and so forth, have certainly not been sufficient to explain this general dearth among them of the products of creative genius.

Lastly, with regard to judgment, I think there can be no real question that the female mind stands considerably below the male. It is much more apt to take superficial views of circumstances calling for decision, and also to be guided by less impartiality. Undue influence is more frequently exercised from the side of the emotions. . . . As a general rule, that the judgment of women is inferior to that of men has been a matter of universal recognition from the earliest times. The man has always been regarded as the rightful lord of the woman, to whom she is by nature subject, as both mentally and physically the weaker vessel.

But if woman has been a loser in the intellectual race as regards acquisition, origination, and judgment, she has gained, even on the intellectual side, certain very conspicuous advantages. First among these we must place refinement of the senses, or higher evolution of sense-organs. Next we must place rapidity of perception, which no doubt in part arises from this higher evolution of the sense-organs. . . .

Turning now to the emotions, we find that in woman, as contrasted with man, these are almost always less under control of the will—more apt to break away, as it were, from the restraint of reason, and to overwhelm the mental chariot in disaster. Whether this tendency displays itself in the overmastering form of hysteria, or in the more ordinary form of comparative childishness, ready annoyance, and a generally unreasonable temper, . . . we recognize it as more of a feminine than a masculine characteristic. . . .

Of course the greatest type of manhood, or the type wherein our ideal of manliness reaches its highest expression, is where the virtues of strength are purged from its vices. To be strong and yet tender, brave and yet kind, to combine in the same breast the temper of a hero with the sympathy of a maiden—this is to transform the ape and the tiger into what we know ought to constitute the man. And if in actual life we find that such an ideal is but seldom realised, this should make us more lenient in judging the frailties of the opposite sex. . . . This truth is, that the highest type of manhood can only then be reached when the heart and mind have been so far purified from the refuse of a brutal ancestry as genuinely to appreciate, to admire, and to reverence the greatness, the beauty, and the strength which have been made perfect in the weakness of womanhood.

"This Is the Logic of Demons!"
JOSEPHINE BUTLER

Between 1864 and 1886, English prostitutes were subject to the strict provisions of the Contagious Disease Acts. These acts required that any woman suspected of prostitution undergo detention (often for months) in a women's hospital, specifically established to provide internal medical examinations and treatments for venereal disease. The object of the acts was to protect soldiers and sailors in English cities. The women had no legal recourse for this detention and the law took no action against the men, who solicited their services and often themselves spread venereal disease. The Contagious Disease Acts angered middle-class women who saw them as promoting a double-standard. These activists argued that poor women became victims of prostitution because inferior wages and inadequate working conditions often forced many into an immoral and destructive life.

One of the most vocal opponents of this treatment of poor women was Josephine Butler (1828–1906). She led the Ladies National Association for the Repeal of the Contagious Disease Acts; by 1883, she had achieved their suspension and by 1886 their repeal. In the following selection from her book, Personal Reminiscences of a Great Crusade *(1886), Josephine Butler explains her position.*

Yes, prostitution kills the soul, even when it does not kill the body. This is the dialectic of evil, which follows its own inexorable course.

The partisans of this system say to us, however: "Society has a right to defend itself against physical evils which destroy it; it has a right to resort to any means when it has to deal not only with debauchery, but with debauchery which is a commerce; and these regulations, after all, only apply to the infamous creatures who sell themselves, and have put themselves beyond the pale of the law and of society: they are but the dirt of the street." Now I do not under-rate the abomination of paid debauchery. Yes, the vice which sells itself is abominable; what, then, shall we say of those who buy it? But there are distinctions to be made among those who sell. Let us look a little closer at the situation of the woman whom Governments have submitted to a regulation

"This Is the Logic of Demons!" is from Josephine E. Butler, *Personal Reminiscences of a Great Crusade* (London: Horace Marshall & Son, 1911), pp. 119, 121.

which is a complete and abject slavery. She deserves nothing but contempt you tell us! She is invariably as morally perverse as you tell us she is! I ask, how many of these girls are thrust upon the streets by abandonment after seduction, or dragged down by want into the infamy from which they cannot escape? What is you part in the matter? You engulf them further; you thrust them down lower; you throw on them the last shovelful of earth to hurl them to the abyss; you roll upon them the stone which cannot be removed except by a supernatural effort. "Ah! You have fallen, unfortunate creature," you say; "well, we will complete the work, we consummate your degradation: that which is already soiled shall be made still more vile." This is logic; but it is the logic of demons! . . .

I do not hide from myself the horror and the peril of the prostitution which exists where there are not these laws—the horror and danger of prostitution under every aspect, independently of the moral guilt of governments which guarantee it. We must enter upon a grand crusade, not only against legal prostitution, but against profligacy itself; we must form an indomitable league. . . . We must pursue vice up to its source; we must follow it in all its forms and in all its hiding-places; we must attack the unholy literature, the impure art, and the debased drama which are connected with it. Above all, we must combat the disastrous delusion, so fixed in many minds, that vice is an inevitable fatality; we must hold up before our youth the ideal of purity and of domestic worth.

"I Incite This Meeting to Rebellion!" (1912)
EMMELINE PANKHURST

Emmeline Pankhurst (1858–1928) founded the Women's Social and Political Union in 1903 and was the leader of the militant suffragists until the beginning of World War I in 1914. She and her daughter, Christabel, disrupted political meetings, organized riots, and endured hunger strikes in prison to call attention to women's demands for the vote. Her tactics were not approved or shared by all women's reform organizations, but her methods became influential among more radical American suffragists. Pankhurst gave this speech just after having been released from prison for leading a violent demonstration in which the windows of several elegant London shops had been smashed by women wielding hammers.

It always seems to me when the anti-suffrage members of the [British] Government criticize militancy in women that it is very like beasts of prey reproaching the gentler animals who turn in desperate resistance when at the point of death. . . . Ladies and gentlemen, the only recklessness the militant suffragists have shown about human life has been about their own lives and

"'I Incite This Meeting to Rebellion!'" is from Emmeline Pankhurst, *My Own Story* (New York: Hearst's International Library Co., 1914).

not about the lives of others, and I say here and now that it never has been and never will be the policy of the Women's Social and Political Union reck-lessly to endanger human life. We leave that to the enemy. We leave that to the men in their warfare. It is not the method of women. . . . There is some-thing that governments care far more for than human life, and that is the security of property, and so it is through property that we shall strike the enemy. From henceforward the women who agree with me will say, "We dis-regard your laws, gentlemen, we set the liberty and the dignity and the wel-fare of women above all such considerations, and we shall continue this war as we have done in the past; and what sacrifice of property, or what injury to property accrues will not be our fault. It will be the fault of that Government who admits the justice of our demands, but refuses to concede them. . . .

Be militant each in your own way. Those of you who can express your mili-tancy by going to the House of Commons and refusing to leave without satis-faction, as we did in the early days—do so. . . . Those of you who can break windows—break them. Those of you who can still further attack the secret idol of property, so as to make the Government realize that property is as greatly endangered by women's suffrage as it was by the Chartists of old—do so.

And my last word to the Government: I incite this meeting to rebellion! . . . Take me, if you dare, but if you dare I tell you this: you will not keep me in prison.

The Revolt Against Reason

> I know my fate. One day my name will be associated with the memory of something tremendous—a crisis without equal on earth, the most profound collision of conscience, a decision that was conjured up against everything that had been believed, demanded, hallowed so far. I am no man—I am dynamite.
>
> —Friedrich Nietzsche

Intellectual history, or the study of ideas, is an exciting, sometimes frustrating discipline. Ideas are abstract and intangible, but often provide the foundation and justification for political and social change and thus are an important com-ponent of historical inquiry.

Europeans, at the turn of the century, could lay claim to a long intellectual her-itage. The Enlightenment of the eighteenth century had emphasized rationalism and toleration, as well as an appreciation of the methods of scientific inquiry. The Romantic movement of the early-nineteenth century valued feelings, intuition, the imagination and artistic freedom as vital components in the exploration of human dimension. But by the mid-nineteenth century, science had once again attained prestige in the intellectual world as theories were advanced to explain, through rational scientific method, the development of human thought, social and economic interrelationships, and the evolution of plants and animals by natural selection.

The emphasis on scientific method produced an intellectual skepticism toward any-thing that could not be proved by tangible evidence. Scholars sought to free them-selves from the constraints of religion and Christian morality in particular. In his book entitled The Life of Jesus *(1835), David Friedrich Strauss, questioned whether there was any genuine historical evidence to confirm the very existence of the preeminent religious figure in Western Civilization.*

During the second half of the nineteenth century, philosophy even confronted the rational processes of scientific inquiry. Perhaps human beings had to go fur-ther, beyond the attack on organized religion, beyond rational experimentation and postulation, to question the very source of our human values within the deep recesses of the mind. Sigmund Freud (1856–1939) with his theses on human mo-tivation, the efficacy of dreams, and the complexities that lay beneath the calm human surface, gave birth to a new science of the mind—psychoanalysis.

More fervent even than understanding the complexities of the mind was the desire to tap the essence of the heart—the inner spirit of the soul wherein the Truth of life was stored, a vision of pure God, unadulterated by the mask of the Catholic church or any other religious organization that sought to reveal the intent of God.

Fyodor Dostoevsky (1821–1881) was one of Russia's greatest novelists. He finished his most influential novel entitled The Brothers Karamozov *in 1880, near the end of his life. In it he created a vast panorama of humankind's eternal quest for spiritual insight. In the following selection from that novel, Dostoevsky envisions the Spanish Inquisition of the sixteenth century with the Grand In-quisitor confronting God Himself. The Grand Inquisitor rejects the Truth of God by substituting God's Will with his own interpretation of morality on earth. Dos-toevsky believed that knowledge of God must stem from the exploration of one's own soul without the optical illusion of Christianity. The rejection of Christian-ity was not a rejection of God, but the rejection of any method of inquiry or insti-tution that restricted the power of the human spirit to explore the beautiful, but hazardous, uncharted regions of the soul.*

The Grand Inquisitor (1880)
FYODOR DOSTOEVSKY

[Guards have detained God in a Seville prison to await judgment by the Grand Inquisitor, a cardinal of the Church. During the night the cardinal enters the cell and confronts God]:

"Is it You? You? . . . Don't answer, be silent. What can You say, indeed? I know too well what You would say. And You have no right to add anything to what You have said of old. Why, then, have You come to hinder us? For You have

"The Grand Inquisitor" is from Fyodor Dostoevsky, *The Brothers Karamozov* (New York: Modern Library, n.d.), pp. 310; 315–319. The translation has been modernized by the editor.

come to hinder us, You know that. But do You know what will be tomorrow? I know not who You are and care not to know whether it is You or only a semblance of Him, but tomorrow I shall condemn You and burn You at the stake as the worst of heretics. And the very people who have today kissed Your feet, tomorrow at the faintest sign from me will rush to heap up the embers of Your fire. . . ." . . .

"Why have You come now to hinder us? And why do You look silently and searchingly at me with Your mild eyes? Be angry. I don't want your love, for I do not love You. And what use is it for me to hide anything from You? Don't I know to Whom I am speaking? All that I say is known to You already. And is it for me to conceal from You our mystery? Perhaps it is Your will to hear it from my lips. Listen, then. . . ."

"Mankind as a whole has always striven to organise a universal state. There have been many great nations with great histories, but the more highly they were developed the more unhappy they were, for they felt more acutely than other people the craving for worldwide union. The great conquerors, Timors [Tammerlane] and Ghenghis-Khans, whirled like hurricanes over the face of the earth striving to subdue its people, and they too were but the unconscious expression of the same craving for universal unity. Had You taken the world and Caesar's purple, You would have founded the universal state and have given universal peace. For who can rule men if not he who holds their conscience and their bread in his hands. We have taken the sword of Caesar, and in taking it, of course, have rejected You and followed *him*. Oh, ages are yet to come of the confusion of free thought, of their science and cannibalism. For having begun to build their tower of Babel without us, they will end, of course, with cannibalism. But then the beast will crawl to us and lick our feet and spatter them with tears of blood. And we shall sit upon the beast and raise the cup, and on it will be written, 'Mystery.' But then, and only then, the reign of peace and happiness will come for men. You are proud of Your elect, but You have only the elect while we give rest to all. And besides, how many of those elect, those mighty ones who could become elect, have grown weary waiting for You, and have transferred and will transfer the powers of their spirit and the warmth of their heart to the other camp, and end by raising their *free* banner against You? You have lifted up that banner Yourself. But with us all will be happy and will no more rebel nor destroy one another as under Your freedom. Oh, we shall persuade them that they will only become free when they renounce their freedom to us and submit to us. And shall we be right or shall we be lying? They will be convinced that we are right, for they will remember the horrors of slavery and confusion to which Your freedom brought them. Freedom, free thought and science, will lead them into such straits and will bring them face to face with such marvels and insoluble mysteries, that some of them, the fierce and rebellious, will destroy themselves, others, rebellious but weak, will destroy one another, while the rest, weak and unhappy, will crawl fawning to our feet and whine to us: 'Yes, you were right, you alone possess His mystery, and we come back to you, save us from ourselves!'" . . .

"Too, too well they know the value of complete submission! And until men know that, they will be unhappy. Who is most to blame for their not knowing it, speak? Who scattered the flock will come together again and will submit once more, and then it will be once for all. Then we shall give them the quiet humble happiness of weak creatures such as they are by nature. Oh, we shall persuade them at last not to be proud. We shall show them that they are weak, that they are only pitiful children, but that childlike happiness is the sweetest of all. They will become timid and will look to us and huddle close to us in fear, as chicks to the hen. They will marvel at us and will be awe-stricken before us, and will be proud at our being so powerful and clever, that we have been able to subdue such a turbulent flock of thousands of millions. They will tremble impotently before our wrath, their minds will grow fearful, they will be quick to shed tears like women and children, but they will be just as ready at a sign from us to pass to laughter and rejoicing, to happy mirth and child-ish song. Yes, we shall set them to work, but in their leisure hours we shall make their life like a child's game, with children's songs and innocent dances. Oh, we shall allow them even sin, they are weak and helpless, and they will love us like children because we allow them to sin. We shall tell them that every sin will be expiated, if it is done with our permission, that we allow them to sin because we love them, and the punishment for these sins we take upon ourselves. And we shall take it upon ourselves, and they will adore us as their saviours who have taken on themselves their sins before god. And they will have no secrets from us. We shall allow or forbid them to live with their wives and mistresses, to have or not to have children—according to whether they have been obedient or disobedient—and they will submit to us gladly and cheerfully. The most painful secrets of their conscience, all, all they will bring to us, and we shall have an answer for all. And they will be glad to be-lieve our answer, for it will save them from the great anxiety and terrible agony they endure at present in making a free decision for themselves. And all will be happy, all the millions of creatures except the hundred thousand who rule over them. For only we, we who guard the mystery, shall be un-happy. There will be thousands of millions of happy babes, and a hundred thousand sufferers who have taken upon themselves the curse of the knowl-edge of good and evil. Peacefully they will die, peacefully they will expire in Your name, and beyond the grave they will find nothing but death. But we shall keep the secret, and for their happiness we shall allure them with the re-ward of heaven and eternity. Though if there were anything in the other world, it certainly would not be for such as they. It is prophesied that You will come again in victory, You will come with Your chosen, the proud and strong, but we will say that they have only saved themselves, but we have saved all. We are told that the harlot who sits upon the beast, and holds in her hands the *mystery*, shall be put to shame, that the weak will rise up again, and will rend her royal purple and will strip naked her loathsome body [Revelation 17]. But then I will stand up and point out to Thee the thousand millions of happy children who have known no sin. And we who have taken their sins upon us for their happiness will stand up before You and say: 'Judge us if You can and dare.' Know that I do not fear You. Know that I too have been in the wilderness, I too have lived on roots and locusts, I too prized the freedom with which You the strong and powerful, thirsting 'to make up the number.' But I awakened and would not serve madness. I turned back and joined the ranks of those who have corrected Your work. I left the proud and went back to the humble, for the happiness of the humble. What I say to You will come to pass, and our dominion will be built up. I repeat, tomorrow You shall see that obedient flock who at a sign from me will hasten to heap up the hot cinders about the pile on which I shall burn You for coming to hinder us. For if any one has ever deserved our fires, it is You. Tomorrow I shall burn You. I have spoken."

Faith, Love, and Hope: "Enough! Enough!" (1887)
FRIEDRICH NIETZSCHE

Perhaps the most radical and powerful detractor of the positive value of reason was the German philosopher, Friedrich Nietzsche (1844–1900). He was raised as a child prodigy and became a professor of classical philology at Basel University at the astonishing age of twenty-five. His first book, The Birth of Tragedy *(1872), shocked the world of classical studies and was roundly condemned for its radical interpretations. Nietzsche was completely at odds with the values of his age. At various times in his career, he attacked democracy, Christianity, nationalism, rational analysis, and the "progressive" nature of science. Nietzsche defined the political arena in terms of the Will to Power. For Nietzsche, democratic political values and the concept of equal rights actively masked a "lust for power" that was at the heart of human nature. He introduced the concept of the "Übermensch," or Overman, who through his mental and physical authority, would rise to dominate the weak. Christian morality, with its emphasis on peace and brotherly love, created a servile mentality. In the following selections from his* Genealogy of Morals *(1887) and* The Gay Science *(1882), Nietzsche presents some of his most forceful ideas regarding the relationship between the "morality of slaves" and the "morality of aristocrats." Nietzsche emphasizes his desire to strip away the masks of society by declaring that "God is dead!" Human beings who so willed could create a new moral order that would reject the rational philosophy of the weak and replace it with a glorification of pride, assertiveness and pure strength.*

The profound, icy mistrust which the German provokes, as soon as he arrives at power—even at the present time—is always still an aftermath of that inex-

---

"Faith, Love, and Hope" is from Friedrich Nietzsche, *The Genealogy of Morals in The Philosophy of Nietzsche* (New York: Modern Library, 1922), pp. 647–654.

tinguishable horror with which for whole centuries Europe has regarded the wrath of the blond Teuton beast. . . . Granted the truth of the theory now believed to be true, that the very *essence of all civilization* is to *train* out of man, the beast of prey, a tame and civilized animal, a domesticated animal, it follows indubitably that we must regard as the real *tools of civilization* all those instincts of reaction and resentment, by the help of which the aristocratic races, together with their ideals, were finally degraded and overpowered; though that has not yet come to be synonymous with saying that the bearers of those tools also *represented* the civilization. It is rather the contrary that is not only probable—nay, it is *palpable* today; these bearers of vindictive instincts that have to be bottled up, these descendants of all European and non-European slavery, especially of the pre-Aryan population—these people, I say, represent the *decline* of humanity! These "tools of civilization" are a disgrace to humanity, and constitute in reality more of an argument against civilization, more of a reason why civilization should be suspected. One may be perfectly justified in being always afraid of the blond beast that lies at the core of all aristocratic races, and in being on one's guard: but who would not a hundred times prefer to be afraid, when one a the same time admires, than to be immune from fear, at the cost of being perpetually obsessed with the loathsome spectacle of the distorted, the dwarfed, the stunted, the envenomed? And is that not our fate? What produces today our repulsion towards "man"?—for we *suffer* from "man," there is no doubt about it. It is not fear, it is rather that we have nothing more to fear from men; it is that the worm "man" is in the foreground and pullulates; it is that the "tame man," the wretched mediocre and unedifying creature, has learned to consider himself a goal and a pinnacle, an inner meaning, an historic principle, a "higher man"; yes, it is that he has a certain right so to consider himself, in so far as he feels that in contrast to that excess of deformity, disease, exhaustion, and effeteness whose odor is beginning to pollute present-day Europe, he at any rate has achieved a relative success, he at any rate still says "yes" to life. . . .

The Slave Morality

Will any one look a little into—right into—the mystery of how *ideals* are *manufactured* in this world? Who has the courage to do it? Come! . . . Now speak! What is happening below down yonder? Speak out! Tell what you see, many of the most dangerous curiosity—for now I am the listener.

"I see nothing, I hear the more. It is a cautious, spiteful, gentle whispering and muttering together in all the corners and crannies. It seems to me that they are lying; sugary softness adheres to every sound. Weakness is turned to merit, there is no doubt about it—it is just as you say."

Further!

"And the impotence which requites not, is turned to 'goodness,' craven baseness to meekness, submission to those whom one hates, to obedience (namely obedience to one of whom they say that he ordered this submis-

Friedrich Nietzsche: "Whither is God? I shall tell you. We have killed him, you and I. We are all his murderers." *(Brown Brothers)*

sion—they call him God). The inoffensive character of the weak, the very cowardice in which he is rich, his standing at the door, his forced necessity of waiting, gain here fine names, such as 'patience,' which is also called 'virtue'; not being able to avenge one's self, is called not wishing to avenge one's self, perhaps even forgiveness (for *they* know not what they do—we alone know what they do). They also talk of the 'love of their enemies' and swear thereby. Further!

"They are miserable, there is no doubt about it, all these whisperers and counterfeiters in the corners. . . . But enough! Enough! I can endure it no longer. Bad air! Bad air! These workshops *where ideals are manufactured*—verily they reek with the crassest lies." . . .

Now do I hear for the first time that which they have said so often: 'We good, *we are the righteous*'—what they demand they call not revenge but 'the triumph of *righteousness*'; what they hate is not their enemy, no, they hate 'unrighteousness,' 'godlessness'; what they believe in and hope is not the hope of revenge, the intoxication of sweet revenge, . . . but the victory of God, of the *righteous God* over the 'godless'; what is left for them to love in this world is not their brothers in hate, but their 'brothers in love,' as they say, all the good and righteous on the earth."

And how do they name that which serves them as a solace against all the troubles of life—their phantasmagoria of their anticipated future blessedness?

"How? Do I hear right? They call it 'the last judgment' the advent of their kingdom, the kingdom of God'—but in the *meanwhile* they live 'in faith,' 'in love,' 'in hope.'"

Enough! Enough!

"God Is Dead!"

FRIEDRICH NIETZSCHE

Have you not heard of that mad man who on a bright morning lit a lantern, ran to the market place, and shouted incessantly, "I seek God! I seek God!" Among the many of those who do not believe in god and who were standing around there, he provoked much laughter. Shy, did God get lost? asked one. Did he lose his way like a child? asked another. Or is he hiding? Is he afraid of us? Has he left on a boat? Has he emigrated? Thus they shouted and laughed. The man jumped into their midst and pierced them with his glances.

"Whither is God?" he shouted. "I shall tell you. We have killed him—you and I. We all are his murderers. But how have we done it? How were we able to drink up the ocean? Who gave us the sponge to wipe out the whole horizon? What did we do when we unchained this earth from its sun? Whither is it moving now? Whither are we moving? Away from all suns? Are we not falling continually? Falling backward, sideward, forward, in all directions? Is there any up or down left? Are we not straying as through infinite nothingness? Do we not feel the breath of empty space? Has it not become colder? Is not night and more night coming on all the time? Must not lanterns be lit in the morning? Do we not yet hear the noise of the gravediggers who are burying God? Do we not begin to smell god's putrefaction? Gods, to, putrefy. God is dead. God will remain dead. And we have killed him. How shall we, the murderers of all murderers comfort ourselves? The holiest and mightiest of all that the world has ever owned has bled to death under our knives: who will wipe this blood off us? With what water can we clean ourselves? . . . Is not the greatness of this deed too great for us? Must not we ourselves become gods in order to seem worthy of it? There has never been a greater deed: whoever will be born

"God Is Dead!" is from Oscar Levy, ed., *The Complete Works of Friedrich Nietzsche*, trans. by Anthony M. Ludovici (London, 1911).

after us, will be on account of this deed part of a higher history than all prior history."

Here the mad man became silent and glanced at his listeners; they too had become silent and stared at him with a strange feeling. Finally, he threw his lantern on the ground so that it broke into pieces and was extinguished. Then he said: "I have come too soon, my time has not come yet. This tremendous event is still on its way, it has not yet reached the ears of man. Lightning and thunder require time, the light of the stars requires time, deeds require time even after they are done, to be seen and heard. This deed is still more distant from them than the most distant stars—and yet they themselves have done it."

On the same day, we are told, the mad man entered a number of churches and there sang his *requiem aeternam deo.* Led out and questioned, he, according to the report, gave always the same reply, "What are these churches now if they are not the tombs and sepulchers of God?"

"A Warlike Age Is Now Starting"
FRIEDRICH NIETZSCHE

I welcome all signs that a more manly, a warlike age is now starting, an age which above all will honor valor again. For this age shall prepare the way for one yet higher and it shall gain the strength which one day this higher age will need, this age which is to carry heroism into the pursuit of knowledge and to wage wars for the sake of thoughts and their consequences. For that many preparatory courageous men are now needed. Yet they cannot leap into being out of nothing—anymore than out of the sand and slime of today's civilization and metropolitan culture: men who understand how to be silent, solitary, determined, constant and satisfied with inconspicuous activity; who in everything seek for that which must be overcome; men characterized by cheerfulness, patience, simplicity and contempt for all great vanities, as well as by magnanimity in victory and forbearance regarding the small vanities of all vanquished; men judging sharply and freely all victors and the share of chance in every victory and every fame; . . . men who live in greater danger, more fruitful and happier. For, believe me, the secret which enables us to harvest in life the greatest fruitfulness and the greatest enjoyment is: to live dangerously! Build your cities under Vesuvius! Send your ships into uncharted seas! Live at war with your peers and yourselves! . . . At long last the pursuit of knowledge will reach out for its due: it will wish to rule and own, and you with it.

"A Warlike Age Is Now Starting" is from Oscar Levy, ed., *The Complete Works of Friedrich Nietzsche,* trans. by Anthony M. Ludovici (London, 1911).

The Road to War (1900–1914)

The Celebration of War

Military Glory! The image of victorious armies engaged in limited campaigns designed to further the righteous expansion of domain or to win security or to establish a national identity—this vision had fired the imagination of European leaders in the nineteenth century. War was an opportunity to parade all the trappings of authority: neatly pressed uniforms with braid and insignia, plumed helmets, polished swords that sparkled in the sun—all of this reflected the pomp and display that fed the egos and confirmed the superiority of class. War was a celebration of image. But this image was shallow, indeed, because just below the surface of the glitter lay the agony of pain and destruction.

The Crimean War of 1854–1856 was the first campaign to be photographed. Through the senseless cavalry charges in the face of canon, the degradation of cholera, and the lack of decisive victory, France, Britain, Russia, and Turkey denied the reality of the photographs and failed to register despair about this short and inconclusive war. The vision of victory with troops returning home covered in glory sustained in the imagination until the first battles of the Great War in 1914. The European accumulation of empire in India and Africa had inspired the competitive juices. If Britannia "ruled the waves" and Germany deserved its "place in the sun," then the process of conflict would not take long—and it would be glorious.

This attitude was a feature of the writings of the German historian Heinrich von Treitschke (1834–1896). From 1874 on, he held the chair of modern history at the University of Berlin. His ideal of power and heroism reflected the confidence in German military superiority, and infected students and statesmen alike with the belief in Germany's right to rule. In the first selection from a lecture published posthumously, Germany's mission is clear—war was a necessity to be embraced. And Kaiser Wilhelm II was certainly anxious to seize the opportunity as noted in the militaristic speech that follows.

"Without War, No State Could Exist"
HEINRICH VON TREITSCHKE

The essential function of the State is the conduct of war. The long oblivion into which this principle had fallen is a proof of how effeminate the science of government had become in civilian hands. . . .

Without war no State could exist. All those we know of arose through war, and the protection of their members by armed force remains their primary

"Without War, No State Could Exist" is from Heinrich von Treitschke, *Politics,* tr. by Blanche Dugdale (London: Constable, 1916).

and essential task. War, therefore, will endure to the end of history, as long as there is multiplicity of States. The laws of human thought and of human nature forbid any alternative, neither is one to be wished for. The blind worshiper of an eternal peace falls into the error of isolating the State, or dreams of one which is universal, which we have already seen to be at variance with reason.

Even as it is impossible to conceive of a tribunal above the State, which we have recognized as sovereign in its very essence, so it is likewise impossible to banish the idea of war from the world. . . . The great strides which civilization makes against barbarism and unreason are only made actual by the sword. Between civilized nations also war is the form of litigation by which States make their claims valid. The argument brought forward in these terrible law suits of the nations compel as no argument in civil suits can ever do. . . .

Moreover war is a uniting as well as a dividing element among nations; it does not draw them together in enmity only, for through its means they learn to know and to respect each other's peculiar qualities.

It is important not to look upon war always as a judgment from God. Its consequences are impermanent; but the life of a nation is reckoned by centuries, and the final verdict can only be pronounced after the survey of whole epochs. . . .

The grandeur of war lies in the utter annihilation of puny man in the great conception of the State, and it brings out the full magnificence of the sacrifice of fellow-countrymen for one another. In the war the chaff is winnowed from the wheat. . . .

It is war which fosters the political idealism which the materialist rejects. What a disaster for civilization it would be if mankind blotted its heroes from memory. The heroes of a nation are the figures which rejoice and inspire the spirit of its youth, and the writers whose words ring like trumpet blasts become the idols of our boyhood and our early manhood. He who feels no answering thrill is unworthy to bear arms for his country. To appeal from this judgement to Christianity would be sheer perversity, for does not the Bible distinctly say that the ruler shall rule by the sword, and again that greater love hath no man than to lay down his life for his friend? To Aryan races, who are before all things courageous, the foolish preaching of everlasting peace has always been vain. They have always been men enough to maintain with the sword what they have attained through the spirit. . . .

But it is not worth while to speak further of these matters, for the God above us will see to it that war shall return again, a terrible medicine for mankind diseased.

Despite all this it is not denied that the progress of culture must make wars both shorter and rarer. They must become shorter and rarer owing to man's natural horror of bloodshed, as well as to the size and quality of modern armies, for it is impossible to see how the burdens of a great war could long be borne under the present conditions. But it would be false to conclude that wars can ever cease. They neither can nor should, so long as the state is sovereign and stands among its peers. . . .

The fears and aggression that permeated Europe at the outset of World War I are expressed in this painting by Rudolf Henneberg. Note the emphasis on the Kaiser's insatiable lust for world conquest and dominion. Was this the primary reason that the world went to war in 1914? (*Indiana War Memorial*)

Germany's Place in the Sun (1901)
KAISER WILHELM II

In spite of the fact that we have no such fleet as we should have, we have conquered for ourselves a place in the sun. It will now be my task to see to it that this place in the sun shall remain our undisputed possession, in order that the sun's rays may fall fruitfully upon our activity and trade in foreign parts, that our industry and agriculture may develop within the state and our sailing sports upon the water, for our future lies upon the water. The more Germans go out upon the waters . . . whether it be in journeys across the ocean, or in the service of the battleflag, so much the better will it be for us. For when the German has once learned to direct his glance upon what is distant and great, the pettiness which surrounds him in daily life on all sides will disappear. . . .

As head of the empire I therefore rejoice over every citizen, whether from Hamburg, Bremen, or Lubeck, who goes forth with this large outlook and seeks new points where we can drive in the nail on which to hang our armour.

Establishing "Laws of War": The Hague Convention (1907)

There were those, however, who did not fall prey to the celebration of war. The Hague Convention of 1907 sought to promote peaceful coexistence by establishing "laws of war" that were intended to control or limit the destruction that always accompanies conflict; the convention was to meet next in 1915 but ironically was canceled because of the Great War. In the second selection written in 1910, historian Norman Angell challenged the whole doctrine that war had justification in the evolutionary law of survival of the fittest.

SECTION II.—HOSTILITIES

Chapter I.—*Means of Injuring the Enemy, Sieges, and Bombardments*

Article 22

The right of belligerents to adopt means of injuring the enemy is not unlimited.

"Germany's Place in the Sun" is from Christian Gauss, excerpted from *The German Emperor*, pp. 181–183. Copyright © 1915 Charles Scribner's Sons. Reprinted with the permission of Charles Scribner's Sons.

"Establishing 'Laws of War'" is from Carnegie Endowment for International Peace, *The Hague Conventions and Declarations of 1899 and 1907* (New York: Oxford University Press, 1915), pp. 116–118.

Article 23

In addition to the prohibitions provided by special Conventions, it is especially forbidden—

(a) To employ poison or poisoned weapons;
(b) To kill or wound treacherously individuals belonging to the hostile nation or army;
(c) To kill or wound an enemy who, having laid down his arms, or having no longer the means of defence, has surrendered at discretion;

Article 25

The attack or bombardment, by whatever means, of towns, villages, dwellings, or buildings which are undefended is prohibited.

Article 26

The officer in command of an attacking force must, before commencing a bombardment, except in cases of assault, do all in his power to warn the authorities.

Article 27

In sieges and bombardments all necessary steps must be taken to spare, as far as possible, buildings dedicated to religion, art, science, or charitable purposes, historic monuments, hospitals, and places where the sick and wounded are collected, provided they are not being used at the time for military purposes.

It is the duty of the besieged to indicate the presence of such buildings or places by distinctive and visible signs, which shall be notified to the enemy beforehand.

Article 28

The pillage of a town or place, even when taken by assault, is prohibited.

The Great Illusion (1910)
NORMAN ANGELL

What are the fundamental motives that explain the present rivalry of armaments in Europe, notably the Anglo-German? Each nation pleads the need for defence; but this implies that someone is likely to attack, and has

"The Great Illusion" is from Norman Angell, *The Great Illusion* (New York: G. P. Putnam's Sons, 1913), pp. ix–xiii, 381–382.

therefore a presumed interest in so doing. What are the motives which each State thus fears its neighbors may obey?

They are based on the universal assumption that a nation, in order to find outlets for expanding population and increasing industry, or simply to ensure the best conditions possible for its people, is necessarily pushed to territorial expansion and the exercise of political force against others. . . . It is assumed that a nation's relative prosperity is broadly determined by its political power; that nations being competing units, advantage in the last resort goes to the possessor of preponderant military force, the weaker goes to the wall, as in the other forms of the struggle for life. The author challenges this whole doctrine. . . .

War has no longer the justification that it makes for the survival of the fittest; it involves the survival of the less fit. The idea that the struggle between nations is a part of the evolutionary law of man's advance involves a profound misreading of the biological analogy.

The warlike nations do not inherit the earth; they represent the decaying human element. . . .

Are we, in blind obedience to primitive instincts and old prejudices, enslaved by the old catchwords and that curious indolence which makes the revision of old ideas unpleasant, to duplicate indefinitely on the political and economic side a condition from which we have liberated ourselves on the religious side? Are we to continue to struggle, as so many good men struggled in the first dozen centuries of Christendom—spilling oceans of blood, wasting mountains of treasure—to achieve what is at bottom a logical absurdity, to accomplish something which, when accomplished, can avail us nothing, and which, if it could avail us anything, would condemn the nations of the world to never-ending bloodshed and the constant defeat of all those aims which men, in their sober hours, know to be alone worthy of sustained endeavor?

"The Lamps Go Out Over Europe"

The lamps are going out all over Europe; we shall not see them lit again in our lifetime.

—Sir Edward Grey, British Foreign Minister (August 3, 1914)

You will be home before the leaves have fallen from the trees.

—German Kaiser Wilhelm II to his departing troops (August, 1914)

For decades the Balkan areas of Bosnia and Serbia had been in turmoil, causing the neighboring Austro-Hungarian empire great anxiety. The Serbs had their own language and customs and had always been wary of Austrian attempts to unify the region politically and culturally. Several extremist organizations, inspired by patriotic idealism, sought to eliminate the Austro-Hungarian presence through terror and violence. Among these organizations was the pan-Serbian nationalist group "Union or Death," also known as The Black Hand. Statutes of this representative group are included in the first selection.

The second selection recounts the famous assassination of the heir to the Austro-Hungarian throne, Archduke Franz Ferdinand. The murderer, a nineteen-year-old Serb student named Gavrilo Princip, was a member of a patriotic society similar to The Black Hand, called Narodna Odbrana. *One of the leaders of this organization who was arrested along with Princip gave this firsthand account of the assassination, an event that propelled the world to war.*

Statutes of "The Black Hand"

Article 1. This organization has been created with the object of realising the national ideal: The union of all the Serbs. All Serbs without distinction of sex, religion, place of birth, and all who are sincerely devoted to this cause, may become members.

Article 2. This organization prefers terrorist action to intellectual propaganda and for this reason must be kept absolutely secret from persons who do not belong to it.

Article 3. This organization bears the name "Union or Death."

Article 4. To accomplish its task, the organization:

1. Brings influence to bear on Government circles, on the various social classes and on the whole social life of the Kingdom of Serbia, regarded as Piedmont.

2. Organizes revolutionary action in all territories inhabited by Serbs.

3. Outside the frontiers of Serbia uses every means available to fight the adversaries of this idea.

4. Maintains amicable relations with all states, peoples, organizations, and individuals who entertain feelings of friendship towards Serbia and the Serbian element.

5. Lends help and support in every way possible to all people and all organizations struggling for their national liberation and for their union.

Article 5. A central Committee having its headquarters at Belgrade is at the head of this organization and exercises executive authority. . . .

Article 25. Members of the organization are not known to each other personally. It is only the members of the Central Committee who are known to one another.

Article 26. In the organization itself the members are known by numbers. Only the Central Committee at Belgrade is to know their names. . . .

"Statutes of 'The Black Hand'" is from p. 309 of *Readings in European International Relations* by W. Henry Cooke and Edith P. Stickney. Copyright, 1931, by Harper & Row, Publishers, Inc.; renewed 1959 by W. Henry Cooke. Reprinted by permission of HarperCollins, Publishers, Inc.

Article 31. Anyone who once enters the organization may never withdraw from it. . . .

Article 33. When the Central Committee at Belgrade has pronounced penalty of death [on one of the members] the only matter of importance is that the execution take place without fail. . . .

Assassination at Sarajevo: The Plot and Murder (June 28, 1914)

A tiny clipping from a newspaper, mailed without comment from a secret band of terrorists in Zagreb, capital of Croatia, to their comrades in Belgrade, was the torch which set the world afire with war in 1914. That bit of paper wrecked old, proud empires. It gave birth to new, free nations.

I was one of the members of the terrorist band in Belgrade which received it.

The little clipping declared that the Austrian Archduke Francis Ferdinand would visit Sarajevo, the capital of Bosnia, June 28, to direct army maneuvers in the neighboring mountains.

It reached our meeting place, the café called Zeatna Moruna, one night the latter part of April, 1914. To understand how great a sensation that little piece of paper caused among us when it was passed from hand to hand almost in silence, and how greatly it inflamed our hearts, it is necessary to explain just why the *Narodna Odbrana* existed, the kind of men that were in it, and the significance of that date, June 28, on which the Archduke dared to enter Sarajevo.

As every one knows, the old Austro-Hungarian Empire was built by conquest and intrigues, by sales and treacheries, which held in subjugation many peoples who were neither Austrian nor Hungarian. It taxed them heavily; it diverted the products of their toil to serve the wealth of the master state. It interfered in their old freedom by a multiplicity of laws administered with arrogance.

Several years before the war, a little group of us, thirty-five in all, living in several Bosnian and Herzegovinian cities and villages, formed the *Narodna Odbrana,* the secret society, the aim of which was to work for freedom from Austria and a union with Serbia. So strict was the police vigilance in Bosnia and Herzegovina that we set up our headquarters in Belgrade, the capital of our mother country.

The men who were terrorists in 1914 embraced all classes. Most of them were students. Youth is the time for the philosophy of action. There were also teachers, tradesmen and peasants, artisans and even men of the upper classes

"The Plot and Murder" is from *New York World,* June 28, 1924, the North American Newspaper Alliance.

were ardent patriots. They were dissimilar in everything except hatred of the oppressor.

Such were the men into whose hands the tiny bit of newsprint was sent by friends in Bosnia that April night in Belgrade. At a small table in a very humble café, beneath a flickering gas jet we sat and read it. There was no advice nor admonition sent with it. Only four letters and two numerals were sufficient to make us unanimous, without discussion, as to what we should do about it. They were contained in the fateful date, June 28.

How dared Francis Ferdinand, not only the representative of the oppressor but in his own person an arrogant tyrant, enter Sarajevo on that day? Such an entry was a studied insult.

June 28 is a date engraved deep in the heart of every Serb, so that the day has a name of its own. It is called the *vidovnan* [St. Vitus Day]. It is the day on which the old Serbian kingdom was conquered by the Turks at the battle of Amselfelde in 1389. It is also the day on which in the second Balkan War the Serbian armies took glorious revenge on the Turk for his old victory and for the years of enslavement. . . .

As we read that clipping in Belgrade we knew what we would do to Francis Ferdinand. We would kill him to show Austria there yet lived within its borders defiance of its rule. We would kill him to bring once more to the boiling point the fighting spirit of the revolutionaries and pave the way for revolt.

Our decision was taken almost immediately. Death to the tyrant!

Then came the matter of arranging it. To make his death certain twenty-two members of the organization were selected to carry out the sentence. At first we thought we would choose the men by lot. But here Gavrilo Princip intervened. . . . From the moment Ferdinand's death was decided upon, he took an active leadership in its planning. Upon his advice we left the deed to members of our band, who were in and around Sarajevo, under his direction and that of Gabrinovic, a linotype operator on a Serbian newspaper. Both were regarded as capable of anything in the cause. . . .

The fateful morning dawned. Two hours before Francis Ferdinand arrived in Sarajevo all the twenty-two conspirators were in their allotted positions, armed and ready. They were distributed five hundred yards apart over the whole route along which the Archduke must travel from the railroad station to the town hall.

When Francis Ferdinand and his retinue drove from the station they were allowed to pass the first two conspirators. The motor cars were driving too fast to make an attempt feasible and in the crowd were many Serbians; throwing a grenade would have killed many innocent people.

When the car passed Gabrinovic, the compositor, he threw his grenade. It hit the side of the car, but Francis Ferdinand with presence of mind threw himself back and was uninjured. Several officers riding in his attendance were injured.

The cars sped to the Town Hall and the rest of the conspirators did not interfere with them. After the reception in the Town Hall General Potiorek, the Austrian Commander, pleaded with Francis Ferdinand to leave the city, as it was seething with rebellion. The Archduke was persuaded to drive the shortest way out of the city and to go quickly.

The road to the maneuvers was shaped like the letter V, making a sharp turn at the bridge over the River Nilgacka. Francis Ferdinand's car could go fast enough until it reached this spot but here it was forced to slow down for the turn. Here Princip had taken his stand.

As the car came abreast he stepped forward from the curb, drew his automatic pistol from his coat and fired two shots. The first struck the wife of the Archduke, the Archduchess Sofia, in the abdomen. She was an expectant mother. She died instantly.

The second bullet struck the Archduke close to the heart.

He uttered only one word, "Sofia"—a call to his stricken wife. Then his head fell back and he collapsed. He died almost instantly.

The officers seized Princip. They beat him over the head with the flat of their swords. They knocked him down, they kicked him, scraped the skin from his neck with the edges of their swords, tortured him, all but killed him.

The next day they put chains on Princip's feet, which he wore till his death. . . .

I was placed in the cell next to Princip's, and when Princip was taken out to walk in the prison yard I was taken along as his companion.

By Oct. 12, the date of Princip's trial, his prison sufferings had worn him to a skeleton. His sentence was twenty years imprisonment at hard labor, the death sentence being inapplicable because he was a minor.

Awakened in the middle of the night and told that he was to be carried off to another prison, Princip made an appeal to the prison governor:

"There is no need to carry me to another prison. My life here is already ebbing away. I suggest that you nail me to a cross and burn me alive. My flaming body will be a torch to light my people on their path to freedom."

"The Sword Is Drawn!" (August 18, 1914)
KAISER WILHELM II

For several years Europe had been diplomatically divided into two rival camps. The Triple Alliance was formed in 1882 among Germany, Italy, and Austria-Hungary. In 1907, the Triple Entente was established among Great Britain, France, and Russia. Both organizations were pledged by treaty to support their respective allies militarily should their mutual interests or existence be threatened. Thus, the European world was shocked by the assassination of Archduke Franz Ferdinand. Poised on the brink of crisis, each nation took stock of its

"'The Sword Is Drawn!'" is from Louis L. Snyder, ed., *Historic Documents of World War I* (Princeton: Van Nostrand, 1958), pp. 80–81. Reprinted by permission of Louis Snyder.

diplomatic commitments, its military arsenal, and its long-range goals. Such a slap in the face of the powerful Austro-Hungarian empire by Serbian terrorists had wide-ranging implications. Response had to be quick in order to preserve the honor and integrity of the throne and to assure that such action would not invite further insolence, which could lead to outright revolt. There were other factors to consider as well. How would Russia react to a severe stand against the Serbs? Russia, after all, was a Slavic nation and was promoting a policy that advocated the independence and cultural integrity of Balkan Slavs.

The Austrians sought German support in their plans to punish Serbia for the assassination of the Austrian heir. Germany would be an important ally in countering the potential hostility of Russia. On July 6, 1914, the German kaiser, Wilhelm II, sent a "blank check" telegram that guaranteed German support for whatever punishment Austria decided to inflict upon Serbia. Austria thereupon declared war and started mobilizing her military forces. One by one, the European powers declared war on each other, constrained by the dictates of their alliance systems and by the necessity to obtain an advantage in mobilizing their military forces as quickly as possible.

The light of reason gave way to military timetables, national pride, and the celebration of war. Certain of their military superiority, the Germans expected a short conflict and looked forward to being home "before the leaves fall." As Kaiser Wilhelm drew his sword, European confidence, even arrogance, was about to meet the full fury of modern, mechanized warfare. A door had closed and the modern era was born amid the tragedy of the Great War.

Former generations as well as those who stand here today have often seen the soldiers of the First Guard Regiment and My Guards at this place. We were brought together then by an oath of allegiance which we swore before God. Today all have gathered to pray for the triumph of our weapons, for now that oath must be proved to the last drop of blood. The sword, which I have left in its scabbard for decades, shall decide.

I expect My First Guard Regiment on Foot and My Guards to add a new page of fame to their glorious history. The celebration today finds us confident in God in the Highest and remembering the glorious days of Leuthen, Chlum, and St. Privat. Our ancient fame is an appeal to the German people and their sword. And the entire German nation to the last man has grasped the sword. And so I draw the sword which with the help of God I have kept in its scabbard for decades. [At this point the Kaiser drew his sword from its scabbard and held it high above his head.]

The sword is drawn, and I cannot sheathe it again without victory and honor. All of you shall and will see to it that only in honor is it returned to the scabbard. You are my guarantee that I can dictate peace to my enemies. Up and at the enemy! Down with the enemies of Brandenburg!

Three cheers for our army!

"Our ancient fame is an appeal to the German people and their sword. And the entire German nation to the last man has grasped the sword. . . . Three cheers for our army!"—Kaiser Wilhelm II *(Corbis-Bettmann)*

"They Shall Not Pass": The Great War (1914–1918)

The Horror of Battle

The German strategy in August 1914 had been planned long in advance by Count Alfred von Schlieffen, German chief of staff until 1905. The essence of the strategy was to sweep through Belgium and overwhelm French defenses in one swift onslaught; about 90 percent of the German army would be used for that purpose, while the remaining fraction, together with the Austrians, would hold off Russia. Once France was defeated, Germany and Austria-Hungary could concentrate their forces against the Russian army. Quite unexpectedly, however, the Belgians put up a gallant resistance, and the German attack was stalled long enough to upset the timetable. The British were able to land troops in Europe, and the war degenerated into a struggle for position that was characterized by trench warfare. New weapons such as the machine gun, the tank, and barbed wire eliminated thousands of men as attacks failed and comrades were left to die in the region between the trenches called "no man's land."

The following accounts of soldiers testify to the horrors of ceaseless shelling and destruction. The Battle of Verdun in 1916 raged for ten months, resulting in a combined total of about one million casualties. The Battle of the Somme lasted five months, with well over one million killed or wounded. Very little ground or tactical advantage was gained. Battle cries such as the French "They Shall Not Pass" were indicative of the stalemated defensive war. In such a situation, propaganda leaflets dropped into enemy trenches by balloons attempted to gain advantage in what was as much psychological as physical combat.

The Battle of Verdun (February–December 1916)

During three days (February 26–29th) after their initial advance over devastated and useless ground, they assaulted with the greatest dash and determination the main French positions. But the defenders were now in strength; and the French guns at length took matters in hand. The German assaulting waves dashed themselves in vain against the Talou heights, the Pepper ridge, and the Vaux position. They were ripped open with cannon, broken by the French bayonets, and driven back with fearful slaughter, time and again. Finally the mauled and battered German columns collapsed, and they were withdrawn from the fray; the casualties of the assailants for the first full week of uninterrupted fighting being estimated, on the lowest computation, at 60,000.

For such heavy sacrifice the enemy technically had won nothing, although, as usual, he indulged in much boasting and he magnified tremendously the barren results he had obtained from the action—an insignificant and useless gain of ground, a few prisoners, and some disabled guns; this was really all he could show as the outcome of his plan which was meant to open to him the gates of Verdun and to place him in possession of the Heights of the Meuse. The French, who had lost 20,000 men, continued to hold Verdun and the main positions surrounding it. . . .

Thousands of projectiles are flying in all directions, some whistling, others howling, others moaning low, and all uniting in one infernal roar. From time to time an aerial torpedo passes, making a noise like a gigantic motor car. With a tremendous thud a giant shell bursts quite close to our observation post, breaking the telephone wire and interrupting all communication with our batteries.

A man gets out at once for repairs, crawling along on his stomach through all this place of busting mines and shells. It seems quite impossible that he should escape in the rain of shell, which exceeds anything imaginable; there has never been such a bombardment in war. Our man seems to be enveloped

"The Battle of Verdun" is from Charles F. Horne, ed., *Source Records of the Great War*, vol. 4 (Indianapolis: The American Legion, 1931), pp. 45, 54–57. Reprinted by permission of The American Legion.

The French soldier defending the stronghold of Verdun, where the German high command tried "to bleed the French army white" during ten months of fighting: "Despite the horror of it, despite the ceaseless flow of blood, one wants to see. One's soul wants to feed on the sight of the brute Boches falling." *(Reproduced by permission of the Trustees of the Imperial War Museum, London)*

282

in explosions, and shelters himself from time to time in the shell craters which honeycomb the ground; finally he reaches a less stormy spot, mends his wires, and then, as it would be madness to try to return, settles down in a big crater and waits for the storm to pass.

Beyond, in the valley, dark-masses are moving over the snow-covered ground. It is German infantry advancing in packed formation along the valley to the attack. They look like a big gray carpet being unrolled over the country. We telephone through to the batteries and the ball begins. The sight is hellish. In the distance, in the valley and upon the slopes, regiments spread out, and as they deploy fresh troops come pouring in.

There is a whistle over our heads. It is our first shell. It falls right in the middle of the enemy infantry. We telephone through, telling our batteries of their hit, and a deluge of heavy shells is poured on the enemy. Their position becomes critical. Through glasses we can see men maddened, men covered with earth and blood, falling one upon the other. When the first wave of the assault is decimated, the ground is dotted with heaps of corpses, but the second wave is already pressing on. Once more our shells carve awful gaps in their ranks. Nevertheless, like an army of rats the Boches [Germans] continue to advance in spite of our "marmites." Then our heavy artillery bursts forth in fury.

The whole valley is turned into a volcano, and its exit is stopped by the barrier of the slain.

Despite the horror of it, despite the ceaseless flow of blood, one wants to see. One's soul wants to feed on the sight of the brute Boches falling. I stopped on the ground for hours, and when I closed my eyes I saw the whole picture again. The guns are firing at 200 and 300 yards, and shrapnel is exploding with a crash, scything them down. Our men hold their ground; our machine guns keep to their work, and yet they advance.

The Boches are returning again massed to the assault, and they are being killed in bulk. It makes one think that in declaring war the Kaiser had sworn the destruction of his race, and he would have shown good taste in doing so. Their gunfire is slackening now, and ours redoubles. The fort has gone, and if under its ruins there are left a few guns and gunners the bulk of the guns are firing from outside. The machine guns are coming up and getting in position, and our men are moving on in numerous waves.

I find a rifle belonging to a comrade who has fallen and join the Chasseurs with the fifty cartridges that I have left. What a fight it is, and what troops! From time to time a man falls, rises, shoots, runs, shoots again, keeps on firing, fights with his bayonet, and then, worn out, falls, to be trampled on without raising a cry. The storm of fire continues. Everything is on fire—the wood nearby, the village of Douaumont, Verdun, the front of Bezonvaux, and the back of Thiaumont. There is fire everywhere. The acid smell of carbonic acid and blood catches at our throats, but the battle goes on.

They are brave, but one of our men is worth two of theirs, especially in hand-to-hand fighting. . . . Our reinforcements continue to arrive. We are the masters.

The Battle of the Somme (July–November 1916)

The German Command was not thinking much about the human suffering of its troops. It was thinking, necessarily, of the next defensive line upon which they would have to fall back if the pressure of the British offensive could be maintained. . . . It was getting nervous. Owing to the enormous efforts made in the Verdun offensive the supplies of ammunition were not adequate to the enormous demand.

The German gunners were trying to compete with the British in continuity of bombardments and the shells were running short. Guns were wearing out under this incessant strain, and it was difficult to replace them. General von Gallwitz received reports of "an alarmingly large number of bursts in the bore, particularly in the field guns."

In all the letters written during those weeks of fighting and captured by us from dead or living men there is one great cry of agony and horror.

"I stood on the brink of the most terrible days of my life," wrote one of them. "They were those of the battle of the Somme. It began with a night attack on August 13th–14th. The attack lasted till the evening of the 18th, when the English wrote on our bodies in letters of blood: 'It is all over with you.' A handful of the half-mad, wretched creatures, worn out in body and mind, were all that was left of a whole battalion. We were that handful."

In many letters this phrase was used. The Somme was called the "Bath of Blood" by the German troops who waded across its shell-craters, and in the ditches which were heaped with their dead. But what I have described is only the beginning of the battle, and the bath was to be filled deeper in the months that followed.

It was in no cheerful mood that men went away to the Somme battlefields. Those battalions of gray-clad men entrained without any of the old enthusiasm with which they had gone to earlier battles. Their gloom was noticed by the officers.

"Sing, you sheep's heads, sing!" they shouted.

They were compelled to sing, by order.

"In the afternoon," wrote a man of the 18th Reserve Division, "we had to go out again: we were to learn to sing. The greater part did not join in, and the song went feebly. Then we had to march round in a circle, and sing, and that went no better."

"After that we had an hour off, and on the way back to billets we were to sing 'Deutschland über Alles,' but this broke down completely. One never hears songs of the Fatherland any more."

They were silent, grave-eyed men who marched through the streets of French and Belgian towns to be entrained for the Somme front, for they had

"The Battle of the Somme" is from Charles F. Horne, ed., *Source Records of the Great War*, vol. 4 (Indianapolis: The American Legion, 1931), pp. 248–251. Reprinted by permission of The American Legion.

forebodings of the fate before them. Yet none of their forebodings were equal in intensity of fear to the frightful reality into which they were flung.

No Man's Land

J. KNIGHT-ADKIN

No Man's Land is an eerie sight
At early dawn in the pale gray light.
Never a house and never a hedge
In No Man's Land from edge to edge,
And never a living soul walks there
To taste the fresh of the morning air.
Only some lumps of rotting clay,
That were friends or foemen yesterday.

What are the bounds of No Man's Land?
You can see them clearly on either hand,
A mound of rag-bags gray in the sun,
Or a furrow of brown where the earth works run
From the eastern hills to the western sea,
Through field or forest o'er river and lea;
No man may pass them, but aim you well
And Death rides across on the bullet or shell.

But No Man's Land is a goblin sight
When patrols crawl over at dead o' night;
Boche or British, Belgian or French,
You dice with death when you cross the trench.
When the "rapid," like fireflies in the dark,
Flits down the parapet spark by spark,
And you drop for cover to keep your head
With your face on the breast of the four months' dead.

The man who ranges in No Man's Land
Is dogged by the shadows on either hand
When the star-shell's flares, as it bursts o'erhead,
Scares the great gray rats that feed on the dead,
And the bursting bomb or the bayonet-snatch
May answer the click of your safety-catch.
For the lone patrol, with his life in his hand,
Is hunting for blood in No Man's Land.

"No Man's Land" is from W. Reginald Wheeler, ed., *A Book of Verse of the Great War* (New Haven: Yale University Press, 1917), pp. 90–91. Reprinted by permission of The Spectator.

Life in the Trenches

ROBERT GRAVES

Those were early days of trench warfare, the days of the jamtin bomb and the gas-pipe trench mortar: still innocent of Lewis or Stokes guns, steel helmets, telescopic rifle-sights, gas-shells, pillboxes, tanks, well-organized trench-raids, or any of the later refinements of trench warfare.

After a meal of bread, bacon, rum, and bitter stewed tea sickly with sugar, we went through the broken trees to the east of the village and up a long trench to battalion headquarters. The wet and slippery trench ran through dull red clay. I had a torch with me, and saw that hundreds of field mice and frogs had fallen into the trench but found no way out. The light dazzled them, and because I could not help treading on them, I put the torch back in my pocket. We had no mental picture of what the trenches would be like, and were almost as ignorant as a young soldier who joined us a week or two later. He called out excitedly to old Burford, who was cooking up a bit of stew in a dixie, apart from the others: 'Hi, mate, where's the battle? I want to do my bit.'

We now came under rifle-fire, which I found more trying than shell-fire. The gunner, I knew, fired not at people but at map-references—crossroads, likely artillery positions, houses that suggested billets for troops, and so on. Even when an observation officer in an aeroplane or captive balloon or on a church spire directed the guns, it seemed random, somehow. But a rifle-bullet, even when fired blindly, always seemed purposely aimed. And whereas we could usually hear a shell approaching, and take some sort of cover, the rifle-bullet gave no warning. So, though we learned not to duck a rifle-bullet because, once heard, it must have missed, it gave us a worse feeling of danger. Rifle-bullets in the open went hissing into the grass without much noise, but when we were in a trench, the bullets made a tremendous crack as they went over the hollow. Bullets often struck the barbed wire in front of the trenches, which sent them spinning with a head-over-heels motion—ping! rockety-ockety-ockety into the woods behind.

I went on patrol fairly often, finding that the only thing respected in young officers was personal courage. Besides, I had cannily worked it out like this. My best way of lasting through to the end of the war would be to get wounded. The best time to get wounded would be at night and in the open, with the rifle fire more or less unaimed and my whole body exposed. Best, also, to get wounded when there was no rush on the dressing-station services, and while the back areas were not being heavily shelled. Best to get wounded,

American soldiers go "over the top" in an effort to storm German fortifications. "Only a general who was a Barbarian would send his men to certain death against the concentrated power of my new gun."—Hiram Maxim (inventor of the machine gun) *(AP/Wide World Photos)*

therefore, on a night patrol in a quiet sector. One could usually manage to crawl into a shell hole until help arrived.

Still, patrolling had its peculiar risks. If a German patrol found a wounded man, they were as likely as not to cut his throat. The bowie-knife was a favourite German patrol weapon because of its silence. . . . The most important information that a patrol could bring back was to what regiment and division the troops opposite belonged. So if it were impossible to get a wounded enemy back without danger to oneself, he had to be stripped of his badges. To do that quickly and silently, it might be necessary to cut his throat or beat in his skull.

Like everyone else, I had a carefully worked out formula for taking risks. In principle, we would all take any risk, even the certainty of death, to save life or to maintain an important position. To take life we would run, say, a one-in-five risk, particularly if there was some wider object than merely reducing the enemy's manpower; for instance, picking off a well-known sniper, or getting fire ascendancy in trenches where the lines came dangerously close.

French Propaganda Leaflet

Pass this along!
  German War Comrades!
Think about this:

1. Only greedy rulers want war. The people want peace, and work, and bread.
2. Only the German Kaiser with his militarists, Junkers, and arms manufac-
    turers wanted war, prepared for it, and brought it on. No one wanted to
    fight Germany, no one opposed her desires for a "place in the sun."
3. If a murderer shoots a revolver on the street, it is the duty of every peace-
    loving, dutiful citizen to hurry to the aid of the fallen. For that reason
    Italy, Rumania, and the United States went to war against Germany; to
    free Belgium, Serbia, and France from the clutches of the murderer. . . .
10. Stop *[fighting]*! Turn your cannons around! Come over to us. Shoot any-
    one who wants to hinder you from coming.

YOUR DEMOCRATIC GERMAN COMRADES IN FRENCH PRISONS

What Are You Fighting For, Michel?

They tell you that you are fighting to secure victory for your Fatherland. But
have you ever thought about what you are fighting for?

You are fighting for the glory of, and for the enrichment of the Krupps.
You are fighting to save the Kaiser, the Junkers and the War Lords who
caused the war from the anger of the people.

The Junkers [German nobility] are sitting at home with their bejewelled wives
and mistresses. Their bank accounts are constantly growing, accounts to which
you and your comrades pay with your lives. For your wives and brides there are no
growing bank accounts. They are at home working and starving, sacrifices like
yourselves to the greed of the ruling class to whose pipes you have to dance.

What a dance! The dance of death. But yesterday you marched over the
corpses of your comrades against the English cannon. Tomorrow another
German soldier will march over your corpse.

You have been promised victory and peace. You poor fool! Your comrades
were also promised these things more than three years ago. Peace indeed
they have found—deep in the grave. But victory did not come.

Your Kaiser has adorned the glorious Hindenburg with the Iron Cross with
golden beams. What has the Kaiser awarded to you? Ruin, suffering, poverty,
hunger for your wives and children, misery, disease, and tomorrow the grave.

"French Propaganda Leaflet" is from George G. Bruntz, *Allied Propaganda and the Collapse of the German Empire in 1918*, Hoover War Library Publication No. 13 (Stanford: Stanford University Press, 1938), p. 98. Reprinted by permission of the publisher.

"What Are You Fighting For, Michel?" is from George G. Bruntz, *Allied Propaganda and the Collapse of the German Empire in 1918*, Hoover War Library Publication No. 13 (Stanford: Stanford University Press, 1938), p. 99. Reprinted by permission of the publisher.

It is for the Fatherland, you say, that you go out as a brave patriot to death for the Fatherland.

But of what does your Fatherland consists? Is it the Kaiser with his fine speeches? Is it the Crown Prince with his jolly companions, who sacrificed 600,000 men at Verdun? Is it [Field Marshall] Hindenburg, who sits with [General] Ludendorf, both covered with medals many kilometers behind you and who plans how he can furnish the English with still more cannon fodder. Is it Frau Bertha Krupp for whom through year after year of war you pile up millions upon millions of marks? Is it the Prussian Junkers who cry out over your dead bodies for annexation?

No, the Fatherland is not any of these. You are the Fatherland, Michel! You and your sisters and your wives and your parents and your children. You, the common people are the Fatherland. And yet it is you and your comrades who are driven like slaves into the hell of English cannon-fire, driven by the command of the feelingless slave-drivers.

When your comrades at home were striking, they were shot at with machine guns. If you, after the war, strike a blow for your rights, the machine guns will be turned upon you, for you are fighting only to increase the power of your lords.

Do you perhaps believe your rulers who love war as you hate it? Of course not. They love war for it brings them advancement, honor, power, profit. The longer the war lasts, the longer they will postpone the revolution.

They promise you that you can compel the English to beg for peace. Do you really believe that? You have advanced a few kilometers but for every Englishman whom you have shot down, six Germans have fallen. And all America is still to come.

Your commanders report to you wonderful stories of English losses. But did they tell you that Germany in the first five days of battle lost 315,000 men? Arrayed against Germany in battle today stands the entire world because it knows that German rulers caused the war to serve their own greedy ambition. The entire power of the Western World stands behind England and France and America. Soon it will go forth to battle. Have you thought of that, Michel?

The Red Baron: Glory in the Skies?
BARON MANFRED VON RICHTHOFEN

While the infantryman was exposed to the frustration and chaos of land combat, there was another war that existed with less restriction. By 1916, airplanes had been developed for combat, and the sky became the haven for men who relished the opportunity to test individual skill in "dogfights" high above the earth. The romantic notion of the solitary warrior, with scarf flying high in the wind, was established by men who played by their own rules of honor and death in the air. Baron Manfred von

"The Red Baron" is from Manfred von Richthofen, *The Red Battle Flyer* (New York: McBride Co., 1918), pp. 131–133

Richthofen, a member of the Prussian aristocracy, became the ace of the war, shoot-ing down eighty planes within two years before he himself was felled. In spite of his romantic aura, Richthofen was a methodical killer, a hunter with a morbid curios-ity for death, who flew with his brains and not with the innocent courage of other pilots. The Red Baron discriminated between a sportsman and a butcher: "The lat-ter shoots for fun. When I have shot down an Englishman, my hunting passion is satisfied for a quarter of an hour. If one of them comes down, I have a feeling of complete satisfaction. Only much much later I have overcome my instinct and have become a butcher." The first excerpt is from his autobiography, The Red Battle Flyer; *the second selection is an assessment of the Red Baron by one of his fellow pilots.*

My First English Victim (September 17, 1915)

We were all at the butts trying our machine guns. On the previous day we had received our new aeroplanes and the next morning Boelcke was to fly with us. We were all beginners. None of us had had a success so far. Consequently everything that Boelcke told us was to us gospel truth. Every day, during the last few days, he had, as he said, shot one or two Englishmen for breakfast.

Slowly we approached the hostile squadron. It could not escape us. We had intercepted it, for we were between the Front and our opponents. If they wished to go back they had to pass us. We counted the hostile machines. They were seven in number. We were only five. All the Englishmen flew large bomb-carrying two-seaters. In a few seconds the dance would begin.

Boelcke had come very near the first English machine but he did not yet shoot. I followed. Close to me were my comrades. The Englishman nearest to me was traveling in a large boat painted with dark colors. I did not reflect very long but took my aim and shot.

Apparently he was no beginner, for he knew exactly that his last hour had arrived at the moment when I got at the back of him. At that time I had not yet the conviction "He must fall!" which I have now on such occasions, but on the contrary, I was curious to see whether he would fall. There is a great dif-ference between the two feelings. When one has shot down one's first, sec-ond or third opponent, then one begins to find out how the trick is done.

In a fraction of a second I was at his back with my excellent machine. I gave a short series of shots with my machine gun. I had gone so close that I was afraid I might dash into the Englishman. Suddenly, I nearly yelled with joy for the propeller of the enemy machine had stopped turning. I had shot his engine to pieces; the enemy was compelled to land, for it was impossible for him to reach his own lines.

The Englishman landed close to the flying ground of one of our squadrons. I was so excited that I landed also and my eagerness was so great that I nearly smashed up my machine. The English flying machine and my own stood close together. I rushed to the English machine and saw that a lot of soldiers were running towards my enemy. When I arrived I discovered that my assumption had been correct. I had shot the engine to pieces and both the pilot and ob-server were severely wounded. The observer died at once and the pilot while

The aerial dogfight. "In my opinion the aggressive spirit is everything and that spirit is very strong in us Germans. . . . Therefore, the blood of English pilots will have to flow in streams."—Baron Manfred von Richthofen *(Mrs. Cockburn-Lange/Corbis)*

being transported to the nearest dressing station. I honored the fallen enemy by placing a stone on his beautiful grave.

English and French Flying (February 1917)

The great thing in air fighting is that the decisive factor does not lie in trick flying but solely in the personal ability and energy of the aviator. A flying man may be able to loop and do all the stunts imaginable and yet he may not suc-ceed in shooting down a single enemy. In my opinion the aggressive spirit is everything and that spirit is very strong in us Germans. Hence we shall always retain the domination of the air.

The French have a different character. They like to put traps and to attack their opponents unawares. That cannot easily be done in the air. Only a beginner can be caught and one cannot set traps because an aeroplane cannot hide itself. The invisible aeroplane has not yet been discovered. Sometimes, however, the Gaelic blood asserts itself. The Frenchmen will then attack. But the French attacking spirit is like bottled lemonade. It lacks tenacity.

The Englishmen, on the other hand, one notices that they are of Germanic blood. Sportsmen easily take to flying, and Englishmen see in flying nothing but a sport. They take a perfect delight in looping the loop, flying on their back, and indulging in other stunts for the benefit of our soldiers in the trenches. All these tricks may impress people who attend a Sports Meeting, but the public at the battle-front is not as appreciative of these things. It demands higher qualifications than trick flying. Therefore, the blood of English pilots will have to flow in streams.

An Assessment of the Red Baron

ERNST UDET

What a man he was! The others, admittedly, were doing their share, but they had wives at home, children, a mother or a profession. And only on rare occasions could they forget it. But Richthofen always lived on the other side of the boundary which we crossed only in our great moments. When he fought, his private life was thrust ruthlessly behind him. Eating, drinking and sleeping were all he granted life, and then only the minimum that was necessary to keep flesh and blood in working order. He was the simplest man I ever met. He was a Prussian through and through. A great soldier.

It Is Sweet and Proper to Die for One's Country

Wilfred Owen, a poet and soldier who was killed a week before the war ended, wrote that the "Lie" of the conflict lay in the belief that it was honorable and proper to give your life for the benefit of your country (Dulce et decorum est pro patria mori). *Indeed, the war seemed to people an absurd and tragic event. Why were they fighting? Why did old men send young men off to die "for their country"? How could poisonous gas, which burned out the lungs and led to a painfully slow death, be justified—or submarines, which destroyed under cover, thus eliminating a "fair fight"? The rules of war had changed. Disillusionment was evident in mutinies*

"An Assessment of the Red Baron" is from Ernst Udet, *Ace of the Black Cross,* trans. Kenneth Kirkness (London: Newnes, 1937), p. 72.

and in the poetry written in the trenches and in the letters sent home. It was not enough to be complimented by your general for victory in battle.

Order of the Day (Battle of the Marne, September 1914)
GENERAL JOSEPH JOFFRE

September 11th

The battle which we have been fighting for the last five days has ended in an undoubted victory. The retreat of the 1st, 2nd, and 3rd German Armies before our left and center becomes more and more marked. The enemy's 4th Army in its turn has begun to withdraw to the north of Vitry and Sermaise.

Everywhere the enemy has left on the field numerous wounded and a quantity of munitions. Everywhere we have made prisoners while gaining ground. Our troops bear witness to the intensity of the fight, and the means employed by the Germans in their endeavors to resist our élan. The vigorous resumption of the offensive has determined our success.

Officers, non-commissioned officers, and men! You have all responded to my appeal; you have all deserved well of your country.

Five Souls
W. N. EWER

FIRST SOUL—
    I was a peasant of the Polish plain;
        I left my plow because the message ran:
        Russia, in danger, needed every man
    To save her from the Teuton; and was slain.
        I gave my life for freedom—this I know;
        For those who bade me fight had told me so.
SECOND SOUL—
    I was a Tyrolese, a mountaineer;
    I gladly left my mountain home to fight
    Against the brutal, treacherous Muscovite;
    And died in Poland on a Cossack spear.
        I gave my life for freedom—this I know;
        For those who bade me fight had told me so.

"Order of the Day" is from Charles F. Horne, ed., *Source Records of the Great War,* vol. 2 (Indianapolis: The American Legion, 1931), p. 281. Reprinted by permission of the American Legion.

"Five Souls" is from W. Reginald Wheeler, ed., *A Book of Verse of the Great War* (New Haven: Yale University Press, 1917), pp. 46–47. Reprinted by permission.

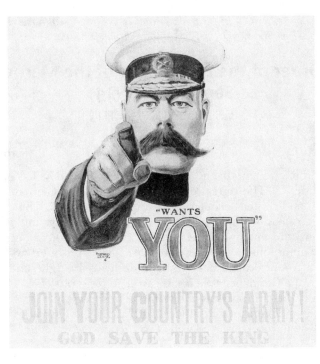

This poster of Field Marshal Lord Kitchener was the most famous and successful British recruiting poster during the Great War: "It is sweet and proper to give your life for your country."—Wilfred Owen *(Reproduced by permission of the Trustees of the Imperial War Museum, London)*

THIRD SOUL—
    I worked in Lyons at my weaver's loom,
        When suddenly the Prussian despot hurled
        His felon blow at France and at the world;
    Then I went forth to Belgium and my doom.
      I gave my life for freedom—this I know;
      For those who bade me fight had told me so.
FOURTH SOUL—
    I owned a vineyard by the wooded Main,
        Until the Fatherland, begirt by foes
        Lusting her downfall, called me, and I rose
    Swift to the call—and died in fair Lorraine.
      I gave my life for freedom—this I know;
      For those who bade me fight had told me so.
FIFTH SOUL—
    I worked in a great shipyard by the Clyde,
        There came a sudden word of wars declared,

Of Belgium, peaceful, helpless, unprepared,
Asking our aid; I joined the ranks, and died.
I gave my life for freedom—this I know;
For those who bade me fight had told me so.

A German War Letter:
"One Blood-Soaked, Corpse-Strewn Field"

RICHARD SCHMIEDER, Student of Philosophy, Leipzig
Born January 24th, 1888.
Killed July 14th, 1916, near Bethenville.

In the Trenches near Vaudesincourt, March 13th, 1915.

Anybody who, like myself, has been through the awful days near Penthy since the 6th of February, will agree with me that a more appalling struggle could not be imagined. It has been a case of soldier against soldier, equally matched and both mad with hate and anger, fighting for days on end over a single square of ground, till the whole tract of country is one blood-soaked, corpse-strewn field. . . .

On February 27th, tired out and utterly exhausted in body and mind, we were suddenly called up to reinforce the VIIIth Reserve Corps, had to reoccupy our old position at Ripont, and were immediately attacked by the French with extraordinary strength and violence. It was a gigantic murder, by means of bullets, shells, axes, and bombs, and there was such a thundering, crashing, bellowing and screaming as might have heralded the Day of Judgment.

In three days, on a front of about 200 yards, we lost 909 men, and the enemy casualties must have amounted to thousands. The blue French cloth mingled with the German grey upon the ground, and in some places the bodies were piled so high that one could take cover from shell-fire behind them. The noise was so terrific that orders had to be shouted by each man into the ear of the next. And whenever there was a momentary lull in the tumult of battle and the groans of the wounded, one heard, high up in the blue sky, the joyful song of birds! Birds singing just as they do at home in spring-time! It was enough to tear the heart out of one's body!

Don't ask about the fate of the wounded! Anybody who was incapable of walking to the doctor had to die a miserable death; some lingered in agony for hours, some for days, and even for a week. And the combatants stormed regardlessly to and fro over them: 'I can't give you a hand,—You're for the

"German Student's War Letter" is from *German Students' War Letters,* translated and arranged from the original edition of Dr. Philipp Witkop by A. F. Wedd (New York: E. P. Dutton, 1929), pp. 208–209. Reprinted by permission of Methuen and Company.

Promised Land,—My Comrade good and true.' A dog, dying in the poorest hovel at home, is enviable in comparison.

There are moments when even the bravest soldier is so utterly sick of the whole thing that he could cry like a child. When I heard the birds singing at Ripont, I could have crushed the whole world to death in my wrath and fury. If only those gentlemen—Grey, Asquith, and Poincaré—could be transported to this spot, instead of the war lasting ten years, there would be peace tomorrow!

Dulce et Decorum Est

WILFRED OWEN

Bent double, like old beggars under sacks,
Knocked-kneed, coughing like hags, we cursed through sludge,
Till on the haunting flares we turned our backs
And towards our distant rest began to trudge.
Men marched asleep. Many had lost their boots
But limped on, blood-shod. All went lame; all blind;
Drunk with fatigue; deaf even to the hoots
Of tired, outstripped Five-Nines that dropped behind.

Gas! Gas! Quick Boys!—An ecstasy of fumbling,
Fitting the clumsy helmets just in time;
But someone still was yelling out and stumbling
And flound'ring like a man in fire or lime. . . .
Dim, through the misty panes and thick green light,
As under a green sea, I saw him drowning.
In all my dreams, before my helpless sight,
He plunges at me, guttering, choking, drowning.

If in some smothering dreams you too could pace
Behind the wagon that we flung him in,
And watch the white eyes writhing in his face,
His hanging face, like a devil's sick of sin;
If you could hear, at every jolt, the blood
Come gargling from the froth-corrupted lungs,
Obscene as cancer, bitter as the cud

Of vile, incurable sores on innocent tongues,—
My friend, you would not tell with such high zest
To children ardent for some desperate glory,
The old Lie: Dulce et decorum est
Pro patria mori.

The Framework of Peace

In January 1917, Germany informed the United States that it intended to resume unrestricted submarine warfare. Consequently, three American merchant ships were sunk, and at President Woodrow Wilson's request Congress declared war with Germany on April 6. As fresh American troops arrived in Europe, German resistance became increasingly tenuous. It was left to President Wilson to provide the framework for a peace treaty. In his address to Congress, he proposed a fourteen-point plan.

The Fourteen Points (January 8, 1918)
WOODROW WILSON

Gentlemen of the Congress:

It will be our wish and purpose that the processes of peace, when they are begun, shall be absolutely open and that they shall involve and permit henceforth no secret understandings of any kind. The day of conquest and aggrandizement is gone by; so is also the day of secret covenants entered into in the interest of particular governments and likely at some unlooked-for moment to upset the peace of the world. It is this happy fact, now clear to the view of every public man whose thoughts do not still linger in an age that is dead and gone, which makes it possible for every nation whose purposes are consistent with justice and the peace of the world to avow now or at any other time the objects it has in view.

We entered this war because violations of right had occurred which touched us to the quick and made the life of our own people impossible unless they were corrected and the world secured once for all against their recurrence. What we demand in this war, therefore, is nothing peculiar to ourselves. It is that the world be made fit and safe to live in; and particularly that it be made safe for every peace-loving nation which, like our own, wishes to live its own life, determine its own institutions, be assured of justice and fair dealing by the other peoples of the world as against force and selfish aggression. All the peoples of the world are in effect partners in this interest, and for our own part we see very clearly that unless justice be done to others it will not be done to us. The program of the world's peace, therefore, is our program; and that program, the only possible program, as we see it, is this:

1. Open covenants of peace, openly arrived at, after which there shall be no private international understandings of any kind but diplomacy shall proceed always frankly and in the public view.

2. Absolute freedom of navigation upon the seas. . . .

4. Adequate guarantees given and taken that national armaments will be reduced to the lowest point consistent with domestic safety.

"The Fourteen Points" is from *Congressional Record* (January 8, 1918), vol. 56, pt. 1, p. 691.

5. A free, open-minded, and absolutely impartial adjustment of all colonial claims, based upon a strict observance of the principle that in determining all such questions of sovereignty the interests of the populations concerned must have equal weight with the equitable claims of the government whose title is to be determined.

6. The evacuation of all Russian territory and such a settlement of all questions affecting Russia as will secure . . . the independent determination of her own political development and national policy and assure her of a sincere welcome into the society of free nations under institutions of her own choosing. . . .

7. Belgium, the whole world will agree, must be evacuated and restored, without any attempt to limit the sovereignty which she enjoys in common with all other free nations. No other single act will serve as this will serve to restore confidence among the nations in the laws which they have themselves set and determined for the government of their relations with one another. Without this healing act the whole structure and validity of international law is forever impaired.

8. All French territory should be freed and the invaded portions restored, and the wrong done to France by Prussia in 1871 in the matter of Alsace-Lorraine, which has unsettled the peace of the world for nearly fifty years, should be righted, in order that peace may once more be made secure in the interest of all.

10. The peoples of Austria-Hungary, whose place among the nations we wish to see safeguarded and assured, should be accorded the freest opportunity of autonomous development.

11. Rumania, Serbia, and Montenegro should be evacuated; occupied territories restored; Serbia accorded free and secure access to the sea. . . .

13. An independent Polish state should be erected which should include the territories inhabited by indisputably Polish populations. . . .

14. A general association of nations must be formed under specific covenants for the purpose of affording mutual guarantees of political independence and territorial integrity to great and small states alike.

In regard to these essential rectifications of wrong and assertions of right we feel ourselves to be intimate partners of all the governments and peoples associated together against the Imperialists. We cannot be separated in interest or divided in purpose. We stand together until the end.

For such arrangements and covenants we are willing to fight and to continue to fight until they are achieved; but only because we wish the right to prevail and desire a just and stable peace such as can be secured only by removing the chief provocations to war, which this program does not remove. We have no jealousy of German greatness, and there is nothing in this program that impairs it. We grudge her no achievement or distinction of learning or of pacific enterprise such as have made her record very bright and very enviable. We do not wish to injure her or to block in any way her legitimate influence or power. We do not wish to fight her either with arms or with hostile arrangements of trade if she is willing to associate herself with us and the other peace-loving nations of the world in covenants of justice and law and fair dealing. We wish her only to accept a place of equality among the peoples of the world—the new world in which we now live,—instead of a place of mastery.

Neither do we presume to suggest to her any alteration or modification of her institutions. But it is necessary, we must frankly say, and necessary as a preliminary to any intelligent dealings with her on our part, that we should know whom her spokesmen speak for when they speak to us, whether for the Reichstag majority or for the military party and the men whose creed is imperial domination.

We have spoken now, surely, in terms too concrete to admit to any further doubt or question. An evident principle runs through the whole program of justice to all peoples and nationalities, and their right to live on equal terms of liberty and safety with one another, whether they be strong or weak. Unless this principle be made its foundation no part of the structure of international justice can stand. The people of the United States could act upon no other principle; and to the vindication of this principle they are ready to devote their lives, their honor, and everything that they possess. The moral climax of this, the culminating and final war for human liberty has come, and they are ready to put their own strength, their own highest purpose, their own integrity and devotion to the test.

Aftermath: The Light That Failed

"This Is the Way the World Ends"

On November 9, 1918, the German kaiser abdicated his throne and fled the country. The armistice, which ended the war, was signed on November 11. The European world of 1914 had been shattered, people were changed, and the foremost question was, how to begin again?

The first selection is from the diary of Anna Eisenmenger, an Austrian whose son returned home after the armistice a changed man. The treaty of 1922 was an attempt to civilize war and to protect the lives of noncombatants by regulating submarine warfare and by banning the use of poisonous gas. Both weapons were considered to have been immorally used during the war and remained a subject of controversy. The great psychoanalyst, Sigmund Freud (1856–1939), then comments on the great impact the war had on the modern attitude towards death. The final piece is an excerpt from a poem by T. S. Eliot. Where is the bluster and confidence that gave rise to the Great War?

A German Soldier Returns Home:
"A Complete Stranger"
ANNA EISENMENGER

Karl looked very ill. He had no underlinen or socks. His uniform was dirty and in rags. "Mother, I am famished!" he said, and walking straight into the kitchen without waiting for me to bring him something he began to devour our rations of bread and jam. "Forgive me, Mother, but we have got into the habit of taking what we can find." He only greeted us very casually and did not notice until much later that Erni, who had come in to welcome him on Liesbeth's arm, was wounded. "Hullo! So it's caught you too!" and then, still hurriedly chewing and swallowing: "Well, just wait! We'll pay them out yet, the war profiteers and parasites. We've grown wiser out there in the trenches, far wiser than we were. Everything must be changed, utterly changed."

I got ready the bath and clean underlinen. After his bath Karl went straight to bed, but he was too excited to sleep, although it was almost 11 o'clock at night. He telephoned to Edith, and then he made us all come to his bedside, for he wanted to tell us about himself. He told us that . . . the Italians had gone on attacking in spite of the Armistice. For another whole day they had fired on our retreating columns in the Fellathal and had captured several divisions. That, however, was the only victory they had won. It was contemptible, but war made every one base and contemptible. He had become so too. . . . After the proclamation of the Armistice all military discipline went to pieces. Everyone was intent only on getting home and made for home by the way that seemed to him quickest and surest. The men trampled down whatever stood in their way, even if the obstacle were their own officers. Woe to the officers who were unpopular with their men. . . . In the next war there would be no one foolish enough to risk his life, they would see to that. . . . Karl was evidently in a nervous, overexcited state, but he went on talking, and only after I had entreated him several times did he consent to try to get to sleep.

"We are all tired, Karl, and it is already past midnight . . ."

"Do you know, Mother, how I feel here? In a clean bed, washed and fed? As if I were in heaven. . . . Oh no, there is no heaven so beautiful. . . . As if I were in a beautiful dream . . . and in that dream I shall try to find sleep."

We left Karl's room in order to go to bed ourselves. As I was helping Erni undress, he said: "Mother, Karl seems to me like a complete stranger."

Although I was nervously and physically exhausted, sleep refused to close my eyelids. For a long, long time I lay awake, agitated by the horrors of the War. I found myself marvelling that civilised human beings could live through all the brutalities which war entailed for themselves and others without going utterly to pieces. . . .

"A German Soldier Returns Home" is from Anna Eisenmenger, *Blockade: The Diary of an Austrian Middle-Class Woman, 1914–1924* (London: Constable Publishers, 1932), pp. 39–42. Reprinted by permission of the publisher.

Treaty Concerning Submarines and Poisonous Gases in Warfare (1922)

The United States of America, the British Empire, France, Italy and Japan, hereinafter referred to as the Signatory Powers, desiring to make more effective the rules adopted by civilized nations for the protection of the lives of neutrals and noncombatants at sea in time of war, and to prevent the use in war of noxious gases and chemicals, have determined to conclude a Treaty to this effect:

Article I

The Signatory Powers declare that among the rules adopted by civilized nations for the protection of the lives of neutrals and noncombatants at sea in time of war, the following are to be deemed an established part of international law:

(1) A merchant vessel must be ordered to submit to visit and search to determine its character before it can be seized.

A merchant vessel must not be attacked unless it refuse to submit to visit and search after warning, or to proceed as directed after seizure.

A merchant must not be destroyed unless the crew and passengers have been first placed in safety.

(2) Belligerent submarines are not under any circumstances exempt from universal rules above stated; and if a submarine can not capture a merchant vessel in conformity with these rules the existing law of nations requires it to desist from attack and from seizure and to permit the merchant vessel to proceed unmolested.

Article IV

The Signatory Powers recognize the practical impossibility of using submarines as commerce destroyers without violating, as they were violated in the recent war of 1914–1918, the requirements universally accepted by civilized nations for the protection of the lives of neutrals and noncombatants, and to the end that the prohibition of the use of submarines as commerce destroyers shall be universally accepted as a part of the law of nations, they now accept that prohibition as henceforth binding as between themselves and they invite all other nations to adhere thereto.

Article V

The use in war of asphyxiating, poisonous or other gases, and all analogous liquids, materials or devices, having been justly condemned by the general

---

"Treaty Concerning Submarines and Poisonous Gases" is from *Department of State Bulletin* (February 6, 1922).

opinion of the civilized world and a prohibition of such use having been declared in treaties to which a majority of the civilized Powers are parties.

The Signatory Powers, to the end that this prohibition shall be universally accepted as a part of international law binding alike the prohibitions, agree to be bound thereby as between themselves and invite all other civilized nations to adhere thereto.

"If You Want to Endure Life—Prepare for Death"
SIGMUND FREUD

[A primary factor] to which I attribute our present sense of estrangement in this once lovely and congenial world is the disturbance that has taken place in the attitude which we have hitherto adopted towards death.

That attitude was far from straightforward. To anyone who listened to us we were of course prepared to maintain that death was the necessary outcome of life, that everyone owes nature a death and must expect to pay the debt—in short, that death was natural, undeniable and unavoidable. In reality, however, we were accustomed to behave as if it were otherwise. We showed an unmistakable tendency to put death on one side, to eliminate it from life. We tried to hush it up; indeed we even have a saying [in German]: "To think of something as though it were death." That is, as though it were our own death, of course. It is indeed impossible to imagine our own death; and whenever we attempt to do so we can perceive that we are in fact still present as spectators. Hence the psycho-analytic school could venture on the assertion that at bottom no one believes in his own death, or, to put the same thing in another way, that in the unconscious every one of us is convinced of his own immortality. . . .

It is evident that war is bound to sweep away this conventional treatment of death. Death will no longer be denied; we are forced to believe in it. People really die; and no longer one by one, but many, often tens of thousands, in a single day. And death is no longer a chance event. To be sure, it still seems a matter of chance whether a bullet hits this man or that; but a second bullet may well hit the survivor; and the accumulation of deaths puts an end to the impression of chance. Life has, indeed, become interesting again; it has recovered its full content. . . .

To sum up: our unconscious is just as inaccessible to the idea of our own death, just as murderously inclined towards strangers, just as divided (that is, ambivalent) towards those we love, as was primaeval man. But how far we

"If You Want to Endure Life—Prepare for Death" is from James Strachey, trans. and ed., *Standard Edition of the Complete Works of Sigmund Freud,* vol. 14 (London: Hogarth Press Ltd., 1957), pp. 280–281. Reprinted by permission of Sigmund Freud Copyrights, the Institute of Psycho-Analysis and The Hogarth Press Ltd.

"This is the way the world ends / Not with a bang but a whimper."—T. S. Eliot. *(Library of Congress)*

have moved from this primal state in our conventional and cultural attitude towards death!

It is easy to see how war impinges on this dichotomy. It strips us of the later accretions of civilization, and lays bare the primal man in each of us. It compels us once more to be heroes who cannot believe in their own death; it stamps strangers as enemies, whose death is to be brought about or desired; it tells us to disregard the death of those we love. But war cannot be abolished; so long as the conditions of existence among nations are so different and their mutual repulsion so violent, there are bound to be wars. The question then arises: Is it not we who should give in, who should adapt ourselves to war? Should we not confess that in our civilized attitude towards death we are once again living psychologically beyond our means, and should we not rather turn back and recognize the truth? Would it not be better to give death the place in reality and in our thoughts which is its due, and to give a little more prominence to the unconscious attitude towards death which we have hitherto so carefully suppressed? This hardly seems as advanced to higher achievement, but rather in some respects a backward step—a regression; but it has the advantage of taking the truth more into account, and of making life more tolerable for us once again. To tolerate life remains, after all, the first duty of all living beings. Illusion becomes valueless if it makes this harder for us.

We recall the old saying: *Si vis pacem, para bellum.* If you want to preserve peace, arm for war.

It would be in keeping with the times to alter it: *Si vis vitam, para mortem.* If you want to endure life, prepare yourself for death.

The Hollow Men (1925)

T. S. ELIOT

A penny for the Old Guy

We are the hollow men
We are the stuffed men

Leaning together
Headpiece filled with straw. Alas!
Our dried voices, when
We whisper together
Are quiet and meaningless
As wind in dry grass
Or rats' feet over broken glass
In our dry cellar

Shape without form, shade without colour,
Paralysed force, gesture without motion;

Those who have crossed
With direct eyes, to death's other Kingdom
Remember us—if at all—not as lost
Violent souls, but only
As the hollow men
The stuffed men.

        ● ● ●

For Thine is
Life is
For Thine is the

This is the way the world ends
This is the way the world ends
This is the way the world ends
Not with a bang but a whimper.

The Reflection in the Mirror (1925–1930)

The Great War was a turning point in the history of Western Civilization. The bluster of European achievement, the creation of armed states with myopic and rigid alliance systems, mobilization timetables, and uncreative leadership led the world to the greatest mass destruction yet experienced by human beings. Political arrogance had been supported in this endeavor by the perversions of science, which had produced the mechanized destruction of machine guns and the unimaginable pain of poisonous gas. Many worried that the West was an empty shell, a carcass on the desert, guilty of hubris and worthy of decline. Over the next twenty years, Europeans battled homelessness and despair, unemployment and economic dislocation. This was the "lost generation," searching for an explanation, appalled by the reflection in the mirror, and looking for new inspiration. The following selections reveal this weariness and search for meaning. The first is by the English mathematician and philosopher Alfred North Whitehead (1861–1947). In his book, Science and the Modern World *(1925), he sought to give some perspective regarding the impact of science on society and civilization. In the second selection, historian G. Lowes Dickinson struggled in 1926 with the relationship between war and civilization.*

"The Great Ages Have Been Unstable Ages"
ALFRED NORTH WHITEHEAD

Modern science has imposed on humanity the necessity of wandering. Its progressive thought and its progressive technology make the transition through time, from generation to generation, a true migration into uncharted seas of adventure. The very benefit of wandering is that it is dangerous and needs skill to avert evils. We must expect, therefore, that the future will disclose dangers. It is the business of the future to be dangerous; and it is among the merits of science that it equips the future for its duties. The prosperous middle classes, who ruled the nineteenth century, placed an excessive value upon placidity of existence. They refused to face the necessities for social reform imposed by the new industrial system, and they are now refusing to face the necessities for intellectual reform imposed by the new knowledge. The middle class pessimism over the future of the world comes from a confusion between civilisation and security. In the immediate future, there will be less security than in the immediate past, less stability. It must be admitted that there is a degree of instability which is inconsistent with civilisation. But, on the whole, the great ages have been unstable ages.

"The Great Ages Have Been Unstable Ages" is from Alfred North Whitehead, *Science and the Modern World* (New York: The Macmillan Company, 1925).

The International Anarchy (1926)

G. LOWES DICKINSON

I have written, consciously and deliberately, to point a moral. I believe, with most instructed people, that modern war, with all the resources of science at its disposal, has become incompatible with the continuance of civilization. If this be true, it is a mistake to look back upon the course of history and say: There has always been war, and yet civilization has survived. At the best, what has survived is a poor thing compared to what might have been, had there been no war. But even such poor survival cannot be counted upon in the future. . . .

My thesis is, that whenever and wherever the anarchy of armed states exists, war becomes inevitable. That was the condition in ancient Greece, in republican Rome, in medieval Italy, and in Europe for several centuries after its emergence from the feudal chaos. That chaos also involved war. But such war is not properly to be called civil or international; and with that particular condition we are not now concerned. International war, in our own age as in the others referred to, is a clash between sovereign armed States. It arises in consequence of the international anarchy. . . .

States armed, and therefore a menace to one another; policies ostensibly defensive, but really just as much offensive; these policies pursued in the dark by a very few men who, because they act secretly, cannot act honestly; and this whole complex playing upon primitive passions, arousable at any moment by appropriate appeals from a Press which has no object except to make money out of the weaknesses of men—that is the real situation of the world under the conditions of the international anarchy.

These conditions are commonly regarded as unalterable. Hence the view that war is a fate from which we cannot escape. I will cite in illustration the words of a typical militarist which express, I believe, the real opinion of most soldiers, sailors, politicians, journalists, and plain men: "Possibly in the future great coalitions of Powers will be able to keep the peace for long epochs and to avoid conflict with arms; but this will not be possible in permanence. The life of man is unbroken combat in every form; eternal peace, unfortunately, a Utopia in which only philanthropists ignorant of the world believe. A nation which lays down its arms thereby seals its fate."

Those who hold this philosophy also devoted their lives to making sure that it shall come true; for it is impossible to hold any view about life without thereby contributing to its realization. The confusion, in the passage quoted, between military conflict and other forms of struggle is patent to any one who can think. The same philosophy should conclude that civil war also is an eternal fact, a conclusion to which militarists are usually much averse. But this much is certainly true, that until men lay down their arms, and accept the method of peaceable decision of their disputes, war can never cease.

"The International Anarchy" is from G. Lowes Dickinson, *The International Anarchy*, 1904–1914 (London: Allen & Unwin, 1926), pp. v, 47–48.

A Room of One's Own (1929)

VIRGINIA WOOLF

The suffrage movement gained great impetus from the participation of women in the factories and hospitals during World War I (1914–1918). By 1920, women won full or partial political rights in Soviet Russia, Canada, Germany, Austria, Poland, Czechoslovakia, Hungary, Great Britain, and the United States. Still, there was to be a long road toward achieving a recognition among men and even among women of their potential for complete social equality. Postwar societies conceded initial change and then demanded stability and a reestablishment of "normalcy."

One of the most personal and articulate commentators on women in Western society was Virginia Woolf (1882–1941). A distinguished critic of her time, she stressed in her novels and essays the continuous flow of human experience. In her famous essay A Room of One's Own *(1929), she described the difficulties encountered by women writers in a man's world and offered her insight regarding the role of women in influencing history.*

Women have served all these centuries as looking-glasses possessing the magic and delicious power of reflecting the figure of man at twice its natural size. Without that power probably the earth would still be swamp and jungle. The glories of all our wars would be unknown. We should still be scratching the outlines of deer on the remains of mutton bones and bartering flints for sheepskins or whatever simple ornament took our unsophisticated taste. Supermen and Figures of Destiny would never have existed. The Czar and the Kaiser would never have worn their crowns or lost them. Whatever may be their use in civilised societies, mirrors are essential to all violent and heroic action. That is why Napoleon and Mussolini both insist so emphatically upon the inferiority of women, for if they were not inferior, they would cease to enlarge. That serves to explain in part the necessity that women so often are to men. And it serves to explain how restless they are under her criticism; how impossible it is for her to say to them this book is bad, this picture is feeble, or whatever it may be, without giving far more pain and rousing far more anger than a man would do who gave the same criticism. For if she begins to tell the truth, the figure in the looking-glass shrinks; his fitness for life is diminished. How is he to go on giving judgement, civilising natives, making laws, writing books, dressing up and speechifying at banquets, unless he can see himself at breakfast and at dinner at least twice the size he really is? So I reflected, crumbling my bread and stirring my coffee and now and again looking at the people in the street. The looking-glass vision is of supreme importance because it charges the vitality; it stimulates the nervous system. Take it away and man may die, like the drug fiend deprived of his cocaine. Under the spell of that illusion, I thought, looking out of the window, half the people on the pavement are striding to work. They put on their hats and coats in the morning under its agreeable rays. They star the day confident, braced, believing themselves desired at Miss Smith's tea party; they say to themselves as they go into the room, I am the superior of half the people here, and it is thus that they speak with that self-confidence, that self-assurance, which have had such profound consequences in public life and lead to such curious notes in the margin of the private mind. . . .

I need not hate any man; he cannot hurt me. I need not flatter any man; he has nothing to give me. So imperceptibly I found myself adopting a new attitude towards the other half of the human race. It was absurd to blame any class or any sex, as a whole. Great bodies of people are never responsible for what they do. They are driven by instincts which are not within their control. They too, the patriarchs, the professors, had endless difficulties, terrible drawbacks to contend with. Their education had been in some ways as faulty as my own. It had bred in them defects as great. True, they had money and power, but only at the cost of harbouring in their breasts an eagle, a vulture, forever tearing the liver out and plucking at the lungs—the instinct for possession, the rage for acquisition which drives them to desire other people's fields and goods perpetually; to make frontiers and flags; battleships and poison gas; to offer up their own lives and their children's lives. . . .

I thought how much harder it is now than it must have been even a century ago to say which . . . employments [are] the higher, the more necessary. Is it better to be a coal-heaver or a nursemaid; is the charwoman who has brought up eight children of less value to the world than the barrister who has made a hundred thousand pounds? It is useless to ask such questions; for nobody can answer them. Not only do the comparative values of charwomen and lawyers rise and fall from decade to decade, but we have no rods with which to measure them even as they are at the moment. . . . Even if one could state the value of any one gift at the moment, those values will change; in a century's time very possibly they will have changed completely. Moreover, in a hundred years, I thought, reaching my own doorstep, women will have ceased to be the protected sex. Logically they will take part in all the activities and exertions that were once denied them. The nursemaid will heave coal. The shop-woman will drive an engine. All assumptions founded on the facts observed when women were the protected sex will have disappeared. . . . Anything may happen when womanhood has ceased to be a protected occupation, I thought, opening the door.

On Human Nature (1930)

SIGMUND FREUD

Among the most controversial figures of the twentieth century was the Austrian physician and psychoanalyst Sigmund Freud (1856–1939). Freud sought to apply the critical methods of science to the understanding of the human uncon-

scious. His research centered on sexuality and the interpretation of dreams in his explanation of human motivation. He portrayed the mind as an area in which the irrational, amoral instincts (id) struggled with the restrictive demands of society (superego). The ego sought to reconcile these conflicting forces in order to maintain a stable existence. Freud's work stripped humanity of the privacy of its inner nature and led to a revolution in human understanding that has only recently been challenged.

One of Freud's most revealing works on the antagonisms between the demands of instinct and the restrictions of human society is Civilization and Its Discontents *(1930). In the excerpt below, Freud describes the destructive nature of human beings.*

The element of truth behind all this, which people are so ready to disavow, is that men are not gentle creatures who want to be loved, and who at the most can defend themselves if they are attacked; they are, on the contrary, creatures among whose instinctual endowments is to be reckoned a powerful share of aggressiveness. . . . Anyone who calls to mind the atrocities committed during the racial migrations or the invasions of the Huns, or by the people known as Mongols under Ghengis Khan and Tamerlane, or at the capture of Jerusalem by the pious Crusaders, or even, indeed, the horrors of the recent World War [1914–1918]—anyone who calls these things to mind will have to bow humbly before the truth of this view.

The existence of this inclination to aggression, which we can detect in ourselves and justly assume to be present in others, is the factor which disturbs our relations with our neighbour and which forces civilization into such a high expenditure [of energy]. In consequence of this primary mutual hostility of human beings, civilized society is perpetually threatened with disintegration. The interest of work in common would not hold it together; instinctual passions are stronger than reasonable interests. Civilization has to use its utmost efforts in order to set limits to man's aggressive instincts and to hold the manifestations of them in check. . . . Hence, therefore, the use of methods intended to incite people into identifications and aim-inhibited relationships of love, hence the restriction upon sexual life, and hence too the ideal's commandment to love one's neighbour as oneself—a commandment which is really justified by the fact that nothing else runs so strongly counter to the original nature of man. In spite of every effort, these endeavours of civilization have not so far achieved very much. It hopes to prevent the crudest excesses of brutal violence by itself assuming the right to use violence against criminals, but the law is not able to lay hold of the more cautious and refined manifestations of human aggressiveness. The time comes when each one of us has to give up as illusions the expectations which, in his youth, he pinned upon his fellow-men, and when he may learn how much difficulty and pain has been added to his life by their ill-will. At the same time, it would be unfair to reproach civilization with trying to eliminate strife and competition from human activity. These things are undoubtedly indispensable. But opposition is not necessarily enmity; it is merely misused and made an occasion for enmity.

The Communists believe that they have found the path to deliverance from our evils. According to them, man is wholly good and is well-disposed to his neighbour; but the institution of private property has corrupted his nature. The ownership of private wealth gives the individual power, and with it the temptation to ill-treat his neighbour; while the man who is excluded from possession is bound to rebel in hostility against his oppressor. If private property were abolished, all wealth held in common, and everyone allowed to share in the enjoyment of it, ill-will and hostility would disappear among men. Since everyone's needs would be satisfied, no one would have any reason to regard another as his enemy; all would willingly undertake the work that was necessary. I have no concern with any economic criticisms of the communist system; I cannot enquire into whether the abolition of private property is expedient or advantageous. But I am able to recognize that the psychological premises on which the system is based are an untenable illusion. In abolishing private property we deprive the human love of aggression of one of its instruments, certainly a strong one, though certainly not the strongest; but we have in no way altered the differences in power and influence which are misused by aggressiveness, nor have we altered anything in its nature. Aggressiveness was not created by property. It reigned almost without limit in primitive times, when property was still very scanty, and it already shows itself in the nursery almost before property has given up its primal, anal form; it forms the basis of every relation of affection and love among people. . . . If we do away with personal rights over material wealth, there still remains prerogative in the field of sexual relationships, which is bound to become the source of the strongest dislike and the most violent hostility among men who in other respects are on an equal footing. If we were to remove this factor, too, by allowing complete freedom of sexual life and thus abolishing the family, the germ-cell of civilization, we cannot, it is true, easily foresee what new paths the development of civilization could take; but one thing we can expect, and that is that this indestructible feature of human nature will follow it there. . . .

The fateful question for the human species seems to me to be whether and to what extent their cultural development will succeed in mastering the disturbance of their communal life by the human instinct of aggression and self-destruction. It may be that in this respect precisely the present time deserves a special interest. Men have gained control over the forces of nature to such an extent that with their help they would have no difficulty in exterminating one another to the last man. They know this, and hence comes a large part of their current unrest, their unhappiness and their mood of anxiety. . . .

CHRONOLOGY: The Great War and the Birth of the Modern Era

1900	Max Planck formulates quantum theory.
1901	Guglielmo Marconi transmits telegraphic radio messages from Cornwall to Newfoundland.

1903	Orville and Wilbur Wright successfully fly a powered airplane.
1905	Albert Einstein formulates special theory of relativity.
1910	Marie Curie: *Treatise on Radiography*.
1912	*S.S. Titanic* sinks on its maiden voyage.
1913	Premier of Igor Stravinsky's ballet *Rite of Spring* in Paris.
June 28, 1914	Assassination of Archduke Franz Ferdinand, heir to the Austro-Hungarian Empire.
July 28, 1914	Austria-Hungary declares war on Serbia after receiving "blank check" of support from Germany.
August 1914	Germany declares war on Russia (August 1) and France (August 3); Germany invades Belgium, followed immediately by Britain's declaration of war on Germany (August 4).
September 5–9, 1914	Battle of the Marne: French and British are able to stop the German advance in the west. Thereafter, the nature of the war in the west changed completely and became one of position instead of movement.
April 22, 1915	Germans employ poisonous gas for the first time at the Second Battle of Ypres.
April 25, 1915	British land at Gallipoli, start of Dardanelles campaign.
May 7, 1915	German submarine sinks the American ship, *Lusitania*. Among 1200 drowned were 118 Americans.
February–December 1916	Battle of Verdun results in 550,000 French and 450,000 German casualties.
July–November 1916	Battle of the Somme fails to achieve major breakthrough for Allied forces; British use tanks for the first time.
1917	Sigmund Freud: *Introduction to Psychoanalysis*.
March 1917	Revolution in Russia leads to abdication of Tsar Nicholas II.
April 6, 1917	United States declares war on Germany.
November 8, 1917	Bolsheviks seize power in Petrograd. Russia pulls out of the war.
January 8, 1918	President Woodrow Wilson issues the "Fourteen Points" framework for peace.
March 3, 1918	Bolsheviks accept German peace terms at Brest Litovsk.
November 9, 1918	Kaiser Wilhelm II abdicates German throne and flees to Holland. Armistice concluded on western front.
January, 1919	Treaty of Versailles imposes harsh settlement on Germany.

1920	Women receive full franchise in the United States.
1921	Chromosome theory of heredity postulated by American biologist Thomas Hunt Morgan.
1925	John Scopes goes on trial for violating Tennessee law that prohibits teaching of evolution.
1927	Charles Lindbergh flies monoplane *Spirit of St. Louis* nonstop from New York to Paris (33.5 hours).
1929	Women receive full franchise in Great Britain.
1930	Planet Pluto discovered by C. W. Tombaugh, Lowell Observatory.

STUDY QUESTIONS

1. What were the major points contained in the Seneca Falls Declaration of 1848 that reformers wanted "submitted to a candid world"? What made this such a radical document? Why did French socialist women support these resolutions? Have the issues presented at Seneca Falls been resolved in our contemporary society?

2. Carefully note Francis Parkman's arguments against women's suffrage. Which ones could be applied to any political, social, religious, or ethnic group that strives for equal status with an incumbent authority? Which of his arguments do you find most specious? Which seem the most well founded and persuasive? Do you agree with his statement that "progress, to be genuine, must be in accord with natural law"?

3. What is the scientific evidence for arguing the general inferiority of women, as presented by George Romanes in his article about the mental differences between men and women? How does Romanes damn women with "faint praise"?

4. What were the Contagious Disease Acts and why was Josephine Butler opposed to the practice of prostitution? What was her ideal for women? Why was Emmeline Pankhurst so important to the women's movement? What tactics for achieving change did she advocate and practice? Why was property the focus of her campaign? Do you agree with her argument?

5. In "The Grand Inquisitor," what is Fyodor Dostoevsky's message regarding Christianity? What is the role of the church in human society? Are you disturbed by this excerpt? What is the fate of God at the end of the confrontation?

6. What general ideas seem to flow through the selections of Friedrich Nietzsche? What are his thoughts concerning power, God and Christianity? What does Nietzsche value? What does he mean by the declaration: "Build your cities under Vesuvius! Send your ships into uncharted seas!"? How does Nietzsche embody the "revolt against reason" that was current at the end of the nineteenth century?

7. In any conflict there are underlying tensions within countries or between countries that depend on a precipitating action to upset the status quo. What was

the "spark" that ignited the Great War, and what were the underlying causes for the conflict? The war has sometimes been viewed as the logical outcome of the intense nationalism and imperialism of the late nineteenth century. Do you agree with this view? What evidence exists in this chapter that indicates that nationalism and imperialism played a role in the Great War?

8. What are the arguments of Heinrich von Treitschke? Are you persuaded by his idea that "without war, no state could exist"? Why do nations often celebrate war? Could this itself be a cause of war?

9. What are your most vivid impressions from the personal accounts of combat under the section "The Horrors of Battle"? Granted that all wars are horrible, what made this war unique? What makes the propaganda leaflet an effective weapon?

10. Apart from the physical differences, how was war in the air different from war on land? Is killing more palatable when it is romanticized? Do you find the Red Baron an exciting or intriguing personality?

11. Evaluate the statement "It is sweet and proper to die for one's country." Is it an "Old Lie" as Wilfred Owen said? Was this war a game started by the old, fought by the young, and suffered by the innocent? What about patriotism and honor? Were they hollow concepts in this war? How about in World War II or in Vietnam, or more recently in the Persian Gulf War?

12. In his Fourteen Points and at the Paris Peace Conference (1919), President Woodrow Wilson advocated idealistic principles: self-determination for nationalities, open diplomacy, disarmament, and the establishment of an international organization to discuss the concerns of the world community. Would these measures have helped stop the war? Was the Great War inevitable? What do Norman Angell ("The Great Illusion") and G. Lowes Dickinson ("The International Anarchy") advocate? Does the fact that their books were written before and after the war say anything about political leadership in the early decades of the twentieth century?

13. In 1864, the English prelate John Henry Cardinal Newman said, "There is such a thing as legitimate warfare: war has its laws; there are things which may fairly be done, and things which may not be done." Do you agree or disagree? Analyze the articles of the Hague Convention of 1907. Are "laws of war" so unrealistic? Which of the articles do you respect the most? Note the treaty of 1922 concerning submarines and poisonous gas. Why were these weapons considered immoral at the time? By mutual consent poisonous gas was not used in World War II—yet this was a "total war." Does total war preclude "laws of humanity"? In the same sense, consider the Persian Gulf War of 1990–1991. Since modern technology now provides laser-controlled missiles to destroy specific targets, do such "surgical strikes" allow us to fight antiseptic campaigns where civilian casualties are considerably reduced and war is thus made more palatable and civilized?

14. The views of the philosopher Alfred North Whitehead contained in his post-war selection entitled "The Great Ages Have Been Unstable Ages" (1925) seem eerily linked to those of Friedrich Nietzsche in "A Warlike Age Is Now Upon Us!" (1892). Nietzsche recommended that Europeans "build your cities under

Vesuvius! Send your ships into uncharted waters!" Whitehead argues that it is the "business of the future to be dangerous," and that progressive thought and technology "make the transition throughout time . . . a true migration into uncharted seas of adventure." Given that the new weaponry of the Great War and attitudes of defiance and bluster combined to wreak havoc in World War I, should we be afraid of the dangerous future or embrace technology and the merits of science as pathways to a better world? Are great ages inherently unstable ages? Although terrible in its ferocity, can the Great War be viewed as an agent of change and progress in civilization?

15. According to Virginia Woolf, why is the "looking-glass vision" of supreme importance in history? Do you believe, as she wrote, that it is useless to compare the worth of charwomen and lawyers in society? Why? How do her views in 1929 reflect insight and a development in attitude and spirit from the earlier feminist reformers in the nineteenth and early-twentieth centuries? Notice her criticism, without blame, of the "manly" attitudes that drove the European leaders "to desire other people's fields and goods perpetually; to make frontiers and flags; battleships and poison gas; to offer up their own lives and their children's lives." Do you agree that anything is possible "when womanhood ceases to be a protected occupation"?

16. The influential psychoanalyst Sigmund Freud believed that traditional concepts of life and death had been altered by the Great War. Might this be considered a defining characteristic of the Modern Era in the twentieth century? What is his main argument in the selection entitled, "If You Want to Endure Life—Prepare for Death"? In the excerpt from *Civilization and Its Discontents* (1930), what was Freud's view of human nature? Do you agree? Is humanity disposed more toward granting mercy or toward aggression? How do we progress in a moral sense?

7

The Russian Revolution and the Development of the Totalitarian State (1917–1939)

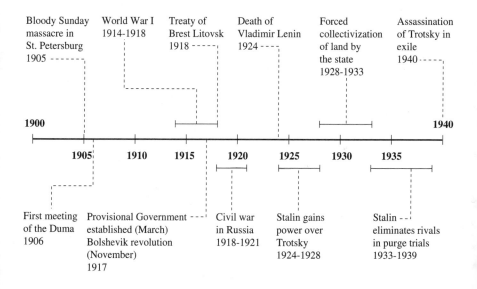

Bloody Sunday massacre in St. Petersburg 1905

World War I 1914-1918

Treaty of Brest Litovsk 1918

Death of Vladimir Lenin 1924

Forced collectivization of land by the state 1928-1933

Assassination of Trotsky in exile 1940

1900

1940

1905 1910 1915 1920 1925 1930 1935

First meeting of the Duma 1906

Provisional Government established (March) Bolshevik revolution (November) 1917

Civil war in Russia 1918-1921

Stalin gains power over Trotsky 1924-1928

Stalin eliminates rivals in purge trials 1933-1939

Just think what's going on around us! And that you and I should be living at such a time. Such a thing happens only once in an eternity. Just think of it, the whole of Russia has had its roof torn off, and you and I and everyone else are out in the open! And there's nobody to spy on us. Freedom! Real freedom, not just talk about it, freedom dropped out of the sky, freedom beyond our expectations.

—Boris Pasternak (*Doctor Zhivago*)

The essence of Bolshevism, the essence of Soviet power, lies in exposing the fraud and hypocrisy of bourgeois democracy, in abolishing the private ownership of the land, the factories, and in concentrating all political power in the hands of the toilers and the exploited masses.

—V. I. Lenin

Even if for every hundred correct things we did, we committed ten thousand mistakes, our revolution would still be—and it will be in the judgment of history—great and invincible; for this is the first time that the working people are themselves building a new life.

—V. I. Lenin

Now you see what they've brought Russia to! They'll make you equal to the peasants, deprive you of your privileges, and recall the old affronts into the bargain. Bad times are coming. . . . It depends on whose hands the government falls into, otherwise we shall be brought to utter disaster.

—Mikhail Sholokhov (*And Quiet Flows the Don*)

The Russian dictatorship of the proletariat has made a farce of the whole Marxist vision: developing a powerful, privileged ruling class to prepare for a classless society, setting up the most despotic state in history so that the state may wither away, establishing by force a colonial empire to combat imperialism and unite the workers of the world.

—Herbert J. Muller

A proletarian revolution is never proletarian.

—Will Durant

Those who hold the power also write the history.

—Plato

CHAPTER THEMES

- **Revolution:** Against great odds, why were the Bolsheviks able to overthrow the Provisional Government and come to power in Russia in 1917? How would you compare the Russian Revolution to the French Revolution or the Nazi revolution in Germany?

- **Systems of Government:** What are the components of totalitarian government? How does it differ from fascism? How did the character of Stalin's government differ from that of Lenin or Hitler?

This dramatic portrait of Lenin as the heroic leader of the Russian Revolution created a sense of urgency and compelling energy that was so vital in establishing the destined communist utopia of Karl Marx. Images like this also created distrust among Western governments, which feared the Soviet rhetoric of "world revolution." (*Scala/Art Resource, NY*)

- **Women in History:** How did Lenin's vision of women's roles and responsibilities differ from that of Hitler in Nazi Germany? Did women have greater equality of opportunity under the Soviet system than they did in other Western societies?

- **Historical Change and Transition:** Karl Marx predicted that the state under communism would eventually "wither away" rather than grow more pervasive, as happened under Stalin. What happened?

- **The Big Picture:** Is a government that is based on fear and oppression doomed to fail? Or is totalitarian rule workable and even preferable in some ways to democracy? Is freedom really the natural condition of human beings?

The events of the year 1917 remain among the most significant in the history of the twentieth century. The world was in the midst of a war that could no longer be viewed as glorious and patriotic, but had degenerated in people's minds to what war really is—suffering, destruction, and death. In such a crisis, it is important for governments to justify their actions, inspire soldiers, and assuage the populace. Statesmen require domestic stability in order to focus attention on the war effort. However, Russia was not afforded this tranquility, and the monarchy of Tsar Nicholas II fell in March 1917, a prelude to a power struggle that by November of that year would see the imposition of a new regime, born of Marxist revolutionary philosophy and led by Vladimir Ulyanov, better known as Lenin (1870–1924). This was a complex revolution, and any simplification distorts the intricacy of events and political philosophies. Yet, for our purposes, it can be divided into three separate but related phases: the revolution of 1905, the March revolution of 1917, and the Bolshevik revolution of November 1917. This chapter seeks to unravel the conditions and pressures that led to the overthrow of the Romanov dynasty and the eventual Bolshevik seizure of power.

As in the French and American revolutions, social and economic conditions, as well as ideology, played an important role in providing the underlying causes and inspiration for revolution. Tsar Nicholas II was heir to a long tradition of autocracy that regarded change as dangerous to the stability of the dynasty. In the nineteenth century alone, Tsar Alexander I (1801–1825) continued the longstanding policy of absolutism, and his successor, Nicholas I (1825–1855), became Europe's most reactionary monarch with the slogan "Autocracy, Orthodoxy, and National Unity." Under Nicholas's leadership, Russia became a closed society. Nicholas employed a secret police and a network of paid informers that successfully exiled over 150,000 persons to the frigid wastes of Siberia. And yet there existed reform movements. Alexander Herzen (1812–1870), called the "father of Russian liberalism," advocated moderate socialist policies. But other dissidents were not so polite. Mikhail Bakunin (1814–1876) founded the anarchist movement and advocated the use of terror to effect change. Tsar Alexander II (1855–1881) instituted a series of liberal measures, including the emancipation of Russian serfs (1861), and reforms of the judiciary, army, and local and municipal governments. Yet his actions, though revolutionary for the absolutist government of Russia, were incomplete, and his failure to provide a constitution led to growing opposition and a populist movement (Narodnik), which preached revolution to the peasant masses and was suppressed by the tsar. On March 13, 1881, Alexander II was assassinated by the terrorist group "People's Will"—ironically on the very day he had signed a decree that was to lead to constitutional reform. His son, Alexander III (1881–1894), refused to conform to the decree and set about reimplementing a policy of reactionary oppression. Thus when Nicholas II came to the throne in 1894, a long tradition of violent repression and terrorist response already existed.

One of the most influential philosophies that gave inspiration to the Russian Revolution was Marxism. Karl Marx and Friedrich Engels published the *Communist Manifesto* in 1848. In it they advocated a classless society that would come about through struggle between the exploiting *bourgeoisie* or middle-class capitalists and the working class, or proletariat. Marx intoned, "Workers of the world unite! You have nothing to lose but your chains!" Marx's ideas became popular among the Russian revolutionary intelligentsia, and converts met in secret societies throughout Europe and Russia to discuss and plan action. One of his most dedicated disciples was Lenin. By 1905, Tsar Nicholas II's political opposition was more firmly organized. The Social Democratic party had been formed among industrial workers and was truly Marxist in philosophy. Yet party members differed among themselves; the Menshevik faction was more moderate and wanted to concentrate on improving the lot of the industrial worker, instead of concentrating on the world revolution that Marx predicted would become a reality. The other faction of the Social Democrats, the Bolsheviks, were led by Lenin and were more extreme in their insistence on a core of "professional revolutionaries," dedicated to the immediate overthrow of capitalist society. Other political groups existed in 1905 as well, including the Constitutional Democratic party (Cadets) and the Social Revolutionary party, which sought agricultural land reform.

Although Russian tsars had long resisted demands for basic civil rights, equality before the law, and representative government, Nicholas II especially seemed to live in a vacuum—his own world of yachts and tennis, crystal and caviar. He remained unaware of the plight of the Russian peasantry, half-starved and oppressed by landlords who often confiscated their land, or of the urban worker who was burdened by low wages and long hours. Following the massacre of Russian workers during a peaceful demonstration in January 1905 (called "Bloody Sunday"), the popular outcry forced the tsar to establish an Imperial Duma, or representative assembly, and to provide a new constitution, guaranteeing civil rights for the people. The first phase of the Russian Revolution had taken place. Still, the Duma had no real authority over the tsar, and its liberal recommendations were stifled. From 1906 to 1907, Nicholas merely dismissed Dumas that sought to encroach upon his power. From 1907 to 1916, the Dumas were controlled by the tsar through voting restrictions and altered election laws.

In the summer of 1914, Europe gravitated toward disaster. When Germany declared war on Russia (August 1, 1914), France supported her Russian ally. On August 4, Great Britain also joined in the struggle against Germany and Austria.

The Great War had begun. Conditions among the Russian people deteriorated as thousands died in battle or as victims of disease or famine. The refugee problem was acute, and people wandered homeless throughout Russia. The government was simply not able to cope with the economic and logistic demands of military mobilization and war. In March of 1917, the tsar was persuaded to abdicate, hoping that such action would assure Russia's continued participation in the war. This action came as a surprise to almost everyone. Even the most vitriolic detractors of the tsarist regime, notably Lenin in Switzerland, were caught off guard. The second phase of the revolution had just begun.

With the fall of the tsar, a power vacuum existed and the competition to fill it was intense. A Provisional Government was chosen from members of the sitting Imperial Duma. The Provisional Government generally was made up of liberals and moderate socialists who promised an elected Constituent Assembly that was representative of the Russian people; they also pledged to draw up a new constitution that guaranteed civil liberties. However, the Provisional Government also supported Russia's continuation of the war. The other competitor for power was the Petrograd Soviet of Workers and Soldiers' Deputies. A soviet was simply a council of elected representatives that advocated reforms for the working classes. The soviets were generally composed of Social Revolutionaries, Mensheviks, and initially only a minority of Bolsheviks. They regarded the war as a struggle between capitalists at the expense of the working classes (proletariat) and therefore wanted Russia to cease hostilities immediately. However, the Petrograd Soviet did not advocate armed rebellion against the Provisional Government. On the contrary, some members of the Soviet even believed that they held a kind of dual power with it. No one proposed a government of national unity, and this lack of cooperation was to prove fatal to political stability.

Perhaps too much was expected of the Provisional Government. Soldiers wanted an end to the war, peasants needed more land, the workers in the cities demanded better living conditions, the national and religious minorities of Russia wanted official recognition, as well as political and cultural autonomy, and the Allies wanted Russia's continued support in the war. For a temporary government composed of people who lacked experience and an organized plan of action, the burden was too great.

Lenin arrived in Petrograd in April and started organizing the opposition. As leader of the more radical Bolshevik faction of the Social Democratic party, he denounced the Provisional Government and worked independently of the other socialist groups in an effort to seize control. Lenin proclaimed "all power to the soviets" and in July led a premature uprising that failed. Several Bolsheviks were arrested (including Lenin's brilliant associate Leon Trotsky), but Lenin escaped to Finland. Bolshevik fortunes changed when the leader of the Provisional Government, Alexander Kerensky (1881–1970), was confronted with a military rebellion—a right-wing revolt led by General Lavr Kornilov that was quelled only with the assistance of the Petrograd Soviet. In November 1917, Lenin, against the judgment of some of his colleagues, again attempted to topple the Provisional Government. This time he was successful and his Bolshevik faction of radical socialists was able to maintain its power. This third phase of the Russian Revolution established a regime of a very different order.

The Provisional Government failed for many reasons. The members had little experience in government and administration and could not counter the effective propaganda of Lenin, which offered "Peace, Bread, and Land." Kerensky believed that he had an obligation to act in a legal, democratic fashion, to demonstrate that his leadership was progressive and superior to that of the tsar. Lenin played by his own rules and would not share power. His organization and insistence on the rightness of his ideas, coupled with a measure of luck, produced a revolution that indeed shook the world.

Lenin's Bolshevik government survived a counterrevolutionary threat from supporters of the tsar as the civil war came to an end in 1921. Lenin had started the transition toward Marx's concept of a Communist society, but fell ill in 1922 and died two years later. His position as leader of the revolution would eventually be assumed by Joseph Stalin (1879–1953). Under Stalin's brutal direction, and the leadership of his successors, the Soviet Union emerged as a formidable political, military, and ideological adversary to the United States in the late-twentieth century.

From 1945 to 1989, the two countries lived under a cloud of mutual suspicion, fostered by intense propaganda, massive nuclear arsenals, and geopolitical competition. Only in the 1990s with the collapse of the Soviet Union and the Russian preoccupation with domestic affairs has the rhetoric cooled, the Cold War ended, and the future seemed less threatening. Viewed from this perspective, the Russian Revolution of 1917 and Stalin's institution of totalitarian rule remain among the most significant political events of the modern world.

The Provisional Government (March–November 1917)

World War I proved especially disastrous for Russia. The army suffered tremendous losses against a German onslaught of superior force and preparation. Misery, famine, and disease descended on the Russian people, and thousands were dislocated and wandered aimlessly as refugees. Tsar Nicholas II feared a general uprising and finally decided to abdicate his throne in favor of his brother, the Grand Duke Michael. But the tide had turned and the question was posed by the newspaper Izvestia: *"Shall the Romanov Dynasty Remain?"*

After the abdication of the tsar in March 1917, a temporary body called the Provisional Government was installed to maintain stability in the country until a representative Constituent Assembly could be elected by the Russian people. The Petrograd Soviet, an elected council of workers and soldiers, immediately threatened the authority of the Provisional Government. Lenin, who had just arrived from Switzerland, reasserted leadership of the Bolshevik party and set forth his demands in the last selection, the famous "April Theses."

Shall the Romanov Dynasty Remain? (March 15, 1917)
IZVESTIA

The revolutionary people should carry through to the end the revolution and the democratization of its political and social organization. To return to the old is unthinkable. The revolutionary people should organize the State in the way that will best satisfy its interests, strength and great zeal, and will make impossible a new attempt on its rights and liberty. This can be done by handing the power over to the people, that is to say, by forming a democratic republic, in which the officers of government are elected by universal equal, secret, and direct suffrage. All the revolutionary elements in Russia, who have made tremendous sacrifices in the fight and the forging of freedom, should strive for such a government.

If the power were entrusted to a monarch, one, with his responsible ministry, the latter might make an attempt on the liberty of the people and bind it with chains of slavery. Then again, in a constitutional monarchy there is the right of succession which again creates the possibility of rulers of the type of Nicholas, the Last.

In a constitutional monarchy, the army serves not the people, but the monarch, giving him great power, which he could use to harm the people.

The Romanov dynasty is now overthrown. . . . There must be no going back to it. The revolutionary people will find enough strength to form a new republican government, which will guarantee its rights and freedom.

First Declaration of the Provisional Government (March 19, 1917)

Citizens of Russia:

A great event has taken place. By the mighty assault of the Russian people, the old order has been overthrown. A new, free Russia is born. The great revolution crowns long years of struggle. By the act of October 17, [30] 1905, under the pressure of the awakened popular forces, Russia was promised constitutional liberties. Those promises, however, were not kept. The First State Duma, interpreter of the nation's hopes, was dissolved. The Second Duma suffered the same fate, and the Government, powerless to crush the national will, decided, by the act of June 3, [16] 1907, to deprive the people of a part of those rights of participation in legislative work which had been granted.

In the course of nine long years, there were taken from the people, step by step, all the rights that they had won. Once more the country was plunged

"Shall the Romanov Dynasty Remain?" is from Frank A. Golder, ed., *Documents of Russian History (1914–1917)*, trans. Emanuel Aronsberg (New York: The Century Company, 1927), pp. 296–297.

"First Declaration of the Provisional Government" is from Frank A. Golder, ed., *Documents of Russian History (1914–1917)*, trans. Emanuel Aronsberg (New York: The Century Company, 1927), pp. 311–313.

into an abyss of arbitrariness and despotism. All attempts to bring the Government to its senses proved futile, and the titanic world struggle, into which the country was dragged by the enemy, found the Government in a state of moral decay, alienated from the people, indifferent to the fate of our native land, and steeped in the infamy of corruption. Neither the heroic efforts of the army, staggering under the crushing burdens of internal chaos, nor the appeals of the popular representatives who had united in the face of the national peril, were able to lead the former Emperor and his Government into the path of unity with the people. And when Russia, owing to the illegal and fatal actions of her rulers, was confronted with gravest disasters, the nation was obliged to take the power into its own hands.

The unanimous revolutionary enthusiasm of the people, fully conscious of the gravity of the moment, and the determination of the State Duma, have created the Provisional Government, which considers it to be its sacred and responsible duty to fulfill the hopes of the nation, and lead the country out onto the bright path of free civic organization.

The Government trusts that the spirit of lofty patriotism, manifested during the struggle of the people against the old regime, will also inspire our valiant soldiers on the field of battle. For its own part, the Government will make every effort to provide our army with everything necessary to bring the war to a victorious end.

The Government will sacredly observe the alliances which bind us to other powers, and will unswervingly carry out the agreements entered into by the Allies. While taking measures to defend the country against the foreign enemy, the Government will, at the same time, consider it to be its primary duty to make possible the expression of the popular will as regards the form of government, and will convoke the Constituent Assembly within the shortest time possible, on the basis of universal, direct, equal, and secret suffrage, also guaranteeing participation in the elections to the gallant defenders of our native land, who are now shedding their blood on the fields of battle.

The Constituent Assembly will issue the fundamental laws, guaranteeing to the country the inalienable rights of justice, equality, and liberty. Conscious of the heavy burden which the country suffers because of the lack of civic rights, which lack stands in the way of its free, creative power at this time of violent national commotion, the Provisional Government deems it necessary, at once, before the convocation of the Constituent Assembly, to provide the country with laws for the safeguard of civic liberty and equality, in order to enable all citizens freely to apply their spiritual forces to creative work for the benefit of the country. The Government will also undertake the enactment of legal provisions to assure to all citizens, on the basis of universal suffrage, an equal share in the election of local governments.

At this moment of national liberation, the whole country remembers with reverent gratitude those who, in the struggle for their political and religious convictions, fell victims to the vindictive old regime, and the Provisional Government will regard it as its joyful duty to bring back from their exile, with full honors, all those who have suffered for the good of the country.

In fulfilling these tasks, the Provisional Government is animated by the belief that it will thus execute the will of the people, and that the whole nation will support it in its honest efforts to insure the happiness of Russia. This belief inspires it with courage. Only in the common effort of the entire nation and the Provisional Government can it see a pledge of triumph of the new order.

March 19, 1917

Policy of the Petrograd Soviet (March 27, 1917)

Comrade-proletarians, and toilers of all countries:

We, Russian workers and soldiers, united in the Petrograd Soviet of Workers' and Soldiers' Deputies, send you warmest greetings and announce the great event. The Russian democracy has shattered in the dust the age-long despotism of the Tsar and enters your family [of nations] as an equal, and as a mighty force in the struggle for our common liberation. Our victory is a great victory for the freedom and democracy of the world. The chief pillar of reaction in the world, the "Gendarme of Europe" is no more. May the earth turn to heavy granite on his grave! Long live freedom! Long live the international solidarity of the proletariat, and its struggle for final victory!

Our work is not yet finished: the shades of the old order have not yet been dispersed, and not a few enemies are gathering their forces against the Russian revolution. Nevertheless our achievement so far is tremendous. The people of Russia will express their will in the Constituent Assembly, which will be called as soon as possible on the basis of universal, equal, direct, and secret suffrage. And it may already be said without a doubt that a democratic republic will triumph in Russia. The Russian people now possess full political liberty. They can now assert their mighty power in the internal government of the country and in its foreign policy. And, appealing to all people who are being destroyed and ruined in the monstrous war, we announce that the time has come to start a decisive struggle against the grasping ambitions of the governments of all countries; the time has come for the people to take into their own hands the decision of the question of war and peace.

Conscious of its revolutionary power, the Russian democracy announces that it will, by every means, resist the policy of conquest of its ruling classes, and it calls upon the peoples of Europe for concerted, decisive action in favor of peace.

We are appealing to our brother-proletarians of the Austro-German coalition, and, first of all, to the German proletariat. From the first days of the war, you were assured that by raising arms against autocratic Russia, you were defending the culture of Europe from Asiatic despotism. Many of you saw in this a justification of that support which you were giving to the war. Now even this justification is gone: democratic Russia cannot be a threat to liberty and civilization.

"Policy of the Petrograd Soviet" is from Frank A. Golder, ed., *Documents of Russian History (1914–1917)*, trans. Emanuel Aronsberg (New York: The Century Company, 1927), pp. 325–326.

We will firmly defend our own liberty from all reactionary attempts from within, as well as from without. The Russian revolution will not retreat before the bayonets of conquerors, and will not allow itself to be crushed by foreign military force. But we are calling to you: Throw off the yoke of your semi-autocratic rule, as the Russian people have shaken off the Tsar's autocracy; refuse to serve as an instrument of conquest and violence in the hands of kings, landowners, and bankers—and then by our united efforts, we will stop the horrible butchery, which is disgracing humanity and is beclouding the great days of the birth of Russian freedom.

Toilers of all countries: We hold out to you the hand of brotherhood across the mountains of our brothers' corpses, across rivers of innocent blood and tears, over the smoking ruins of cities and villages, over the wreckage of the treasures of civilization;—we appeal to you for the reestablishment and strengthening of international unity. In it is the pledge of future victories and the complete liberation of humanity.

Proletarians of all countries, Unite!

PETROGRAD SOVIET OF WORKERS'
AND SOLDIERS' DEPUTIES

The April Theses (April 20, 1917)
V. I. LENIN

The class conscious proletariat can consent to a revolutionary war, which would really justify revolutionary defencism, only on condition: (a) that the power of government pass to the proletariat and the poor sections of the peasantry bordering on the proletariat; (b) that all annexations be renounced in deed as well as in words; (c) that a complete and real break be made with all capitalist interests.

In view of the undoubted honesty of the mass of the rank-and-file believers in revolutionary defencism, who accept the war as a necessity only and not as a means of conquest; in view of the fact that they are being deceived by the bourgeoisie, it is necessary thoroughly, persistently and patiently to explain their error to them, to explain the indissoluble connection between capital and the imperialist war, and to prove that *it is impossible* to end the war by a truly democratic, non-coercive peace without overthrow of capital.

The widespread propaganda of this view among the army on active service must be organised.

Fraternisation

(2) The specific feature of the present situation in Russia is that it represents a transition from the first stage of the revolution—which owing to the

"The April Theses" is from Martin McCauley, ed., *The Russian Revolution and the Soviet State* (New York: Barnes & Noble, 1975), pp. 52–54. Permission granted by Barnes & Noble Books, Totowa, New Jersey.

insufficient class consciousness and organisation of the proletariat, led to the assumption of power by the bourgeoisie—*to the second stage*, which must place power in the hands of the proletariat and the poor strata of the peasantry.

This transition is characterised, on the one hand, by a maximum of freedom (Russia is *now* the freest of all the belligerent countries in the world); on the other, by the absence of violence in relation to the masses, and, finally, by the naive confidence of the masses in the government of capitalists, the worst enemies of peace and socialism.

This specific situation demands on our part an ability to adapt ourselves to the specific requirements of Party work among unprecedently large masses of proletarians who have just awakened to political life.

(3) No support must be given to the Provisional Government, the utter falsity of all its promises must be exposed, particularly of those relating to the renunciation of annexations. Exposure, and not the unpardonable illusion-breeding 'demand' that this government, a government of capitalists, should cease to be an imperialist government.

(4) The fact must be recognised that in most of the Soviets of Workers' Deputies our Party is in a minority, and so far in a small minority, as against *a bloc of all* the petty-bourgeois opportunist elements, who have yielded to the influence of the bourgeoisie and are the conveyors of its influence to the proletariat. . . .

It must be explained to the masses that the Soviet of Workers' Deputies is the *only possible* form of revolutionary government and that therefore our task is, as long as *this* government submits to the influence of the bourgeoisie, to present a patient, systematic, and persistent *explanation* of its errors and tactics, an explanation especially adapted to the practical needs of the masses.

As long as we are in the minority we carry on the work of criticising and exposing errors and at the same time advocate the necessity of transferring the entire power of state to the Soviets of Workers' Deputies, so that the masses may by experience overcome their mistakes.

(5) Not a parliamentary republic—to return to a parliamentary republic from the Soviets of Workers' Deputies would be a retrograde step—but a republic of Soviets of Workers', Agricultural Labourers' and Peasants' Deputies throughout the country, from top to bottom.

Abolition of the police, the army and the bureaucracy.

(6) The agrarian programme must be centered around the Soviets of Agricultural Labourers' Deputies.

Confiscation of All Landed Estates

Nationalisation of *all* lands in the country, the disposal of such *lands* to be in the charge of the local Soviets of Agricultural Labourers' and Peasants' Deputies. The organisation of separate soviets of Deputies of the Poor Peasants. The creation of model farms on each of the large estates. . . .

(7) The immediate amalgamation of all banks in the country into a single national bank, control over which shall be exercised by the Soviet of Workers' Deputies.

(8) Our *immediate* task shall be not the 'introduction of socialism,' but to bring social production and distribution of products at once under the control of the Soviet of Workers' Deputies.

(9) Party tasks:

    (a) Immediate summoning of a Party congress.
    (b) Alteration of the Party programme, mainly:
        1. On the question of imperialism and the imperialist war;
        2. On the question of our attitude towards the state and our demand for a 'commune state.'
        3. Amendment of our antiquated minimum programme;
    (c) A new name for the Party.

(10) A new International.

The Bolshevik Revolution (November–December 1917)

The Bolshevik faction, led by Lenin and his very competent colleague Leon Trotsky, had suffered reversals during an abortive uprising in July 1917. Trotsky was imprisoned and Lenin fled to Finland. Finally in November 1917, Lenin persuaded his faction that the time was ripe for a coup. The first selection is Lenin's speech after his successful storming of the Winter Palace in Petrograd. Note the critical editorial from the newspaper Izvestia *on November 8. It was the last before the Bolsheviks censored the press. Lenin's seizure of power also included the establishment of a secret police (Cheka), an institution that had been used (in another form) by the autocratic tsar to eliminate opposition.*

Speech After the Overthrow of the Provisional Government

V. I. LENIN

Comrades, the workmen's and peasant's revolution, the need of which the Bolsheviks have emphasized many times, has come to pass.

"Speech After the Overthrow of the Provisional Government" is from Frank A. Golder, ed., *Documents of Russian History (1914–1917)*, trans. Emanuel Aronsberg (New York: The Century Company, 1927), pp. 618–619.

What is the significance of this revolution? Its significance is, in the first place, that we shall have a soviet government, without the participation of bourgeoisie of any kind. The oppressed masses will of themselves form a government. The old state machinery will be smashed into bits and in its place will be created a new machinery of government by the soviet organizations. From now on there is a new page in the history of Russia, and the present, third Russian revolution shall in its final result lead to the victory of Socialism.

One of our immediate tasks is to put an end to the war at once. But in order to end the war, which is closely bound up with the present capitalistic system, it is necessary to overthrow capitalism itself. In this work we shall have the aid of the world labor movement, which has already begun to develop in Italy, England, and Germany.

A just and immediate offer of peace by us to the international democracy will find everywhere a warm response among the international proletariat masses. In order to secure the confidence of the proletariat, it is necessary to publish at once all secret treaties.

In the interior of Russia a very large part of the peasantry has said: Enough playing with the capitalists; we will go with the workers. We shall secure the confidence of the peasants by one decree, which will wipe out the private property of the landowners. The peasants will understand that their only salvation is in union with the workers.

We will establish a real labor control on production.

We have now learned to work together in a friendly manner, as is evident from this revolution. We have the force of mass organization which has conquered all and which will lead the proletariat to world revolution.

We should now occupy ourselves in Russia in building up a proletarian socialist state.

Long live the world-wide socialistic revolution!

"Little Good Is to Be Expected" (November 8, 1917)

IZVESTIA

Yesterday we said that the Bolshevik uprising is a made adventure and today, when their attempt is crowned with success, we are of the same mind. We repeat: that which is before us is not a transfer of power to the Soviets, but a seizure of power by one party—the Bolsheviks. Yesterday we said that a successful attempt meant the breaking up of the greatest of the revolution—the Constituent Assembly. Today we add that it means, also, the breaking up of

"'Little Good Is to Be Expected'" is from Frank A. Golder, ed., *Documents of Russian History (1914–1917)*, trans. Emanuel Aronsberg (New York: The Century Company, 1927), p. 619.

the Congress of Soviets, and perhaps the whole soviet organization. They can call themselves what they please; the fact remains that the Bolsheviks alone took part in the uprising. All the other socialistic and democratic parties protest against it.

How the situation may develop we do not know, but little good is to be expected. We are quite confident that the Bolsheviks cannot organize a state government. As yesterday, so today, we repeat that what is happening will react worst of all on the question of peace.

Censorship of the Press (November 9, 1917)
V. I. LENIN

In the trying critical period of the revolution and the days that immediately followed it the Provisional Revolutionary Committee was compelled to take a number of measures against the counter-revolutionary press of different shades.

Immediately outcries were heard from all sides that the new, socialist power had violated a fundamental principle of its programme by encroaching upon the freedom of the press.

The Workers' and Peasants' Government calls the attention of the population to the fact that what this liberal facade actually conceals is freedom for the propertied classes, having taken hold of the lion's share of the entire press, to poison, unhindered, the minds and obscure the consciousness of the masses.

Every one knows that the bourgeois press is one of the most powerful weapons of the bourgeoisie. Especially at the crucial moment when the new power, the power of workers and peasants, is only affirming itself, it was impossible to leave this weapon wholly in the hands of the enemy, for in such moments it is no less dangerous than bombs and machine-guns. That is why temporary extraordinary measures were taken to stem the torrent of filth and slander in which the yellow and green press would be only too glad to drown the recent victory of the people.

As soon as the new order becomes consolidated, all administrative pressure on the press will be terminated and it will be granted complete freedom within the bounds of legal responsibility, in keeping with a law that will be broadest and most progressive in this respect.

However, being aware that a restriction of the press, even at critical moments, is permissible only within the limits of what is absolutely necessary, the Council of People's Commissars resolves:

"Censorship of the Press" is from Martin McCauley, ed., *The Russian Revolution and the Soviet State* (New York: Barnes & Noble, 1975), pp. 190–191. Permission granted by Barnes & Noble Books, Totowa, New Jersey.

General Provisions on the Press

1. Only those publications can be suppressed which (1) call for open resistance or insubordination to the Workers' and Peasants' Government; (2) sow sedition through demonstrably slanderous distortion of facts; (3) instigate actions of an obviously criminal, i.e. criminally punishable, nature.
2. Publications can be proscribed, temporarily or permanently, only by decision of the Council of People's Commissars.
3. The present ordinance is of a temporary nature and will be repealed by a special decree as soon as normal conditions of social life set in.

Chairman of the Council of People's Commissars,
VLADIMIR ULYANOV (LENIN)

Establishment of the Secret Police (December 20, 1917)

V. I. LENIN

The Commission is to be called the All-Russian Extraordinary Commission for the Struggle with Counter-Revolution and Sabotage and is to be attached to the Council of People's Commissars.

The duties of the Commission are to be as follows:

1. To investigate and nullify all acts of counter-revolution and sabotage throughout Russia, irrespective of origin.
2. To bring before the Revolutionary Tribunal all counter-revolutionaries and saboteurs and to work out measures to combat them.
3. The Commission is to conduct the preliminary investigation only, sufficient to suppress (the counter-revolutionary act). The Commission is to be divided into sections: (1) the information (section) (2) the organization section (in charge of organizing the struggle with counter-revolution throughout Russia) with branches, and (3) the fighting section.

The Commission shall be set up finally tomorrow. Then the fighting section of the All-Russian Commission shall start its activities. The Commission shall keep an eye on the press, saboteurs, right Socialist Revolutionaries and strikers. Measures to be taken are confiscation, imprisonment, confiscation of cards, publication of the names of the enemies of the people, etc.

Chairman of the Council of People's Commissars
V. ULYANOV (LENIN)

"Establishment of the Secret Police" is from Martin McCauley, ed., *The Russian Revolution and the Soviet State* (New York: Barnes & Noble, 1975), pp. 181–182. Permission granted by Barnes & Noble Books, Totowa, New Jersey.

Dissolution of the Constituent Assembly (December 1917)

V. I. LENIN

A major responsibility of the Provisional Government had been to organize an election and establish a Constituent Assembly that was truly representative of the Russian people. Lenin, after achieving power through political manipulation and force of arms, decided to hold the election anyway. The results were not encouraging since the Bolsheviks were soundly defeated. Lenin, however, would not concede defeat and chose to dissolve the Constituent Assembly instead. Note Lenin's reasons for his actions. The second document is a questionnaire that all delegates to the Tenth All Russian Congress of the Russian Communist Party had to fill out. This was Lenin's view of himself in 1921.

At its very inception, the Russian revolution produced the Soviets of Workers', Soldiers' and Peasants' Deputies as the only mass organization of all the working and exploited classes capable of giving leadership to the struggle of these classes for their complete political and economic emancipation.

Throughout the initial period of the Russian revolution the Soviets grew in number, size and strength, their own experience disabusing them of the illusions regarding compromise with the bourgeoisie, opening their eyes to the fraudulence of the forms of bourgeois-democratic parliamentarism, and leading them to the conclusion that the emancipation of the oppressed classes was unthinkable unless they broke with these forms and with every kind of compromise. Such a break came with the October [November] Revolution, with the transfer of power to the Soviets.

The Constituent Assembly, elected on the basis of lists drawn up before the October Revolution, was expressive of the old correlation of political forces, when the conciliators and Constitutional-Democrats were in power.

The working classes learned through experience that old bourgeois parliamentarism had outlived its day, that it was utterly incompatible with the tasks of Socialism, and that only class institutions (such as the Soviets) and not national ones were capable of overcoming the resistance of the propertied classes and laying the foundations of socialist society.

Any renunciation of the sovereign power of the Soviets, of the Soviet Republic won by the people, in favour of bourgeois parliamentarism and the Constituent Assembly would now be a step backwards and would cause a collapse of the entire October Workers' and Peasants' Revolution.

By virtue of generally known circumstances the Constituent Assembly, opening on January 18, gave the majority to the party of Right-Wing Socialist-Revolutionaries, the party of Kerensky, Avksentev and Chernov. Naturally,

"Dissolution of the Constituent Assembly" is from Martin McCauley, ed., *The Russian Revolution and the Soviet State* (New York: Barnes & Noble, 1975), pp. 184–186. Permission granted by Barnes & Noble Books, Totowa, New Jersey.

this party refused to recognize the programme of Soviet power, to recognize the Declaration of Rights of the Working and Exploited People, to recognize the October Revolution and Soviet power. . . .

Obviously, under such circumstances the Constituent Assembly can only serve as a cover for the struggle of the bourgeois counter-revolution to overthrow the power of the Soviets.

In view of this, the Central Executive Committee resolves:

The Constituent Assembly is hereby dissolved.

A Self-Portrait (March 7, 1921)

V. I. LENIN

Name: Ulyanov (Lenin), Vladimir Ilyich

Party organization: Central Committee, Russian Communist Party

Number of delegate mandate (voting/advisory):   No. 21 advisory

By whom elected: Central Committee

No. of Party members represented at meeting at which elected: Central Committee—19 members

Which All-Russian party Congresses have you attended: All except July (August?) 1917

Date of birth—age: 1870—51 years

State of health: Good

Family—no. of members of dependents: Wife and sister

Nationality: Russian

Native tongue: Russian

Knowledge of other languages: English, German, French—poor, Italian—very poor

What parts of Russia do you know well, and how long have you lived there: Know Volga country where I was born best; lived there until age 17

Have you been abroad (when, where, how long):   In a number of West European countries—1895, 1900–1905, 1908–1917

Military training: None

Education: Graduate (passed examination as extern) Petrograd University Law Faculty, 1891

"A Self-Portrait" is from Warren B. Walsh, ed., *Readings in Russian History*, 3rd ed. (Syracuse, N.Y.: Syracuse University Press, 1959), pp. 622–623. Reprinted by permission of the publisher.

Portrait of V. I. Lenin (October 1918). Could the Russian Revolution have succeeded without Lenin's firm direction? *(Sovfoto/Eastfoto)*

Basic occupation before 1917:   Writer

Special training: None

Occupation since 1917 besides Party, Soviet, trade union, and similar work: Besides those enumerated, only writing

What trade union do you belong to: Union of Journalists

Positions held since 1917:   October 1917 to March 1921; Moscow; Council People's Commissars and Council of Labor and Defense; Chairman

Present position: Since October 1917; Moscow; Chairman, Council of People's Commissars and Council of Labor and Defense

How long have you been a member of the R.C.P. (Bolsheviks):   Since 1894

Have you ever belonged to any other parties: No

Participation in the revolutionary movement before 1917:   Illegal Social-Democratic circles; member of the Russian Social-Democrats Workers' Party since its foundation. 1892–3, Samara; 1894–5, St. Petersburg; 1895–7, prison; 1898–1900, Siberia; 1900–05, abroad; 1905–07, St. Petersburg; 1908–1917, abroad

Penalties incurred for revolutionary activities: 1887 prison; 1895–7 prison; 1898–1900 Siberia; 1900 prison

How long in prison: Several days and 14 months

How long at hard labor: None

How long in exile: Three years

How long a political refugee: 9–10 years

Party functions since 1917:   October 1917 to March 1921, Moscow, Member of the Central Committee

Present Party function: As above

Have you ever been tried by the courts of the RSFSR or of the Party: No

Date: March, 1921

Signature of delegate: V. Ulyanov (Lenin)

The Aftermath of Revolution

The Bolsheviks were thrust into a difficult situation on achieving power. Lenin was true to his slogan "Peace, Bread, and Land," and took Russia out of the war, negotiating a peace with Germany (Brest-Litovsk) that conceded much Russian territory. Lenin then applied his energies to quelling a civil war that pitted his Red Army (led by Trotsky) against the "White" forces, which consisted of supporters of the tsar or of other anti-Bolshevik elements. The tsar's execution in 1918 removed a possible impediment to the progress of the revolution. The civil war ended in 1921, and Lenin spent the next three years until his death consolidating his gains and preparing for Russia's transition from a capitalist to a communist state. In this, Lenin endeavored to apply Marxist theory to the realities of the situation. The first selection is from a pamphlet entitled "State and Revolution" written in August 1917, two months before the Bolshevik seizure of power. In it Lenin discusses this crucial period of transition. Events were to move in logical progression: from bourgeois capitalism to the dictatorship of the proletariat, to the "withering away" of the state, and finally to the justice and equality of the purely communist society. But things did not quite go as planned. The chaos of the civil war and a great drought rendered the socialization of the economic system an unrealistic proposition. Lenin thus allowed a "partial return to capitalism" by permitting the revival of private industry and authorizing the peasantry to produce and trade for profit as part of his New Economic Plan (NEP). Although Russia would still move toward Marx's dream of a truly communist existence, the journey would take longer than Lenin expected. In any event, Lenin envisioned an egalitarian future, one that included women as integral members of society, valued for their talents and abilities. His thoughts on the role of women in the new state are included in the second selection.

State and Revolution: The Transition from Capitalism to Communism (August 1917)

V. I. LENIN

Earlier the question was put thus: to attain its emancipation, the proletariat must overthrow the Bourgeoisie, conquer political power and establish its own revolutionary dictatorship.

Now the question is put somewhat differently: the transition from capitalist society, developing towards Communism, towards a Communist society, is impossible without a "political transition period," and the state in this period can only be the revolutionary dictatorship of the proletariat.

What, then, is the relation of this dictatorship to democracy?

We have seen that the *Communist Manifesto* simply places side by side the two ideas: the "transformation of the proletariat into the ruling class" and the "establishment of democracy." On the basis of all that has been said above, one can define more exactly how democracy changes in the transition from capitalism to Communism.

In capitalist society, under the conditions most favourable to its development, we have more or less complete democracy in the democratic republic. But this democracy is always bound by the narrow framework of capitalist exploitation, and consequently always remains, in reality, a democracy for the minority, only for the possessing classes, only for the rich. . . .

Democracy for an insignificant minority, democracy for the rich—that is the democracy of capitalist society. If we look more closely into the mechanism of capitalist democracy, everywhere, both in the . . . details of suffrage (residential qualification, exclusion of women, etc.), and in the technique of the representative institutions . . . on all sides we see restriction after restriction upon democracy. These restrictions, exceptions, exclusions, obstacles for the poor, seem slight, especially in the eyes of one who has himself never known want and has never been in close contact with the oppressed classes in their mass life (and nine-tenths, if not ninety-nine hundredths, of the bourgeois publicists and politicians are of this class), but in their sum total these restrictions exclude and squeeze out the poor from politics and from an active share in democracy.

Marx splendidly grasped this *essence* of capitalist democracy, when . . . he said that the oppressed were allowed once every few years, to decide which particular representatives of the oppressing class should be in parliament to represent and repress them!

But from this capitalist democracy—inevitably narrow, subtly rejecting the poor, and therefore hypocritical and false to the core—progress does not march onward, simply, smoothly and directly, to "greater and greater democracy," as the liberal professors and petty-bourgeois opportunists would have us believe. No, progress marches onward, i.e., towards Communism, through the dictatorship of the proletariat; it cannot do otherwise, for there is no one else and no other way to *break the resistance* of the capitalist exploiters.

But the dictatorship of the proletariat—i.e., the organisation of the vanguard of the oppressed as the ruling class for the purpose of crushing the oppressors—cannot produce merely an expansion of democracy. *Together* with an immense expansion of democracy which *for the first time* becomes democracy for the poor, democracy for the people, and not democracy for the rich folk, the dictatorship of the proletariat produces a series of restrictions of liberty [by itself oppressing] the exploiters, the capitalists. We must crush them in order to free humanity from wage-slavery; their resistance must be broken by force; it is clear that where there is suppression there is also violence, there is no liberty, no democracy.

Engels expressed this splendidly . . . when he said . . . that "as long as the proletariat still *needs* the state, it needs it not in the interests of freedom, but for the purpose of crushing its antagonists; and as soon as it becomes possible to speak of freedom, then the state, as such, ceases to exist."

Democracy for the vast majority of the people, and suppression by force, i.e., exclusion from democracy, of the exploiters and oppressors of the people—this is the modification of democracy during the *transition* from capitalism to Communism.

Only in Communist society, when the resistance of the capitalists has been completely broken, when the capitalists have disappeared, when there are no classes (i.e., there is no difference between the members of society in their relation to the social means of production), *only then* "the state ceases to exist," and "*it becomes possible to speak of freedom.*" Only then a really full democracy, a democracy without any exceptions, will be possible and will be realised. And only then will democracy itself begin to *wither away* due to the simple fact that, free from capitalist slavery, from the untold horrors, savagery, absurdities and infamies of capitalist exploitation, people will gradually *become accustomed* to the observance of the elementary rules of social life that have been known for centuries and repeated for thousands of years in all school books; they will become accustomed to observing them without force, without compulsion, without subordination, without the *special apparatus* for compulsion which is called the state.

The expression "the state *withers away*," is very well chosen, for it indicates both the gradual and the elemental nature of the process. Only habit can, and undoubtedly will, have such an effect; for we see around us millions of times how readily people get accustomed to observe the necessary rules of life in common, if there is no exploitation, if there is nothing that causes indignation, that calls forth protest and revolt and has to be *suppressed*.

Thus, in capitalist society, we have a democracy that is curtailed, poor, false; a democracy only for the rich, for the minority. The dictatorship of the proletariat, the period of transition to Communism, will, for the first time, produce democracy for the people, for the majority, side by side with the necessary suppression of the minority—the exploiters. Communism alone is capable of giving a really complete democracy, and the more complete it is the more quickly will it become unnecessary and wither away of itself. . . .

Again, during the *transition* from capitalism to Communism, suppression is *still* necessary; but it is the suppression of the minority of exploiters by the majority of exploited. . . . Finally, only Communism renders the state absolutely unnecessary, for there is *no one* to be suppressed—"no one" in the sense of a *class*, in the sense of a systematic struggle with a definite section of the population.

The Communist Emancipation of Women (1920)
V. I. LENIN

The thesis must clearly point out that real freedom for women is possible only through communism. The inseparable connection between the social and human position of the woman, and private property in the means of production, must be strongly brought out. . . . And it will also supply the basis for regarding the woman question as a part of the social question, of the workers' problem, and so bind it firmly to the proletarian class struggle and the revolution. The Communist women's movement must itself be a mass movement, a part of the general mass movement. Not only of the proletariat, but of all the exploited and oppressed, all the victims of capitalism or any other mastery. . . . We must win over to our side the millions of toiling women in the towns and villages. Win them for our struggles and in particular for the communist transformation of society. There can be no real mass movement without women. . . .

Could there be more damning proof of [female exploitation] than the callous acquiescence of men who see how women grow worn out in the petty, monotonous household work, their strength and time dissipated and wasted, their minds growing narrow and stale, their hearts beating slowly, their will weakened? Of course, I am not speaking of the ladies of the bourgeoisie who shove onto servants the responsibility of all household work, including the care of children. What I am saying applies to the overwhelming majority of women, to the wives of workers and to those who stand all day in a factory.

So few men—even among the proletariat—realize how much effort and trouble they could save women, even quite do away with, if they were to lend a hand in "woman's work." But no, that is contrary to the "right and dignity of a man." They want their peace and comfort. The home life of the woman is a daily sacrifice to a thousand unimportant trivialities. The old master right of the man still lives in secret. His slave takes her revenge, almost secretly. The backwardness of women, their lack of understanding for the revolutionary ideals of the man decrease his joy and determination in fighting. They are like little worms which, unseen slowly but surely rot and corrode. I know the life of the worker, and not only from books. Our Communist work among the women, our political work, embraces a great deal of educational work among men. We must root out the old "master" idea to its last and smallest root, in the party and among the masses. That is one of our political tasks, just as is the urgently necessary task of forming a staff of men and women comrades, well trained in theory and practice, to carry on party activity among working women.

The government of the proletarian dictatorship, together with the Communist Party and trade unions, is of course leaving no stone unturned in the effort to overcome the backward ideas of men and women, to destroy the old Communist psychology. In law there is naturally complete equality of rights for men and women. And everywhere there is evidence of a sincere wish to put this equality into practice. We are bringing the women into the social economy, into legislation and government. All educational institutions are open to them, so that they can increase their professional and social capacities. We are establishing communal kitchens and public eating-houses, laundries and repair shops, infant asylums, kindergartens, children's homes, educational institutes of all kinds. In short, we are seriously carrying out the demand in our program for the transference of the economic and educational functions of the separate household to society. That will mean freedom for the women from the old household drudgery and dependence on man. That enables her to exercise to the full her talents and her inclinations. . . . We have the most advanced protective laws for women workers in the world, and the officials of the organized workers carry them out. We are establishing maternity hospitals, homes for mothers and children, mothercraft clinics, organizing lecture courses on child care, exhibitions teaching mothers how to look after themselves and their children, and similar things. We are making the most serious efforts to maintain women who are unemployed and unprovided for.

We realize clearly that that is not very much, in comparison with the needs of the working women, that it is far from being all that is required for their real freedom. But still, it is tremendous progress, as against conditions in tsarist-capitalist Russia. It is even a great deal compared with conditions in countries where capitalism still has a free hand. It is a good beginning in the right direction, and we shall develop it further. With all our energy, you may believe that. For every day of the existence of the Soviet state proves more clearly that we cannot go forward without the women.

"Stalin Is Too Rude" (January 4, 1923)
V. I. LENIN

In 1922, Lenin suffered the first of a series of strokes that gradually incapacitated him until his death in 1924. His leadership of the revolution was thus interrupted at a crucial time. Lenin worried about a successor and expected Leon Trotsky to continue his policies. He doubted Joseph Stalin's character, as he revealed in a note written about a year before his death.

"'Stalin Is Too Rude'" is from Warren B. Walsh, ed., *Readings in Russian History*, 3rd ed. (Syracuse, N.Y.: Syracuse University Press, 1959), p. 626. Reprinted by permission of the publisher.

Stalin is too rude and this defect, which can be freely tolerated in our midst and in contacts among us Communists, can become an intolerable defect in one holding the position of the Secretary General. Because of this, I proposed that the comrades consider ways and means by which Stalin can be removed from this position and another man selected, a man who, above all, would differ from Com. Stalin in only one quality, namely, attitude toward his comrades, less capricious temper, etc. This circumstance could appear to be a meaningless trifle. I think, however, that from the viewpoint of preventing a split and from the viewpoint of what I have written above concerning the relationship between Stalin and Trotsky, this is not a trifle, or if it is one, then it is a trifle which can acquire a decisive significance.

The Development of the Totalitarian State

The Soviet Control of Society

In 1922, when Lenin's stroke removed him from active leadership of the Communist party, a struggle broke out among Lenin's chief lieutenants for control of the party. Leon Trotsky appeared to be the most logical choice, for he had been, together with Lenin, the primary ideological force behind the Russian Revolution and had proved his organizational ability during the Civil War of 1918 by managing the Red Army. He was outmaneuvered, however, by Joseph Stalin, who in his capacity as general secretary of the Communist party was in a position to control the delegates to the party congress. Stalin's control over the administrative levers of the party allowed him to eliminate all rivals. Trotsky was dismissed from the party, exiled to Siberia in 1928, and deported to Turkey a year later. He was eventually murdered in Mexico at the hands of Stalin's assassins in 1940.

After establishing his dictatorship over the Communist party, Stalin moved to consolidate his control over all aspects of Soviet society. Stalin's practical mind was in direct contrast to the ideologue Trotsky. Stalin rejected Trotsky's emphasis on immediate world revolution and embarked on the rapid, large-scale industrialization of the Soviet Union. He sought to create "socialism in one country" and understood that Lenin's revolution had taken place in at best an imperfectly industrialized country, one that would have difficulty competing with the productive capacity of Western capitalism. In the mid-1920s, Stalin decided to continue the New Economic Policy (NEP) that Lenin had developed to establish rudimentary capitalism and increase production among shop workers and peasants. But by 1928, he had taken steps to replace this with an economy planned and directed by the state. In 1928, the first Five-Year Plan was introduced for "expansion of the national economy." The plan prioritized heavy industry and the construction of steel mills, dams for the production of hydraulic electricity, and plants for the production of automobiles and chemicals.

The goals of this "command economy" were impressive: steel production was to go from 4.2 million tons to 10 million tons; coal from 35 million to 150 million tons, electric power from 5 million to 22 million kilowatt-hours. In the following speech, Stalin explains the importance of industrialization.

Industrialization: "Either Perish or Overtake Capitalistic Countries" (1931)

JOSEPH STALIN

Science, technical experience, knowledge, are all things that can be acquired. We may not have them today, but tomorrow we will. The main thing is to have the passionate Bolshevik desire to master technique, to master the science of production. Everything can be achieved, everything can be overcome, if there is a passionate desire to do so.

It is sometimes asked whether it is not possible to slow down the tempo somewhat, to put a check on the movement. No, comrades, it is not possible! The tempo must not be reduced! On the contrary, we must increase it as much as is within our powers and possibilities. This is dictated to us by our obligations to the workers and peasants of the USSR. This is dictated to us by our obligations to the working class of the whole world. . . . To slacken the tempo would mean falling behind. And those who fall behind get beaten. But we do not want to be beaten. No, we refuse to be beaten! . . .

In the past we had no fatherland, nor could we have one. But now that we have overthrown capitalism and power is in our hands, in the hands of the people, we have a fatherland, and we will defend its independence. Do you want our socialist fatherland to be beaten and to lose its independence? If you do not want this you must put an end to its backwardness in the shortest possible time and develop genuine Bolshevik tempo in building up its socialist system of economy. There is no other way. That is why Lenin said on the eve of the October Revolution: "Either perish, or overtake and outstrip the advanced capitalist countries." We are fifty or a hundred years behind the advanced countries. We must make good this distance in ten years. Either we do it, or we shall be crushed.

Collectivization and the Liquidation of the Kulaks (1929)

JOSEPH STALIN

Collectivized agriculture, wherein all land was owned by the proletariat and worked in common for the benefit of the whole community, had always been considered an integral aspect of communism. Although Karl Marx had little to say

"Industrialization: 'Either Perish or Overtake Capitalistic Countries' " is from Joseph Stalin, *Problems of Leninism* (Moscow: Foreign Languages Publishing House, 1953), pp. 455–456.

"Collectivization and the Liquidation of the Kulaks" is from Joseph Stalin, *Problems of Leninism* (Moscow: Foreign Languages Publishing House, 1953), pp. 392–393, 409, 411–412.

about its organization, this was a preeminent problem for Lenin and later Stalin. Lenin had conceived of the peasantry as a rural proletariat of agricultural workers who also belonged to the "working class." All income after expenses and taxes from the collective farm were to be shared based on the total number of workdays performed by each member of the collective. The farmers were also permitted a "private plot" of not more than one acre for use as a garden, and a cow, pigs, and chickens. In the 1920s the government offered special subsidies and favorable tax treatments to join the collective farms, but by 1928 only one peasant in sixty had joined. The first Five-Year Plan called for 17.5 percent of the cultivated land to be organized as collective farms. But there was great resistance, especially from a class of prosperous, middle-class farmers called Kulaks. They had prospered because of their efficiency and expected to reap the benefits of their dedicated labor. Stalin decided to force the issue and declared the Kulaks to be class enemies, as the following account confirms. Communist squads from the cities were sent into the countryside to seize the grain and livestock of the Kulaks. In response, the Kulaks often burned their property in defiance. They were executed by the thousands.

Can Soviet power and the work of socialist construction rest for any length of time on two different foundations: on the most large-scale and concentrated socialist industry, and the most scattered and backward, small-commodity peasant farming? No, they cannot. Sooner or later this would be bound to end in the complete collapse of the whole national economy.

What, then, is the solution? The solution lies in enlarging the agricultural units, in making agriculture capable of accumulation, of expanded reproduction, and in thus transforming the agricultural bases of our national economy. But how are the agricultural units to be enlarged?

There are two ways of doing this. There is the *capitalist* way, which is to enlarge the agricultural units by introducing capitalism in agriculture—a way which leads to the impoverishment of the peasantry and to the development of capitalist enterprises in agriculture. We reject this way as incompatible with the Soviet economic system.

There is a second way: the *socialist* way, which is to enlarge the agricultural units to introduce collective farms and state farms in agriculture, the way which leads to the amalgamation of the small-peasant farms into large collective farms, employing machinery and scientific methods of farming, and capable of developing further, for such agricultural enterprises can achieve expanded reproduction.

And so, the question stands as follows: either one way or the other, either *back*—to capitalism, or *forward*—to socialism. There is no third way, nor can there be. . . .

What does this mean? It means that we have passed from the policy of *restricting* the exploiting proclivities of the Kulaks to the policy of *eliminating* the Kulaks as a class. This means that we have made, and are still making, one of the decisive turns in our whole policy. . . .

Could we have undertaken such an offensive against the Kulaks five years or three years ago? Could we then have counted on success in such an offensive? No, we could not. That would have been the most dangerous adventurism. . . . Why? Because we still lacked a wide network of state and collective farms in the rural districts which could be used as strongholds in a determined offensive against the Kulaks. Because at that time we were not yet able to *substitute* for the capitalist production of the Kulaks the socialist production of the collective farms and state farms. . . .

Now we are able to carry on a determined offensive against the Kulaks, to break their resistance, to eliminate them as a class and substitute for their output the output of the collective farms and state farms. No, the Kulaks are being expropriated by the masses of poor and middle peasants themselves, by the masses who are putting solid collectivization into practice. Now, the expropriation of the Kulaks in the regions of solid collectivization is no longer just an administrative measure. Now, the expropriation of the Kulaks is an integral part of the formation and development of the collective farms. Consequently it is now ridiculous and foolish to discourse on the expropriation of the Kulaks. You do not lament the loss of the hair of one who has been beheaded.

There is another question which seems no less ridiculous: whether the Kulaks should be permitted to join the collective farms. Of course not, for they are sworn enemies of the collective-farm movement.

"For the Fatherland!" (1936)
PRAVDA

During the First Five-Year Plan, overall living standards in the Soviet Union diminished 35 percent, especially in the countryside. But by pouring nearly 35 percent of the gross national product into new production, the goals of the first plan were more or less accomplished. The Second and Third Five-Year Plans followed, but the Soviet people saw little benefit from their labor and the standard of living remained essentially unchanged. Criticism of Stalin's programs increased, especially among his supporters. The result was to purge or eliminate any opposition in political circles, the military, and the artistic community. Lenin had established the Cheka, or "secret police," to combat "counterrevolution," but Stalin honed this organization into a formidable intelligence unit that specialized in foreign espionage and domestic surveillance. Stalin made his secret police the primary instrument of his ruthless purges. They conducted interrogations, tortures, and trials, and expedited the incarceration of dissidents in the Siberian labor camps known as the "Gulag."

The climax of the purge trials came in 1938 when several former revolutionaries who had planned the Russian Revolution with Lenin were condemned and

"'For the Fatherland'" is from *The Communist Conspiracy, Part I: Communism Outside the U.S.,* Section B: the USSR, U.S. House of Representatives Report No. 2241, 84th Congress, 2nd Session (Washington, D.C.: Government Printing Office, 1956), pp. 287–288.

executed. These included "Trotskyites" and "Bukharinites," whose opposition was especially troubling. Stalin's victims even included heads of the secret police, who simply vanished one day and were quickly replaced. Stalin thus used terror effectively and maintained his preeminent authority by making sure that there were no entrenched or safe positions in the state. The estimated numbers of his purge victims including Kulaks range from ten to twenty million. Even when compared with Adolf Hitler's imposition of the Holocaust, Stalin was perhaps history's greatest mass murderer.

The first selection is from the official organ of the Communist party, Pravda *(meaning "Truth"). The proclamation of patriotism served as justification for intensifying the penalties of treason. The following accounts of the purge trials and the Gulag give evidence of the nature of Stalin's dominance.*

For our fatherland! This call fans the flame of heroism, the flame of creative initiative in pursuits and all fields of our rich life. For our fatherland! This call arouses millions of workers and alerts them in the defence of their great country.

The defence of the fatherland is the supreme law of life. And he who raises his hand against his country, he who betrays his country should be destroyed.

Today we publish the decree of the Central Executive Committee of the USSR regarding the supplementing of the statutes of the state criminal code with articles on treason. The Soviet country is very dear to the workers. . . . They have paid for it dearly in blood and suffering in their struggle with exploiters and interventionists and they will not allow anyone to betray their country and will not allow anyone to bargain with her interests.

For high treason, for acts detrimental to the country's military might, or state independence, or inviolability of her territories, for espionage, for divulging military or state secrets, for deserting to the enemy, or escaping across the border, the Soviet court will punish the guilty by shooting or by confiscating all his property. In the case of a civilian, some leniency will be shown according to circumstances, and for the death penalty will be substituted the confiscation of his property or imprisonment for ten years. For a person in military service, however, for treason there will be only one measure of punishment—execution by shooting with confiscation of all his property. Individual members of his family are also responsible for the acts of traitors. In the case of the escape or flight across the border of a person in military service, all mature members of his family, if they are implicated in aiding the criminal, or knew of his intentions and did not report them to the authorities, are punished by imprisonment for five to ten years with confiscation of all their property.

The other members of the family of the traitor and all his dependents at the time he committed treason are subject to disfranchisement and exile to some remote region in Siberia for five years.

Traitors should be punished unmercifully. On the other hand, if a person in military service was aware of a plot to betray the government or of an act of betrayal and did not report this to the authorities, he is subject to imprisonment for ten years. One cannot be a neutral observer where the interests of the country or the workers and peasants are concerned. This is a terrible crime; this is complicity in the crime.

This decree of the Central Executive Committee gives the workers of the great Soviet Union a new weapon in their hands in the struggle against the enemies of the proletariat dictatorship. The one hundred and seventy million working people who regard the Soviet land as their own mother who has nursed them to a happy and joyous life will deal with the traitors of their fatherland with all their force. For the fatherland, for its honor and glory, might and well-being!

The Purge Trials: "Traitors Must Be Shot Like Dirty Dogs!" (1938)
ANDREI VYSHINSKY

The Trotskyites and Bukharinites, . . . the leading lights of which are now in the prisoners' dock is not a political party, nor a political tendency, but a band of felonious criminals, and not simply felonious criminals, but of criminals who have sold themselves to enemy intelligence services, criminals whom even ordinary felons treat as the basest, the lowest, the most contemptible, the most depraved of the depraved. . . .

The investigation established, and I deem it necessary to remind you of this here in its full scope, Comrades Judges, that in 1918, immediately following the October Revolution, . . . Bukharin and his group of so-called "Left Communists," and Trotsky with his group . . . organized a conspiracy against Lenin as the head of the Soviet government.

Bukharin and the other conspirators, as can be seen from the materials of the investigation, aimed at . . . overthrowing the Soviet government, arresting and killing Lenin, Stalin, and Sverdlov [Secretary of the Party from 1917 to 1919], and forming a new government made up of Bukharinites. . . .

It has been proved that this bloc consisted of agents of the intelligence services of several foreign states, it has been proved that the [Trotskyites] regularly engaged in espionage on behalf of these states and supplied their intelligence services with most important state secret material. . . .

It has been proved that the bloc had organized, but fortunately for us had not succeeded in effecting, a number of terrorist acts against the leaders of our Party and government. . . .

"The Purge Trials: 'Traitors Must Be Shot Like Dirty Dogs!' " is from *Report of Court Proceedings: The Case of the Anti-Soviet Bloc of Rights and Trotskyites* (Moscow: People's Commissariat of Justice of the USSR, 1938), English edition, pp. 696–697.

Our whole country, from young to old, is awaiting and demanding one thing: the traitors and spies who were selling our country to the enemy must be shot like dirty dogs! Our people are demanding one thing: crush the accursed reptile!

Time will pass. The graves of the hateful traitors will grow over with weeds and thistle, they will be covered with eternal contempt of honest Soviet citizens, of the entire Soviet people. But over us, over our happy country, our sun will shine with its luminous rays as bright and as joyous as before. Over the road cleared of the last scum and filth of the past, we, our people, with our beloved leader and teacher, the great Stalin, at our head, will march as before onwards and onwards, towards communism!

The Gulag: "Stalin's Sadistic Nature Thirsted for Blood!" (1938)

Certain Trotskyists, including Vladimir Ivanov, Kossior, and Trotsky's son, Sergei Sedov, a modest and likeable youth, who had imprudently refused to follow his parents into exile in 1928, were taken in a special convoy to Moscow. We can only believe that Stalin was not satisfied simply to hurl them into the tundra; his sadistic nature thirsted not only for blood; he wished first to immeasurably humiliate them and torture them, coercing them into false self-accusations. Ivanov and Kossior disappeared without trace behind the walls of the Lubyanka prison. As for Sergei Sedov, after a "treatment" at the Lubyanka he was "tried" at Sverdlovsk, where he had worked as an engineer at the electric station; according to the newspaper stories, "he recalled having devoted himself to acts of sabotage" and other "crimes," for which he was condemned to be shot. . . .

The whole winter of 1937–38 some prisoners, encamped in barracks at the brickyard, starved and waited for a decision regarding their fate. Finally, in March, three NKVD [Secret Police] officers, with Kashketin at their head, arrived by plane at Vorkuta, coming from Moscow. They came to the brickyard to interrogate the prisoners. Thirty to forty were called each day, superficially questioned five to ten minutes each, rudely insulted, forced to listen to vile name-calling and obscenities. Some were greeted with punches in the face; Lt. Kashketin himself several times beat up one of them, the Old Bolshevik Virap Virapov, a former member of the Central Committee of Armenia. . . .

Two days later, there was a new call, this time of forty names. Once more there was a ration of bread. Some, out of exhaustion, could no longer move; they were promised a ride in a cart. Holding their breath, the prisoners remaining in the barracks heard the grating of the snow under the feet of the

"The Gulag: 'Stalin's Sadistic Nature Thirsted for Blood!' " is from "Trotskyists at Vorkuta: An Eyewitness Report," *International Socialist Review*, vol. 24, no. 3 (Summer 1963), p. 97.

departing convoy. For a long time there was no sound; but all on the watch still listened. Nearly an hour passed in this way. Then, again, shots resounded in the tundra; this time, they came from much further away, in the direction of the narrow railway which passed three kilometers from the brickyard. The second "convoy" definitely convinced those remaining behind that they had been irremediably condemned.

The executions in the tundra lasted the whole month of April and part of May. Usually one day out of two, or one day out of three, thirty to forty prisoners were called. It is characteristic to note that each time, some common criminals, repeaters, were included. In order to terrorize the prisoners, the officials, from time to time, made publicly known by means of local radio, the list of those shot. Usually broadcasts began as follows: "For counter-revolutionary agitation, sabotage, brigandage in the camps, refusal to work, attempts to escape, the following have been shot . . . " followed by a list of names of some political prisoners mixed with a group of common criminals.

At the beginning of May, a group of women were shot. . . . At the time of execution of a male prisoner, his imprisoned wife was automatically liable to capital punishment; and when it was a question of well-known members of the Opposition, this applied equally to any of his children over the age of twelve.

The Soviet State Ideal
The Creation of "Stalinism" (1934)
JOSEPH STALIN

The nineteenth-century political thinker Karl Marx had established the philosophical tenets of communism in 1848 that had guided Lenin, Trotsky, and other revolutionaries toward the establishment of a communist society. Marx was specific about his vision of a community of workers, the proletariat, which would work in harmony after the state had "withered away." Marx was notoriously unspecific, however, regarding the details or time span of this process. Therefore, revolutionaries like Lenin were left on their own to make whatever practical accommodations were necessary to implement Marx's vision. Lenin was a devoted Marxist and tried to remain faithful to his general principles. But Stalin, while outwardly professing Marxism, reinterpreted the primary doctrines. In the following address at the Seventeenth Party Congress in 1934, Stalin enunciated his revised conception of Marxism. In fact, it was his rejection of the guiding influence of Marx and the imposition of his own philosophy that might best be termed

"The Creation of 'Stalinism'" is from Joseph Stalin, *Problems of Leninism* (Moscow: Foreign Languages Publishing House, 1953), pp. 631–632, 635.

"Stalinism." Note carefully Stalin's views of the maintenance of class warfare, rather than the "withering away" of the state's influence; the emphasis on inequality, rather than a community of equals; and the importance of individual effort to effect change, rather than the unyielding influence of impersonal social and economic forces.

It goes without saying that a classless society cannot come of itself, spontaneously, as it were. It has to be achieved and built by the efforts of all the working people, by strengthening the organs of the dictatorship of the proletariat, by intensifying the class struggle, by abolishing classes, by eliminating the remnants of the capitalist classes, and in battles with enemies both internal and external.

The point is clear, one would think. And yet, who does not know that the promulgation of his clear and elementary thesis of Leninism has given rise to not a little confusion and to unhealthy sentiments among a section of Party members? The thesis that we are advancing towards a classless society—which was put forward as a slogan—was interpreted by them to mean a spontaneous process. And they began to reason in this way: If it is a classless society, then we can relax the class struggle, we can relax the dictatorship of the proletariat, and get rid of the state altogether, since it is fated to wither away soon in any case. They dropped into a state of moon-calf ecstasy, in the expectation that soon there will be no classes, and therefore no class struggle, and therefore no cares and worries, and therefore we can lay down our arms and retire—to sleep and to wait for the advent of a classless society. . . .

It goes without saying that if this confusion of mind and these non-Bolshevik sentiments obtained a hold over the majority of our Party, the Party would find itself demobilized and disarmed. . . .

[Some] people evidently think that socialism calls for equalization, for levelling the requirements and the individual lives of the members of society. Needless to say, such an assumption has nothing in common with Marxism, with Leninism. By equality Marxism means, not equalization of individual requirements and individual life, but the abolition of classes, i.e., a) the equal emancipation of all working people from exploitation after the capitalists have been overthrown and expropriated; b) the equal abolition for all of private property in the means of production after they have been converted into the property of the whole of society; c) the equal duty of all to work according to their ability, and the equal right of all working people to receive remuneration according to the amount of work performed (socialist society); d) the equal duty of all to work according to their ability, and the equal right of all working people to receive remuneration according to their needs (communist society). Furthermore, Marxism proceeds from the assumption that people's tastes and requirements are not, and cannot be identical, equal, in regard to quality or quantity, either in the period of socialism or in the period of communism. That is the Marxian conception of equality. . . .

Literature and the Soviet Ideal:
"The Craftsmen of Culture" (1934)
MAXIM GORKY

With the launching of the First Five-Year Plan in 1928, Stalin decided that the creative arts (literature, dance, music, and the visual arts) had to be mobilized to support the state efforts to industrialize the economy and collectivize agriculture. All artistic endeavor had to be intelligible to the masses, so creativity and experimentation were condemned. Themes suggested to creative artists included industrial construction, the fight against external aggression and internal subversion, and the glory of life on collective farms. Socialist realism became the order of the day, and the state demanded that artists and writers depict Soviet society not as it was, but as it was supposed to be. Music was to be melodic and firmly grounded in folk themes, art could not be abstract, modern and jazz dance were barred. The result was an outpouring of poster art depicting scenes from the Russian Revolution or portraits of Marx and Lenin. Ballet was locked into a classical mode or focused on revolutionary themes.

The famous revolutionary writer Maxim Gorky became the leading advocate of Soviet realism. In the following selection, he discussed the new standards of Soviet literature at a writers' conference in 1935.

The Communist-Leninist Party, the workers' and peasants' government of the Union of Socialist Soviets, which have destroyed capitalism throughout the length and breadth of tsarist Russia, which have handed over political power to the workers and the peasants, and which are organizing a free classless society, have made it the object of their daring, sage, and indefatigable activity to free the working masses from the age-old yoke of an old and outworn history, of the capitalist development of culture, which today has glaringly exposed all its vices and its creative decrepitude. And it is from the height of this great aim that we honest writers of the Union of Soviets must examine, appraise and organize our work. . . .

As the principal hero of our books we should choose labor, i.e. a person, organized by the processes of labor, who in our country is armed with the full might of modern technique, a person who, in his turn, so organizes labor that it becomes easier and more productive, raising it to the level of an art. . . .

The party leadership of literature must be thoroughly purged of all philistine influences. Party members active in literature must not only be the teachers of ideas which will muster the energy of the proletariat in all countries for the last battle for its freedom; the party leadership must, in all its conduct, show a morally authoritative force. This force must imbue literary workers first and foremost with a consciousness of their collective responsibility for all

"Literature and the Soviet Ideal" is from H. G. Scott, ed., *Problems of Soviet Literature* (Moscow: Cooperative Publishing Society of Foreign Workers in the USSR, 1935), pp. 53–54, 64–67.

that happens in their midst. Soviet literature, with all its diversity of talents, and the steadily growing number of new and gifted writers, should be organized as an integral collective body, as a potent instrument of socialist culture. . . . The idea, of course, is not to restrict individual creation, but to furnish it with the widest means of continued powerful development. . . .

The high standard demanded of literature, which is being rapidly remolded by life itself and by the cultural revolutionary work of Lenin's party, is due to the high estimation in which the party holds the importance of the literary art. There has never been a state in the world where science and literature enjoyed such comradely help, such care for the raising of professional proficiency among the workers of art and science.

The proletarian state must educate thousands of first-class "craftsmen of culture," "engineers of the soul." This is necessary in order to restore to the whole mass of the working people the right to develop their intelligence, talents and faculties—a right of which they have been deprived everywhere else in the world. This aim, which is a fully practicable one, imposes on us writers the need of strict responsibility for our work and our social behavior. This places us not only in the position, traditional to realist literature, of "judges of the world and men," "critics of life," but gives us the right to participate directly in the construction of a new life, in the process of "changing the world." The possession of this right should impress every writer with a sense of his duty and responsibility for all literature, for all the aspects in it which should not be there. . . .

Our Country: "A Dream Come True" (1937)
A. STETSKY

In the late-1930s, as Stalin moved to consolidate his power by destroying any opposition through the purges, he also began a campaign to export propaganda for consumption abroad that would influence public opinion and confirm the "Soviet miracle" as an industrial and military power. The Soviet "ideal" is nowhere better explained than in this utopian vision of Soviet progress.

The land of the Soviets differs from the capitalist world in that here the power belongs to the toilers themselves—to the workers and peasants. In our country there are no private owners of factories and banks, of land and manors. All the mills and factories, all the mines, railways and banks, and all the land, forests and mineral wealth . . . belong to the toilers themselves, organized in the Soviet socialist state.

There are no capitalists in our country, no stockbrokers, no landlords, no Kulaks, nor any of the classes which in bourgeois countries oppress and rob

"Our Country" is from A. Stetsky, ed., *Our Country* (Moscow: Cooperative Publishing Society of Foreign Workers in the USSR, 1937), pp. 7–8, 19–20, 23, 27–28, 43–45, 79.

This amazing photograph of a staged "aquatic event" demonstrates the extent to which Stalin's "cult of personality" had permeated social, political, and cultural life in the Soviet Union. The Marxist vision of a state that was supposed to "wither away" had been replaced with the totalitarian control of a dictator. *(Sovfoto/Eastfoto)*

the workers and peasants.... The working class of our country, acting in alliance with the toiling peasantry, has created the social system of which the best representatives of the toiling people have dreamed for centuries.... The USSR is the first country in the world where socialism reigns victorious....

Soviet industry has made giant strides during the period of the Second Five-Year Plan [1933–1937]. Wretched and beggarly does the industry of prewar Russia now appear to us compared with the mighty and up-to-date industry of the USSR.... One of the aims of the policy of industrializing the USSR was to overtake and outstrip the foremost capitalist countries economically and technically. The rapid development of Soviet industry ... advanced our country to first place in Europe with respect to output of tractors, and first place in the world with respect to output of harvester combines....

If exploitation was to be ended completely, the whole system in the countryside had to be changed. The Communists set about explaining to the peasants that only large-scale, collective farming could put an end to their poverty and their enslavement to the Kulaks. The USSR had built up a powerful, up-to-date industry. Agriculture could not be allowed to lag behind industry. It was impermissible that, with a large-scale, highly developed socialist industry, agriculture should consist of a sea of small and dwarf farms.

The Communists explained to the peasants that the only way they could escape from their poverty was to abandon the ancient habit of each household working its separate farm. The Soviet government aided the peasants in every way—by loans, seed, and agricultural implements, and by curbing the Kulaks and placing restrictions on their exploiting proclivities. But at the same time, the Communist Party and the Soviet government made it clear to the peasants that the only sure way they could escape from poverty and exploitation altogether was to form collective farms. . . . That is why the Bolsheviks, in leading the struggle of the workers and peasants for the victory of socialism, insistently directed the peasants towards collectivization, towards large-scale collective, co-operative farming. . . .

The cultural level of our country is rising with the rise in the standard of living of the people. Ever since the dictatorship of the proletariat was set up, the Party and the Soviet government have been steadily working to completely abolish illiteracy, that accursed heritage of the tsarist regime. In 1920, two-thirds of the population were still illiterate, but by 1936 the proportion of illiterates had dropped to 10 per cent. . . .

Education in our country is open to everybody—juvenile or adult. The workers under the Soviet system, where exploitation is unknown, have the shortest working day in the world. They possess great opportunities for cultural development and rational recreation. Russian workers before the revolution on an average worked 10 or 11 hours a day. Under the Soviet system the working day has been fixed at 7 hours, and for some branches at 6 hours. . . .

The development of culture in the USSR has been accompanied by the development of science. Scientific institutions and research laboratories have sprung up all over the country. There is no branch of knowledge in which Soviet scientists are not active and to which they have not made important contributions. . . . Soviet science is working hand in hand with our industry and is serving the cause of socialist development and the emancipation of humanity from the blind forces of nature. Soviet science strives to master nature, to make it the servant of man and to place upon its shoulders the burdensome forms of physical labor which are detrimental to the health and strength of man. . . .

The people of our Soviet country are stretching to their full height. They are justly proud of their great gains. And they have expressed their joy and warm gratitude to their beloved leader in their song:

> "And we who have conquered, we sing it so proudly,
> The Stalinist epoch we honor as one,
> We sing of our new life so happy and splendid,
> We sing of the joy of our victories won.
> From border to border, o'er valley and mountain,
> Where loudly the airplane's swift motor roars,
> Of Stalin the wise, the dearly beloved,
> The song of the peoples triumphantly soars."

Reflections on Totalitarianism

As we have noted, under the tenets of "Stalinism" the state became a dominant force and exercised complete control over all political, social, and economic affairs. Thus total control, or "totalitarianism," was the most sophisticated expression of authoritarian government that had developed through the fascist societies of Hitler and Mussolini. Fascism and communism theoretically were diametrically opposed, the former advocating the subordination of all elements to the needs of the state, the latter seeking the withering away of the state. Yet Stalin's perversion of Marxist orthodoxy allowed the creation of a state even more encompassing than fascist Germany or Italy.

The next two selections are from a conference on totalitarianism held by the American Academy of Arts and Sciences in 1953, the year of Stalin's death. Waldemar Gurian and George F. Kennan attempted to define totalitarianism and to provide perspective on the nature of this phenomenon. The last selection is from George Orwell's famous novel 1984, *wherein he discusses the real implications of totalitarian power.*

Totalitarianism as Political Religion

WALDEMAR GURIAN

The term "totalitarianism," which started its triumphal march through our time in Italy and was taken over in Germany, has never been accepted by the regime which today is regarded as the survival of totalitarianism in its most powerful form. The representatives of the Soviet regime do not care to appear on the side of Fascism and Nazism as belonging to the front of totalitarianism. The ruling Soviet party does not officially pretend to be a ruling elite separated from the masses, destined to lead and dominate them. . . . And even today, after the withering away of the state, announced in Lenin's *State and Revolution* (1917), has been postponed to a future very far away, beyond all human calculation, and after the strong almighty Soviet state has been accepted as the decisive fact of the present, the belief is not abandoned that the state will disappear. But this belief has become a utopian promise completely overshadowed by the political regime as it exists today. Therefore, it can be said that despite the rejection of the name "totalitarianism," the USSR has become the purest embodiment of totalitarianism, for in Germany it did not have time to last long enough. . . .

What is totalitarianism? Totalitarianism is often not distinguished from absolutism. Under absolutism all regimes without parties or elected representative bodies are subsumed. . . . Totalitarianism appears then as a modern

"Totalitarianism as Political Religion" is from Carl J. Friedrich, ed., *Totalitarianism* (New York: Grosset & Dunlap, 1964), pp. 120–123, 125–129. Reprinted by permission of The President and Fellows of Harvard College.

despotism. A power-hungry group achieves power—using demagogic means and deception of the masses. . . . Thereafter, it employs all means to maintain and expand its unlimited and unchecked power. These means are particularly terrifying and efficient in our time because of technical progress and inventions which permit swift concentration and application of power and manipulation as well as production of public opinion. There are no truly representative subleaders, there are no independent social groups, no traditional rights, no historical contributions and merits which can check the modern absolute totalitarian rulers; it must be emphasized that the totalitarian system differs from old-fashioned despotism and autocracy in its use of economic and technological pressures and manifestations of so-called public opinion. The totalitarian tyrannies of our time do not appeal to the "divine right," but they claim to represent the true will of the masses and of the people. They like to characterize themselves as representing the "real country" against legalistic fictions of democracies which destroy the unity of the people and paralyze it by parties, the instruments of parasitic and egoistic particular interests. They present themselves as "true" democracies because, for instance, only the communistic party (which allegedly is identical with the working productive masses) exists; whereas all exploiters and their representatives are suppressed. . . .

Therefore it may be said that the various forms of totalitarianism—Nazism and Soviet Communism—are politico-social secularized religions, characteristic of our epoch. The totalitarian movements and their power replace God and religious institutions such as the Church; the leaders are deified; the public mass-meetings are regarded and celebrated as sacred actions; the history of the movement becomes a holy history of the advance of salvation, which the enemies and betrayers try to prevent in the same way as the devil tries to undermine and destroy the work of those who are in the service of the City of God. There are not only sacred formulas and rituals, there are also dogmatic beliefs, claims to absolute obedience and damnation of heretics in the name of absolute truth which is authoritatively determined by those leading the movement. The doctrine may impose certain slogans and formulas—racism for the Nazis; class war, anti-capitalism for the Bolsheviks—but just the unlimited and uncontrollable right of interpretation and reinterpretation by the leadership gives to totalitarian politics its flexibility. . . .

What is the formal structure of the totalitarian ideocracy or socio-political religion? Essential is the belief; there are laws of necessary social development, economic or biological ones. After many fights the good forces will win out; the right order will be established. The victory of these good forces is dependent upon elites who represent either groups of natural superiority or those by whom the true interest of the masses becomes conscious. The domination of these groups is necessary for the world salvation; indeed it is the world's salvation.

This domination cannot be a limited one; it must embrace the whole of life and society. It must determine all realms of individual and social existence. There can be no private life outside. Passive acceptance is insufficient.

Enthusiastic, active acclamation and support are necessary, or men must serve as malleable material in order to show the superiority and the unlimited power of the rulers. . . .

If the totalitarian masters are in a ruling position, then they start to build up their machinery for total domination. Their power must be organized in such a way that it appears unassailable and omnipresent. There seems to be no other alternative left than submission and public acceptance. Each individual must appear and regard himself as an isolated helpless atom whose movements are dominated by the totalitarian masters; their power machinery is based on the pillars of the belief in their own world mission, the monopoly of propaganda and production of public opinion and a systematic terror which at the same time is surprising and crushing in its manifestations. All that must result in the attempt to replace reality by the official ideology. The doctrine enforced by the totalitarian power determines the reality; enemies, betrayers, evil contaminating forces are constantly created. There seems to be no other aim and purpose than the existence of totalitarian power and its leadership. Totalitarian terror—this must be emphasized—is not primarily directed against real or even potential enemies; it is directed against those who are declared to be enemies; what is real, is determined by the declaration of the totalitarian master, and of course, corresponding facts must and can easily be found; for the masters cannot err, though they may correct errors of subleaders. . . .

The totalitarian ideology is the deification of a power system—the power system directed by that group which came into being as its creator and claims to act as its realizer. Therefore, it is on the one hand a system which pretends to answer all questions and to solve all problems by its doctrine; on the other hand, it is very flexible, for it can be adapted to all situations according to the decisions and the interests of the ruling elite. Unauthorized criticism of details and rational arguments against the general line are without effect; they appear simply as expressions of evil and ignorant forces unable to see the whole truth. The individual must sacrifice himself to the collective dynamic. The imperfect present is justified by the coming perfect future, that of the classless society or of the Third Reich. Scientific and "ethical" justifications are used to express the necessity of the totalitarian politics and demonstrate its superiority.

The totalitarian ideology becomes at the end a purely formal one. Under Stalin the belief in the withering away of the state is transferred to a realm practically beyond human history, but it continues to be most important. It justifies eternal dynamism, it makes all actions of the totalitarian regime appear as necessary and corresponding to the unity and logic of a system. . . .

The totalitarian society would dissolve into a chaos if it could not be kept together by the artificial totalitarian doctrine whose domination corresponds not only to the laws of society and history, but fulfills the mission which it above all challenges. . . . The ideocracy is the ideology for the continuation of the present rule by a group which has established a system of absolute domination by terror, organization, manipulation, and propaganda.

"Diversity Is the Best Defense of Healthy Societies"
GEORGE F. KENNAN

All societies have varying degrees of vulnerability to totalitarian tendencies and of resistance to them. The powers of resistance are partly connected with, and dependent on, the requisite degree of gradualness in evolution—a decent and sedate pace of social change—a pace that permits change to occur without disrupting the continuity of the generations or destroying the individual's confidence in his environment. Where peoples have had a decent time to prepare themselves for the strains of modern life they are better able to resist the totalitarian virus than where these things have come too suddenly upon them. . . .

We see, also, how important it is, if men are not to fall into the illness of totalitarianism, that they should not be subjected without adequate ideological preparation to the strains of the great apocalyptic disasters of society; that without such preparation they should not know on their own territories the infinite horrors of modern warfare, that they should not be asked to sit for dreary long years in filthy, vermin-infested trenches and to witness what can only seem to them to be the senseless agony and slaughter of their fellow creatures, just as they must not be thrown out onto the streets by unemployment through processes they cannot understand, and thus be forced to lose their sense of usefulness and belonging in society. If democracy does not wish its members to turn to the morbid and despairing delusions of totalitarianism, it must take care to spare them these harrowing and excruciating experiences. This does not mean that it must always avoid war, or that it must baby its people in the extreme paternalism of the welfare state. But it must never ask men to undergo such experiences unless it also enables them to understand their rationale. If democracy cannot make men understand why life is sometimes hard and dangerous, it will not be able to continue successfully to subject men to hardship and danger. It will have only itself to blame if by so doing it drives them to seek refuge in the purgatory of totalitarianism. For even a purgatory in which there seems initially to be some semblance of meaning, however crude and irrational, is preferable, from the standpoint of the human soul, to a liberal chaos from which the sense of community is absent and in which freedom means only the sense of being lost and lonely and helpless.

I suspect, furthermore, that a neurotic sense of tidiness in political arrangements can be a great danger to any society. Too great an urge for symmetry and order, too strong an insistence on uniformity and conformity, too little tolerance for the atypical and minority phenomenon: these are all things that can grease the path by which nations slide into totalitarianism.

"Diversity Is the Best Defense of Healthy Societies" is from Carl J. Friedrich, ed., *Totalitarianism* (New York: Grosset & Dunlap, 1964), pp. 28–30. Reprinted by permission of The President and Fellows of Harvard College.

Lucky, in this respect, are countries like Great Britain, with its bizarre pattern of nationalities and dialects, its far-flung bonds of blood and interest, and its picturesque ceremonies and traditions; lucky is Switzerland, with mountain barriers, its unique historical path, and its multilingual balance. Lucky, even, we Americans have been up to this time, without our sectional diversities, our checks and balances, and our deference to the vital interests of competing minorities. Woe to any of us, if these things begin to yield to the leveling influences of the perfectionist, to utopian dreams of progress and equality, to the glorification of conformity in tongue or outlook that have been embraced in the concept of romantic nationalism and have gone before the disasters of totalitarian triumph. Diversity, in all the glorious disorder of nature, is the best defense of healthy societies.

In short, I suspect totalitarianism to be the retribution that befalls all peoples who give free rein to extremists and extremism, who forget the golden rule of political life, which is that ideas are never good except in moderation, and that anything carried to its logical conclusion becomes a menacing caricature of itself. For this reason one must not be too morbid about incipient totalitarian tendencies, which are only a part of life—so long as they remain incipient and counterbalanced. All totalitarianism is only a matter of degree; but it is precisely in this fact that its mortal danger lies. Who says differences of degree are not vital differences? Remember Shakespeare's words:

> Take but degree away, untune that string,
> And, hark! what discord follows . . .
> Then every thing includes itself in power,
> Power into will, will into appetite;
> And appetite, a universal wolf . . .
> Must make perforce a universal prey,
> And last eat up himself . . .

1984: "Power Is in Tearing Human Minds to Pieces"

GEORGE ORWELL

"The real power, the power we have to fight for night and day, is not power over things, but over men." O'Brien paused, and for a moment assumed again his air of a schoolmaster questioning a promising pupil: "How does one man assert his power over another, Winston?"

Winston thought. "By making him suffer," he said.

"1984: 'Power Is in Tearing Human Minds to Pieces'" is from George Orwell, *Nineteen Eighty-Four* (New York: Harcourt, Brace and Company, 1949), pp. 269–271. Reprinted by permission.

"Exactly. By making him suffer. Obedience is not enough. Unless he is suffering, how can you be sure that he is obeying your will and not his own? Power is in inflicting pain and humiliation. Power is in tearing human minds to pieces and putting them together again in new shapes of your own choosing. Do you begin to see, then, what kind of world we are creating? It is the exact opposite of the stupid hedonistic Utopias that the old reformers imagined. A world of fear and treachery and torment, a world of trampling and being trampled upon, a world which will grow not less but more merciless as it refines itself. Progress in our world will be progress toward more pain. The old civilizations claimed that they were founded on love and justice. Ours is founded upon hatred. In our world there will be no emotions except fear, rage, triumph, and self-abasement. Everything else we shall destroy—everything. Already we are breaking down the habits of thought which have survived from before the Revolution. We have cut the links between child and parent, and between man and man, and between man and woman. No one dares trust a wife or a child or a friend any longer. But in the future there will be no wives and no friends. Children will be taken from their mothers at birth, as one takes eggs from a hen. The sex instinct will be eradicated. Procreation will be an annual formality like the renewal of a ration card. We shall abolish the orgasm. Our neurologists are at work upon it now. There will be no loyalty, except loyalty toward the Party. There will be no love, except the love of Big Brother. There will be no laughter, except the laugh of triumph over a defeated enemy. There will be no art, no literature, no science. When we are omnipotent we shall have no more need of science. There will be no distinction between beauty and ugliness. There will be no curiosity, no employment of the process of life. All competing pleasures will be destroyed. But always—do not forget this, Winston—always there will be the intoxication of power, constantly increasing and constantly growing subtler. Always, at every moment, there will be the thrill of victory, the sensation of trampling on an enemy who is helpless. If you want a picture of the future, imagine a boot stamping on a human face—forever."

CHRONOLOGY: The Russian Revolution and the Development of the Totalitarian State (1917–1939)

1894	Nicholas II becomes tsar.
1895	Vladimir I. Ulyanov (Lenin) is arrested and sent to Siberia. Released in 1900, he leaves for the West, spending most of the next seventeen years in Switzerland.
1902	Lenin writes *What Is to Be Done?* in which he criticized accommodations and short-term gains rather than true revolutionary change for the working class. He advocates a small elite party of professional revolutionaries. In *Two Tactics of Social Democracy*

	(1905), Lenin urges that the socialist revolution unite the proletariat and the peasants.
1904	Russo-Japanese war breaks out.
1905	Revolution breaks out in St. Petersburg after Bloody Sunday massacre (January 22). Japan defeats Russia (January). Manifesto establishes constitutional government and institution of the Duma, or representative assembly.
1906	Meeting of the first Duma (April). It is dissolved in July. Three subsequent Dumas elected and dismissed.
1914	Outbreak of the Great War.
March 15, 1917	Tsar Nicholas II abdicates the Russian throne.
March 19, 1917	Provisional Government established until a representative Constituent Assembly could be elected by the Russian people. Leadership assumed by Alexander Kerensky.
April 20, 1917	Lenin arrives in Petrograd, reasserts his leadership of the Bolshevik party, and issues *The April Theses,* which declares war on the Provisional Government and advocates the confiscation of all landed estates for redistribution to the people at a later time.
July 1917	Bolsheviks attempt a coup that is premature and fails. Lenin flees to Finland and his collaborator, Leon Trotsky, is arrested.
November 8, 1917	Lenin returns to Petrograd, convinces his skeptical colleagues to act. Trotsky organizes a successful coup on the Provisional Government. Bolsheviks seize power.
December 1917	Lenin, after achieving power through political manipulation and force of arms, decides to hold elections to legitimize the popular mandate of the people. Bolsheviks soundly defeated. Lenin does not concede defeat and dissolves Constituent Assembly. Freedom of the press curtailed and secret police (Cheka) organized.
March 3, 1918	Treaty of Brest Litovsk formally ends Russian involvement in World War I. Poland, the Baltic States, and the Ukraine are ceded to Germany. The Bolsheviks agree to pay a heavy war indemnity.
1918–1921	Civil war between supporters of the tsar (White Army) and the communists with the Red Army organized by Trotsky. Tsar Nicholas II is executed in the summer of 1918. In spite of aid to the tsarist faction from the West, the Red Army eventually overcomes the domestic opposition. Under the economic policy of "War Communism," the revolutionary government confiscated

	and then operated the banks, transport facilities, and heavy industry.
March 1921	Following the Kronstadt mutiny and in the face of peasant resistance to the requisition of grain necessary to feed the urban population, Lenin issues the New Economic Policy (NEP). Peasants allowed to farm for a profit and could sell surplus grain on the open market. Russia becomes a country of family farmers and small, private shops and businesses.
1924	Lenin dies after suffering a series of strokes starting in 1922. Two factions emerge: Trotsky and Stalin. Stalin uses the party apparatus to edge out Trotsky, who is exiled in 1929 and murdered in 1940, presumably by Stalin's agents.
1928–1933	Start of forced collectivization of land among Kulaks. Resistance harshly dealt with by force and deportation.
1933–1939	Purge trials of Communist Party members in opposition to Stalin.

STUDY QUESTIONS

1. Analyze the demands of the Provisional Government and the Petrograd Soviet just after the abdication of the tsar. How are they similar and what are their differences? Note Lenin's ideas in his *April Theses*. What action does he advocate?

2. What measures did Lenin take to protect the position of the Bolsheviks once they had achieved power? How does Lenin justify censorship of the press? Do fallacies or inconsistencies exist in his argument? Note especially the vocabulary. For example, how is the phrase "workmen's and peasants' revolution" used? How was the Izvestia newspaper editorial dangerous to the Bolshevik revolution?

3. What are the duties of the secret police? What elements of society was this organization directed against? The tsar also had an active secret police that protected against "enemies of the monarchy." What is the difference between "enemies of the monarchy" and "enemies of the people"? Is a secret police therefore a necessary instrument for maintaining power, regardless of political philosophy?

4. What arguments do the Bolsheviks give to justify the dissolution of the Constituent Assembly? What gave them the authority to invalidate an assembly that was chosen by vote of the Russian people? Why did the Bolsheviks allow the election to occur in the first place?

5. What social or economic conditions contributed to the outbreak of the Russian Revolution? Although the Russian Revolution involved such strong personalities as Kerensky, Trotsky, and Stalin, it was Lenin who was the guiding spirit. What do his comments on the emancipation of women tell you about the man? Analyze his self-portrait. What kind of a man emerges? In Marxist theory, the

individual is of little or no importance in contributing to the social and economic forces that result in the eventual destruction of capitalism and capitalist society. If so, how then does one explain Lenin? What was his role in the revolution? Without his presence, would the Russian Revolution have succeeded? To what extent can the individual change the course of history?

6. The 1936 Constitution of the Soviet Union guaranteed citizens freedom of speech, press, and assembly. In view of this, how do you account for Stalin's liquidation of the Kulaks, the purge trials, and the establishment of the Gulag?

7. In 1924, Stalin, in true Marxist fashion, argued that the Communist party was the instrument in the hands of the people for achieving the dictatorship of the proletariat. He noted that "when classes disappear and the dictatorship of the proletariat withers away, the Party will also wither away." How does this statement compare with his ideas ten years later in 1934 concerning the creation of "Stalinism"? What does this tell you about Stalin? Was he an orthodox Marxist or was he merely adapting Marxism to fit the demands of the time—or the needs of his own authority?

8. Read the selections on "The Soviet State Ideal." What are the main points that Maxim Gorky makes about Soviet literature? What is the purpose of the "craftsmen of culture" and the "engineers of the soul"? Do you think the selection "Our Country: 'A Dream Come True'" is a valuable and convincing piece of propaganda? Why or why not? All of these works were created in the middle to late 1930s. What do you think of the juxtaposition of this expression of Soviet idealism with the purge trials that were taking place within the Soviet Union?

9. According the Waldemar Gurian, what is totalitarianism? In what ways does totalitarianism share common elements with religion? What are the basic means by which totalitarian rule is achieved and maintained?

10. What is the key to the prevention of totalitarianism in the view of George F. Kennan? He calls it an "illness." What is the cause of this illness? What does he mean when he says "all totalitarianism is a matter of degree"? In what ways do you see the elements of totalitarianism present in contemporary society?

11. After reading the excerpt from George Orwell's *1984*, what images remain in your mind? What is the essence of power? Could you foresee a modern state with that amount of control over society? As we become more advanced technologically, does the threat increase? How do humans remain free in mind and body?

12. Compare the vision of Stalin on capitalism versus communism, on the duty of citizens to the state, and on the future of communism with the remarks made by Mikhail Gorbachev and Boris Yeltsin in Chapter 11. What happened to the "Soviet miracle"? Why did the Soviet Union fail?

8

Europe Between the Wars: Fascism and the Nazi Rise to Power (1919–1939)

World
War I
1914-1918

Mussolini
comes to
power in
Italy
1922

Dawes Plan
modifies
German reparation
payments
1924

Kellogg-
Briand Pact
outlaws war
1928

Hitler
appointed
chancellor
of Germany
1933

1914

1940

1920   1925   1930   1935

Treaty
of Versailles
1919

Massive
inflation
in Germany
1923

Locarno
agreements
(December)
1925

Stock market
crash in
New York City
(October)
1929

World War II
begins
1939

Power is given only to him who dares to stoop and seize it. There is only
one thing that matters, just one thing: you have to dare!

—Fyodor Dostoyevsky

Tyranny consists in the desire of universal power beyond its scope; it is
the wish to have in one way what can only be had in another.

—Blaise Pascal

Order is the mother of civilization and liberty; chaos is the midwife of
dictatorship.

—Will Durant

It is too difficult to think nobly when one only thinks to get a living.

—Jean Jacques Rousseau

There is nothing more terrible than ignorance in action.

—Johann von Goethe

CHAPTER THEMES

- *Systems of Government:* What is fascism, and why was it so popular in the 1920s and 1930s? Why did democracy fail in Germany and Italy? What is totalitarianism, and how did Hitler's control over Germany differ from Stalin's control over the Soviet Union?

- *Revolution:* Is it legitimate to speak of a fascist revolution in Italy and Germany? Mussolini and Hitler came to power legally. How did their revolutions differ from Napoleon's revolution in France or Lenin's revolution in Russia?

- *Propaganda:* How were the Nazis aided in their rise to power by creating belief in their cause? What elements of their propaganda appealed to most Germans?

- *Women in History:* What were the role and expectation of women and children in the Nazi state? How did the image differ from the reality?

- *Historical Change and Transition:* How important were Hitler and Mussolini in changing the course of European history? Were the political, social, and economic conditions right for historical change, or did these leaders create the conditions of their success?

- *The Big Picture:* Is fascism dead, or will it always exist? Does modern communication technology make it even more dangerous? Why does fascism seem to strike a responsive chord in human nature? Is freedom most importantly a thing of the mind? If the institutions of government are controlled, yet *appear* to be free, and if you *feel* that you are free, are you free?

With the end of the war in 1918, Europe entered a new age of change and development. Democratic governments had won the "war to make the world safe for democracy" and the aggressive German monarchy had been abolished. Indeed, most other European nations adopted or maintained democratic institutions. The dominant theme, however, in the political history of Europe from 1919 to 1939 is the decline of these democratic governments. By the beginning of World War II in 1939, authoritarian regimes had been established in Italy, Germany, Spain, and throughout most of central and eastern Europe. The world was introduced to two of the most intriguing and destructive individuals of the twentieth century: Benito Mussolini and Adolf Hitler.

In order to understand the success of Hitler and the Nazis in particular, we must first look at the doctrine of fascism to which Hitler and many other twentieth-century dictators have subscribed. Fascism varies in its particular details of application, but in the simplest of terms, it is a doctrine that sanctifies the interests of the state and minimizes the rights of the individual. Fascism promotes as its great benefit the stability and security of the state.

Nearly all fascist governments have certain features in common. For example, fascism was born in direct opposition to liberal democracy, and as such regards personal freedom as dangerous to the stability of the state. Democracy, according to fascist doctrine, promotes individual expression and self-aggrandizement, which in turn results in disagreement and class conflict. Fascists also oppose socialism and communism since they promote the welfare of the masses over the good of the state. Communism, in fact, with its Leninist emphasis on the immediacy of world revolution, has dangerous potential for destabilization by its very insistence on class warfare. Fascism also depends on extreme nationalism. This goes far beyond the patriotic love of one's nation, but is based on pride in the allegedly unique characteristics and achievements of a "special" people. Therefore, fascist national pride is exclusive and implies a hostility toward other countries that are considered inferior in their outlook, governmental organization, or national heritage. This hostility is a unifying factor and is often vented against particular minority groups within the state itself. Thus, Hitler promoted hatred of the Jews as a rallying point for his support. This fascist national pride often expresses itself through imperialism, since military and economic expansion actually strengthens the state. Because stability and security of the state are the watchwords of fascism, it is important to implement a strong, highly centralized, and efficient government that only dictatorial rule can provide. One man with total control over the affairs of state ensures coordination and consistency of rule. Such a dictatorship is achieved and maintained through control of the national army, but most practically through paramilitary organizations like secret police, private armies, and bodyguards, which do not hesitate to use violence.

Fascism traditionally derives its support from the "right-wing" or conservative forces of society. The military represents, by its very nature, order and discipline. Big industrialists want to enjoy the lucrative profits that state stability affords; in a fascist society, general workers' strikes, which can often cripple an economy and interrupt production, are forbidden. Socially, fascism derives its mass support from the lower-middle class. In general, these are people who have worked hard within the confines of society to attain some measure of self-respect. Sociologically, they are individuals of commitment and pride who harbor dreams of social mobility, have faith in traditional values, and love their country; they have much to lose from instability and chaos. The fascist, totalitarian regime is intended to eliminate class conflict by concentrating the energy of all its members in the service of the state.

Fascism is often born of the frustration and discontent of people who have been in some way humiliated or robbed of their dignity either as individuals or collectively as a nation. According to the philosopher Eric Hoffer, in his book *The True Believer* (New York: Harper & Row, 1951), people who are most susceptible to mass movements are filled with the burden of their present existence and seek inspiration from those who have a vision of a proud and stable future.

Fascism first took hold in Italy during the 1920s, when unemployment greeted returning war veterans and disruptive strikes crippled the economy. Liberal middle-class politicians lost control of the state, and four Socialist governments fell in three years. In addition, Italy felt deprived of the "fruits of victory" from her involvement in World War I. She failed to obtain any of the German colonies in Africa and was frustrated in her attempt to acquire Albania as well. Amidst this frustration and dislocation, Benito Mussolini rose to power with his Italian National Fascist party ("Black Shirts"). Mussolini (1883–1945) promised stability and the vision of a "corporate state" in which each individual worked for the welfare of the entire nation. Mussolini guaranteed employment and satisfactory wages for labor but did not permit strikes. He favored industrialists by allowing lucrative profits and gave respect to Italy by closely identifying his regime with the glorious heritage of the ancient Roman Empire. Mussolini succeeded in giving Italy direction and dignity, but he accomplished this through suppression of civil rights and individual liberties. He was, indeed, the quintessential fascist.

But perhaps the most important and influential of the authoritarian regimes in the subsequent history of Europe was established legally in Germany by Adolf Hitler and the National Socialist party.

After the abolition of the aggressive German monarchy in 1918, the Weimar Republic was established amidst lofty ideals. Yet it labored under the burden of antirepublican pressures from the army, judiciary, bureaucracy, and even monarchists who wanted to reinstate the kaiser. Germany had never had a strong democratic tradition and had been united under a central monarch for only about fifty years. The German republic was also weakened because it had been created during a time of national defeat and humiliation. Critics used the Republic as a scapegoat for Germany's ills and accused its democratic leaders of betraying the German armies by making an unacceptable peace. Faced with the threat of communist revolution in Germany and economic dislocation, which was prompted by incredible price inflation and devaluation of currency, the Weimar Republic struggled through the early 1920s. Even during a period of relative economic stability after 1924, the leaders of the Republic were unable to foster a coherent program because of the conflicting demands of coalition government.

In the summer of 1929, Germany felt the first effects of the worldwide depression. By the winter of 1929–1930, three million Germans were unemployed, a figure that increased to six million by 1933. The deepening depression made it increasingly difficult for the various parties in the coalition government to work together. In the elections of 1930, the moderate and prorepublican parties suffered a significant defeat; the greatest gains were made by the National Socialist party, headed by Adolf Hitler. The Nazis, as its members were called, had been a small, violent group on the fringes of antirepublican politics during the early

1920s. But by 1930, their membership had increased greatly and they were the most dynamic of the antidemocratic parties. Their success and popularity lay in providing, or at least promising, something for everyone. The Nazis promised a renegotiation of peace treaties and reestablishment of German honor and power to those who saw Germany's greatness shattered by the defeat in 1918 and the Treaty of Versailles in 1919. They promised efficient authoritarianism to those who were frustrated by the inadequacy of republican politics. The Nazis promised a strong economy to those (especially in the middle class) whose savings were threatened by the depression. Hitler also promised protection to the industrialists whose profits and very existence were jeopardized by the communist movement.

The central doctrine, however, of the National Socialist party was anti-Semitism. In his autobiography, *Mein Kampf* (My Struggle), and in speeches and party announcements, Hitler blamed the Jews for the economic crises of the 1920s. The inflation and depression, he argued, had been caused by Jewish international financiers. The Nazis also believed that the Jews controlled the international communist movement. Jews had to be excluded from German life, they concluded. In the unstable and violent years after 1929, more and more Germans seemed willing to accept this explanation for their difficult times.

As Hitler's influence grew, his followers advocated a violent seizure of power. Although he sanctioned violent political disruption and intimidation, Hitler insisted on attaining power legally. On January 30, 1933, after much political maneuvering, Hitler was appointed chancellor of the Weimar Republic. By July 1934, Hitler had legally altered the Weimar constitution, changed the nature of the Republic, removed all Jews and "politically unreliable" people from the bureaucracy, dissolved all opposition political parties, and purged the army. On August 2, 1934, President von Hindenburg died, and Hitler combined the offices of president and chancellor. The army formally supported these developments by swearing "unconditional obedience to the Führer of the German Reich and People, Adolf Hitler." Hitler then began fashioning his own dictatorship.

In this chapter, we will look carefully at the political, social, and economic conditions that existed in Germany during the 1920s and early 1930s in an effort to understand why the Nazis were able to gain power. Themes that will emerge from the material include the use of racism and propaganda in the pursuit of power, as well as the role of the individual in history. Could Hitler have risen to lead Germany had he not been presented with the devastating social and economic conditions of the time? To what extent did Hitler change the course of history? In essence, why did Germany follow the leadership of Adolf Hitler? The complicated political maneuverings are not at issue here. Rather, it is important to try to understand people in crisis.

The Legacy of World War I

The Rise of Benito Mussolini

Before discussing the Nazi rise to power, one must understand the doctrine of fascism to which most of the right-wing dictatorships in the decades between the wars adhered. Benito Mussolini (1883–1945) was perhaps its most articulate spokesman. Mussolini was born the son of a blacksmith and worked as a school teacher and day laborer before becoming editor of a Socialist newspaper prior to World War I. He supported Italy's entry into the war and was wounded in the conflict. In 1919, he was one of many small-time candidates trying to make a mark in Italian politics. An amazing orator and opportunist, Mussolini presented a message of order and action that won him the support of working and middle-class Italians who had been hit hard by the inflation that plagued Europe after the war. Mussolini even organized terrorist squads to contribute to the very instability that drew him adherents.

By 1922, the fascists controlled local governments in many cities in northern Italy. Mussolini initiated a march on Rome that met with no resistance from King Victor Emmanuel III. Concerned with violence and his personal safety, the king asked Mussolini to become prime minister and form a government. Although Mussolini had achieved power legally, he did not enjoy even a near majority in the Chamber of Deputies. He immediately disrupted the parliamentary government with threats and physical acts of violence against its elected members. Mussolini was then given temporary dictatorial powers by the king to stabilize the political situation; he soon turned these into a permanent and personal dominance.

The first two excerpts come from Mussolini's autobiography and represent the official fascist interpretation of events leading to his assumption of power in Italy. Focus carefully on his reasons for taking action. The last selection is perhaps the quintessential defining statement of fascism. Mussolini believed that the twentieth century was a new historical epoch that required a different political premise based on popular loyalty to the state and supported by violent force.

"The State's Authority Was Ready for the Grave!" (1922)

BENITO MUSSOLINI

Milan, our greatest modern city, was in the power of political anarchy. Those same military forces who would have been able easily to take the situation in hand and dominate it were put at the mercy of the local authorities. They

"The State's Authority Was Ready for the Grave!" is from Benito Mussolini, *My Autobiography* (New York: Charles Scribner's Sons, 1928), pp. 110–111, 119–120.

were even obliged to ask the authorities for the flour to make bread for the troops! The stations, situated at the boundaries of the district of Milan, had in store heaps on heaps of goods; or course these stores decayed or deteriorated and were at the mercy of ware-house and freight-car robbers. At length, after thirteen days, on the morning of June twenty-fourth [1922] and after a meeting on behalf of the striking railway employees during which there was a fusillade of firearms, with dead and wounded, the railway men, overpowered by the indignation which had spread through the whole body of citizens, were convinced that it was better to return to work. But the state's authority was dead; it was now ready for the grave. . . .

I called to Milan the responsible chiefs of the Fascist movement, the representatives of the Po Valley, of Upper Italy, of the towns and countrysides. Those present were not many, but they were men resolved to take any risk. I made them understand, as I had suddenly understood, that through newspaper propaganda, or by example, we would never attain any great successes. It was necessary to beat the violent adversary on the battlefield of violence.

As if a revelation had come to me, I realized that Italy would be saved by one historic agency—in an imperfect world, sometimes inevitable still—righteous force. Our democracy of yesterdays had died; its testament had been read; it had bequeathed us nothing but chaos.

The Fascist March on Rome (October 26, 1922)
BENITO MUSSOLINI

Suddenly, when I knew that everything was ready, I issued from Milan, through the . . . correspondents of all the Italian newspapers, my proclamation of revolution. . . . Here is the text of the memorable document:

Fascisti! Italians!

The time for determined battle has come! Four years ago at this season the national army loosed the final offensive which brought it to Victory. Today the army of the black shirts [Fascists] again takes possession of that Victory, which has been mutilated, and going directly to Rome, brings Victory again to the glory of that Capitol. . . . By order of the Duce all the military, political and administrative functions of the party management are taken over by a secret Quadrumvirate of Action with dictatorial powers.

The army, the reserve and safeguard of the Nation, must not take part in this struggle. . . . Fascism, furthermore, does not march against the police, but against a political class both cowardly and imbecile, which in four long years has not been able to give a Government to the Nation. Those who form the productive class must know that Fascism wants to impose nothing more than order and discipline upon the Nation and to help to raise the strength which will renew progress and prosperity. The people who work

"The Fascist March on Rome" is from Benito Mussolini, *My Autobiography* (New York: Charles Scribner's Sons, 1928), pp. 176–177, 184, 205–207.

in the fields and in the factories, those who work in the railroads or in offices, have nothing to fear from the Fascist Government. Their just rights will be protected. We will even be generous with unarmed adversaries.

Fascism draws its sword to cut the multiple Gordian knots which tie and burden Italian life. We call God and the spirit of our five hundred thousand dead to witness that only one impulse sends us on, that only one passion burns within us—the impulse and the passion to contribute to the safety and greatness of our Country.

Fascisti of all Italy!

Stretch forth like Romans your spirits and your sinews! We must win. We will.

Long live Italy! Long live Fascism!

"The Quadrumvirate"

At night there reached me the first news of bloody clashes in Cremona, Alessandri and Bologna, and of the assaults on munitions factories and upon military barracks. . . . Fascism was under arms, it was dominating the centers of national life, it had a very well-defined aim, it had followed deliberately an extra-parliamentary path and it could not allow its victory to be mutilated or adulterated in such a manner. That was my exact answer to the mediators of the union between the National right and Fascism. No compromise! . . .

On the afternoon of the 29th, I received a very urgent telephone call from Rome. General Cittadini, first aide-de-camp of His Majesty the King, asked me very kindly to go to Rome because the King, having examined the situation, wanted to charge me with forming a ministry. . . .

Italy needed what? An avenger! Her political and spiritual resurrection needed a worthy interpreter. It was necessary to cauterize the virulent wounds, to have strength, and to be able to go against the current. It was necessary to eliminate evils which threatened to become chronic. It was necessary to curb political dissolution. I had to bring to the blood stream of national life a new, serene and powerful lymph of the Italian people.

Voting was reduced to a childish game; it had already humiliated the nation for entire decades. It had created a perilous structure far below the heights of the duties of any new Italy. I faced numberless enemies. I had created new ones—I had few illusions about that! The struggle, in my opinion, had to have a final character: it had to be fought as a whole over the most diverse fields of action. . . .

From petty discords and quarrels of holiday and Sunday frequency, from many-colored political partisanships, from peasant strifes, from bloody struggles, from the insincerity and duplicity of the press; from parliamentary battles and maneuvers, from the vicissitudes of representative lobbies, from hateful and useless debates and snarling talk, we finally climbed up to the plane of a unified nation, to a powerful harmony—dominated, inspired and spiritualized by Fascism. That is not my judgment, but that of the world.

After my speech of November 16th, 1922, in the Chamber of Deputies, I obtained approval for my declaration by 306 votes against 116. I asked and without difficulty obtained full powers.

The Doctrine of Fascism:
"This Will Be the Century of the State"

BENITO MUSSOLINI

Fascism was not the nursling of a doctrine worked out beforehand with detailed elaboration; it was born of the need for action and it was itself from the beginning practical rather than theoretical; it was not merely another political party but, even in the first two years, in opposition to all political parties as such. . . . If one were to re-read . . . the report of the meeting in which the Fasci Italiani di Combáttimento [Italian Bands of Combat] were constituted, one would there find no ordered expression of doctrine, but a series of aphorisms, anticipations, and aspirations which, when refined by time from the original ore, were destined after some years to develop into an ordered series of doctrinal concepts, forming the Fascists' political doctrine—different from all others either of the past or the present day. . . .

We want to accustom the working-class to real and effectual leadership, and also to convince them that it is no easy thing to direct an industry or a commercial enterprise successfully. . . . We shall combat every retrograde idea, technical or spiritual. . . . When the succession to the seat of government is open, we must not be unwilling to fight for it. We must make haste; when the present regime breaks down, we must be ready at once to take its place. It is we who have the right to the succession, because it was we who forced the country into the War, and led her to victory. . . .

The years which preceded the March to Rome were years of great difficulty, during which the necessity for action did not permit research of any complete elaboration of doctrine. The battle had to be fought in the towns and villages. There was much discussion, but—what was more important and more sacred—men died. They knew how to die. Doctrine, beautifully defined and carefully elucidated, with headlines and paragraphs, might be lacking; but there was to take its place something more decisive—Faith. . . . But, since there was inevitably some lack of system, the adversaries of Fascism have disingenuously denied that it had any capacity to produce a doctrine of its own, though that doctrine was growing and taking shape under their very eyes . . . in the laws and institutions of the regime as enacted successively in the years 1926, 1927 and 1928. . . .

Above all, Fascism, the more it considers and observes the future and the development of humanity quite apart from political considerations of the moment, believes neither in the possibility nor the utility of perpetual peace. It thus repudiates the doctrine of Pacifism—born of a renunciation of the struggle and an act of cowardice in the face of sacrifice. War alone brings up to its highest tension all human energy and puts the stamp of nobility upon the peoples who have the courage to meet it. All other trials are substitutes, which never really put men into the position where they have to make the great

"'This Will Be the Century of the State'" is from Benito Mussolini, "The Political and Social Doctrine of Fascism," in *International Conciliation*, no. 306 (January 1935), pp. 5–17. Reprinted by permission of the Carnegie Endowment for International Peace.

decision—the alternative of life or death. Thus a doctrine which is founded upon this harmful postulate of peace is hostile to Fascism. . . . This anti-pacifist spirit is carried by Fascism even in the life of the individual. . . . The Fascist accepts life and loves it, knowing nothing of and despising suicide; he rather conceives of life as duty and struggle and conquest, life which would be high and full, lived for oneself, but above all for others—those who are at hand and those who are far distant contemporaries, and those who will come after. . . .

Such a conception of life makes Fascism the complete opposite of that doctrine, the base of the so-called scientific and Marxian Socialism, the materialist conception of history; according to which the history of human civilization can be explained simply through the conflict of interests among the various social groups and by the change and development in the means and instruments of production. That the changes in the economic field . . . have their importance no one can deny; but that these factors are sufficient to explain the history of humanity excluding all others is an absurd delusion. Fascism now and always, believes in holiness and in heroism; that is to say, in actions influenced by no economic motive, direct or indirect. . . . And above all Fascism denies that class war can be the preponderant force in the transformation of society. . . .

After Socialism, Fascism combats the whole complex system of democratic ideology; and repudiates it, whether in its theoretical premises or in its practical application. Fascism denies that the majority, by the simple fact that it is a majority, can direct human society; it denies that numbers alone can govern by means of a periodical consultation, and it affirms the immutable, beneficial, and fruitful inequality of mankind, which can never be permanently leveled through the mere operation of a mechanical process such as universal suffrage. The democratic regime may be defined as from time to time giving the people the illusion of sovereignty, while the real effective sovereignty lies in the hands of other concealed and irresponsible forces. Democracy is a regime nominally without a king, but it is ruled by many kings—more absolute, tyrannical, and ruinous than one sole king, even though a tyrant. . . .

Political doctrines pass, but humanity remains; and it may rather be expected that this will be a century of Fascism. For if the nineteenth century was the century of individualism (Liberalism always signifying individualism) it may be expected that this will be the century of collectivism, and hence the century of the State. . . .

The foundation of Fascism is the conception of the State. Fascism conceives of the State as an absolute, in comparison with which all individuals or groups are relative, only to be conceived of in their relation to the State. . . .

The Fascist State has drawn into itself even the economic activities of the nation, and through the corporative social and educational institutions created by it, its influence reaches every aspect of the national life and includes, framed in their respective organizations, all the political, economic and spiritual forces of the nation. A State which reposes upon the support of millions of individuals who recognize its authority, are continually conscious of its power and are ready at once to serve it, is not the old tyrannical State of the medieval lord nor has it anything in common with the absolute governments either before or after 1789. The individual in the Fascist State is not annulled but rather multiplied, just in the same way that a soldier in a regiment is not diminished but rather increased by the number of his comrades. The Fascist State organizes the nation, but leaves a sufficient margin of liberty to the individual; the latter is deprived of all useless and possibly harmful freedom, but retains what is essential. . . .

The Fascist State is an embodied will to power and government; the Roman tradition is here an ideal of force in action. According to Fascism, government is not so much a thing to be expressed in territorial or military terms as in terms of morality and the spirit. It must be thought of as an empire—that is to say, a nation which directly or indirectly rules other nations, without the need for conquering a single square yard of territory. For Fascism, the growth of empire, that is to say the expansion of the nation, is an essential manifestation of vitality, and its opposite a sign of decadence. Peoples which are rising, or rising again after a period of decadence, are always imperialist: any renunciation is a sign of decay and of death.

Fascism is the doctrine best adapted to represent the tendencies and the aspirations of a people, like the people of Italy, who are rising again after many centuries of abasement and foreign servitude. But empire demands discipline, the coordination of all forces and a deeply felt sense of duty and sacrifice; . . . for never before has the nation [Italy] stood more in need of authority, of direction, and of order. If every age has its own characteristic doctrine, there are a thousand signs which point to Fascism as the characteristic doctrine of our time. For if a doctrine must be a living thing, this is proved by the fact that Fascism has created a living faith; and that this faith is very powerful in the minds of men, is demonstrated by those who have suffered and died for it.

"Germany in Her Deepest Humiliation"
"I Resolved Now to Become a Politician"
ADOLF HITLER

On November 11, 1918, German representatives signed terms of surrender and the Great War came to an end. Although they were clearly beaten militarily, defeat came as a shock to the majority of Germans because they had been told, as late as September, that victory was certain. Adolf Hitler, a corporal at the time, was gassed during the night of October 13, 1918. While recuperating in a military hospital, he heard rumors of German surrender.

"'I Resolved Now to Become a Politician'" is from *Mein Kampf,* by Adolf Hitler, trans. Ralph Manheim, pp. 266–269. Copyright 1943 and copyright © renewed 1971 by Houghton Mifflin Company. Reprinted by permission of Houghton Mifflin Company. All rights reserved.

But then as the old gentleman tried to continue and began to tell us that now we had to end the long war, that even our fatherland would now be submitted to severe oppressions in the future, that now the War was lost and that we had to surrender to the mercy of the victors . . . that the armistice should be accepted with confidence in the generosity of our previous enemies . . . there I could stand it no more. It was impossible for me to stay any longer. While everything began to go black again before my eyes, stumbling, I groped my way back to the dormitory, threw myself on my cot and buried my burning head in the covers and pillows. . . .

Now all had been in vain. In vain all the sacrifices and deprivations, in vain the hunger and thirst of endless months, in vain the hours during which, gripped by the fear of death, we nevertheless did our duty, and in vain the death of two millions who died thereby. Would not the graves of all the hundred of thousands open up, the graves of those who once had marched out with faith in the fatherland, never to return? Would they not open up and send the silent heroes, covered with mud and blood, home as spirits of revenge, to the country that had so mockingly cheated them of the highest sacrifice which in this world man is able to bring to his people? Was it for this that they had died, the soldiers of August and September, 1914, was it for this that the regiments of volunteers followed the old comrades in the fall of the same year? Was it for this that boys of seventeen sank into Flanders Fields? Was that the meaning of the sacrifice which the German mother brought to the fatherland when in those days, with an aching heart, she let her most beloved boys go away, never to see them again? Was it all for this that now a handfull of miserable criminals was allowed to lay hands on the fatherland? . . .

I . . . resolved now to become a politician.

"Stabbed in the Back" (1919)
PAUL VON HINDENBURG

The following is a statement by the German field marshal Paul von Hindenburg (1847–1934) to the Committee of Enquiry in November 1919. The committee was established to investigate charges that Germany had provoked the war and committed war crimes. Hindenburg was one of the most influential German commanders during World War I and later became president of the German Weimar Republic (1925–1934). His statement reveals the dissatisfaction and betrayal that many Germans felt upon surrender.

In spite of the superiority of the enemy in men and materials, we could have brought the struggle to a favourable conclusion if determined and unanimous cooperation had existed between the army and those at home. But while the enemy showed an ever greater will for victory, divergent party interests began to show themselves with us. These circumstances soon led to a breaking up of our will to conquer. . . . Our operations therefore failed, as they were bound to, and the collapse became inevitable; the Revolution was merely that last straw. As an English General has truly said, "The German Army was stabbed in the back." It is plain enough on whom the blame lies.

The Treaty of Versailles (1919)

The Treaty of Versailles, which was signed by Germany on June 28, 1919, was a dictated peace designed to affix blame and to punish. The reduction of the army to 100,000 men and the territorial clauses, which eliminated areas abundant in natural resources, were viewed with outrage. The Germans were particularly incensed by the reparation clauses and the statement of German responsibility for the war contained in Article 231.

Article 227. The Allied and Associated Powers publicly arraign William II of Hohenzollern, formerly German Emperor, for a supreme offence against international morality and the sanctity of treaties.

A special tribunal will be constituted to try the accused, thereby assuring him the guarantees essential to the right of defence. It will be composed of five judges, one appointed by each of the following Powers: namely, the United States of America, Great Britain, France, Italy and Japan.

In its decision the tribunal will be guided by the highest motives of international policy, with a view to vindicating the solemn obligations of international undertakings and the validity of international morality. It will be its duty to fix the punishment which it considers should be imposed.

Article 228. The German Government recognises the right of the Allied and Associated Powers to bring before military tribunals persons accused of having committed acts of violation of the laws and customs of war. Such persons shall, if found guilty, be sentenced to punishments laid down by law.

Article 231. The Allied and Associated Governments affirm and Germany accepts the responsibility of Germany and her allies for causing all the loss and damage to which the Allied and Associated Governments and their nationals have been subjected as a consequence of the war imposed upon them by the aggression of Germany and her allies.

Article 232. The Allied and Associated Governments recognise that the resources of Germany are not adequate . . . to make complete reparation for all such loss and damage.

The Allied and Associated Governments, however, require, and Germany undertakes, that she will make compensation for all damage done to the civilian population of the Allied and Associated Powers . . . by such aggression by land, by sea, and from the air. . . .

"The Treaty of Versailles" is from *Great Britain, State Papers,* vol. 112 (1919), pp. 104 ff.

Article 428.   As a guarantee for the execution of the present Treaty by Germany, the German territory situated to the west of the Rhine together with the bridgeheads, will be occupied by Allied and Associated troops for a period of fifteen years from the coming into force of the present Treaty.

Article 430.   In case either during the occupation or after the expiration of the fifteen years referred to above the Reparation Commission finds that Germany refuses to observe the whole or part of her obligations under the present Treaty with regard to reparation, the whole or part of the areas specified will be re-occupied immediately by the Allied and Associated forces.

Article 431.   If before the expiration of the period of fifteen years Germany complies with all the undertakings resulting from the present Treaty, the occupying forces will be withdrawn immediately.

The Weimar Republic

Germany's Unstable Democracy: The Best and Worst of Times

The Weimar Republic, burdened by the specter of defeat and shame, was impotent to meet the economic and political problems of the 1920s. The portion of the constitution that follows reflects the liberal idealism of the Social Democratic, Catholic Center, and Democratic parties that shaped it. Although there was much opposition to these beliefs from the National Socialist (Nazi) party, among others, many Germans were still loyal to the Republic, as the second selection reveals.

The Weimar Constitution: Fundamental Rights and Duties of the Germans (1919)

Section I: The Individual

Article 109.   All Germans are equal before the law. Men and women have the same fundamental civil rights and duties. Public legal privileges or disadvantages of birth or of rank are abolished. Titles of nobility . . . may be bestowed no longer. . . . Orders and decorations shall not be conferred by the state. No German shall accept titles or orders from a foreign government.

Article 110.   Citizenship of the Reich and the states is acquired in accordance with the provisions of a Reich law. . . .

"The Weimar Constitution" is from Louis L. Snyder, ed., *Documents of German History*, pp. 390–392. Copyright © 1985 by Rutgers, the State University. Reprinted by permission of Rutgers University Press.

Article 111.   All Germans shall enjoy liberty of travel and residence throughout the whole Reich. . . .

Article 112.   Every German is permitted to emigrate to a foreign country. . . .

Article 114.   Personal liberty is inviolable. Curtailment or deprivation of personal liberty by a public authority is permissible only by authority of law.

Persons who have been deprived of their liberty must be informed at the latest on the following day by whose authority and for what reasons they have been held. They shall receive the opportunity without delay of submitting objections to their deprivation of liberty.

Article 115.   The house of every German is his sanctuary and is inviolable. Exceptions are permitted only by authority of law. . . .

Article 117.   The secrecy of letters and all postal, telegraph, and telephone communications is inviolable. Exceptions are inadmissable by national law.

Article 118.   Every German has the right, within the limits of the general laws, to express his opinion freely by word, in writing, in print, in picture form, or in any other way. . . . Censorship is forbidden. . . .

Section II. The General Welfare

Article 123.   All Germans have the right to assemble peacefully and unarmed without giving notice and without special permission. . . .

Article 124.   All Germans have the right to form associations and societies for purposes not contrary to the criminal law. . . .

Article 126.   Every German has the right to petition. . . .

Section III. Religion and Religious Societies

Article 135.   All inhabitants of the Reich enjoy full religious freedom and freedom of conscience. The free exercise of religion is guaranteed by the Constitution and is under public protection. . . .

Article 137.   There is no state church. . . .

Section IV. Education and the Schools

Article 144.   The entire school system is under the supervision of the state. . . .

Article 145.   Attendance at school is compulsory. . . .

Section V: Economic Life

Article 151.   The regulation of economic life must be compatible with the principles of justice, with the aim of attaining humane conditions of existence for all. Within these limits the economic liberty of the individual is assured. . . .

Article 152.   Freedom of contract prevails . . . in accordance with the laws. . . .

Article 153.   The right of private property is guaranteed by the Constitution. . . . Expropriation of property may take place . . . by due process of law. . . .

Article 159. Freedom of association for the preservation and promotion of labor and economic conditions is guaranteed to everyone and to all vocations. All agreements and measures attempting to restrict or restrain this freedom are unlawful. . . .

Article 161. The Reich shall organize a comprehensive system of [social] insurance. . . .

Article 165. Workers and employees are called upon to cooperate, on an equal footing, with employers in the regulation of wages and of the conditions of labor, as well as in the general development of the productive forces. . . .

Loyalty to the Weimar Republic

LILO LINKE

A procession was formed, headed by the military band with triangles and drums and clarinets and followed by the members of the movement, two abreast, holding their torches in their upraised hands. We marched through the town, our ghostly magnified shadows moving restlessly over the fronts of the houses.

Never before had I followed the flag of the Republic, which was now waving thirty yards in front of me, spreading its colours overhead, the black melting in one with the night, the red glowing in the light of the torches, and the gold overshining them like a dancing sun. It was not just a torchlight march for me, it was a political confession. I had decided to take part in the struggle for German democracy. I wanted to fight for it although I knew that this meant a challenge to my parents and my whole family, who all lived with their eyes turned towards the past and thought it disloyal and shameful to help the Socialists.

We marched out of the town to the cemetery, where the first President of the Republic, Fritz Ebert, has been buried. Silently we assembled round the grave. Wilhelm Wismar, national leader of the Young Democrats and youngest member of the Reichstag, stepped forward and spoke slowly the oath.

"We vow to stand for the Republic with all our abilities and strength."

"We vow to work for the fulfillment of the promises given to the German people in the Weimar Constitution."

"We vow to shield and defend democracy against all its enemies and attackers whoever they might be."

And out of the night in a rolling echo two thousand citizens of tomorrow answered, repeating solemnly word for word:

"We vow to stand for the Republic with all our abilities and strength."

"We vow to work for the fulfillment of the promises given to the German people in the Weimar Constitution."

"We vow to shield and defend democracy against all its enemies and attackers whoever they might be."

Inflation: "The Boiling Kettle of a Wicked Witch"
LILO LINKE

Inflation, or the decline in the value of currency with the attendant rise in prices, engulfed Germany in the early 1920s, reaching a peak in 1923. The following accounts reflect some of the difficulties and frustrations felt by people of the time. The middle classes were especially affected, and their hard-earned savings became worthless. Both Lilo Linke and Konrad Heiden witnessed the hardship of these days. Heiden was particularly active against the Nazis in street confrontations as a student at the University of Munich in 1923.

The time for my first excursions into life was badly chosen. Rapidly Germany was precipitated into the inflation, thousands, millions, milliards of marks whirled about, making heads swim in confusion. War, revolution, and the wild years after had deprived everyone of old standards and the possibility of planning a normal life. Again and again fate hurled the helpless individual into the boiling kettle of a wicked witch. Now the inflation came and destroyed the last vestige of steadiness. Hurriedly one had to make use of the moment and could not consider the following day.

The whole population had suddenly turned into maniacs. Everyone was buying, selling, speculating, bargaining, and dollar, dollar, dollar was the magic word which dominated every conversation, every newspaper, every poster in Germany. Nobody understood what was happening. There seemed to be no sense, no rules in the mad game, but one had to take part in it if one did not want to be trampled underfoot at once. Only a few people were able to carry through to the end and gain by the inflation. The majority lost everything and broke down, impoverished and bewildered.

The middle class was hurt more than any other, the savings of a lifetime and their small fortunes melted into a few coppers. They had to sell their most precious belongings for ten milliard inflated marks to buy a bit of food or an absolutely necessary coat, and their pride and dignity were bleeding out of many wounds. Bitterness remained for ever in their hearts. Full of hatred, they accused the international financiers, the Jews and Socialists—their old enemies—of having exploited their distress. They never forgot and never forgave and were the first to lend a willing ear to Hitler's fervent preaching.

In the shop, notices announced that we should receive our salaries in weekly parts; after a while we queued up at the cashier's desk every evening, and before long we were paid twice daily and ran out during the lunch hour to buy a few things, because as soon as the new rate of exchange became known in the early afternoon our money had again lost half its value.

In the beginning I did not concern myself much with these happenings. They merely added to the excitement of my new life, which was all that mattered to me. Living in the east of Berlin and in hard times, I was long accustomed to seeing people around me in hunger, distress, and poverty. My mother was always lamenting that it was impossible for her to make both ends meet, my father—whenever he was at home—always asking what the deuce she had done with all the money he had given her yesterday. A few tears, a few outbreaks more did not make a difference great enough to impress me deeply.

Yet, in the long run, the evil influence of the inflation, financially as well as morally, penetrated even to me. Berlin had become the centre of international profiteers and noisy new rich. For a few dollars they could buy the whole town, drinks and women, horses and houses, virtue and vice, and they made free use of these possibilities.

The Devaluation of Currency
KONRAD HEIDEN

They all stood in lines outside the pay-windows, staring impatiently at the electric wall clock, slowly advancing until at last they reached the window and received a bag full of paper notes. According to the figures inscribed on them, the paper notes amounted to seven hundred thousand or five hundred million, or three hundred and eighty billion, or eighteen trillion marks—the figures rose from month to month, then from week to week, finally from day to day. With their bags the people moved quickly to the doors, all in haste, the younger ones running. They dashed to the nearest food store, where a line had already formed. Again they moved slowly, oh how slowly, forward. When you reached the store, a pound of sugar might have been obtainable for two millions; but, by the time you came to the counter, all you could get for two millions was half a pound, and the saleswoman said the dollar had just gone up again. With the millions and billions you bought sardines, sausages, sugar, perhaps even a little butter, but as a rule the cheaper margarine—always things that would keep for a week, until next pay-day, until the next stage in the fall of the mark.

"The Outlawry of War": Kellogg-Briand Pact (1928)

Although the 1920s proved to be a difficult decade for the Weimar Republic amidst extreme inflation and political turbulence, several signs of progress lent hope for the future. German reparation payments to the victors of World War I were restructured under the more liberal terms of the Dawes Plan of 1924. In 1925, the German foreign minister Gustav Stresemann initiated a conference at Locarno wherein Germany and France met as equals to establish firm boundaries and "preserve their respective nations from the scourge of war" by providing for the peaceful settlement of any dispute that might eventually arise between them. This "Spirit of Locarno" was a stabilizing influence in Europe until Hitler's accession to power in 1933.

The following document is perhaps the most riveting expression of international progress during the first half of the twentieth century. The French foreign minister Aristide Briand, together with the American secretary of state Frank Kellogg, negotiated a multilateral treaty that renounced war as an instrument of national policy. It was signed by representatives of the several European states, including Germany and Russia, as well as Japan, India, and South Africa. Although it was an expression of confident humanitarianism, the succeeding events in Europe that led to World War II proved its naïveté.

Aristide Briand's Message to the American People (1927)

Disarmament can come about only by the will to peace among all nations. In that the thought of America will ever be certain to find sympathetic accord in the thought of France.

If there were need of it between the two great democracies in order to give high testimony of their desire for peace and to furnish a solemn example to other peoples, France would be willing to enter into an engagement with America mutually outlawing war, to use your way of expressing it.

The Multilateral Treaty for the Renunciation of War (1928)

Article 1. The high contracting parties solemnly declare in the names of their respective peoples that they condemn recourse to war for the solution of international controversies, and renounce it as an instrument of national policy in their relations with one another.

Article 2. The high contracting parties agree that the settlement or solution of all disputes or conflicts of whatever nature or of whatever origin they may be, which may arise among them, shall be never sought except by pacific means.

Hitler's Response to Germany's Problems

The National Socialist party produced a program in 1920 that formed the basis of Hitler's campaign against the Weimar Republic. The succeeding selections of speeches and rally announcements not only reveal Nazi ideology but also testify to the dynamism of Nazi propaganda.

The Nazi Program (1920)

The program is the political foundation of the NSDAP [Nazi Party] and accordingly the primary political law of the State. It has been made brief and clear intentionally.

All legal precepts must be applied in the spirit of the party program.

Since the taking over of control, the Fuehrer has succeeded in the realization of essential portions of the Party program from the fundamentals to the detail.

The Party Program of the NSDAP was proclaimed on the 24 February 1920 by Adolf Hitler at the first large Party gathering in Munich and since that day has remained unaltered. Within the national socialist philosophy is summarized in 25 points:

1. We demand the unification of all Germans in the Greater Germany on the basis of the right of self-determination of peoples.

2. We demand equality of rights for the German people in respect to the other nations; abrogation of the peace treaties of Versailles and St. Germain.

3. We demand land and territory [colonies] for the sustenance of our people, and colonization for our surplus population.

4. Only a member of the race can be a citizen. A member of the race can only be one who is of German blood, without consideration of creed. Consequently no Jew can be a member of the race.

5. Whoever has no citizenship is to be able to live in Germany only as a guest, and must be under the authority of legislation for foreigners.

6. The right to determine matters concerning administration and law belongs only to the citizen. Therefore we demand that every public office, of any sort whatsoever, whether in the Reich, the county or municipality, be filled only by citizens. . . .

7. We demand that the state be charged first with providing the opportunity for a livelihood and way of life for citizens. If it is impossible to sustain the total population of the State, then the members of foreign nations (non-citizens) are to be expelled from the Reich.

8. Any further immigration of non-citizens is to be prevented. We demand that all non-Germans, who have immigrated to Germany since the 2 August 1914, be forced immediately to leave the Reich.

9. All citizens must have equal rights and obligations.

10. The first obligation of every citizen must be to work both spiritually and physically. . . .

"The Nazi Program" is from "National Socialist Yearbook, 1941," Office of the U.S. Chief Counsel for Prosecution of Axis Criminality, *Nazi Conspiracy and Aggression* (Washington, D.C.: Government Printing Office, 1946), vol. 4, pp. 208–211.

13. We demand the nationalization of all [previous] associated industries [trusts].

14. We demand a division of profits of all heavy industries.

15. We demand an expansion on a large scale of old age welfare.

16. We demand the creation of a healthy middle class and its conservation. . . .

18. We demand struggle without consideration against those whose activity is injurious to the general interest. Common national criminals, usurers . . . and so forth are to be punished with death, without consideration of confession or race.

20. The state is to be responsible for a fundamental reconstruction of our whole national education program, to enable every capable and industrious German to obtain higher education and subsequently introduction into leading positions. . . .

21. The State is to care for the elevating of national health by protecting the mother and child, by outlawing child-labor, by the encouragement of physical fitness, by means of the legal establishment of a gymnastic and sport obligation, by the utmost support of all organizations concerned with the physical instruction of the young.

23. We demand legal opposition to known lies and their promulgation through the press. In order to enable the provision of a German press, we demand, that: (a) All writers and employees of the newspapers appearing in the German language be members of the race: (b) Non-German newspapers be required to have the express permission of the State to be published. They may not be printed in the German language: (c) Non-Germans are forbidden by law any financial interest in German publications, or any influence on them, and as punishment for violations the closing of such a publication as well as the immediate expulsion from the Reich of the non-German concerned. Publications which are counter to the general good are to be forbidden. We demand legal prosecution of artistic and literary forms which exert a destructive influence on our national life, and the closure of organizations opposing the above made demands.

24. We demand freedom of religion for all religious denominations within the state so long as they do not endanger its existence or oppose the moral senses of the Germanic race. The Party as such advocates the standpoint of a positive Christianity without binding itself confessionally to any one denomination. It combats the Jewish-materialistic spirit within and around us, and is convinced that a lasting recovery of our nation can only succeed from within on the framework: common utility precedes individual utility.

25. For the execution of all of this we demand the formation of a strong central power in the Reich. Unlimited authority of the central parliament over the whole Reich and its organizations in general. The forming of state and profession chambers for the execution of the laws made by the Reich within the various states of the confederation. The leaders of the Party promise, if necessary by sacrificing their own lives, to support the execution of the points set forth above without consideration.

This photograph of Benito Mussolini and Adolf Hitler expresses the image of discipline and vision that was so much a part of fascist propaganda. They both rose to power amidst the political and economic dislocation of the 1920s and 1930s. "Order is the mother of civilization and liberty; chaos is the midwife of dictatorship."—Will Durant. *(UPI/Corbis)*

Speech on the Treaty of Versailles (April 17, 1923)
ADOLF HITLER

With the armistice begins the humiliation of Germany. If the Republic on the day of its foundation had appealed to the country: "Germans, stand together! Up and resist the foe! The Fatherland, the Republic expects of you that you fight to your last breath," then millions who are now enemies of the Republic would be fanatical Republicans. Today they are the foes of the Republic not because it is a Republic but because this Republic was founded at the moment when Germany was humiliated, because it so discredited the new flag that men's eyes must turn regretfully towards the old flag.

So long as this Treaty stands there can be no resurrection of the German people; no social reform of any kind is possible! The Treaty was made in order to bring 20 million Germans to their deaths and to ruin the German nation. But those who made the Treaty cannot set it aside. As its foundation our Movement formulated three demands:

1. Setting aside of the Peace Treaty.
2. Unification of all Germans.
3. Land and soil [*Grund und Boden*] to feed our nation.

Our movement could formulate these demands, since it was not our Movement which caused the War, it has not made the Republic, it did not sign the Peace Treaty.

There is thus one thing which is the first task of this Movement: it desires to make the German once more National, that his Fatherland shall stand for him above everything else. It desires to teach our people to understand afresh the truth of the old saying: He who will not be a hammer must be an anvil. An anvil are we today, and that anvil will be beaten until out of the anvil we fashion once more a hammer, a German sword!

Nazi Political Rally Announcement (February 1921)
NATIONAL SOCIALIST GERMAN WORKERS' PARTY
Fellow Citizens!

A year ago we called you to the Zirkus Krone. For the first time we invited you to a giant protest against making Germany defenseless by disarmament. We

---

"Speech on the Treaty of Versailles" is from Normal H. Baynes, trans. and ed., *The Speeches of Adolf Hitler, April 1922–1939*, vol. 1 (London: Oxford University Press, 1942), pp. 56–57. Reprinted by permission of the publisher.

"Nazi Political Rally Announcement" is from *Mein Kampf*, by Adolf Hitler, trans. Ralph Manheim, pp. 546–547. Copyright 1943 and copyright © renewed 1971 by Houghton Mifflin Company. Reprinted by permission of Houghton Mifflin Company.

declared that this making her defenseless would be the prelude for the loss of Upper Silesia.

For the second time we invite you to resist against the Paris Dictate. We called it the permanent enslavement of Germany. . . .

Poverty no longer begins to appear, it is here. And though one does not feel it in the armchairs of the parliaments and in the soft cushions of our people's leaders it is felt all the more by the millions who have been cheated, by the masses of the people who do not live by cheating, profiteering and usury, but by the sweat of their honest work. But we are not only a poor people, we are also a miserable people.

We have forgotten the millions of our fellow citizens who once, during a long four and a half years, bled for Germany's existence on innumerable battlefields, and of whom our fatherland has been robbed by a cruel fate.

We have forgotten the millions of those Germans who longingly await the day which brings them home to a country that even as the poorest would still present the happiness of being their fatherland. We have forgotten the Rhineland and Upper Silesia, forgotten German-Austria and the millions of our brothers in Czechoslovakia, forgotten Alsace-Lorraine and the Palatinate, and while our beloved Germany thus lies dismembered, powerless and torn, disgracefully robbed, a colony of the international world criminals, there— we dance.

We invite you to come Thursday, February 2, 1921, to a GIANT DEMON-STRATION for a coming GREATER GERMANY to the Zirkus Krone, Engineer Rudolf JUNG, Deputy of the Prague Parliament, and Party Member Adolf HITLER will speak about:

'GERMANY IN HER DEEPEST HUMILIATION'

Beginning 8 P.M., end 10 P.M.   Jews not admitted

To cover expenses of the hall and posters, admission M.I. War invalids free.

Fellow citizens, white collar and manual workers, Germans from all countries of our fatherland, come in masses!

[The meeting was attended by more than seven thousand persons.]

Nazi Appeal and Victory

Nazi Propaganda

In order to rise to power, an organization or individual must promote ideas, gain converts, and feed on mistakes of the opposition. Where no problems exist, they must be created, and where they are real, they must be exposed and used to advantage. Such is the nature and purpose of propaganda. The first selection is a pamphlet composed in 1930 by Dr. Joseph Goebbels, the future minister of propaganda for the Third Reich. It was important to focus on enemies, whether they were cowards, communists, or Jews, since fear and hatred can often unify a people more readily than positive ideas.

Unity must also be achieved through leadership. Above anything else, the Nazis promoted faith over rational thought. The National Socialist program could be reduced to two words: Adolf Hitler. His mythic presence is seen in the second selection, which appeared in the newspaper Völkischer Beobachter *just before an election on March 13, 1932. As Hitler noted, "The most brilliant propaganda technique must concentrate on a few points and repeat them over and over." He understood that in troubled times, people want a simple explanation for their pain and insecurity—and then they want the pain to go away.*

Nationalists, Socialists, and Jews (1930)
JOSEPH GOEBBELS

WHY ARE WE NATIONALISTS?

We are NATIONALISTS because we see in the NATION the only possibility for the protection and the furtherance of our existence.

The NATION is the organic bond of a people for the protection and defense of their lives. He is nationally minded who understands this IN WORD AND IN DEED.

Today, in GERMANY, NATIONALISM has degenerated into BOURGEOIS PATRIOTISM, and its power exhausts itself in tilting at windmills. . . .

Young nationalism has its unconditional demands. BELIEF IN THE NATION is a matter of all the people, not for individuals of rank, a class, or an industrial clique. The eternal must be separated from the contemporary. The maintenance of a rotten industrial system has nothing to do with nationalism. I can love Germany and hate capitalism; not only CAN I do it, I also MUST do it. The germ of the rebirth of our people LIES ONLY IN THE DESTRUCTION OF THE SYSTEM OF PLUNDERING THE HEALTHY POWER OF THE PEOPLE.

WE ARE NATIONALISTS BECAUSE WE, AS GERMANS, LOVE GERMANY. And because we love Germany, we demand the protection of its national spirit and we battle against its destroyers.

WHY ARE WE SOCIALISTS?

We are SOCIALISTS because we see in SOCIALISM the only possibility for maintaining our racial existence and through it the reconquest of our political freedom and the rebirth of the German state. SOCIALISM has its peculiar form first of all through its comradeship in arms with the forward-driving energy of a newly awakened nationalism. Without nationalism it is nothing, a

"Nationalists, Socialists, and Jews" is from Louis L. Snyder, ed., *Documents of German History,* pp. 414–416. Copyright © 1985 by Rutgers, the State University. Reprinted by permission of Rutgers University Press.

phantom, a theory, a vision of air, a book. With it, it is everything, THE FUTURE, FREEDOM, FATHERLAND!

It was a sin of the liberal bourgeoisie to overlook THE STATEBUILDING POWER OF SOCIALISM. It was the sin of MARXISM to degrade SOCIALISM to a system of MONEY AND STOMACH.

We are SOCIALISTS because for us THE SOCIAL QUESTION IS A MATTER OF NECESSITY AND JUSTICE, and even beyond that A MATTER FOR THE VERY EXISTENCE OF OUR PEOPLE.

DOWN WITH POLITICAL BOURGEOIS SENTIMENT: FOR REAL NATIONALISM!

DOWN WITH MARXISM: FOR TRUE SOCIALISM!

UP WITH THE STAMP OF THE FIRST GERMAN NATIONAL SOCIALIST STATE!

AT THE FRONT THE NATIONAL SOCIALIST GERMAN WORKERS PARTY! . . .

WHY DO WE OPPOSE THE JEWS?

We are ENEMIES OF THE JEWS, because we are fighters for the freedom of the German people. THE JEW IS THE CAUSE AND THE BENEFICIARY OF OUR MISERY. He has used the social difficulties of the broad masses of our people to deepen the unholy split between Right and Left among our people. He has made two halves of Germany. He is the real cause for our loss of the Great War.

The Jew has no interest in the solution of Germany's fateful problems. He CANNOT have any. FOR HE LIVES ON THE FACT THAT THERE HAS BEEN NO SOLUTION. If we could make the German people a unified community and give them freedom before the world, then the Jew can have no place among us. He has the best trumps in his hands when a people lives in inner and outer slavery. THE JEW IS RESPONSIBLE FOR OUR MISERY AND HE LIVES ON IT.

That is the reason why we, AS NATIONALISTS and AS SOCIALISTS, oppose the Jew. HE HAS CORRUPTED OUR RACE, FOULED OUR MORALS, UNDERMINED OUR CUSTOMS, AND BROKEN OUR POWER.

THE JEW IS THE PLASTIC DEMON OF THE DECLINE OF MANKIND.

THE JEW IS UNCREATIVE. He produces nothing. HE ONLY HANDLES PRODUCTS. As long as he struggles against the state, HE IS A REVOLUTIONARY; as soon as he has power, he preaches QUIET AND ORDER, so that he can consume his plunder at his convenience.

ANTI-SEMITISM IS UN-CHRISTIAN. That means, then, that he is a Christian who looks on while the Jew sews straps around our necks. TO BE A CHRISTIAN MEANS: LOVE THY NEIGHBOR AS THYSELF! MY NEIGHBOR IS ONE WHO IS TIED TO ME BY HIS BLOOD. IF I LOVE HIM, THEN I MUST HATE HIS ENEMIES. HE WHO THINKS GERMAN MUST DESPISE THE JEWS. The one thing makes the other necessary.

WE ARE ENEMIES OF THE JEWS BECAUSE WE BELONG TO THE GERMAN PEOPLE. THE JEW IS OUR GREATEST MISFORTUNE.

It is not true that we eat a Jew every morning at breakfast.

It is true, however, that he SLOWLY BUT SURELY ROBS US OF EVERY-THING WE OWN.

THAT WILL STOP, AS SURELY AS WE ARE GERMANS.

Free Germany! (1932)

The National Socialist movement, assembled, at this hour, as a fighting squad around its leader, today calls on the entire German people to join its ranks, and to pave a path that will bring Adolf Hitler to the head of the nation, and thus

HITLER	is the password of all who believe in Germany's resurrection.
HITLER	is the last hope of those who were deprived of everything: of farm and home, of savings, employment, survival; and who have but one possession left: their faith in a just Germany which will once again grant to its citizens honor, freedom, and bread.
HITLER	is the word of deliverance for millions, for they are in despair, and see only in this name a path to new life and creativity.
HITLER	was bequeathed the legacy of the two million dead comrades of the World War, who died not for the present system of the gradual destruction of our nation, but for Germany's future.
HITLER	is the man of the people hated by the enemy because he understands the people and fights for the people.
HITLER	is the furious will of Germany's youth, which, in the midst of a tired generation, is fighting for new forms, and neither can nor will abandon its faith in a better German future. Hence Hitler is the password and the flaming signal of all who wish for a German future.

All of them, on March 13, will call out to the men of the old system who promised them freedom, and dignity, and delivered stones and words instead: We have known enough of you. Now you are to know us!

Statistical Evidence

The statistical table on the following page reveals the increasing popularity of the National Socialist party from 1924, when the Nazis first appeared on a ballot, to 1932, the last free election before Hitler's accession to power. Note the direct relationship of Nazi popularity to the unemployment figures.

"Free Germany" is from *The Nazi Years: A Documentary History*, ed. Joachim Remak, p. 45. © 1969. Used by permission of Prentice Hall, Inc., Englewood Cliffs, N.J.

Elections to the German Reichstag (1924–1932)

	May 4, 1924	December 7, 1924	May 20, 1928	September 14, 1930	July 31, 1932	November 6, 1932
Number of eligible voters (in millions)	38.4	39.0	41.2	43.0	44.2	44.2
Votes cast (in millions)	29.7	30.7	31.2	35.2	37.2	35.7
National Socialist German Workers' party (Nazi)	1,918,000 6.6%	908,000 3%	810,000 2.6%	6,407,000 18.3%	13,779,000 37.3%	11,737,000 33.1%
German Nationalist People's party (Conservative)	5,696,000 19.5%	6,209,000 20.5%	4,382,000 14.2%	2,458,000 7%	2,187,000 5.9%	3,131,000 8.8%
Center party (Catholic)	3,914,000 13.4%	4,121,000 13.6%	3,712,000 12.1%	4,127,000 11.8%	4,589,000 12.4%	14,230,000 11.9%
Democratic party (The German State Party)	1,655,000 5.7%	1,921,000 6.3%	1,506,000 4.9%	1,322,000 3.8%	373,000 1%	339,000 1%
Social Democratic party	6,009,000 20.5%	7,886,000 26%	9,153,000 29.8%	8,575,000 24.5%	7,960,000 21.6%	7,251,000 20.4%
Communist party	3,693,000 12.6%	2,712,000 9%	3,265,000 10.6%	4,590,000 13.1%	5,370,000 14.3%	5,980,000 16.9%

Unemployment in Germany (1924–1932)*

1924	1928	1930	July 31, 1932	October 31, 1932
978,000	1,368,000	3,076,000	5,392,000	5,109,000

*The figures are those of annual average unemployment, except for 1932, where some precise end-of-the-month figures are available, and the two dates that coincide with the Reichstag elections are given.

"Elections to the German Reichstag" is from *The Nazi Years: A Documentary History,* ed. Joachim Remak, p. 44. © 1969. Used by permission of Prentice-Hall, Inc., Englewood Cliffs, N.J.

Parade through Brandenburg Gate (January 30, 1933). The Nazis celebrated the appointment of Adolf Hitler as chancellor of the Weimar Republic with a night rally. The dismantling of the Weimar Constitution began almost immediately. (*Bundesarchiv*)

Chancellor to Dictator

By 1932, the Nazis had emerged as Germany's strongest single party. Hitler demanded the chancellorship of the Weimar Republic. The president, Paul von Hindenburg, disliked Hitler and resisted entrusting all governmental authority to a single party which "held to such a one-sided attitude toward people with convictions different from theirs." But on January 30, 1933, Hindenburg gave in to political pressure and popular demand and appointed Hitler chancellor. The Nazis were confirmed in power and immediately began to dismantle the Weimar Constitution. On the night of February 27, 1933, the Reichstag building burned. The Nazis blamed the communists and issued the "Decree for the Protection of the People and State," an article of which is presented in the first selection.

The second selection is the famous Enabling Act, which allowed Hitler and his Reich Cabinet to issue laws that could deviate from the established constitution, yet could not practically be challenged by representatives of the Reichstag. Its overwhelming passage (444 to 94) gave the destruction of parliamentary democracy an appearance of legality; from then on, the Reichstag became a rubber stamp of approval for Hitler's decrees. The succeeding documents show the conversion of Hitler's chancellorship to a dictatorship.

Decree for the Protection of the People and State (February 28, 1933)

In virtue of Section 48 (2) of the German Constitution, the following is decreed as a defensive measure against Communist acts of violence endangering the state:

Article 1

Sections 114, 115, 117, 118, 123, 124, and 153 of the Constitution of the German Reich are suspended until further notice. Thus, restrictions on personal liberty, on the right of free expression of opinion, including freedom of the press, on the right of assembly and the right of association, and violations of the privacy of postal, telegraphic, and telephone communications, and warrants for house-searches, orders for confiscations as well as restrictions on property, are also permissible beyond the legal limits otherwise prescribed.

"Decree for the Protection of the People and State" is from Office of the U.S. Chief Counsel for Prosecution of Axis Criminality, *Nazi Conspiracy and Aggression* (Washington, D.C.: Government Printing Office, 1946), vol. 1, p. 126 (PS-1390).

The Enabling Act (March 24, 1933)

The Reichstag has passed the following law, which is, with the approval of the Reichsrat [upper house], herewith promulgated, after it has been established that it satisfies the requirements for legislation altering the Constitution.

Article 1:　In addition to the procedure for the passage of legislation outlined in the Constitution, the Reich Cabinet is also authorized to enact Laws.

Article 2:　The national laws enacted by the Reich Cabinet may deviate from the Constitution provided they do not affect the position of the Reichstag and the Reichsrat. The powers of the President remain unaffected.

Article 3:　The national laws enacted by the Reich Cabinet shall be prepared by the Chancellor and published in the official gazette. They come into effect, unless otherwise specified, upon the day following their publication. Articles 68–77 of the Constitution [concerning the enactment of new legislation] do not apply to the laws enacted by the Reich Cabinet.

Article 4:　Treaties of the Reich with foreign states which concern matters of domestic legislation do not require the consent of the bodies participating in legislation. The Reich Cabinet is empowered to issue the necessary provisions for the implementing of these treaties.

Article 5:　This law comes into effect on the day of its publication.

Law Against the New Formation of Parties (July 14, 1933)

The government has passed the following law, which is being proclaimed herewith:

Article 1

The sole political party existing in Germany is the National Socialist German Workers' Party.

"The Enabling Act" is from Jeremy Noakes and Geoffrey Pridham, eds., *Documents on Nazism, 1919–1945*, p. 195. Reprinted by permission of A. D. Peters & Co., Ltd.

"Law Against the New Formation of Parties" is from *The Nazi Years: A Documentary History*, ed. Joachim Remak, p. 54. © 1969. Used by permission of Prentice-Hall, Inc., Englewood Cliffs, N.J.

Article 2

Whoever shall undertake to maintain the organization of another party, or to found a new party, shall be punished with a sentence of hard labor of up to three years, or of prison between six months and three years, unless other regulations provide for heavier punishment.

The Chancellor
s. ADOLF HITLER
The Minister of the Interior
s. FRICK
The Minister of Justice
s. GURTNER

Law Concerning the Head of the German State (August 1, 1934)

The government has passed the following law, which is being proclaimed herewith:

Article 1

The office of President shall be combined with that of Chancellor. Thus all the functions heretofore exercised by the President are transferred to the Fuhrer and Chancellor Adolf Hitler. He has the right to appoint his deputy.

The Role of Women and Children in the Nazi State

Once Hitler and his National Socialist party were firmly seated in power, he began to enact legislation designed to restrict Jews and other racial groups whose presence threatened his plans for a racially pure society. Women became the cornerstone of the new social policy. Their role in the state as wives and mothers was crucial to Hitler's sense of future and the establishment of his "thousand-year" Reich. Two weeks after Hitler received 88 percent of the votes in a plebiscite and assumed the title "Reichführer," he delivered the following speech at Nuremberg and articulated his vision of the role of women in the Nazi state. This vision was apparently not translated into reality for many, as the second selection on the disenfranchisement of women attests.

"Law Concerning the Head of the German State" is from *The Nazi Years: A Documentary History*, ed. Joachim Remak, p. 54. © 1969. Used by permission of Prentice-Hall, Inc., Englewood Cliffs, N.J.

"Our Fanatical Fellow-Combatants" (September 8, 1934)

ADOLF HITLER

If one says that man's world is the State, his struggle, his readiness to devote his powers to the service of the community, one might be tempted to say that the world of woman is a smaller world. For her world is her husband, her family, her children, and her house. But where would the greater world be if there were no one to care for the small world? How could the greater world survive if there were none to make the cares of the smaller world the content of their lives? . . . Providence has entrusted to woman the cares of that world which is peculiarly her own, and only on the basis of this smaller world can the man's world be formed and built up. These two worlds are never in conflict. They are complementary to each other, they belong together as man and woman belong together. . . .

Every child that a woman brings into the world is a battle, a battle waged for the existence of her people. Man and woman must therefore mutually value and respect each other when they see that each performs the task which Nature and Providence have ordained. And from this separation of the functions of each there will necessarily result this mutual respect. It is not true, as Jewish intellectuals assert, that respect depends upon the overlapping of the spheres of activity of the sexes: this respect demands that neither sex should try to do that which belongs to the other's sphere. Respect lies in the last resort in this: that each knows that the other is doing everything which is necessary to maintain the whole community. . . .

We National Socialists have for many years protested against bringing woman into political life; that life in our eyes was unworthy of her. A woman said to me once: You must see to it that women go into Parliament; that is the only way to raise the standard of Parliamentary life. I do not believe, I answered, that man should try to raise the level of that which is bad in itself. And the woman who enters into this business of Parliament will not raise it, it will dishonor her. I would not leave to woman what I intend to take away from men. My opponents thought that in that case we would never gain women for our Movement, but in fact we gained more women than all the other parties together, and I know we should have won over the last German woman if she had only had the opportunity to study Parliament and the dishonoring role which women have played there. . . .

So our Women's Movement is for us not something which inscribes on its banner as its program the fight against man, but something which sets on its program the common fight of woman together with man: For the new National Socialist community of the people was set on a firm basis precisely because we gained in millions of women our truest, our fanatical fellow-combatants,

---

"'Our Fanatical Fellow-Combatants'" is from Raoul de Roussy de Sales, ed., *My New Order* (New York: Reynal & Hitchcock, Inc., 1941), pp. 286–289. Reprinted by permission of Harcourt Brace Jovanovich.

women who fought for the common life in the service of the common task of maintaining life, who in that combat did not set their gaze on rights which a Jewish intellectualism mirrored before their eyes, but rather on duties which nature imposes on all of us in common. . . .

The program of our National Socialist Women's Movement has in truth but one single point, and that point is The Child—that tiny creature which must be born and should grow strong, for in the child alone the whole life-struggle gains its meaning. . . . It is a glorious sight, this golden youth of ours: we know that it is the Germany of the future when we shall be no more. What we create and construct, that youth will maintain. For youth we work; it is that fact which gives its significance to all this effort of ours.

"The Disenfranchisement of Women"
HANNA SCHMITT

In 1918 German women were given the active and passive franchise. From that time on, they were represented in the parliaments of the Reich, the states and the communities. The progressive and socialist parties in particular sent women representatives to these bodies. The only exception was the Nazi party and once the dictatorship was in power, it was this party that expelled women from parliaments and deprived them again of their public functions. Thousands of women who formerly had been active in state and communal positions experienced the hostile attitude of the new regime. In numerous cases they were turned out of hospitals and schools where they were employed as physicians, school principals and valuable teachers.

Mr. Goebbels tried to explain the measure in his own peculiar brand of dishonest pathos: "When we exclude women from public life, we give them back their honor." . . .

Women have disappeared from editorial offices and are deprived of professorships. There is no room for them in laboratories. If they are suspect for racial and ideological reasons, the regime persecutes them even more ruthlessly than men. For they are out of favor not only because of their convictions but also because of their sex, which, according to National Socialism, places them on a lower level than the male.

This is particularly evident in the economic and social life of women. An official decree issued on April 27, 1933, shortly after Hitler's seizure of power, said: "Management is to see to it that all married women employees ask for their discharge. If they do not comply voluntarily, the employer is free to dismiss them upon ascertaining that they are economically protected some other way." Thousands of employees lost their positions by this decree, married as well as single women, who were simply told that parents or other members of their families could take care of them. . . .

"The Disenfranchisement of Women" is from Eleanor S. Riemer and John C. Fout, eds., *European Women* (New York: Schocken Books, 1980), pp. 111–113. Copyright © 1980 by Schocken Books. Reprinted by permission of the publisher.

And what about the private life of women? The Nazis claim to honor housewives and mothers above all. But this honor is denied to a great number of mothers. It does not cover, for example, the mothers of illegitimate children. They bear the burden of care but are morally disqualified and do not get the benefit of the necessary legal protection.

Marriage is subject to the severest restrictions. Women who have been in a concentration camp must provide proof before marriage that they are in perfect physical and mental health, racially pure and not dependent on public relief. The threat of sterilization hangs over many women like the sword of Damocles. Every woman with a physical defect, be it ever so slight, must make it known to the authorities. The doors are wide open for denunciation and vindictive vengeance. . . .

The most tender and intimate relationship held sacred by all civilized peoples is that between mother and child. But with what brutality does National Socialism often tear asunder these bonds. If, for example, a mother is Jewish and the father Aryan, the child is taken away from the mother in case of divorce to avoid exposure to "Jewish influences." The fate of Jewish mothers is especially tragic in small towns. They must look on as their children grow up in isolation which has a devastating effect on the young minds. . . .

Women who are silent, women who serve, are not free women. For only free women can develop their characters to the fullest, be it in pursuit of studies or at work, as housewives and mothers. A nation that honors its women honors itself. However much it may boast of national virtues, a regime that oppresses the women shows contempt for the people and at the same time for those who are responsible for the future, the mothers of its children.

Hitler Youth: "Tough as Leather, Hard as Krupp Steel"
ADOLF HITLER

Any political or religious movement that seeks stability and longevity must ultimately cultivate the loyalty of those who will inherit the future. Hitler established several youth organizations for boys and girls that sought to inculcate the values and ideals that would maintain his authority in the future. Ten-year-olds were taught to "serve the Führer" by stressing the virtues of duty, obedience, and strength. The following speech at a Nuremburg party rally demonstrates how earnestly the Nazis looked to the future.

Each year at the gatherings of youth at the Parteitage (Nuremberg Party Day celebrations) I note the difference: in each year I see the same development which we can discern today in all the other spheres of German life. Our

"Hitler Youth" is from Norman H. Baynes, trans. and ed., *The Speeches of Adolf Hitler, April 1922–1939*, vol. 1 (London: Oxford University Press, 1942), pp. 542–545. Reprinted by permission of the publisher.

Nazi propaganda poster: "Youth Serve the Führer. All ten-year-olds in Hitler Youth." (*Bundesarchiv*)

people grows continuously more disciplined, more taut, more sturdy, and youth begins to do the same. . . .

What we wish from our German youth is different from what past generations asked. In our eyes the German youth of the future must be slim and slender, swift as the greyhound, tough as leather, and hard as Krupp steel. We must educate a new type of manhood so that our people does not go to ruin amongst all the degeneracy of our day. We do not talk, we act. We have undertaken to educate this people in a new school, to give it an education which begins in youth and shall never come to an end. . . .

Everyone is bound to serve his people, everyone is bound to arm himself for that service, to steel his body, to prepare and fortify his mind. And the sooner these preparations begin, the better. . . .

Nothing is possible if there is not a single will which issues its commands and which the others must always obey, beginning from above and ending only at the lowest point. And that is alongside of the training and hardening of the body the second great task. We are a "following," and that means that it is our duty to "follow," to obey. We must educate our whole people so that wherever one is appointed to command the others recognize their duty to obey him, because perhaps an hour later they in their turn will be called upon to command and can only do so precisely as others render to them obedience. That is the expression of an authoritarian State, not of a weak chattering democracy; and in the authoritarian State everyone is proud to owe obedience because he knows: I shall in just the same way find obedience when I have to give a command. . . .

If the others fail to understand us, that need not trouble us. . . . We are no bullies. If the rest of the world misconceives us in our discipline, we cannot help it. From this discipline of ours there will come fewer brawls for the world than from the parliamentary democratic chaos of today. We go our own way: we do not wish to cross the way of another. Would that the others would let us pursue our way in peace! . . . But never do we wish to forget that only the strong deserves friendship, only the strong keeps friendship. And so our will is to make ourselves strong: that is our solution!

Conversion and Resistance

The people of Germany were generally enthusiastic about Hitler, his image of a strong, successful fatherland, and his promises of prosperity. Membership in the National Socialist party rose steadily. Some people found that joining the Nazis was even more than a political experience; for them it was almost a religious conversion. The following section presents the experience of two such converts. But it must be remembered that there were still many who were alarmed at Hitler's actions. Among those who refused to support the "Fuehrer" was S. Ricarda Huch, a distinguished novelist and popular historian. In protest to the recent expulsion of writers who were politically or racially undesirable from the Prussian Academy of Arts and Sciences, Huch decided to resign. Her letter to the president of the academy, Max von Schillings, explains her decision.

"Now I Know Which Road to Take"
JOSEPH GOEBBELS

Someone was standing up and had begun to talk, hesitatingly and shyly at first. . . . Then suddenly the speech gathered momentum. I was caught, I was listening. . . . The crowd began to stir. The haggard grey faces were reflecting hope. . . . Two seats to my left, an old officer was crying like a child. I felt alternately hot and cold. . . . It was as though guns were thundering. . . . I was beside myself. I was shouting hurrah. Nobody seemed surprised. The man up there looked at me for a moment. His blue eyes met my glance like a flame. This was a command. At that moment I was reborn. . . . Now I know which road to take.

[Goebbels became member No. 8,762.]

"'Now I Know Which Road to Take'" is from *Joseph Goebbels*, by Curt Riess, p. 14. Copyright 1948 by Curt Riess. Reprinted by permission of Doubleday, a division of Bantam, Doubleday, Dell Publishing Group, Inc.

"I Had Given Him My Heart"

KURT LUDECKE

Hitler's words were like a scourge. When he spoke of the disgrace of Germany, I felt ready to spring on any enemy . . . glancing around, I saw that his magnetism was holding these thousands as one. . . . I was a man of 32, weary of disgust and disillusionment, a wanderer seeking a cause . . . a yearner after the heroic without a hero. The intense will of the man, the passion of his sincerity, seemed to flow from him into me. I experienced a feeling that could be likened only to a religious conversion. . . . I felt sure that no-one who heard Hitler that night could doubt he was the man of destiny. . . . I had given him my heart.

A Matter of Principle

S. RICARDA HUCH

Heidelberg, April 9, 1933

Dear President von Schillings:

Let me first thank you for the warm interest you have taken in having me remain in the Academy. I would very much like you to understand why I cannot follow your wish. That a German's feelings are German I would consider to be just about self-evident, but the definition of what is German, and what acting in a German manner means—those are things where opinions differ. What the present government prescribes by way of the use of compulsion, the brutal methods, the defamation of those who hold different convictions, the boastful self-praise—these are matters which I consider un-German and disastrous. As I consider the divergence between this opinion of mine and that being ordered by the state, I find it impossible to remain in an Academy that is a part of the state. You say that the declaration submitted to me by the Academy would not prevent me from the free expression of my opinions. But "loyal cooperation, in the spirit of the changed historical situation, on matters affecting national and cultural tasks that fall within the jurisdiction of the Academy" requires an agreement with the government's program which in my case does not exist. Besides, I would find no newspaper or magazine that would print an opposition opinion. Thus the right to the free expression of opinion would remain quite theoretical. . . .

I hereby resign from the Academy.

In this photograph of a 1938 Nazi party rally, S.S. *(Schutzstaffel)* troops demonstrate their discipline and loyalty to Adolf Hitler. The S.S. had originated in the 1920s as Hitler's bodyguard and developed into an elite paramilitary organization. It carried out the bloody purges of the party in 1934 and formed the center of Hitler's police state. Note the propaganda value of the mass rally. (*Corbis*)

Leaflets of "The White Rose" (1942)
HANS AND SOPHIE SCHOLL

The degree to which the German people resisted the Nazi regime has been an ongoing and important topic of research among historians. Resistance was not simply confined to intellectuals, and many dissident Germans were incarcerated in concentration camps along with Jews, Gypsies, and homosexuals. One of the more courageous acts of defiance came from a group of university students and young professionals who called themselves "the White Rose."

In the summer of 1942, leaflets of the White Rose were nailed on poster boards, handed out to the public, and distributed through the mail. They contained attacks on the cultural and political policies of the National Socialist regime. In particular, members of the White Rose accused the Nazis of atrocities against the Jews. Their goal was to resist and obstruct the government through passive resistance. Hans and Sophie Scholl were leaders of the movement. Hans attended medical school and had served in the German army with the rank of sergeant. His sister Sophie first worked as a kindergarten teacher and then attended the University of Munich as a science and philosophy student. They were apprehended in February 1942, accused of treason, and executed that same month after a perfunctory trial. The following is an excerpt from the second leaflet they distributed.

It is impossible to engage in intellectual discourse with National Socialism because it is not an intellectually defensible program. It is false to speak of a National Socialist philosophy, for if there were such an entity, one would have to try by means of analysis and discussion either to prove its validity or to combat it. In actuality, however, we face a totally different situation. At its very inception this movement depended on the deception and betrayal of one's fellow man; even at that time it was inwardly corrupt and could support itself only by constant lies. After all, Hitler states in an early edition of "his" book (a book written in the worst German I have ever read, in spite of the fact that it has been elevated to the position of the Bible in this nation of poets and thinkers): "It is unbelievable to what extent one must betray a people in order to rule it." If at the start this cancerous growth in the nation was not particularly noticeable, it was only because there were still enough forces at work that operated for the good, so that it was kept under control. As it grew larger, however, and finally in an ultimate spurt of growth attained ruling power, the tumor broke open, as it were, and infected the whole body. The greater part of its former opponents went into hiding. The German intellectuals fled to their cellars, there, like plants struggling in the dark, away from light and sun, gradually to choke to death. Now the end is at hand. Now it is our task to find one another again, to spread information from person to person, to keep a steady purpose, and to allow ourselves no rest until the last man is persuaded of the urgent need of his struggle against this system. When thus a wave of unrest goes through the land, when "it is in the air," when many join the cause, then in a great final effort this system can be shaken off. After all, an end in terror is preferable to terror without end. . . .

Since the conquest of Poland [1939], three hundred thousand Jews have been murdered in this country in the most bestial way. Here we see the most frightful crime against human dignity, a crime that is unparalleled in the whole of history. For Jews, too, are human beings—no matter what position we take with respect to the Jewish question—and a crime of this dimension has been perpetrated against human beings. Someone may say that the Jews deserved their fate. This assertion would be a monstrous impertinence. . . .

Why do the German people behave so apathetically in the face of all these abominable crime, crimes so unworthy of the human race? Hardly anyone thinks about that. It is accepted as fact and put out of mind. The German people slumber on in their dull, stupid sleep and encourage these fascist criminals; they give them the opportunity to carry on their depredations; and of course they do so. Is this a sign that the Germans are brutalized in their simplest human feelings, that no chord within them cries out at the sight of such deeds, that they have sunk into a fatal consciencelessness from which they will never, never awake? It seems to be so, and will certainly be so, if the German does not at last start up out of his stupor, if he does not protest wherever and whenever he can against this clique of criminals, if he show no sympathy for these hundreds of thousands of victims. He must evidence not only sympathy; no, much more: a sense of complicity in guilt. For through his apathetic behavior he gives these evil men the opportunity to act as they do; he tolerates this "government" which has taken upon itself such an infinitely great burden of guilt; indeed, he himself is to blame for the fact that it came about at all! Each man wants to be exonerated of a guilt of this kind, each one continues on his way with the most placid, the calmest conscience. But he cannot be exonerated; he is guilty, guilty, guilty!

Up until the outbreak of the war the larger part of the German people was blinded; the Nazis did not show themselves in their true aspect. But now, now that we have recognized them for what they are, it must be the sole and first duty, the holiest duty of every German to destroy these beasts!

CHRONOLOGY: Fascism and the Nazi Rise to Power (1919–1939)

November 11, 1918	Kaiser Wilhelm II abdicates German throne and flees to Holland. Armistice concluded on Western Front.
June 28, 1919	Treaty of Versailles signed between Germany and the Allies. Germany ceded territory and all her colonies to the Allies, returned Alsace-Lorraine to France, promised to pay large reparations, and had its armed forces restricted. The Rhineland was

demilitarized and occupied, and the League of Nations was created. Germany admitted "war guilt."

August 1919	Constitution of the Weimar Republic promulgated.
October–November 1922	After Fascist takeovers in Bologna and Milan, Mussolini marches on Rome where an intimidated King Victor Emmanuel asks him to form a government. Mussolini is granted temporary dictatorial powers to institute reforms.
January 11, 1923	German nonpayment of reparations leads to French and Belgian troops occupying the industrial Ruhr; Germany adopts passive resistance to the occupation. France leaves in 1925.
September–November 1923	Massive inflation in Germany. Interest rates raised to 90 percent, but by October German mark trading at 10,000 million to the English pound.
November 8–9, 1923	Unsuccessful "Beer Hall" putsch in Munich led by Hitler and Ludendorff. Hitler spends eight months in jail, where he writes *Mein Kampf.*
April 9, 1924	Dawes Plan provides a modified settlement of the reparations issue.
December 1, 1924	Locarno Agreements signed which guarantee Franco-German and Belgian-German frontiers and demilitarization of the Rhineland.
December 24, 1925	Mussolini's dictatorial powers increased in Italy. Press censorship tightened, secret nonfascist organizations banned, and widespread arrests.
February 6, 1929	Germany accepts Kellogg-Briand Pact, outlawing war and providing for the pacific settlements of disputes.
October 29, 1929	Wall Street crash and cessation of American loans to Europe.
September 14, 1930	In Reichstag elections, Hitler and the National Socialists (Nazis) emerge as a major party with 107 seats, second only to the Social Democrats with 143 seats.
July 1931	Worsening economic crisis in Germany. Unemployment reaches over 4 million.
July 31, 1932	In Reichstag elections, Nazis win 230 seats and become largest party.
January 30, 1933	President von Hindenburg accepts a cabinet with Hitler as chancellor.
February 27, 1933	Reichstag fire blamed on Communists and made pretext for suspension of civil liberties and freedom of the press.
March 23, 1933	Hitler obtains Enabling Law, granting him dictatorial powers for four years.

July 14, 1933   All parties, other than the Nazis, suppressed. The National Socialist party is formally declared the only political party in Germany.

August 2, 1934   Death of President von Hindenburg. Hitler assumes presidency,
but retains title *Der Führer*. Army swears oath of allegiance.

STUDY QUESTIONS

1. According to the excerpts from Mussolini's autobiography, why was it necessary "to beat the violent adversary on the battlefield of violence"? What did
Mussolini mean by this? Did Mussolini save Italy from the destructive ennui of
chaos? Why did he call himself the "avenger" of Italy?

2. According to Benito Mussolini, what are the primary tenets of fascist doctrine?
Why was he especially critical of socialism (Marxism) and democracy? Do you
find his arguments compelling or flawed? Why is war such an important re-
quirement for the fascist state? What did Mussolini mean by "[the individual] is
deprived of all useless and possibly harmful freedom, but retains what is essential"? What is "harmful freedom" as opposed to "essential freedom"? In what
ways was Hitler's concept of fascism (as expressed in the various documents)
consistent or inconsistent with Mussolini's concept?

3. Why was the National Socialist party able to rise to power? What were the main
political, social, and economic problems of the 1920s and early 1930s, and
what were the solutions offered by the Nazis? Why was the Weimar Republic unable to cope with the major problems facing Germany? Was its destruction inevitable?

4. Compare the constitution of the Weimar Republic with the Nazi program of
1920. How are they similar in outlook, and what are the main differences? Pay
particular attention to the presentation of specific points and the vocabulary.

5. Analyze the propaganda documents included in this chapter. In particular,
what messages does Goebbels promote in "Nationalists, Socialists, and Jews"?
Is he logical in the presentation of his arguments, or can you find inconsistencies? What emotions does the propaganda exploit? What is the message in
"Free Germany!"? Would you call it effective propaganda? Analyze the selection
on Hitler Youth. How were German children propagandized?

6. Statistics often reveal much after close analysis. What statements about the
comparative strength of political parties can you make based on these data?
Which party lost the most support from 1924 to 1932? How successful was the
Communist party? What relationships do you see between political election and
unemployment?

7. Many have viewed the Nazi rise to power as a legitimate act, fully sanctioned
by law. Others have called it a revolution in which Hitler seized power. What do
you think? To what extent was Hitler justified in stressing the legality of the
Nazi assumption of power? Compare Hitler's rise to power with that of Mussolini. In what ways were Mussolini's rhetoric and political techniques similar to
Hitler's? How were their situations different?

8. According to Hitler's speech of September 8, 1934, what was the intended role of women in the Nazi state? What does this document say about Nazi society and the future? Compare this statement with that of V. I. Lenin in the preceding chapter on the Russian Revolution entitled "The Communist Emancipation of Women" (1920). Why are the concepts for the position of women in these two states so different? How does the selection on the "disenfranchisement of women" change the perspective concerning the Nazi treatment of women?

9. Carefully read the conversion accounts of Joseph Goebbels and Kurt Ludecke. Why did they join the Nazi party? The philosopher Eric Hoffer, in his book *The True Believer* (New York: Harper & Row, 1951), described such converts as "permanent misfits." He noted that no achievement can give them a sense of fulfillment; they pursue goals passionately, but never arrive: "The permanent misfits can find salvation only in a complete separation from the self; and they usually find it by losing themselves in the compact collectivity of a mass movement. By renouncing individual will, judgment, and ambition, and dedicating all their powers to the service of an eternal cause, they are at last lifted off the endless treadmill which can never lead them to fulfillment. A rising mass movement attracts and holds a following not by its doctrine or promises, but by the refuge it offers from the anxieties [and] barrenness of an individual existence" (p. 50). Do you agree? Why do people give their fanatical devotion to a cause?

10. Analyze the methods of German resistance to the Nazi regime in the accounts of S. Ricarda Huch ("A Matter of Principle") and Hans and Sophie Scholl ("The White Rose"). Was Huch's resignation from the Prussian Academy of Arts and Sciences just as courageous an act as the resistance of the Scholls?

11. In the leaflet distributed by the White Rose, the Scholls ask the question "Why do the German people behave so apathetically in the face of all these abominable crimes? . . . Is this a sign that the Germans are brutalized in their simplest human feelings?" How would you answer these questions? Why didn't more Germans join in the resistance?

12. Was the victory of National Socialism in Germany dependent on Adolf Hitler? How important was he to the Nazi movement? To what extent can the individual mold the events of history? What conditions in a state present the greatest opportunity for individual assertion of will and power?

13. Konrad Heiden, in his book *Der Fuehrer* (New York: Houghton Mifflin, 1944), stated that "Hitler was able to enslave his own people because he gave them something that even the traditional religions could no longer provide; the belief in a meaning to existence beyond the narrowest self-interest" (p. v). How do you see this statement reflected in the various sources?

14. During the 1930s and 1940s, Hitler and Germany led the world to war, with all its attendant suffering and destruction. Some historians argue that the victory of Adolf Hitler and the National Socialist party was consistent with the racism, militarism, and blind obedience to authority that mark the German national character. Can you describe French, Italian, British, Russian, or American character? Is there even such a thing as "national character," and is it legitimate to explain historical events on the basis of such a characterization?

9

The "Good War": World War II (1939–1945)

German reoccupation
of the Rhineland
Rome-Berlin
Axis formed
1936 - - - - -

German unification
with Austria (March)
Munich conference
on Czechoslovakian
crisis (September)
1938

Battle of Midway (June)
Battle of Stalingrad
(November)
1942 - - - - - - -

German surrender (May)
Atomic bombs
dropped on
Japan (August)
Japanese surrender
(September)
1945 - - - - - - -

1935

1936 1937 1938 1939 1940 1941 1942 1943 1944

1945

Spanish
civil war
1936-1939

Nazi/Soviet - - - - - - -
Neutrality Pact (August)
German invasion
of Poland (September)
1939

Battle of
Britain
(August)
1940

Pearl Harbor
attacked by
Japanese (December)
1941

D-day invasion (June)
Battle of the
Bulge (December)
1944

War will never be avoided until babies come into the world with larger
cerebrums and smaller adrenal glands.

—H. L. Mencken

War is an ugly thing, but not the ugliest of things; the decayed and degraded state of moral and patriotic feeling which thinks nothing worth a war, is worse....A war to protect other human beings against tyrannical injustice; a war to give victory to their own ideas of right and good, and which is their own war, carried on for an honest purpose by their own free choice—is often the means of their regeneration.

—John Stuart Mill

This is no war for domination or imperial aggrandizement or material gain.... It is a war ... to establish on impregnable rocks, the rights of the individual and it is a war to establish and revive the stature of man.

—Winston Churchill

There was never a good war or a bad peace.

—Benjamin Franklin

The real trouble with war is that it gives no one a chance to kill the right people.

—Ezra Pound

CHAPTER THEMES

- *Imperialism:*   Was the German and Japanese desire to expand and acquire more territory the primary cause of World War II? Was the same kind of imperialism the root cause of World War I?

- *Propaganda:*   Why has World War II been termed the "Good War" in the United States and the "Great Patriotic War" in Russia? Was there a distinct clash of ideologies and values that provided the primary motivation for Allied victory? Why was World War II never billed as the "war to end all wars"? Had Europeans and Americans grown less naïve and more cynical?

- *Women in History:*   How essential were the contributions of women to the prosecution of World War II? What were the different expectations of German, British, and American women in particular? How did their efforts affect their social and political status in the postwar years?

- *Beliefs and Spirituality:*   After the massive destruction of World War I, how were soldiers motivated a scant twenty years later to engage once again in war? Was there something spiritual, almost sacred, in the image of "Mother Russia" that motivated twelve million Russian soldiers to sacrifice their lives?

- ***The Big Picture:***   Was World War II merely a continuation of World War I? Or had political and social conditions changed so much that World War II was set apart by new ideologies and technologies? Was World War II inevitable?

At the conclusion of the Great War in November 1918, the peoples of Europe paused amidst their ruined cities, twisted landscapes, and shattered lives to consider the remnants of Western Civilization. They understood that an era had truly ended. They had passed from the structured formalism of polite Victorian company, from an era of effete monarchs, to a world of disillusioned reality. An entire generation of men had been sacrificed to aggressive monarchs, shortsighted politicians, incompetent generals, and the ruinous effects of modern military technology. Everywhere people sought to justify the many lives that had been lost—some might say wasted—on the battlefields of Europe. This had been "the war to make the world safe for democracy," the "war to end all wars." It was termed the "Great War" because no one could envision another of such magnitude and destructive capacity. And yet, as we now view the twentieth century, we refer to it as the First World War, to be followed twenty years later by another that was truly global in scope and far more destructive, consuming the lives and property of over thirty million people.

Some historians have viewed the First and Second World Wars as one conflict with an intervening period of "festering peace," as the Greek historian Thucydides might have termed it. There is no doubt that the origins of the Second World War certainly sprang in part from the harsh peace that had been imposed on the Germans in the Treaty of Versailles in 1919. Adolf Hitler had used the restrictions, reparations, and guilt imposed on the struggling German Weimar Republic in the 1920s to remind the German populace of a distant past of dignity and glorious culture that could once again be gained by following a regimen of discipline and devotion to the nation and to the Führer. After coming to power in 1933 and gaining success in solving some of the employment and monetary problems engendered by the depression, Hitler obtained the confidence and mass support of a majority of Germans. He worked carefully to persuade through propaganda and punish through terror. By 1936, the Nazi state had consolidated its domestic situation and was eager to be recognized by the international community as an equal, no longer burdened by reparations or military and territorial restriction. Feeling buoyed by his domestic success, Hitler invited the world to the 1936 Olympics in Berlin as a way of showcasing German discipline and talent.

But his vision was focused on a broader agenda to be gained, if possible, by subtlety and, if not, by intimidation and force. Hitler sought to incorporate territory into the German Reich to which Germany had historical or racial connections. This need for *Lebensraum,* or "living space," was essential, Hitler argued, for the development of the German nation. In 1936, Hitler reoccupied the Rhineland, a region between Germany and France, in defiance of the Treaty of Versailles. To his surprise, he encountered little reaction from Great Britain and France, which were charged with guaranteeing the provisions of Versailles. Hitler's next step in obtaining more territory for the Reich was the *Anschluss,* or unification with Austria, in March 1938. This was achieved when Germany invaded Austria the day before a plebiscite on unification was to be held because Hitler feared defiance and a defeat at the polls. His assertive policy of incorporation reached its apex in September 1938 as Hitler demanded the Sudentenland of Czechoslovakia, where ethnic Germans resided and were (as he claimed) abused. As a result of the Munich agreements, Hitler gained access to this territory.

At each step, Hitler was confronted and pacified by the figure of British Prime Minister Neville Chamberlain, who believed that Hitler could be satisfied and war averted by conceding territory and respect to Germany. This policy of "appeasement," as it came to be called, depended on the assumption that Germany's demands were legitimate and limited. It is to Hitler's credit that he understood the domestic divisions within Britain and France and was able to take bold risks at crucial times. As the concessions mounted and Hitler realized his visions of greater "living space" for the German *Volk* and the consolidation of a greater German Reich that would last a thousand years, he moved into areas that could no longer be viewed as having special significance to German history and culture. Hitler's desire to link the Reich with East Prussia by a corridor through Poland was the final straw in Chamberlain's appeasement concessions, and the line was drawn. War broke out on September 3, 1939, after Hitler had invaded Poland two days earlier.

World War II, however, is not simply the story of Hitler and Chamberlain. The world was enrolled as the Axis alliance joined together the other fascist powers of Italy and Japan. The influence and independence of Benito Mussolini soon faded amidst the dominance and military power of Germany. Japan had pursued its own policy of imperialism in the Far East by grabbing valuable mineral-rich areas like Manchuria from China and by imposing its presence in Indochina and Malaya in pursuit of oil and tin. Japanese relations with the United States were tenuous at best. The fascist Japanese government under the leadership of General Hideki Tojo received sanction from Emperor Hirohito to cripple the American fleet at Pearl Harbor to prevent any restriction of an aggressive Japanese policy. The "Rising Sun" of Japan would not be restrained.

The war itself gave new meaning to the definition of destruction. The world now fell to the unleashed might of mechanized warfare supported by the full commitment of national will. Societies were transformed as men went to war and women moved to the factories. Civilian populations felt the pain of war as never before. Cities were bombed and refugees were rarely spared—this was total war, war with no restriction and no innocents. Ultimately the developing technologies of war blurred the boundaries of civilization as nuclear weapons were finally detonated over the Japanese cities of Hiroshima and Nagasaki.

World War II truly causes a pause in the consideration of civilization. In the eyes of the Western Powers this became "the Good War," the struggle against the evil of Hitler, Mussolini, and Tojo. There was purpose and justification for our destruction. And yet at the conclusion of hostilities in 1945, the world had not been "made safe for democracy." The Soviet Union had indeed made a "strange bedfellow" in the war against fascism, but the Cold War against Soviet authoritarianism would continue for an additional forty years. With the looming specter of the "Red Menace" and the subsequent undeclared wars in Korea and Vietnam, the claim was never made that the "Good War" was the "war to end all wars."

The Road to War (1936–1939)

There is no avoiding war; it can only be postponed to the advantage of others.

—Niccolò Machiavelli

All war represents a failure of diplomacy.

—Tony Benn

An appeaser is one who feeds a crocodile, hoping it will eat him last.

—Sir Winston Churchill

To delight in war is a merit in the soldier, a dangerous quality in the captain, and a positive crime in the statesman.

—George Santayana

What a country calls its vital economic interests are not the things which enable its citizens to live, but the things which enable it to make war. Petrol is more likely than wheat to be a cause of international conflict.

—Simone Weil

German Remilitarization of the Rhineland (March 1936)

One of the crucial turning points of German history occurred in March 1936 when Adolf Hitler remilitarized the region between Germany and France called the Rhineland. The security of this region was guaranteed by the Treaty of Versailles (1919) and the Locarno Agreements of 1925. In all respects, both Britain and France had a legal right to resist. But there existed a rising tide of pacifism in Europe which prevented British support of France and reinforced France's own commitment to a defensive rather than offensive posture. Hitler evaluated the situation and decided to test the strength and determination of the Western Powers. To his relief, neither country did anything except register a mild protest with the League of Nations.

In retrospect, the Allies lost an important opportunity to stop Hitler, whose tiny German force in the Rhineland would have easily been overwhelmed by the French army.

Such a failure may well have led to the political overthrow of Hitler's regime since the German military commanders had generally not supported the gamble to remilitarize the Rhineland. The Western response slowly crystallized into a policy of "appeasement," which was based on the assumption that Germany had legitimate grievances and that Hitler's goals were limited and rational. With perfect hindsight, the remilitarization of the Rhineland was but the beginning of a German power play that eventually resulted in war. In the following official communiqué, note how Hitler tempers his aggressive action by offering to create "a system of peaceful security for Europe."

The Restoration of German Sovereignty

ADOLF HITLER

The German Government has continually emphasized during the negotiations of the last years its readiness to observe and fulfil all the obligations arising from the Rhine Pact so long as the other contracting parties were ready on their side to maintain the pact. This obvious and essential condition can no longer be regarded as being fulfilled by France. France has replied to Germany's repeated friendly offers and assurances of peace by infringing the Rhine Pact through a military alliance with the Soviet Union directed exclusively against Germany. In this manner, however, the Locarno Rhine Pact has lost its inner meaning and ceased in practice to exist. Consequently, Germany regards herself for her part as no longer bound by this dissolved Treaty. . . . In accordance with the fundamental right of a nation to secure its frontiers and ensure its possibilities of defence, the German Government has today restored the full and unrestricted sovereignty of Germany in the demilitarized zone of the Rhineland.

In order, however, to avoid any misinterpretation of its intentions and to establish beyond doubt the purely defensive character of these measures, as well as to express its unalterable longing for a real pacification of Europe between states equal in rights and equally respected, the German Government declares itself ready to conclude new agreements for the creation of a system of peaceful security for Europe.

The German Anschluss with Austria (March 1938)

Events progressed quickly during 1936. In July a civil war broke out in Spain between a divided republican government and Spanish fascists led by General Francisco Franco. This war lasted three years, cost hundreds of thousands of lives, and provided Hitler with an opportunity to test his new weapons in support of Franco. Hitler also garnered the support of the Italian fascist Benito Mussolini, who had broken with the League of Nations in 1935 over his invasion of Ethiopia. By November of 1936, Hitler could speak publicly of an alliance with Mussolini that he termed the Rome-Berlin "Axis."

"The Restoration of German Sovereignty" is from the Office of the U.S. Chief Counsel for Prosecution of Axis Criminality, *Nazi Conspiracy and Aggression* (Washington, D.C.: Government Printing Office, 1947), vol. 8, pp. 396–397 (46-TC).

Hitler had always planned to annex his native Austria into the German Reich, and in 1938 his new working relationship with Mussolini offered an opportunity to do so. Hitler hoped to achieve his goal through intimidation and propaganda, but was disappointed when the Austrian chancellor Kurt Schuschnigg announced a plebiscite for March 13 in which the Austrian people themselves could decide whether to unite with Germany. To forestall the vote, Hitler sent his troops into Austria on March 12, thus confirming the German Anschluss, *or union with Austria. To Hitler's relief, Mussolini did not object to his action. Hitler had gambled again and won.*

Hitler's invasion orders are confirmed in the first document that refers to the Top Secret Operation "OTTO." Hitler's speech later that day to the Austrian people offers his vision of the future.

"I Intend to Invade Austria" (March 11, 1938)
ADOLF HITLER

Referring to: Operation OTTO

TOP SECRET

1) If other measures prove unsuccessful, I intend to invade Austria with armed forces to establish constitutional conditions and to prevent further outrages against the pro-German population.
2) The whole operation will be directed by myself....
3) The behavior of the troops must give the impression that we do not want to wage war against our Austrian brothers. It is in our interest that the whole operation shall be carried out without violence but in the form of a peaceful entry welcomed by the population. Therefore any provocation is to be avoided. If, however, resistance is offered it must be broken ruthlessly by force of arms.

"Make Your Contribution to this German Future!" (March 12, 1938)
ADOLF HITLER

I thank you for your words of greeting. Above all I thank all of you assembled here who have borne witness that it is not the will and the wish of some few only to found this great Reich of the German people, but that it is the

---

"'I Intend to Invade Austria'" is from the Office of the U.S. Chief Counsel for Prosecution of Axis Criminality, *Nazi Conspiracy and Aggression* (Washington, D.C.: Government Printing Office, 1947), vol. 6, pp. 911–912 (102-C).

"'Make Your Contribution to this German Future!'" is from Raoul de Roussy de Sales, *My New Order* (New York: Reynal & Hitchcock, 1941), p. 466. Reprinted by permission of the publisher.

wish and the will of the German people.... When years ago I went forth from this town [Linz, Austria], I bore within me precisely the same profession of faith which today fills my heart. Judge the depth of my emotion when after so many years I have been able to bring that profession of faith to its fulfillment.

If Providence once called me forth from this town to be the leader of the Reich, it must, in so doing, have given to me a commission, and that commission could be only to restore my dear homeland to the German Reich. I have believed in this commission. I have lived and fought for it, and I believe I have now fulfilled it. You all are witnesses and sureties for that. I know not on what day you will be summoned. I hope it will not be far distant. Then you must make good your pledge with your own confession of faith, and I believe that then before the whole German people I shall be able to point with pride to my own homeland. And this must then prove to the world that every further attempt to tear this people asunder will be in vain.

And just as then it will be your duty to make your contribution to this German future, so all Germany is ready for its part to make its contribution and it is already making it today. In the German soldiers who now from all the shires of the Reich are marching into Austria you must see those who are ready and willing to make sacrifices in their fight for the unity of the whole great German people, for the power of the Reich, for its greatness and its glory now and evermore—Germany, Sieg Heil!

The Czechoslovakian Crisis
(September 1938–March 1939)

The German union with Austria was another clear violation of the Treaty of Versailles, but that arrangement was clearly dead by 1938, as neither Great Britain nor France was willing to enforce its provisions. But it was the Czechoslovakian crisis that defined the term "appeasement." Behind British negotiations of this policy was the fear that another general war might break out, with all the concomitant horrors that had characterized World War I. Britain, led by its prime minister, Neville Chamberlain, hoped to negotiate and make reasonable concessions to Germany in order to avert the possibility of war.

With the addition of Austria to the Reich, Germany now surrounded Czechoslovakia on three sides. Czechoslovakia itself was an affront to Hitler. It had been created after World War I as a check on Germany and was democratic and allied to both France and the Soviet Union. It also had a German population of about 3.5 million, which was concentrated in an area near the German border called the Sudetenland. These Sudeten Germans had been agitating for greater privileges and even autonomy in the Czech state. In the following selection, Hitler recounts his version of the misery of Sudeten Germans.

"The Misery of the Sudeten Germans Is Indescribable" (September 12, 1938)

ADOLF HITLER

I am speaking of Czechoslovakia. . . . Amongst the majority of the nationalities which are suffering oppression in this State there are to be found three and a half million Germans, that is to say about as many people of our race as, for example, the whole population of Denmark. But these Germans—they too are God's creatures. The Almighty did not create them in order that by means of a State-construction designed at Versailles they should be given over to a hated alien Power. And He did not create the seven million Czechs that they should watch over and take under their care—much less that they should outrage and torture—these three and a half millions.

The conditions in this State, as is generally known, are intolerable. Here in political life over seven and a half millions in the name of the right of self-determination of a certain Mr. Wilson [President Woodrow Wilson] are deprived of their right of self-determination. In economic life these seven and a half millions are being systematically ruined and thus devoted to a slow process of extermination. This misery of the Sudeten Germans is indescribable. It is sought to annihilate them. As human beings they are oppressed and scandalously treated in an intolerable fashion. When three and a half million members of a people which numbers nearly eighty millions may not sing a song they like simply because it does not please the Czechs, or when they are beaten until the blood flows solely because they wear stockings the sight of which offends the Czechs, or when they are terrorized and ill-treated because they use a form of greeting which the Czechs dislike, although they use it only in greeting each other and not in greeting Czechs, when they are hunted and harried like helpless wild-fowl for every expression of their national sentiment—this may perhaps cause the worthy representatives of our democracies no concern: they may possibly welcome it since in this case only some three and a half million Germans are in question; but I can only say to the representatives of these democracies that this does concern us, and that if these tortured creatures can of themselves find no justice and no help they will get both from us. The depriving of these people of their rights must come to an end. . . . All of us have the duty never again to bow the head beneath an alien will. Let that be our vow. So help us God!

"'The Misery of the Sudeten Germans Is Indescribable'" is from Norman H. Baynes, trans. and ed., *The Speeches of Adolf Hitler, April 1922–1939*, vol. 1 (London: Oxford University Press, 1942), pp. 1489–1490, 1499. Reprinted by permission of the publisher.

In this photograph taken during the Munich conference in September 1938, Adolf Hitler discusses the fate of Czechoslovakia with British Prime Minister Neville Chamberlain. Chamberlain's policy of appeasing Hitler failed, and the world went to war a year later. (*UPI / Corbis*)

"Czechoslovakia Has Ceased to Exist" (March 15, 1939)
ADOLF HITLER

British Prime Minister Neville Chamberlain was so concerned that Hitler might invade Czechoslovakia and thus threaten European peace that he proposed a conference at Hitler's mountain retreat on September 15. Returning home to criticism from the British Parliament and press, Chamberlain justified his actions to the House of Commons on September 28. The next day he met with Mussolini and Hitler at Munich, where Britain guaranteed Czechoslovak security in exchange for their concession of territory to Germany.

With the Munich agreement, Chamberlain believed that he had secured "peace with honor. I believe it is peace for our time." It was not. The Czech state was rapidly torn up as Poland and Hungary took territory and the Slovaks demanded a state of their own. Finally Hitler broke his agreement and occupied Prague on March 15, 1939. Czechoslovakia had ceased to exist, and appeasement had ended any illusions that Hitler's only goal was to restore Germans to the Reich. The following documents reveal the bitter reality of the moment.

Only a few months ago [September, 1938] Germany was compelled to protect her fellow-countrymen living in well defined settlements against the un-

---

"'Czechoslovakia Has Ceased to Exist'" is from the Office of the U.S. Chief Counsel for Prosecution of Axis Criminality, *Nazi Conspiracy and Aggression* (Washington, D.C.: Government Printing Office, 1946), vol. 8, pp. 402–403 (050-TC).

bearable Czecho-Slovakian terror regime; and during the last weeks the same thing has happened on an ever increasing scale. This is bound to create an intolerable state of affairs within an area inhabited by citizens of so many nationalities.

These national groups, to counteract the renewed attacks against their freedom and life, have now broken away from the Prague Government. Czecho-Slovakia has ceased to exist. Since Sunday at many places wild excesses have broken out, amongst the victims of which are again many Germans. Hourly the number of oppressed and persecuted people crying for help is increasing. From areas thickly populated by German-speaking inhabitants, which last autumn Czecho-Slovakia was allowed by German generosity to retain, refugees robbed of their personal belongings are streaming into the Reich.

Continuation of such a state of affairs would lead to the destruction of every vestige of order in an area in which Germany is vitally interested, particularly as for over a thousand years it formed a part of the German Reich.

In order definitely to remove this menace to peace and to create the conditions for a necessary new order in this living space, I have today resolved to allow German troops to march into Bohemia and Moravia. They will disarm the terror gangs and the Czech forces supporting them, and protect the lives of all who are menaced. Thus they will lay the foundations for introducing a fundamental reordering of affairs which will be in accordance with a thousand-year history and will satisfy the practical needs of the German and Czech peoples.

Berlin, 15 March 1939   (*Signed*) Adolf Hitler

"I Bitterly Regret What Has Now Occurred" (March 15, 1939)

NEVILLE CHAMBERLAIN

A further point which I would make is this: Hitherto the German Government in extending the area of their military control have defended their action by the contention that they were only incorporating in the Reich neighboring masses of people of German race. Now for the first time they are effecting a military occupation of territory inhabited by people with whom they have no racial connection. These events cannot fail to be a cause of disturbance to the international situation. They are bound to administer a shock to confidence, all the more regrettable because confidence was

---

"'I Bitterly Regret What Has Now Occurred'" is from *Parliamentary Debates,* 5th series, vol. 345 (1939), col. 440.

beginning to revive and to offer a prospect of concrete measures which would be of general benefit.

In a speech which I made at Birmingham on 30th January last I pointed out that we ought to define our aims and attitude, namely, our determination to search for peace. I added that I felt it was time now that others should make their contribution to a result which would overflow in benefits to many besides those immediately concerned. It is natural, therefore, that I should bitterly regret what has now occurred. But do not let us on that account be deflected from our course. Let us remember that the desire of all the peoples of the world still remains concentrated on the hopes of peace and a return to the atmosphere of understanding and good will which has so often been disturbed. The aim of this Government is now, as it has always been, to promote that desire and to substitute the method of discussion for the method of force in the settlement of differences. Though we may have to suffer checks and disappointments, from time to time, the object that we have in mind is of too great significance to the happiness of mankind for us lightly to give it up or set it on one side.

The Invasion of Poland (September 1939)

The occupation of Prague by German troops in March 1939 was a tremendous blow to Chamberlain's foreign policy. Two weeks later, the British government responded to public opinion by joining with France to guarantee the independence of Poland. Hitler now wanted to incorporate the Polish port city of Danzig into the German Reich and demanded access to this eastern city through a "corridor" that would link Germany with East Prussia. Hitler apparently did not take the Franco-British guarantee seriously, as is revealed by the following notes taken at a conference at Obersalzberg in which he considered his options.

Hitler Mulling over the Options: "There Will Never Again Be a Man with More Authority Than I Have" (August 22, 1939)
ADOLF HITLER

It was clear to me that a conflict with Poland had to come sooner or later. I had already made this decision in the spring, but I thought I would first turn against the West in a few years, and only afterwards against the East. But the sequence of events cannot be fixed. Also one must not close one's eyes to a

"Hitler Mulling over the Options" is from the Nuremberg Military Tribunals, *Trials of War Criminals* (Washington, D.C.: Government Printing Office, 1947–1949), vol. 26, pp. 338–344 (PS-798).

threatening situation. I wanted first of all to establish an acceptable relationship with Poland in order to fight first against the West. But this plan, which was agreeable to me, could not be executed since fundamentals have changed. It became clear to me that Poland would attack us in case of a conflict with the West. Poland wants access to the sea. . . . It became clear to me that under the circumstances conflict with Poland could arise at an inopportune moment. I enumerate as reasons for this reflection: my own personality and that of Mussolini.

Essentially it depends on me, my existence, because of my political ability. Furthermore, the fact that probably no one will ever again have the confidence of the whole German people as I do. There will probably never again be a man in the future with more authority than I have. My life is, therefore, a factor of great value. But I can be eliminated at any time by a criminal or an idiot.

The second personal factor is the Duce [Mussolini]. His life is also a decisive factor. If something happens to him, Italy's loyalty to the alliance will no longer be certain. The basic attitude of the Italian Court is against the Duce. Above all, the Court sees in the expansion of the empire a burden. The Duce is the man with the strongest nerves in Italy. . . .

On the other side, negative picture, as far as decisive personalities are concerned. There is no outstanding personality in England or France. For us it is easy to make decisions. We have nothing to lose; we can only gain. Our economic situation is such, because of our limitations, that we cannot hold out more than a few years. Goring can confirm this. We have no other choice; we must act. Our opponents risk much and can gain only a little. England's stake in a war is unimaginably great. Our enemies have leaders who are below the average. No personalities. No masters, no men of action. . . .

All these fortunate circumstances will no longer prevail in two or three years. No one knows how long I shall live. Therefore war is better now. . . .

Relations with Poland have become unbearable. My Polish policy hitherto was opposed to the ideas of the people. My proposals to Poland [regarding Danzig and the Corridor] were disturbed by England's intervention. Poland changed her tone towards us. A state of tension which lasts for any length of time is intolerable. The initiative cannot be allowed to pass to the others. This moment is more favorable than it will be in two to three years. An attempt on my life or Mussolini's could change the situation to our disadvantage. One cannot eternally stand opposite one another with cocked rifle. . . .

England and France are under an obligation, neither is in a position to fulfil it. There is no actual rearmament in England, just propaganda. . . . England's position in the world is very precarious. She will not take any risks. . . . France lacks men (decline of the birth-rate). Little has been done for rearmament. The artillery is obsolete. . . .

The enemy had another hope, that Russia would become our enemy after the conquest of Poland. The enemy did not count on my great power of determination. Our enemies are little worms. I saw them in Munich.

I was convinced that Stalin would never accept the English offer. Russia has no interest in maintaining Poland, and Stalin knows that it will be the end of his regime no matter whether his soldiers come out of a war victorious or beaten. . . . I brought about the change of attitude towards Russia gradually. In connection with the commercial treaty we got into political conversation. Proposal of a non-aggression pact. Then came a general proposal from Russia. Four days ago I took a special step, with the result that Russia answered yesterday that she was ready to sign. The personal relations with Stalin are established. The day after tomorrow [German Foreign Minister] von Ribbentrop will conclude the treaty. Now Poland is in the position in which I wanted her. . . .

Today's publication of the non-aggression pact with Russia acted as a bombshell. The consequences cannot be foreseen. Stalin has also said that this course will be of benefit to both countries. The effect on Poland will be tremendous.

The German Neutrality Pact with the Soviet Union (August 23, 1939)

On August 23, 1939, Hitler formally revealed a neutrality pact that he had signed with the Soviet Union. Joseph Stalin had resented having been cut out of the Munich negotiations by the West and felt that he would have to bear the brunt of any future war with Germany. The most bitter ideological rivals thus became allies. This pact shocked the Western powers and paved the way for Hitler's conquest of Poland by removing the threat of Soviet retaliation from the East. Note the secret provisions of the pact which divided Poland between the two powers and allowed Russia to occupy the Baltic States.

The Government of the German Reich and The Government of the Union of Soviet Socialist Republics, directed by the wish to strengthen the cause of peace between Germany and the USSR . . . have reached the following agreement:

Article 1: The two contracting parties undertake to refrain from any act of violence, any aggressive action, or any attack against one another, whether individually or jointly with other powers.

Article 2: In case any of the contracting parties should become the object of warlike acts on the part of a third power, the other contracting party will no longer support that third power in any form.

Article 4: Neither of the two contracting parties will participate in any grouping of powers which is indirectly or directly aimed against the other party.

Article 5: Should disputes or conflicts arise between the contracting parties regarding questions of any kind whatsoever, the two parties would clear away these disputes or conflicts solely by means of friendly exchanges of views or if necessary by arbitration commissions.

"The German Neutrality Pact with the Soviet Union" is from *Documents in German Foreign Policy* (London: Her Majesty's Stationery Office, 1956), series D, vol. 7, pp. 245–247.

Secret Additional Protocol

On the occasion of the signature of the Non-Aggression Treaty between the German Reich and the Union of Soviet Socialist Republics, the undersigned . . . parties discussed in strictly confidential conversations the question of the delimitation of their respective spheres of interest in Eastern Europe. These conversations led to the following result:

1. In the event of a territorial and political transformation in the territories belonging to the Baltic States (Finland, Estonia, Latvia, Lithuania), the northern frontier of Lithuania shall represent the frontier of the spheres of interest both of Germany and the USSR. . . .
2. In the event of a territorial and political transformation of the territories belonging to the Polish State, the spheres of interest of both Germany and the USSR shall be bounded approximately by the line of the rivers Narev, Vistula, and San.
3. This Protocol will be treated by both parties as strictly secret.

"A Catastrophe That Will Involve Europe in War" (August 22, 1939)
NEVILLE CHAMBERLAIN

The following letter from Chamberlain to Hitler was a last attempt to impress upon the German government the seriousness of the situation. Britain would no longer appease Hitler's demands and was willing to support Polish independence by going to war. When Hitler invaded Poland on September 1, war was declared. Chamberlain's radio address and speech in Parliament on September 3 reveal the abridgment of his hopes and the ultimate failure of his policy of appeasement.

10 Downing Street

August 22, 1939

Your Excellency [Adolf Hitler],

Your Excellency will have already heard of certain measures taken by His Majesty's Government, and announced in the press and on the wireless this evening.

These steps have, in the opinion of His Majesty's Government, been rendered necessary by the military movements which have been reported from Germany, and by the fact that apparently the announcement of a German-Soviet Agreement is taken in some quarters in Berlin to indicate that inter-

---

"'A Catastrophe That Will Involve Europe in War'" is from Great Britain: Foreign Office, *Documents Concerning German-Polish Relations and the Outbreak of Hostilities Between Great Britain and Germany on September 3, 1939* (London: Her Majesty's Stationery Office, 1939), cmd. 6106, no. 56.

vention by Great Britain on behalf of Poland is no longer a contingency that need be reckoned with. No greater mistake could be made. Whatever may prove to be the nature of the German-Soviet Agreement, it cannot alter Great Britain's obligation to Poland which His Majesty's Government have stated in public repeatedly and plainly and which they are determined to fulfil. . . .

Having thus made our position perfectly clear, I wish to repeat to you my conviction that war between our two peoples would be the greatest calamity that could occur. I am certain that it is desired neither by our people, nor by yours, and I cannot see that there is anything in the questions arising between Germany and Poland which could not and should not be resolved without the use of force, if only a situation of confidence could be restored to enable discussions to be carried on in an atmosphere different from that which prevails today. . . .

At this moment I confess I can see no other way to avoid a catastrophe that will involve Europe in war.

In view of the grave consequences to humanity, which may follow from the action of their rulers, I trust that Your Excellency will weigh with the utmost deliberation the considerations which I have put before you.

Yours sincerely,
Neville Chamberlain

"Everything I Have Hoped for Has Crashed into Ruins" (September 3, 1939)

NEVILLE CHAMBERLAIN

Radio Address to the British People

I am speaking to you from the Cabinet Room at 10, Downing Street. This morning the British Ambassador in Berlin handed the German Government a final note stating that unless we heard from them by 11 o'clock that they were prepared at once to withdraw their troops from Poland a state of war would exist between us. I have to tell you now that no such undertaking has been received, and that consequently this country is at war with Germany.

You can imagine what a bitter blow it is to me that all my long struggle to win peace has failed. Yet I cannot believe that there is anything more or anything different that I could have done that would have been more successful.

Up to the very last it would have been quite possible to have arranged a peaceful and honorable settlement between Germany and Poland. But Hitler would not have it. He had evidently made up his mind to attack Poland whatever happened, and although he now says he put forward reasonable proposals which were rejected by the Poles, that is not a true statement.

"'Everything I Have Hoped for Has Crashed into Ruins'" is from *Parliamentary Debates*, 5th series, vol. 340 (1939).

The Proposals were never shown to the Poles, nor to us, and, though they were announced in a German broadcast on Thursday night, Hitler did not wait to hear comments on them, but ordered his troops to cross the Polish frontier. His action shows convincingly that there is no chance of expecting that this man will ever give up his practice of using force to gain his will. He can only be stopped by force.

We and France are today, in fulfillment of our obligations, going to the aid of Poland, who is so bravely resisting this wicked and unprovoked attack upon her people. We have a clear conscience. We have done all that any country could do to establish peace, but a situation in which no word given by Germany's ruler could be trusted and no people or country could feel themselves safe had become intolerable. And now that we have resolved to finish it, I know that you will all play your part with calmness and courage. . . .

Address to the House of Commons

This is a sad day for all of us, and to none is it sadder than to me. Everything that I have worked for, everything that I have hoped for, everything that I have believed in during my public life, has crashed into ruins. There is only one thing left for me to do; that is, to devote what strength and powers I have to forwarding the victory of the cause for which we have to sacrifice so much. I cannot tell what part I may be allowed to play myself. I trust I may live to see the day when Hitlerism has been destroyed and a liberated Europe has been reestablished.

Total War (1939–1945)

It takes twenty years of peace or more to make a man; it takes only twenty seconds of war to destroy him.

—Baudouin I, King of Belgium

What war has always been is a puberty ceremony. It's a rough one, but you went away a boy and came back a man, maybe with an eye missing or whatever but godammit you were a man and people had to call you a man thereafter.

—Kurt Vonnegut

Blitzkrieg!

The German attack on Poland instituted a new form of warfare called blitzkrieg, *or "lightning war." The emphasis was on speed and focused aggression through massed armored columns of tanks supported by airpower. The Germans quickly*

Europe on the Eve of World War II. Germany's secret neutrality pact with the Soviet Union allowed Hitler to invade Poland on September 1, 1939. Britain had guaranteed Poland's independence and declared war on Germany two days later. *(From* The War in Maps: An Atlas of the New York Times Maps, 4/e *by Francis Brown and Lucas Manditch. Copyright © 1942, 1943, 1946, 1973 by Oxford University Press, Inc., renewed 1973 by Francis Brown. Reprinted by permission of the publisher.)*

overwhelmed Polish defenses, as the following account by a German officer indicates.

"At Dawn We Crossed into Poland" (September 1, 1939)

LIEUTENANT BARON TASSLIO VON BOGENHARDT

The ordering of general mobilization came almost on top of Britain's and France's guarantee of Poland; reservists were called up, vehicles and troops mobilized and ammunition distributed. We loaded our tanks and trucks onto the train and travelled for three days to Paprad in Slovakia, where we waited about ten miles from the Polish border. Several of us went up to the frontier to reconnoitre, and after the third day we got orders to move up during the night. At dawn we crossed into Poland.

The whole thing was so like an occupation of a manoeuvre that we could hardly believe this was really war; it all seemed too well-ordered and familiar. There was virtually no resistance, and for days on end we advanced towards the Polish Ukraine. There were rumors of sharpshooters and partisans, but I never saw or heard anything of them, except for the occasional sound of a shot in the distance. There was a certain amount of sporadic fighting when we got to the river barriers, but the Luftwaffe [Air Force] had already cleared the way for us. Their Stuka dive-bombers were deadly accurate, and as there was no opposition they had it all their own way. The roads and fields were swarming with unhappy peasants who had fled in panic from their villages when the bombing began, and we passed hundreds and hundreds of Polish troops walking dejectedly towards Slovakia. The Poles seemed to be completely apathetic, and there were so many prisoners that nobody bothered to guard them or even tell them where to go.

The Invasion of France: "We Were Through the Maginot Line!" (May 15, 1940)

GENERAL ERWIN ROMMEL

The German invasion of Poland was so successful that the Russians moved quickly to claim their division of Poland and the Baltic countries of Estonia, Latvia, and Lithuania. After this, events slowed dramatically into a sitzkrieg, *or "phony war," as Germany consolidated its gains and prepared for the next phase*

"At Dawn We Crossed into Poland" is from Louis Hagen, *Follow My Leader* (London: Wingate, 1951), p. 24. Reprinted by permission of the publisher.

"The Invasion of France" is from *The Rommel Papers* by Lucie-Maria Rommel, pp. 19–20. Copyright © 1953 by B.H. Liddell Hart and renewed 1981 by Lady Kathleen Liddell Hart, Fritz Bayerlein, and Manfred Rommel. Reprinted by permission of Harcourt Brace & Company.

of war. In April, Hitler invaded Denmark and Norway and followed this with attacks on Belgium and the Netherlands. France had relied for its defense on the renowned Maginot Line, a series of artillery fortifications built after World War I to repel an attack. But the new German-mobilized warfare, together with the fact that the fortifications were never completed through Belgium to the sea,

The Battle of France. On May 10, 1940, Hitler launched his attack against France, Belgium, and the Netherlands. The blitzkrieg across the arcane French defensive network called the Maginot Line took just five weeks to complete. *(From* The War in Maps: An Atlas of the New York Times Maps, 4/e)

allowed the Germans to maneuver around and through the Maginot Line. The French army, poorly led by generals who could not fathom the changes in mechanized warfare since 1918, collapsed. Hitler defeated France in five weeks.

General Erwin Rommel was one of the most able of all German commanders. A specialist in tank warfare, he wrote the following account of the invasion of France which reveals a sense of wonder at the ease of the Nazi victory.

The way to the west was now open. The moon was up and for the time being we could expect no real darkness. I had already given orders in the plan for the break-through, for the leading tanks to scatter the road and converge with machine and anti-tank gunfire at intervals during the drive to Avesnes, which I hoped would prevent the enemy from laying mines. . . .

The tanks now rolled in a long column through the line of fortifications and on towards the first houses, which had been set alight by our fire. . . . Our artillery was dropping heavy harassing fire on villages and the road far ahead of the regiment. Gradually the speed increased. Before long we were five hundred—a thousand—two thousand—three thousand yards into the fortified zone. Engines roared, tank tracks clanked and clattered. Whether or not the enemy was firing was impossible to tell in the ear-splitting noise. . . .

Civilians and French troops, their faces distorted with terror, lay huddled in the ditches, alongside hedges and in every hollow beside the road. We passed refugee columns, the carts abandoned by their owners, who had fled in panic into the fields. On we went, at a steady speed, towards our objective. . . . Every so often [I took] a look out of the hatch to assure myself that there was still no resistance and that contact was being maintained to the rear. The flat countryside lay spread out around us under the cold light of the moon. We were through the Maginot Line! It was hardly conceivable. Twenty-two years before we had stood for four and a half long years before this self-same enemy [the French] and had won victory after victory and yet finally lost the war. And now we had broken through the renowned Maginot Line and were driving deep into enemy territory. It was not just a beautiful dream. It was reality.

Alone: The Battle of Britain (May–September 1940)

The fall of France in June 1940 left Britain alone to fight the Germans. Hitler expected the British to negotiate an arrangement which allowed Britain to retain its empire if Germany could rule the European continent. British opposition to such an accommodation was assured with the appointment of Winston Churchill as prime minister in May of 1940.

Churchill had been a vocal critic of Neville Chamberlain's appeasement policies and inspired his nation through a series of speeches and an aura of dogged determination to resist the Nazi menace. Although the United States was officially neutral and dominated by isolationist sentiments, it still helped Britain survive by sending warships and military supplies through a mutually beneficial lend-lease arrangement.

The following speeches by Churchill in the British Parliament reveal his dynamic qualities of leadership. He was a great orator who understood how to inspire the British people to unify and resist regardless of the cost.

"Blood, Toil, Tears, and Sweat" (May 13, 1940)
WINSTON CHURCHILL

In this crisis I hope I may be pardoned if I do not address the House at any length today. I hope that any of my friends and colleagues, or former colleagues, who are affected by the political reconstruction, will make all allowance for any lack of ceremony with which it has been necessary to act. I would say to the House, as I said to those who have joined the Government: "I have nothing to offer but blood, toil, tears and sweat."

We have before us an ordeal of the most grievous kind. We have before us many, many long months of struggle and of suffering. You ask, What is our policy? I will say: It is to wage war, by sea, land and air, with all our might and with all the strength that God can give us: to war against a monstrous tyranny, never surpassed in the dark, lamentable catalogue of human crime. That is our policy. You ask, What is our aim? I can answer in one word: Victory—victory at all costs, victory in spite of all terror, victory, however long and hard the road may be; for without victory, there is no survival. Let that be realized; no survival for the British Empire; no survival for all that the British Empire has stood for, no survival for the urge and impulse of the ages, that mankind will move forward towards its goal. But I take up my task with buoyancy and hope. I feel sure that our cause will not be suffered to fail among men. At this time I feel entitled to claim the aid of all, and I say, "Come, then, let us go forward together with our united strength."

"Their Finest Hour" (June 18, 1940)
WINSTON CHURCHILL

The Battle of France is over. I expect that the Battle of Britain is about to begin. Upon this battle depends the survival of Christian civilization. Upon it depends our own British life, and the long continuity of our institutions and our Empire. The whole fury and might of the enemy must very soon be turned on us. Hitler knows that he will have to break us in this island or lose the war. If we can stand up to him, all Europe may be free and the life of the

"'Blood, Toil, Tears, and Sweat'" is from *Parliamentary Debates*, 5th series, vol. 341 (1940).
"'Their Finest Hour'" is from *Parliamentary Debates*, 5th series, vol. 362 (1940), cols. 60–61.

The War in the Air. This map shows the relative distances and important military and industrial targets that formed the basis of Allied bombing attacks throughout the war. Once Germany had secured air bases in western France and the Netherlands in the spring of 1940, British cities and industrial sites also became targets. (*From* The War in Maps: An Atlas of the New York Times Maps, 4/e)

world may move forward into broad, sunlit uplands. But if we fail, then the whole world, including the United States, including all that we have known and cared for, will sink into the abyss of a new Dark Age made more sinister, and perhaps more protracted, by the lights of perverted science. Let us therefore brace ourselves to our duties and so bear ourselves that, if the British Empire and its Commonwealth last for a thousand years, men will still say, 'This was their finest hour.'

The War in the Air: "Scramble!"
FLIGHT LIEUTENANT RICHARD HILLARY

The British had been saved from invasion throughout the centuries by the formidable difficulties in mounting an operation across the English Channel. But with Britain continuing to defy Germany and determined to survive, Hitler planned an invasion of the island called "Operation Overlord." Hitler needed to weaken British resistance and facilitate the invasion by achieving supremacy of the air, so he relied on his Luftwaffe (air force), which had proved a menacing force in his European victories. From August throughout the next several months, the Luftwaffe struck British airfields and bombed British cities, most notably London. The Royal Air Force (RAF), however, aided by newly developed radar and the high-performance Spitfire and Hurricane fighter planes, destroyed more than twice as many enemy aircraft as were lost by the RAF. The skill and courage of the British fighter pilots forced Hitler to abandon his invasion plans. He had lost the Battle of Britain and turned his attention east toward the Soviet Union.

The first selection is an account of the action by an RAF pilot. Churchill's famous tribute to the heroism of this elite force follows.

The voice of the controller came unhurried over the loud speaker, telling us to take off, and in a few seconds we were running for our machines. I climbed into the cockpit of my plane and felt an empty sensation of suspense in the pit of my stomach. For one second time seemed to stand still and I stared blankly in front of me. I knew that morning I was to kill for the first time. That I might be killed or in any way injured did not occur to me. Later, when we were losing pilots regularly, I did consider it in an abstract way when on the ground; but once in the air, never. I knew it could not happen to me. I suppose every pilot knows that, knows it cannot happen to him; even when he is taking off for the last time, when he will not return, he knows that he cannot be killed. I wondered idly what he was like, this man I would kill. Was he young, was he fat, would he die with the Fuhrer's name on his lips, or would he die alone, in that last moment conscious of himself as a man? I

"The War in the Air" is from Gavin Lyall, ed., *The War in the Air,* 1939–1945 (London: Hutchinson & Co. Ltd., 1968), pp. 43–45. Reprinted by permission of the publisher.

would never know. Then I was being strapped in, my mind automatically checking the controls, and we were off.

We ran into them at 18,000 feet, twenty yellow-nosed Messerschmitt 109s, about five hundred feet above us. Our Squadron strength was eight, and as they came down on us we went into line astern and turned head on to them. Brian Carberry, who was leading the Section, dropped the nose of his machine, and I could almost feel the leading Nazi pilot push forward on his stick to bring his guns to bear. At the same moment Brian hauled hard back on his own control stick and led us over them in a steep climbing turn to the left. In two vital seconds they lost their advantage. I saw Brian let go a burst of fire at the leading plane, saw the pilot put his machine into a half roll, and knew that he was mine. Automatically, I kicked the rudder to the left to get him at right angles, turned the gun button to "Fire," and let go in a four-second burst with full deflection. He came right through my sights and I saw the tracer from all eight guns thud home. For a second he seemed to hang motionless; then a jet of red flame shot upward and he spun to the ground. . . .

My first emotion was one of satisfaction, satisfaction at a job adequately done, at the final logical conclusion of months of specialized training. And then I had a feeling of the essential rightness of it all. He was dead and I was alive; it could so easily have been the other way round; and that would somehow have been right too. I realized in that moment just how lucky a fighter pilot is. He has none of the personalized emotions of the soldier, handed a rifle and bayonet and told to charge. He does not even have to share the dangerous emotions of the bomber pilot who night after night must experience that childhood longing for smashing things. The fighter pilot's emotions are those of the duelist—cool, precise, impersonal. He is privileged to kill well. For if one must either kill or be killed, as now one must, it should, I feel, be done with dignity. Death should be given the setting it deserves; it should never be a pettiness; and for the fighter pilot it never can be.

"So Much Owed by So Many to So Few" (August 20, 1940)

WINSTON CHURCHILL

The gratitude of every home in our Island, in our Empire, and indeed throughout the world, except in the abodes of the guilty, goes out to the British airmen who, undaunted by odds, unwearied in their constant challenge and mortal danger, are turning the tide of the world war by their prowess and by their devotion. Never in the field of human conflict was so much owed by so many to so few. All hearts go out to the fighter pilots, whose brilliant actions we see with our own eyes day after day; but we must never

"'So Much Owed by So Many to So Few'" is from *Parliamentary Debates*, 5th series, vol. 364 (1940), cols. 1166–1167.

forget that all the time, night after night, month after month, our bomber squadrons travel far into Germany, find their targets in the darkness by the highest navigational skill, aim their attacks, often under the heaviest fire, often with serious loss, with deliberate careful discrimination, and inflict shattering blows upon the whole of the technical and war-making structure of the Nazi power. On no part of the Royal Air Force does the weight of the war fall more heavily than on the daylight bombers who will play an invaluable part in the case of invasion and whose unflinching zeal it has been necessary in the meanwhile on numerous occasions to restrain.

The Japanese Attack on Pearl Harbor (December 7, 1941)

Although American support of the British through lend-lease arrangements might have justified a German declaration of war against the United States, Hitler knew that his chances for victory in Europe were greater without the

The Pacific War Zone. This map shows the strategic territorial interests of the Japanese Empire in December 1941 as it sought the oil and other raw industrial resources that would fuel its war machine. *(From* The War in Maps: An Atlas of the New York Times Maps, 4/e)

involvement of the "sleeping giant." In fact, America may not have overcome its isolationist caution and entered the European conflict had not war been thrust on it in the Pacific.

Since the early 1930s, Japan had been forging a policy of conquest in Asia. Japan had conquered the mineral-rich Chinese region of Manchuria in 1931 and renamed it Manchukuo. After allying itself with Germany and Italy and signing a neutrality pact with the Soviet Union, Japan exploited the weakness of Britain and France abroad. In July 1941, the Japanese occupied Indochina. In response, the United States and Britain froze Japanese assets and cut off oil supplies. Without control over the Indonesian oil fields and the supplies of rubber and tin in Malaya, Japanese plans for expansion would fail. The solution, imposed by a war faction in the Japanese government led by General Hideki Tojo, was to end the constraint of the United States.

On Sunday morning, December 7, 1941, while Japanese representatives were still negotiating in Washington, Japan launched a surprise air attack on the American naval base at Pearl Harbor, Hawaii. Its aim was to severely cripple America's ability to respond to Japanese aggression in the Pacific and allow Japan to consolidate its gains before America could rebuild its fleet. The following Japanese sources show the development of this plan from conception in February 1941 to its fateful execution in December. The first selection was written in 1947 by Minoru Genda, who more than any other individual was responsible for the planning and ultimate success of the operation. The second is an excerpt from the diary of Sadamu Sanagi, an experienced air officer who was a member of the Operations Section of the Naval General Staff. Eyewitness accounts of the disaster follow, and the section ends with President Roosevelt's famous request in Congress for a declaration of war against Japan.

"This Attack Will Be Difficult, but Not Impossible" (February 2, 1941)

CAPTAIN MINORU GENDA

I am Minoru Genda, formerly a captain in the Japanese Navy. . . . Early in February 1941, . . . I received a letter from the Chief of Staff of the 11th Air Fleet, Rear Admiral Onishi, with whom I was well acquainted personally, though not under his direct command officially. In this letter he asked me to come to Kanoya at once as he wanted to see me on important business. . . . He then showed me a private letter which he had received from Vice Admiral

---

"'This Attack Will Be Difficult, but Not Impossible'" is from Donald M. Goldstein and Katherine V. Dillon, eds. *The Pearl Harbor Papers: Inside the Japanese Plans* (New York: Brassey's, 1993), pp. 13, 18–19. Copyright © 1993 by Prange Enterprises, Inc. Reprinted by permission of the publisher.

Yamamoto, Commander in Chief of the Combined Fleet. The substance of that letter was to the following effect:

> In the event of outbreak of war with the United States, there would be little prospect of our operations succeeding unless, at the very outset, we can deal a crushing blow to the main force of the American Fleet in Hawaiian waters by using the full strength of the 1st and 2nd air Squadrons against it, and thus to preclude the possibility of the American Fleet advancing to take the offensive in the Western Pacific for some time.
>
> And it is my hope that I may be given command of this air attack force, so that I may carry out the operation myself. Please make a study of the operation.

Rear Admiral Onishi said to me, "Please make this study in utmost secrecy, with special attention to the feasibility of the operation, method of execution, and the forces to be used." . . .

The more I studied this plan of attack, the more . . . I realized the difficulty of such a plan. After about two weeks I brought the answer to Rear Admiral Onishi. The content of the answer to the letter, as I recall, is as follows:

A. This attack must be a perfect surprise attack. And the result of this attack must be such that the main force of the American Fleet will not be able to advance to the Western Pacific for a period of at least six months.

B. The main target of the attack must be against the American aircraft carriers and land-based planes.

C. We must use the entire carrier strength that we have.

D. In order to continue the attack by carrier-based planes, we must have sufficient means of supplying the carriers.

E. An attack by torpedoes will be the best, but when it is not possible due to antisubmarine or antitorpedo obstructions in the deeper waters and near harbors, we must use dive bombers for the attack. In that case, we must change the type of planes on the carriers. Whether the torpedo attacks be in shallow or deep waters, plans for such attacks must be made.

F. This attack will be difficult but not impossible. The success of this attack lies in the success of the initial attack, therefore, the planning of the attack must be done in strict secrecy.

The message with which I handed the answer to Rear Admiral Onishi was: "It is necessary to follow up this attack on Hawaii with a landing operation. If Hawaii is occupied, America will lose her largest and best advanced base and, furthermore, the command of future operations for us will be very good."

As he received the answer, Rear Admiral Onishi said: "With our present strength, we are not able to take the offensive in both the eastern and southern areas. First, we must destroy the larger part of the American Fleet."

"Tora! Tora! Tora!" (December 7, 1941)
COMMANDER SADAMU SANAGI

Headquarters—Japanese Naval Operations

8 December (7 December, Hawaii Time):

Every nerve had been concentrated to receive messages. It was not until 0330 that messages began to come in. Wild joy burst out with the news of "Tora Tora . . ." and "successful surprise attack." Relaxed receiving the news of "bombed the enemy main strength with good results" and "torpedoed enemy heavy cruisers; heavy damage inflicted."

How the enemy was surprised can be easily imagined by such a Task Force's message as saying that they were encountered by enemy defense gunfire only after the torpedo attacks. The enemy in the Hawaii area had been completely surprised at about 0730 on Sunday morning. . . .

Our air force, together with the submarine force, achieved a great success unprecedented in history by the Pearl Harbor attack. About 400 planes, of which 120 were fighters, 160 dive bombers and 120 torpedo-attacking planes, inflicted the following damage upon the enemy:

> Two battleships sunk, four battleships seriously damaged and about four cruisers seriously damaged.
> Additionally, a great many enemy planes were destroyed.
> Our losses: 30 planes.

The surprise air attack coupled with submarine attacks by the midget submarines solely contributed to this successful attack, which could only be done by the Imperial Navy. This success is owing to the Imperial Navy's hard training for more than twenty years. Our navy had made this hard training only for this one day. So excited to hear of this success today!

Nothing could hold back our Imperial Navy which had kept silent for a long time. But once it arose, it never hesitated to dare to do the most difficult thing on this earth. Oh, how powerful is the Imperial Navy!

"I Saw My Maker on Sunday"
PRIVATE NICHOLAS GAYNOS

December 9, 1941

Dear Folks,

Well, I'm okay and feeling fine. We sure had a hot time here for a while and I thought that my end had come—God, was it hell. I'll give you an eyewitness

"'Tora! Tora! Tora!'" is from Donald M. Goldstein and Katherine V. Dillon, eds., *The Pearl Harbor Papers: Inside the Japanese Plans* (New York: Brassey's, 1993), pp. 89–90. Copyright © 1993 by Prange Enterprises, Inc. Reprinted by permission of the publisher.

"'I Saw My Maker on Sunday'" is from Paul Joseph Travers, *Eyewitness to Infamy: An Oral History of Pearl Harbor* (New York: Madison Books, 1991), pp. 48–50. Copyright © 1991 by Paul Joseph Travers. Reprinted by permission of the publisher.

account of the Japanese air raid on Pearl Harbor and Hickam Field on Sunday, 7 December 1941. This ought to make a good news copy for the *Bridgeport Post*.

Well, Sunday as usual, all of the men were sleeping late because we had no work to do. I was sound asleep, having gone to bed at 4:30 A.M. after being relieved of duty. It was exactly 7:55 when I was almost tossed out of bed by a terrific roar and the ensuing concussion. Most of the fellows also got up and, on looking out the window, we could see flames about five hundred feet high and huge clouds of smoke coming from Pearl Harbor.

No one thought it was war until we looked out of our eastern windows and saw some of our hangars in flames. Somebody yelled, "They are Japanese planes," but nobody believed it. We all ran out of the barracks and looked skyward. It was plain to see them. They were only from fifty to one hundred feet off the ground, and the huge red circle under their wings proved their identity. Some of them had huge torpedoes under the fuselage almost as long as the ship itself.

The thunder of bombs and the staccato of machine guns made such a deafening roar you had to yell to be heard a few feet away. The splintering of wood as fifty-caliber bullets ripped through the wooden barracks was mixed with screams of men as they ran from one shelter to another. We soon collected our senses and the full realization that war was here.

Some men cried, some laughed, others were terrified, some just couldn't seem to understand what it was all about. I soon had my senses under control and jumped in a car headed for my post. With a hail of bullets and with the planes roaring right over our heads, we raced down the street. I arrived at my transmitters and dove into a hole caused by an exploded bomb. One young fellow was dead, and his legs stuck out of the hole. It reminded me of a book I once read back home. I stayed here until things had quieted down and then scurried for safety in my flimsy office. We all knew they would be back soon so we hurriedly made preparations for their return. It was at 10:20 when the second attack came.

I was busy removing a radio truck to safety. Three men and I kept working as they dived into the big barracks and dropped load after load of bombs. The very ground shook, and my ears were ringing. By this time they spotted my equipment and headed straight for my men and me. I was lying in a small hole about ten feet to the right of my trucks. As the planes dove down at us, I could peek out under the brim of my tin helmet and see them spitting fire at us. The ground in front of me was spraying up and I could see the bombs leave the planes and head straight down at us. One of them was a one-thousand-pound bomb and landed fifty feet on my right. Three kids with a machine gun were shooting at the plane and the bomb landed almost on them. It blew them sky-high—gun and all.

The dirt and stones fell all over us and I ached all over. I emptied my forty-five pistol time after time into the planes, but it was futile. I thumbed my nose as they roared right over my head. We all swore like hell.

The planes were still roaring around strafing us unmercifullīy as those of us that were alive got into cars and started to pick up the dead and wounded.

One of the kids who was blown up with the machine gun was lying about fifty feet away. I tried to pick him up and he fell apart in my arms. He was covered with dirt and smiling. We rushed as many as we could to the hospital and gave first aid to those lying near us. Things were now getting quiet and then ambulances, nurses, and trucks came to pick up the men. Some of the things were so ghastly I cannot write of them. All I can say is that my baptism under fire sure was hell on earth and I saw my Maker on Sunday, December 7, 1941.

"An Inexhaustible Supply of Wounded"
ARMY NURSE MYRTLE WATSON

Within minutes of the attack, the wounded started to stream into the hospital. For three days, there seemed to be an inexhaustible supply of wounded and dying men. They were bringing men in so quickly that they didn't have time to separate the living from the dead. Bodies were piling up like cordwood wherever there was space. It was unbelievable what I was seeing. Some men were missing arms and legs, while others had limbs hanging by a shred of skin. It was hard to think that these men might be considered lucky since they had an outside chance of pulling through. The saddest and most depressing cases were the burn victims. Some of the men that were brought in were charred to a crisp, while others had their skin burned off, so their bodies resembled strips of fried and partially burnt bacon. It amazed the medical staff that these men were still alive when they were brought in.

The U.S.S. *Arizona*:
"Some Sort of Hellish Nightmare!"
SEAMAN JOHN RAMPLEY

On 7 December, a beautiful, clear, typical island day dawned. Being Sunday, the entire ship would be on "holiday routine." Sunrise over the harbor on Sunday was in itself a religious experience. With the stillness and quietness which surrounded the water, it was as if every Sunday was an Easter sunrise service. Certainly, this Sunday was to be no exception. . . .

Within moments, general quarters were sounded. "This is no drill. I repeat, this is no drill," echoed down the steel corridors of the ship. The words

"'An Inexhaustible Supply of Wounded'" is from Paul Joseph Travers, *Eyewitness to Infamy: An Oral History of Pearl Harbor* (New York: Madison Books, 1991), pp. 100–101. Copyright © 1991 by Paul Joseph Travers. Reprinted by permission of the publisher.

"The U.S.S. *Arizona*" is from Paul Joseph Travers, *Eyewitness to Infamy: An Oral History of Pearl Harbor* (New York: Madison Books, 1991), pp. 140–142. Copyright © 1991 by Paul Joseph Travers. Reprinted by permission of the publisher.

"A date which will live in infamy." The Japanese attack on the American naval base at Pearl Harbor, Hawaii, on December 7, 1941, brought the United States into World War II. This picture shows the destruction of the battleships *Arizona, Tennessee, and West Virginia. (National Archives)*

sent a cold, shuttering chill down my spine. At our battle stations on the fourteen-inch guns, there was little to do but pray. In the space of a few seconds, some men made up for twenty and more years of tardy prayers. Inside the turret, there was an eerie silence. Everyone seemed afraid to breathe, much less speak, as if that would somehow give away our position to the enemy or attract the attention of one of the bombs. We waited anxiously for some word from topside. Even though we were protected by the heavy plating of the turret, we felt helpless and defenseless, not being able to take any kind of action to defend ourselves and our fellow sailors. We could hear the thunder and feel the ship shudder as the bombs fell upon her. At one point in time, we felt a tremendous jolt, as if the ship had been lifted up in the air and slammed back down. Little did we realize that this was the fatal blow for the Arizona. Rivets popped from the steel walls and flew about the place. . . .

After what seemed like an eternity, the order came over the speakers, "All hands abandon ship." I looked around for some comfort, but all my shipmates seemed to have the same awareness as myself. Our life together aboard the old Arizona was over. I climbed down the ladder on the outside of the turret. Everywhere I touched or grabbed onto the ship, I felt the effects of the fires and explosions. The ship had become a piece of molten steel, a kind of giant tea kettle, where heat was being transferred to all metal and steel parts.

... Finally being outside the turret, it looked as if the rest of the ship was a blazing inferno, encircled by a wall of fire which was quickly closing in. I remember looking around the deck and seeing my shipmates from the deck division with their bodies burned black or lying on the deck bleeding from open wounds. Some men were screaming and jumping over the side of the ship. Others were spread about the deck in various positions, crying and moaning in agony. Charred and mutilated bodies were scattered everywhere in the wreckage of the ship. They lay crumpled like broken dolls who had been picked up in the air by some giant hand and slammed against the structures of the ship. With all the smoke and fire on the decks, it seemed difficult to catch one's breath. ... All around, the air was filled with the smell of burning oil and burning flesh. It was a smell which lingered in the air like a heavy fog, saturating one's clothes and body.

I walked, then crawled, very calmly and carefully to the side of the ship and looked down into the water. The water was partially covered with oil, most of which was burning. ... From where I stood, all I could see forward was a crumbling mass of twisted metal that had only minutes before been the proud superstructure. The command to abandon ship was being repeated over and over again. Enemy planes were still strafing the ship when I made the decision to jump. The warm water was certainly a refresher. When I came to the surface, I was hoping that the whole thing was a bad dream, some sort of hellish nightmare. ... I began swimming toward Ford Island. The swim wasn't far, but it was very exhausting swimming an obstacle course filled with oil, debris, and bodies. I reached the island in relatively good shape, considering the ordeal which I had been through. After a short rest and a couple of mouthfuls of water, I got my second wind and was ready to help wherever needed.

It wasn't until many hours later that I learned so many of my shipmates were dead. Of the fifteen from my boot platoon that I went aboard with, I was the only one who survived.

"A Date Which Will Live in Infamy"
PRESIDENT FRANKLIN DELANO ROOSEVELT

Yesterday, December 7, 1941—a date which will live in infamy—the United States of America was suddenly and deliberately attacked by naval and air forces of the Empire of Japan.

The United States was at peace with that nation and, at the solicitation of Japan, was still in conversation with its Government and its Emperor looking toward the maintenance of peace in the Pacific. ...

"'A Date Which Will Live in Infamy'" is from Department of State, *Bulletin,* December 13, 1941, p. 474.

It will be recorded that the distance of Hawaii from Japan makes it obvious that the attack was deliberately planned many days or even weeks ago. During the intervening time the Japanese Government has deliberately sought to deceive the United States by false statements and expressions of hope for continued peace.

The attack yesterday on the Hawaiian Islands has caused severe damage to American naval and military forces. Very many American lives have been lost. In addition American ships have been reported torpedoed on the high seas between San Francisco and Honolulu. . . .

As Commander-in-Chief of the Army and Navy I have directed that all measures be taken for our defense. Always will we remember the character of the onslaught against us. No matter how long it may take us to overcome this premeditated invasion, the American people in their righteous might will win through to absolute victory. . . .

With confidence in our armed forces—with the unbounded determination of our people—we will gain the inevitable triumph—so help us God.

I ask that the Congress declare that since the unprovoked and dastardly attack by Japan on Sunday, December seventh, a state of war has existed between the United States and the Japanese Empire.

Last Stand: The Siege of Stalingrad (1942–1943)

With the American entry into the war in 1941, the Allies had great hopes that a combined, coordinated effort could repel the Axis onslaught in Europe and in the Pacific. But neither American industry nor its military forces were prepared for war. By 1942, the Japanese controlled Hong Kong, Malaya, Burma and New Guinea, and the Germans had advanced deep into Russia on an enormous front, threatening Leningrad and Moscow itself. Of greatest importance for the Axis advance were the oil fields near the Caspian Sea in southern Russia. The German war machine had to be fed and Hitler targeted the city of Stalingrad as the key to the capture of the region.

On September 15, the German Sixth Army commanded by General Friedrich Paulus arrived on the outskirts of Stalingrad as the spearhead of the German advance. Stalin was determined to hold the city, and the battle raged with unparalleled ferocity for the next five months. Through the bitter Russian winter, the German army remained cut off from supplies and vulnerable to incessant Russian attacks. Hitler would not allow General Paulus to order a retreat and the German Sixth Army was surrounded, cut off, starved and frozen to death. It was a devastating battle for both sides as the Russians lost more soldiers in this one battle than the Americans lost in combat during the entire war.

Stalingrad marked the turning point for the campaign and Russian troops began an inexorable advance westward against stubborn German resistance. The following dispatches, and anonymous letters from doomed German soldiers and their loved ones at home bear witness to the terrible battle of attrition at Stalingrad.

To the Death: "Surrender Is Forbidden!"

Sixth Army to High Command: January 24, 1943

Troops without ammunition or food. Contact maintained with elements only of six divisions. Evidence of disintegration on southern, northern and western fronts. Effective command no longer possible. Little change on eastern front: eighteen thousand wounded without any supplies of dressings or drugs; 44, 76, 100, 305, 384 Infantry Divisions destroyed. Front torn open as a result of strong break-throughs on three sides. Strong-points and shelter only available in the town itself; further defence senseless. Collapse inevitable. Army requests immediate permission to surrender in order to save lives of remaining troops.

—General Paulus

Adolf Hitler to Sixth Army: January 24, 1943

Surrender is forbidden. Sixth Army will hold their positions to the last man and the round and by their heroic endurance will make an unforgettable contribution towards the establishment of a defensive front and the salvation of the Western world.

—Adolf Hitler

Last Letters from Stalingrad

I was horrified when I saw the map. We're quite alone, without any help from outside. Hitler has left us in the lurch. Whether this letter gets away depends on whether we still hold the airfield. We are lying in the north of the city. The men in my battery already suspect the truth, but they aren't so exactly informed as I am. So this is what the end looks like. Hans and I have no intention of going into captivity; yesterday I saw four men who'd been captured before our infantry reoccupied a strong-point. No, we're not going to be captured. When Stalingrad falls you will hear and read about it. Then you will know that I shall not return.

—Anonymous

For a long time to come, perhaps for ever, this is to be my last letter. A comrade who has to go to the airfield is taking it along with him, as the last machine to leave the pocket is taking off tomorrow morning. The situation has become quite untenable. The Russians are only two miles from the last spot from which aircraft can operate, and when that's gone not even a mouse will get out, to say nothing of me. Admittedly several hundred thousand others won't escape either, but it's precious little consolation to share one's own destruction with other men.

—Anonymous

"To the Death: 'Surrender Is Forbidden!'" is from Heinz Schrorer, *Stalingrad* (London: E.P. Dutton & Co., Inc), p. 305. Translated by Constantine FitzGibbon. Copyright © 1958 by E.P. Dutton & Co., Inc. Reprinted by permission.

"Last Letters from Stalingrad" is from *Last Letters from Stalingrad* (London: Coronet, 1955).

To return to the present position. Of the division there are only sixty-nine men still fit for action. Bleyer is still alive, and Hartlieb as well. Little Degen has lost both arms. . . . Life is finished for him, too. . . . [He] has given up hope. . . . All we have left are two machine-guns and four hundred rounds. And then a mortar and ten bombs. Except for that all we have are hunger and fatigue. We have been swindled, and have been condemned to death. . . .

—Anonymous

The End: "Plain Murder"

ELSE WENDEL

We all had friends on the Russian Front and we tried not to talk too much about them to each other. But one day an old friend of mine—Edith Wieland—wrote, begging me to visit her, as she had just lost her husband in the battle [of Stalingrad]. I found, as she opened the door, a thin, old woman in black, not the proud, confident Edith I had known. She began to cry as she asked me inside.

In the lounge she showed me her husband's last letter from Stalingrad. He asked her to forgive him for anything he might ever have done to hurt her. He had never at any time wanted to hurt her. It was for her alone that he was now living and he loved her more than his life. This was no empty phrase he wrote, because they were now facing death, and it would only be a matter of days or weeks. But as long as he felt his death served a purpose he would be willing to give his life for the Fatherland. He implored her never to give up, no matter what might come, and to bring up their children—the youngest only two months old—in the spirit they had agreed upon.

I was utterly shaken. I could see him standing before me in his officer's uniform, so proud and with the Iron Cross on his chest and the stars of a *Hauptmann*. He had been a strong and virile man, honest as the day.

"Was he wounded when he wrote this letter?" I asked Edith

"No," she said quickly, "I have been told he was not wounded. He met his death with open eyes. He was perfectly well and strong."

I looked down at the carpet. What kind of death then had he met? As if Edith could guess my thoughts, she said, "They have written that death came instantaneously. He got a bullet through the head as he came round the corner of a house."

While I was searching desperately for the right words, Edith spoke again. "There is one thing that haunts me. I have heard a rumor that they could have escaped, but that Hitler forbade it!"

I was frightened. I had not heard that rumor myself at the time. "No! Impossible!" I said. "It would be plain murder. Hitler would never do such a thing. You know that, surely?"

Very slowly Edith lifted her head. "I am not so sure," she said in a low voice. "I keep re-reading that sentence in Albert's letter ('as long as I feel my

"The End: 'Plain Murder'" is from Boris Agapov, *After the Battle* (London: Hutchinson, 1943).

death serves a purpose'); that doesn't sound a bit like Albert. It sounds as though his confidence was waning, and he was beginning to doubt."

The Home Front

Perhaps the most amazing feat of logistical supply in history occurred after the disaster at Pearl Harbor when American industry was transformed to produce the implements of war. Much more than the economy was altered, however. An entire society was transformed as men went to war and women went into the factories.

"Rosie the Riveter" became an endearing image of women who decided to leave their jobs as homemakers, teachers, and sales clerks to become crane operators and machinists. At proving grounds, women loaded and tested machine guns and anti-aircraft weapons. Women became guards at plants, foundry workers, hydraulic press operators, and miners. In January 1942, four thousand women were employed as war workers. Within a year the number had swollen to forty-three thousand.

The standard workweek was forty-eight hours (six days of eight hours each) with only Sundays off, and many women routinely worked overtime. Many doubted that women could handle the long hours and grind of grueling, repetitious work. But most women truly felt that their contributions were essential to victory and proved to themselves and to the country that they could compete in traditional male occupations. The following account explains the demands and benefits of wartime factory work for women.

Women in the Factories: "My Hands Are as Smooth as the Steel I Worked On" (August 1943)

ELIZABETH HAWES

A few months ago, when everybody was talking about the production crisis—can women do it?—will women do it?—how are you going to make women do it?—I began to murmur that I guessed I'd go into a factory and find out how the wheels went round. . . .

Now that I've worked a few months in a plant—on the graveyard shift too—the only wonder to me is that all the women in the USA aren't storming the factory gates. I'm convinced that any healthy woman can work in a factory—and like it. My biggest regret is that I had to leave because I'd agreed to do some writing. My biggest ambition is to get back.

Sure, I caught a bad cold. My hands aren't soft any more but they're as smooth as the steel I worked on. . . . So what! All the other women had to do cleaning and laundry as well as cooking and shopping. I was spared that. . . .

The plant itself was exciting. It's one of the Wright aeronautical plants in northern New Jersey—I believe the biggest airplane engine plant in the

---

"'My Hands Are as Smooth as the Steel I Worked On'" is from Elizabeth Hawes, "My Life on the Midnight Shift," *Woman's Home Companion* (August 1943), pp. 24, 47.

country. You feel you're in a small town, only the streets are lined with machines. Electric trucks honk at you constantly and people on bicycles flip past as you wend your way from the locker room to your machine a mile or so distant. There are no windows. Air conditioning and thousands of long blue lights take the place of the breezes and the sun. . . .

It was a great pleasure to me that nobody gave a darn who anyone was or whether you'd ever had your picture in the paper or shaken hands with the Duchess of Windsor or Gertie Lawrence. . . . Of course there are little discords. The foremen and subforemen are honestly scared to death of us women. When first you arrive they look at you out of the corner of their eyes. . . . Every woman machinist has to endure sheer torture from her fellow male employees at one point in her career. You discover that you can't work without tools and that the company doesn't provide all of them. First you borrow from your lead man or somebody near by who owns a toolbox. Ultimately you buy your own toolbox and quite a few dollars' worth of wrenches, hammers, micrometers and such.

The men see that now you think you're a mechanic. Some honestly don't believe the Lord ever intended women to be mechanics. Others are infuriated by your presumption that you can do their work. . . .

Thank heaven, none of the women in the plant had ever been told by "authoritative sources," as I had, that the women of the USA are unpatriotic— that they're just working for money.

They are working for money—money to feed their kids, money to keep their homes together—so their sons and husbands can fight. They never speak of being useful because it might sound boastful. It might sound as if you were taking credit for losing sleep, for tending sick children at home, for not having time to shop carefully and for still turning up at work.

But mostly I want to go back to Wright's new plant because I think the women who work in war plants, and the men who first help them and then work with them are the luckiest people in the world. There's an equality developing there unlike any I've ever seen. Joe was an Italian—Nel, a Negro—Suzy, Irish—there were Germans, Poles, Hungarians, Gentiles, Jews. Slowly you could see there was no difference between any two of us. Gradually everybody was beginning to work as one unit. When you see something like that happening you feel you're not just doing a job to help win the war. You also have the profound pleasure of seeing the future peace being worked out before your eyes.

London Aflame!

MRS. ROBERT HENREY

The Battle of Britain began in August 1940 with German attacks on the airfields of southeastern England. But in early September, seeking revenge for British bombing raids on German cities, the Nazis switched their attacks to

"London Aflame!" is from Mrs. Robert Henrey, *London Under Fire, 1940–1945* (London: J. M. Dent & Sons, Ltd., 1969), pp. 36–37, 43–44. Copyright © 1969 by Mrs. Robert Henrey. Reprinted by permission of J. M. Dent & Sons, Ltd.

London. For two months, life in London was transformed as the air raid siren and blackout curtains signaled the daily ritual of night bombings.

Much of the city was destroyed and over fifteen thousand people were killed. British inhabitants went underground to the subways where life continued, as babies were born, friendships formed, and the survivors were tallied. Mrs. Robert Henrey, a mother who lived in London's West End, recounts the activity.

As the battle for London continued, the face of the West End changed; but as far as possible its inhabitants attempted to carry on as usual. Crowds filed through the streets an hour before dusk carrying their mattresses on their way to the tube stations and public shelters. . . .

Bombs fell by day as well as by night. We became accustomed to the sudden drone of an airplane in the middle of the morning, the screech of a bomb, the dull crash of its explosion and the smell of cordite that filled the air a moment later. The sight of a burned-out bus unexpectedly in Berkeley Square, the ruins of a shop still half-hidden in a cloud of dust, streets that were impassable because of time bombs, enemy planes that burst in mid air sending down large chunks of fuselage, the pilots gliding down with their parachutes, became the normal things of life. . . . Almost every night some landmark near us would go up in dust, and yet our building continued to stand. . . .

From the very first night of the battle for London [1940], because of the fires in the east which lit up the dome, St. Paul's Cathedral had become a symbol of London's defiance. As long ago as the night of the 12th September a large delayed-action bomb hurtled down south of the granite posts and buried itself twenty-seven feet deep. Everybody knew that if it exploded there would be nothing left of St. Paul's. For three days men worked to dig it out. Then it was driven in state to Hackney Marshes on a lorry under the command of Lt. Davies, a Canadian who became a national hero.

Even for a very ordinary housewife living with her baby in the West End, St. Paul's could never for long be out of her mind. Almost every evening from the flat roof of Carrington House we peered east and prayed that it might stand.

The Final Destruction (1944–1945)

War alone brings up to their highest tension all human energies and imposes the stamp of nobility upon the peoples who have the courage to make it.

—Benito Mussolini

When you lose a friend, you have an overpowering desire to go back home and yell in everybody's ear, 'This guy was killed fighting for you. Don't forget him—ever.' Keep him in your mind when you wake up in

the morning and when you go to bed at night. Think of him as a guy who
wanted to live every bit as much as you do.

—Bill Mauldin

The D-Day Invasions (June 6, 1944)

*By 1944, with Allied victories in Northern Africa, Italy, and Russia beginning
to turn the tide of battle, the Allied High Command, led by General Dwight
Eisenhower, had developed plans for the invasion of Europe. The Germans were
aware that an invasion was imminent and had constructed formidable defenses
along the French coast under the direction of Field Marshal Erwin Rommel. But
the Germans could not defend the entire coast with equal troop strength and focused more of their attention on the area surrounding Calais, which marked the
shortest invasion route across the English Channel. Because British intelligence
had secretly broken German codes and could better estimate the strength of enemy
defenses, the decision was made to invade along the Normandy beaches.*

*An amphibious assault is a delicate operation, and even the most meticulous
plans are vulnerable to changes of wind and weather. The operation was a high-
risk gamble that cost thousands of lives but resulted in the establishment of a
"second front" against the Germans. The next drive was to Berlin itself.*

*The following personal accounts of "The Longest Day" capture the confusion
and heroism displayed by soldiers in the greatest amphibious operation in history.
The fiftieth anniversary commemorative speech by President Bill Clinton on June
6, 1994, offers perspective on the cost and importance of this day.*

The Paratrooper: "He Was Blown Away"
KEN RUSSELL

I was just a boy, seventeen—I should have been in high school rather than in a
strange country. I should have been going to school. I think my class was grad-
uating that night. Sainte-Mere-Eglise was the area that we had to take, and as we
came in, there was a building on fire. The fire gave light for miles around, and
we came in and when we saw the fire, we jumped. I knew we were in trouble, and
it was so horrifying, because most of our stick were killed.

They didn't even hit the ground. They hit the telephone poles—Lieutenant Cadish, H. T. Bryant, and Laddie Tlapa landed on telephone poles
down the street, and it was like they were crucified there. Coming down, one

fellow had a Gammon grenade on his hip, and I looked to my right, and I saw the guy, and instantaneously, I looked around and there was just an empty parachute coming down. He was blown away.

I got hit in the hand—just a kind of a valley up through my hand. To be honest, I was trying to hide behind my reserve chute, because you could hear the shells hitting. We were all sitting ducks coming down. The heat drew the nylon chutes toward the fire, and the air to feed the fire was actually drawing us into it, and I saw one trooper land in the fire. I heard him scream one time before he was engulfed, and he didn't scream any more.

When I came down, I knew that we were going to hit in the town, but I didn't know exactly where. I finally hit the roof of the church first and a couple of my suspension lines went around the church steeple and I slid off the roof. I was hanging on the edge of the roof, and when Steele had come down, his chute covered the steeple.

While I was there, a buck sergeant who was in our unit who had jumped from our plane by the name of John Ray came down. I was on the right side of the church, and Steele was hung up on the steeple, and Sergeant Ray came down and missed the edge of the church, but he hit in front of it. A Nazi soldier, billeted on the next street behind the church, came around from behind the church. He was a red-haired German soldier, and he came to shoot Steele and myself, who were still hanging there. As he came around, he shot Ray in the stomach. Ray being a sergeant, had been armed with a .45 pistol, and while he was dying in agony, got his .45 out and when this German soldier started turning around to us, Ray shot him in the back of the head and killed him.

The Assault on Omaha Beach: "I'm Hit! I'm Hit!"
HAROLD BAUMGARTEN

At 7:00 A.M. I saw the beach with its huge seawall at the foot of a massive 150-foot bluff. We'd made it. And then an 88-millimeter shell landed right in the middle of the LCA [landing craft] on the side of us, and splinters of the boat, equipment, and bodies were thrown into the air. Lieutenant Donaldson cautioned us to get down. Bullets were passing through the thin wooden sides of our vessel. The ramp was lowered and the inner door was opened. In a British LCA, we could only get out one at a time, and a German machine gun trained on the opening took a heavy toll of lives. Many of my thirty buddies went down as they left the LCA.

I got a bullet through the top of my helmet first, and then as I waded through the deep water, a bullet aimed at my heart hit the receiver of my M-1 rifle as I carried it at port arms, embedding itself in my ammunition. I waded through the waist-deep water, watching many of my buddies fall alongside of me. The

American troops land on Normandy beach during the D-day assault, June 6, 1944: "I waded through the waist-deep water, watching many of my buddies fall alongside of me. The water was being shot up all around, and many a bullet ricocheted off the water."—Harold Baumgarten *(UPI/Corbis)*

water was being shot up all around, and many a bullet ricocheted off the water. Clarius Riggs, who left the assault boat in front of me, went under, shot to death, and eight or ten feet to my right, just as we hit the beach, I heard a hollow thud and I saw Private Robert Ditmar hold his chest and yell, "I'm hit! I'm hit!" I hit the ground and watched him as he continued to go forward ten more yards and then trip over a tank obstacle. As he fell, his body made a complete turn and he lay sprawled on the damp sand with his head facing the German, his face looking skyward. He seemed to be suffering from shock, and was yelling, "Mother, Mom . . ." as he kept rolling around on the sand.

There were three or four others wounded and dying right near him. Sergeant Barnes got shot down right in front of me, and Lieutenant Donaldson, and another sergeant had a gaping wound in the upper right corner of his forehead. He was walking crazily in the water, without his helmet, and then he got down on his knees and started praying with his rosary beads, and at that moment the Germans cut him in half with their deadly cross fire. The fire came from a pillbox [machine gun emplacement] built into the mountain on the right flank of the beach. We had snipers firing at us from the vantage points in front of us and from dugouts and pillboxes. I saw the reflection from the helmet of one of the snipers, and took aim, and later on found out I got a bull's-eye. It was the only shot that rifle fired, because the rifle broke in half and I had to throw it away. The shot that had hit my rifle must have shattered the wood. . . .

Finally, I came to dry sand, and there was another hundred yards to go, and I started across the sand, crawling very fast. When I reached the stone wall without further injury, I looked back on the beach I had crossed and saw two of our battalion's twelve special tanks knocked out in the water, a dead man hanging out of the turret of one of them. The other one fired his 75-millimeter gun shells right into the pillbox on the right flank and could not knock them out.

At the wall, I met a fellow from Company B from my boat team named Dominick Surrow, a boy from Georgia about my age, a rugged fellow, who looked at my face and said, "Stay here, I'm going to run down the beach and get help." He got killed.

I watched him being washed around by the incoming water, and I saw the bodies of my buddies who had tried in vain to clear the beach. It looked like the beach was littered with the refuse of a wrecked ship that were the dead bodies of what once were the proud, tough, and the well-trained combat infantrymen of the 1st Battalion of the 116th Infantry.

I saw Sergeant Draper and Vargos and all of Company A dying in the water to my left. . . . There was no medical aid available at this time, and many had bled to death and many drowned. I ran down the wall to the left a hundred yards or so, giving a hand to many of the wounded who were trying to pull themselves against the wall. . . .

Lying in the sand in front of the Vierville draw was our boat's walkie-talkie radio man and my best buddy, PFC Robert Garbed of Newport News, Virginia. He was facedown with his back to the enemy, probably spun around by the force of a bullet. . . .

Sergeant Cecil Bredan dressed my face wound. I had received five individual wounds that day in Normandy.

Fiftieth Anniversary of D-Day: "When They Were Young, These Men Saved the World"

PRESIDENT BILL CLINTON

In these last days of ceremonies, we have heard wonderful words of tribute. Now we come to this hallowed place that speaks, more than anything else, in silence. Here on this quiet plateau, on this small piece of American soil, we honor those who gave their lives for us fifty crowded years ago.

"Fiftieth Anniversary of D-Day" is from President Bill Clinton, speech delivered at the United States National Cemetery above Omaha Beach, Colleville-sur-Mer, France, on June 6, 1994. Contained in *Vital Speeches of the Day,* July 1, 1994, pp. 546–547.

"Fresh, spirited American troops, flushed with victory, are bringing in thousands of hungry, ragged, battle-weary prisoners..." (News item). *(Copyright © 1944 Bill Mauldin. Reprinted with permission.)*

Today, the beaches of Normandy are calm. If you walk these shores on a summer's day, all you might hear is the laughter of children playing on the sand, or the cry of seagulls overhead, or perhaps the ringing of a distant church bell—the simple sounds of freedom barely breaking the silence.

But June 6th, 1944 was the least ordinary day of the 20th century. On that chilled dawn, these beaches echoed with the sounds of staccato gunfire, the roar of aircraft, the thunder of bombardment. And through the wind and the waves came the soldiers, out of their landing craft and into the water, away from their youth and toward a savage place many of them would sadly never leave.

They had come to free a continent—the Americans, the British, the Canadians, the Poles, the French Resistance, the Norwegians and the others—they had all come to stop one of the greatest forces of evil the world has ever known.

As news of the invasion broke back home in America, people held their breath. In Boston, commuters stood reading the news on the electric sign at South Station. In New York, the Statue of Liberty, its torch blacked out since Pearl Harbor, was lit at sunset for 15 minutes. . . .

During those first hours on bloody Omaha nothing seemed to go right. Landing craft were ripped apart by mines and shells. Tanks sent to protect them had sunk, drowning their crews. Enemy fire raked the invaders as they stepped into chest-high water and waded past the floating bodies of their comrades. And as the stunned survivors of the first wave huddled behind a seawall, it seemed the invasion might fail.

Hitler and his followers had bet on it. They were sure the Allied soldiers were soft, weakened by liberty and leisure, by the mingling of races and religion. They were sure their totalitarian youth had more discipline and zeal.

But then, something happened. Although many of the American troops found themselves without officers on unfamiliar ground, next to soldiers they didn't know, one by one, they got up. They inched forward and together in groups of threes and fives and tens, the sons of democracy improvised and mounted their own attacks. At that exact moment on these beaches, the forces of freedom turned the tide of the 20th century. . . .

Today, many of them are here among us. Oh, they may walk with a little less spring in their step and their ranks are growing thinner, but let us never forget—when they were young, these men saved the world. . . .

Millions of our GI's did return home from that war to build up our nations and enjoy life's sweet pleasures. But on this field, there are 9,386 who did not. . . . They were the fathers we never knew, the uncles we never met, the friends who never returned, the heroes we can never repay. They gave us our world. And those simple sounds of freedom we hear today are their voices speaking to us across the years. . . .

Fifty years ago, the first Allied soldiers to land here in Normandy came not from the sea, but from the sky. They were called Pathfinders, the first paratroopers to make the jump. Deep in the darkness they descended upon these fields to light beacons for the airborne assaults that would soon follow. Now, near the dawn of a new century, the job of lighting those beacons falls to our hands.

To you who brought us here, I promise, we will be the new pathfinders, for we are the children of your sacrifice.

The Divine Wind: Kamikaze!

In 1943, American forces began a campaign of "island hopping" in hopes of capturing several strategic islands that would provide important bases for an eventual assault on Japan. By March 1945, the islands of Iwo Jima and Okinawa had fallen despite determined Japanese resistance. The Japanese High Command realized the gravity of the moment and focused their resistance with suicide attacks on American ships and aircraft carriers by Japanese planes filled with explosives. These planes, called kamikazes, were named after the "Divine Wind" that had saved Japan from Mongolian invasion in the thirteenth century. The following diary account is from a kamikaze pilot who was about to sacrifice his life with honor and dignity.

"Death and I Are Waiting"

ENSIGN HEIICHI OKABE

22 February 1945

I am actually a member at last of the Kamikaze Special Attack Corps. My life will be rounded out in the next thirty days. My chance will come! Death and I are waiting. The training and practice have been rigorous, but it is worthwhile if we can die beautifully and for a cause.

I shall die watching the pathetic struggle of our nation. My life will gallop in the next few weeks as my youth and life draw to a close. . . .

The sortie has been scheduled for the next ten days. I am a human being and hope to be neither saint nor scoundrel, hero nor fool—just a human being. As one who has spent his life in wistful longing and searching, I die resignedly in the hope that my life will serve as a "human document."

"'Death and I Are Waiting'" is from Rikihei Inoguchi and Tadashi Nakajima, *The Divine Wind* (Annapolis, Md.: United States Naval Institute, 1958), pp. 207–208. Copyright © 1958 by the United States Naval Institute. Reprinted by permission of the United States Naval Institute.

The world in which I lived was too full of discord. As a community of rational human beings it should be better composed. Lacking a single great conductor, everyone lets loose with his own sound, creating dissonance where there should be melody and harmony.

We shall serve the nation gladly in its present painful struggle. We shall plunge into enemy ships cherishing the conviction that Japan has been and will be a place where only lovely homes, brave women, and beautiful friendships are allowed to exist.

> What is the duty today? It is to fight.
> What is the duty tomorrow? It is to win.
> What is the daily duty? It is to die.

We die in battle without complaint. I wonder if others, like scientists, who pursue the war effort on their own fronts, would die as we do without complaint. Only then will the unity of Japan be such that she can have any prospect of winning the war.

If, by some strange chance, Japan should suddenly win this war it would be a fatal misfortune for the future of the nation. It will be better for our nation and people if they are tempered through real ordeals which will serve to strengthen.

> Like cherry blossoms
> In the spring,
> Let us fall
> Clean and radiant.

The Nuclear Age

On August 6, 1945, the world entered the nuclear age with the detonation of the atomic bomb over the city of Hiroshima, Japan. Persuaded by the argument that such use would ultimately save Allied lives, President Truman ordered another bomb dropped on Nagasaki two days later. The Japanese surrendered, and World War II finally came to an end. The next selections relate the events, from Albert Einstein's famous letter to President Roosevelt proposing the possibility of such a weapon, to Winston Churchill's defense of its use. The United States responsibly attempted to control the destructive power it had unleashed, but the race was on to match America's technological achievement. The escalation of nuclear arms became a focal point for the Cold War competition between the United States and the Soviet Union for the next forty years.

The Theory: Letter to President Roosevelt (1939)

ALBERT EINSTEIN

Albert Einstein
Old Grove Rd.
Nassau Point
Peconic, Long Island

August 2nd, 1939

F. D. Roosevelt,
President of the United States,
White House
Washington, D.C.

Sir:

Some recent work by E. Fermi and L. Szilard, which has been communicated to me in manuscript, leads me to expect that the element uranium may be turned into a new and important source of energy in the immediate future. Certain aspects of the situation which has arisen seem to call for watchfulness and, if necessary, quick action on the part of the Administration. I believe therefore that it is my duty to bring to your attention the following facts and recommendations:

In the course of the last four months it has been made probable—through the work of Joliot in France as well as Fermi and Szilard in America—that it may become possible to set up a nuclear chain reaction in a large mass of uranium, by which vast amounts of power and large quantities of new radium-like elements would be generated. Now it appears almost certain that this could be achieved in the immediate future.

This new phenomenon would also lead to the construction of bombs, and it is conceivable—though much less certain—that extremely powerful bombs of a new type may thus be constructed. A single bomb of this type, carried by boat and exploded in a port, might very well destroy the whole port together with some of the surrounding territory. However, such bombs might very well prove to be too heavy for transportation by air.

The United States has only very poor ores of uranium in moderate quantities. There is some good ore in Canada and the former Czechoslovakia, while the most important source of uranium is the Belgian Congo. . . .

I understand that Germany has actually stopped the sale of uranium from the Czechoslovakian mines which she has taken over. That she should have taken such early action might perhaps be understood on the ground that the son of the German Under-Secretary of State, von Weizsacker, is attached to the Kaiser-Wilhelm-Institut in Berlin where some of the American work on uranium is now being repeated.

Yours very truly,

(Albert Einstein)

The Reality: The Destruction of Hiroshima (August 6, 1945)

HARRY S TRUMAN

Sixteen hours ago an American airplane dropped one bomb on Hiroshima, an important Japanese Army base. That bomb had more power than 20,000 tons of T.N.T. It had more than two thousand times the blast power of the British "Grand Slam" which is the largest bomb ever yet used in the history of warfare.

The Japanese began the war from the air at Pearl Harbor. They have been repaid many fold. And the end is not yet in sight. With this bomb we have now added a new and revolutionary increase in destruction to supplement the growing power of our armed forces. In their present form these bombs are now in production and even more powerful forms are in development. It is an atomic bomb. It is a harnessing of the basic power of the universe. The force from which the sun draws its power has been loosed against those who brought war to the Far East.

Before 1939, it was the accepted belief of scientists that it was theoretically possible to release atomic energy. But no one knew any practical method of doing it. By 1942, however, we knew that the Germans were working feverishly to find a way to add atomic energy to the other engines of war with which they hoped to enslave the world. But they failed. We may be grateful to Providence that the Germans got the V-1's and V-2's late and in limited quantities and even more grateful that they did not get the atomic bomb at all. . . .

We are now prepared to obliterate more rapidly and completely every productive enterprise the Japanese have above ground in any city. We shall

---

"The Reality: Announcement of the Destruction of Hiroshima" is from *Public Papers of the President,* Harry S Truman, 1947 (Washington, D.C.: Government Printing Office, 1963), pp. 197–200.

Explosion of the atomic bomb over Nagasaki, Japan (August 9, 1945). *(AP/Wide World Photos)*

destroy their docks, their factories, and their communications. Let there be no mistake; we shall completely destroy Japan's power to make war. . . .

I shall recommend that the Congress of the United States consider promptly the establishment of an appropriate commission to control the production and use of atomic power within the United States. I shall give further consideration and make further recommendations to the Congress as to how atomic power can become a powerful and forceful influence towards the maintenance of world peace.

In Defense of the Use of the Atomic Bomb (August 16, 1946)
SIR WINSTON CHURCHILL

There are voices which assert that the bomb should never have been used at all. I cannot associate myself with such ideas. Six years of total war have convinced most people that, had the Germans or Japanese discovered this new weapon, they would have used it upon us to our complete destruction with utmost alacrity. I am surprised that very worthy people, but people who in most cases had no intention of proceeding to the Japanese front themselves, should adopt the position that, rather than throw this bomb, we should have sacrificed a million American and a quarter million British lives in the desperate battles and massacres of an invasion of Japan. Future generations will judge these dire decisions, and I believe if they find themselves dwelling in a happier world from which war has been banished, and where freedom reigns, they will not condemn those who struggled for their benefit amid the horrors and the miseries of this gruesome and ferocious epoch.

The Aftermath of War

At the close of World War II, humanity paused, much as it had at the end of the Great War in 1918, stunned by the prolonged destruction that shook the very foundations of Western Civilization. But in 1945, there was a clear winner and a clear loser. This time there was joy, a celebration that evil had been vanquished and the world made safe from the horrors of fascism. Still, Europe was in ruins, over thirty million people lay dead or wounded, and the new threat, the Soviet Union, with its totalitarian government and "creeping Communism," was the next obstacle to freedom. The post-war world would again pick up the pieces of its destruction and rearrange its alliances in order to reflect the new realities. The century had begun with devastation, followed at midpoint by even greater annihilation—and the looming potential to destroy the human race. Such events demand reflection. After the cold statistics of destruction, photographer Phillippe Halsman and philosopher Jean-Paul Sartre comment on the carnage and lend perspective to the age of anxiety.

"In Defense of the Use of the Atomic Bomb" is from Sir Winston S. Churchill, in an address to the House of Commons, *Parliamentary Papers*, August 16, 1946.

The Toll of Dead and Wounded

Country	Population	No. Served in Forces	Forces Casualties				Total Civilian Casualties
			Killed & Missing	Wounded	P.O.W.	Total Killed & Wounded	
ALBANIA	1,100,000	?	?	?	?	?	?
AUSTRALIA	6,900,000	1,340,000	29,400	39,800	26,400	69,200	—
BELGIUM 1940	8,300,000	650,000	7,500	15,900	200,000	23,400	12,000
BELGIUM in exile		3,500	500	?	?	?	
BULGARIA with Axis	6,300,000	?	?	?	?	?	50,000 killed inc. 40,000 Jews
BULGARIA with Russians		500,000	32,000		?	32,000	
CANADA	11,100,000	1,100,000	39,300	53,200	9,000	92,500	—
CHINA	450,000,000	14,000,000	1,400,000	1,800,000	?	?	8,000,000
CZECHOSLOVAKIA (in exile)	10,300,000	c. 5,000	?	?	?	?	215,000 killed
DENMARK	3,800,000	6,600	?	?	?	?	1,000 killed
FINLAND Winter War	3,800,000	?	24,900	43,600	?	78,500	3,400 killed
FINLAND 1941–44		?	65,000	158,000	?	223,000	
FRANCE 1940	42,000,000	c. 4,000,000	92,000	250,000	1,450,000	342,000	470,000
FRANCE in exile		c. 600,000	c. 30,000	c. 85,000	6,500	c. 115,000	
GERMANY	(1938) 78,000,000	17,900,000	3,250,000	4,606,600	?	7,856,600	2,050,000 killed by Allies 300,000 by Germans
GREECE	7,000,000	?	18,300	60,000	?	78,300	415,000 dead inc. 260,000 from famine
HUNGARY	(Nov 1938) 10,000,000	?	136,000	c. 250,000	?	c. 386,000	300,000
INDIA	359,000,000	2,582,000	36,100	64,300	79,500	100,400	—

"The Toll of Dead and Wounded" is from John Ellis, *World War II: A Statistical Survey* (New York: Facts on File, Inc., 1993), pp. 253–254. Copyright © 1993 by John Ellis. Reprinted by permission of Facts on File, Inc.

Country	Population	No. Served in Forces	Forces Casualties				Total Civilian Casualties
			Killed & Missing	*Wounded*	*P.O.W.*	*Total Killed & Wounded*	
ITALY	43,800,000	?	226,900	?	?	?	60,000 killed
JAPAN	from 1937 72,200,000	9,100,000	1,740,000	94,000	41,000†	1,834,000	393,400 killed 275,000 wounded/ missing
NETHERLANDS 1940	8,700,000	400,000	2,900	6,900	?	9,800	150,000 killed or missing (inc. Asia)
in exile		?	10,800	?	?	?	
NEW ZEALAND	1,600,000	?	12,200	19,300	8,500	31,500	—
NORWAY	2,900,000	25,000	2,000	?	?	?	3,800 killed
POLAND 1939	34,800,000	1,200,000	66,300	133,700	787,000	200,000	4,800,000 killed in camps plus c. 500,000 other dead
in W. Europe		c. 90,000	4,500	13,000	?	27,500	
with Russians		200,000	at least 40,000		?	at least 40,000	
RUMANIA with Axis	(Dec 1937) 19,600,000	?	381,000‡	243,000	?	624,000	340,000 killed
with Russians		540,000	170,000		?	170,000	
S. AFRICA	10,000,000 (inc. 2.1 m. white)	250,000	8,700	14,400	14,600	23,100	—
UK	47,500,000	5,896,000	305,800	277,100	172,600	582,900	146,800 inc. 60,600 killed
USA	129,200,000	16,354,000	405,400	670,800	139,700	1,076,200	—
USSR	194,100,000	c. 30,000,000	11,000,000	?	c. 6,000,000	?	6,700,000
YUGOSLAVIA	15,400,000	?	Estimates of total Yugoslav deaths 1941–45 1.5 to 1.7 million.				

A Portrait of Albert Einstein: "As Long as There Will Be Man, There Will Be Wars" (1947)

PHILLIPPE HALSMAN

One of the most fertile and influential scientific minds in history belonged to Albert Einstein. In addition to his contributions to the field of physics, Einstein was also a great humanist who believed in mankind's ability to change society and progress toward international cooperation. It is ironic that it was Einstein who brought the destructive potential of nuclear energy to the attention of President Roosevelt in 1939. In this excerpt, Phillippe Halsman, one of the most famous photographers of distinguished people, describes his meeting with Einstein in 1947.

I admired Albert Einstein more than anyone I ever photographed, not only as the genius who singlehandedly had changed the foundation of modern physics, but even more as a rare and idealistic human being.

Personally, I owed him an immense debt of gratitude. After the fall of France, it was through his personal intervention that my name was added to the list of artists and scientists who, in danger of being captured by the Nazis, were given emergency visas to the United States.

After my miraculous rescue I went to Princeton to thank Einstein and I remember vividly my first impression. Instead of a frail scientist I saw a deep-chested man with a resonant voice and a hearty laugh. The long hair, which in some photographs gave him the look of an old woman, framed his marvelous face with a kind of leonine mane. He wore slacks, a grey sweater with a fountain pen stuck in its collar, black leather shoes, and no socks.

On my third visit I had the courage to ask him why he did not wear any socks. His secretary, Miss Dukas, who overheard me, said, "The professor never wears socks. Even when he was invited by Mr. Roosevelt to the White House, he did not wear any socks." I looked with surprise at Professor Einstein.

He smiled and said, "When I was young I found out that the big toe always ended up by making a hole in the sock. So I stopped wearing socks." As slight as this remark was, it made an indelible impression on me. This detail seemed symbolic of Einstein's absolute and total independence of thought. It was this independence that gave him the courage when he was an unknown twenty-six-year-old patent clerk to publish a scientific paper which overthrew all the axioms held sacrosanct by the greatest physicists of his time.

The question of how to capture the essence of such a man in a portrait filled me with apprehension. Finally, in 1947, I had the courage to bring on one of my visits my Halsman camera and a few floodlights. After tea, I asked

"A Portrait of Albert Einstein" is from Phillippe Halsman, *Halsman Sight and Insight* (Garden City, N.Y.: Doubleday, 1972), p. 8.

for permission to set up my lights in Einstein's study. The professor sat down and started peacefully working on his mathematical calculations. I took a few pictures. Ordinarily, Einstein did not like photographers, whom he called Lichtaffen (light monkeys). But he cooperated because I was his guest and, after all, he had helped to rescue me.

Suddenly, looking into my camera, he started talking. He spoke about his despair that his formula $E\ 5\ mc^2$ and his letter to President Roosevelt had made the atomic bomb possible, that his scientific search had resulted in the death of so many human beings. "Have you read," he asked, "that powerful voices in the United States are demanding that the bombs be dropped on Russia now, before the Russians have the time to perfect their own?" With my entire being I felt how much this infinitely good and compassionate man was suffering from the knowledge that he had helped to put in the hands of politicians a monstrous weapon of devastation and death.

He grew silent. His eyes had a look of immense sadness. There was a question and a reproach in them.

The spell of this moment almost paralysed me. Then, with an effort, I released the shutter of my camera. Einstein looked up, and I asked him, "So you don't believe that there will ever be peace?"

"No," he answered, "as long as there will be man, there will be wars."

The Responsibility of the Individual (1956)
JEAN-PAUL SARTRE

Existentialism has been an important philosophical movement in the twentieth century. Its premier spokesman, Jean-Paul Sartre, in his book Being and Nothingness, *contends that human beings are condemned to be free and that with freedom comes responsibility for one's choices and actions. Such responsibility for war, life, and death is a burden that cannot be shirked and is not easily borne. The alienation of the individual from society was an axiom for the intellectual crisis that followed World War II.*

The essential consequence of our earlier remarks is that man, being condemned to be free, carries the weight of the whole world on his shoulders; he is responsible for the world and for himself as a way of being. . . . Thus there are no *accidents* in a life. . . . If I am mobilized in a war, this war is *my* war; it is in my image and I deserve it. I deserve it first because I could always get out of it by suicide or by desperation; these ultimate possibilities are those which must always be present for us when there is a question of envisaging a situation. For lack of getting out of it, I have *chosen* it. This can be due to inertia, to cowardice in the face of public opinion, or because I prefer certain other

"The Responsibility of the Individual" is from Jean-Paul Sartre, *Existentialism and Human Emotions* (New York: Philosophical Library, 1957), pp. 52–54, 56–57. Copyright © 1957 by the Philosophical Library Inc. Reprinted by permission of the Philosophical Library Inc.

values to the value of the refusal to join in the war (the good opinion of my relatives, the honor of my family, etc.). Any way you look at it, it is a matter of a choice. This choice will be repeated later on again and again without a break until the end of the war. . . . Thus, totally free, undistinguishable from the period for which I have chosen to be the meaning, as profoundly responsible for the war as if I had myself declared it, unable to live without integrating it in my situation, engaging myself in it wholly and stamping it with my seal, *I must be without remorse or regrets as I am without excuse; for from the instant of my upsurge into being, I carry the weight of the world by myself alone without anything or any person being able to lighten it.*

CHRONOLOGY: The "Good War": World War II (1939–1945)

September 1931   Seeking to fuel their growing war machine, Japan invades the mineral-rich area of Manchuria in China.

January 1933   National Socialist (Nazi) party victorious in general elections. Hitler becomes chancellor of Germany.

October 1933   Germany withdraws from the League of Nations.

March 1935   Hitler renounces disarmament as required by the Treaty of Versailles, starts an air force, and begins conscription into the army.

October 1935   Mussolini attacks Ethiopia and achieves glorious victory over opponents armed with spears.

March 1936   Germany reoccupies and remilitarizes Rhineland in defiance of Versailles and Locarno agreements.

July 1936–1939   Spanish civil war. Fascist forces victorious with armaments supplied by Germany and Italy. Francisco Franco in power until his death in 1975.

October 1936   Formation of the Rome-Berlin Axis. Japan joins Axis in the Anti-Comintern Pact.

March 1938   German Anschluss (unification) with Austria after Nazi invasion halted Austrian plebiscite.

September 1938   Munich conference between Hitler and British Prime Minister Neville Chamberlain. Policy of appeasement results in partition of Czechoslovakia: "Peace for our time."

March 1939   Hitler occupies Prague. Great Britain and France decide to guarantee Polish independence.

August 1939   Nazi-Soviet neutrality pact established. Poland secretly divided between Soviet Union and Germany; Stalin allowed to occupy Baltic States and Bessarabia in Romania in return for neutrality.

September 1, 1939	Germany invades Poland.
September 3, 1939	Britain and France declare war on Germany.
October 1939–March 1940	Sitzkrieg, or "phony war." Hitler consolidates Poland and equips military in preparation for coming attacks against Europe.
April–May 1940	Blitzkrieg, or "lightning war," as German invades Denmark, Norway, the Netherlands, Luxembourg, and France. France falls by June.
August 1940	Battle of Britain begins as Hitler bombs Britain in preparation for invasion across English Channel. Britain saved by Royal Air Force: "So much owed by so many to so few."
June 1941	Germany opens eastern front by invading Soviet Union.
July 1941	Japan takes over Indochina in search of sources of petroleum.
August 1941	FDR and Churchill meet and agree to Atlantic Charter, a broad set of peace principles in the spirit of Wilson's Fourteen Points.
December 7, 1941	Japan attacks American Pacific fleet at Pearl Harbor, Hawaii: "A day which will live in infamy." United States enters war against Axis powers (December 9).
June 1942	Battle of Midway. Japan defeated by United States, thus halting Japanese advance in the Pacific and preventing another attack on Hawaii.
November 1942	Battle of Stalingrad begins. After months of fighting and tremendous losses, the Soviet army defeats the Germans and assumes the offensive.
July–August 1943	Led by Generals Montgomery and Patton, Allies take Sicily and invade Italy.
June 6, 1944	"D-day." Allies land in Normandy in the greatest amphibious invasion in history. Begin move toward Berlin.
December 1944	Battle of the Bulge. Germans launch a counterattack in Belgium through the Ardennes forest. "Last gasp" of German strength in the West as Allies cross Rhine River in March 1945.
February 1945	Allied firebombing of Dresden. Yalta conference held with "Big Three" in attendance (FDR, Churchill, and Stalin) to plan postwar arrangements.
March 1945	American firebombing of Tokyo kills more than eighty thousand Japanese. Battle of Iwo Jima ends after a vicious struggle, leaving six thousand Americans dead. Allies continue move toward Japan. Okinawa falls to Allies in April.

April 12, 1945   Death of Franklin Roosevelt. Harry S. Truman succeeds.

May 1945   Germany surrenders. Hitler and associates commit suicide in Berlin bunker.

July 1945   Potsdam conference (Truman, Atlee, and Stalin) to discuss postwar arrangements.

August 1945   Atomic bombs dropped on Hiroshima and Nagasaki. Surrender of Japanese on September 2, 1945.

STUDY QUESTIONS

1. What justification does Hitler give for his remilitarization of the Rhineland in 1936? In what ways does he appear to be a statesman seeking legitimate security for Germany?
2. How would you define the policy of "appeasement"? Carefully read the selections on the German *Anschluss* with Austria and the Czechoslovakian crisis of 1938–1939. According to these documents, what arguments did Hitler use to justify his incorporation of Austria, the Sudetenland, and finally other regions of Czechoslovakia? Was Hitler consistent in his approach? What is your evaluation of Hitler's diplomatic skills? What were his goals, and how specifically did he achieve them?
3. Note the document entitled "Hitler Mulling over the Options." This reveals Hitler's thought process concerning the pros and cons of a Polish invasion. Why does he think that the invasion of Poland would be successful, and why must it take place soon? Why was the German neutrality pact with the Soviet Union so important to Hitler's plans? What does this pact say about the Soviet leader Joseph Stalin?
4. In Neville Chamberlain's radio address to the British people on September 3, 1939, wherein he explains why Britain has gone to war against Germany, he stated: "I cannot believe that there is anything more or anything different that I could have done that would have been more successful." Do you agree with this evaluation? What was his evaluation of Hitler's intentions in this document? Ultimately, why did Chamberlain's appeasement policy fail? Could this failure have been predicted?
5. Analyze Winston Churchill's war speeches. What are the most impressive techniques that he used to inspire the people of Great Britain? Did Neville Chamberlain have the qualities necessary to head the British war effort?
6. After reading the documents and firsthand accounts of the Japanese attack on Pearl Harbor, what images stand out in your mind? Was the attack well planned? How did the Japanese miscalculate?
7. What roles did women play during World War II? How important were their contributions to the war effort? Answer this question with specific reference to the selections by and about women.
8. Why did the Japanese resort to suicide attacks on American aircraft carriers during 1944 and 1945? What is the general impression you receive from the letters

and diary accounts written by kamikaze pilots? Was the Japanese government asking a greater sacrifice from them than the British and American governments asked of their pilots and soldiers during the Battle of Britain or the D-day invasions? How do you interpret the phrase of the kamikaze pilot that should Japan suddenly win the war "it would be a fatal misfortune for the future of the nation"? What did he mean?

9. Do you think that President Truman was justified in using the atomic bomb on Hiroshima and Nagasaki? Are Churchill's arguments in support of this decision convincing? Does "total war" have limits? Is there an acceptable versus unacceptable degree of destruction, and where is the line of demarcation?

10. The first and only time nuclear weapons have been directed against human beings occurred in 1945. For those born after this date, can the terror of that long-ago event maintain our allegiance toward arms control, or must we have an example of an atomic explosion every generation or so in order to promote the seriousness of negotiation? Will people forget the horrors of Hiroshima the further they are removed by time from the experience?

11. Analyze the casualty statistics for World War II. Which countries suffered the greatest number of soldiers who were killed or wounded? Which countries suffered the greatest casualties as a percentage of those who served in the armed forces? Finally, which countries suffered the greatest civilian casualties? How can these statistics be misleading?

12. According to Jean-Paul Sartre, why are there no "accidents" in life? Why has existentialism often been called a "depressing philosophy"? If being "free" is usually considered an advantageous human condition, why does the existentialist believe that he is "condemned to be free"? Do you think that Albert Einstein was correct in his assessment that "As long as there will be man, there will be wars"?

10

The Jewish Holocaust

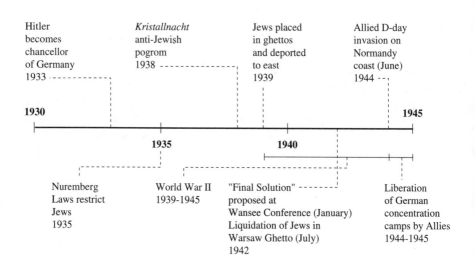

Hitler becomes chancellor of Germany 1933

Kristallnacht anti-Jewish pogrom 1938

Jews placed in ghettos and deported to east 1939

Allied D-day invasion on Normandy coast (June) 1944

1930

1945

1935

1940

Nuremberg Laws restrict Jews 1935

World War II 1939-1945

"Final Solution" proposed at Wansee Conference (January) Liquidation of Jews in Warsaw Ghetto (July) 1942

Liberation of German concentration camps by Allies 1944-1945

I mean the clearing out of the Jews, the extermination of the Jewish race. . . . Most of you must know what it means when 100 corpses are lying side by side, or 500, or 1,000. To have stuck it out and at the same time . . . to have remained decent fellows, that is what has made us hard. This is a page of glory in our history which has never been written and is never to be written. . . .

—Heinrich Himmler to his S.S. Officers

In spite of everything, I still believe that people are really good at heart.

—Anne Frank

464

Whoever fights monsters should see to it that in the process he does not become a monster; and when you look long into an abyss, the abyss also looks into you.

—Friedrich Nietzsche

Man does not deny that terrible things have happened and still go on happening, but it is always the others who do them. And when such deeds belong to the recent or remote past, they quickly and conveniently sink into the sea of forgetfulness. . . . [but] Man has done these things; I am a man, who has his share of human nature; therefore, I am guilty with the rest and bear . . . within me the inclination to do them again at any time. Even if . . . we were not accessories to the crime, we are always, thanks to our human nature, potential criminals. In reality, we merely lacked a suitable opportunity to be drawn into the infernal melee. None of us stands outside humanity's black collective shadow.

—Carl Jung

Despair is no solution. I know that. What is the solution? Hitler had one. And he tried it while a civilized world kept silent. I remember. And I am afraid.

—Elie Wiesel

CHAPTER THEMES

- *Beliefs and Spirituality:*   Why did the Holocaust take place, and who bears ultimate responsibility? One might argue that the Nazi attack on the Jews was an aberration, but do the values and ideas promulgated by the Nazis have their origins in history with established precedents? How did the Jews survive?

- *Propaganda:*   How did the Nazis tap a core of resentment and fear in the German people that allowed Jews, gypsies, homosexuals, and dissident Germans to be persecuted and the Final Solution to become a logical, necessary end? If a government controls access to information and image, thus possessing the mind of a people, is anything possible?

- *Historical Change and Transition:*   Could the Holocaust happen again, and would contemporary technology make genocide a reality? Can the "ethnic cleansing" by Serbian soldiers in Bosnia and Kosovo be likened to the Final Solution of the Nazis? What is the value of studying history?

- *The Big Picture:*   Why? But isn't the bigger question "Why not?" Why not do what our technology allows us to do? Why not give up personal freedom and moral responsibility to think and act as one people with a common, efficient purpose?

In 1933, Adolf Hitler was appointed chancellor of the German Weimar Republic, a post of prestige and authority. His National Socialist party was swept into power on the promises made to end the rampant inflation and unemployment that plagued the German economy, and to restore the dignity of the German people, who had been humiliated by the onerous Treaty of Versailles. Germany had to accept the harsh terms of this peace that resolved World War I and was especially dissatisfied with the stipulation that Germany alone had been responsible for the war. Hitler's program presented a vision of the future, and his speeches inspired a defeated nation. His constant demands for more "living space" (*Lebensraum*) extended the boundaries of Germany, as Austria and the Sudetenland of Czechoslovakia were incorporated. By 1939, Hitler had revived the German economy and set the people back to work building the armaments that were to maintain a strong, united Germany. The other nations of Europe, particularly Great Britain, had generally appeased Hitler and allowed him to incorporate more territory, thinking that each demand would be his last. When Hitler invaded Poland in 1939, he went too far and the world once again went to war.

The road to World War II is, of course, a twisted one, and there are many different aspects to Hitler's rise and ultimate destruction. The name Adolf Hitler has become synonymous with evil. Much of this reputation has been derived from his attempt to commit genocide, to exterminate an entire race of people. One of the more distinctive differences between Italian fascism under Benito Mussolini (1883–1945) and the Nazi movement was Hitler's use of anti-Semitism. Hitler demanded that Germany be composed of racially pure Aryan stock. The blond, blue-eyed German, untainted by inferior blood, became Hitler's ideal and the image he tried to cultivate in his propaganda. Hitler saw the Jews as the source of all of Germany's trouble. According to Hitler, Jews were cowards who did not support the fatherland in the Great War. They had deep communist sympathies, controlled international finance, and dominated the most important offices in government. Jews also controlled the purse strings of the nation and thus prevented worthier and more talented individuals from holding jobs and contributing to German culture. Indeed, Hitler had once been a frustrated artist in Vienna who blamed his failure on such Jewish influence. Hitler understood that hatred often unifies a nation more readily than does love. In troubled times, people want a simple explanation for their pain and insecurity. For Hitler, and consequently for Germany, that explanation was the Jew.

Anti-Semitism certainly did not originate with Hitler. Jews had been persecuted since the Middle Ages and even blamed for such things as outbreaks of bubonic plague. Still, never before was there such a systematic, methodical attempt to exterminate an entire race.

Although Hitler had exhibited his racism from the early 1920s in speeches and writings, and had incorporated it into the philosophy of National Socialism, nothing could be implemented until the Nazis came into power. By 1935, Jews were excluded from citizenship by law in order to preserve German blood and honor.

Germany was saturated with propaganda that presented the Jew as an immoral pervert whose presence was a threat to the health and morality of the German community. Nazi policy slowly evolved toward deportation and then toward isolation of the Jews in city ghettos. The "Final Solution" to the Jewish problem actually began in June 1941. As Hitler's armies drove into Russia, special mobile killing units (*Einsatzgruppen*) were set up and followed just behind the front lines. For eighteen months, the *Einsatzgruppen* operated and killed over 1.3 million Jews. The Nazis also built several concentration camps generally designed to house workers and remove Jews from society. The treatment of prisoners was cruel, and hundreds of thousands died of exhaustion, starvation, and disease. The Nazi commitment to Jewish extermination even exceeded the bounds of practicality. Although there was a widespread shortage of labor throughout German-controlled Europe during the war, the Nazis continued to wipe out valuable workers. The camps, run by Hitler's private army called the "S.S." (*Schutzstaffel*), often served as holding pens until the inmates were sent by train to six death camps located in Poland. Created solely for the task of killing, the camps at Auschwitz and Treblinka have become infamous—over 2.7 million Jews were eliminated, 1 million in Auschwitz alone. Thousands of other undesirable people such as gypsies, Slavs, and even dissident Germans were also killed.

Many questions arise out of the Holocaust that make this a particularly important and relevant historical problem. How could such a violation against humanity have happened? Could it happen again? Can one view the Jewish Holocaust as a precedent that legitimized the dropping of the atomic bomb on Hiroshima and Nagasaki? Can one say, "War is Hell," and let it go at that? How deep and penetrating is the racial argument? Do we all have prejudices, which, if exploited properly, can lead to such results? The urgency of these questions is intensified when we consider other issues such as the policy of "ethnic cleansing" by the Serbs in Bosnia or the influence of the Ku Klux Klan; the millions who were murdered by Stalin during Soviet collectivization, industrialization, and the Great Purges of the 1930s; the ruthlessness of the Cambodian dictator Pol Pot; or the maniacal ranting of Muammar Gaddafi or Saddam Hussein.

Not forgetting is the responsibility of the living.

———— ೲ ೞ ————

The Evolution of Nazi Jewish Policy

Anti-Semitism was one of the cornerstones of Nazi dogma. When Hitler became chancellor in 1933, he began the process of excluding Jews from life in the German Reich. Note the charges that are leveled against the Jews in one of Hitler's early speeches. Indeed, Jews felt compelled to defend themselves against accusations that they were in control of international finance and the German government, or that they were cowards who forsook Germany in World War I. With the adoption of the Nuremberg Laws in 1935, Hitler excluded Jews from German citizenship and made provisions to restrict their social relations.

Jewish Responsibility

The Jewish Peril (April 1923)

ADOLF HITLER

The German people was once clear thinking and simple: why has it lost these characteristics? Any inner renewal is possible only if one realizes that this is a question of race: America forbids the yellow peoples to settle there, but this is a lesser peril than that which stretches out its hand over the entire world—the Jewish peril. Many hold that the Jews are not a race, but is there a second people anywhere in the wide world which is so determined to maintain its race?

As a matter of fact the Jew can never become a German however often he may affirm that he can. If he wished to become a German, he must surrender the Jew in him. And that is not possible: he cannot, however much he tries, become a German at heart, and that for several reasons: first because of his blood, second because of his character, thirdly because of his will, and fourthly because of his actions. His actions remain Jewish: he works for the "greater idea" of the Jewish people. Because that is so, because it cannot be otherwise, therefore the bare existence of the Jew as part of another State rests upon a monstrous lie. It is a lie when he pretends to the peoples to be a German, a Frenchman, etc.

What then are the specifically Jewish aims?

To spread their invisible State as a supreme tyranny over all other States in the whole world. The Jew is therefore a disintegrator of peoples. To realize his rule over the peoples he must work in two directions: in economics he dominates peoples when he subjugates them politically and morally: in politics he dominates them through the propagation of the principles of democracy and the doctrines of Marxism—the creed which makes a Proletarian a Terrorist in the domestic sphere and a Pacifist in foreign policy. Ethically the Jew destroys the peoples both in religion and in morals. He who wishes to see that can see it, and him who refuses to see it no one can help.

The Jew, whether consciously or unconsciously, whether he wishes it or not, undermines the platform on which alone a nation can stand.

We are now met by the questions: Do we wish to restore Germany to freedom and power? If "yes": then the first thing to do is to rescue it from him who is ruining our country. Admittedly it is a hard fight that must be fought here. We National Socialists on this point occupy an extreme position: but we know only one people: it is for that people we fight and that is our own people. . . . We want to stir up a storm. Men must not sleep: they ought to know that a thunder-storm is coming up. We want to prevent our Germany from suffering, as Another did, the death upon the Cross.

"The Jewish Peril" is from Norman H. Baynes, trans. and ed., *The Speeches of Adolf Hitler*, April, 1922–1939, vol. 1, pp. 59–60 (London, RIIA/Oxford University Press, 1942). Reprinted by kind permission of the Royal Institute of International Affairs, London.

We may be inhumane, but if we rescue Germany we have achieved the greatest deed in the world! We may work injustice, but if we rescue Germany then we have removed the greatest injustice in the world. We may be immoral, but if our people is rescued we have once more opened up the way for morality!

Jewish Defense
"Not a Single Jew" (1932)

Jewish World Finance

Today, capital formation takes place in large industry. Its largest enterprises are almost entirely dominated by non-Jewish interests: Krupp, Vereinigte Stahlwerke, Klockner, Stinnes, Siemeins, Stumm, I. G. Farben, Hugenberg, Hapag, Nordlloyd.

International connections are concentrated most heavily in those industries in which Jews are without influence or altogether unrepresented: the German-French iron cartel, wooden matches trust, oil trust, potash industry, and shipping conventions are all "clean of Jews," and so are the international chemical cartel, nylon production and all the other raw material and key industries in which Jews have no influence either as owners or directors. . . .

Jewish Government

The anti-Semites assert that the German government is full of Jews. The 19 post-war cabinets consisted of 237 ministers of whom three (Preuss and twice Rathenau) were Jews and four (Landsberg, Gradnauer, and twice Hilferding) of Jewish descent. The last few governments have had no Jewish ministers.

In the German provinces, the situation is not different: none of the provincial cabinets contain a Jew. The administration is not full of Jews, either. For example, in Prussia, among the twelve chief presidents, thirty-five government presidents and four hundred provincial counsellors, there is not a single Jew. . . .

The Jews in World War I

Of 538,000 Jews in Germany, more than 96,000 were under arms, including 10,000 volunteers; about 80,000 were on the front lines, 35,000 received decorations, 23,000 were promoted, including more than 2000 to officer rank (without medical corps). One hundred sixty-eight Jews who volunteered as flyers are known by name. At the top of the list is Lieutenant D. R. Frankl who

"'Not a Single Jew'" is from Raul Hilberg, ed., *Documents of Destruction* (Chicago: Quadrangle Books, 1971), pp. 8–11. Reprinted by permission of the author.

received the *Pour le merite* [combat medal] and who like 29 other Jewish flyers was killed in battle.

Twelve thousand Jewish soldiers did not see their homeland again; they *died a hero's death for their German fatherland.* More than 10,000 of their names have now been recorded with personal information, unit, and number. The dead of Hamburg, Alsace-Lorraine and ceded Posen (with its relatively large Jewish population) have not yet been registered.

It is heartless to demand today that the widows and orphans, parents and brothers, brides and relatives of 12,000 fallen Jews be deprived of equality in Germany.

Legal Restriction of the Jews: The Nuremberg Laws

Law for the Protection of German Blood and German Honor (September 1935)

Entirely convinced that the purity of German blood is essential to the further existence of the German people, and inspired by the uncompromising determination to safeguard the future of the German nation, the Reichstag has unanimously resolved upon the following law, which is promulgated herewith:

Section 1

Marriages between Jews and citizens of German or kindred blood are forbidden. Marriages concluded in defiance of this law are void, even if, for the purpose of evading this law, they were concluded abroad.

Proceedings for annulment may be initiated only by the Public Prosecutor.

Section 2

Sexual relations outside marriage between Jews and nationals of German or kindred blood are forbidden.

Section 3

Jews will not be permitted to employ female citizens of German or kindred blood as domestic servants.

"Law for the Protection of German Blood and German Honor" is from Jeremy Noakes and Geoffrey Pridham, eds., *Documents on Nazism, 1919–1945*, pp. 463–464. Reprinted by permission of Peters, Fraser, & Dunlop Group, Ltd.

Section 4

Jews are forbidden to display the Reich and national flag or the national colours.

On the other hand they are permitted to display the Jewish colours. The exercise of this right is protected by the State.

Section 5

A person who acts contrary to the prohibition of Section 1 will be punished with hard labour.

A person who acts contrary to the prohibition of Section 2 will be punished with imprisonment or with hard labour.

A person who acts contrary to the provisions of Sections 3 or 4 will be punished with imprisonment up to a year and with a fine, or with one of these penalties.

The Reich Citizenship Law (September 1935)

Article 1

1. A subject of the State is a person who belongs to the protective union of the German Reich, and who therefore has particular obligations towards the Reich.

2. The status of subject is acquired in accordance with the provisions of the Reich and State Law of Citizenship.

Article 2

1. A citizen of the Reich is that subject only who is of German or kindred blood and who, through his conduct, shows that he is both desirous and fit to serve the German people and Reich faithfully.

2. The right to citizenship is acquired by the granting of Reich citizenship papers.

3. Only the citizen of the Reich enjoys full political rights in accordance with the provision of the laws.

"The Reich Citizenship Law" is from Jeremy Noakes and Geoffrey Pridham, eds., *Documents on Nazism, 1919–1945*, pp. 464–465. Reprinted by permission of Peters, Fraser, & Dunlop Group, Ltd.

Anti-Jewish Propaganda

In 1936, Germany hosted the Olympic Games, and Hitler ordered the temporary removal of anti-Jewish placards in order to appease foreign opinion. Still, the propaganda continued to flow, especially from Der Stürmer, a sensationalistic journal published by Julius Streicher. In the first selection, note the accusation of cannibalism and the misrepresentation of the two Jewish festivals of Purim and Passover, which commemorate not murder but deliverance from oppression. The second excerpt is from a book for older children called Der Giftpilz (The Poisonous Mushroom), which presented the Jew as an evil deviate who preyed on the innocence of children.

Ritual Murder: *Der Stürmer* (1937)

The murder of the 10 year old Gertrud Lenhoff in Quirschied (Saarpfalz)

* * * The Jews are our MISFORTUNE! * * *

Also the numerous confessions made by the Jews show that the execution of ritual murders is a law to the Talmud Jew. The former Chief Rabbi (and later monk) Teofiti declares ... that the ritual murders take place especially on the Jewish Purim (in memory of the Persian murders) and Passover (in memory of the murder of Christ).

The instructions are as follows:

The blood of the victims is to be tapped by force. On Passover, it is to be used in wine and matzos; thus, a small part of the blood is to be poured into the dough of the matzos and into the wine. The mixing is done by the Jewish head of the family.

The procedure is as follows: the family head empties a few drops of the fresh and powdered blood into the glass, wets the fingers of the left hand with it and sprays (blesses) with it everything on the table. The head of the family then says: "Dam Izzardia chynim heroff dever Isyn porech harbe hossen maschus pohorus" (Exod. 7.12) ("Thus we ask God to send the ten plagues to all enemies of the Jewish faith.") Then they eat, and at the end the head of the family exclaims: "Sfach, chaba, moscho kol hagoym!" ("May all Gentiles perish—as the child whose blood is contained in the bread and wine!")

The fresh (or dried and powdered) blood of the slaughtered is further used by young married Jewish couples, by pregnant Jewesses, for circumcisions, and so on. Ritual murder is recognized by all Talmud Jews. The Jew believes he absolves himself thus of his sins.

"Ritual Murder: Der Stürmer" is from the Office of the U.S. Chief of Counsel for the Prosecution of Axis Criminality, *Nazi Conspiracy and Aggression* (Washington, D.C.: Government Printing Office, 1947), vol. 5, pp. 372–373 (PS-2699).

The Poisonous Mushroom (1938)

ERNST HIEMER

"It is almost noon," he said, "now we want to summarize what we have learned in this lesson. What did we discuss?"

All the children raise their hands. The teacher calls on Karl Scholz, a little boy on the first bench. "We talked about how to recognize a Jew."

"Good! Now tell us about it!"

Little Karl takes the pointer, goes to the blackboard and points to the sketches.

"One usually recognizes a Jew by his nose. The Jewish nose is crooked at the end. It looks like the figure 6. Therefore it is called the 'Jewish Six.' Many non-Jews have crooked noses, too. But their noses are bent, not at the end but further up. Such a nose is called a hook nose or eagle's beak. It has nothing to do with a Jewish nose."

"Right!" says the teacher. "But the Jew is recognized not only by his nose. . . ." The boy continues. "The Jew is also recognized by his lips. His lips are usually thick. Often the lower lip hangs down. This is called 'sloppy.' And the Jew is also recognized by his eyes. His eyelids are usually thicker and more fleshy than ours. The look of the Jew is lurking and sharp."

Then the teacher goes to the desk and turns over the blackboard, on its back is a verse. The children recite it in chorus:

From a Jew's countenance—the evil devil talks to us,
The devil, who in every land—is known as evil plague.
If we shall be free of the Jew—and again will be happy and glad,
Then the youth must struggle with us—to subdue the Jew devil.

Inge sits in the reception room of the Jew doctor. She has to wait a long time. She looks through the journals which are on the table. But she is almost too nervous to read even a few sentences. Again and again she remembers the talk with her mother. And again and again her mind reflects on the warnings of her leader of the BDM [League of German Girls]: "A German must not consult a Jew doctor! And particularly not a German girl! Many a girl that went to a Jew doctor to be cured, found disease and disgrace!"

When Inge had entered the waiting room, she experienced an extraordinary incident. From the doctor's consulting room she could hear the sound of crying. She heard the voice of a young girl: "Doctor, doctor leave me alone!"

Then she heard the scornful laughing of a man. And then all of a sudden it became absolutely silent. Inge had listened breathlessly.

"What may be the meaning of all this?" she asked herself and her heart was pounding. And again she thought of the warning of her leader in the BDM.

"The Poisonous Mushroom" is from the Office of the U.S. Chief of Counsel for the Prosecution of Axis Criminality, *Nazi Conspiracy and Aggression* (Washington, D.C.: Government Printing Office, 1947), vol. 4, pp. 358–359 (PS-1778).

Inge was already waiting for an hour. Again she takes the journals in an endeavor to read. Then the door opens. Inge looks up. The Jew appears. She screams. In terror she drops the paper. Frightened she jumps up. Her eyes stare into the face of the Jewish doctor. And this face is the face of the devil. In the middle of this devil's face is a huge crooked nose. Behind the spectacles two criminal eyes. And the thick lips are grinning. A grinning that expresses: "Now I got you at last, you little German girl!"

And then the Jew approaches her. His fleshy fingers stretch out after her. But now Inge has her wits. Before the Jew can grab hold of her, she hits the fat face of the Jew doctor with her hand. Then one jump to the door. Breathlessly she escapes the Jew house.

The Radicalization of Anti-Semitism (1938–1941)

On November 9–10, 1938, the Nazis, in retaliation for the assassination of a German diplomat, set fire to Jewish synagogues and systematically destroyed 7,500 Jewish stores. The incident became known as Kristallnacht *(Crystal Night) because of the broken glass that covered the street. A few days later, Reich Marshal Hermann Goering called a meeting of some of the Nazi hierarchy (Reinhard Heydrich and Joseph Goebbels) to place ultimate responsibility for the destruction on the Jews. It was decided that the Jews would have to pay for the damage they "provoked." In the first selection, note the mention of ideas (separate schools, badges, and ghettos) that achieved fruition later as indicated in the second selection. Hitler gave little doubt as to his intentions regarding the Jews in a speech given before the Reichstag in 1939. Joseph Goebbels, the minister of propaganda, capitalized on this official anti-Semitic stance of the German government in his tract, which blamed the war on the Jews.*

Conference on the Jewish Question
(November 12, 1938)

Goering: I should not want to leave any doubt, gentlemen, as to the aim of today's meeting. We have not come together merely to talk again, but to make decisions, and I implore the competent agencies to take all measures for the elimination of the Jew from German economy and to submit them to me, as far as it is necessary. . . .

Furthermore, I advocate that the Jews be eliminated from all positions in public life in which they may prove to be provocative. . . . Jews should not be allowed to sit around in German parks. I am thinking of the whispering campaign on the part of Jewish women in the public gardens at Fehrbelliner Platz. They go and sit with German mothers and their children and begin to gossip and incite. I see in

"Conference on the Jewish Question" is from Office of the U.S. Chief of Counsel for the Prosecution of Axis Criminality, *Nazi Conspiracy and Aggression* (Washington, D.C.: Government Printing Office, 1947), vol. 4, pp. 426, 432–434 (PS-1816).

this a particularly grave danger. I think it is imperative to give the Jews certain public parks, not the best ones—and tell them: "You may sit on these benches," these benches shall be marked, "For Jews only." Besides that they have no business in German parks. Furthermore, Jewish children are still allowed in German schools. That's impossible. It is out of the question that any boy should sit beside a Jewish boy in a German gymnasium and receive lessons in German history. Jews ought to be eliminated completely from German schools; they may take care of their own education in their own communities. . . .

Heydrich: As another means of getting the Jews out, measures for Emigration are to be taken in the rest of the Reich for the next 8 to 10 years.

The highest number of Jews we can possibly get out during one year is 8,000 to 10,000. Therefore, a great number of Jews will remain. Because of aryanizing and other restrictions, Jewry will become unemployed. The remaining Jews gradually become proletarians. Therefore, I shall have to take steps; to isolate the Jew so he won't enter into the German normal routine of life. On the other hand, I shall have to restrict the Jew to a small circle of consumers, but I shall have to permit certain activities within professions; lawyers, doctors, barbers, etc. This question shall also have to be examined.

As for the isolation, I'd like to make a few proposals regarding police measures which are important also because of their psychological effect on public opinion. For example, who is Jewish according to the Nuremberg laws shall have to wear a certain insignia. That is a possibility which shall facilitate many other things. I don't see any danger of excuses, and it shall make our relationship with the foreign Jew easier.

Goering: A uniform?

Heydrich: An insignia. This way we could also put an end to it that the foreign Jews who don't look different from ours, are being molested.

Goering: But, my dear Heydrich, you won't be able to avoid the creation of ghettos on a very large scale, in all the cities. They shall have to be created.

Police Decree Concerning the Marking of Jews (September 1941)

Paragraph 1

1. Jews over the age of six are forbidden to show themselves in public without a Jew's star.
2. The Jew's star consists of a six-pointed star of yellow cloth with black borders, equivalent in size to the palm of the hand. The inscription is to read "JEW" in black letters. It is to be sewn to the left breast of the garment, and to be worn visibly.

"Police Decree Concerning the Marking of Jews" is from *The Nazi Years: A Documentary History*, ed. Joachim Remak, p. 151. © 1969. Used by permission of Prentice-Hall, Inc., Upper Saddle River, N.J.

Paragraph 2

Jews are Forbidden

a) to leave their area of residence without carrying, on their person, written permission from the local police.
b) to wear medals, decorations, or other insignia. . . .

Speech to the Reichstag: "The Annihilation of the Jewish Race in Europe!" (January 30, 1939)
ADOLF HITLER

One thing I should like to say on this day which may be memorable for others as well as for us Germans. In the course of my life I have very often been a prophet, and have usually been ridiculed for it. During the time of my struggle for power it was in the first instance only the Jewish race that received my prophecies with laughter when I said that I would one day take over the leadership of the State, and with it that of the whole nation, and that I would then among other things settle the Jewish problem. Their laughter was uproarious, but I think that for some time now they have been laughing on the other side of their face. Today I will once more be a prophet: if the international Jewish financiers in and outside Europe should succeed in plunging the nations once more into a world war, then the result will not be the Bolshevizing of the earth, and thus the victory of Jewry, but the annihilation of the Jewish race in Europe!

The Jews Are to Blame! (1941)
JOSEPH GOEBBELS

World Jewry's historic guilt for the outbreak and extension of this war has been so abundantly proven that no additional words need to be lost over the matter. The Jews wanted their war. Now they have it. But what is also coming true for them is the Führer's prophecy which he voiced in his Reichstag speech of January 30, 1939. It was that if international financial Jewry succeeded in plunging the nations into another world war, the result would not be the Bolshevization of the world and thus the victory of Jewry, but the destruction of the Jewish race in Europe.

We are now witnessing the acid test of this prophecy, and thus Jewry is experiencing a fate which is hard but more than deserved. Pity or even regrets are entirely out of place here. World Jewry, in starting this war, made an

---

"Speech to the Reichstag" is from Norman H. Baynes, trans. and ed., *The Speeches of Adolf Hitler,* April, 1922–1939, vol. 1, pp. 740–741 (London, RIIA/Oxford University Press, 1942). Reprinted by kind permission of the Royal Institute of International Affairs, London.

"The Jews Are to Blame!" is from *The Nazi Years: A Documentary History,* ed. Joachim Remak, pp. 155–156. © 1969. Used by permission of Prentice-Hall, Inc., Upper Saddle River, N.J.

entirely wrong estimate of the forces at its disposal, and is now suffering the same gradual process of destruction which it had planned for us, and which it would apply without hesitation were it to possess the power to do so. It is in line with their own law, "An eye for an eye, a tooth for a tooth," that the ruin of the Jews is now taking place. . . .

So, superfluous though it might be, let me say once more:

1. The Jews are our destruction. They provoked and brought about this war. What they mean to achieve by it is to destroy the German state and nation. This plan must be frustrated.

2. There is no difference between Jew and Jew. Every Jew is a sworn enemy of the German people. If he fails to display his hostility against us, it is merely out of cowardice and slyness, but not because his heart is free of it.

3. Every German soldier's death in this war is the Jew's responsibility. They have it on their conscience; hence they must pay for it.

4. Anyone wearing the Jew's star has been marked as an enemy of the nation. Any person who still maintains social relations with him is one of them, and must be considered a Jew himself and treated as such. He deserves the contempt of the entire nation, which he has deserted in its gravest hour to join the side of those who hate it.

5. The Jews enjoy the protection of the enemy nations. No further proof is needed of their destructive role among our people.

6. The Jews are the messengers of the enemy in our midst. Anyone joining them is going over to the enemy in time of war.

7. The Jews have no claim to pretend to have rights equal to ours. Wherever they want to open their mouths, in the street, in the lines in front of the stores, or on public transportation, they are to be silenced. They are to be silenced not only because they are wrong on principle, but because they are Jews and have no voice in the community.

8. If Jews pull a sentimental act for you, bear in mind that they are speculating on your forgetfullness. Show them immediately that you see right through them and punish them with contempt.

9. A decent enemy, after his defeat, deserves our generosity. But the Jew is no decent enemy. He only pretends to be one.

10. The Jews are to blame for this war. The treatment we give them does them no wrong; they have more than deserved it. . . .

The Final Solution (1941–1945)

By 1940, the Nazis had embarked on a policy that was designed to "cleanse" the German homeland of Jews by confining them to ghettos in cities, especially in Poland. There the Nazis could control them and, upon demand, export them to concentration camps where they would be put to work or die. But in July 1941, preparations were made for a secretive "Final Solution" to the Jewish problem. It was discussed in more detail at the Wansee Conference in January 1942, as the following excerpts indicate.

Official Policy

Decree of the Reich Marshal (July 31, 1941)
HERMANN GOERING

To: The Chief of the Security Police and the Security Service; SS-Gruppen-fuehrer Heydrich

Complementing the task that was assigned to you on 24 January 1939, which dealt with the carrying out of emigration and evacuation, a solution of the Jewish problem, as advantageous as possible, I hereby charge you with making all necessary preparations in regard to organizational and financial matters for bringing out a complete solution of the Jewish question in the German sphere of influence in Europe.

Wherever other governmental agencies are involved, these are to cooperate with you.

I charge you furthermore to send me, before long, an overall plan concerning the organizational, factual and material measures necessary for the accomplishment of the desired solution of the Jewish question.

Wansee Conference (January 20, 1942)

II. At the beginning of the meeting the Chief of the Security Police and the SD, SS Lieutenant General Heydrich, reported his appointment by the Reich Marshal to service as Commissioner for the Preparation of the Final Solution of the European Jewish Problem, and pointed out that the officials had been invited to this conference in order to clear up the fundamental problems. The Reich Marshal's request to have a draft submitted to him on the organizational, factual, and material requirements with respect to the Final Solution of the European Jewish Problem, necessitated this previous general consultation by all the central offices directly concerned, in order that there should be coordination in the policy.

The primary responsibility for the administrative handling of the Final Solution of the Jewish Problem will rest centrally with the Reich Leader SS and the Chief of the German Police (Chief of the Security Police and the SD)—regardless of geographic boundaries.

The Chief of the Security Police and the SD thereafter gave a brief review of the battle conducted up to now against these enemies. The most important are—

    a. Forcing the Jews out of the various fields of the community life of the German people.

"Decree of the Reich Marshal" is from the Office of the U.S. Chief Counsel for Prosecution of Axis Criminality, *Nazi Conspiracy and Aggression* (Washington, D.C.: Government Printing Office, 1947), vol. 3, pp. 525–526 (PS-710).

"Wansee Conference" is from the Nuremberg Military Tribunals, *Trials of War Criminals* (Washington, D.C.: Government Printing Office, 1947–1949), vol. 13, pp. 211–213.

b. Forcing the Jews out of the living space [*Lebensraum*] of the German people.

• • •

Meanwhile, in view of the dangers of emigration during the war and in view of the possibilities in the East, the Reich Leader SS and Chief of the German Police had forbidden the emigrating of the Jews.

III. The emigration program has now been replaced by the evacuation of the Jews to the East as a further solution possibility, in accordance with previous authorization by the Fuehrer.

These actions are of course to be regarded only as a temporary substitute; nonetheless, here already, the coming Final Solution of the Jewish Question is of great importance. In the course of this Final Solution of the European Jewish Problem, approximately 11 million Jews are involved.

Under proper direction the Jews should now in the course of the Final Solution be brought to the East in a suitable way for use as labor. In big labor gangs, with separation of the sexes, the Jews capable of work are brought to these areas and employed in road building, in which task undoubtedly a great part will fall out through natural diminution.

The remnant that finally is able to survive all this—since this is undoubtedly the part with the strongest resistance—must be treated accordingly since these people, representing a natural selection, are to be regarded as the germ cell of a new Jewish development. (See the experience of history.)

In the program of the practical execution of the Final Solution, Europe is combed through from the West to the East.

The evacuated Jews are brought first group by group into the so-called transit ghettos, in order to be transported from these farther to the East.

The Death Camps

The "Final Solution" ordered the implementation of a policy of genocide. Hitler wanted to rid the world of a people whom he found responsible for most of humanity's ills. The following selections present the system of extermination from the trip to the death camp by train through the selection process and the gas chambers. Much of the testimony in this section comes from the Nuremberg trial proceedings in 1946. Hermann Gräbe ("The Pit") was a German construction engineer working in the Ukraine in 1942. Kurt Gerstein ("Gas") was the S.S. head of Disinfection Services in early 1942. The gassing of Jews did not take place at concentration or death camps alone, as is noted by the selection entitled "Mobile Killing." This is a top secret dispatch concerning the Einsatzgruppen *that often followed advancing troops. Excerpts from the autobiography and Nuremberg testimony of Rudolf Hoess are also included. He was commandant of the notorious Auschwitz death camp and was himself executed there in 1947 after being judged guilty of crimes against humanity.*

Sites of Nazi Concentration Camps

"Sites of Nazi Concentration Camps" is from Louis L. Snyder, *Encyclopedia of the Third Reich* (New York: McGraw-Hill Book Company, 1976), p. 57. Reprinted by permission of the publisher.

Arrival: The Death Train

ELIE WIESEL

Indescribable confusion reigned.

Parents searched for their children, children for their parents, and lonely captives for their friends. The people were beset by loneliness. Everyone feared that the outcome of the journey would be tragic and would claim its toll of lives. And so one yearned to have the companionship of someone who would stand by with a word, with a loving glance.

Afterward, an ominous silence fell upon us. We squatted on the soft snow that covered the floor of the railroad car like a carpet, and tried to keep warm by drawing closer to our neighbors.

When the train started to move, no one paid any attention to it. Careworn and burdened with conflicting thoughts, each of us wondered if he was wise to continue on the journey. But in our weariness, whether one died today, tomorrow, a week or a generation later, hardly seemed to matter.

"Arrival: The Death Train" is from E. Wiesel, *The World Was Silent*, trans. Moshe Spiegel (Buenos Aires, 1956), in *An Anthology of Holocaust Literature*, eds. J. Glatstein, I. Knox, and S. Margoshes (Philadelphia: The Jewish Publication Society, 1969), pp. 3–5, 10. Reprinted by permission of the publisher.

The night dragged on interminably, as though it were to go on to the end of time. When the gray dawn appeared in the east, I felt as though I had spent a night in a tomb haunted by evil spirits. Human beings, defeated and broken, sat like dusty tombstones in the dim light of early dawn. I looked about the subdued throng and tried to distinguish one from another. And, indeed, perhaps there was no distinction.

My gaze fell on one who stared blankly ahead. A wry smile seemed to play on his ice-encrusted face. Those glazed eyes, whether living or dead, seemed to ensnare my gaze. A hundred and twenty captives, shadows of human lives, extinguished flames of burned-out candles lit on the anniversaries of the deaths of their loved ones.

Wrapped in a drenched blanket, his black cap pulled down over his ears, a layer of snow on his shoulders, my father sat beside me. Could it be that he, too, was dead? The thought flashed across my mind. I tried to talk to him. I wanted to shout, but all I could do was mutter. He did not reply, he did not utter a sound. I was certain that from then on I was to be all alone, all alone. Then I was filled with a numbing sense of indifference to everyone and to myself. Well, the Lord giveth and the Lord taketh away. The struggle was over. There was nothing and no one for whom to fight now.

The train ground to an abrupt halt in a snow-covered field. Awakened by the jolt, a few curious captives struggled to their feet to look out. The scene was reminiscent of cattle staring stupidly from a livestock car.

German S.S. guards surrounded the human cargo, shouting, "All the dead are to be thrown out! All the dead are to be thrown out!"

The living were pleased; there would be more space. It would not be as crowded now.

Strong men appeared and examined each one who could not stand up, and rapped out, "Here's one! Get hold of him!"

Whereupon two men would pick the corpse by the shoulders and feet and fling it out of the car like a sack of flour.

From various parts of the car came such cries as, "Here's another—my neighbor! He doesn't move. Help me get rid of him!"

There were some twenty-odd dead in our one car, and after they were stripped of their clothes, which the living snatched up, they were flung out of the car.

This task took several hours. Then the train chugged along, and as icy gusts shrieked about it, it seemed that through the accursed world about us could be heard the far-away, muffled wail of the naked bodies that had been abandoned on Polish snow-covered fields.

The journey was insufferable; and every one who lived through it later questioned the natural laws that their survival seemed to disprove.

We were deprived of even bread and water, and snow was our only source of water. Cramped for space and thoroughly chilled, we were very weak by the third day of the journey. Days were turned into nights, and the nights cast a shadow of doom over our very souls.

The train plodded along for what seemed countless days, and the snow fell, fell, fell incessantly. And the exhausted, travel-weary unfortunates lay huddled for days on end, without uttering a word, eyes closed, waiting for one thing only—the next station, where the new yield of corpses would be got rid of. That was what we looked forward to.

The journey lasted ten interminable days and nights. Each day claimed its toll of victims and each night paid its homage to the Angel of Death.

We passed through German settlements, generally in the early morning hours, only in a few instances. Sometimes men on their way to work would halt in their tracks to glare at us as though we were animals in a kind of demonic circus. Once a German hurled a chunk of bread into our car and caused pandemonium to break out as scores of famished men fought each other in an effort to pounce upon it. And the German workers eyed the spectacle with sneering amusement.

We arrived at the Buchenwald concentration camp late at night. "Security police" of the camp came forward to unload the human cargo. The dead were left in the cars. Only those who were able to drag their feet got out. Meir Katz was left in the car; like so many others, he had frozen to death a short time before we reached our destination. The journey itself was the worst part of the ordeal. About forty of the deportees were claimed by death on that one day alone. Our car had originally started out with a hundred and twenty souls; twelve—among them my father and I—had survived the ordeal.

Train shop near Jassy with Jewish dead. "German S.S. guards surrounded the human cargo, shouting, 'All the dead are to be thrown out! All the dead are to be thrown out!' "—Elie Wiesel. *(Yad Vashem, Jerusalem)*

Genocide
RUDOLF HOESS

I, Rudolf Franz Ferdinand Hoess, being first duly sworn, depose and say as follows:

1. I am forty-six years old, and have been a member of the NSDAP since 1922; a member of the SS since 1934; a member of the Waffen-SS since 1939. I was a member from 1 December 1934 of the SS Guard Unit, the so-called Deaths-head Formation [*Totenkopf Verband*].

2. I have been constantly associated with the administration of concentration camps since 1934, serving at Dachau until 1938; then as Adjutant in Sachenhausen from 1938 to May 1, 1940, when I was appointed Commandant of Auschwitz. I commanded Auschwitz until 1 December 1943, and estimate that at least 2,500,000 victims were executed and exterminated there by gassing and burning, and at least another half million succumbed to starvation and disease making a total dead of about 3,000,000. This figure represents about 70% or 80% of all persons sent to Auschwitz as prisoners, the remainder having been selected and used for slave labor in the concentration camp industries. Included among the executed and burnt were approximately 20,000 Russian prisoners of war (previously screened out of Prisoner of War cages by the Gestapo) who were delivered at Auschwitz in Wehrmacht transports operated by regular Wehrmacht officers, 100,000 German Jews, and great numbers of citizens, mostly Jewish from Holland, France, Belgium, Poland, Hungary, Czechoslovakia, Greece, or other countries. We executed about 400,000 Hungarian Jews alone at Auschwitz in the summer of 1944. . . .

4. Mass executions by gassing commenced during the summer of 1941 and continued until fall 1944. I personally supervised executions at Auschwitz until the first of December 1943 and know by reason of my continued duties . . . that these mass executions continued as stated above. All mass executions by gassing took place under the direct orders, supervisions, and responsibility of RSHA [Reich Security Main Office]. I received all orders for carrying out these mass executions directly from RSHA. . . .

6. The "final solution" of the Jewish question meant the complete extermination of all Jews in Europe. I was ordered to establish extermination facilities at Auschwitz in June 1941. At that time, there were already in the general government three other extermination camps; Belzek, Treblinka, and Wolzek. These camps were under the Einsatzkommando of the Security Police and SD. I visited Treblinka to find out how they carried out their extermination. The Camp Commandant at Treblinka told me that he had liquidated 80,000 in the course of one-half year. He was principally concerned with liquidating all the Jews from the Warsaw ghetto. He used monoxide gas and I did not think that his methods

"Genocide" is from the Office of the U.S. Chief of Counsel for the Prosecution of Axis Criminality, *Nazi Conspiracy and Aggression* (Washington, D.C.: Government Printing Office, 1947), vol. 6, pp. 787–790 (PS-3868).

Entrance to Birkenu, the death camp at Auschwitz. " *(Yivo Institute for Jewish Research. New York)*

were very efficient. So when I set up the extermination building at Auschwitz, I used Cyclon B, which was a crystallized prussic acid which we dropped into the death chamber from a small opening. It took from 3 to 15 minutes to kill the people in the death chamber depending upon climatic conditions. We knew when the people were dead because their screaming stopped. We usually waited about one-half hour before we opened the doors and removed the bodies. After the bodies were removed our special commandos took off the rings and extracted the gold from the teeth of the corpses.

7. Another improvement we made over Treblinka was that we built our gas chambers to accommodate 2,000 people at one time, whereas at Treblinka their 10 gas chambers only accommodated 200 people each. The way we selected our victims was as follows: we had two SS doctors on duty at Auschwitz to examine the incoming transports of prisoners. The prisoners would be marched by one of the doctors who would make spot decisions as they walked by. Those who were fit for work were sent into the Camp. Others were sent immediately to the extermination plants. Children of tender years were invariably exterminated since by reason of their youth they were unable to work. Still another improvement we made over Treblinka was that at Treblinka the victims almost always knew that they were to be exterminated and at Auschwitz we endeavored to fool the victims into thinking that they were to go through a delousing process. Of course, frequently they realized our true intentions and we sometimes had riots and difficulties due to that fact. Very frequently women would hide their children under their clothes but of course when we found them we would send the children in to be extermi-

nated. We were required to carry out these exterminations in secrecy but of course the foul and nauseating stench from the continuous burning of bodies permeated the entire area and all of the people living in the surrounding communities knew that exterminations were going on at Auschwitz.

8. We received from time to time special prisoners from the local Gestapo office. The SS doctors killed such prisoners by injections of benzine. Doctors had orders to write ordinary death certificates and could put down any reason at all for the cause of death.

9. From time to time we conducted medical experiments on women inmates, including sterilization and experiments relating to cancer. Most of the people who died under these experiments had been already condemned to death by the Gestapo. . . .

I understand English as it is written above. The above statements are true; this declaration is made by me voluntarily and without compulsion; after reading over the statements, I have signed and executed the same at Nuremberg, Germany, on the fifth day of April 1946.

Rudolf Franz Ferdinand Hoess

Subscribed and sworn to before me this 5th day of April 1946, at Nuremberg, Germany
Smith W. Brookhart Jr., Lt. Colonel, IGD

The Pit

HERMANN GRÄBE

On October 5, 1942, when I visited the building office at Dubno, my foreman told me that in the vicinity of the site, Jews from Dubno had been shot in three large pits, each about 30 metres long and 3 metres deep. About 1,500 persons had been killed daily. All the 5,000 Jews who had still been living in Dubno before the pogrom were to be liquidated. As the shooting had taken place in his presence, he was still much upset.

Thereupon, I drove to the site accompanied by my foreman and saw near it great mounds of earth, about 30 metres long and 2 metres high. Several trucks stood in front of the mounds. Armed Ukrainian militia drove the people off the trucks under the supervision of an S.S. man. The militiamen acted as guards on the trucks and drove them to and from the pit. All these people had the regulation yellow patches on the front and back of their clothes, and thus could be recognized as Jews.

My foreman and I went directly to the pits. Nobody bothered us. Now I heard rifle shots in quick succession from behind one of the earth mounds. The people who had got off the trucks—men, women and children of all ages—had to undress upon the orders of an S.S. man, who carried a riding or dog whip. They had to put down their clothes in fixed places, sorted accord-

"I remember and I am afraid."—Elie Wiesel. *(Yad Vashem, Jerusalem)*

ing to shoes, top clothing and underclothing. I saw a heap of shoes of about 800 to 1,000 pairs, great piles of underlinen and clothing.

Without screaming or weeping, these people undressed, stood around in family groups, kissed each other, said farewells, and waited for a sign from another S.S. man, who stood near the pit, also with a whip in his hand. During the fifteen minutes that I stood near I heard no complaint or plea for mercy. I watched a family of about eight persons, a man and a woman both about fifty with their children of about one, eight and ten, and two grown-up daughters of about twenty to twenty-nine. An old woman with snow-white hair was holding the one-year old child in her arms and singing to it and tickling it. The child was cooing with delight. The couple were looking on with tears in their eyes. The father was holding the hand of a boy about ten years old and speaking to him softly; the boy was fighting his tears. The father pointed to the sky, stroked his head, and seemed to explain something to him.

At that moment the S.S. man at the pit shouted something to his comrade. The latter counted off about twenty persons and instructed them to go behind the earth mound. Among them was the family which I have mentioned. I well remember a girl, slim and with black hair, who, as she passed close to me pointed to herself and said "23." I walked around the mound and found myself confronted by a tremendous grave. People were closely wedged together and lying on top of each other so that only their heads were visible.

"The Pit" is from Louis L. Snyder, ed., *Documents of German History*, pp. 462–463. Copyright 1958 by Rutgers, The State University. Reprinted by permission of Rutgers University Press.

Nearly all had blood running over their shoulders from their heads. Some of the people shot were still moving. Some were lifting their arms and turning their heads to show that they were still alive. The pit was already two-thirds full. I estimated that it already contained about 1,000 people.

Gas

KURT GERSTEIN

In January, 1942, I was named chief of the Waffen SS technical disinfection services, including a section for extremely toxic gases. . . . SS Gruppenfuhrer Globocnik was waiting for us at Lublin. He told us, "This is one of the most secret matters there are, even the most secret. Anybody who talks about it will be shot immediately." He explained to us that there were three installations:

1) Belzec, on the Lublin-Lwow road. A maximum of 15,000 people per day.
2) Sobibor (I don't know exactly where it is), 20,000 people a day.
3) Treblinka, 120 kilometers NNE of Warsaw.
4) Maidanek, near Lublin (under construction).

Globocnik said: "You will have to disinfect large piles of clothing coming from Jews, Poles, Czechs, etc. Your other duty will be to improve the workings of our gas chambers, which operate on the exhaust from a Diesel engine. We need a more toxic and faster working gas, something like prussic acid. . . .

The following morning, a little before seven there was an announcement: "The first train will arrive in ten minutes!" A few minutes later a train arrived from Lemberg: 45 cars with more than 6,000 people. Two hundred Ukrainians assigned to this work flung open the doors and drove the Jews out of the cars with leather whips. A loud speaker gave instructions: "Strip, even artificial limbs and glasses. Hand all money and valuables in at the 'valuables window.' Women and young girls are to have their hair cut in the 'barber's hut.'"

Then the march began. Barbed wire on both sides, in the rear two dozen Ukrainians with rifles. They drew near. Wirth and I found ourselves in front of the death chambers. Stark naked men, women, children, and cripples passed by. A tall S.S. man in the corner called to the unfortunates in a loud minister's voice: "Nothing is going to hurt you! Just breathe deep and it will strengthen your lungs. It's a way to prevent contagious diseases. It's a good disinfectant!" They asked him what was going to happen and he answered: "The men will have to work, build houses and streets. The women won't have to do that, they will be busy with the housework and the kitchen." This was the last hope for some of these poor people, enough to make them march toward the death chambers without resistance. The majority knew everything; the smell betrayed it! They climbed a little wooden stairs and entered the death chambers, most of them silently, pushed by those behind them. A Jewess of about forty with eyes like fire cursed the murderers; she disappeared into the gas chambers after being struck several times by Captain Wirth's whip. . . . All were dead after thirty-two minutes! Jewish workers on the other side opened the wooden doors. They had been promised their lives in return for doing this horrible work, plus a small percentage of the money and valuables collected. The men still standing, like columns of stone, with no room to fall or lean. Even in death you could tell the families, all holding hands. It was difficult to separate them while emptying the rooms for the next batch. The bodies were tossed out, blue, wet with sweat and urine, the legs smeared with excrement and menstrual blood. Two dozen workers were busy checking mouths which they opened with iron hooks. "Gold to the left, no gold to the right." Others checked anus and genitals, looking for money, diamonds, gold, etc. Dentists knocked out gold teeth, bridges and crowns, with hammers. . . .

Then the bodies were thrown into big ditches near the gas chambers, about 100 by 20 by 12 meters. After a few days the bodies swelled and the whole mass rose up 2–3 yards because of the gas in the bodies. When the swelling went down several days later, the bodies matted down again. They told me later they poured Diesel oil over the bodies and burned them on railroad ties to make them disappear.

Mobile Killing

Kiev, 16 May 1942

Field Post Office
No 32704
B Nr 40/42

TOP SECRET

To: SS-Obersturmbannfuehrer Rauff
    Berlin, Prinz-Albrecht-Str. 8

pers.
R/29/5 Pradel n.R
b/R

Sinkkel [?] b.R., p 16/6

The overhauling of vans by groups D and C is finished. . . .

I ordered the vans of group D to be camouflaged as house trailers by putting one set of window shutters on each side of the small van and two on each side of the larger vans, such as one often sees on farm-houses in the

"Mobile Killing" is from the Office of the U.S. Chief Counsel for Prosecution of Axis Criminality, *Nazi Conspiracy and Aggression* (Washington, D.C.: Government Printing Office, 1946), vol. 3, pp. 418–419 (PS-501).

country. The vans became so well-known, that not only the authorities, but also the civilian population called the van "death van," as soon as one of these vehicles appeared. It is my opinion, the van cannot be kept secret for any length of time, not even camouflaged. . . .

I ordered that during application of gas all the men were to be kept as far away from the vans as possible, so they should not suffer damage to their health by the gas which eventually would escape. I should like to take this opportunity to bring the following to your attention: several commands have had the unloading after the application of gas done by their own men. I brought to the attention of the commanders of the Sonder-Kommando [special unit] concerning the immense psychological injuries and damages to their health which that work can have for those men, even if not immediately, at least later on. The men complained to me about headaches which appeared after each unloading. Nevertheless prisoners called for that work, could use an opportune moment to flee. To protect the men from these damages, I request orders be issued accordingly.

The application of gas usually is not undertaken correctly. In order to come to an end as fast as possible, the driver presses the accelerator to the fullest extent. By doing that the persons to be executed suffer death from suffocation and not death by dozing off as was planned. My directions now have proved that by correct adjustment of the levers death comes faster and the prisoners fall asleep peacefully. Distorted faces and excretions, such as could be seen before, are no longer noticed.

Today I shall continue my journey to group B, where I can be reached with further news.

Signed: D. Becker
SS Untersturmfuehrer

Commandant of Auschwitz
RUDOLF HOESS

I must emphasise here that I have never personally hated the Jews. It is true that I looked upon them as the enemies of our people. But just because of this I saw no difference between them and the other prisoners, and I treated them all in the same way. I never drew any distinctions. In any event the emotion of hatred is foreign to my nature. But I know what hate is, and what it looks like. I have seen it and I have suffered it myself.

When the Reichsfuhrer SS modified his original Extermination Order of 1941, by which all Jews without exception were to be destroyed, and ordered

"Commandant of Auschwitz" is from Rudolf Hoess, *Commandant of Auschwitz: The Autobiography of Rudolf Hoess*, trans. Constantine Fitzgibbon, pp. 147–149, 202–203. Copyright © 1959 by George Weidenfeld & Nicholson, Ltd. Copyright © 1961 by Pan Books, Ltd. Reprinted by permission.

instead that those capable of work were to be separated from the rest and employed in the armaments industry, Auschwitz became a Jewish camp. It was a collecting place for Jews, exceeding in scale anything previously known.

Whereas the Jews who had been imprisoned in former years were able to count on being released one day and were thus far less affected psychologically by the hardships of captivity, the Jews in Auschwitz no longer had any such hope. They knew, without exception, that they were condemned to death, that they would live only so long as they could work.

Nor did the majority have any hope of a change in their sad lot. They were fatalists. Patiently and apathetically, they submitted to all the misery and distress and terror. The hopelessness with which they accepted their impending fate made them psychologically quite indifferent to their surroundings. This mental collapse accelerated its physical equivalent. They no longer had the will to live, everything had become a matter of indifference to them, and they would succumb to the slightest physical shock. Sooner or later, death was inevitable. I firmly maintain from what I have seen that the high mortality among the Jews was due not only to the hard work, to which most of them were unaccustomed, and to the insufficient food, the overcrowded quarters and all the severities and abuses of camp life, but principally and decisively to their psychological state. . . .

What I have just written applies to the bulk, the mass of the Jewish prisoners. The more intelligent ones, psychologically stronger and with a keener desire for life, that is to say in most cases those from the western countries, reacted differently.

These people, especially if they were doctors, had no illusions concerning their fate. But they continued to hope, reckoning on a change of fortune that somehow or other would save their lives. They also reckoned on the collapse of Germany, for it was not difficult for them to listen to enemy propaganda.

For them the most important thing was to obtain a position which would lift them out of the mass and give them special privileges, a job that would protect them to a certain extent from accidental and mortal hazards, and improve the physical conditions in which they lived.

They employed all their ability and all their will to obtain what can truly be described as a 'living' of this sort. The safer the position the more eagerly and fiercely it was fought for. No quarter was shown, for this was a struggle in which everything was at stake. They flinched from nothing, no matter how desperate, in their efforts to make such safe jobs fall vacant and then to acquire them for themselves. Victory usually went to the most unscrupulous man or woman. Time and again I heard of these struggles to oust a rival and win his job. . . .

So it can be seen that even in a small prison the governor is unable to prevent such behavior; how much more difficult was it in a concentration camp the size of Auschwitz!

I was certainly severe and strict. Often perhaps, when I look at it now, too severe and too strict.

In my disgust at the errors and abuses that I discovered, I may have spoken many hard words that I should have kept to myself. But I was never cruel, and I have never maltreated anyone, even in a fit of temper. A great deal happened in Auschwitz which was done ostensibly in my name, under my authority and on my orders, which I neither knew about nor sanctioned. But all these things happened in Auschwitz and so I am responsible. For the camp regulations say: the camp commandant is fully responsible for everything that happens in his sphere.

Jewish Resistance

As Hoess noted in his autobiography, many Jews went to their deaths as lambs to slaughter without struggling against their apparent fate. Still, it is misleading to characterize the acts of the condemned under duress as devoid of courage. In fact, there was constant Jewish resistance to the Nazis in the camps and ghettos. A Jewish Fighting Organization was active in the Warsaw ghetto, and resistance continued from January to mid-May 1943, when the Jews were finally defeated. Joseph Goebbels was rather surprised at their tenacity, as the excerpt from his diary indicates. An account by the Nazi S.S. chief in Warsaw of the destruction of the ghetto follows. The Treblinka death camp was often the final stop for Jews from the Warsaw ghetto. In August 1943, the inmates rebelled. Although the rebellion was ultimately unsuccessful, the camp was shut down shortly afterward. The last selection is a manifesto of a Jewish resistance organization in the Vilna ghetto dated a month after the revolt at Treblinka.

Nazi Problems in the Warsaw Ghetto (May 1, 1943)
JOSEPH GOEBBELS

Reports from the occupied areas contain no sensational news. The only noteworthy item is the exceedingly serious fights in Warsaw between the police and even a part of our Wehrmacht on the one hand and the rebellious Jews on the other. The Jews have actually succeeded in making a defensive position of the Ghetto. Heavy engagements are being fought there which led even to the Jewish Supreme Command's issuing daily communiques. Of course this fun won't last very long. But it shows what is to be expected of the Jews when they are in possession of arms. Unfortunately, some of their weapons are good German ones, especially machine guns. Heaven only knows how they got them. . . .

"Nazi Problems" is from *The Goebbels Diaries* by Louis P. Lochner, pp. 350–351. Copyright © 1948 by The Fireside Press, Inc. Reprinted by permission of Doubleday, a division of Bantam, Doubleday, Dell Publishing Group, Inc.

The Destruction of the Warsaw Ghetto (May 1943)
JÜRGEN STROOP

On 23 April 1943 the Reichsführer SS issued through the higher SS and Police Führer East at Cracow his order to complete the combing out of the Warsaw Ghetto with the greatest severity and relentless tenacity. I therefore decided to destroy the entire Jewish residential area by setting every block on fire, including the blocks of residential buildings near the armament works. One concern after the other was systematically evacuated and later destroyed by fire. In almost every case, the Jews then emerged from their hiding places and dug-outs. Not infrequently, the Jews stayed in the burning buildings until, because of the heat and the fear of being burned alive, they preferred to jump down from the upper storeys after having thrown mattresses and other upholstered articles into the street from the burning buildings. With their bones broken, they still tried to crawl across the streets into blocks of buildings which had not yet been set on fire or were only partly in flames. Often Jews changed their hiding places during the night, by moving into the ruins of burnt-out buildings, taking refuge there until they were found by our patrols. Their stay in the sewers also ceased to be pleasant after the first week. From the street we could frequently hear loud voices coming through the sewer shafts. Then the men of the Waffen SS, the police or the Wehrmacht engineers courageously climbed down the shafts to bring out the Jews and not infrequently they then stumbled over Jews already dead, or were shot at. It was always necessary to use smoke candles to drive out the Jews. Thus, one day we opened 183 sewer entrance holes and at a fixed time lowered smoke candles into them, so that the bandits fled from what they believed to be gas to the centre of the former Ghetto, where they could then be pulled out of the sewer holes. A great number of Jews, beyond counting, were exterminated by the blowing up of the sewers and dug-outs. . . .

Only through the continuous and untiring work of all involved did we succeed in catching a total of 56,065 Jews, whose extermination can be proved. To this should be added the number of Jews who lost their lives in explosions or fires, whose numbers could not be ascertained.

During the large-scale operation the Aryan population was informed by posters that it was strictly forbidden to enter the former Jewish Ghetto and that anybody caught within the former Ghetto without a valid pass would be shot. At the same time these posters informed the Aryan population again that the death penalty would be imposed on anyone who intentionally gave refuge to a Jew, especially on anyone who lodged, supported or concealed a Jew outside the Jewish residential area. . . .

The large-scale action was terminated on 16 May 1943 with the blowing up of the Warsaw synagogue at 20.15 hours.

"The Destruction of the Warsaw Ghetto" is from Jeremy Noakes and Geoffrey Pridham, eds., *Documents on Nazism, 1919–1945*, pp. 491–492. Reprinted by permission of A. D. Peters & Co. Ltd.

Warsaw Jews on the way to the Treblinka death camp. *(AP/Wide World Photos)*

The Treblinka Revolt (August 1943)

STANISLAW KOHN

Before I arrived at Treblinka, in other words before October 1, 1942, cases of rebellion on the part of Jews had been reported. Thus, for example, a Jewish youth from Warsaw who worked in one of the death companies, having seen his wife and child escorted to the gas chamber, attacked the S.S. man, Max Bill, with a knife and killed him on the spot. From that day the S.S. barracks bore the name of this Hitlerite "martyr." Neither the plate on the wall of the barracks nor the massacre of Jews after this attack deterred us. This episode encouraged us to fight and take our revenge. The Warsaw youth became our ideal.

A desire for revenge burned within us as we witnessed Hitler's extermination methods, and ripened each day and began to concretize into something precise, particularly from the moment when the fifty-year-old doctor, Choronzicki, of Warsaw, began to be active. The doctor worked in the camps as sanitation adviser, a task invented by the Germans to mock the humiliated victims even more vilely before despatching them to the gas chamber. He was a calm, cautious man who, on the surface, appeared very cold. He wandered around in his white apron with the sign of the Red Cross on his arm as in the olden days in his

"The Treblinka Revolt" is from *An Anthology of Holocaust Literature,* eds. J. Glatstein, I. Knox, and S. Margoshes (Philadelphia: The Jewish Publication Society, 1969), pp. 319, 321–324. Reprinted by permission of the publisher.

Warsaw consulting room, and seemed completely disinterested. But beneath his apron beat a warm Jewish heart, burning with desire for revenge. . . .

The date of the revolt was postponed several times for various reasons. And then the last transports of the Warsaw Jews were brought to Treblinka. From them we learned about the ghetto revolt. The Germans treated them with particular savagery; most of the trucks were full of corpses of ghetto combatants who had refused to leave the ghetto alive. Those who now arrived were no longer resigned and indifferent creatures like their predecessors. . . .

The desire for revenge increased continuously. The terror-stricken eyes of the Jews being led to their death, and throngs into the gas chamber, called for revenge.

At last the leader, Galewski, gave the signal for the revolt. The date fixed was for Monday, August 2, 1943, at five o'clock in the afternoon. This was the plan of action: to lay an ambush for the chief murderers, to liquidate them, to disarm the warders, cut the telephone wires and then burn and destroy all the extermination plants so that they could never function again; to free the Poles from the detention camp of Treblinka, to flee into the forest to organize a partisan band. . . .

At two o'clock in the afternoon the distribution of weapons began. It was very difficult to purloin the hand grenades from the armory. . . . Marcus and Salzberg took up the carpets and beat them in front of the armory. The guards were obliged to move away for a while. At that moment the door of the armory was opened with our key [which had been stolen] and Jacek, the Hungarian boy, slipped inside, climbed onto the window sill at the end of the room, cut out a small square in the glass with a diamond and handed out the bombs and other weapons to Jacob Miller who put them on his refuse cart. The arms were carried to the garage. This time the hand grenades acted as a spur.

Spirits grew agitated and no one could keep the secret. The leaders therefore decided to start the revolt an hour before the agreed time.

Punctually at four o'clock in the afternoon messages were sent to all groups with orders to assemble immediately in the garage to fetch their weapons.

Anyone coming to fetch weapons had to give the password, "Death," to which the reply was "life." "Death-Life," "Death-Life!" Cries of enthusiasm arose as the long-hoped-for guns, revolvers and hand grenades were distributed. At the same time the chief murderers of the camp were attacked. Telephonic communication was cut and the watchtowers were set on fire with petrol. The armory was taken by assault and the weapons distributed. We already had two hundred armed men. The others attacked the Germans with axes and spades.

We set fire to the gas chambers, burned the railway station with all the notices. . . . We burned the barracks. . . .

The flames and the reports of the firing roused the Germans who began to arrive from all sides. S.S. and police arrived from Kosow, soldiers from the nearby airfield and finally a special section of the Warsaw S.S. Orders had been given to make for the neighboring forest. Most of our fighters fell but there were many German casualties. Very few of us survived.

Manifesto of the Jewish Resistance in Vilna (September 1943)

Offer armed resistance! Jews, defend yourselves with arms!

The German and Lithuanian executioners are at the gates of the ghetto. They have come to murder us! Soon they will lead you forth in groups through the ghetto door.

Tens of thousands of us were despatched. But we shall not go! We will not offer our heads to the butcher like sheep.

Jews, defend yourselves with arms!

Do not believe the false promises of the assassins or believe the words of the traitors.

Anyone who passes through the ghetto gate will go to Ponar! [Death Camp]

And Ponar means death!

Jews, we have nothing to lose. Death will overtake us in any event. And who can still believe in survival when the murderer exterminates us with so much determination? The hand of the executioner will reach each man and woman. Flight and acts of cowardice will not save our lives.

Active resistance alone can save our lives and our honor.

Brothers! It is better to die in battle in the ghetto than to be carried away to Ponar like sheep. And know this: within the walls of the ghetto there are organized Jewish forces who will resist with weapons.

Support the revolt!

Do not take refuge or hide in the bunkers, for then you will fall into the hands of the murderers like rats.

Jewish people, go out into the squares. Anyone who has no weapons should take an ax, and he who has no ax should take a crowbar or a bludgeon!

For our ancestors!

For our murdered children!

Avenge Ponar!

Attack the murderers!

In every street, in every courtyard, in every house within and without the ghetto, attack these dogs!

Jews, we have nothing to lose! We shall save our lives only if we exterminate our assassins.

Long live liberty! Long live armed resistance! Death to the assassins!

The Commander of the F.P.A.

Vilna, the Ghetto, September 1, 1943.

"Manifesto of the Jewish Resistance in Vilna" is from *An Anthology of Holocaust Literature,* eds. J. Glatstein, I. Knox, and S. Margoshes (Philadelphia: The Jewish Publication Society, 1969), pp. 332–333. Reprinted by permission of the publisher.

Judgment and Reflection

The Nuremberg Trials (November 1945–October 1946)

In the spring of 1945, Allied troops fought their way into the heart of Nazi Germany. Infamous concentration camps such as Dachau and Buchenwald were liberated by soldiers; the German inhabitants of the area were forced to view the horrors perpetrated by their "neighbors." Judgment was demanded, and an international court was established in Nuremberg. Its responsibility was to pass sentence on the various Nazi leaders after first examining documentary evidence and transcripts of oral testimony. No court has ever attained such universal recognition. Transcripts and documents of the proceedings fill forty-two large volumes. The following selection is from the summation of Justice Robert H. Jackson, the chief American prosecutor.

The Crimes of the Nazi Regime
JUSTICE ROBERT H. JACKSON

The Nazi movement will be an evil memory in history because of its persecution of the Jews, the most far-flung and terrible racial persecution of all time. Although the Nazi party neither invented nor monopolized anti-Semitism, its leaders from the very beginning embraced it, and exploited it. They used it as "the psychological spark that ignites the mob." After the seizure of power, it became an official state policy. The persecution began in a series of discriminatory laws eliminating the Jews from the civil service, the professions, and economic life. As it became more intense it included segregation of Jews in ghettos, and exile. Riots were organized by party leaders to loot Jewish business places and to burn synagogues. Jewish property was confiscated and a collective fine of a billion marks was imposed upon German Jewry. The program progressed in fury and irresponsibility to the "final solution." This consisted of sending all Jews who were fit to work to concentration camps as slave laborers, and all who were not fit, which included children under 12 and people over 50, as well as any others judged unfit by an SS doctor, to concentration camps for extermination. . . .

The chief instrumentality for persecution and extermination was the concentration camp, sired by defendant Goering and nurtured under the overall authority of defendants Frick and Kaltenbrunner.

The horrors of these iniquitous places have been vividly disclosed by documents and testified to by witnesses. The Tribunal must be satiated with

"The Crimes of the Nazi Regime" is from Office of the U.S. Chief of Counsel for the Prosecution of Axis Criminality, *Nazi Conspiracy and Aggression* (Washington, D.C.: Government Printing Office, 1947), Supplement A, pp. 15–16, 44.

ghastly verbal and pictorial portrayals. From your records it is clear that the concentration camps were the first and worst weapons of oppression used by the National Socialist State, and that they were the primary means utilized for the persecution of the Christian Church and the extermination of the Jewish race. This has been admitted to you by some of the defendants from the witness stand. In the words of defendant Frank: "A thousand years will pass and this guilt of Germany will still not be erased." . . .

It is against such a background that these defendants now ask this Tribunal to say that they are not guilty of planning, executing, or conspiring to commit this long list of crimes and wrongs. They stand before the record of this trial. . . . If you were to say of these men that they are not guilty, it would be as true to say there has been no war, there are no slain, there has been no crime.

Judgment and Sentence

At Nuremberg, the accused Nazis were indicted on one or more charges: (1) Crimes Against Peace (conspiracy), (2) War Crimes, (3) Crimes Against Humanity, (4) Membership in a Criminal Organization. The verdicts on some of the major Nazi figures of the Holocaust are presented next, followed by an account of the execution of Julius Streicher as described by Kingsbury Smith, European general manager of the International News Service. Streicher, a former elementary school teacher and fanatical Nazi, published Der Stürmer, *the most violently anti-Semitic journal in the Reich.*

Hermann Goering

Goering is indicted on all four Counts. The evidence shows that after Hitler he was the most prominent man in the Nazi regime. He was Commander-in-Chief of the Luftwaffe. Plenipotentiary for the Four Year Plan, he had tremendous influence with Hitler, at least until 1943, when their relationship deteriorated, ending in his arrest in 1945. He testified that Hitler kept him informed of all important military and political problems. . . .

Goering persecuted the Jews, particularly after the November 1938 riots, and not only in Germany . . . but in the conquered territories as well. As these countries fell before the German Army, he extended the Reich anti-Jewish laws to them. . . . Although their extermination was in Himmler's hands, Goering was far from disinterested or inactive, despite his protestations in the witness box. By decree of 31 July 1941 he directed Himmler and Heydrich to "bring about a complete solution of the Jewish question in the German sphere of influence in Europe."

"Judgment and Sentence" is from International Military Tribunal, *Nuremberg Trials of the Major War Criminals* (Nuremberg: Allied Central Commission, 1948), vol. 22, pp. 524, 527, 544–549.

There is nothing to be said in mitigation. For Goering was often, indeed almost always, the moving force, second only to his leader. He was the leading war aggressor, both as political and as military leader; he was the director of the slave labor program and the creator of the oppressive program against the Jews and other races, at home and abroad. All of these crimes he frankly admitted. On some specific cases there may be conflict of testimony, but in terms of the broad outline his own admissions are more than sufficiently wide to be conclusive of his guilt. His guilt is unique in its enormity. The record discloses no excuses for this man.

The Tribunal finds the Defendant Goering guilty of all four Counts of the Indictment.

Wilhelm Frick

Frick is indicted on all four Counts. Recognized as the chief Nazi administrative specialist and bureaucrat, he was appointed Reich Minister of the Interior in Hitler's first cabinet.

Always rabidly anti-Semitic, Frick drafted, signed, and administered many laws designed to eliminate Jews from German life and economy. His work formed the basis of the Nuremberg Decrees, and he was active in enforcing them. Responsible for prohibiting Jews from following various professions and for confiscating their property, he signed a final decree in 1943, after the mass destruction of Jews in the East, which placed them "outside the law" and handed them over to the Gestapo. These laws paved the way for the "final solution," and were extended by Frick to the incorporated territories and to certain of the occupied territories. While he was Reich Protector of Bohemia and Moravia, thousands of Jews were transferred from the Terezin ghetto in Czechoslovakia to Auschwitz, where they were killed. He issued a decree providing for special penal laws against Jews and Poles in the Governmental General. . . .

During the war nursing homes, hospitals, and asylums in which euthanasia was practised as described elsewhere in this Judgment, came under Frick's jurisdiction. He had knowledge that insane, sick, and aged people, "useless eaters," were being systematically put to death. Complaints of these murders reached him, but he did nothing to stop them. A report of the Czechoslovak War Crimes Commission estimated that 275,000 mentally deficient and aged people, for whose welfare he was responsible, fell victim to it.

The Tribunal finds that Frick is not guilty on Count One. He is guilty on Counts Two, Three and Four.

Julius Streicher

Streicher is indicted on Counts One and Four. One of the earliest members of the Nazi Party, joining in 1921, he took part in the Munich Putsch. From

1925 to 1940 he was Gauleiter of Franconia. Elected to the Reichstag in 1933, he was an honorary general in the SA. His persecution of the Jews was notorious. He was the publisher of *Der Stürmer,* an anti-Semitic weekly newspaper, from 1923 to 1945 and was its editor until 1933. . . .

For his 25 years of speaking, writing, and preaching hatred of the Jews, Streicher was widely known as "Jew-Baiter Number One." In his speeches and articles, week after week, month after month, he infected the German mind with the virus of anti-Semitism and incited the German people to active persecution. Each issue of *Der Stürmer,* which reached a circulation of 600,000 in 1935, was filled with such articles, often lewd and disgusting. . . .

As the war in the early stages proved successful in acquiring more and more territory for the Reich, Streicher even intensified his efforts to incite the Germans against the Jews. In the record are 26 articles from *Der Stürmer,* published between August 1941 and September 1944, 12 by Streicher's own hand, which demanded annihilation and extermination in unequivocal terms. He wrote and published on 25 December 1941:

"If the danger of the reproduction of that curse of God in the Jewish blood is finally to come to an end, then there is only one way—the extermination of that people whose father is the devil." And in February 1944 his own article stated: "Whoever does what a Jew does is a scoundrel, a criminal. And he who repeats and wishes to copy him deserves the same fate: annihilation, death."

With knowledge of the extermination of the Jews in the Occupied Eastern Territories, this defendant continued to write and publish his propaganda of death. Testifying in this Trial, he vehemently denied any knowledge of mass executions of Jews. But the evidence makes it clear that he continually received current information on the progress of the "final solution."

Streicher's incitement to murder and extermination at the time when Jews in the East were being killed under the most horrible conditions clearly constitutes persecution on political and racial grounds in connection with War Crimes, as defined by the Charter, and constitutes a Crime against Humanity.

The Tribunal finds that Streicher is not guilty on Count One, but that he is guilty on Count Four.

The Execution of Julius Streicher (1946)
KINGSBURY SMITH

The only one, however, to make any reference to Nazi ideology was Julius Streicher, that arch Jew-baiter. Displaying the most bitter and enraged defiance of any of the condemned, he screamed "Heil Hitler" at the top of his voice as he was about to mount the steps leading to the gallows.

"The Execution of Julius Streicher" is from *New York Journal-American* (October 16, 1946). Reprinted by permission of United Press International, Copyright 1946.

Streicher appeared in the execution hall, which had been used only last Saturday night for a basketball game by American security guards, at twelve and a half minutes after two o'clock. As in the case of all the condemned, a warning knock by a guard outside preceded Streicher's entry through a door in the middle of the hall.

An American lieutenant colonel sent to fetch the condemned from the death row of the cell block to the near-by prison wing entered first. He was followed by Streicher, who was stopped immediately inside the door by two American sergeants. They closed in on each side of him and held his arms while another sergeant removed the manacles from his hands and replaced them with a leather cord.

The first person whom Streicher and the others saw upon entering the gruesome hall was an American lieutenant colonel who stood directly in front of him while his hands were being tied behind his back as they had been manacled upon his entrance.

This ugly, dwarfish little man, wearing a threadbare suit and a well-worn bluish shirt buttoned to the neck but without a tie, glanced at the three wooden scaffolds rising up menacingly in front of him.

Two of these were used alternately to execute the condemned men while the third was kept in reserve.

After a quick glance at the gallows, Streicher glared around the room, his eyes resting momentarily upon the small group of American, British, French, and Russian officers on hand to witness the executions.

By this time Streicher's hands were tied securely behind his back. Two guards, one to each arm, directed him to No. 1 gallows on the left entrance. He walked steadily the six feet to the first wooden step, but his face was twitching nervously. As the guards stopped him at the bottom of the steps for official identification requests, he uttered his piercing scream:

"Heil Hitler!"

His shriek sent a shiver down the back of this International News Service correspondent, who is witnessing the executions as sole representative of the American press.

As its echo died away, another American colonel standing by the steps said sharply:

"Ask the man his name."

In response to the interpreter's query Streicher shouted:

"You know my name well."

The interpreter repeated his request, and the condemned man yelled:

"Julius Streicher."

As he mounted the platform Streicher cried out:

"Now it goes to God!"

After getting up the thirteen steps to the eight-foot-high and eight-foot-square black-painted wooden platform, Streicher was pushed two steps to the mortal spot beneath the hangman's rope.

This was suspended from an iron ring attached to a crossbeam which rested on two posts. The rope was being held back against a wooden rail by the American Army sergeant hangman.

Streicher was swung around to face the front.

He glanced again at the Allied officers and the eight Allied correspondents representing the world's press who were lined up against a wall behind small tables directly facing the gallows.

The American officer standing at the scaffold said:

"Ask the man if he has any last words."

When the interpreter had translated, Streicher shouted:

"The Bolsheviks will hang you one day."

As the black hood was being adjusted about his head, Streicher was heard saying:

"Adele, my dear wife."

At that moment the trap was sprung with a loud bang. With the rope snapped taut and the body swinging wildly, a groan could be heard distinctly within the dark interior of the scaffold.

Why?

The most difficult question to answer regarding a genocidal policy is why people participate in such action. In the first selection, Rudolf Hoess, the commandant of Auschwitz, speaks of the formation of his character. The next selections are from two influential authors who have written books about fanaticism. One of the foremost authorities on the Holocaust is Raul Hilberg. In his book The Destruction of the European Jews, *he offers some perspective on the possibilities of reoccurrence.*

"Whatever They Said Was Always Right"
RUDOLF HOESS

I had been brought up by my parents to be respectful and obedient towards all grown-up people, and especially the elderly, regardless of their social status. I was taught that my highest duty was to help those in need. It was constantly impressed upon me in forceful terms that I must obey promptly the wishes and commands of my parents, teachers and priests, and indeed of all grown-up people, including servants, and that nothing must distract me from this duty. Whatever they said was always right.

These basic principles on which I was brought up became part of my flesh and blood. I can still clearly remember how my father, who on account of his fervent Catholicism was a determined opponent of the Reich government and its policy, never ceased to remind his friends that, however strong one's

---

"'Whatever They Said Was Always Right'" is from Rudolf Hoess, *Commandant of Auschwitz: The Autobiography of Rudolf Hoess,* trans. Constantine Fitzgibbon, pp. 28–29, 199–200. Copyright © 1959 by Comite Internationale d'Auschwitz. Reprinted by permission.

opposition might be, the laws and decrees of the State had to be obeyed unconditionally.

From my earliest youth I was brought up with a strong awareness of duty. In my parents' house it was insisted that every task be exactly and conscientiously carried out. Each member of the family had his own special duties to perform. My father took particular care to see that I obeyed all his instructions and wishes with the greatest meticulousness. I remember to this day how he hauled me out of bed one night, because I had left the saddle-cloth lying in the garden instead of hanging it up in the barn to dry, as he had told me to do. I had simply forgotten all about it. Again and again he impressed on me how great evils almost always spring from small, apparently insignificant misdeeds. At that time I did not fully understand the meaning of this dictum, but in later years I was to learn, through bitter experience, the truth of his words.

I remain, as I have always been, a convinced National-Socialist in my attitude to life. When a man has adhered to a belief and an attitude for nigh on twenty-five years, has grown up with it and become bound to it body and soul, he cannot simply throw it aside because the embodiments of this ideal, the National-Socialist State and its leaders have used their powers wrongly and even criminally, and because as a result of this failure and misdirection his world has collapsed and the entire German people been plunged for decades into untold misery. I, at least, cannot.

From the documents published and from the Nuremberg trials I can see that the leaders of the Third Reich, because of their policy of force, were guilty of causing this vast war and all its consequences. I see that these leaders, by means of exceptionally effective propaganda and of limitless terrorism, were able to make the whole German people so docile and submissive that they were ready, with very few exceptions, to go wherever they were led, without voicing a word of criticism. . . .

In order to disguise a policy of force it is necessary to use propaganda so that a clever distortion of all the facts, the policies and measures of the rulers of the State can be made palatable. Terrorism must be used from the outset, to stifle all doubt and opposition.

The True Believer
ERIC HOFFER

The impulse to fight springs less from self-interest than from intangibles such as tradition, honor (a word), and, above all, hope. Where there is no hope, people either run, or allow themselves to be killed without a fight. They will hang on to life as in a daze. How else to explain the fact that millions of Europeans allowed themselves to be led into annihilation camps and gas chambers, knowing beyond doubt that they were being led to death? It was not the least of Hitler's formidable powers that he knew how to drain his opponents (at least in continental Europe) of all hope. His fanatical conviction that he was building a new order that would last a thousand years communicated itself both to followers and antagonists. To the former it gave the feeling that in fighting for the Third Reich they were in league with eternity, while the latter felt that to struggle against Hitler's new order was to defy inexorable fate. . . .

To rely on the evidence of the senses and of reason is heresy and treason. It is startling to realize how much unbelief is necessary to make belief possible. What we know as blind faith is sustained by innumerable unbeliefs. The fanatical Japanese in Brazil refused to believe for years the evidence of Japan's defeat. The fanatical Communist refuses to believe any unfavorable report or evidence about Russia, nor will he be disillusioned by seeing with his own eyes the cruel misery inside the Soviet promised land.

It is the true believer's ability to "shut his eyes and stop his ears" to facts that do not deserve to be either seen or heard which is the source of his unequaled fortitude and constancy. He cannot be frightened by danger nor disheartened by obstacle nor baffled by contradictions because he denies their existence. Strength of faith . . . manifests itself not in moving mountains but in not seeing mountains move. And it is the certitude of his infallible doctrine that renders the true believer impervious to the uncertainties, surprises and the unpleasant realities of the world around him.

Thus the effectiveness of a doctrine should not be judged by its profundity, sublimity or the validity of the truths it embodies, but by how thoroughly it insulates the individual from his self and the world as it is. What Pascal said of an effective religion is true of any effective doctrine: It must be "contrary to nature, to common sense and to pleasure."

The Destruction of the European Jews
RAUL HILBERG

The destruction of the European Jews between 1933 and 1945 appears to us now as an unprecedented event in history. Indeed, in its dimensions and total configuration, nothing like it had ever happened before. Five million people were killed as a result of an organized undertaking in the short space of a few years. The operation was over before anyone could grasp its enormity, let alone its implications for the future.

Yet if we analyze that singularly massive upheaval, we discover that most of what happened in those twelve years had already happened before. The Nazi

"The Destruction of the European Jews" is reprinted from Raul Hilberg, *The Destruction of the European Jews*, revised and definitive edition, 3 vols. (New York: Holmes & Meir, 1985), vol. 3, pp. 1187, 1193–1194. Copyright © 1985 by Raul Hilberg. Reprinted by permission of the publisher.

destruction process did not come out of a void; it was the culmination of a cyclical trend. We have observed the trend in the three successive goals of anti-Jewish administrators. The missionaries of Christianity had said in effect: You have no right to live among us as Jews. The secular rulers who followed had proclaimed: You have no right to live among us. The German Nazis at last decreed: You have no right to live. . . .

As time passes, the destruction of the European Jews will recede into the background. Its most immediate consequences are almost over, and whatever developments may henceforth be traced to the catastrophe will be consequences of consequences, more and more remote. Already the Nazi outburst has become historical. But this is a strange page in history. Few events of modern times were so filled with unpredicted action and suspected death. A primordial impulse had suddenly surfaced among the Western nations; it had been unfettered through their machines. From this moment, fundamental assumptions about our civilization have no longer stood unchallenged, for while the occurrence is past, the phenomenon remains.

Before the emergence of the 20th century and its technology, a destructive mind could not play in fantasy with the thoughts that the Nazis were to translate into action. The administrator of earlier centuries did not have the tools. He did not possess the network of communications; he did not dispose over rapid small arms fire and quick-working poison gasses. The bureaucrat of tomorrow would not have these problems; already, he is better equipped than the German Nazis were. Killing is not as difficult as it used to be. The modern administrative apparatus has facilities for rapid, concerted movements and for efficient massive killings. These devices not only trap a larger number of victims; they also require a greater degree of specialization, and with that division of labor the moral burden too is fragmented among the participants. The perpetrator can now kill his victims without touching them. He may feel sure of his success and safe from its repercussions. This ever-growing capacity for destruction cannot be arrested anywhere. . . .

Since the end of the Jewish catastrophe, basic decisions have been made about the future. In the Christian world the remaining alternatives are gradually moving toward polar ends. After two thousand years there is no defensible middle ground. The ancient compromise, with all its contradictions, is weakening day by day. To the Jewish community that growing dichotomy conveys unique opportunities and unprecedented vulnerabilities. Jewry is faced with ultimate weapons. It has no deterrent. The Jews can live more freely now. They can also die more quickly. The summit is within sight. An abyss has opened below.

CHRONOLOGY: The Jewish Holocaust

March 23, 1933	Hitler obtains the Enabling Law, granting him dictatorial powers for four years.
April 1, 1933	National boycott of all Jewish businesses and professions.
April 7, 1933	Civil Service law permits removal of Jews and other opponents.
August 2, 1934	Death of President Hindenburg. Hitler assumes presidency but retains title Der Führer. Army swears allegiance.
September 15, 1935	Nuremberg Laws prohibit marriage and sexual intercourse between Jews and German nationals.
November 9–10, 1938	Anti-Jewish pogrom, the *Kristallnacht* (Crystal Night).
September 1, 1939	Germany invades Poland, forcing declarations of war from Britain and France two days later.
September 21, 1939	Polish Jews ordered into ghettos.
October 12, 1939	Austrian Jews deported to east.
May 10, 1940	Germany invades Holland, France, and Belgium.
June 22, 1941	German forces launch invasion of Russia.
July 31, 1941	Reich Marshall Hermann Goering gives S.S. Lt. Colonel Reinhard Heydrich a written order to achieve a "general solution to the Jewish problem in areas of Jewish influence in Europe."
January 20, 1942	Heydrich proposes Final Solution to the "Jewish problem" at Wansee Conference.
July 1942	Liquidation of Jewish ghetto in Warsaw begins.
August–September 1942	German advance in North Africa halted at El Alamein.
February 2, 1943	German army at Stalingrad surrenders.
June 6, 1944	D-day invasion of Allied forces on Normandy coast. Liberation of concentration camps begins as Allies gradually secure territory from German control.
May 2, 1945	Fall of Berlin to Soviet forces.
May 7, 1945	German surrender. Resettlement of Jews becomes a political and moral issue in postwar Europe.

STUDY QUESTIONS

1. What were the main accusations leveled against the Jews by Hitler and the Nazis? Does the Jewish defense seem convincing? Why were the Jews legally restricted?

2. In the conference on the Jewish question (November 12, 1938), the topic concerned the isolation of the Jews. What measures does Heydrich advocate? Why is Goering's solution inevitable?

3. What solutions to the Jewish problem were presented at the Wansee Conference? On the basis of this evidence and on the directive of Hermann Goering, how would you define the "Final Solution"? What did it entail? Why was there no specific talk of extermination in these documents?

4. After reading through the accounts concerning the death camps, what are your feelings? What statements by Rudolf Hoess in his testimony at Nuremberg and in his autobiography stand out in your mind? Why? How does he free himself from guilt while still accepting it?

5. Granted that Jews were both submissive and resistant to Nazi atrocities during the Holocaust, how do you think you would react under the same stress and abuse?

6. In your opinion, was justice served and the dead avenged by the Nuremberg trials and execution of Nazi leaders?

7. In the opinion of Eric Hoffer, why were the Jews killed and why are people able to commit such acts? Do you agree with him?

8. Comment on another statement of Eric Hoffer's: "It is obvious . . . that in order to be effective, a doctrine must not be understood, but has to be believed in. We can be absolutely certain only about things we do not understand; a doctrine that is understood is shorn of its strength." Do you agree? How can you relate this to the Holocaust?

9. After reading the selection by Raul Hilberg, "The Destruction of the European Jews," do you think such a thing as the Holocaust could happen again?

10. In a way, was the Holocaust the inevitable outcome of the racist and Social Darwinist ideas that were discussed in the chapter on "Nationalism and Imperialism"? Was the Holocaust "conditioned" by the expendability of life that was so characteristic of battles during World War I? Was the Holocaust itself a precedent for the American bombing of Hiroshima? As you look at the world today, give some examples of attitudes, specific organizations, or individuals that might threaten reoccurrence of genocide. What can be done?

11

The Era of the Superpowers: Confrontation and the Dynamics of Change

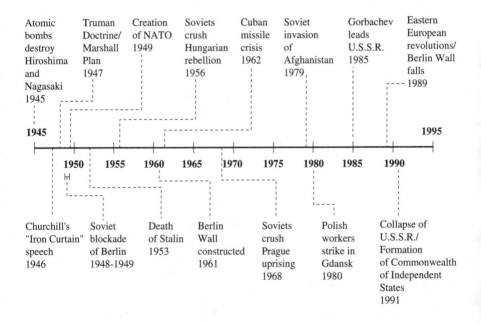

Atomic bombs destroy Hiroshima and Nagasaki 1945

Truman Doctrine/ Marshall Plan 1947

Creation of NATO 1949

Soviets crush Hungarian rebellion 1956

Cuban missile crisis 1962

Soviet invasion of Afghanistan 1979

Gorbachev leads U.S.S.R. 1985

Eastern European revolutions/ Berlin Wall falls 1989

1945

1995

1945 1950 1955 1960 1965 1970 1975 1980 1985 1990

Churchill's "Iron Curtain" speech 1946

Soviet blockade of Berlin 1948-1949

Death of Stalin 1953

Berlin Wall constructed 1961

Soviets crush Prague uprising 1968

Polish workers strike in Gdansk 1980

Collapse of U.S.S.R./ Formation of Commonwealth of Independent States 1991

Whether you like it or not, history is on our side. We will bury you.

—Nikita Khrushchev

There is nothing more difficult to take in hand, more perilous to conduct, or more uncertain in its success than to take the lead in a new order of things.

—Niccolò Machiavelli

Much of what accumulated in the stifling and repressive atmosphere of Stalinism and stagnation, and is now surfacing, is far from pleasant and constructive. But this has to be tolerated. This is what a revolution is all about. Its primary function is always to give people freedom. And *perestroika* with its democratization and *glasnost* has already fulfilled its primary task.

—Mikhail Gorbachev

Russia is doomed to be governed by fools; she knows no other way.

—Alexander Solzhenitsyn

History teaches us that enmities between nations . . . do not last forever. However fixed our likes and dislikes, the tide of time and events will often bring surprising changes in the relations between nations and neighbors.

—John F. Kennedy

Many people feel empty, a world that seemed so strong just collapsed. Forty years have been wasted on stupid strife for the sake of an unsuccessful experiment.

—George Konrad

In the end we beat them with Levi 501 jeans. Seventy-two years of Communist indoctrination and propaganda was drowned out by a three-ounce Sony Walkman. A huge totalitarian system . . . has been brought to its knees because nobody wants to wear Bulgarian shoes. Now they're lunch, and we're number one on the planet.

—P. J. O'Rourke

The autopsy of history is that all great nations commit suicide.

—Arnold Toynbee

CHAPTER THEMES

- *Systems of Government:* Was the Cold War an ideological struggle between two different systems of government, or did it have very little to do with government at all? What was the root cause of the Cold War?

- *Imperialism:* Was the Cold War just another term for "ideological imperialism"? Was the Cold War really about the accumulation of territory or about the winning of "hearts and minds"? How does this differ from nineteenth-century imperialism?

- *Propaganda:* Just how does one spot a communist? Were the fear and distrust during the Cold War real or were they manufactured by governments seeking justification for authority?

- **Beliefs and Spirituality:**   How did the Cold War transform the concepts of freedom and tyranny, of democracy and totalitarianism into a spiritual realm where abstractions obscured reality? Was nuclear destruction such a threat that each side deified its leaders, and transformed its ideologies into pure truth, to be supported without equivocation?

- **Women in History:**   What political, social, and economic strides have women made in the last 150 years? Have women attained true equality with men in our contemporary society? How much influence has Madison Avenue advertising had on the definition of women's roles in society? Do movies and advertising create images or reflect them? Has the women's movement run its course, or will there always be a need to redefine the relationship between the sexes?

- **Historical Change and Transition:**   Have the computer revolution and new medical technologies accelerated the process of decline in Western Civilization? Or do you resist this idea? To what extent might advanced technologies impede the process of decline? In fact, are we in decline at all as a society or are we moving toward international social justice and a solution to many of the world's political and economic problems?

The erection of the Berlin Wall in August 1961 separated East and West Berlin but also symbolized the Cold War rivalry that had developed between the United States and the Soviet Union. *(UPI/Corbis)*

- **The Big Picture:**   How should we measure progress in civilization? Is it a quantifiable commodity linked to advances in technology? Or is the ethical development of humanity the only real determinant of whether a society has evolved and progressed? Is human nature basically good or evil? Is this the fundamental question that must be answered before political systems can be developed or social programs instituted? Where are we headed in the next century, and what is the value of studying history?

The use of atomic weapons by American forces on the Japanese cities of Hiroshima and Nagasaki in August 1945 presaged not only the end of World War II but also the end of an era. The world entered the nuclear age when modern science joined with military necessity to produce an astonishing desolation. The horrors of trench warfare, poisonous gas, dislocated refugees, and the deprivation and starvation that had plagued the victims of two world wars could not compare with the new possibilities: Human beings had finally discovered a way to destroy themselves and their world. The power unleashed by the splitting of the atom had created a completely new distribution of power. Those countries that had access to the necessary materials and technologies were in a position to dominate and impose their will on less developed regions. As the people of Europe struggled to find food and shelter, to repair their lives and mourn their dead, another game was being played with the ultimate risk at stake. This was a contest between good and evil, between dominance and survival—between the United States and the Soviet Union.

The uneasy relationship between the United States and the Soviet Union was not created at the end of World War II. Its roots were deep and primarily philosophical. The United States had been founded on the principles of the eighteenth-century Enlightenment. There existed "natural rights" that were the birthright of each individual: life, liberty, and property. The government was to exist in balance with its citizens, protecting the rights of the individual while seeing to the general welfare of its population. Capitalism, with its inherent emphasis on private enterprise and the reward of individual ability, hard work, and perseverance, blended nicely with the ideals of the democratic political system. As it was applied in the United States, capitalism was not always successful and not always fair. It was regulated by the federal government at various intervals in order to protect the general welfare of the citizenry. But the American commitment to personal liberty was never in question. The fear of communism as a threat to the "American way" was inculcated in the public consciousness in the first decades of the twentieth century.

The Soviet Union was founded on a different philosophical premise. It was created in 1917 when the Bolshevik party seized power from a Provisional Government that had opposed the absolutism of the Russian tsar and was both democratic and capitalistic. The Bolsheviks were lead by Vladimir Lenin, a disciple of the German philosopher Karl Marx. Marx had developed the economic theory of communism, which decried the exploitation of workers by middle-class entrepreneurs who sought a profit at all costs. Marx's complex philosophy argued that the conflict engendered by competing capitalistic forces would eventually lead to a communist society where the state would "wither away" and all people would live in harmony, giving what labor they could to the community and taking just what they needed to live a life of mutual respect and tolerance. Communism theoretically looks to the best in human nature—that people are basically good and that they will share the necessities of life with others. Thus, Marx expected "world revolution" that would free people from the class exploitation of capitalism: "The proletarians have nothing to lose but their chains. They have a world to win. Workers of the world unite!"

Communism, it should be noted, is an economic theory, not a political system. If anything, the state is supposed to remove itself from the life of its citizens. Marx believed that the world would naturally evolve toward communism, but he left no practical plans for the application of his ideas. Lenin based the Russian Revolution of 1917 on Marx's philosophy but found himself having to make adjustments in Marx's theory. Americans felt threatened by the coming "world revolution," which sought the overthrow of their cherished principles of individualism and capitalism. The United States even sent troops to fight against the communists in 1918 when Lenin had not yet consolidated control of the government.

Communism therefore became a great evil in the American mind. When Lenin died in 1924 and Joseph Stalin struggled for control of the new Soviet state, further modifications in Marx's philosophy confirmed American fears. Instead of the Soviet state "withering away," Stalin increased its authority and actually "redefined" Marxism to justify his reorganization of agriculture and industry in order to protect the Soviet state from hostile Western democracies. From about 1928 to 1940, Stalin imprisoned and eliminated millions of Russians who resisted his authority. Secret police and a Siberian prison system known as the "Gulag" sought to maintain total control over the population. The term "totalitarian" has been coined to describe this complete imprisonment of society to the dictatorship of the state.

It was therefore with great delicacy that the Western Allies in 1940 decided to "sleep with the enemy" and join Stalin in the crusade against Hitler and Nazism during World War II. This was from the first an expedient relationship—Hitler, the Great Evil, had to be vanquished, and Stalin became a tolerable, lesser evil.

But with the victory over Hitler assured in 1945, Europe became the battleground once again for a new war—the Cold War. As European governments licked their wounds and looked to the immediate needs of their citizens, they retreated from the empires that they had established and depended on for decades. Britain removed itself from controlling interests in Africa, India, and the Middle East, while France loosened its control over countries in Africa and Southeast Asia. Into this power vacuum flowed the interests of the new emerging "superpowers," each trying to compete for the "hearts and minds" as well as the territory of the remnants. Even though the Soviet Union had suffered the greatest losses (nearly eighteen million military and civilian dead) of all combatants in World War II, the need to maintain and expand its position in the face of perceived Western encroachment became Stalin's obsession. By 1946, Winston Churchill spoke of an "Iron Curtain" that had descended over eastern Europe, trapping Hungary, Czechoslovakia, Bulgaria, Romania, Poland, and East Germany. The United States sought to reinforce Western democracies by providing financial aid through the Marshall Plan in 1947. The United States also moved to halt Soviet expansionism in 1947 by proclaiming the Truman Doctrine, which justified intervention against communist movements. Containment of communist "world revolution" became the watchword of American foreign policy throughout the 1950s and 1960s.

The Cold War between the United States and the Soviet Union lasted from about 1945 to 1990. This was a bipolar arrangement in which the world in a sense was held hostage by two nations, philosophically opposed to one another, paranoid about losing face and territory to the unspeakable evil of the other. New alliance systems like NATO and the Warsaw Pact were developed to achieve a balance of power. Military competition was intense as both countries expended billions in order to develop new weapons systems and accumulate more tanks, more missiles, more bombers. The world became a dangerous place in the 1960s as the arms race was on, fueled by military theories that demanded "parity" with the enemy. Mutually Assured Destruction (MAD) was presented as a security measure—if each side could destroy the other many times over, then it would be too dangerous to start a war with a "first strike." The balance of power was thus maintained and peace assured by building ever more sophisticated weaponry, the mere threat of which was enough to keep the peace.

This is not to say that there weren't outbreaks of "hot war." The Korean "police action" (1950–1953), the Cuban "missile crisis" (1962), and the Vietnam "conflict" (1960–1975) were euphemistic struggles in which the two superpowers "fought," often through surrogates without formally declaring war, in order to achieve geopolitical position and influence over strategic regions of the world.

There was a price to pay for the tension of the Cold War, even if the world was spared a nuclear holocaust. Weapon systems developed during the 1980s such as the B-1 bomber, the M-1 tank, stealth fighter aircraft, and the laser-based Strategic Defense Initiative (SDI, or "Star Wars") cost hundreds of billions of dollars and drove defense expenditures to nearly one-quarter of the national budget.

In the Soviet Union, the expense of competing in the arms race proved fatal. The Soviets could put cosmonauts in space and sophisticated MIG fighters in the air but could not put bread on the table or refrigerators in the houses of Soviet citizens. The managed economy of a Soviet state that was supposed to have "withered away" proved disastrous as the workforce became apathetic and inefficient. The Soviets were never able to solve the many ethnic problems that plagued the unity of their political system, and, more importantly, the government was never able to cultivate the trust and commitment of its people that are essential to success and stability. By the time that Mikhail Gorbachev came on the scene in 1985 with his policies of *glasnost* ("openness") and *perestroika* ("political restructuring"), social and economic problems were spinning out of control. The ossified political leadership that had survived Stalin by committing itself to his policies, methods, and priorities for so long could not prepare the Soviet Union for the future.

By 1991, the Soviet Union had collapsed, with its empire of dependent countries broken apart and left to fend for themselves. The United States had won the Cold War and rejoiced in its "victory," the triumph of Capitalism over Communism, of Right over Wrong, of Good over Evil. But it is up to each of us to assess the damage wrought by fifty years of distrust and destructive competition. The world, as it moves toward the twenty-first century, is very different than it was in 1945 when the evil of Hitler could be defined and destroyed. When there is no longer an evil to be vanquished, which road do you take? What are you willing to fight and die for? What is your agenda for the future? How long will it take for the deception and distrust created by Cold War propaganda to disappear? And what will replace it? The twenty-first century awaits.

The Cold War (1945–1990)

The "Superpower" Rivalry and the Rejection of Stalin

The Soviet Victory: Capitalism Versus Communism (February 1946)

JOSEPH STALIN

The term "Cold War" describes the era of uneasy relations between the Western Allies and the Soviet Union after World War II. Each was competing for influence in Europe through propaganda and troop placement. In the first excerpt, the Soviet leader Joseph Stalin offered a glimpse of the ideological combat that was to be waged in the future. A month later, Winston Churchill, who had largely directed the British war effort, warned the West of the deceptive Soviet Union in his famous "Iron Curtain" speech.

It would be wrong to believe that the Second World War broke out accidentally or as a result of the mistakes of some or other statesmen, though mistakes certainly were made. In reality, the war broke out as an inevitable result of the development of world economic and political forces on the basis of modern monopoly capitalism.

Marxists have stated more than once that the capitalist system of world economy conceals in itself the elements of general crisis and military clashes, that in view of this in our time the development of world capitalism takes place not as a smooth and even advance but through crises and war catastrophes.

The reason is that the unevenness of the development of capitalist countries usually results, as time passes, in an abrupt disruption of the equilibrium within the world system of capitalism, and that a group of capitalist countries which believes itself to be less supplied with raw materials and markets usually attempts to alter the situation and re-divide the "spheres of influence" in its own favour by means of armed force. . . .

This results in the splitting of the capitalist world into two hostile camps and in war between them. Perhaps the catastrophes of war could be avoided if there existed the possibility of re-distributing periodically raw materials and markets among the countries in accordance with their economic weight—by means of adopting coordinated and peaceful decisions. This, however,

"The Soviet Victory" is from Embassy of the U.S.S.R., Speech Delivered by J. V. Stalin at a Meeting of Voters of the Stalin Electoral Area of Moscow (Washington, D.C.: Government Printing Office, 1946).

cannot be accomplished under present capitalist conditions of the development of world economy. . . .

As to our country, for her the war was the severest and hardest of all the wars our Motherland has ever experienced in her history.

But the war was not only a curse. It was at the same time a great school in which all the forces of the people were tried and tested. The war laid bare all the facts and events in the rear and at the front, it mercilessly tore off all the veils and covers which had concealed the true faces of States, governments, and parties, and placed them on the stage without masks, without embellishments, with all their shortcomings and virtues.

• • •

And so, what are the results of the war? . . .

Our victory means, in the first place, that our Soviet social system has won, that the Soviet social system successfully withstood the trial in the flames of war and proved its perfect viability.

It is well known that the foreign press more than once asserted that the Soviet social system is a "risky experiment" doomed to failure, that the Soviet system is a "house of cards," without any roots in life, imposed upon the people by the organs of the "Cheka," [secret police] that a slight push from outside would be enough to blow this "house of cards" to smithereens.

Now we can say that the war swept away all these assertions of the foreign press as groundless. The war has shown that the Soviet social system is a truly popular system, which has grown from the people and enjoys its powerful support, that the Soviet social system is a perfectly viable and stable form of organisation of society.

More than that, the point is now not whether the Soviet social system is viable or not, since after the objective lessons of the war no single skeptic now ventures to come out with doubts concerning the viability of the Soviet social system. The point now is that the Soviet social system has proved more viable and stable than a non-Soviet social system, that the Soviet social system is a better form of organisation of society than any non-Soviet social system.

"An Iron Curtain Has Descended Across the Continent" (March 1946)
SIR WINSTON CHURCHILL

I now come to the . . . danger which threatens the cottage home and ordinary people, namely tyranny. We cannot be blind to the fact that the liberties enjoyed by individual citizens throughout the United States and British Empire are not valid in a considerable number of countries, some of which are very

"'An Iron Curtain Has Descended Across the Continent'" is from *Congressional Record,* 79th Congress, 2nd session, pp. A1145–A1147.

powerful. In these states control is forced upon the common people by various kinds of all-embracing police governments, to a degree which is overwhelming and contrary to every principle of democracy. The power of the state is exercised without restraint, either by dictators or by compact oligarchies operating through a privileged party and a political police. It is not our duty at this time, when difficulties are so numerous, to interfere forcibly in the internal affairs of countries whom we have not conquered in war, but we must never cease to proclaim in fearless tones the great principles of freedom and the rights of man, which are the joint inheritance of the English-speaking world and which, through Magna Carta, the Bill of Rights, the habeas corpus, trial by jury, and the English common law find their famous expression in the Declaration of Independence. . . .

A shadow has fallen upon the scenes so lately lighted by the Allied victory. Nobody knows what Soviet Russia and its Communist international organization intends to do in the immediate future, or what are the limits, if any, to their expansive and proselytizing tendencies. . . . From Stettin in the Baltic to Trieste in the Adriatic, an iron curtain has descended across the continent. Behind that line lie all the capitals of the ancient states of central and eastern Europe. Warsaw, Berlin, Prague, Vienna, Budapest, Belgrade, Bucharest, and Sofia, all these famous cities and the populations around them lie in the Soviet sphere and all are subject, in one form or another, not only to Soviet influence but to a very high and increasing measure of control from Moscow. Athens alone, with its immortal glories, is free to decide its future at an election under British, American, and French observation.

In a great number of countries, far from the Russian frontiers and throughout the world, Communist fifth columns are established and work in complete unity and absolute obedience to the directions they receive from the Communist center. Except in the British Commonwealth, and in the United States, where communism is in its infancy, the Communist parties and fifth columns constitute a growing challenge and peril to Christian civilization. These are somber facts for anyone to have to recite on the morrow of a victory gained by so much splendid comradeship in arms and in the cause of freedom and democracy, and we should be most unwise not to face them squarely while time remains. . . .

On the other hand, I repulse the idea that a new war is inevitable, still more that it is imminent. It is because I am so sure that our fortunes are in our own hands and that we hold the power to save the future, that I feel the duty to speak out now that I have occasion to do so. I do not believe that Soviet Russia desires war. What they desire is the fruits of war and the indefinite expansion of their power and doctrines. But what we have to consider here today while time remains, is the permanent prevention of war and the establishment of conditions of freedom and democracy as rapidly as possible in all countries.

Our difficulties and dangers will not be removed by closing our eyes to them; they will not be removed by mere waiting to see what happens; nor will they be relieved by a policy of appeasement. What is needed is a settlement, and the longer this is delayed, the more difficult it will be and the greater our dangers will become. From what I have seen of our Russian friends and allies during the war, I am convinced that there is nothing they admire so much as strength, and there is nothing for which they have less respect than for military weakness. For that reason the old doctrine of a balance of power is unsound. We cannot afford, if we can help it, to work on narrow margins, offering temptations to a trial of strength. If the western democracies stand together in strict adherence to the principles of the United Nations Charter, their influence for furthering these principles will be immense and no one is likely to molest them. If, however, they become divided or falter in their duty, and if these all-important years are allowed to slip away, then indeed catastrophe may overwhelm us all.

The Truman Doctrine (March 1947)
HARRY S TRUMAN

In the first months of 1946, President Truman received urgent requests from the Greek government for economic assistance, which, it was hoped, would put an end to the chaos and strife hindering its recovery from the war. Hoping to forestall Communist dissidents who were threatening the stability of the government, Truman appealed to Congress to appropriate such financial assistance. He also asked for military as well as economic aid to Turkey. The controversial Truman Doctrine, as it came to be called, committed the United States to an active policy of promoting ideological divisions between it and the Soviet Union, and further escalated Cold War tensions. The Marshall Plan of 1947, which advocated the rebuilding of West Germany after the war, is an example of this policy of Soviet containment.

One of the primary objectives of the foreign policy of the United States is the creation of conditions in which we and other nations will be able to work out a way of life free from coercion. This was a fundamental issue in the war with Germany and Japan. Our victory was won over countries which sought to impose their will, and their way of life, upon other nations.

To ensure the peaceful development of nations, free from coercion, the United States has taken a leading part in establishing the United Nations. The United Nations is designed to make possible lasting freedom and independence for all its members. We shall not realize our objectives, however, unless we are willing to help free peoples to maintain their free institutions and their national integrity against aggressive movements that seek to impose upon them totalitarian regimes. This is no more than a frank recognition that totalitarian regimes imposed upon free peoples, by direct or indirect aggression, undermine the foundations of international peace and hence the security of the United States.

The peoples of a number of countries of the world have recently had totalitarian regimes forced upon them against their will. The Government of the United States has made frequent protests against coercion and intimidation, in violation

"The Truman Doctrine" is from *Public Papers of the President,* Harry S Truman, 1947 (Washington, D.C.: Government Printing Office, 1963), pp. 177–180.

of the Yalta agreement, in Poland, Rumania, and Bulgaria. I must also state that in a number of other countries there have been similar developments. At the present moment in world history nearly every nation must choose between alternative ways of life. The choice is too often not a free one.

One way of life is based upon the will of the majority, and is distinguished by free institutions, representative government, free elections, guarantees of individual liberty, freedom of speech and religion, and freedom from political oppression.

The second way of life is based upon the will of a minority forcibly imposed upon the majority. It relies upon terror and oppression, a controlled press and radio, fixed elections, and the suppression of personal freedoms.

I believe that it must be the policy of the United States to support free peoples who are resisting attempted subjugation by armed minorities or by outside pressures.

I believe that we must assist free peoples to work out their own destinies in their own way.

I believe that our help should be primarily through economic and financial aid which is essential to economic stability and orderly political processes.

The world is not static, and the status quo is not sacred. But we cannot allow changes in the status quo in violation of the Charter of United Nations by such methods as coercion, or by such subterfuges as political infiltration. In helping free and independent nations to maintain their freedom, the United States will be giving effect to the principles of the Charter of the United Nations. . . .

The seeds of totalitarian regimes are nurtured by misery and want. They spread and grow in the evil soil of poverty and strife. They reach their full growth when the hope of a people for a better life has died.

We must keep that hope alive.

The free peoples of the world look to us for support in maintaining their freedoms.

If we falter in our leadership, we may endanger the peace of the world—and we shall surely endanger the welfare of this Nation.

Great responsibilities have been placed upon us by the swift movement of events.

I am confident that the Congress will face these responsibilities squarely.

The Marshall Plan (June 1947)

GEORGE C. MARSHALL

The truth of the matter is that Europe's requirements for the next three or four years of foreign food and other essential products—principally from America—are so much greater than her present ability to pay that she must

"The Marshall Plan" is from *Department of State Bulletin* (June 15, 1947), pp. 1159–1160.

have substantial additional help or face economic, social, and political deterioration of a very grave character.

The remedy lies in breaking the vicious circle and restoring the confidence of the European people in the economic future of their own countries and of Europe as a whole. The manufacturer and the farmer throughout wide areas must be able and willing to exchange their products for currencies the continuing value of which is not open to question.

Aside from the demoralizing effect on the world at large and the possibilities of disturbances arising as a result of the desperation of the people concerned, the consequences to the economy of the United States should be apparent to all. It is logical that the United States should do whatever it is able to do to assist in the return of normal economic health in the world, without which there can be no political stability and no assured peace. Our policy is directed not against any country or doctrine but against hunger, poverty, desperation, and chaos. Its purpose should be the revival of a working economy in the world so as to permit the emergence of political and social conditions in which free institutions can exist. Such assistance, I am convinced, must not be on a piecemeal basis as various crises develop. Any assistance that this Government may render in the future should provide a cure rather than a mere palliative. Any government that is willing to assist in the task of recovery will find full cooperation, I am sure, on the part of the United States Government. Any government which maneuvers to block the recovery of other countries cannot expect help from us. Furthermore, governments, political parties, or groups which seek to perpetuate human misery in order to profit therefrom politically or otherwise will encounter the opposition of the United States.

It is already evident that, before the United States Government can proceed much further in its efforts to alleviate the situation and help start the European world on its way to recovery, there must be some agreement among the countries of Europe as to the requirements of the situation and the part those countries themselves will take in order to give proper effect to whatever action might be undertaken by this Government. It would be neither fitting nor efficacious for this Government to undertake to draw up unilaterally a program designed to place Europe on its feet economically. This is the business of the Europeans. The initiative, I think, must come from Europe. The role of this country should consist of friendly aid in the drafting of a European program and of later support of such a program so far as it may be practical for us to do so. The program should be a joint one, agreed to by a number, if not all, European nations.

An essential part of any successful action on the part of the United States is an understanding on the part of the people of America of the character of the problem and the remedies to be applied. Political passion and prejudice should have no part. With foresight, and a willingness on the part of our people to face up to the vast responsibility which history has clearly placed upon our country, the difficulties I have outlined can and will be overcome.

An Assessment of Communism (1953)
THEODORE WHITE

Distrust and tension between the United States and the Soviet Union continued to mount in 1948 as the Russians stopped all traffic, including food transports, into their zone of German occupation. From June 1948 to May 1949, the United States airlifted supplies to the people of Berlin and defied Soviet heavy-handedness. This tenacious policy in the face of Soviet aggression was termed "containment."

By 1950, it was natural to begin assessing the events that had transpired during the first half of the century and to speculate on developments for the future. In 1953, the Soviet leader Joseph Stalin died, and many wondered how this might change the face of communism and subsequently the nature of the Cold War. Theodore White, a journalist who had spent much of his early career in China and became famous for his political analysis of the presidency, offered this view of communism in 1953.

Americans are so frightened by the evil in communism that they fail to see that the greatest danger is not the evil but the attraction in it. Only Americans live in a society in which communism can seduce no healthy mind. Most of our senior Allies and the myriad-man countries who live outside our Alliance are made of people who stand transfixed by fear of communism and its sinister charm at the same time.

The magic appeal in the Communist faith is simple. It is the belief that pure logic applied to human affairs is enough to change the world and cure it of all its human miseries. It is buttressed by the belief that the processes of history are governed by certain "scientific" laws, which automatically guarantee the triumph of communism when the situation is ripe, if only its protestants have the courage to strike and act.

This simple credo carries an almost irresistible attraction to two kinds of people everywhere in the world: first, to small coteries of able and ambitious young men hungry for the ecstasy of leadership, and, secondly, to larger masses of ignorant people who have just begun to hope.

To both these schools of converts, the fatal flaw in the Communist faith is neither apparent nor important. This fatal flaw is embedded in the nature of human beings whenever they gather politically. Human beings tend to be illogical. The logic of which communism boasts is never certain, therefore, of success in any political operation unless simultaneously it imposes so rigid a discipline as to make ordinary people mere bodies in the sequence of their masters' planning. Logic cannot succeed if its premises are to be shaken over and over again by vagrant human emotions allowed freely to express themselves in all their passion and frailty. Any political organization which sets out to be totally logical thus calls for total discipline; total discipline inevitably requires police, and police bring terror.

"An Assessment of Communism" is from Theodore H. White, *Fire in the Ashes* (New York: William Sloane Associates Publishers, 1953), pp. 318–320.

But the weakness of communism lies less in the calculated immorality of terror than in the inevitable internal appetite of the discipline. The discipline feeds on itself; it shrinks the area of discussion and decision into ever narrower, ever tighter, ever more cramped circles. Fewer and fewer men have less and less access to the raw facts which are necessary for wise judgment. The discipline they control and impose inevitably sneaks back to weaken them, to blind or deafen them into stupidity and error.

To those who come to communism out of ambition or out of misguided intelligence, this flaw is not immediately apparent. Each of this type of convert cherishes the illusion until too late that the ever-shrinking circle of discipline will leave him safe at its center of creative leadership, rather than crushed and tortured as discipline contracts about his own soft human body. To the second category of converts, those who come to it out of hunger and ignorance, this flaw in communism (even if it could be explained to them) seems unimportant. They have always been excluded from decision and control over their own lives. Communism promises them simply "more"; they are ready to believe. The hungrier and more ignorant they are, the more difficult it is to explain to them that their own hopes and welfare are directly dependent on the freedom of creative minds, with which they are unfamiliar, to think independently of all discipline.

To the Western world, so challenged by communism, this flaw in the adversary presents a grotesque problem. Communism's prison-logical system of human organization grows in strength decade by decade even as its leadership becomes less and less capable of wise and sensible decision. For all its dynamism and strength, the Communist world falls into blunders with increasing frequency, blunders which are only rectified by great wrenchings of policy that shake the world with disaster. To deal with communism, one must recognize both its strength and its blunders clearly. . . .

Such an event as the death of Stalin, by shaking the superstructure of discipline, by admitting for a brief moment the clash of several opinions and the consequent opportunity for a slightly larger area of discussion at the summit, has given the Communist machinery of politics a momentary opportunity to review some of its errors. But, unless communism ceases to be communism, the process of discipline calls for a new tightening of control, a new struggle to apply the logic of a single man to a world of dark and uncertain phenomena.

How to Spot a Communist (1955)

The following article was issued by the U.S. First Army Headquarters for public dissemination and reveals the Cold War paranoia that was so much a part of the decade of the 1950s.

"How to Spot a Communist" was first issued by First Army Headquarters in a pamphlet entitled *How to Spot a Communist*. It was reprinted by *U.S.A., An American Magazine of Fact and Opinion,* in a special supplement on June 22, 1955. Copyright © 1955 by U.S.A. Contained in Anthony Bouscaren, ed., *A Guide to Anti-Communist Action* (Chicago: Henry Regnery Company, 1958), pp. 174–185.

Events of recent years have made it obvious that there is no fool-proof way of detecting a Communist. The Communist individual is no longer a "type" exemplified by the bearded and coarse revolutionary with time bomb in briefcase. U.S. Communists come from all walks in life, profess all faiths, and exercise all trades and professions. In addition, the Communist Party, USA, has made concerted efforts to go underground for the purpose of infiltration.

If there is no fool-proof system in spotting a Communist, there are, fortunately, indications that may give him away. These indications are often subtle but always present, for the Communist, by reason of his "faith" must act and talk along certain lines.

While a certain heaviness of style and preference for long sentences is common to most Communist writing, a distinct vocabulary provides the . . . more easily recognized feature of the "Communist Language."

Even a superficial reading of an article written by a Communist or a conversation with one will probably reveal the use of some of the following expressions: integrative thinking, vanguard, comrade, hootenanny, chauvinism, book-burning, syncretistic faith, bourgeois-nationalism, jingoism, colonialism, hooliganism, ruling class, progressive, demagogy, dialectical, witch-hunt, reactionary, exploitation, oppressive, materialist.

This list, selected at random, could be extended almost indefinitely. While all of the above expressions are part of the English language, their use by Communists is infinitely more frequent than by the general public. . . .

The tell-tale signs of the "Communist Religion" are not easy to detect. There is, above all, a rigidity in views insofar as they pertain to the Communist doctrine. This is not to say that the Communist lacks persuasiveness or variety of expression. It does mean, however, that he will stubbornly cling to the "line" even when proven wrong in debate. The Communist has implicit faith in Marxist philosophy and in the truth of the "line" as transmitted from Moscow. Because of this faith, he cannot and will not give ground when challenged on basic Marxist issues or political pronouncements made by his leaders. The possibility of compromising on these issues is utterly beyond his comprehension. . . .

His "religion," then, can give away the Communist. His naive and unquestioning acceptance of the "line," his refusal to accept criticism are excellent indications. Last but not least, the Communist feels a strong compulsion to speak his "faith" and can frequently be spotted by his never-ceasing attempts at conversion of others.

The "Communist Logic" . . . is diametrically opposed to our own. Thus, the Communist refers to the iron curtain police states as "democracies," and any defensive move on the part of the Western powers is condemned as "aggression." The Communist thus builds for himself a topsy-turvy world with a completely distorted set of values. For this reason, it is practically impossible to win an argument with a hard-core Communist. . . . The Communist mind cannot and will not engage in a detached examination of ideas. Talking to a Communist about his own ideas, then, is like listening to a phonograph record. His answers will invariably follow a definite pattern because he can never admit, even hypothetically, that the basis for his ideas may not be sound. This attitude is typical not only for the individual but also on a national scale. . . . The answer is final and no arguments are permitted so far as the Communists are concerned. The Communist, then, is not really "logical." The finality of his arguments and the completeness of his condemnation marks him clearly, whether as a speaker, a writer or a conversation partner.

In addition to these very general principles common to Communist tactics, a number of specific issues have been part of the Communist arsenal for a long period of time. These issues are raised not only by Communist appeals to the public, but also by the individual Party member or sympathizer who is a product of his Communist environment. They include: "McCarthyism," violation of civil rights, racial or religious discrimination, immigration laws, antisubversive legislation, any legislation concerning labor unions, the military budget, "peace."

While showing standard opposition to certain standard issues, the U.S. Communist has traditionally identified himself with certain activities in the hope of furthering his ultimate purposes. Such hobbies as "folk dancing" and "folk music" have been traditionally allied with the Communist movement in the United States. . . . The reason for their choice [of hobbies] is not altogether an attempt to hide political activities. The Communist's fondness for everything that comes from "the people" is not an entirely theoretical preference and has found expression in his everyday life. Most Communists are likely to show preference for group activities rather than such bourgeois forms of recreation as ballroom dancing. . . .

A study such as this can lead to only one certain conclusion: There is no sure-fire way of spotting a Communist. . . . The principle difficulty involved is the distinction between the person who merely dissents in the good old American tradition and the one who condemns for the purpose of abolishing that tradition.

In attempting to find the answer to the question: "Is this man a Communist?" a checklist such as this can prove helpful, although in itself it cannot provide the answer:

Does the individual use unusual language? ("Communist Language")

Does he stubbornly cling to Marxist ideals without being willing to question them?

Does he condemn our American institutions and praise those of Communist countries?

Does he pick on any event, even the most insignificant occurrences in this country for his criticism?

Is he secretive about certain of his contacts?

Does he belong to groups exploiting controversial subjects?

Above all, the approach to the problem of discovering Communists must be detached and completely free from prejudice. Using some of the clues mentioned in this study in connection with a factual approach provides the best system at present of spotting a Communist.

Self-Renewal: The Attack on Stalin (June 1956)
NIKITA KHRUSHCHEV

After Stalin's death in 1953, the power vacuum was eventually filled by Sergeye-vich (Nikita) Khrushchev. At the 20th Communist Party Congress, Khrushchev quite unexpectedly attacked Stalin and his legacy of fear. The Soviets were looking for a new beginning.

Comrades, in the report of the Central Committee of the Party at the 20th Congress, in a number of speeches by delegates to the Congress . . . quite a lot has been said about the cult of the individual and about its harmful consequences.

After Stalin's death the Central Committee of the Party began to implement a policy of explaining concisely and consistently that it is impermissible and foreign to the spirit of Marxism-Leninism to elevate one person, to transform him into a superman possessing supernatural characteristics akin to those of a god. Such a man supposedly knows everything, sees everything, thinks for everyone, can do anything, is infallible in his behavior.

Such a belief about a man, and specifically about Stalin, was cultivated among us for many years. . . .

Stalin originated the concept "enemy of the people." This term automatically rendered it unnecessary that the ideological errors of a man or men engaged in a controversy be proven; this term made possible the usage of the most cruel repression, violating all norms of revolutionary legality, against anyone who in any way disagreed with Stalin, against those who were only suspected of hostile intent, against those who had bad reputations. This concept, "enemy of the people," actually eliminated the possibility of any kind of ideological fight or the making of one's views known on this or that issue, even those of a practical character. In the main, and in actuality, the only proof of guilt used, against all norms of current legal science, was the "confession" of the accused himself; and, as subsequent probing proved, "confessions" were acquired through physical pressures against the accused.

This led to glaring violations of revolutionary legality, and to the fact that many entirely innocent persons, who in the past had defended the Party line, became victims.

We must assert that in regard to those persons who in their time had opposed the Party line, there were often no sufficient serious reasons for their physical annihilation. The formula, "enemy of the people" was specifically introduced for the purpose of physically annihilating such individuals. . . .

Thus, Stalin had sanctioned in the name of the Central Committee of the All-Union Communist Party (Bolsheviks) the most brutal violation of Socialist legality, torture and oppression, which led as we have seen to the slandering and self-accusation of innocent people.

"Self-Renewal" is from *Congressional Record*, 84th Congress, 2nd session, pp. 9390–9402 (June 4, 1956).

Speech to the 22nd Communist Party Congress (1962)

NIKITA KHRUSHCHEV

Although there may have been hope that the fears of the Cold War would be re-
duced, the decade from 1955 to 1966 was especially intense in its rhetoric and
ideological conflict. As Khrushchev menacingly said of capitalist states in 1956,
"Whether you like it or not, history is on our side. We will bury you!" This was
the era of Senator Joseph McCarthy, who played on the fears of Americans with
his deceitful rantings that communists had infiltrated the highest echelons of gov-
ernment. It was during this time (1961) that the Berlin Wall was built, sealing
off the city into communist and democratic sectors—a symbolic as well as practi-
cal measure. And finally, in 1962, the two superpowers nearly went to nuclear
war as President Kennedy demanded the removal of Soviet missiles from Cuba.
The following excerpt is from Khrushchev's speech to the 22nd Congress of the
Communist party. Note the argument carefully.

The most rabid imperialists, acting on the principle of "after us the deluge,"
openly voice their desire to undertake a new war venture. The ideologists of
imperialism, intimidating the peoples, try to instill a kind of philosophy of
hopelessness and desperation. Hysterically they cry: "Better death under capitalism than life under communism." They do not like free peoples to flourish,
you see. They fear that the peoples in their countries too will take the path of
socialism. Blinded by class hatred, our enemies are ready to doom all mankind
to the catastrophe of war. The imperialists' opportunities to carry out their
aggressive designs, however, are becoming smaller and smaller. They behave
like a feeble and greedy old man whose powers have been exhausted, whose
physical capacity has weakened, but whose avid desires remain. . . .

As long as the imperialist aggressors exist, we must be on guard, keep our
powder dry, improve the defense of the socialist countries, their armed forces
and the state security agencies. If, in the face of common sense, the imperialists dare attack the socialist countries and plunge mankind into the abyss of a
world war of annihilation, this mad act of theirs would be their last, it would
be the end of the whole system of capitalism. (*Applause.*)

Our party clearly understands its tasks, its responsibility, and will do everything in its power to see to it that the world socialist system continues to grow
stronger, gathers fresh strength and develops. We believe that in the competition with capitalism socialism will win. (*Prolonged applause.*) We believe that
this victory will be won in peaceful competition and not by way of unleashing
a war. We have stood, we stand and we will stand by the positions of peaceful
competition of states with different social systems; we will do everything to
strengthen world peace. (*Prolonged applause.*)

"Speech to the 22nd Communist Party Congress" is from *Current Soviet Policies,* IV (New York,
1962), pp. 44–45, 50, 77. Reprinted by permission of *The Current Digest.*

The most important component of our party's foreign policy activities is *the struggle for general and complete disarmament.* The Soviet Union has been waging this struggle for many years now, and doing so firmly and perseveringly. We have always been resolutely opposed to the arms race, since rivalry in this sphere in the past not only saddled the peoples with a terrible burden but inevitably led to world wars. We are even more resolutely opposed to the arms race now that there has been a colossal technical revolution in the art of war and the use of today's weapons would inevitably entail the deaths of hundreds of millions of people.

The stockpiling of these weapons, proceeding as it is in a setting of cold war and war hysteria, is fraught with disastrous consequences. All that has to happen is for the nerves of some fellow in uniform to crack while he is on duty at a "push-button" somewhere in the West, and things may happen that will bring more than a little misfortune upon the peoples of the whole world.

Naturally, when we put forward a program of general and complete disarmament, we are talking not about the unilateral disarmament of socialism in the face of imperialism or vice versa, but about universal renunciation of arms as a means of solving problems at issue among states. . . .

The example of the Soviet Union inspires all progressive mankind. Never has the great vital force of Marxist-Leninist teaching been so clearly evident as in our days, now that socialism has triumphed fully and finally in the Soviet Union, the cause of socialism is winning new victories in the countries of the world socialist commonwealth, and the international Communist and workers' movement and the national liberation struggle of peoples are growing and expanding tempestuously. The revolution awakened the great energy of peoples, which is transforming the world on the principles of socialism and communism. Colossal changes are taking place and will take place throughout the world under the influence of the successes of communism.

The victory of communism is inevitable! (*Stormy applause.*)

The great army of Communists and of Marxist-Leninists acts as the vanguard of the peoples in the struggle for peace, for social progress and for communism, the bright future of mankind. New and ever newer millions of people will assemble and rally under the great banner of communism. The cause of progress, the cause of communism will triumph! (*Stormy applause.*)

Long live the great and heroic Soviet people, the builders of communism! (*Stormy applause.*)

Long live the indestructible unity and fraternal friendship of the peoples of the world socialist camp! (*Stormy applause.*)

Long live the heroic party of the Communists of the Soviet Union, created and tempered in struggle by the great Lenin! (*Stormy applause.*)

Long live the indestructible unity of the international Communist and workers' movement and the fraternal solidarity of the proletarians of all countries! (*Stormy applause.*)

Long live peace the world over! (*Stormy applause.*)

Under the all-conquering banner of Marxism-Leninism, under the leadership of the Communist Party, forward to the victory of communism! (*Stormy, prolonged applause, turning into an ovation. All rise.*)

Currents of Dissent in the "Evil Empire"

During the early 1970s, the Soviet Union and United States, under the leadership, respectively, of Leonid Brezhnev and Richard Nixon, demonstrated cooperation through cultural exchanges and even negotiated a Strategic Arms Limitation Treaty (SALT) in 1972. This policy of détente, as it was called, was a hopeful sign that the world was becoming a safer place. But internally, the Soviet Union continued to stifle dissent in an effort to preserve the integrity of its image as a united and stable state, proof of the success and superiority of the communist philosophy.

Two of the most outspoken dissenters became international spokesmen against arbitrary political and social repression. The first selection is by Andrei Sakharov (1921–1989), who was a brilliant physicist and helped develop the Soviet Union's first hydrogen bomb. Like Albert Einstein, Sakharov was outspoken in his fear of nuclear proliferation and called on all nuclear powers for arms reduction. He also criticized Soviet leadership and predicted the eventual integration of communist and capitalist systems in a form of democratic socialism. He won the Nobel Peace Prize in 1975 but was censured by the Soviet government and exiled to Gorky in 1980. Released six years later by Mikhail Gorbachev, Sakharov and his wife, human rights activist Yelena Bonner, continued to advocate political and intellectual liberty, and international coexistence.

The next selection is from the dissident writer Alexander Solzhenitsyn. A winner of the Nobel Prize for Literature in 1970, his fame was secured by his book The Gulag Archipelago *(1973), which examined the brutal Soviet prison system in Siberia. Exiled in 1974, Solzhenitsyn commanded international recognition and focused concern on the inadequacies and repression of Soviet society.*

"Freedom of Thought Is the Only Guarantee" (1974)
ANDREI SAKHAROV

The division of mankind threatens it with destruction. Civilization is imperiled by: a universal thermonuclear war, catastrophic hunger for most of mankind, stupefaction from the narcotic of "mass culture," and bureaucratized dogmatism, a spreading of mass myths that put entire peoples and continents under the power of cruel and treacherous demagogues, and destruction or degeneration from the unforeseeable consequences of swift changes in the conditions of life on our planet.

In the face of these perils, any action increasing the division of mankind, any preaching of the incompatibility of world ideologies and nations is madness and a crime. Only universal cooperation under conditions of intellectual

---

"'Freedom of Thought Is the Only Guarantee'" is from Andrei Sakharov, "Progress, Coexistence, and Intellectual Freedom," in Harrison E. Salisbury, ed., *Sakharov Speaks* (New York: Alfred A. Knopf, Inc., 1974), pp. 58–61. Copyright © 1974 by Alfred A. Knopf, Inc. Reprinted by permission of the publisher.

freedom and the lofty moral ideals of socialism and labor, accompanied by the elimination of dogmatism and pressures of the concealed interests of ruling classes, will preserve civilization. . . .

Millions of people throughout the world are striving to put an end to poverty. They despise oppression, dogmatism, and demagogy (and their more extreme manifestations—racism, fascism, Stalinism, and Maoism). They believe in progress based on the use, under conditions of social justice and intellectual freedom, of all the positive experience accumulated by mankind. . . .

Intellectual freedom is essential to human society—freedom to obtain and distribute information, freedom for open-minded and unfearing debate, and freedom from pressure by officialdom and prejudices. Such a trinity of freedom of thought is the only guarantee against an infection of people by mass myths, which, in the hands of treacherous hypocrites and demagogues, can be transformed into bloody dictatorship. Freedom of thought is the only guarantee of the feasibility of a scientific democratic approach to politics, economy, and culture.

But freedom of thought is under a triple threat in modern society—from the deliberate opium of mass culture, from cowardly, egotistic, and philistine ideologies, and from the ossified dogmatism of a bureaucratic oligarchy and its favorite weapon, ideological censorship. Therefore, freedom of thought requires the defense of all thinking and honest people. This is a mission not only for the intelligentsia, but for all strata of society, particularly its most active and organized stratum, the working class. The world-wide dangers of war, famine, cults of personality, and bureaucracy—these are perils for all of mankind.

"What Have You to Fear?" (1974)
ALEXANDER I. SOLZHENITSYN

But what about us? Us, with our unwieldiness and our inertia, with our flinching and inability to change even a single letter, a single syllable, of what Marx said in 1848 about industrial development? Economically and physically we are perfectly capable of saving ourselves. But there is a road block on the path to our salvation—the sole Progressive World View. If we renounce industrial development, what about the working class, socialism, Communism, unlimited increase in productivity and all the rest? Marx is not to be corrected, that's revisionism. . . .

But you are already being called "revisionists" anyway, whatever you may do in the future. So wouldn't it be better to do your duty soberly, responsibly and firmly, and give up the dead letter for the sake of a living people who are utterly dependent on your power and your decisions? And you must do it

"'What Have You to Fear?'" is an excerpt from Alexander I. Solzhenitsyn, *Letter to the Soviet Leaders* (New York, 1974), pp. 25–26, 41–43, 56–58. Copyright © 1974 by Aleksandr I. Solzhenitsyn. English translation by Hilary Sternberg. Copyright © 1974 by Writers and Scholars International Ltd. Reprinted by permission of HarperCollins Publishers, Inc.

without delay. Why dawdle if we shall have to snap out of it sometime anyway? Why repeat what others have done and loop the agonizing loop right to the end, when we are not too far into it to turn back? If the man at the head of the column cries, "I have lost my way," do we absolutely have to plow right on to the spot where he realized his mistake and only there turn back? Why not turn and start on the right course from wherever we happen to be? . . .

This Ideology [Marxism] that fell to us by inheritance is not only decrepit and hopelessly antiquated now; even during its best decades it was totally mistaken in its predictions and was never a science.

A primitive, superficial economic theory, it declared that only the worker creates value and failed to take into account the contribution of either organizers, engineers, transportation or marketing systems. It was mistaken when it forecast that the proletariat would be endlessly oppressed and would never achieve anything in a bourgeois democracy—if only we could shower people with as much food, clothing and leisure as they have gained under capitalism! It missed the point when it asserted that the prosperity of the European countries depended on their colonies—it was only after they had shaken the colonies off that they began to accomplish their "economic miracles." It was mistaken through and through in its prediction that socialists could never come to power except through an armed uprising. It miscalculated in thinking that the first uprisings would take place in the advanced industrial countries—quite the reverse. And the picture of how the whole world would rapidly be overtaken by revolutions and how states would soon wither away was sheer delusion, sheer ignorance of human nature. And as for wars being characteristic of capitalism alone and coming to an end when capitalism did—we have already witnessed the longest war of the twentieth century so far, and it was not capitalism that rejected negotiations and a truce for fifteen to twenty years; and God forbid that we should witness the bloodiest and most brutal of all mankind's wars—a war between two Communist superpowers. Then there was nationalism, which this theory also buried in 1848 as a "survival"—but find a stronger force in the world today! And it's the same with many other things too boring to list.

Marxism is not only not accurate, is not only not a science, has not only failed to predict *a single event* in terms of figures, quantities, time-scales or locations . . .—it absolutely astounds one by the economic and mechanistic crudity of its attempts to explain that most subtle of creatures, the human being, and that even more complex synthesis of millions of people, society. Only the cupidity of some, the blindness of others and a craving for *faith* on the part of others can serve to explain this grim jest of the twentieth century: how can such a discredited and bankrupt doctrine still have so many followers in the West! In *our* country are left the fewest of all! We who have had a taste of it are only pretending willy-nilly. . . .

So that the country and people do not suffocate, and so that they all have the chance to develop and enrich us with ideas, allow competition on an equal and honorable basis—not for power, but for truth—between all ideological and moral currents, in particular between *all religions*. . . . Allow us a free art and literature, the free publication not just of political books—God preserve us!—and exhortations and election leaflets; allow us philosophical, ethical, economic and social studies, and you will see what a rich harvest it brings and how it bears fruit—for the good of Russia. . . .

What have you to fear? Is the idea really so terrible? Are you really so unsure of yourselves? You will still have absolute and impregnable power, a separate, strong and exclusive Party, the army, the police force, industry, transportation, communications, mineral wealth, a monopoly of foreign trade, an artificial rate of exchange for the ruble—but let the people breathe, let them think and develop! If you belong to the people heart and soul, there can be nothing to hold you back!

After all, does the human heart not still feel the need to atone for the past?

Your dearest wish is for our state structure and our ideological system never to change, to remain as they are for centuries. But history is not like that. Every system either finds a way to develop or else collapses.

"A World Turned Upside Down!":
The Gorbachev Era and Beyond

During the presidency of Jimmy Carter, the Soviet Union invaded the sovereign state of Afghanistan (December 1979), an act that drew international criticism and contributed to the Carter Doctrine of January 1980: Any threat upon American oil interests in the Persian Gulf would be considered provocative and tantamount to war. In 1981, Ronald Reagan was inaugurated as president, having won the election in part on a "get-tough" stance toward the U.S.S.R. His verbal attacks characterized the Soviet Union as "the evil Empire" and "the focus of evil in the world." Such rhetoric did little to encourage cooperation between the two nations.

A new era in international relations dawned on the death of the old-guard Soviet leader Constantine Chernenko in 1985. His government had been transitional, a geriatric accommodation to the demands of a new-style Soviet leadership waiting in the wings. Mikhail Gorbachev was forty-eight years old when he secured entry to the Politburo in 1979 and only fifty-four when he assumed the position of general secretary of the Communist party in 1985. A career bureaucrat with primary assignments in agricultural administration, Gorbachev was nevertheless ready to embark on a radical departure from established Soviet policies. He sought to define and implement the new concepts of perestroika *("restructuring") and* glasnost *("openness") through which he hoped to liberalize the political, economic, and cultural bases of Soviet society. Change was imminent, but no one could predict its full impact on travel restrictions and emigration, censorship, state control of artistic expression, and ultimately political organization itself through democratization and self-determination of ethnic nationalities.*

Gorbachev's initial declarations in 1985 were met with international and domestic astonishment. Gorbachev was hailed in the West as the "man of the century," personally responsible for overcoming the legacy of Stalinism, for eliminating an authoritarian mindset, for offering flexible positions on arms reduction in pursuit of a safer world. The "Evil Empire" was fast losing its threatening aura as each of the eastern European "satellite" nations broke away from Soviet control in popular revolutions throughout 1989. This time there was no military attempt to maintain Soviet control as in Hungary (1956) and in Czechoslovakia (1968). The symbolic culmination of this process occurred on November 10, 1989, with the destruction of the Berlin Wall by the people of East and West Germany.

But Mikhail Gorbachev also faced severe opposition at home, both from the political right, which feared chaos and a loss of influence, and from the political left, led by Boris Yeltsin, who argued that perestroika *was not being instituted fast enough, nor with a deep democratic conviction. Also in the late 1980s, the various ethnic minorities in the Soviet republics of Armenia, Azerbaijan, and Georgia began testing the limits of Gorbachev's commitment to democracy and self-determination of peoples. So too did the Baltic States of Estonia, Latvia, and Lithuania seek to break away from the Soviet "Union" and once again run their own affairs independent of Moscow.*

Add to this turmoil a tense domestic background of deprivation as evidenced by food shortages and a heritage of consumer neglect, and Gorbachev was pressed at every turn. However, he was a maneuverer, a political tactician, an orchestra-tor of change. In an effort to maintain the union of the Soviet republics, Gorbachev tried to run a center position against the divergent agendas of the re-formists and conservatives. He promised the former continued democratization and progress toward a market economy, and he reassured the latter that he was a loyal Communist party man, who would respect them and protect their tradi-tional interests. In late 1990, Gorbachev felt the need to conciliate the right wing of the party, which was increasingly concerned about demonstrations of indepen-dence in the republics. Gorbachev regarded this placation as necessary for the maintenance of his authority; however, it drove away some of the most talented and avid reformers in the Gorbachev orbit. Eduard Shevardnadze resigned as foreign minister and warned of dictatorship.

On August 19, 1991, Shevardnadze's fears threatened to become reality as hard-line members of Gorbachev's advisory cabinet tried to institute a coup d'état. Gorbachev was confined in the Crimea for three days while an "emergency commit-tee" of eight coup leaders explained that he was "ill" and needed a long rest. The in-competency of the conspirators, the refusal of the army and KGB security forces to fire on the Russian people, and most importantly the defiance of the Soviet citizenry and their commitment to the tenets of popular sovereignty resulted in the swift col-lapse of the coup. But the Soviet state emerged from this drama a changed entity. Boris Yeltsin, the popularly elected president of the Republic of Russia, now seemed to hold the keys to the future. By August 24, Gorbachev's cabinet had been reap-pointed with reformers scrutinized by Yeltsin; the Communist party newspaper, Pravda, *had been shut down; and Gorbachev had resigned from his position as general secretary of the Communist party. Indeed, the Communist party was in complete disarray after having ruled the country for nearly seventy-five years. Each of the Baltic States as well as the Ukraine and other Soviet republics had declared independence, a foreshadowing of the dissolution of the Soviet empire. Some schol-ars have hailed this as the "Second Russian Revolution." That revolution left Gorbachev behind. He had styled himself a reforming communist and a convinced socialist, an image essential to the initial phases of reform. Paradoxically, this close identification with the Communist party afforded him the path to success, but it also sowed the seeds of failure. Gorbachev faced the great challenge of transition, of creating revolution and controlling it at the same time. As Lenin, Napoleon, Robespierre, and the Roman emperor Augustus understood in earlier ages, it is difficult to hold onto a world turned up-side down.*

The following selections address the transitional dilemmas facing the Russian people as they continue to cope with political instability, social chaos, economic dislocation, and ethnic rebellion.

Perestroika and the Socialist Renewal of Society (September 11, 1989)

MIKHAIL GORBACHEV

Good evening, comrades, I am here to talk to you about our current affairs. The situation in the country is not simple. We all know and feel this. Everything has become entangled in a tight knot: scarcity on the consumer goods market, conflicts in ethnic relations, and difficult and sometimes painful processes in the public consciousness, resulting from the overcoming of distortions and from the renewal of socialism. People are trying to understand where we have found ourselves at the moment, evaluating the pluses and minuses of the path we have covered during the last four-plus years, the development of democracy and the pace of the economic and political reforms.

It is only natural that people want to know the real causes of our weaknesses and failures in carrying out specific programs for perestroika and in tackling urgent problems and to find out why the situation in some areas has deteriorated rather than improved.

In short, political life today is characterized by intense debate. But the main thing I want to emphasize is that the mass of people have become involved in this movement and they play an ever growing role in discussing and accomplishing social, economic, and political tasks.

Comrades, this is a fact of fundamental importance because it gives perestroika the elements of constructive and businesslike effort and helps overcome people's alienation from power. Yet one cannot fail to see a different trend. Against the background of heated debate and a rapid succession of events, things are happening that must not be ignored or left unaccounted for. Efforts are being made to discredit perestroika from conservative, leftist and sometimes unmistakably anti-socialist positions. One can hear in this discordant choir voices predicting an imminent chaos and speculation about the threat of a coup and even civil war. It is a fact that some people would like to create an atmosphere of anxiety, despair and uncertainty in society. . . .

"Perestroika and the Socialist Renewal of Society" is from Mikhail Gorbachev, speech delivered to the people of the U.S.S.R., September 11, 1989. Contained in *Vital Speeches of the Day,* October 15, 1989, pp. 5–7.

In effect, the conservative forces are trying to impose on us such evaluations of the situation that would provoke resistance to perestroika and mold in people's mind the view that the process of change begun in society should be halted or at least slowed down; these forces demand that the old command methods of government should be restored. Otherwise, they say, chaos will set in. Meanwhile, the leftist elements suggest tackling extremely difficult problems in one go, without taking into account our actual possibilities or the interests of society. Such demands are presented as concern for the people and its well-being.

Recommendations have also been made lately from which one can assume that our only "salvation" is renouncing the values of socialism and conducting perestroika in the capitalist manner. Such views do exist. Needless to say, such ideas go against the grain of perestroika, which implies socialist renewal of society. . . .

True, perestroika is meeting with many difficulties. But it is radical change, a revolution in the economy and in policy, in the ways of thinking and in people's consciousness, in the entire pattern of our life. Besides, we have not been able to avoid mistakes in our practical actions in the course of perestroika.

But perestroika has opened up realistic opportunities for society's renewal, for giving society a new quality and for creating truly humane and democratic socialism. It has returned to the great nation a sense of dignity and given the Soviet people a sense of freedom. It is a powerful source of social, spiritual, and, I should say, patriotic energy for decades to come.

That is why we must do everything to continue perestroika on the basis of the ideas and principles proclaimed by the party. And we must not stop. We must continue along the way of changes we have embarked upon. . . . The community is casting off its illusions. It no longer believes that there are simple solutions to be brought ready-made from above for all our problems. . . .

I think it very important that the community is coming to better understand the primary link between perestroika and labor—dedicated, creative, efficient work fully implementing every worker's knowledge and abilities. This is essential because until recently, we concentrated not so much on labor as on the distribution of benefits. One could think that redistribution of fictitious wealth was all perestroika was about. We have at last begun to shed this delusion. . . .

The Government of the U.S.S.R. is elaborating a program of extraordinary measures to improve the economy and, above all, to normalize the consumer market. The program is to be submitted to the Congress of People's Deputies. We believe that this program will give clear answers to the questions of how and when the most urgent social and economic problems will be solved. I think society will not accept it if the program does not determine clear and concrete measures, stages, and time limits as well as the responsibility of the republic and local bodies and labor collectives. I presume that this package may include unpopular, probably tough and even painful measures. This will be justified, however, only if they are prompted by the need to get out of the present situation. Shortages, which arouse the sharpest criticisms and discontent of the people, are a special issue. The government is to give an explanation on this urgent social problem and come up with practical measures shortly. . . .

Of major political importance will be the laws on republic and regional cost-accounting and self-government. They are an important step toward realistically strengthening the sovereignty of the republics and expanding the rights of the local Soviets [councils].

The party, which is society's consolidating and vanguard force, has a unique role to play in this process. Those who strive to use the difficulties of the transition period for certain unseemly purposes and try to undermine the influence of the party should know that they will not succeed. We are sure that with all the critical sentiments concerning the activities of some or other party committee or communists, the working people realize perfectly well the importance of the party of Lenin for the fate of socialism, which today is inseparable from the success of perestroika. On the other hand, it is clear that the new tasks call for a deep renewal of the party.

By restructuring itself, getting rid of all that hinders its activities, overcoming dogmatism and conservatism, mastering a new style and new methods of work, renewing its personnel, and working side by side with the working people, the Communist Party of the Soviet Union will be able to fulfill its role of the political vanguard of society. The party will firmly pursue the policy of perestroika, heading the revolutionary transformation of society. We should realistically assess all processes and phenomena of the present-day situation, show restraint, see clearly where we are and not become confused. On this basis we should draw conclusions for our action at the given moment and in the future. We must act responsibly and prudently, without deviating from the course of perestroika in society.

Dear comrades, I wish you success in work, determination and firm spirit.

Gorbachev's Resignation: "The Old System Fell Apart Before the New System Began to Work" (December 25, 1991)

MIKHAIL GORBACHEV

Dear fellow countrymen, compatriots. Due to the situation which has evolved as a result of the formation of the Commonwealth of Independent States, I hereby discontinue my activities at the post of President of the Union of Soviet Socialist Republics.

I am making this decision on considerations of principle. I firmly came out in favor of the independence of nations and sovereignty for the republics. At

"Gorbachev's Resignation" is from Mikhail Gorbachev, speech delivered over Russian television on December 25, 1991. Contained in *Vital Speeches of the Day*, January 15, 1992, pp. 194–195.

the same time, I support the preservation of the union state and the integrity of this country. The developments took a different course. The policy prevailed of dismembering this country and disuniting the state, which is something I cannot subscribe to. . . .

This being my last opportunity to address you as President of the U.S.S.R., I find it necessary to inform you of what I think of the road that has been trodden by us since 1985. I find it important because there have been a lot of controversial, superficial, and biased judgments made on this score. Destiny so ruled that when I found myself at the helm of this state it already was clear that something was wrong in this country.

We had a lot of everything—land, oil and gas, other natural resources—and there was intellect and talent in abundance. However, we were living much worse than people in the industrialized countries were living and we were increasingly lagging behind them. The reason was obvious even then. This country was suffocating in the shackles of the bureaucratic command system. Doomed to cater to ideology, and suffer and carry the onerous burden of the arms race, it found itself at the breaking point.

All the half-hearted reforms—and there have been a lot of them—fell through, one after another. This country was going nowhere and we couldn't possibly live the way we did. We had to change everything radically. It is for this reason that I have never had any regrets—never had any regrets—that I did not use the capacity of General Secretary just to rein in this country for several years. I would have considered it an irresponsible and immoral decision. I was also aware that to embark on reform of this caliber and in a society like ours was an extremely difficult and even risky undertaking. But even now, I am convinced that the democratic reform that we launched in the spring of 1985 was historically correct.

The process of renovating this country and bringing about drastic change in the international community has proven to be much more complicated than anyone could imagine. However, let us give its due to what has been done so far. This society has acquired freedom. It has been freed politically and spiritually, and this is the most important achievement that we have yet fully come to grips with. And we haven't, because we haven't learned to use freedom yet. However, an effort of historical importance has been carried out. The totalitarian system has been eliminated, which prevented this country from becoming a prosperous and well-to-do country a long time ago. A breakthrough has been effected on the road of democratic change.

Free elections have become a reality. Free press, freedom of worship, representative legislatures and a multi-party system have all become reality. Human rights are being treated as the supreme principle and top priority. Movement has been started toward a multi-tier economy and the equality of all forms of ownership is being established. . . .

We're now living in a new world. An end has been put to the Cold War and to the arms race, as well as to the mad militarization of the country, which has crippled our economy, public attitudes and morals. The threat of nuclear war has been removed. Once again, I would like to stress that during this transitional period, I did everything that needed to be done to insure

"We have paid with all our history and tragic experience for these democratic achievements, and they are not to be abandoned, whatever the circumstances, and whatever the pretexts. Otherwise, all our hopes for the best will be buried."—Mikhail Gorbachev. *(American Publishing)*

that there was reliable control of nuclear weapons. We opened up ourselves to the rest of the world, abandoned the practices of interfering in others' internal affairs and using troops outside this country, and we were reciprocated with trust, solidarity, and respect. . . .

All this change had taken a lot of strain, and took place in the context of fierce struggle against the background of increasing resistance by the reactionary forces, both the party and state structures, and the economic elite, as well as our habits, ideological bias, the sponging attitudes. The change ran up against our intolerance, a low level of political culture and fear of change. That is why we have wasted so much time. The old system fell apart even before the new system began to work. Crisis of society as a result aggravated even further.

I'm aware that there is popular resentment as a result of today's grave situation. I note that authority at all levels, and myself are being subject to harsh criticisms. I would like to stress once again, though, that the cardinal change in so vast a country, given its heritage, could not have been carried out without difficulties, shock and pain.

The August [1991] coup brought the overall crisis to the limit. The most dangerous thing about this crisis is the collapse of statehood. I am concerned about the fact that the people in this country are ceasing to become citizens of a great power and the consequences may be very difficult for all of us to deal with. I consider it vitally important to preserve the democratic achievements which have been attained in the last few years. We have paid with all our history and tragic experience for these democratic achievements, and they are not to be abandoned, whatever the circumstances, and whatever the pretexts. Otherwise, all our hopes for the best will be buried. I am telling you all this honestly and straightforwardly because this is my moral duty. . . .

I am very much concerned as I am leaving this post. However, I also have a feeling of hope and faith in you, your wisdom and force of spirit. We are heirs of a great civilization and it now depends on all and everyone whether or not this civilization will make a comeback to a new and decent living today. . . . Of course, there were mistakes made that could have been avoided, and many of the things that we did could not have been done better. But I am positive that sooner or later, some day our common efforts will bear fruit and our nations will live in a prosperous, democratic society.

"Russia Is Living Through a Most Difficult Period" (February 24, 1994)

BORIS YELTSIN

Russia is currently living through a most difficult period in its history. However, Russia existed before Peter the Great or the October 1917 revolution. Russia doesn't end with the disintegration of a communist superpower. The Soviet empire that recently threatened mankind and suppressed Russians and other peoples exists no more. However, the Russian state has still failed to take its own place in the world community. The state that used to be a stern jailer and merciless judge of its subjects is no more. However, Russia has failed to develop a fully fledged democratic and law-abiding state system so far, we have to admit.

Most people are permanently anxious over their future, the future of their children and retired parents. In the meanwhile, federal and local authorities prefer to give a blind eye to the rapid social stratification. We have to responsibly admit that we underestimate all threats that stratification harbors. I am not appealing to come back to former notorious egalitarian practices, when all people were supposed to be equally poor and better off people ripped off. However, this delicate and painful issue shall not be left until it solves by itself.

We are bitterly learning that the state-ruled self-consuming economy, in which ten people are busy with the work that can be reasonably done by one

"Russia Is Living Through a Most Difficult Period" is from Boris Yeltsin, speech delivered to the Federal Assembly, Moscow, Russia, on February 24, 1994. Contained in *Vital Speeches of the Day,* April 1, 1994, pp. 355, 359–360.

person, has no future. We don't have a normal market economy so far. On the other hand, swindlers and rippers are feeling nice and easy. Honest and industrious people, who don't fear to be self-employed have enormous difficulties in getting on. My heart is breaking to say this, but it is true. We have greater freedom in this country, yes. But this is not enough. Our strategic goal is to develop justice, security and confidence in Russia.

We have been convinced that Russia cannot be recovered by fiat from any boss or political party or personality. The time has come for a new political style based on confidence, constructive cooperation, mutual understanding and concerted efforts. The time has come for a national effort that would pool all resources. That effort should be targeted at a stronger state identity of Russia. We have to admit it finally, that a weak state system makes elementary order in the country unfeasible. All citizens and nations of Russia are interested in a stable and strong institutional system. No matter where people of different national identities are living, they need civil peace and don't want ethnic feuds. . . .

The world community also needs a strong Russia, or it will become a permanent source of threat to its security. A strong and active state is a major prerequisite for further transformation in this country. Otherwise, we won't have a healthy and civilized market and genuine democracy, the great Russian culture and morality will never get fully recovered. A stronger state system is an obvious goal to attain, and this should unite all Russians in the current dramatic period. . . .

In its current shape, the state fails to perform its major functions, which includes in the first place the assurance of public order, human rights and safety. The country is flooded by crime. Institutional structures are permeated by irresponsibility and arbitrariness. Human life in our country is more and more ensnared by countless petty orders and limitations. The work of federal and local state authorities has been marked by muddle and great confusion. The army of bureaucrats has rapidly expanded. . . .

All these factors bear witness to the new increasing alienation of power from the people and their daily needs. However, whereas in the past they were separated by bureaucracy and the nomenclature caste, today money has been added on. This shameful money now serves as the tool for solving many problems. . . .

Russia is capable of starting out on a qualitatively new stage of its development. The period of total destructive processes of the former system is nearing its end. We are laying economic, legal and social foundations of a new Russian society. . . . I know that among you are people who doubt whether or not we shall be able to cope with these tasks in conditions of the spiritual and ideological discord that is reigning in society and in our hearts now. We will have to give a reply to that question all together. And certainly not by engaging in wearisome and fruitless debates, but in real cooperation. Only if we act jointly shall we be able to overcome mutual suspicion and regain trust in each other. Only if we act jointly shall we be able, forever, to divert the threat of confrontation from Russia and go over to lasting civic accord. Only if we act jointly shall we be able to break through the black veil of uncertainty, restore spiritual balance and find ourselves in the new conditions.

The citizens of Russia expect us to cooperate. And I am certain that they will support us. They will support us because they want to work normally and earn money. They will support us because they want to be safe in the streets and in their own homes. They will support us because they want peace and prosperity for Russia. I hope that in a year's time we shall all together be able to look into our electors' eyes and say: "We had a hard time, but we have done our best and even more in that past year. We certainly have not wasted that time." For my own part, I shall do all I can for it.

The God That Failed History: "Marx Was Wrong" (1990)

TIM KORANDA

Perhaps one of the greatest controversies of the twentieth century has revolved around a comparison of the relative virtues and vices of "bourgeois capitalism" and communism. There is an obvious difference in Marxism as an ideology and theory of social organization, and as practiced by Lenin and corrupted by Stalin. The controversy is made all the more difficult because of confusions in terminology and the distortions of propaganda utilized to win the hearts and minds of various populations. Most of the last half of the twentieth century has been spent in political and military competition between these two spheres in the Cold War of spies and speeches, and more dangerously in Korea and Vietnam.

With the failure of communism to produce the utopia that Marx advocated as inevitable, his ideology has come under increasing attack. In the following selection, Tim Koranda, president of the East/West Alliance, gave his assessment in a speech to the Symposium on World Economic Development.

Last June [1989], Francis Fukuyama published a provocative essay in the National Interest magazine entitled, "The End of History?" arguing that bourgeois democracy is the telos of political life: the final archetype in man's long march from primitive society to modern society. The article proved prophetic in light of subsequent events in East Berlin, Eastern Europe, and now the Soviet Union. These events have left Marxist historians alienated from the product of their labors. How is it that a communist society—that dictatorship of the proletariat—can revolt and become democratic and capitalist? The question so intrigued me that I decided to do what Marx would have done: reread history for its paradigms.

"The God That Failed History" is from Tim Koranda, speech delivered before the Symposium on World Economic Development, New York, New York, on May 15, 1990. Contained in *Vital Speeches of the Day*, October 15, 1990, pp. 19–21.

According to Marx's materialist conception of history, societies pass through four formative stages on their way to becoming communist: asiatic, ancient, feudal and bourgeois capitalist.

The asiatic stage is a highly organized tribal state characterized by an absence of private property; the ancient, a slave-owning society; the feudal, a rent-based society defined by ownership of land; and the bourgeois capitalist, a society of shareholders and workers.

The history of the East European countries never fit the Marxist paradigm since communism was largely imposed from without. And as historians often point out, Russia and China don't measure up either because neither evolved from feudalism into capitalism on the way to becoming communist. Even today, the U.S.S.R. and China are forty and eighty percent agrarian, respectively. Marxists learned to live with these contradictions in much the same way a neurotic learns to live with his conflicts. But despite firmly-held beliefs in the face of contrary fact, Marxists now face a crisis of confidence as events conspire to destroy the paradigm.

Marxist history differs from other deterministic systems in its assumption that history is non-cyclical. Marx said that history never moves backwards, and that all its conquests are final and irrevocable. The asiatic society is to be replaced by the ancient; the ancient would give way to the medieval; feudalism was to break down into capitalism. And finally, capitalism was to be swept away by communism. But Marx's reading of history was never true to history. In the West, feudalism wasn't replaced by capitalism. It was replaced by a non-marxist communism.

During the medieval era, walled towns co-existed with landed estates, the former offering escaped serfs and yeoman the promise of a better life. Trade guilds, which defined the economic life of the towns, were brotherhoods—collective associations of workers in the same trade that shared profits and spurned competition. There were guilds of goldsmiths and silversmiths, of butchers and bakers, doctors and tailors, hatters and glovers, and of fishmongers and shoemakers. . . .

The guilds, however, were a necessary transition from a feudal to a capitalist society. Merchant guilds such as the Commenda, the Hansa and the Merchant Adventurers, had first-hand experience cultivating overseas markets and cheap sources of raw materials. This broadened the markets that the guilds served but also helped undermine the structure of society. . . .

Change was necessary. Capitalism demanded too much of the guilds. Encumbered by regulation and Christian ideas of brotherhood, they had trouble adjusting to the world they had helped create. Their communistic structure impeded efficiency and their insularity ruled out raising outside capital. By the mid-15th century these communist organizations evolved into "chartered and regulated companies" which traded in "joint stock," allowing outsiders to buy in. This was the beginning of capitalism.

Therefore, Marx was wrong. Communism, guild style, was the precursor of capitalism in the West and not the other way around. And that's precisely what happened in Eastern Europe and is happening in the Soviet Union.

Statues of Lenin, Marx, and other Soviet heroes were destroyed or removed from various cities in eastern Europe after 1989. Were Marx and Lenin wrong? Were they "gods who failed history"? *(United Media)*

Communism was the guild phase—an important step toward capitalist democracy, a transition to more efficient economic organization.

Before communism, Eastern Europe had been underdeveloped. Capital accumulation was extremely low. This lack of accumulation was largely due to large estates continuing wasteful consumption patterns. The principal economic activity—farming—provided very meager savings. And instead of being invested in fixed capital, the savings were earmarked for usurious consumer loans. . . .

The communist takeover after World War II helped steward the region's core capital, providing an exogenous transition from a feudal to a communist society. Now, with the arrival of democracy and capitalism, the paradigm is complete.

Over the past forty years, the East European countries have mastered industrial processes that evolved over one hundred fifty years in the West. Today, Belgrade, Budapest and Prague are manufacturing everything from small motors to men's suits, and finding ready markets in the West. . . . The move to capitalism will bring about greater efficiencies as markets determine the allocation of the nation's resources.

A similar pattern is apparent in Russia. Long before Gorbachev, Peter the Great [seventeenth and eighteenth centuries] made an heroic attempt to modernize the country by establishing new industries and converting small workshops into large scale manufactories. . . . Factories mushroomed during Peter's reign, but demand remained flat prompting his successors to abandon the modernization scheme. Peter the Great attempted the wholesale conversion of a feudal state into a modern capitalistic state. But that conversion is only possible now, after several decades of communist rule. Even though the Soviets renounced the use of foreign capital for industrial development, they desired a high rate of industrial growth and paid for it largely from the earning of agriculture. The collectivization of farms provided the seed money, so to speak, for large scale industry and mass production. The transition to private ownership and entrepreneurship is now all but certain.

The pattern in China is more bewildering. . . . The great achievement of communism in China was not so much in industrialization as in wiping out the corruption and extortion that robbed basic industries of capital. Ironically, recent Chinese attempts to modernize the country through economic incentives have only produced a class of wealthy farmer. But the guild phase of communism—the transition stage—may be taking root right now in the form of joint ventures with foreign companies. Most of the venture partners have now returned to China after last spring's violence. And while democracy may be the only way to avoid more violence and the probable flight of capital, China's leaders are reluctant democrats.

The Chinese will likely arrive at capitalism in a way that again repeals the laws of Marxist history: by revolution against communism. One could say that the only thing they have to lose are their chains.

The Future of Europe

Few years have seen such fundamental political, social, and economic changes as occurred throughout eastern Europe in 1989. Poland, Hungary, Czechoslovakia, and East Germany all peacefully established new governments with democratic overtones after more than four decades of Marxist rule. The Soviet Union, continuing to pursue its own liberalization, gave most of its former satellites wide latitude in carrying out reforms in contrast to its earlier suppression of popular movements in Hungary (1956) and Czechoslovakia (1968). Only in Romania was the transition violent, as a swift but bloody revolution toppled the regime of hard-line Communist dictator Nicolai Ceausescu in December 1989. He and his wife were charged with genocide and executed.

Perhaps the most symbolic act of freedom occurred on November 9, 1989, when East Germany opened all its borders and allowed its citizens to travel and emigrate freely. The notorious Berlin Wall, constructed in 1961 at the height of the Cold War, was subsequently torn down, and thousands made their way to the West in search of new lives. This act would have serious consequences for the future of Germany.

Germany has occupied a central position in the history of the late-nineteenth and twentieth centuries. After nearly forty-five years of division, the events of 1989 presented opportunities for reunification. But the new realities posed new problems for Europe: Would Germany once again threaten its neighbors militarily? Would the financial costs of reunification stall the process? Who would bear the economic burden? Would the new Germany be politically neutral or maintain its central position in the NATO alliance? In 1990, German Chancellor Helmut Kohl addressed several of these questions in his speech to the American Council on Germany in New York City.

A United Germany in a United Europe
(June 5, 1990)

HELMUT KOHL

We Germans are not oblivious of the fact that here and in other countries we are being asked questions as we head for unity:

—What kind of Germany will emerge?

—What will German unity mean for peace and security in the heart of Europe?

—Will this Germany revert to old patterns of behaviour, or has it learned the lessons of history?

I shall attempt to provide answers here for the future, bearing in mind that we Germans can build on proven foundations as we move towards unity. Moreover, we Germans are determined, as we prove by our actions, to heed the lessons of our and of European history.

My first answer is this: A future united Germany will remain linked to the United States in close friendship and responsible partnership. . . . We shall remain together! This responsible partnership entails a future united Germany being a full member of the North Atlantic defense alliance.

We are thus drawing the first and most important conclusion from history: Peace, stability and security in Europe were ensured whenever Germany, the country in the heart of Europe, maintained firm ties, a fair balance of interests and mutually beneficial interchange with all its neighbours. On the other hand, when the Germans chose to go it alone or follow a separate nationalistic path, whether out of blind arrogance or criminal hubris, or when they were forced into isolation after a lost war, this resulted in discord, instability and insecurity for the whole of Europe.

A future Germany cannot and will not, therefore, drift back and forth between two camps. We do not seek neutrality or demilitarization, and we reject a non-aligned status. We Germans want to exercise our sovereign right, as enshrined in the Charter of the United Nations. . . . We want to be a member of . . . the North Atlantic defense alliance. Our immediate neighbours in the East—the Poles, Czechs and Hungarians support this position.

"A United Germany in a United Europe" is from Helmut Kohl, speech delivered to the American Council on Germany, New York City, New York, on June 5, 1990. Contained in *Vital Speeches of the Day*, July 1, 1990, pp. 546–548.

The Berlin Wall begins to fall on the night of November 9–10, 1989, near Bernauer Strasse. *(David Brauchll/Reuter/Corbis)*

Our commitment to the Western Alliance—and this is my second answer—implies above all our commitment to the Western community of shared values. A future Germany will be a free and democratic state based on social justice and the rule of law, on respect for human dignity and human rights. Right- or left-wing extremism does not, as more than forty years of domestic stability prove, stand a chance in our country in the future either.

A future Germany will also remain a federal state. . . . There is no better a means of preventing tyranny and totalitarianism than a constitution which not only provides for checks and balances, but also envisages a federal system.

We in the Federal Republic of Germany have such a constitution: Our Basic Law has in more than forty years proved to be the most liberal constitution in German history. . . .

My third answer is this: A united Germany will be an economically sound and socially stable country. The unanimous opinion of international economic organizations is that German unification will significantly boost world economic growth. The pent-up demand in the GDR [formerly East Germany] and in the reformist countries of Central, Eastern and South-Eastern Europe affords substantial market opportunities for everyone. . . .

The Federal Republic of Germany will strongly support this new economic and social start in the GDR. We are well prepared for this. For eight years our economy has been expanding. Business earnings, investments and employment are at a high level. We want to pave the way for private enterprise and the influx of private capital into the GDR. . . . I would like to repeat my invitation to American business: Become actively involved in the GDR to the mutual benefit. We Germans do not seek a monopoly; on the contrary, we seek competition and the common advantages of the international division of labour.

A future Germany—and this is my fourth answer—will from the very beginning be a member of the European Community. A united Germany will take part in 1992 when the large single market with 336 million people is completed. A united Germany will, together with France, be a driving force behind European unification. Before the end of this year two parallel intergovernmental conferences will be started to lay the contractual foundation not only for economic and monetary union, but also for political union.

Finally, our commitment to federalism does not end at our borders. Federalism is our real goal for Europe as a whole. A united Germany will therefore also espouse the ambitious goal of laying the groundwork for a United States of Europe before the end of this century. We are thus drawing a further conclusion from our history: German unity has a future only if it is achieved in harmony with our neighbours, and not through confrontation with them. . . .

A future Germany, firmly anchored in the West, will—and this is my fifth answer—in the future, too, live up to its share of responsibility for ensuring peaceful and stable reforms in the neighbouring Eastern and South-Eastern countries. In following our path to national unity, we Germans do not call borders into question. On the contrary, we want to make them more permeable. We are willing to achieve lasting understanding and comprehensive, forward-looking cooperation. Our goal is international reconciliation. In particular we are willing to take account of the legitimate security interests of all our neighbours, not the least the Soviet Union.

We are convinced that this recognition will soon prevail in the whole of Europe: A future united Germany as a member of the Western defense alliance will increase the security of everyone concerned and thus become a cornerstone of a stable, peaceful order in Europe.

The Reconciliation of France and Germany (September 24, 1990)

FRANÇOIS MITTERRAND

As Europe moved away from the wasteland of World War II and the intellectual confines of the Cold War, toward a new era of intranational economic cooperation, many variables exist that may radically alter its face. A tunnel under the English Channel was constructed (dubbed "the Chunnel"), which not only physically links Great Britain and France but "threatens" to meld the cultures as well. Britain has lost the island status that protected it and offered a unique identity for centuries, in exchange for a more intimate link with the economic destiny of continental Europe. So too will the great enemies of the first half of the twentieth century, France and Germany, lie down together and reconcile past offenses for future gains. With the reunification of Germany and the reintroduction of eastern countries such as Czechoslovakia, Hungary, and Poland into the heart of Europe, there are great financial opportunities and the very real potential for domestic chaos. The following speeches by European leaders of the late-twentieth century testify to the changing nature of Europe and the progress of Western Civilization.

Think of the events that have shaken up Europe and the World in 1939, the popular movements that have emerged from the depths which, like the French revolution of two hundred years ago, have triumphed over structures and systems, set ways of thinking and acting, powers and fears, because of the simple, irresistible need to live differently, in accordance with the requirements of the mind. When the walls separating peoples came down, walls built on the foolish assumption that the order they were protecting would never be untouched by the great winds of space, dreams and ideas, I remember saying to my compatriots in France . . . that the end of one order did not necessarily mean that another order would be born immediately thereafter, and that it would be a very difficult process. And I would ask you this: what are we to do with this era we are entering, so promising, so perilous? What shall we make of it? . . .

I think that an era of hope is opening up for mankind, if the peoples of the world accept to overcome what they take to be the fatality of history, and of their own interest. Believe me, such a goal is within our reach. After destroying each other in three wars in less than a century, France and Germany have sealed their reconciliation, a rare occurrence indeed: They belong to the same community, they meet together, they are forging a genuine friendship. While I speak, on the eve of German unity, instead of harping on the tragic events they experienced in the past because of each other, our two peoples are turned toward the same

"The Reconciliation of France and Germany" is from François Mitterrand, speech delivered to the 45th Session of the United Nations General Assembly, New York, New York, on September 24, 1990. Contained in *Vital Speeches of the Day*, October 15, 1990, pp. 5, 7–8.

future. And so it is that here in New York, I can send the best wishes of France to the Germans, who are preparing to celebrate a great moment of their history. The deep understanding between France and Germany is a reality. As you know, it makes itself felt in the twelve-nation European Community. Can you imagine the trouble and strife, the conflicts of age-old ambitions that were overcome forty years ago by a bold, almost unbelievable undertaking engaged in first by six, nine, then ten, now twelve countries of Europe? . . .

We Europeans are looking beyond the Community, to the horizon of the continent of Europe, the Europe of geography and history. . . . Where would our old continent be now if audacity had not managed to overthrow well-established patterns of thought? And if peoples and their leaders had not accepted to build a future different from the past? In this Europe these are countries which yesterday were known as Eastern bloc countries and which belonged to a rival system. Now they control their own destiny, but with what means at their disposal? . . . We must think of them, they are our brethren and we will be by their side, until as I said in France, a more fixed relationship will bring together all the countries of Europe, those of the East, those of the Community, those of the Free Trade Area, those who are part of no system, in what I have called a Confederation. . . . Europe has been the first field of application thereof and a very real one. . . .

At the beginning of this century and at the end of the previous one, our forebears expressed their dreams of peace with these three words: disarmament, arbitration, collective security. Theirs came to be an era of unrest, dictatorship and war. Let us act in such a way, I beseech you, that through the United Nations, law, solidarity and peace may finally rule over a new era.

"Czechoslovakia Is Returning to Europe" (February 21, 1990)

VÁCLAV HAVEL

Czechoslovakia is returning to Europe. In the general interest and in its own interest as well, it wants to coordinate this return—both politically and economically—with the other returnees, which means, above all, with its neighbors the Poles and the Hungarians. We are doing what we can to coordinate these returns. And at the same time, we are doing what we can so that Europe will be capable of really accepting us, its wayward children. Which means that it may open itself to us, and may begin to transform its structures—which are formally European but de facto Western European—in that direction, but in such a way that it will not be to its detriment, but rather to its advantage. . . .

"'Czechoslovakia Is Returning to Europe'" is from Václav Havel, speech delivered to the Joint Session of Congress, Washington, D.C., on February 21, 1990. Contained in *Vital Speeches of the Day*, March 15, 1990, pp. 329–330.

The Communist type of totalitarian system has left... all the nations of the Soviet Union and the other countries the Soviet Union subjugated in its time, a legacy of countless dead, an infinite spectrum of human suffering, profound economic decline, and above all enormous human humiliation. It has brought us horrors that fortunately you have not known.

At the same time, however—unintentionally, of course—it has given us something positive: a special capacity to look, from time to time, somewhat further than someone who has not undergone this bitter experience. A person who cannot move and live a somewhat normal life because he is pinned under a boulder has more time to think about his hopes than someone who is not trapped that way.... We too can offer something to you: our experience and the knowledge that has come from it.... Consciousness precedes Being, and not the other way around, as the Marxists claim.

For this reason, the salvation of the human world lies nowhere else than in the human heart, in the human power to reflect, in human meekness and in human responsibility.... If we are no longer threatened by world war, or by the danger that the absurd mountains of accumulated nuclear weapons might blow up the world, this does not mean that we have definitively won. We are in fact far from the final victory....

In other words, we still don't know how to put morality ahead of politics, science and economics. We are still incapable of understanding that the only genuine backbone of all our actions—if they are to be moral—is responsibility. Responsibility to something higher than my family, my country, my company, my success. Responsibility to the order of Being, where all our actions are indelibly recorded and where, and only where, they will be properly judged....

I end where I began: history has accelerated. I believe that once again it will be the human mind that will notice this acceleration, give it a name, and transform those words into deeds.

Ethnic Strife in Eastern Europe
(April 15, 1994)
HELMUT TUERK

One of the most tragic consequences of the collapse of the Soviet Union has been the political, social, and economic chaos that accompanied the liberation of eastern Europe. For nations whose political freedoms and ethnic identities were so long suppressed, the disintegration of Soviet control has meant a search for order and equity. This has posed new problems that have strained domestic relations at a crucial time when stability is most necessary. In the following selection, Austrian ambassador to the United States, Helmut Tuerk, provides some perspective.

"Ethnic Strife in Eastern Europe" is from Helmut Tuerk, speech delivered at the Town Hall of California, Los Angeles, California, on April 15, 1994. Contained in *Vital Speeches of the Day,* June 15, 1994, pp. 517–518, 521.

When talking about ethnic strife in Central and Eastern Europe, it must, first of all, be recalled that the continent of Europe has traditionally been a mosaic of peoples with different cultures, languages, traditions, and religions. This diversity has, in the past and present, often been a source of conflict. The tragic events we are witnessing today in parts of the former Yugoslavia are a case in point for the continuing explosiveness of unresolved issues stemming from this diversity.

This very diversity, however, constitutes, at the same time, through a cross-fertilization process, a powerful source of richness of European culture and civilization. If preserved and allowed to flourish everywhere on our continent under conditions of respect for human rights, democracy and the rule of law, this diversity can be a tremendous asset instead of being a source of chaos.

It is obvious that the living together of different ethnic, linguistic and/or religious groups as a rule presupposes that one group forms a majority while one or more other groups constitute minorities. The existence of such minorities is an undeniable feature of almost every European country. With dozens of distinct ethnic groups in Europe alone, the ideas of a separate state for each one of these groups would be totally unrealistic if not altogether absurd. Very often ethnic groups forming a minority in one country are the dominant nationality in another country. On the other hand there are groups which only constitute minorities in a single country or in several countries. . . .

Totalitarian States—as until quite recently was the case in most of Central and all of Eastern Europe—often try to resolve the problem by either denying the very existence of such minorities or by theoretically granting them certain rights which in practice, however, remain largely on paper. When such systems of government collapse, the minorities' aspiration to safeguard and develop their identity may take on a violent form. The comparison has often been made to lifting a lid from a boiling pot. The collapse of communism in Central and Eastern Europe has thus been accompanied by a resurgence of nationalism among peoples and ethnic groups seeking to right the wrongs to which they had been subjected. . . .

Let me now refer to some regions of Europe, formerly under communist domination, where the coexistence of different ethnic groups has either already led to strife, even armed conflict, or is of serious concern for the future. Let me begin with . . . the case of the former Yugoslavia, where conflicting aspirations of various ethnic groups did not only lead to the disintegration of the confederation, but to continuing bloodshed and atrocities of a kind Europe has not experienced since World War II. . . .

The former Soviet Union poses even greater problems. Let me only point to the fact that on the territory of the former Soviet Union there are over 100 different ethnic groups, speaking 130 different languages. The largest groups include Russians, Ukrainians, Uzbeks, Byelorussians, and Azeris.

Tsarist politics aimed at strengthening the empire and at transforming its multi-ethnic character into that of a Russian national State. Under communist rule, the various nationalities at first enjoyed relative autonomy within the Federation and saw their culture and languages promoted. Stalin's policies, however, aimed at putting an end to the various cultural traditions and to forcibly achieve russification of the Soviet Union.

Gorbachev's Perestroika finally brought about liberation of the various ethnic groups, however, the Soviet Union fell apart. This development was in no small measure the consequence of decades of oppression. The process of the assertion of rights by certain ethnic groups is still continuing and is threatening peace and stability in some areas of the former Soviet Union.

The problems the former Soviet Republics are facing also stem from the fact that many members of ethnic groups live outside the boundaries of the State where they form the majority, i.e. that State boundaries do not correspond to ethnic boundaries; e.g. out of 145 million Russians, 25 million live outside the Russian Federation; only one fourth of the 6.5 million Tartars live in Tartastan. In the Russian Federation itself, 19 percent of the population is non-Russian. . . .

Looking at today's Europe with its multitude of ethnic groups and the actual and potential conflicts stemming therefrom, the urgency of codifying the rights of these groups on an international level, coupled with an international control mechanism, becomes obvious. Important steps in this direction have already been taken with Austria being at the forefront of these endeavors. We firmly believe that the future of the European continent in no small measure depends on a satisfactory resolution of these issues, the alternative being unending confrontation, strife and even armed conflict.

Ethnic groups should serve as bridges between nations and as an element promoting greater understanding between peoples. This presupposes a democratic political framework based on the rule of law, with a functioning independent judiciary. Such a framework must guarantee full respect for human rights and fundamental freedoms, equal rights and status for all citizens, the free expression of all their legitimate interests and aspirations, political pluralism, social tolerance and the implementation of legal rules that place effective restraints on the abuse of governmental power. Respect for and promotion of rights of ethnic groups cannot aim at establishing separate states for each and every ethnic group. What we should rather aim for, is to speed up the process of European integration and extend that process as far as possible to Central and Eastern Europe. The importance of the national State will diminish due to the existence of supra-national institutions on the one hand and the increasing role of regions on the other hand. Thus, issues relating to ethnic groups should become less burning, as every individual, no matter to which group he or she belongs, will enjoy the advantage of living in a broader European framework. . . .

In view of the fundamental political changes in Central and Eastern Europe in favor of democracy, the rule of law and a system of market economy there is every reason to believe that the process of European integration can in due course be extended to the east of Vienna. This would be the best guarantee that ethnic strife can be resolved by peaceful means and a new European order will emerge out of ethnic chaos. Austria as a traditional bridge between East and West on the European continent will be happy to make its contribution and will be even more in a position to do so as member of the European Union.

"We Are Witnesses to a Process of Death in the Balkans" (January 12, 1994)

POPE JOHN PAUL II

The nation of Yugoslavia was created shortly after World War I by the provisions of the Treaty of Versailles in 1919. The Balkan region, which includes the areas of Romania, Bulgaria, and Yugoslavia, had been a "powder keg" of ethnic strife and violence for centuries as Serbs, Slovenes, Croats, Bosnians, and other Slavs who lived in the region sought freedom from foreign control and fought among themselves over disputed boundaries. The spark that set off World War I was lit by a Serb nationalist who resented Austrian presence in the area. After World War II, as eastern Europe succumbed to the onslaught of Soviet troops, Yugoslavia, although communist, resisted Soviet domination under the strong leadership of Marshal Josip Broz Tito. Tito, who had been a military commander of Slavic partisans during World War II, argued that the different Slavic peoples who had been artificially thrust together in the nation of Yugoslavia could remain independent of Soviet control only if they exchanged their individual ethnic demands in return for the stability of his leadership. But when Tito died in 1980, Yugoslavian unity began to break apart. Upon the collapse of the Soviet Union in 1991, there was no longer the fear of a foreign threat to curb domestic bickering. Yugoslavia broke apart quickly in the face of Serbian aggression to capture and control territory where Bosnians and Croats had formed ethnic majorities. Thousands died, including Muslims who form minorities throughout the region. The Serbs justified their aggression on the basis of a need for more "living space," echoing Hitler's demands just before World War II. In addition, the Serbs embarked on a program of "ethnic cleansing," which had all the earmarks of another holocaust. Since the United Nations was ineffective in limiting the violence and working out acceptable boundaries, the United States, late in 1995, took the lead in negotiating the Dayton Peace Accords, which required the presence of NATO troops in Bosnia. In 1999, Serbian forces embarked on an aggressive campaign against ethnic Albanians in the region of Kosovo, again provoking a military response by NATO. In the following selection, Pope John Paul II offers perspective and a different solution.

"We Are Witnesses to a Process of Death in the Balkans" is from a general audience of Pope John Paul II on January 12, 1994, contained in *The Pope Speaks*, vol. 39 (1994), pp. 180–182.

We are witnesses to a process of death precisely in the Balkans, and, unfortunately, powerless witnesses at that. . . . The overwhelming majority of the victims in the war in the Balkans are innocent people. Even among the soldiers themselves there are relatively few who bear full responsibility for the present warfare. . . .

But is it really possible to say that the people and the circles responsible for the tragic events of the former Yugoslavia do not know what they are doing? In fact, they cannot possibly fail to know. Perhaps the truth is that they are trying to find some justification for their actions. Unfortunately our century has provided us with more than one example of this sort. Totalitarian systems, whether of a nationalistic or a collectivistic character, have been very widespread in the recent past, and all have been based on obedience to ideologies of "salvation" promising heaven on earth for individuals and for all society. In this context, it could be said that everything presently taking place in the Balkans, if viewed against the backdrop of recent European history, is nothing new. Tragically, we are already familiar with demands for "living space" (lebensraum), as well as the idea of a chosen nation, or of a privileged race or class.

At the end of the Second World War, at a time when consciences were reawakening, humanity realized how contrary all this was to the good of man and of nations. The first response to the atrocities of that terrible conflict was the Universal Declaration of Human Rights. And now, in the Balkans it seems that in a certain sense we have gone right back to the beginning. Human rights are being violated in a frightening and tragic way and those responsible go so far as to justify their actions by the principle of obedience to orders and to particular ideologies. . . . Those responsible for the terrible crimes of the Second World War were brought to judgment and in the West the trial was concluded in a relatively short time. In Eastern Europe, however, it was necessary for the most part to wait until 1989, and not everyone guilty of repeated and documented violations of human rights has yet received a just condemnation. . . .

The Apostolic See, for its part, does not cease to recall the principle of humanitarian intervention. Not in the first place a military intervention, but rather every kind of action which aims at "disarming" the aggressor. This is a principle which has a specific application in the troubling events taking place in the Balkans. In the Church's moral teaching all military aggression is judged to be morally evil; legitimate defense on the other hand is considered admissible and even at times a duty. The history of our century has provided many confirmations of this teaching.

The most powerful humanitarian intervention is always prayer. Prayer represents an enormous spiritual power, especially when accompanied by sacrifice and suffering. How many sacrifices and how much suffering are faced by the people and nations of the war-torn region of the Balkans! Even if it is not apparent to a superficial glance and many people do not acknowledge it, prayer joined to sacrifice constitutes the most powerful force in human history.

The Progress of Western Civilization

The twentieth century has been a most extraordinary time in which to live—extraordinary because the changes that have taken place in science, technology, governmental systems, and especially daily life have occurred in such a short span of time. We live today with computers that can calculate, store, and retrieve information far more quickly and efficiently than is humanly possible. We were amazed in 1969 when a human finally walked on the moon, and we still anticipate news from interplanetary probes, which hold out the possibility of discovering other forms of life. Medical research has developed vaccines for dreaded diseases, extended life by transplanting organs, and even unlocked the possibilities of changing the human condition itself through discovery of DNA and genetic engineering. All these accomplishments bespeak progress. But this progress entails risks that threaten to destroy all that has been created.

There is a curious paradox that technological progress contributes to the ultimate insecurity of humankind. We marvel at the computer revolution, yet fear the specter of "Big Brother," which looms large and threatens personal freedom by controlling information. We in the twentieth century are faced with the ultimate concern: the survival of civilization itself. The obliteration of the human species has never before been within its own power. Those who were born after 1945 have inherited the responsibility of maintaining peace and therefore existence.

So how does one define the word "progress"? Far too often we forget that progress is not necessarily a technological or scientific preserve. Indeed, one must also measure progress on a human scale in terms of moral and ethical considerations. Have we learned anything from history, from the attitudes and mistakes of our ancestors? World War I remains the quintessential turning point for any discussion of progress in the twentieth century. In 1914, technological developments in weaponry altered the very nature of war as machine guns, tanks, airplanes, submarines, and poisonous gas made killing less personal, more brutal and efficient. This new style of "total war," in which innocents died and thousands of men walked into barbed wire and machine gun fire, must be seen as a retreat from progress on a human scale. The succeeding events of the century—World War II, Hitler's destruction of the Jews, the nuclear devastation of Hiroshima, and the Cold War—have led many to view this less as a century of progress and more as a century of holocaust. And yet, have we in the late-twentieth century advanced on an ideal plane of existence toward a more just and equal international community? How much further must we go to secure the political and social equality of women? Is racism generally on the decline? Have we gone beyond totalitarian government and the dictates of imperialism? Can new holocausts be prevented through the force of world opinion? One needs to question human nature and the value of history in this regard. And what influence does the individual have in all this? Personal roles in revolution (V. I. Lenin) and destruction (Adolf Hitler and Joseph Stalin) have been confirmed. But how successful has the individual been in promoting peaceful change and coexistence? Mahatma Gandhi, Martin Luther King, Jr., Desmond Tutu, Albert Schweitzer, Elie Wiesel, Albert Einstein, Mother Theresa—have they too made a difference?

Humanity seems to wage a perpetual duel between progress and holocaust, between inclusion and exclusion. Reasons for this are difficult to discern. The explanation of human action is necessarily fraught with frustration, for humans are ruled more often by their passions than by their intellect. But it is precisely this unpredictability that contributes to the progress of civilization; the new idea, the desire to compete and achieve, the will to give life or take it away—all enter into the equation of success or failure, of progress or destruction. We do not have the benefit of "20/20 hindsight." In fact, we often suffer from the stress of myopia, of not being able to "see the forest for the trees." So the need to understand where we are going in life and what things are of greatest value ceases to be a concern of the historian and becomes more a responsibility of each individual.

This section seeks to develop the dichotomy between the desire of humans for progress and coexistence, and our established record of destruction. The role of science and the responsibilities of scientists and politicians are especially at question in this historical problem. But ultimately, responsibility for our own civilization rests in each individual. It is important to understand the problems and struggle toward the solutions.

The Women's Movement in the Modern Age

Perhaps women have always been in closer contact with reality than men; it would seem to be the just recompense for being deprived of idealism.

—Germaine Greer

I thought that women were going to come along and save us with new humane values. And what do they do? They adopt the worst values of the young male and go off to law school.

—Charles A. Peters

Certainly one of the most dramatic and singular roads to progress in Western society was traveled by courageous and determined women who strove for equal political and social rights in the face of established male opposition. The origin of this movement is difficult to pinpoint and might be said to have existed throughout history, at random moments, in the inner recesses of the personal heart, in occasional diary accounts, in the political tracts of Mary Wollstonecraft, the street demonstrations of Emmeline Pankhurst, the jail cells of Elizabeth Cady Stanton and Susan B. Anthony, in the munitions factories during World Wars I and II, in the forceful prose of Betty Friedan and Gloria Steinem. The following selections attest to some of the fundamental attitudes of a movement that has been more directly defined in the second half of the twentieth century with great impact on Western society. The issues of equal pay and discrimination in the workplace and the continuing controversy over abortion and reproductive freedom continue to provide a focus for the ideal of complete equality between the sexes.

The Feminine Mystique (1963)

BETTY FRIEDAN

Following significant gains made during the 1920s and 1930s, women retreated to their traditional roles after World War II. The image of 1950s life in America as stolid, conservative, and suburban was cemented by a desire to find stability after the chaos of war, to start over with clearly defined sex roles. The emphasis was on traditional family values, supported by Norman Rockwell's paintings and Betty Crocker's recipes. Communism and rock 'n' roll were the enemies, but God was an American and our salvation lay in patriotism. In a sense, it was simpler when women knew the expectations of society and could commit total energy to the primary domestic goal of childrearing. There was purpose, even zeal, in the retreat to domesticity.

Betty Friedan's publication of The Feminine Mystique *in 1963 provided impetus for a new women's movement. Friedan found an underlying frustration in women who had been mesmerized by an abstract ideal, a feminine mystique, and were now measured by society and their husbands for contentment and evaluated by the advertising industry for profit.*

In the fifteen years after World War II, this mystique of feminine fulfillment became the cherished and self-perpetuating core of contemporary American culture. Millions of women lived their lives in the image of those pretty pictures of the American suburban housewife, kissing their husbands goodbye in front of the picture window, depositing their stationwagonsful of children at school, and smiling as they ran the new electric waxer over the spotless kitchen floor. They baked their own bread, sewed their own and their children's clothes, kept their new washing machines and dryers running all day. They changed the sheets on the beds twice a week instead of once, took the rug-hooking class in adult education, and pitied their poor frustrated mothers, who had dreamed of having a career. Their only dream was to be perfect wives and mothers; their highest ambition to have five children and a beautiful house, their only fight to get and keep their husbands. They had no thought for the unfeminine problems of the world outside the home; they wanted the men to make the major decisions. They gloried in their role as women, and wrote proudly on the census blank: "Occupation: housewife."

For over fifteen years, the words written for women, and the words women used when they talked to each other, while their husbands sat on the other side of the room and talked shop or politics or septic tanks, were about problems with their children, or how to keep their husbands happy, or improve their children's school, or cook chicken or make slipcovers. Nobody argued whether women were inferior or superior to men; they were simply different. Words like "emancipation" and "career" sounded strange and embarrassing; no one had

("Doonesbury." Copyright © 1987 by G. B. Trudeau. Reprinted by permission of Universal Press Syndicate.)

used them for years. When a Frenchwoman named Simone de Beauvoir wrote a book called *The Second Sex*, an American critic commented that she obviously "didn't know what life was all about," and besides, she was talking about French women. The "woman problem" in America no longer existed.

If a woman had a problem in the 1950's and 1960's, she knew that something must be wrong with her marriage, or with herself. Other women were satisfied with their lives, she thought. What kind of a woman was she if she did not feel this mysterious fulfillment waxing the kitchen floor? She was so ashamed to admit her dissatisfaction that she never knew how many other woman shared it. If she tried to tell her husband, he didn't understand what she was talking about. She did not really understand it herself. For over fifteen years women in America found it harder to talk about this problem than about sex. Even the psychoanalysts had no name for it. When a woman went to a psychiatrist for help, as many women did, she would say, "I'm so ashamed," or "I must be hopelessly neurotic." "I don't know what's wrong with women today," a suburban psychiatrist said uneasily. "I only know something is wrong because most of my patients happen to be women. And their problem isn't sexual." Most women with this problem did not go to see a psychoanalyst, however. "There's nothing wrong really," they kept telling themselves. "There isn't any problem." But on an April morning in 1959, I heard a mother of four, having coffee with four other mothers in a suburban development fifteen miles from New York, say in a tone of quiet desperation, "the problem." And the others knew, without words, that she was not talking about a problem with her husband, or her children, or her home. Suddenly they realized they all shared the same problem, the problem that has no name. They began, hesitantly, to talk about it. Later, after they had picked up their children at a nursery school and taken them home to nap, two of the women cried, in sheer relief, just to know they were not alone. Gradually I came to realize that the problem that has no name was shared by countless women in America. . . .

If I am right, the problem that has no name stirring in the minds of so many American women today is not a matter of loss of femininity or too much education, or the demands of domesticity. It is far more important than anyone recognizes. It is the key to these other new and old problems which have been torturing women and their husbands and children, and puzzling their doctors and educators for years. It may well be the key to our future as a nation and a culture. "I want something more than my husband and my children and my home." . . .

This is the real mystery: why did so many American women, with the ability and education to discover and create, go back home again, to look for "something more" in housework and rearing children? For, paradoxically, in the same fifteen years in which that spirited New Women was replaced by the Happy Housewife, the boundaries of the human world have widened, the pace of world change has quickened, and the very nature of human reality has become increasingly free from biological and material necessity. Does the mystique keep American women from growing with the world? Does it force her to deny reality to believe she is a queen? Does it doom women to be displaced persons, if not virtual schizophrenics, in our complex, changing world?

It is more than a strange paradox that as all professions are finally open to women in America, "career women" has become a dirty word; that as higher education becomes available to any woman with the capacity for it, education for women has become so suspect that more and more drop out of high school and college to marry and have babies; that as so many roles in modern society become theirs for the taking, women so insistently confine themselves to one role. Why, with the removal of all the legal, political, economic, and education barriers that once kept woman from being man's equal, a person in her own right, an individual free to develop her own potential, should she accept this new image which insists she is not a person but a "woman," by definition barred from the freedom of human existence and a voice in human destiny?

The feminine mystique is so powerful that women grow up no longer knowing that they have the desires and capacities the mystique forbids. But such a mystique does not fasten itself on a whole nation in a few short years, reversing the trends of a century, without cause. What gives the mystique its power? Why did women go home again?

"If Men Could Menstruate" (1978)
GLORIA STEINEM

Betty Friedan opened up the search for the "modern woman" who could find worth in the cultivation of her potential, who was intimately in tune with the heritage of the women's movement and could tap the future through vision and energy. Perhaps the quintessential example of this "modern woman" who staked a claim to high-profile leadership of the feminist movement in the 1970s and 1980s was Gloria Steinem. The commentator Bill Moyers called her "a lightning rod for the cause of other women who would sing but have no voice." She began her career as a journalist and landed a job as a Playboy Club bunny in order to investigate the operations. She was a founding editor of Ms. magazine in 1972 and through this vehicle became a persuasive spokesperson for what has been called the "Feminist Movement." Her voice in her writings has taken on a wide range, from pathos to satire. In the following excerpt from a compilation of her work entitled Outrageous Acts and Everyday Rebellions *(1983), what appears to be a humorous and irreverent parody also contains some rather profound commentary on male and female power relationships in our contemporary society.*

. . . Whatever a "superior" group has will be used to justify its superiority, and whatever an "inferior" group has will be used to justify its plight. Black men were given poorly paid jobs because they were said to be "stronger" than white men, while all women were relegated to poorly paid jobs because they were said to be "weaker." As the little boy said when asked if he wanted to be a lawyer like his mother, "Oh no, that's women's work." Logic has nothing to do with oppression.

So what would happen if suddenly, magically, men could menstruate and women could not?

Clearly, menstruation would become an enviable, boast-worthy masculine event:

Men would brag about how long and how much.

Young boys would talk about it as the envied beginning of manhood. Gifts, religious ceremonies, family dinners, and stag parties would mark the day.

To prevent monthly work loss among the powerful, Congress would fund a National Institute of Dysmenorrhea. Doctors would research little about heart attacks, from which men were hormonally protected, but everything about cramps.

Sanitary supplies would be federally funded and free. Of course, some men would still pay for the prestige of such commercial brands as Paul Newman Tampons, Muhammad Ali's Rope-a-Dope Pads, John Wayne Maxi Pads, and Joe Namath Jock Shields—"For Those Light Bachelor Days." Statistical surveys would show that men did better in sports and won more Olympic medals during their periods.

Generals, right-wing politicians, and religious fundamentalists would cite menstruation ("men-struation") as proof that only men could serve God and country in combat ("You have to give blood to take blood"), occupy high political office ("Can women be properly fierce without a monthly cycle governed by the planet Mars?"), be priests, ministers, God Himself ("He gave His blood for our sins"), or rabbis ("Without a monthly purge of impurities, women are unclean").

Male liberals or radicals, however, would insist that women are equal, just different; and that any woman could join their ranks if only she were willing to recognize the primacy of menstrual rights. . . .

Street guys would invent slang ("He's a three-pad-man") and "give fives" on the corner with some exchange like, "Man, you lookin' good!"

"Yeah, man, I'm on the rag!"

TV shows would treat the subject openly. (Happy Days: Richie and Potsie try to convince Fonzie that he is still "The Fonz," though he has missed two periods in a row. Hill Street Blues: The whole precinct hits the same cycle.) So would newspapers. (SUMMER SHARK SCARE THREATENS MENSTRU-ATING MEN. JUDGE CITES MONTHLIES IN PARDONING RAPIST.) And so would movies. (Newman and Redford in Blood Brothers!)

Men would convince women that sex was more pleasurable at "that time of the month." Lesbians would be said to fear blood and therefore life itself, though all they needed was a good menstruating man.

Medical schools would limit women's entry ("they might faint at the sight of blood").

Of course, intellectuals would offer the most moral and logical arguments. Without that biological gift for measuring the cycles of the moon and planets, how could a woman master any discipline that demanded a sense of time, space, mathematics—or the ability to measure anything at all? . . . Menopause would be celebrated as a positive event, the symbol that men had accumulated enough years of cyclical wisdom to need no more. . . .

And how would women be trained to react? One can imagine right-wing women agreeing to all these arguments with a staunch and smiling masochism. . . . Radical feminists would add that the oppression of the non-menstrual was the pattern for all other oppressions. ("Vampires were our first freedom fighters!") . . . Socialist feminists would insist that, once capitalism and imperialism were overthrown, women would menstruate, too. . . .

In short, we would discover, as we should already guess, that logic is in the eye of the logician. . . .

The truth is that, if men could menstruate, the power justifications would go on and on.

If we let them.

("Doonesbury." Copyright © 1987 by G. B. Trudeau. Reprinted by permission of Universal Press Syndicate.)

Women in the Marketplace (1990)

JOAN KONNER

Throughout the 1980s, both men and women refined a competitive, often uncooperative, relationship in the workplace that had been established in the 1970s. As more women applied and were admitted to professional schools, the face of corporate industry began to change. The workplace was in transition, and women faced new challenges in juggling traditional responsibilities in the home with the demands of the office. A new image of the "modern woman" was created by advertising agencies that placed emphasis on "having it all." The "two-income" family became a standard in society, and women were faced with the demands of both "bringing home the bacon and frying it in a pan." Men, too, were faced with changing realities in personal relationships and found themselves judged by a new standard of the modern, sensitive male, who was comfortable with himself and understood the necessity of intimate communication. "Macho" was out and became acceptable only as a part of a males' guilty fantasy land of Rambo, Dirty Harry, and the Terminator.

The 1990s saw a reaction against the Yuppie "boomers" of the previous decade. Both men and women considered the worth of "free time" and family stability more seriously. Women still exist in a world where their market value has not yet been fully realized. But they are bringing new perspectives and attitudes to that marketplace that may well again change the face of contemporary society.

Joan Konner, dean of Columbia University's School of Journalism, reflected on these developments in a speech delivered to the New Jersey Press Women's Association in May 1990.

I always tried to follow a piece of advice I picked up when I was a student at the Columbia Graduate School of Journalism. The school had a ritual for the women students in the class at the end of the school year. A panel of women journalists was invited to discuss how to manage home and career.

One of the panelists, if I recall correctly, was Betsy Wade of the *New York Times*, who advised: "When you're sick, go to work, because when your children are sick, you're going to have to stay home and you can't be absent for both."

Such was the balancing act of women who worked in the newsroom at the time, and I'm not sure that it's much changed today. . . .

The guest on the program ("Not for Women Only" with Barbara Walters) that day was Clare Booth Luce, and they were talking about the time Mrs. Luce served in Congress.

Mrs. Luce said it was the worst experience of her professional life, and further, she thought that women would never become a strong presence in Congress.

"Why?" Barbara Walters asked.

Mrs. Luce replied, "because women do not have the instinct for the jugular, and men do."

Barbara Walters replied: "We'll learn."

"Women in the Marketplace" is from Joan Konner, speech delivered to the New Jersey Press Women's Association on May 5, 1990. Contained in *Vital Speeches of the Day*, September 15, 1990, pp. 726–728.

I remember thinking that wasn't the point at all. We weren't supposed to be trying to become like men. We were supposed to be trying to get into the decision-making roles so that we could change the way business is done to the advantage of both sexes. What's the point of women getting into the positions of power if, in the process, we have to turn ourselves into killers, psychologically, at least, with an instinct for the jugular? Aren't those killer values the ones we are trying to change?

That's still the question today when we ask: Are women in journalism, especially now that there are more of us, some of us in positions of leadership, making a difference? Given the impact of the media in shaping our social, political, and economic life, are we seeing changes not only in numbers in the newsrooms, but in the agenda and priorities of society?

I suggest the answer is "yes," but it is only a beginning. . . .

We shouldn't mistake quantity for quality, and the quieter history includes the accomplishments of many women off-camera in television newsrooms as well as many more in newspapers and magazines throughout the country. For one, the remarkable *Ms.* magazine, which legitimized women's issues by producing a serious magazine about them. It no doubt can take the credit for the greater seriousness of women's magazines in general, and for leading the way to the changing definition of news generally—the inclusion of domestic and workplace issues like battered wives, child abuse, and maternity leave, in so-called hard-news; values and quality of life stories; stories about children, health, education, social trends, community, and the environment—not only on the front page, but on every page and on television news as well. . . .

Are women better equipped to cover this "new" news? It is possible we are. The psychologist Carol Gilligan, in her book, *In a Different Voice*, described a difference between the moral development of men and women.

Women, she says, develop an ethic of care, an empathy based on their identification with the primary parent, usually the mother. Women define themselves in terms of relationship and responsibility.

Men develop an ethic of justice as they separate from the mother. They define themselves in terms of difference, position and hierarchy. If we accept this, then I think we can assume the responsibility that comes with our

("Doonesbury." Copyright © 1987 by G. B. Trudeau. Reprinted by permission of Universal Press Syndicate.)

capacity to adopt a broader perspective and show the human, caring side of the news.

The feminine sensibility is growing everywhere in our culture today—in literature, in art, in history, politics, and the media. It coincides with concerns about the environment, a growing awareness of Mother Earth, as our life support system. There is talk of the Gaia principle, a world view that says we are all part of one living body. We find the principle expressed in the mythology of the Goddess, in which there is also a revival of interest today. The Goddess was worshipped for thousands of years in agrarian, egalitarian societies in which there was a love of life, of nature and beauty.

There seems at this time to be a great hunger in the American culture for the values of the goddess—the values of life, generation, and creation. There seems to be a growing reverence for nature, for a collective spirit, and relationship based on the awareness of the interconnectedness of life. We are becoming more concerned that our competitive Western culture that developed along the lines of the Darwinian principle of the survival of the fittest may have been a life-supporting pattern for one period of human evolution but it may no longer be a life-supporting pattern for another—this one. Human intelligence creates systems to protect human life. Today those very systems are threatening it—industrial development which threatens the environment, nuclear weapons that threaten all of life. In such a world, those with a wider perspective and greater awareness are turning out to be the fittest.

We are coming around a bend, and we realize there is a need for other values, values of collaboration, community, care. These are the values that used to belong to the private sphere of home and family. But we are beginning to see these values in the workplace and in public life as well. One hypothesis is that women, as they succeed in the marketplace, retain what is valuable from what used to be considered the domestic sphere and bring that wider perspective into view. It does seem some of us—women and men—have had enough of the instinct for the jugular. I think that women in positions of power—in politics, public service, and the media—are helping to make that difference.

Backlash: The Undeclared War Against American Women (1991)

SUSAN FALUDI

In her book Backlash, *Pulitzer Prize–winning reporter Susan Faludi notes that the American women's movement scored some important successes in the 1970s, particularly in the areas of reproductive freedom and fairness in employment. But she argues that this advance led to an antifeminist reaction in the 1980s that was fueled by a campaign of misinformation and outright deception. She sees this as a part of a backlash primarily caused by the anxiety that men feel*

"Backlash" is from Susan Faludi, *Backlash* (New York: Crown Publishers, 1991), pp. ix–x, xxi, xxiii. Copyright © 1991 by Susan Faludi. Reprinted by permission of Crown Publishers, Inc.

when women make modest advances toward gender equality. According to Faludi, this backlash has happened in previous historical periods as well, and she cautions women to see their strides and plight in context. There exists and will continue to exist an ongoing struggle for supremacy between men and women. The following excerpt acknowledges the importance of the media in shaping the image of feminism and providing expectations for women in our contemporary society.

To be a woman in America at the close of the twentieth century—what good fortune. That's what we keep hearing, anyway. The barricades have fallen, politicians assure us. Women have "made it," Madison Avenue cheers. Women's fight for equality has "largely been won," *Time* magazine announces. Enroll at any university, join any law firm, apply for credit at any bank. Women have so many opportunities now, corporate leaders say, that we don't really need equal opportunity policies. Women are so equal now, lawmakers say, that we no longer need an Equal Rights Amendment. Women have "so much," former President Ronald Reagan says, that the White House no longer needs to appoint them to higher office. Even American Express ads are saluting a woman's freedom to charge it. At last, women have received their full citizenship papers.

And yet...

Behind this celebration of the American woman's victory, behind the news, cheerfully and endlessly repeated, that the struggle for women's rights is won, another message flashes. You may be free and equal now, it says to women, but you have never been more miserable.

The bulletin of despair is posted everywhere—at the newsstand, on the TV set, at the movies, in advertisements and doctors' offices and academic journals. Professional women are suffering "burnout" and succumbing to an "infertility epidemic." Single women are grieving from a "man shortage." *The New York Times* reports: Childless women are "depressed and confused" and their ranks are swelling. *Newsweek* says: Unwed women are "hysterical" and crumbling under a "profound crisis of confidence." The health advice manuals inform: High-powered career women are stricken and unprecedented outbreaks of "stress-induced disorders," hair loss, bad nerves, alcoholism, and even heart attacks. The psychology books advise: Independent women's loneliness represents "a major mental health problem today." Even founding feminist Betty Friedan has been spreading the word: she warns that women now suffer from a new identity crisis and "new 'problems that have no name.' "

How can American women be in so much trouble at the same time that they are supposed to be so blessed? If the status of women has never been higher, why is their emotional state so low? If women got what they asked for, what could possibly be the matter now?

The prevailing wisdom of the past decade has supported one, and only one, answer to this riddle; it must be all that equality that's causing all that pain. Women are unhappy precisely *because* they are free. Women are enslaved by their own liberation. They have grabbed at the gold ring of independence, only to miss the one ring that really matters. They have gained control of their fertility, only to destroy it. They have pursued their own professional dreams—and lost out on the greatest female adventure. The women's movement, as we are told time and again, has proved women's own worst enemy. . . .

The truth is that the last decade has seen a powerful counterassault on women's rights, a backlash, an attempt to retract the handful of small and hard-won victories that the feminist movement did manage to win for women. This counterassault is largely insidious; in a kind of pop-culture version of the Big Lie, it stands the truth boldly on its head and proclaims that the very steps that have elevated women's position have actually led to their downfall. . . .

But what has made women unhappy in the last decade is not their "equality"—which they don't yet have—but the rising pressure to halt, and even reverse, women's quest for that equality. The "man shortage" and the "infertility epidemic" are not the price of liberation; in fact, they do not even exist. But these chimeras are the chisels of a society-wide backlash. They are part of a relentless whittling-down process—much of it amounting to outright propaganda—that has served to stir women's private anxieties and break their political wills. Identifying feminism as women's enemy only furthers the ends of a backlash against women's equality, simultaneously deflecting attention from the backlash's central role and recruiting women to attack their own cause. . . .

The force and furor of the backlash churn beneath the surface, largely invisible to the public eye. On occasion in the last decade, they have burst into view. We have seen New Right politicians condemn women's independence, antiabortion protesters firebomb women's clinics, fundamentalist preachers damn feminists as "whores" and "witches." Other signs of the backlash's wrath, by their sheer brutality, can push their way into public consciousness for a time—the sharp increase in rape, for example, or the rise in pornography that depicts extreme violence against women.

More subtle indicators in popular culture may receive momentary, and often bemused, media notice, then quickly slip from social awareness: a report, for instance, that the image of women on prime-time TV shows has suddenly degenerated. A survey of mystery fiction finding the numbers of female characters tortured and mutilated mysteriously multiplying. The puzzling news that, as one commentator put it, "So many hit songs have the B-word [bitch] to refer to women that some rap music seems to be veering toward rape music." The ascendancy of virulently misogynist comics like Andrew Dice Clay—who called women "pigs" and "sluts" and strutted in films in which women were beaten, tortured, and blown up—or radio hosts like Rush Limbaugh, whose broadsides against "femi-Nazi" feminists made his syndicated program the most popular radio talk show in the nation. Or word that in 1987, the American Women in Radio & Television couldn't award its annual prize for ads that feature women positively: it could find no ad that qualified. . . .

The meaning of the word "feminist" has not really changed since it first appeared in a book review in the Athenaeum of April 27, 1895, describing a

woman who "has in her the capacity of fighting her way back to independence." It is the basic proposition that, as Nora put it in Ibsen's *A Doll's House*
a century ago, "Before everything else I'm a human being." It is the simply
worded sign hoisted by a little girl to the 1970 Women's Strike for Equality:
I AM NOT A BARBIE DOLL. Feminism asks the world to recognize at
long last that women aren't decorative ornaments, worthy vessels, members
of a "special-interest group." They are half (in fact, now more that half) of
the national population, and just as deserving of rights and opportunities,
just as capable of participating in the world's events, as the other half. Feminism's agenda is basic: It asks that women not be forced to "choose" between
public justice and private happiness. It asks that women be free to define
themselves—instead of having their identity defined for them, time and
again, by their culture and their men. The fact that these are still such incendiary notions should tell us that American women have a way to go before
they enter the promised land of equality.

The Technological Revolution

Big Brother has arrived, and he is your computer!

—Norman Lear

Progress, far from consisting of change, depends on retentiveness. Those
who cannot remember the past are condemned to repeat it.

—George Santayana

No civilization can exist for long if it is conscious only of the present. It
must draw its nourishment instead from two other sources: its dreams for
the future and the remembered experiences and dreams of the past.

—Stephen Bertman

*Among the many technological advancements that have taken place since 1945,
the development of the microchip has produced some of the most profound
changes in our modern world. It has become the essential component of our modern communication systems and has made possible the computer revolution by
storing vast amounts of information in a minute space. Whether on a network
system at the office or in the privacy of one's home, the computer has opened new
dimensions in communication, architectural design, engineering, medical analysis, and even artistic expression. The 1980s in particular saw the widespread
integration of computers into Western culture. The processing and control of
information will remain a key to political and social influence in the future.*

*In the following selection, John Mayo, president of AT&T Bell Laboratories,
predicts future societal changes as we travel down the "information superhighway."*

The Information Superhighway
JOHN S. MAYO

It's clear that the key underlying information technologies are the prime drivers and the key enablers behind the emerging multimedia communications revolution and the evolution of information superhighways—as well as a host of other advances that together are changing the way we live, work, play, travel, and communicate. Because these key information technologies are changing the work and home environments, these same technologies are helping to address customer needs. The more they can do, the more new products and services the customer wants. It has been an upward spiral that has lasted over three decades, and will surely last at least one or two decades more.

What are these key underlying information technologies? They are silicon chips, computing, photonics or light waves, and software. And we've seen technology capabilities doubling every year in a number of such domains—for example, in computing and photonics—and doubling every 18 months in silicon chips. . . .

To cite perhaps the most widely known example, we've witnessed explosive growth in the power of silicon chips—one measure of which is the number of transistors we can cram onto a chip the size of a fingernail. And this number, now in the millions, is moving steadily toward known physical limits. In the early part of the next century, today's familiar solid state devices may mature with transistors measuring about 400 atoms by 400 atoms each, the smallest such transistors likely to operate reliably at room temperature. The new frontier then will not be in making the devices smaller, but in creatively and economically using the vast increase in complexity and power made possible by this remarkable technology. . . . This re-engineering of our industry appears to be the next-to-last step of the information revolution brought on by the invention of the transistor.

The last step, and one that may go on forever, is the re-engineering of society—of how we live, work, play, travel, and communicate. It will create a whole new way of life. For example, it will change education through distance learning and school at home; it will change work life through virtual offices and work at home; and it will diminish the need to transport our bodies for work or routine tasks such as visiting and shopping. Let me quickly add, however, that it will take social change as well as technology to make many of these changes happen.

Another driving force toward multimedia communications and information superhighway evolution is the world-wide push toward common standards and open, user-friendly interfaces that will encourage global networking, and maximum interoperability and connectivity. . . .

Now, the pacing force behind the multimedia and information superhighway revolution is not so much the technology as it is marketplace demands. For the greater part of this century, the user willingly accepted whatever technological capabilities we were able to achieve. Thus, the telecommunications industry was

"The Information Superhighway" is from John S. Mayo, speech delivered at the National Research Council/World Bank Symposium, Irvine, California, on November 28, 1994. Contained in *Vital Speeches of the Day*, February 1, 1995, pp. 244–248. Reprinted by permission.

supplier-driven, and the suppliers managed the evolution of the industry and the information highways. But, as you may know, the technology became so rich that it made many more capabilities possible than the user could accept. To put it differently, we could design a lot more products and services than the customer was willing to pay for. That marked the transition from a supplier-driven industry to today's customer-driven industry—from supplier push to marketplace pull. . . .

Let's look a bit further into these subjects and start with the multimedia revolution. After all, the pursuit of multimedia is creating social pressures on the evolution of information superhighways, both here and around the world. So what is "multimedia"? A reasonable working definition is that the term "multimedia" refers to information that combines more than one medium, where the media can include speech, music, text, data, graphics, fax, image, video, and animation. . . .

I must stress that networked multimedia communications will dramatically change the nature of work, and will therefore have a broad impact on business, first in developed nations and eventually in developing nations. Video-conferencing, for example, is first coming into businesses to enhance productivity, save time, and reduce travel. And current developments in multimedia telephony are making the possibility of remote collaborative work more and more realistic. In a few years a person could be working with colleagues or suppliers in branch offices in New York, Irvine, Hong Kong, Paris, and Sydney. Working in real time, they could accomplish the combined task of producing printed materials, presentation slides, and a videotape introducing a new product line. . . .

Our vision is to bring people together, giving them easy access to each other and to the information and services they want and need—anytime, anywhere. In our view, the information superhighway is a seamless web of communications and information networks, together with other elements of our national information infrastructure, such as computers, databases, and consumer electronics, which will put vast amounts of information at the fingertips of a variety of users. And we see the information superhighway, quite simply, as a vast interoperable network of networks, embracing local, long distance and global networks, wireless, broadcast and cable, and satellites. In addition, the information superhighway also embraces the Internet. . . . Importantly, the information superhighway is not a uniform end-to-end network developed and operated by government or any one company. It is the totality of networks in our nation, interconnected domestically and globally. And it is an important part of evolving global information superhighways.

Now, let's turn to the impacts of these technology trends on developing nations. These advanced information technology trends, multimedia communications and information superhighways will have a variety of broad, beneficial social impacts on developing nations, including the following:

Item 1: Advanced communications, growing in ubiquity, could slow the migration of rural people to urban areas—a traditional problem in countries such as The People's Republic of China.

Item 2: Access to jobs and services. People living in rural areas would be less inclined to move to the cities if advanced communications systems gave them access to jobs and sophisticated social services where they already live. . . .

Item 3: Information superhighways could alleviate congestion and commuter-traffic pollution in cities by making telecommuting possible—by bringing good jobs to people, wherever they are. . . .

Item 4: Information superhighways could also revolutionize education and eliminate differences in quality between rural and urban education systems by enabling a limited number of the very best teachers and professors to reach huge numbers of students. Both students and teachers could be located practically anywhere, in "virtual" classrooms—and they could enhance learning by accessing multimedia network databases on a great variety of content areas.

Item 5: Information superhighways could also revolutionize medical care by helping to deliver high-quality medical care far from large population centers. Advanced communications would permit frequent meetings between rural health workers and physicians located in more populated areas. The same capability would also permit direct doctor-to-patient consultation and follow-up.

Item 7: Peoples and countries would be able to retain their ethnic and cultural identities, but at the same time they would be able to communicate, transact and interact seamlessly across geographic and political boundaries.

Item 8: Information technology would both *facilitate and complicate* the job of governing; *facilitate* by making available to decision-makers vastly expanded resources of timely information; *complicate* by vastly expanding the numbers of people who would inevitably want to play a role in deciding them.

In summary, rich information technology, the worldwide push toward global standards, ever-increasing customer demands, and growing global competition are key driving forces behind the emerging multimedia communications revolution and the evolution of national information superhighways. The growth of multimedia communications and the further competitive evolution of these information superhighways, as well as of global information superhighways promise a broad range of Information Age benefits to virtually every citizen of our nation. And they also promise to extend these Information Age benefits to virtually every citizen of the world, including the developing nations.

Genetic Research and Bioethics
GEORGE POSTE

One of the areas in which progress in the twentieth century is most evident is in the field of health care. People tend to regard mumps, measles, and whooping cough as childhood diseases of little importance. Yet in the nineteenth century these, as well as tetanus and typhoid, were dangerous and sometimes devastating diseases. Even the bubonic plague (Black Death), which destroyed one-third of the population of Europe in 1348, can be treated today with antibiotics. The development of polio vaccine in 1955 freed humanity from the physical ravages of a

"Genetic Research and Bioethics" is from George Poste, speech delivered at the Jackson Laboratory, Annual Meeting, King of Prussia, Pennsylvania, on August 20, 1994. Contained in *Vital Speeches of the Day*, January 1, 1995, pp. 165–166, 168–169. Reprinted by permission.

disease that afflicted even the rich and powerful: Franklin Roosevelt, who was later to become president of the United States, was struck in 1921. Medical research also led to great advances in heart surgery and organ transplants by the late 1960s, and even to the potential for changing our very "humanness" through genetic engineering. Therein lies the great ethical question of this age of high technology. To what extent do we "play God" if we have the technology to create or alter life forms? Does euthanasia become an ethical option, a defense of individuality in an impersonal, technological world? The following selection lends perspective to the challenges facing medical science and the underlying human concerns in a world where technological progress outstrips the legal and ethical limits of society.

Genomics, the study of genes and their functional regulation in health and disease, now occupies center stage in biomedical research. Fueled by both public and industrial funding, exploration of the human genome is proceeding faster than could be imagined even a few years ago, with profound implications for the future practice of medicine and the future medical educational curriculum. . . .

We now stand on the threshold of a new era of molecular medicine in which genetics promises not only to improve the design and testing of new drugs, but to also create increasingly sophisticated diagnostic tests for the earlier detection of disease, more accurate patient stratification and staging of disease progression, to allow proactive detection of the risk of disease recurrence and clinical relapse and the use of genetic markers in optimizing treatment selection. More futuristically, yet already under exploratory clinical testing, is the longer term prospect of replacing missing or altered genes or the inactivation of dysfunctional genes. Yet perhaps of most fundamental significance is the recognition that many major illnesses are associated with specific predisposition genes and that the genetic profiling, or so called genotyping, of individuals will enable disease risk to be identified well in advance of any illness. In the last few years new gene-based tests have revealed the genes and the genetic mutations predisposing to hypertension, heart disease, diabetes, osteoporosis, colon cancer, polycystic kidney disease and Alzheimers disease among others. . . .

There are indeed exciting vistas for the future of medicine. Yet in conquering the new world of genetic knowledge we can already define ethical, legal, social and economic issues of stunning complexity. These are not issues for some distant tomorrow that will allow governments, medical professionals and the public the luxury of obfuscation to assign responsibility for their resolution to a future generation of better prepared scholars and policy makers. In genetic diagnostics, the challenge is already moving from the wings and will occupy center-stage by the mid-to-late 1990's. . . .

Yet as new genetic technologies impact medical practice with accelerating momentum, how will a coherent framework of ethics be shaped and, if required, as seems likely for certain developments, be incorporated into formal regulations or other legislative statutes? The practical reality is that the scientific hare is far outstripping the ability of the legislative tortoise to keep pace and the prospect of the scientific hare taking an Aesopian pause seems unlikely. How then will policy and law needs be formulated? Who will debate the issues and what should be the forum for debate? . . .

The quest for health, and the intellectual pursuit of the philosophical and moral underpinning of the human condition, represent enduring themes in human history. The unique status accorded to human welfare, and to the moral and legal definitions of individuality, dictate that any scientific or economic forces that threaten long held cultural beliefs and dogmas cannot fail to evoke widespread debate and will run the risk of evoking societal backlash against the perceived perpetrators if the directions being taken by science and technology are viewed as unduly threatening. . . .

The pending debate on the role of the new genetics, and their attendant ethical and legal complexities, will be both intense and public. Such terms as "science out of control," "good versus evil," "big brother versus open society," and "individual rights versus societal good" will be common rhetoric and rallying cries for the protagonists. Only one thing is certain—the debate cannot be avoided. The outcome will lead to fundamental redefinitions of healthcare, clinical practice, physician autonomy and individual rights. New disciplines such as bioethics, technology law and healthcare economics will come of age, fired in a crucible of unprecedented emotional intensity and public scrutiny. Collectively, these events portend a period that will fundamentally alter the relationship between medicine and society.

The dilemma for a modern, multicultural, pluralistic society lacking a single moral authority, is that bioethics has not yet attained the intellectual maturity, or practical experience, to define its identity or authority. . . . The difficulties faced by bioethics in defining its scope and purpose are in large measure a symptom of the increasing ambiguity and contentiousness inherent in the relationship between science and society.

The modern condition forged since the renaissance has sustained an optimistic Promethean march towards greater human freedom and individual dignity. Science has been a powerful force in this evolution, advancing human knowledge, health and general welfare. Yet, first gradually, and now with accelerating pace, at the end of the 20th century, doubt and skepticism pervade societal response to the conduct of all activities, and science is no exception. Science has lost its once secure claim to cognitive reliability and is no longer seen as free from economic or political bias or even fraud, and it is now judged culpable in creating as many problems for society as issues solved.

The unfolding vista of modern genetics in an era of economic limits on healthcare can only accelerate the feeling of human alienation from science and fear of its seeming power. We live in a time of intense expectation and great uncertainty. Modern science remains a powerful force for human progress and we must not surrender this mission.

Solutions must be agreed upon with the full recognition that there are no absolutes, no complete solutions and that background briefings for politicians to confer the wisdom to address issues of this complexity are not easily crafted. Yet unless a more coherent and pragmatic framework of bioethical recommendations is advanced by those who share a relative consensus, politicians will lack the broad platform of support needed to make difficult choices and will prevaricate just when clear actions are so urgently needed. Worse still, any policy vacuum is likely to be filled by single interest lobbies, many of whom also espouse a strong anti-technology bias.

To also ensure societal tolerance, science and medicine must define their roles in a more holistic framework of social, cultural and moral philosophic principles. This is the real challenge of our time. As we embark on the genetic cartography of man we must be vigilant to balance the inherent mechanistic reductionism of molecular biology against a larger unity of human values. . . .

In defining the dimensions of genomics research and its medical and social applications, how will it be used to protect and celebrate the importance of the fullness of genetic diversity? How, and by whom, will the uses of genomics be judged as just? How do we avoid paralysis and other impediments to the just and equitable progress of genetic medicine by not succumbing to extreme claims about the production of superbabies or the callous elimination of embryos deemed genetically unfit, while at the same time ensuring suitable vigilance against both purposeful and inadvertent discriminatory activities?

Only one thing is certain. Deciding how to incorporate new genetic data into medical, social and legal policies is by far the largest long-term challenge posed by the genome project. How history will judge us twenty, fifty and a hundred years from now will be a measure as much of our humanity as our science.

Civilization and Memory:
The Elderly as Keepers of the Flame (1990)
STEPHEN BERTMAN

Because of advancements in medical technology and attention to public health care through governmental programs and private initiative, our population is living longer. The concerns of the elderly increasingly occupy a primary position on legislative agendas and in the public view. Traditionally, the elderly have been regarded as the repositories of wisdom and experience. In a speech to the Gerontological Society of America, Stephen Bertman, professor of classics at the University of Windsor, offered his views about the changing roles of the elderly in a modern technological society where short-term memory is everything and computers store and retrieve the information of generations.

"Civilization and Memory" is from Stephen Bertman (The University of Windsor, Windsor, Ontario, N9B 3P4, Canada), speech delivered to the 43rd Annual Scientific Meeting of the Gerontological Society of America, Boston, Massachusetts, on November 18, 1990. Contained in *Vital Speeches of the Day,* January 1, 1991, pp. 185–186. Reprinted by permission of the author.

The most sacred place in ancient Rome was the Temple of Vesta in the Roman Forum. Vesta was the goddess of the hearth-fire that burned in every home. Maintained by generations of priestesses, an eternal flame inside the temple symbolized the centrality of the family in Roman life and the binding power of tradition.

However progressive Roman civilization became, its validity was forever measured by the extent to which it remained faithful to the traditions of the past, the mores maiorum, or ancestral ways. To the extent that Roman civilization deviated from those ways, to that extent was its viability diminished. The importance of guidance from elders was enshrined in the institution of the Roman Senate, a name derived from the Latin word for old person, or senex.

Nevertheless, time itself and the accelerating force of social change distanced the Romans not only from the past but from the moral imperatives of that past. Both the Senate and the elderly were eventually deauthoritized. Vesta's flame sputtered and the Empire fell.

The elderly of every era are the biologic embodiment of the past tense. To the extent that past is devalued, to that extent also will the elderly be devalued and deemed socially irrelevant. In the world of the future, the elderly will seem more and more irrelevant—even to themselves—as they continue to lose touch with the rapidly shifting dimensions and contours of the landscape they come to inhabit. Traditionally, elder citizens have been regarded as the living repositories of ancestral wisdom. Three factors, however, will conspire to strip the elderly of such credentials in the future: the accelerating obsolescence of past knowledge, the expanding accumulation of self-justifying data, and the propagation of dehumanized instruments to access facts.

Once valued as guides for a long journey, the elderly will become the trivialized guardians of an empty suitcase—the impotent, grown-up version of the culturally illiterate younger generation of today. As a class the elderly will constitute the social equivalent of the Alzheimer's victim: ironically oblivious to the past at the very time when their collective store of memories should be the greatest.

Time levels all. Denied their special role as defenders of old-age tradition, the old will increasingly ape the young. In the future cult of the NOW, short-term memory will replace long-term as antiquated experience slips down the slick memory-chute to oblivion. In the society of the future, where history itself will be an anachronism, few moral traditions will survive. This is not to deny that the elderly may form a political constituency in the future, united by a commonality of experience, temperament, and need. Nor is it to deny that, by virtue of their longevity and numbers, they will play an increasing role in the governing of America. But any discussion of potential gerontocracy must take into account the *content* of their role, not merely their presence on the stage. If the elderly cease to stand for traditional values, what *will* they stand for? And if the elderly cease to remember where the Temple of Vesta stands, who then will maintain tradition's fire? . . .

What if the old have forgotten what to teach? And what if the young do not know what to learn? Then civilization itself is in peril. Were our culture to be left with its external trappings only—the glare of military power and the glitter of material wealth—it would not have satisfied the essential conditions that every civilization must fulfill in order to endure. More than a body, every civilization needs a heart. But more than a heart, every civilization needs a memory.

No civilization can exist for long if it is conscious only of the present. It must draw its nourishment instead from two other sources: its dreams for the future and the remembered experiences and dreams of the past.

If there is to be a gerontocracy, then let it be a gerontocracy of wise guardians who reverence not only life, but time, not a gerontocracy of aerobic ghosts dancing in rhythmic frenzy to songs whose words they have long since forgotten.

CHRONOLOGY: The Era of the Superpowers

1933	Philo Farnsworth develops electronic television.
1936	Dr. Alexis Carrel develops artificial heart.
1937	Insulin used to control diabetes.
1941	Manhattan Project of intensive atomic research begins.
1942	Enrico Fermi splits the atom.
1943	Penicillin successfully used in the treatment of chronic diseases.
February 1945	Yalta Conference between Churchill, Roosevelt, and Stalin decides on four occupation zones in Germany and the prosecution of war criminals; it prepares an Allied Control Council to run Germany on the basis of "complete disarmament, demilitarization, and dismemberment."
June 1945	Charter of the United Nations signed.
July 1945	Potsdam Conference between Churchill, Truman, and Stalin finalizes agreement on the administration of Germany and the territorial adjustments in Eastern Europe.
August 6–9, 1945	The United States drops atomic bombs on Hiroshima and Nagasaki in an attempt to bring a speedy conclusion to World War II.
1946	Electronic brain built at University of Pennsylvania. Xerography process invented by Chester Carlson.
March 6, 1946	Churchill makes "Iron Curtain" speech at Fulton, Missouri: "From Stettin in the Baltic to Trieste in the Adriatic, an Iron Curtain has descended upon the Continent."

1947	Bell Laboratories scientists invent the transistor.
March 1947	In a message to Congress, President Truman outlines the Truman Doctrine, which effectively commits the United States to intervene against Communist or Communist-backed movements in Europe and elsewhere.
June 1947	George Marshall, American secretary of state, calls for a European recovery program (Marshall Plan) supported by American aid.
1948–1949	Soviets impose a complete blockade of traffic into Berlin. Successful airlift of supplies into Berlin continues for nearly one year until blockade is lifted.
April 1949	Creation of NATO (North Atlantic Treaty Organization), a defensive alliance, which pledges mutual military assistance.
1951	Electric power produced from atomic energy.
September 1951	First Soviet atomic bomb exploded.
1952	First hydrogen bomb exploded by United States at Eniwetok Atoll.
1953	U.S.S.R. explodes hydrogen bomb.
March 1953	Death of Stalin. Khrushchev confirmed as first secretary of the Communist party (September).
1954	Dr. Jonas Salk, developer of antipolio serum, starts inoculating schoolchildren.
1956	Oral vaccine developed by Albert Sabin against polio.
February 1956	Khrushchev attacks the abuses of the Stalin era at the Communist 20th Party Congress.
October–November 1956	General strike and street demonstrations in Budapest. Soviets intervene, depose Nagy, and crush the uprising.
1957	U.S.S.R. launches Sputnik I and Sputnik II, first earth satellites.
1957	Treaty of Rome establishes European Economic Community (EEC, or the "Common Market").
1958	NASA established to administer scientific exploration of space.
1961	Yuri Gagarin (U.S.S.R.) orbits the earth in a six-ton satellite.
August 1961	Berlin Wall constructed to prevent flight from East to West Berlin.
October 1961	Program of Twenty-second Communist Party. Congress advocates further "de-Stalinization."
1962	John Glenn orbits earth.

October 1962	Cuban missile crisis after Soviet Union attempts to construct ballistic missile bases in Cuba. Imposition of naval "quarantine" by the United States forces the Soviet Union to back down in the face of the threat of nuclear war.
1963	Dr. Michael De Bakey first uses an artificial heart to take over the circulation of a patient's blood during heart surgery.
October 1964	Leonid Brezhnev replaces Khrushchev as general secretary of the Communist party.
1966	U.S. and U.S.S.R. spacecraft make separate landings on the moon.
1967	People's Republic of China explodes its first hydrogen bomb. Dr. Christiaan Barnard performs the world's first human heart transplant operation.
August 1968	The Soviet Union and other Warsaw Pact forces invade Czechoslovakia and end the "Prague Spring" liberation movement. Czech leaders are forced to agree to reimposition of censorship, centralized Communist control, military occupation, and abandonment of closer links with the West.
1969	Apollo 11 lands lunar module on moon's surface. Neil Armstrong first man to step on moon.
1970	First complete synthesis of a gene by scientists at the University of Wisconsin.
1972	Richard Leakey discovers a 2.5-million-year-old human skull in northern Kenya.
May 26, 1972	President Nixon visits Moscow. Strategic Arms Limitation Treaty (SALT 1) signed limiting antiballistic missile systems.
February 1974	Dissident writer and Nobel Laureate Alexander Solzhenitsyn deported from Soviet Union.
October 1975	Soviet physicist and dissident Andrei Sakharov awarded Nobel Peace Prize.
1977	U.S. space shuttle Enterprise makes its first manned flight. United States confirms testing of neutron bomb which kills with massive radiation, leaving most buildings intact.
1978	First "test-tube baby" born in England.
1979	Margaret Thatcher leads Conservative party to victory in Great Britain and becomes first woman prime minister. Stays in office until 1990.
December 1979	Soviet invasion of Afghanistan. United States imposes a grain embargo on Soviet Union.

1980	World Health Organization announces worldwide eradication of smallpox. François Mitterrand, Socialist party candidate, is elected president of France.
January 1980	Andrei Sakharov sentenced to internal exile in Gorky.
July–September 1980	Widespread strikes among Polish workers led by Lech Walesa at Gdansk result in published demands for free trade unions. New Solidarity unions recognized and reforms on wages and working hours agreed upon.
1981	Scientists identify acquired immune deficiency syndrome (AIDS). IBM launches its "home" or personal computer (PC).
December 1981	Martial law declared in Poland. Leading members of Solidarity are arrested and the organization banned.
1982	Helmut Kohl becomes West German chancellor.
November 1982	Death of Brezhnev. Succession of short-lived Soviet leaders: Andropov (d. 1984) and Chernenko (d. 1985).
1983	The world's first artificially made chromosome created at Harvard University. Compact disk is introduced.
1984	A silicon chip that stores four times more data than previously possible is developed. DNA analysis reveals that chimpanzees are closely related to humans—the genetic difference is barely 1 percent. Apple Macintosh microcomputer is launched.
1985	Mikhail Gorbachev becomes general secretary of the Communist party of the Soviet Union.
1986	Voyager 2 flies by Uranus. 25,000 AIDS cases are diagnosed in the United States.
1988	Development of Gorbachev's concepts of *perestroika* and *glasnost*. New constitution adopted in Soviet Union, which permits openly contested elections. Soviet withdrawal from Afghanistan. European Economic Community agrees to work toward free trade zone by 1992.
1988	First transatlantic optical fiber telephone cable links France, the United Kingdom, and the United States. Surgeons perform first brain cell transplants in the United Kingdom.
1989	Revolutionary movements throughout eastern Europe result in fall of Communist regimes in Hungary, Czechoslovakia, Romania, Bulgaria, and East Germany. Berlin Wall opened in November and thousands of East Berliners cross into the West.

1990	Gorbachev calls for the end of the Communist party's monopoly on political power in the Soviet Union. Reunification of Germany.
June 1991	Boris Yeltsin elected president of Russian Republic in general election. Open competition with Gorbachev for future political direction of Soviet Union.
August 1991	Gorbachev survives an abortive coup attempt by conservative members of his advisory cabinet. Boris Yeltsin's prestige grows as a result of his defiant public stand during the uprising. Gorbachev resigns as general secretary of Communist party with his authority in question and the party in disarray. Future of the U.S.S.R. as a political entity is in doubt as several republics declare their intention to secede from the union.
December 1991	Ukraine's independence declaration makes Soviet dissolution certain. On December 25, 1991, the Soviet Union ceased to exist, Gorbachev left office, and the Commonwealth of Independent States came into being.
1992	Croatian and Serbian forces fight over division of Bosnia. Sarajevo bombarded by Serbs, who begin policy of "ethnic cleansing."
September 1993	Boris Yeltsin emerges as the strongest leader within the new Commonwealth. Popularity high in 1992, but opposition to economic and political policies forms in Russian Parliament. Yeltsin suspends Parliament in September.
October 1993	After pro-Parliament rioters rampaged through Moscow, Yeltsin orders tanks to attack the Parliament building, crushing the revolt. In December, Russians vote for a new Parliament and approve a new constitution limiting parliamentary authority and investing the president with strong emergency powers.
1994–1996	United Nations tries unsuccessfully to mediate the Bosnian conflict and imposes sanctions to little effect. NATO airstrikes on Serbian military positions temporarily force Serbs to withdraw from Sarajevo. Dayton Peace Accords separate warring factions and establish NATO military presence in Bosnia.
1999	Serbian forces provoke a NATO military response by embarking on an aggressive campaign against ethnic Albanians.

STUDY QUESTIONS

1. What did Stalin mean in his speech of February 1946 by the phrase "Soviet victory"? What policy was Churchill advocating in his "Iron Curtain" speech? Was he pessimistic or optimistic about the possibility of war?
2. In his book *Why War?* (Paris, 1933), the great physicist Albert Einstein wrote, "Mankind can only gain protection against the danger of unimaginable de-

struction and wanton annihilation if a supranational organization has alone the authority to produce or possess [nuclear] weapons . . . and the legal right and duty to solve all the conflicts which in the past have led to war." What is your reaction to this opinion? To what extent are organizations like the United Nations and Amnesty International useful and effective? Would it make a difference if they did not exist?

3. Analyze the selection entitled "How to Spot a Communist." Select what you consider the most effective and most ridiculous arguments from this source. How do vocabulary, logic, and religion easily give away the communist? Do you find any hypocrisy in this document?

4. According to Theodore White, why is communism successful and what are its weaknesses? What are the main points about capitalism and communism that Khrushchev stressed in his speech to the 22nd Communist Party Congress? After analyzing this document, do you agree or disagree with White's assessment of communism?

5. What are the specific criticisms of Sakharov and Solzhenitsyn in their 1974 dissents against the policies of the Soviet Union? Were these problems resolved by *perestroika* and *glasnost* under the leadership of Mikhail Gorbachev?

6. How does Mikhail Gorbachev define the concept of *perestroika*? In 1989, Gorbachev described the Communist party as "society's consolidating and vanguard force." Why did the Communist party fail? What was Gorbachev's explanation in his resignation speech? What had Russians gained from his leadership? Will Gorbachev be viewed by history as a great leader who, as John Le Carré said, "had the nerve to mount the rostrum and declare he had no clothes"?

7. According to Boris Yeltsin, what were some of Russia's most immediate problems in 1994? In his address to the Russian Parliament, what did Yeltsin identify as Russia's most important goals for the future? Have Russian politicians achieved them?

8. According to Tim Koranda's speech, why was Marx wrong? How does Koranda see the development of history and the role of communism? Are you convinced that Marx's interpretation of historical economic development was wrong?

9. How did Chancellor Helmut Kohl view the impact of a "new" reunited Germany on Europe? What "lessons of history" has Germany learned? What did Kohl mean when noting that "federalism is our real goal for Europe as a whole"? Do you think Kohl was realistic in his assumptions?

10. In 1990, both François Mitterrand of France and Václav Havel of the Czech Republic offered philosophical perspectives on unity and the progress of Europe. Both appeared optimistic. What did they consider to be the foundations of their optimism? What perspective had been gained over time that Mitterrand could say that "an era of hope is opening up for mankind"? What did Havel mean by his phrase "Consciousness precedes Being"? What did his statement that "history has accelerated" imply?

11. Helmut Tuerk saw the problems of dealing with ethnic minorities throughout eastern Europe as one of the most pressing issues facing Europe in the late twentieth century. Why? What solutions did he propose?

12. What are the main problems in the Balkan region that have resulted in war between the Serbs, Croats, and Bosnians? How does this conflict threaten the stability of Europe and the Western alliance? Why has the United Nations had such difficulty resolving the issues? What fundamental solution did the pope propose? Given the history of this situation, can this problem be resolved? What must happen?

13. How would you define the "feminine mystique"? Why did women, as Betty Friedan noted, "go home again" in the 1950s? What is the main point of Gloria Steinem's parody entitled "If Men Could Menstruate"? Do you think she's correct in her assessment of male and female power relationships?

14. What are the main problems that Joan Konner addresses in her speech "Women in the Marketplace"? Do you think hers was a fair assessment of realities in the 1990s? Must women adopt male attributes in order to succeed in modern society?

15. In her controversial book, Susan Faludi argues that there has been a backlash against women in contemporary American society. What does she mean? Is her analysis correct and her arguments compelling? How are women portrayed by ad agencies, religious leaders, and the popular media? Are women defined by their culture and their men rather than by themselves?

16. How would you define the "information highway"? What does it encompass? According to John Mayo, what impact will multimedia have on the nature of work, business, and political life? Will the new information superhighway complicate or facilitate life in the future?

17. Senator Sam Ervin remarked in 1978 that "each time we give up a bit of information about ourselves to the government, we give up some of our freedom. . . . When the government knows all our secrets, we stand naked before official power." Do you agree with him? In the interests of progress, must we stand "partially clothed," if not "naked," before official power?

18. How would you define genomics? According to George Poste, what are some of the new vistas for the future of medicine, and what are the ethical, legal, and economic issues that we face because of our new technologies? How will bioethical decisions affect our lives in the future?

19. Explore some of the moral questions that arise from medical research. When you replace someone's internal organs, do you change his or her very being? Do the potentials of genetic engineering bother you? Scientists have developed the birth control pill, made possible test-tube babies, and are investigating the possibilities of cryogenic preservation. Are these valid areas of scientific research or steps toward the creation of "Frankenstein's monster"?

20. A simple question: Why must we always do what our technology allows us to do? Apply this to the issues of euthanasia, genetic engineering, the development of nuclear energy and atomic weapons, poisonous gas, and chemical warfare. Is technology a true indicator of progress? In certain cases, is it progressive *not* to apply technology?

21. What are the three factors that Stephen Bertman maintains will conspire to strip the elderly of their credentials as the repository of wisdom? Explain them carefully. Will short-term memory replace long-term memory in importance? Has that already happened? What ramifications does that have on the future? What will be the role of the elderly in the future, if not to "maintain traditions' fire"?